Linux Sound
Programming

Jan Newmarch

Apress®

Linux Sound Programming

Jan Newmarch
Oakleigh, Victoria, Australia

ISBN-13 (pbk): 978-1-4842-2495-3
DOI 10.1007/978-1-4842-2496-0

ISBN-13 (electronic): 978-1-4842-2496-0

Library of Congress Control Number: 2017931692

Managing Director: Welmoed Spahr
Acquisitions Editor: Steve Anglin
Development Editor: Matthew Moodie
Technical Reviewer: Jeff Tranter
Coordinating Editor: Mark Powers
Copy Editor: Kim Wimpsett
Compositor: SPi Global
Indexer: SPi Global
Artist: SPi Global
Cover image designed by Freepik

Distributed to the book trade worldwide by Springer Science+Business Media New York, 233 Spring Street, 6th Floor, New York, NY 10013. Phone 1-800-SPRINGER, fax (201) 348-4505, e-mail orders-ny@springer-sbm.com, or visit www.springeronline.com. Apress Media, LLC is a California LLC and the sole member (owner) is Springer Science + Business Media Finance Inc (SSBM Finance Inc). SSBM Finance Inc is a **Delaware** corporation.

For information on translations, please e-mail rights@apress.com, or visit http://www.apress.com/rights-permission.

Apress titles may be purchased in bulk for academic, corporate, or promotional use. eBook versions and licenses are also available for most titles. For more information, reference our Print and eBook Bulk Sales web page at http://www.apress.com/bulk-sales.

Any source code or other supplementary material referenced by the author in this book is available to readers via the book's product page, located at www.apress.com/9781484224953. For more detailed information, please visit http://www.apress.com/source-code.

Printed on acid-free paper

Contents at a Glance

iii

Contents

About the Author

Jan Newmarch is the head of ICT (Higher Education) at Box Hill Institute, adjunct professor at Canberra University, and adjunct lecturer in the School of Information Technology, Computing, and Mathematics at Charles Sturt University. He is interested in more aspects of computing than he has time to pursue, but the major thrust over the last few years has developed from user interfaces under Unix into Java and the Web and then into general distributed systems. Jan developed a number of publicly available software systems in these areas. For the last few years he has been looking at sound for Linux systems and programming the Raspberry Pi's GPU. He is now exploring aspects of the IoT. He lives in Melbourne, Australia, and enjoys the food and culture there but is not so impressed by the weather.

About the Technical Reviewer

Jeff Tranter has been using Linux since 1992 and has written and contributed to a number of open source and commercial Linux applications and tools. He has written about Linux and multimedia in numerous magazine articles, Linux HOWTOs, and books, including *Linux Multimedia Guide* way back in 1996. Jeff received his bachelor's degree in electrical engineering from the University of Western Ontario. He currently works as an engineering manager for a software consulting company, telecommuting from Ottawa in Ontario, Canada.

CHAPTER 1

■■■

Basic Concepts of Sound

This chapter looks at some basic concepts of audio, both analog and digital. Here are some resources:

- *The Scientist and Engineer's Guide to Digital Signal Processing* (`www.dspguide.com/`) by Steven W. Smith

- *Music and Computers: A Theoretical and Historical Approach* (`http://music.columbia.edu/cmc/MusicAndComputers/`) by Phil Burk, Larry Polansky, Douglas Repetto, Mary Roberts, Dan Rockmore

Sampled Audio

Audio is an analog phenomenon. Sounds are produced in all sorts of ways, through voice, instruments, and natural events such as trees falling in forests (whether or not there is anyone to hear). Sounds received at a point can be plotted as amplitude against time and can assume almost any functional state, including discontinuous.

The analysis of sound is frequently done by looking at its spectrum. Mathematically this is achieved by taking the Fourier transform, but the ear performs almost a similar transform just by the structure of the ear. "Pure" sounds heard by the ear correspond to simple sine waves, and harmonics correspond to sine waves, which have a frequency that's a multiple of the base sine wave.

Analog signals within a system such as an analog audio amplifier are designed to work with these spectral signals. They try to produce an equal amplification across the audible spectrum.

Computers, and an increasingly large number of electronic devices, work on digital signals, comprised of bits of 1s and 0s. Bits are combined into bytes with 256 possible values, into 16-bit words with 65,536 possible values, or even into larger combinations such as 32- or 64-bit words.

Sample Rate

Digitizing an analog signal means taking samples from that signal at regular intervals and representing those samples on a discrete scale. The frequency of taking samples is the sample rate. For example, audio on a CD is sampled at 44,100Hz, that is, 44,100 times each second. On a DVD, samples may be taken up to 192,000 times per second, with a sampling rate of 192kHz. Conversely, the standard telephone sampling rate is 8kHz.

Figure 1-1 illustrates sampling.

© Jan Newmarch 2017
J. Newmarch, *Linux Sound Programming*, DOI 10.1007/978-1-4842-2496-0_1

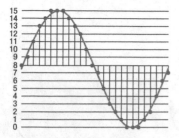

Figure 1-1. *Analog and sampled signal (Wikipedia:* http://en.wikipedia.org/wiki/Pulse-code_
modulation)

The sampling rate affects two major factors. First, the higher the sampling rate, the larger the size of the data. All other things being equal, doubling the sample rate will double the data requirements. On the other hand, the Nyquist-Shannon theorem (http://en.wikipedia.org/wiki/Nyquist_theorem) places limits on the accuracy of sampling continuous data: an analog signal can be reconstructed only from a digital signal (in other words, be distortion-free) if the highest frequency in the signal is less than one-half the sampling rate.

This is often where the arguments about the "quality" of vinyl versus CDs end up, as in "Vinyl vs. CD myths refuse to die" (www.eetimes.com/electronics-blogs/audio-designline-blog/4033509/Vinyl-vs-CD-myths-refuse-to-die). With a sampling rate of 44.1kHz, frequencies in the original signal above 22.05kHz may not be reproduced accurately when converted back to analog for a loudspeaker or headphones. Since the typical hearing range for humans is only up to 20,000Hz (and mine is now down to about 10,000Hz), then this should not be a significant problem. But some audiophiles claim to have amazingly sensitive ears!

Sample Format

The sample format is the other major feature of digitizing audio: the number of bits used to discretize the sample. For example, telephone signals use an 8kHz sampling rate and 8-bit resolution so that a telephone signal can only convey 2^8 (in other words, 256) levels (see "How Telephones Work" at http://electronics.howstuffworks.com/telephone3.htm).

Most CDs and computer systems use 16-bit formats, giving a very fine gradation of the signal and allowing a range of 96dB (see "Audacity: Digital Sampling" at http://manual.audacityteam.org/man/Digital_Audio).

Frames

A frame holds all the samples from one time instance. For a stereo device, each frame holds two samples, while for a five-speaker device, each frame holds five samples.

Pulse-Code Modulation

Pulse-code modulation (PCM) is the standard form of representing a digitized analog signal. According to Wikipedia (http://en.wikipedia.org/wiki/Pulse-code_modulation), "Pulse-code modulation is a method used to digitally represent sampled analog signals. It is the standard form for digital audio in computers and various Blu-ray, DVD, and CD formats, as well as other uses such as digital telephone systems. A PCM stream is a digital representation of an analog signal, in which the magnitude of the analog signal is sampled regularly at uniform intervals, with each sample being quantized to the nearest value within a range of digital steps."

PCM streams have two basic properties that determine their fidelity to the original analog signal: the sampling rate, which is the number of times per second that samples are taken, and the bit depth, which determines the number of possible digital values that each sample can take.

However, even though this is the standard, there are variations (http://wiki.multimedia.cx/index.php?title=PCM). The principal one concerns the representation as bytes in a word-based system: little-endian or big-endian (http://searchnetworking.techtarget.com/definition/big-endian-and-little-endian). The next variation is signed versus unsigned (http://en.wikipedia.org/wiki/Signedness).

There are a number of other variations that are less important, such as whether the digitization is linear or logarithmic. See the MultimediaWiki at http://wiki.multimedia.cx/index.php?title=PCM for a discussion of these.

Overrun and Underrun

According to "Introduction to Sound Programming with ALSA" (www.linuxjournal.com/article/6735?page=0,1), "When a sound device is active, data is transferred continuously between the hardware and application buffers. In the case of data capture (recording), if the application does not read the data in the buffer rapidly enough, the circular buffer is overwritten with new data. The resulting data loss is known as *overrun*. During playback, if the application does not pass data into the buffer quickly enough, it becomes starved for data, resulting in an error called *underrun*."

Latency

Latency is the amount of time that elapses from when a signal enters a system to when it (or its equivalent such as an amplified version) leaves the system.

According to Ian Waugh's "Fixing Audio Latency Part 1" (www.practicalpc.co.uk/computing/sound/latency1.htm), "Latency is a delay. It's most evident and problematic in computer-based music audio systems where it manifests as the delay between triggering a signal and hearing it, for example, pressing a key on your MIDI keyboard and hearing the sound play through your sound card."

It's like a delayed reaction, and if the delay is large, it becomes impossible to play anything in time because the sound you hear is always a little bit behind what you're playing, which is distracting.

This delay does not have to be large before it causes problems. Many people can work with a latency of about 40ms even though the delay is noticeable, although if you are playing pyrotechnic music lines, it may be too long.

The ideal latency is 0, but many people would be hard-pressed to notice delays less than 8ms or 10ms, and many people can work quite happily with a 20ms latency.

A Google search for *measuring audio latency* will turn up many sites. I use a crude but simple test. I installed Audacity on a separate PC and used it to record simultaneously a sound I made and that same sound when picked up and played back by the test PC. I banged a spoon against a bottle to get a sharp percussive sound. When magnified, the recorded sound showed two peaks, and selecting the region between the peaks showed me the latency in the selection start/end. In Figure 1-2, these are 17.383 and 17.413 seconds, with a latency of 30ms.

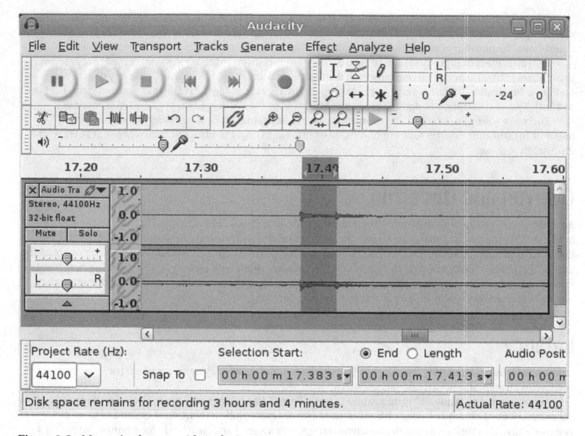

Figure 1-2. *Measuring latency with Audacity*

Jitter

Sampling an analog signal will be done at regular intervals. Ideally, playback should use exactly those same intervals. But, particularly in networked systems, the periods may not be regular. Any irregularity is known as *jitter* (http://en.wikipedia.org/wiki/Jitter). I don't have a simple way of testing for jitter; I'm still stuck on latency as my major problem!

Mixing

Mixing means taking inputs from one or more sources, possibly doing some processing on these input signals and sending them to one or more outputs. The origin, of course, is in physical mixers, which would act on analog signals. In the digital world, the same functions would be performed on digital signals.

A simple document describing analog mixers is "The Soundcraft Guide to Mixing" (`www.soundcraft.com/support/gtm_booklet.aspx`). It covers the following functions:

- Routing inputs to outputs

- Setting gain and output levels for different input and output signals

- Applying special effects such as reverb, delay, and pitch shifting

- Mixing input signals to a common output

- Splitting an input signal into multiple outputs

Conclusion

This short chapter has introduced some of the basic concepts that will occupy much of the rest of this book. *The Scientist and Engineer's Guide to Digital Signal Processing* (`www.dspguide.com/`) by Steven W. Smith has a wealth of further detail,

CHAPTER 2

■ ■ ■

User-Level Tools

This chapter looks at the user-level tools that are typical under a Linux system, including players, various sound manipulation tools, and editors.

Players

The following sections talk about players.

MPlayer

I think MPlayer is fantastic and probably use it more than any other player. I usually run it from the command line, but there are GUI versions available. It will play almost any media type—video as well as audio. I use it for both. It will also accept HTTP URLs, DVD URLs, and VCD URLs, among others.

The man page for MPlayer is at www.mplayerhq.hu/DOCS/man/en/mplayer.1.html, and the reference page is at www.mplayerhq.hu/DOCS/HTML/en/index.html.

There is a GUI version of MPlayer called MPlayerGUI, but it is broken under current versions of Ubuntu (such as 16.04) and apparently won't be fixed. There is a Gnome version called GNOME MPlayer that looks like Figure 2-1.

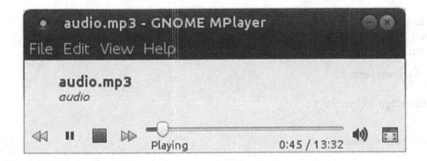

Figure 2-1. *GNOME MPlayer*

VLC

VLC is my second favorite player. It too will play almost anything and accepts HTTP, DVD, and VCD URLs. It has a default GUI but can be run without one with the command cvlc. The GUI looks like Figure 2-2.

© Jan Newmarch 2017
J. Newmarch, *Linux Sound Programming*, DOI 10.1007/978-1-4842-2496-0_2

Figure 2-2. *VLC*

Its main page is VideoLAN(`www.videolan.org/vlc/index.html`), and you can find some documentation at Welcome to VideoLAN's Documentation (`http://wiki.videolan.org/Documentation:D ocumentation`).

Totem

Totem is commonly used, but it is not one of my favorites.

Sound Tools

There are a number of sound tools capable of multiple tasks such as converting formats and applying effects. Some of these are described in the following sections.

SOX

`sox` is the Swiss Army knife of sound-processing programs. The simplest usage is to change file formats as follows:

```
sox audio.mp3 audio.ogg
```

This converts an MP3 file to an Ogg-Vorbis file (you may need to install the `libsox-fmt-all` package to be able to handle all file formats).

However, it can also perform many other functions such as the following:

- Convert to mono, as shown here:

  ```
  sox audio.mp3 audio.ogg channels 1
  ```

- Double the volume, as shown here:

  ```
  sox audio.mp3 audio.ogg vol 2
  ```

- Change the sampling rate, as shown here:

  ```
  sox audio.mp3 audio.ogg rate 16k
  ```

It can also perform more complex effects such as merging files, splitting files when it detects silence, and many others.

Its home page is at http://sox.sourceforge.net/.

FFmpeg/avconv

FFmpeg is generally used as a converter from one format to another. There is a nice series of tutorials at the site A FFmpeg Tutorial For Beginners (http://linuxers.org/tutorial/ffmpeg-tutorial-beginners) by shredder12.

It can also be used to record from ALSA devices such as hw:0 or the default device. Recording from hw:0 can be done with the following:

```
ffmpeg -f alsa -i hw:0 test.mp3
```

It can be done from the default ALSA input with the following:

```
ffmpeg -f alsa -i default test.mp3
```

There was a fork some years ago of FFmpeg that produced avconv, which is the default on Ubuntu systems. There are some differences between the two, but not enough to justify the nuisance factor to users. FFmpeg and avconv are discussed extensively in Chapter 12.

GStreamer

GStreamer allows you to build "pipelines" that can be played using gst-launch. For example, to play an MP3 file using ALSA, you would have the following pipeline:

```
gst-launch-1.0 filesrc location="concept.mp3" | decodebin | alsasink
```

The pipelines can do more complex tasks such as format conversion, mixing, and so on. Check out the tutorial "Multipurpose Multimedia Processing with GStreamer" (www.ibm.com/developerworks/aix/library/au-gstreamer.html?ca=dgr-lnxw07GStreamer) by Maciej Katafiasz.

GStreamer can also play MIDI files with the following:

```
gst-launch-1.0 filesrc location="rehab.mid" ! wildmidi ! alsasink
```

Audacity

According to its web site (http://audacity.sourceforge.net/), "Audacity is a free, easy-to-use, and multilingual audio editor and recorder for Windows, Mac OS X, GNU/Linux, and other operating systems." This is a fantastic tool and well worth using. Examples will be demonstrated in later chapters.

Conclusion

This short chapter has looked at some of the user-level tools available under Linux. These are the ones I use on a regular basis. While I have listed several of the major tools, a casual search will turn up far more. The Wikipedia "List of Linux audio software" page (https://en.wikipedia.org/wiki/List_of_Linux_audio_software) has an exhaustive list.

CHAPTER 3

▪ ▪ ▪

Sound Codecs and File Formats

There are many different ways of representing sound data. Some of these involve compressing the data, which may or may not lose information. Data can be stored in the file system or transmitted across the network, which raises additional issues. This chapter considers the major sound codecs and container formats.

Overview

Audio and video data needs to be represented in digital format to be used by a computer. Audio and video data contains an enormous amount of information, so digital representations of this data can occupy huge amounts of space. Consequently, computer scientists have developed many different ways of representing this information, sometimes in ways that preserve all the information (*lossless*) and sometimes in ways that lose information (*lossy*).

Each way of representing the information digitally is known as a *codec*. The simplest way, described in the next section, is to represent it as "raw" pulse-code modulated (PCM) data. Hardware devices such as sound cards can deal with PCM data directly, but PCM data can use a lot of space.

Most codecs will attempt to reduce the memory requirements of PCM data by *encoding* it to another form, called *encoded data*. It can then be *decoded* back to PCM form when required. Depending on the codec algorithms, the regenerated PCM may have the same information content as the original PCM data (lossless) or may contain less information (lossy).

Encoded audio data may or may not contain information about the properties of the data. This information may be about the original PCM data such as the number of channels (mono, stereo), the sampling rate, the number of bits in the sample, and so on. Or it may be information about the encoding process itself, such as the size of framed data. The encoded data along with this additional information may be stored in a file, transmitted across the network, and so on. If this is done, the encoded data plus the additional information is amalgamated into a *container*.

It is important at times to know whether you are dealing with just the encoded data or with a container that holds this data. For example, files on disk will normally be containers, holding additional information along with the encoded data. But audio data manipulation libraries will typically deal with the encoded data itself, after the additional data has been removed.

PCM

This definition comes from Wikipedia: "Pulse-code modulation is a method used to digitally represent sampled analog signals. It is the standard form for digital audio in computers and various Blu-ray, DVD, and CD formats, as well as other uses such as digital telephone systems. A PCM stream is a digital representation of an analog signal, in which the magnitude of the analog signal is sampled regularly at uniform intervals, with each sample being quantized to the nearest value within a range of digital steps."

© Jan Newmarch 2017
J. Newmarch, *Linux Sound Programming*, DOI 10.1007/978-1-4842-2496-0_3

PCM streams have two basic properties that determine their fidelity to the original analog signal: the sampling rate, which is the number of times per second that samples are taken, and the bit depth, which determines the number of possible digital values that each sample can take.

PCM data can be stored in files as "raw" data. In this case, there is no header information to say what the sampling rate and bit depth are. Many tools such as sox use the file extension to determine these properties.

According to `http://sox.sourceforge.net/soxformat.html`, "f32 and f64 indicate files encoded as 32- and 64-bit (IEEE single and double precision) floating-point PCM, respectively; s8, s16, s24, and s32 indicate 8, 16, 24, and 32-bit signed integer PCM, respectively; u8, u16, u24, and u32 indicate 8, 16, 24, and 32-bit unsigned integer PCM, respectively."

But it should be noted that the file extension is only an aid to understanding some of the PCM codec parameters and how they are stored in the file.

WAV

WAV is a file format wrapper around audio data as a container. The audio data is often PCM. The file format is based on the Resource Interchange File Format (RIFF). While it is a Microsoft/IBM format, it does not seem to be encumbered by patents.

A good description of the format is given by Topherlee (`www.topherlee.com/software/pcm-tut-wavformat.html`). The WAV file header contains information about the PCM codec and also about how it is stored (for example, little- or big-endian).

Because WAV files usually contain uncompressed audio data, they are often huge, around 50Mb for a three-minute song.

MP3

The MP3 and related formats are covered by a patent (actually, a whole lot of patents). For using an encoder or decoder, users should pay a license fee to an organization such as the Fraunhofer Society. Most casual users neither do this nor are aware that they should, but it is reported by Fraunhofer (`www.itif.org/files/2011-fraunhofer-boosting-comp.pdf`) that in 2011 the MP3 patent "generates annual tax revenue of about $300 million." The Fraunhofer Society has currently chosen not to pursue free open source implementations of encoders and decoders for royalties.

The codec used by MP3 is the MPEG-1 Audio Layer III (`http://en.wikipedia.org/wiki/MP3`) audio compression format. This includes a header component that gives all the additional information about the data and the compression algorithm. There is no need for a separate container format.

Ogg Vorbis

Ogg Vorbis is one of the "good guys." According to Vorbis.com, "Ogg Vorbis is a completely open, patent-free, professional audio encoding and streaming technology with all the benefits of open source."

The names break down as follows:

- *Ogg*: Ogg is the name of Xiph.org's container format for audio, video, and metadata. This puts the stream data into *frames* that are easier to manage in files and other things.

- *Vorbis*: Vorbis is the name of a specific audio compression scheme that's designed to be contained in Ogg. Note that other formats are capable of being embedded in Ogg such as FLAC and Speex.

The extension .oga is preferred for Ogg audio files, although .ogg was previously used.

At times it is necessary to be closely aware of the distinction between Ogg and Vorbis. For example, OpenMAX IL has a number of standard audio components including one to decode various codecs. The LIM component with the role "audio decoder ogg" can decode Vorbis streams. But even though the component includes the name *ogg*, it cannot decode Ogg files, which are the containers of Vorbis streams. It can only decode the Vorbis stream. Decoding an Ogg file requires using a different component, referred to as an "audio decoder with framing."

WMA

From the standpoint of open source, WMA files are evil. WMA files are based on two Microsoft proprietary formats. The first is the Advanced Systems Format (ASF) file format, which describes the "container" for the music data. The second is the Windows Media Audio 9 codec.

ASF is the primary problem. Microsoft has a published specification (www.microsoft.com/en-us/download/details.aspx?id=14995) that is strongly antagonistic to anything open source. The license states that if you build an implementation based on that specification, then you:

- Cannot distribute the source code

- Can only distribute the object code

- Cannot distribute the object code except as part of a "solution" (in other words, libraries seem to be banned)

- Cannot distribute your object code for no charge

- Cannot set your license to allow derivative works

And what's more, you are not allowed to begin any new implementation after January 1, 2012, and (at the time of writing) it is already 2017!

Just to make it a little worse, Microsoft has patent 6041345, "Active stream format for holding multiple media streams" (www.google.com/patents/US6041345), which was filed in the United States on March 7, 1997. The patent appears to cover the same ground as many other such formats that were in existence at the time, so the standing of this patent (were it to be challenged) is not clear. However, it has been used to block the GPL-licensed project VirtualDub (www.advogato.org/article/101.html) from supporting ASF. The status of patenting a file format is a little suspect but may become a little clearer now that Oracle has lost its claim to patent the Java API.

The FFmpeg project (http://ffmpeg.org/) has nevertheless done a clean-room implementation of ASF, reverse-engineering the file format and not using the ASF specification at all. It has also reverse-engineered the WMA codec. This allows players such as MPlayer and VLC to play ASF/WMA files. FFmpeg itself can also convert from ASF/WMA to better formats such as Ogg Vorbis.

There is no Java handler for WMA files, and given the license, there is unlikely to be one unless it is a native-code one based on FFmpeg.

Matroska

According to the Matroska web site (http://matroska.org/), Matroska aims to become the standard of multimedia container formats. It was derived from a project called MCF but differentiates from it significantly because it is based on Extensible Binary Meta Language (EBML), a binary derivative of XML. It incorporates features you would expect from a modern container format, such as the following:

- Fast seeking in the file

- Chapter entries

- Full metadata (tags) support
- Selectable subtitle/audio/video streams
- Modularly expandable
- Error resilience (can recover playback even when the stream is damaged)
- Streamable over the Internet and local networks (HTTP, CIFS, FTP, and so on)
- Menus (like DVDs have)

I hadn't come across Matroska until I started looking at subtitles,[1] which can be (optionally) added to videos, where it seems to be one of the major formats.

A GUI tool to create and manage subtitles in Matroska file format (MKV) files is mkvmerge, in the Ubuntu repositories. HYPERLINK "https://mkvtoolnix.download/" MKVToolNix is a GUI tool to handle MKV files.

Conclusion

There are many codecs for sound, and more are being devised all the time. They vary between being codecs, containers, or both, and they come with a variety of features, some with encumbrances such as patents.

---

[1]Subtitles and closed captions are similar but distinct. According to https://www.accreditedlanguage.com/2016/08/18/subtitles-and-captions-whats-the-difference/, "Subtitling is most frequently used as a way of translating a medium into another language so that speakers of other languages can enjoy it. Captioning, on the other hand, is more commonly used as a service to aid deaf and hearing-impaired audiences."

CHAPTER 4

■ ■ ■

Overview of Linux Sound Architecture

The Linux sound system, like most of Linux, has evolved from a simple system to a much more complex one. This chapter gives a high-level overview of the components of the Linux sound system and which bits are best used for which use cases.

Resources

Here are some resources:

- *A Guide Through The Linux Sound API Jungle* by Lennart Poettering (http://0pointer.de/blog/projects/guide-to-sound-apis.html).

- "How it works: Linux audio explained" by TuxRadar (http://tuxradar.com/content/how-it-works-linux-audio-explained).

- Insane Coder posted an article in favor of OSSv4 State of sound in Linux not so sorry after all (http://insanecoding.blogspot.com.au/2009/06/state-of-sound-in-linux-not-so-sorry.html), which drew a lot of comments.

Components

Figure 4-1 indicates the different layers of the Linux sound system.

© Jan Newmarch 2017
J. Newmarch, *Linux Sound Programming*, DOI 10.1007/978-1-4842-2496-0_4

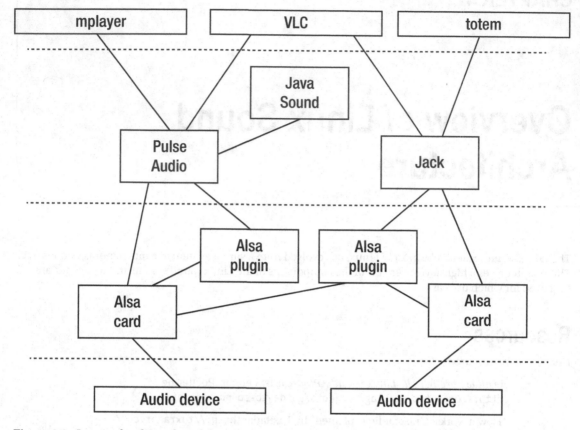

Figure 4-1. *Layers of audio tools and devices*

Device Drivers

At the bottom layer is the hardware itself, the audio device. These devices are the audio cards made by a variety of manufacturers, all with different capabilities, interfaces, and prices. Just like any piece of hardware, in order for it to be visible and useful to the operating system, there must be a device driver. There are, of course, thousands of device drivers written for Linux. Writing Linux device drivers is a specialty in itself, and there are dedicated sources for this, such as *Linux Device Drivers, Third Edition* (http://lwn.net/Kernel/LDD3/) by Jonathan Corbet, Alessandro Rubini, and Greg Kroah-Hartman.

Device drivers must have standardized APIs "at the top" so that users of the device have a known interface to code to. The OSS device driver API was used for audio devices until it was made closed source, at which point developers switched to the ALSA API. While OSS v4 has become open again, the ALSA interface is supported in the kernel, while OSS is not.

Ideally, a device driver API should expose all of the features of hardware while not adding additional baggage. For audio, it is not always so easy to set boundaries for what an audio driver should do. For example, some sound cards will support the mixing of analog signals from different sources, while others will not, and some sound cards will have MIDI synthesizers, while others will not. If the API is to expose these capabilities for sound cards that support them, then it might have to supply them in software for those sound cards that do not.

There is a limited amount of documentation on writing ALSA device drivers. The "ALSA Driver Documentation" page at `www.alsa-project.org/main/index.php/ALSA_Driver_Documentation` points to some documents, including the 2005 document on writing ALSA device drivers (`www.alsa-project.org/~tiwai/writing-an-alsa-driver/`) by Takashi Iwai. There is also a 2010 blog by Ben Collins at `http://ben-collins.blogspot.com.au/2010/05/writing-alsa-driver-basics.html`, "Writing an ALSA driver." Otherwise, there seems to be little help.

Sound Servers

Linux is a multitasking, multithreaded operating system. It is possible that concurrent processes might want to write sounds to the audio cards concurrently. For example, a mail reader might want to "ding" the user to report new mail, even if they are in the middle of a noisy computer game. This is distinct from sound card capabilities of being able to mix sounds from different ports, such as an HDMI input port and an analog input port. It requires the ability to mix (or otherwise manage) sounds from different processes. As an example of the subtlety of this, should the volume of each process be individually controllable, or should the destination port (headphones or speaker) be individually controllable?

Such capabilities are beyond the scope of a device driver. Linux resolves this by having "sound servers," which run above the device drivers and manage these more complex tasks. Above these sound servers sit applications that talk to the sound server, which in turn will pass the resultant digital signal to the device driver.

Here is where a significant difference occurs between sound servers. For professional audio systems, the sound server must be able to process and route audio with a minimal amount of latency or other negative effects. For consumer audio, control over volumes and destinations may be more important than latency; you probably won't care if a new message "ding" takes an extra half-second. Between these may be other cases such as games requiring synchronization of audio and visual effects and karaoke players requiring synchronization of analog and digital sources.

The two major sound servers under Linux are Jack for professional audio and PulseAudio for consumer systems. They are designed for different use cases and consequently offer different features.

Lennart Poettering in "A Guide Through the Linux Sound API Jungle" (`http://0pointer.de/blog/projects/guide-to-sound-apis.html`) offers a good summary of these different use cases:

- "I want to write a media-player-like application!"

  Use GStreamer (unless your focus is only KDE, in which cases Phonon might be an alternative).

- "I want to add event sounds to my application!"

  Use libcanberra, and install your sound files according to the XDG sound theming/naming specifications (unless your focus is only KDE, in which case KNotify might be an alternative, although it has a different focus).

- "I want to do professional audio programming, hard-disk recording, music synthesizing, MIDI interfacing!"

  Use Jack and/or the full ALSA interface.

- "I want to do basic PCM audio playback/capturing!"

  Use the safe ALSA subset.

- "I want to add sound to my game!"

- Use the audio API of SDL for full-screen games, and use libcanberra for simple games with standard UIs such as Gtk+.

- "I want to write a mixer application!"

Use the layer you want to support directly: if you want to support enhanced desktop software mixers, use the PulseAudio volume control APIs. If you want to support hardware mixers, use the ALSA mixer APIs.

- "I want to write audio software for the plumbing layer!"

    Use the full ALSA stack.

- "I want to write audio software for embedded applications!"

    For technical appliances, usually the safe ALSA subset is a good choice. This, however, depends highly on your use case.

Complexities

Figure 4-1 hides the real complexities of Linux sound. Mike Melanson (an Adobe engineer) in 2007 produced the diagram shown in Figure 4-2.

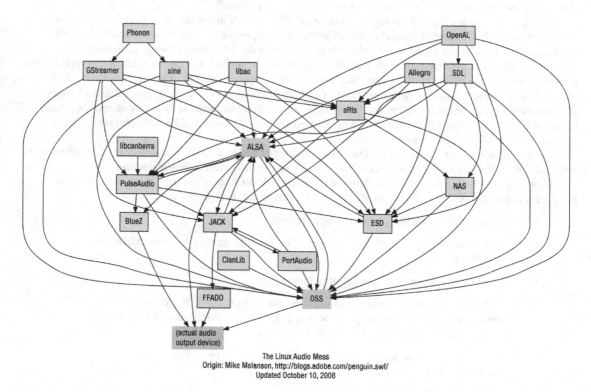

The Linux Audio Mess
Origin: Mike Melanson, http://blogs.adobe.com/penguin.swf/
Updated October 10, 2008

Figure 4-2. *Linux audio relationships*

The figure is not up-to-date. For example, OSS is no longer a major part of Linux. Some special-case complexities are, for example, that PulseAudio sits above ALSA, and it also sits *below* ALSA, as in Figure 4-3 (based on the one at http://insanecoding.blogspot.com.au/2009/06/state-of-sound-in-linux-not-so-sorry.html).

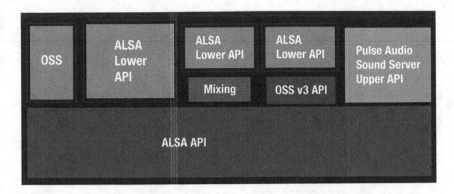

Figure 4-3. *ALSA and PulseAudio. This diagram is upside down compared to mine*

The explanation is as follows:

- PulseAudio is able to do things such as mixing application sounds that ALSA cannot do.

- PulseAudio installs itself as the default ALSA output device.

- An application sends audio to the ALSA default device, which sends it to PulseAudio.

- PulseAudio mixes it with any other audio and then sends it back to a particular device in ALSA.

- ALSA then plays the mixed sound.

Complex, yes, but it accomplishes tasks that would be difficult otherwise.

Conclusion

The architecture of the Linux sound system is complex, and new wrinkles are being added on a regular basis. However, this is the same for any audio system. Successive chapters will flesh out the details of many of these components.

Conclusion

CHAPTER 5

ALSA

ALSA is a low-level interface to the sound cards. If you are building your own sound server system or writing device drivers, then you will be interested in ALSA. It sits at the bottom of most of the current Linux systems, so to understand them, you may need to understand aspects of ALSA. If you are not interested, you can move on.

Resources

Here are some resources:

- "Introduction to Sound Programming with ALSA" (www.linuxjournal.com/article/6735?page=0,1) by Jeff Tranter

- A close look at ALSA (www.volkerschatz.com/noise/alsa.html) by Volker Schatz

- ALSA API (www.alsa-project.org/alsa-doc/alsa-lib/)

- ALSA Programming HOWTO (www.suse.de/~mana/alsa090_howto.html) by Matthias Nagorni

- Linux sound HOWTO for ALSA users (http://techpatterns.com/forums/about1813.html) from Tech Patterns

User Space Tools

ALSA is both a set of APIs to talk to sound cards and a set of user-level applications, built of course using the ALSA API. It includes commands to query and control sound cards and to record from and play to the cards. This section considers the command-line tools.

alsamixer

alsamixer runs within a terminal window and allows you to select sound cards and control interfaces on those cards. It looks like Figure 5-1.

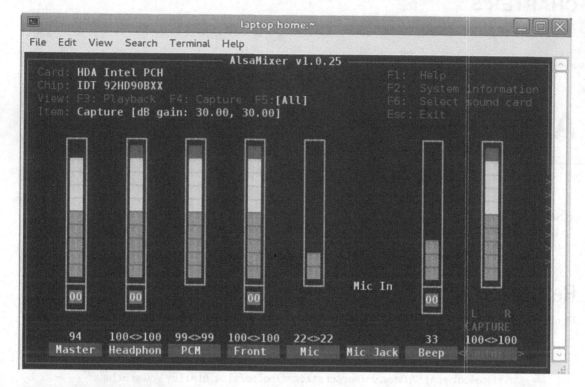

Figure 5-1. *alsamixer display*

`amixer` is a command-line application with similar functions.

Compared to the general mixer functions described in Chapter 1, the mixer functions are quite limited:

- Setting the playback and capture volumes on output and input channels

- Muting or unmuting a card

The document "Sound configuration on Raspberry Pi with ALSA" (http://blog.scphillips.com/2013/01/sound-configuration-on-raspberry-pi-with-alsa/) by Stephen C. Phillips is applicable to all other ALSA systems and not just the Raspberry Pi.

alsactl

This is a simple control program for ALSA configurations.

speaker-test

This command allows you to test which outputs go where. For example, for five-channel sound, run the following:

```
speaker-test -t wav -c 5
```

This will produce on my default sound card the following text and audio:

```
speaker-test 1.0.25

Playback device is default
Stream parameters are 48000Hz, S16_LE, 5 channels
WAV file(s)
Rate set to 48000Hz (requested 48000Hz)
Buffer size range from 39 to 419430
Period size range from 12 to 139810
Using max buffer size 419428
Periods = 4
was set period_size = 104857
was set buffer_size = 419428
 0 - Front Left
 1 - Front Right
 2 - Rear Left
 3 - Rear Right
 4 - Center
Time per period = 12.948378
```

It will also play the phrases "Front Left," and so on, to the relevant speaker.

aplay/arecord

This plays a file or records to a file. To play the microphone to the speaker, use this:

```
arecord -r 44100 --buffer-size=128 | aplay --buffer-size=128
```

To record it to a file, use this:

```
arecord -f dat -d 20 -D hw:0,0 test.wav
```

This will record a 20-second WAV file at DAT quality on your first available sound card (hw:0,0). DAT quality is defined as stereo digital audio recorded with a 48kHz sampling rate and 16-bit resolution.

Identifying ALSA Cards

The simplest ways are to run aplay and arecord with the -l option, as shown here:

```
arecord -l
     **** List of CAPTURE Hardware Devices ****
     card 0: PCH [HDA Intel PCH], device 0: STAC92xx Analog [STAC92xx Analog]
       Subdevices: 1/1
       Subdevice #0: subdevice #0
     card 2: Pro [SB X-Fi Surround 5.1 Pro], device 0: USB Audio [USB Audio]
       Subdevices: 1/1
       Subdevice #0: subdevice #0
aplay -l
     **** List of PLAYBACK Hardware Devices ****
     card 0: PCH [HDA Intel PCH], device 0: STAC92xx Analog [STAC92xx Analog]
       Subdevices: 1/1
       Subdevice #0: subdevice #0
```

```
card 1: NVidia [HDA NVidia], device 3: HDMI 0 [HDMI 0]
  Subdevices: 1/1
  Subdevice #0: subdevice #0
card 1: NVidia [HDA NVidia], device 7: HDMI 1 [HDMI 1]
  Subdevices: 1/1
  Subdevice #0: subdevice #0
card 1: NVidia [HDA NVidia], device 8: HDMI 2 [HDMI 2]
  Subdevices: 1/1
  Subdevice #0: subdevice #0
card 2: Pro [SB X-Fi Surround 5.1 Pro], device 0: USB Audio [USB Audio]
  Subdevices: 1/1
  Subdevice #0: subdevice #0
card 2: Pro [SB X-Fi Surround 5.1 Pro], device 1: USB Audio [USB Audio #1]
  Subdevices: 1/1
  Subdevice #0: subdevice #0
```

Device Names

The cards are often given names such as hw:0 or hw:2.2 in programs such as qjackctl (see Chapter 7). The term hw refers to hardware devices. The major number refers to the card number, and the minor number refers to the device number. The name of the device is in brackets.

Devices may also be known by aliases. The command aplay -L lists device aliases. For example, the hdmi alias is defined on my system in the configuration file /etc/asound.conf.

```
pcm.hdmi0 {
        type hw
        card 1
        device 3 }

pcm.hdmi1 {
        type hw
        card 1
        device 7 }

pcm.hdmi2 {
        type hw
        card 1
        device 8 }
```

So, hdmi:0 is really hw:1,3: card 1, device 3.

Other aliases can be defined to cover a range of devices, parameterized by card and device. For example, /usr/share/alsa/pcm/surround40.conf defines the following:

```
pcm.!surround40 {
        @args [ CARD DEV ]
        @args.CARD {
                type string
                default {
                        @func getenv
                        vars [
                                ALSA_SURROUND40_CARD
                                ALSA_PCM_CARD
```

```
                                ALSA_CARD
                        ]
                        default {
                                @func refer
                                name defaults.pcm.surround40.card
                        }
                }
        }
        @args.DEV {
                type integer
                default {
                        @func igetenv
                        vars [
                                ALSA_SURROUND40_DEVICE
                        ]
                        default {
                                @func refer
                                name defaults.pcm.surround40.device
                        }
                }
        }
        ...
}
```

This defines, for example, surround40:CARD=PCH,DEV=0 as an alias for hw:0,0 on my system (PCH is card 0).
I don't know an easy programmatic way to go from card 1, device 3 to hdmi:0.
You can show the set of aliases using aplay and arecord.
The output from aplay -L on my system is as follows:

```
default
    Default
sysdefault:CARD=PCH
    HDA Intel PCH, STAC92xx Analog
    Default Audio Device
front:CARD=PCH,DEV=0
    HDA Intel PCH, STAC92xx Analog
    Front speakers
surround40:CARD=PCH,DEV=0
    HDA Intel PCH, STAC92xx Analog
    4.0 Surround output to Front and Rear speakers
surround41:CARD=PCH,DEV=0
    HDA Intel PCH, STAC92xx Analog
    4.1 Surround output to Front, Rear and Subwoofer speakers
surround50:CARD=PCH,DEV=0
    HDA Intel PCH, STAC92xx Analog
    5.0 Surround output to Front, Center and Rear speakers
surround51:CARD=PCH,DEV=0
    HDA Intel PCH, STAC92xx Analog
    5.1 Surround output to Front, Center, Rear and Subwoofer speakers
surround71:CARD=PCH,DEV=0
    HDA Intel PCH, STAC92xx Analog
    7.1 Surround output to Front, Center, Side, Rear and Woofer speakers
```

```
hdmi:CARD=NVidia,DEV=0
    HDA NVidia, HDMI 0
    HDMI Audio Output
hdmi:CARD=NVidia,DEV=1
    HDA NVidia, HDMI 1
    HDMI Audio Output
hdmi:CARD=NVidia,DEV=2
    HDA NVidia, HDMI 2
    HDMI Audio Output
sysdefault:CARD=Pro
    SB X-Fi Surround 5.1 Pro, USB Audio
    Default Audio Device
front:CARD=Pro,DEV=0
    SB X-Fi Surround 5.1 Pro, USB Audio
    Front speakers
surround40:CARD=Pro,DEV=0
    SB X-Fi Surround 5.1 Pro, USB Audio
    4.0 Surround output to Front and Rear speakers
surround41:CARD=Pro,DEV=0
    SB X-Fi Surround 5.1 Pro, USB Audio
    4.1 Surround output to Front, Rear and Subwoofer speakers
surround50:CARD=Pro,DEV=0
    SB X-Fi Surround 5.1 Pro, USB Audio
    5.0 Surround output to Front, Center and Rear speakers
surround51:CARD=Pro,DEV=0
    SB X-Fi Surround 5.1 Pro, USB Audio
    5.1 Surround output to Front, Center, Rear and Subwoofer speakers
surround71:CARD=Pro,DEV=0
    SB X-Fi Surround 5.1 Pro, USB Audio
    7.1 Surround output to Front, Center, Side, Rear and Woofer speakers
iec958:CARD=Pro,DEV=0
    SB X-Fi Surround 5.1 Pro, USB Audio
    IEC958 (S/PDIF) Digital Audio Output
```

The output from arecord -L is as follows:

```
default
    Default
sysdefault:CARD=PCH
    HDA Intel PCH, STAC92xx Analog
    Default Audio Device
front:CARD=PCH,DEV=0
    HDA Intel PCH, STAC92xx Analog
    Front speakers
surround40:CARD=PCH,DEV=0
    HDA Intel PCH, STAC92xx Analog
    4.0 Surround output to Front and Rear speakers
surround41:CARD=PCH,DEV=0
    HDA Intel PCH, STAC92xx Analog
    4.1 Surround output to Front, Rear and Subwoofer speakers
surround50:CARD=PCH,DEV=0
    HDA Intel PCH, STAC92xx Analog
```

```
      5.0 Surround output to Front, Center and Rear speakers
surround51:CARD=PCH,DEV=0
      HDA Intel PCH, STAC92xx Analog
      5.1 Surround output to Front, Center, Rear and Subwoofer speakers
surround71:CARD=PCH,DEV=0
      HDA Intel PCH, STAC92xx Analog
      7.1 Surround output to Front, Center, Side, Rear and Woofer speakers
sysdefault:CARD=Pro
      SB X-Fi Surround 5.1 Pro, USB Audio
      Default Audio Device
front:CARD=Pro,DEV=0
      SB X-Fi Surround 5.1 Pro, USB Audio
      Front speakers
surround40:CARD=Pro,DEV=0
      SB X-Fi Surround 5.1 Pro, USB Audio
      4.0 Surround output to Front and Rear speakers
surround41:CARD=Pro,DEV=0
      SB X-Fi Surround 5.1 Pro, USB Audio
      4.1 Surround output to Front, Rear and Subwoofer speakers
surround50:CARD=Pro,DEV=0
      SB X-Fi Surround 5.1 Pro, USB Audio
      5.0 Surround output to Front, Center and Rear speakers
surround51:CARD=Pro,DEV=0
      SB X-Fi Surround 5.1 Pro, USB Audio
      5.1 Surround output to Front, Center, Rear and Subwoofer speakers
surround71:CARD=Pro,DEV=0
      SB X-Fi Surround 5.1 Pro, USB Audio
      7.1 Surround output to Front, Center, Side, Rear and Woofer speakers
iec958:CARD=Pro,DEV=0
      SB X-Fi Surround 5.1 Pro, USB Audio
      IEC958 (S/PDIF) Digital Audio Output
```

ALSA Configuration Files

This tutorial by Volker Schatz explains what is going on in ALSA configuration files and is really good: "A close look at ALSA" (www.volkerschatz.com/noise/alsa.html).

Just note that the default ALSA device is hw:0. This is hard-coded into ALSA. But it can be overridden in configuration files. This is done, for example, by PulseAudio (see the next chapter).

alsa-info

This will collect information about your system and save it in a file. It is a shell script that gives an enormous amount of information. Here is a heavily elided subset of the information:

```
upload=true&script=true&cardinfo=
!!##############################
!!ALSA Information Script v 0.4.60
!!##############################

!!Script ran on: Tue Jun 12 04:50:22 UTC 2012
```

```
!!Linux Distribution
!!------------------

Fedora release 16 (Verne) Fedora release 16 (Verne) Fedora release 16 (Verne) Fedora release
16 (Verne)


...


!!ALSA Version
!!------------

Driver version:    1.0.24
Library version:   1.0.25
Utilities version: 1.0.25

!!Loaded ALSA modules
!!-------------------

snd_hda_intel
snd_hda_intel

!!Sound Servers on this system
!!----------------------------

Pulseaudio:
     Installed - Yes (/usr/bin/pulseaudio)
     Running - Yes

Jack:
     Installed - Yes (/usr/bin/jackd)
     Running - No

!!Soundcards recognised by ALSA
!!-----------------------------

 0 [PCH            ]: HDA-Intel - HDA Intel PCH
                      HDA Intel PCH at 0xe6e60000 irq 47
 1 [NVidia         ]: HDA-Intel - HDA NVidia
                      HDA NVidia at 0xe5080000 irq 17

!!PCI Soundcards installed in the system
!!--------------------------------------

00:1b.0 Audio device: Intel Corporation 6 Series/C200 Series Chipset Family High Definition
Audio Controller (rev 04)
01:00.1 Audio device: nVidia Corporation HDMI Audio stub (rev a1)


...


!!HDA-Intel Codec information
!!---------------------------
```

```
...

Default PCM:
    rates [0x5e0]: 44100 48000 88200 96000 192000
    bits [0xe]: 16 20 24
    formats [0x1]: PCM

Node 0x0a [Pin Complex] wcaps 0x400583: Stereo Amp-In
  Control: name="Mic Jack Mode", index=0, device=0
    ControlAmp: chs=0, dir=In, idx=0, ofs=0
  Control: name="Mic Capture Volume", index=0, device=0
    ControlAmp: chs=3, dir=In, idx=0, ofs=0
  Control: name="Mic Jack", index=0, device=0
  Amp-In caps: N/A
  Amp-In vals:  [0x01 0x01]
  Pincap 0x0001173c: IN OUT HP EAPD Detect
    Vref caps: HIZ 50 GRD 80
  EAPD 0x2: EAPD
  Pin Default 0x03a11020: [Jack] Mic at Ext Left
    Conn = 1/8, Color = Black
    DefAssociation = 0x2, Sequence = 0x0
  Pin-ctls: 0x24: IN VREF_80
  Unsolicited: tag=03, enabled=1
  Power: setting=D0, actual=D0
  Connection: 3
     0x13* 0x14 0x1c

!!ALSA configuration files
!!-----------------------

!!System wide config file (/etc/asound.conf)

#
# Place your global alsa-lib configuration here...
#

@hooks [
        {
                func load
                files [
                        "/etc/alsa/pulse-default.conf"
                ]
                errors false
        }
]

pcm.hdmi0 {
        type hw
        card 1
        device 3 }
```

```
pcm.hdmi1 {
        type hw
        card 1
        device 7 }

pcm.hdmi2 {
        type hw
        card 1
        device 8 }
```

!!Aplay/Arecord output
!!------------

APLAY

**** List of PLAYBACK Hardware Devices ****
card 0: PCH [HDA Intel PCH], device 0: STAC92xx Analog [STAC92xx Analog]
  Subdevices: 1/1
  Subdevice #0: subdevice #0
card 1: NVidia [HDA NVidia], device 3: HDMI 0 [HDMI 0]
  Subdevices: 1/1
  Subdevice #0: subdevice #0
card 1: NVidia [HDA NVidia], device 7: HDMI 1 [HDMI 1]
  Subdevices: 1/1
  Subdevice #0: subdevice #0
card 1: NVidia [HDA NVidia], device 8: HDMI 2 [HDMI 2]
  Subdevices: 1/1
  Subdevice #0: subdevice #0

ARECORD

**** List of CAPTURE Hardware Devices ****
card 0: PCH [HDA Intel PCH], device 0: STAC92xx Analog [STAC92xx Analog]
  Subdevices: 1/1
  Subdevice #0: subdevice #0

!!Amixer output
!!-------------

!!-------Mixer controls for card 0 [PCH]

Card hw:0 'PCH'/'HDA Intel PCH at 0xe6e60000 irq 47'
  Mixer name   : 'IDT 92HD90BXX'
  Components   : 'HDA:111d76e7,10280494,00100102'
  Controls   : 19
  Simple ctrls : 10
Simple mixer control 'Master',0
  Capabilities: pvolume pvolume-joined pswitch pswitch-joined penum
  Playback channels: Mono
  Limits: Playback 0 - 64
  Mono: Playback 62 [97%] [-1.50dB] [on]
Simple mixer control 'Headphone',0

```
  Capabilities: pvolume pswitch penum
  Playback channels: Front Left - Front Right
  Limits: Playback 0 - 64
  Mono:
  Front Left: Playback 64 [100%] [0.00dB] [on]
  Front Right: Playback 64 [100%] [0.00dB] [on]
Simple mixer control 'PCM',0
  Capabilities: pvolume penum
  Playback channels: Front Left - Front Right
  Limits: Playback 0 - 255
  Mono:
  Front Left: Playback 254 [100%] [0.20dB]
  Front Right: Playback 254 [100%] [0.20dB]
Simple mixer control 'Front',0
  Capabilities: pvolume pswitch penum
  Playback channels: Front Left - Front Right
  Limits: Playback 0 - 64
  Mono:
  Front Left: Playback 64 [100%] [0.00dB] [on]
  Front Right: Playback 64 [100%] [0.00dB] [on]
Simple mixer control 'Mic',0
  Capabilities: cvolume penum
  Capture channels: Front Left - Front Right
  Limits: Capture 0 - 3
  Front Left: Capture 1 [33%] [10.00dB]
  Front Right: Capture 1 [33%] [10.00dB]
Simple mixer control 'Mic Jack Mode',0
  Capabilities: enum
  Items: 'Mic In' 'Line In'
  Item0: 'Mic In'
Simple mixer control 'Beep',0
  Capabilities: pvolume pvolume-joined pswitch pswitch-joined penum
  Playback channels: Mono
  Limits: Playback 0 - 3
  Mono: Playback 1 [33%] [-12.00dB] [on]
Simple mixer control 'Capture',0
  Capabilities: cvolume cswitch penum
  Capture channels: Front Left - Front Right
  Limits: Capture 0 - 46
  Front Left: Capture 46 [100%] [30.00dB] [on]
  Front Right: Capture 46 [100%] [30.00dB] [on]
Simple mixer control 'Dock Mic',0
  Capabilities: cvolume penum
  Capture channels: Front Left - Front Right
  Limits: Capture 0 - 3
  Front Left: Capture 0 [0%] [0.00dB]
  Front Right: Capture 0 [0%] [0.00dB]
Simple mixer control 'Internal Mic',0
  Capabilities: cvolume penum
  Capture channels: Front Left - Front Right
  Limits: Capture 0 - 3
  Front Left: Capture 0 [0%] [0.00dB]
```

```
   Front Right: Capture 0 [0%] [0.00dB]

!!-------Mixer controls for card 1 [NVidia]

Card hw:1 'NVidia'/'HDA NVidia at 0xe5080000 irq 17'
   Mixer name    : 'Nvidia GPU 1c HDMI/DP'
   Components    : 'HDA:10de001c,10281494,00100100'
   Controls      : 18
   Simple ctrls  : 3
Simple mixer control 'IEC958',0
   Capabilities: pswitch pswitch-joined penum
   Playback channels: Mono
   Mono: Playback [on]
Simple mixer control 'IEC958',1
   Capabilities: pswitch pswitch-joined penum
   Playback channels: Mono
   Mono: Playback [off]
Simple mixer control 'IEC958',2
   Capabilities: pswitch pswitch-joined penum
   Playback channels: Mono
   Mono: Playback [off]

!!Alsactl output
!!-------------

--startcollapse--
state.PCH {
        control.1 {
                iface MIXER
                name 'Front Playback Volume'
                value.0 64
                value.1 64
                comment {
                        access 'read write'
                        type INTEGER
                        count 2
                        range '0 - 64'
                        dbmin -4800
                        dbmax 0
                        dbvalue.0 0
                        dbvalue.1 0
                }
        }
...
```

Applications Using ALSA

Many applications can directly use ALSA by using the appropriate command-line arguments.

MPlayer

To play a file to an ALSA device using MPlayer, use code such as the following:

```
mplayer -ao alsa:device=hw=1.0 -srate 48000  bryan.mp3
```

VLC

To play a file to an ALSA device using VLC, use code such as the following:

```
vlc --aout alsa ...
```

TiMidity

To play a file to an ALSA device using TiMidity, use code such as the following:

```
timidity -Os ...
```

Programming ALSA

There are several tutorials about programming ALSA, including "A Tutorial on Using the ALSA Audio API" (http://equalarea.com/paul/alsa-audio.html) by Paul Davis (who is the lead on Jack).

You can find an overview of the API at www.alsa-project.org/alsa-doc/alsa-lib/pcm.html. Jeff Tranter has an "Introduction to Sound Programming with ALSA." The ALSA API is large and complex, and it is not always clear how it all hangs together or what part to use where. From the ALSA library API (www.alsa-project.org/main/index.php/ALSA_Library_API).

The currently designed interfaces are as follows:

- Information interface (/proc/asound)
- Control interface (/dev/snd/controlCX)
- Mixer interface (/dev/snd/mixerCXDX)
- PCM interface (/dev/snd/pcmCXDX)
- Raw MIDI interface (/dev/snd/midiCXDX)
- Sequencer interface (/dev/snd/seq)
- Timer interface (/dev/snd/timer)

The Information interface is what ALSA uses for device information and for some control purposes.

The Control interface is used to adjust volumes and other control functions that the sound card offers.

The Mixer interface allows applications to share the use of audio devices in a transparent manner and is one of the major features of ALSA.

The PCM interface allows the definition of virtual and hardware devices via a configuration mechanism. It is the usual interface for digital audio applications.

The raw MIDI interface is used for low-level interaction with MIDI devices and deals directly with MIDI events.

The Sequencer interface is used for MIDI applications at a higher level than the raw MIDI interface.

The Timer interface is designed to use internal timers in sound hardware and allows synchronization of sound events.

Hardware Device Information

Finding information about hardware cards and devices is a multistep operation. The hardware cards first have to be identified. This is done using the Control interface (www.alsa-project.org/alsa-doc/alsa-lib/group___control.html) functions. The ones used are as follows:

```
snd_card_next
snd_ctl_open
snd_ctl_pcm_next_device
snd_ctl_card_info_get_id
snd_ctl_card_info_get_name
```

Cards are identified by an integer from 0 upward. The next card number is found using snd_card_next, and the first card is found using a seed value of -1. The card is then opened using its ALSA name such as hw:0, hw:1, and so on, by snd_ctl_open, which fills in a handle value. In turn, this handle is used to fill in card information using snd_ctl_card_info, and fields are extracted from that using functions such as snd_ctl_card_info_get_name. In the program that follows, this gives information such as the following:

```
card 0: PCH [HDA Intel PCH]
```

For further information, you need to switch to the PCM functions for the card. The function linking the control and PCM interfaces is snd_ctl_pcm_info, which fills in a structure of type snd_pcm_info_t with PCM-related information. Unfortunately, this function is documented neither in the Control interface nor the PCM interface sections of the ALSA documentation but is instead in the Files section under control.c. The structure snd_pcm_info_t is barely documented in the PCM interface (www.alsa-project.org/alsa-doc/alsa-lib/group___p_c_m.html#g2226bdcc6e780543beaadc319332e37b) section and has only a few fields of interest. (See this site for the structure: www.qnx.com/developers/docs/6.4.0/neutrino/audio/libs/snd_pcm_info_t.html.) These fields are accessed using the PCM functions snd_pcm_info_get_id and snd_pcm_info_get_name.

The main value of the snd_pcm_info_t structure is that it is the principal parameter into the functions of the PCM stream (www.alsa-project.org/alsa-doc/alsa-lib/group___p_c_m___info.html). In particular, this allows you to get devices and subdevices and information about them.

The program to find and display card and hardware device information is aplay-1.c, as shown here:

```
/**
 * aplay-1.c
 *
 * Code from aplay.c
 *
 * does the same as aplay -1
 * http://alsa-utils.sourcearchive.com/documentation/1.0.15/aplay_8c-source.html
 */

/*
 * Original notice:
 *
 *  Copyright (c) by Jaroslav Kysela <perex@perex.cz>
 *  Based on vplay program by Michael Beck
 *
 *
 *   This program is free software; you can redistribute it and/or modify
 *   it under the terms of the GNU General Public License as published by
```

```
 *    the Free Software Foundation; either version 2 of the License, or
 *    (at your option) any later version.
 *
 *    This program is distributed in the hope that it will be useful,
 *    but WITHOUT ANY WARRANTY; without even the implied warranty of
 *    MERCHANTABILITY or FITNESS FOR A PARTICULAR PURPOSE.  See the
 *    GNU General Public License for more details.
 *
 *    You should have received a copy of the GNU General Public License
 *    along with this program; if not, write to the Free Software
 *    Foundation, Inc., 59 Temple Place, Suite 330, Boston, MA   02111-1307 USA
 *
 */

#include <stdio.h>
#include <stdlib.h>
#include <alsa/asoundlib.h>
#include <locale.h>

// used by gettext for i18n, not needed here
#define _(STR) STR

static void device_list(snd_pcm_stream_t stream)
{
      snd_ctl_t *handle;
      int card, err, dev, idx;
      snd_ctl_card_info_t *info;
      snd_pcm_info_t *pcminfo;
      snd_ctl_card_info_alloca(&info);
      snd_pcm_info_alloca(&pcminfo);

      card = -1;
      if (snd_card_next(&card) < 0 || card < 0) {
            error(_("no soundcards found..."));
            return;
      }
      printf(_("**** List of %s Hardware Devices ****\n"),
            snd_pcm_stream_name(stream));
      while (card >= 0) {
            char name[32];
            sprintf(name, "hw:%d", card);
            if ((err = snd_ctl_open(&handle, name, 0)) < 0) {
                  error("control open (%i): %s", card, snd_strerror(err));
                  goto next_card;
            }
            if ((err = snd_ctl_card_info(handle, info)) < 0) {
                  error("control hardware info (%i): %s", card, snd_strerror(err));
                  snd_ctl_close(handle);
                  goto next_card;
            }
            dev = -1;
            while (1) {
```

```
                    unsigned int count;
                    if (snd_ctl_pcm_next_device(handle, &dev)<0)
                            error("snd_ctl_pcm_next_device");
                    if (dev < 0)
                            break;
                    snd_pcm_info_set_device(pcminfo, dev);
                    snd_pcm_info_set_subdevice(pcminfo, 0);
                    snd_pcm_info_set_stream(pcminfo, stream);
                    if ((err = snd_ctl_pcm_info(handle, pcminfo)) < 0) {
                            if (err != -ENOENT)
                                    error("control digital audio info (%i): %s", card, snd_
                                    strerror(err));
                            continue;
                    }
                    printf(_("card %i: [%s,%i] %s [%s], device %i: %s [%s]\n"),
                            card, name, dev, snd_ctl_card_info_get_id(info), snd_ctl_card_info_
                            get_name(info),
                            dev,
                            snd_pcm_info_get_id(pcminfo),
                            snd_pcm_info_get_name(pcminfo));
                    count = snd_pcm_info_get_subdevices_count(pcminfo);
                    printf( _("  Subdevices: %i/%i\n"),
                            snd_pcm_info_get_subdevices_avail(pcminfo), count);
                    for (idx = 0; idx < (int)count; idx++) {
                            snd_pcm_info_set_subdevice(pcminfo, idx);
                            if ((err = snd_ctl_pcm_info(handle, pcminfo)) < 0) {
                                    error("control digital audio playback info (%i): %s", card,
                                    snd_strerror(err));
                            } else {
                                    printf(_("  Subdevice #%i: %s\n"),
                                            idx, snd_pcm_info_get_subdevice_name(pcminfo));
                            }
                    }
            }
            snd_ctl_close(handle);
        next_card:
            if (snd_card_next(&card) < 0) {
                    error("snd_card_next");
                    break;
            }
        }
    }

main (int argc, char *argv[])
{
    device_list(SND_PCM_STREAM_CAPTURE);
    device_list(SND_PCM_STREAM_PLAYBACK);
}
```

The following is the output from running aplay-l on my system:

```
**** List of CAPTURE Hardware Devices ****
card 0: [hw:0,0] PCH [HDA Intel PCH], device 0: STAC92xx Analog [STAC92xx Analog]
  Subdevices: 1/1
  Subdevice #0: subdevice #0
**** List of PLAYBACK Hardware Devices ****
card 0: [hw:0,0] PCH [HDA Intel PCH], device 0: STAC92xx Analog [STAC92xx Analog]
  Subdevices: 1/1
  Subdevice #0: subdevice #0
card 1: [hw:1,3] NVidia [HDA NVidia], device 3: HDMI 0 [HDMI 0]
  Subdevices: 1/1
  Subdevice #0: subdevice #0
card 1: [hw:1,7] NVidia [HDA NVidia], device 7: HDMI 1 [HDMI 1]
  Subdevices: 1/1
  Subdevice #0: subdevice #0
card 1: [hw:1,8] NVidia [HDA NVidia], device 8: HDMI 2 [HDMI 2]
  Subdevices: 1/1
  Subdevice #0: subdevice #0
```

PCM Device Information

You can get PCM alias information from the devices by using aplay -L. This uses the "hints" mechanism from the device API. Note that the program is responsible for freeing memory allocated by the ALSA library. This means that if a string or table is returned, then not only do you have to walk through the string/table but you have to retain a pointer to the start of the string/table so that it can be freed.

The source for this is aplay-L.c, as shown here:

```
/**
 * aplay-L.c
 *
 * Code from aplay.c
 * does aplay -L
 * http://alsa-utils.sourcearchive.com/documentation/1.0.15/aplay_8c-source.html
 */


/*
 * Original notice:
 *
 *  Copyright (c) by Jaroslav Kysela <perex@perex.cz>
 *  Based on vplay program by Michael Beck
 *
 *
 *    This program is free software; you can redistribute it and/or modify
 *    it under the terms of the GNU General Public License as published by
 *    the Free Software Foundation; either version 2 of the License, or
 *    (at your option) any later version.
 *
 *    This program is distributed in the hope that it will be useful,
 *    but WITHOUT ANY WARRANTY; without even the implied warranty of
 *    MERCHANTABILITY or FITNESS FOR A PARTICULAR PURPOSE.  See the
 *    GNU General Public License for more details.
 *
```

```
 *    You should have received a copy of the GNU General Public License
 *    along with this program; if not, write to the Free Software
 *    Foundation, Inc., 59 Temple Place, Suite 330, Boston, MA  02111-1307 USA
 *
 */

#include <stdio.h>
#include <stdlib.h>
#include <alsa/asoundlib.h>
#include <locale.h>

#define _(STR) STR

static void pcm_list(snd_pcm_stream_t stream )
{
        void **hints, **n;
        char *name, *descr, *descr1, *io;
        const char *filter;

        if (snd_device_name_hint(-1, "pcm", &hints) < 0)
                return;
        n = hints;
        filter = stream == SND_PCM_STREAM_CAPTURE ? "Input" : "Output";
        while (*n != NULL) {
                name = snd_device_name_get_hint(*n, "NAME");
                descr = snd_device_name_get_hint(*n, "DESC");
                io = snd_device_name_get_hint(*n, "IOID");
                if (io != NULL && strcmp(io, filter) == 0)
                        goto __end;
                printf("%s\n", name);
                if ((descr1 = descr) != NULL) {
                        printf("    ");
                        while (*descr1) {
                                if (*descr1 == '\n')
                                        printf("\n    ");
                                else
                                        putchar(*descr1);
                                descr1++;
                        }
                        putchar('\n');
                }
                __end:
                        if (name != NULL)
                                free(name);
                if (descr != NULL)
                        free(descr);
                if (io != NULL)
                        free(io);
                n++;
        }
        snd_device_name_free_hint(hints);
}
```

```
main (int argc, char *argv[])
{
  printf("********** CAPTURE **********\n");
  pcm_list(SND_PCM_STREAM_CAPTURE);

  printf("\n\n********** PLAYBACK **********\n");
  pcm_list(SND_PCM_STREAM_PLAYBACK);
}
```

The following is the output from running aplay-L on my system:

```
********** CAPTURE **********
default
    Default
sysdefault:CARD=PCH
    HDA Intel PCH, STAC92xx Analog
    Default Audio Device
front:CARD=PCH,DEV=0
    HDA Intel PCH, STAC92xx Analog
    Front speakers
surround40:CARD=PCH,DEV=0
    HDA Intel PCH, STAC92xx Analog
    4.0 Surround output to Front and Rear speakers
surround41:CARD=PCH,DEV=0
    HDA Intel PCH, STAC92xx Analog
    4.1 Surround output to Front, Rear and Subwoofer speakers
surround50:CARD=PCH,DEV=0
    HDA Intel PCH, STAC92xx Analog
    5.0 Surround output to Front, Center and Rear speakers
surround51:CARD=PCH,DEV=0
    HDA Intel PCH, STAC92xx Analog
    5.1 Surround output to Front, Center, Rear and Subwoofer speakers
surround71:CARD=PCH,DEV=0
    HDA Intel PCH, STAC92xx Analog
    7.1 Surround output to Front, Center, Side, Rear and Woofer speakers
hdmi:CARD=NVidia,DEV=0
    HDA NVidia, HDMI 0
    HDMI Audio Output
hdmi:CARD=NVidia,DEV=1
    HDA NVidia, HDMI 1
    HDMI Audio Output
hdmi:CARD=NVidia,DEV=2
    HDA NVidia, HDMI 2
    HDMI Audio Output

********** PLAYBACK **********
null
    Discard all samples (playback) or generate zero samples (capture)
pulse
    PulseAudio Sound Server
default
    Default
```

```
sysdefault:CARD=PCH
    HDA Intel PCH, STAC92xx Analog
    Default Audio Device
front:CARD=PCH,DEV=0
    HDA Intel PCH, STAC92xx Analog
    Front speakers
surround40:CARD=PCH,DEV=0
    HDA Intel PCH, STAC92xx Analog
    4.0 Surround output to Front and Rear speakers
surround41:CARD=PCH,DEV=0
    HDA Intel PCH, STAC92xx Analog
    4.1 Surround output to Front, Rear and Subwoofer speakers
surround50:CARD=PCH,DEV=0
    HDA Intel PCH, STAC92xx Analog
    5.0 Surround output to Front, Center and Rear speakers
surround51:CARD=PCH,DEV=0
    HDA Intel PCH, STAC92xx Analog
    5.1 Surround output to Front, Center, Rear and Subwoofer speakers
surround71:CARD=PCH,DEV=0
    HDA Intel PCH, STAC92xx Analog
    7.1 Surround output to Front, Center, Side, Rear and Woofer speakers
```

Note that this does not include the "plug" devices such as plughw:0. The list of plug devices does not seem to be accessible.

Configuration Space Information

In addition to general characteristics, each PCM device is able to support a range of parameters such as the number of channels, sampling rates, and so on. The full set and range of parameters form the "configuration space" of each device. For example, a device may support between two and six channels and a number of different sampling rates. These two parameters form a two-dimensional space. The full set forms an n-dimensional space.

ALSA has functions to query this space and to set values within this space. The space is initialized by snd_pcm_hw_params_any. To find the possible values of parameters, there are functions called snd_pcm_hw_params_get and so on.

The different parameters are as follows:

Channels

> This is the number of channels supported (zero for mono, and so on).

Rate

> This is the sampling rate in hertz, that is, samples per second. Typically CD audio has a sampling rate of 44,100Hz per channel so that each channel has 44,100 samples per second.

Frames

> Each frame contains one sample for each channel. Stereo audio will contain two samples in each frame. The frame rate is the same as the sampling rate. That is, suppose the sampling rate for stereo audio is 44,100Hz. Then each channel will have 44,100 samples per second. But there will also be 44,100 frames per second so that the overall density of the two channels will be 88,200 samples per second.

Period time

>This is the time in microseconds between hardware interrupts to refresh the buffer.

Period size

>This is the number of frames in between each hardware interrupt. These are related in the following way:

```
Period time = period size x time per frame
            = period size x time per sample
            = period size / sampling rate
```

So, for example, if the sampling rate is 48000Hz stereo and the period size is 8,192 frames, then the time between hardware interrupts is 8192 / 48000 seconds = 170.5 milliseconds.

Periods

>This is the number of periods per buffer.

Buffer time

>This is the time for one buffer.

Buffer size

>This is the size of the buffer in frames. Again, there is a relationship.

```
Time of one buffer = buffer size in frames x time for one frame
                   = buffer size x number of channels x time for one sample
                   = buffer size x number of channels / sample rate
```

The buffer size should be a multiple of the period size and is typically twice as big.

For further examples, see FramesPeriods (www.alsa-project.org/main/index.php/FramesPeriods).

The following is a program to find the range of values of various parameters from the initial state; it is called device-info.c:

```c
/**
 * Jan Newmarch
 */

#include <stdio.h>
#include <stdlib.h>
#include <alsa/asoundlib.h>

void info(char *dev_name, snd_pcm_stream_t stream) {
  snd_pcm_hw_params_t *hw_params;
  int err;
  snd_pcm_t *handle;
  unsigned int max;
  unsigned int min;
  unsigned int val;
  unsigned int dir;
  snd_pcm_uframes_t frames;
```

```
if ((err = snd_pcm_open (&handle, dev_name, stream, 0)) < 0) {
  fprintf (stderr, "cannot open audio device %s (%s)\n",
            dev_name,
            snd_strerror (err));
  return;
}

if ((err = snd_pcm_hw_params_malloc (&hw_params)) < 0) {
  fprintf (stderr, "cannot allocate hardware parameter structure (%s)\n",
            snd_strerror (err));
  exit (1);
}

if ((err = snd_pcm_hw_params_any (handle, hw_params)) < 0) {
  fprintf (stderr, "cannot initialize hardware parameter structure (%s)\n",
            snd_strerror (err));
  exit (1);
}

if ((err = snd_pcm_hw_params_get_channels_max(hw_params, &max)) < 0) {
  fprintf (stderr, "cannot  (%s)\n",
            snd_strerror (err));
  exit (1);
}
printf("max channels %d\n", max);

if ((err = snd_pcm_hw_params_get_channels_min(hw_params, &min)) < 0) {
  fprintf (stderr, "cannot get channel info  (%s)\n",
            snd_strerror (err));
  exit (1);
}
printf("min channels %d\n", min);

/*
if ((err = snd_pcm_hw_params_get_sbits(hw_params)) < 0) {
    fprintf (stderr, "cannot get bits info  (%s)\n",
              snd_strerror (err));
    exit (1);
}
printf("bits %d\n", err);
*/

if ((err = snd_pcm_hw_params_get_rate_min(hw_params, &val, &dir)) < 0) {
  fprintf (stderr, "cannot get min rate (%s)\n",
            snd_strerror (err));
  exit (1);
}
printf("min rate %d hz\n", val);

if ((err = snd_pcm_hw_params_get_rate_max(hw_params, &val, &dir)) < 0) {
  fprintf (stderr, "cannot get max rate (%s)\n",
            snd_strerror (err));
```

```
  exit (1);
}
printf("max rate %d hz\n", val);

if ((err = snd_pcm_hw_params_get_period_time_min(hw_params, &val, &dir)) < 0) {
  fprintf (stderr, "cannot get min period time  (%s)\n",
           snd_strerror (err));
  exit (1);
}
printf("min period time %d usecs\n", val);

if ((err = snd_pcm_hw_params_get_period_time_max(hw_params, &val, &dir)) < 0) {
  fprintf (stderr, "cannot  get max period time  (%s)\n",
           snd_strerror (err));
  exit (1);
}
printf("max period time %d usecs\n", val);

if ((err = snd_pcm_hw_params_get_period_size_min(hw_params, &frames, &dir)) < 0) {
  fprintf (stderr, "cannot  get min period size  (%s)\n",
           snd_strerror (err));
  exit (1);
}
printf("min period size in frames %d\n", frames);

if ((err = snd_pcm_hw_params_get_period_size_max(hw_params, &frames, &dir)) < 0) {
  fprintf (stderr, "cannot  get max period size (%s)\n",
           snd_strerror (err));
  exit (1);
}
printf("max period size in frames %d\n", frames);

if ((err = snd_pcm_hw_params_get_periods_min(hw_params, &val, &dir)) < 0) {
  fprintf (stderr, "cannot  get min periods  (%s)\n",
           snd_strerror (err));
  exit (1);
}
printf("min periods per buffer %d\n", val);

if ((err = snd_pcm_hw_params_get_periods_max(hw_params, &val, &dir)) < 0) {
  fprintf (stderr, "cannot  get min periods (%s)\n",
           snd_strerror (err));
  exit (1);
}
printf("max periods per buffer %d\n", val);

if ((err = snd_pcm_hw_params_get_buffer_time_min(hw_params, &val, &dir)) < 0) {
  fprintf (stderr, "cannot get min buffer time (%s)\n",
           snd_strerror (err));
  exit (1);
}
printf("min buffer time %d usecs\n", val);
```

```
  if ((err = snd_pcm_hw_params_get_buffer_time_max(hw_params, &val, &dir)) < 0) {
    fprintf (stderr, "cannot get max buffer time  (%s)\n",
             snd_strerror (err));
    exit (1);
  }
  printf("max buffer time %d usecs\n", val);

  if ((err = snd_pcm_hw_params_get_buffer_size_min(hw_params, &frames)) < 0) {
    fprintf (stderr, "cannot get min buffer size (%s)\n",
             snd_strerror (err));
    exit (1);
  }
  printf("min buffer size in frames %d\n", frames);

  if ((err = snd_pcm_hw_params_get_buffer_size_max(hw_params, &frames)) < 0) {
    fprintf (stderr, "cannot get max buffer size  (%s)\n",
             snd_strerror (err));
    exit (1);
  }
  printf("max buffer size in frames %d\n", frames);
}

main (int argc, char *argv[])
{
  int i;
  int err;
  int buf[128];
  FILE *fin;
  size_t nread;
  unsigned int rate = 44100;

  if (argc != 2) {
    fprintf(stderr, "Usage: %s card\n", argv[0]);
    exit(1);
  }

  printf("********** CAPTURE **********\n");
  info(argv[1], SND_PCM_STREAM_CAPTURE);

  printf("********** PLAYBACK **********\n");
  info(argv[1], SND_PCM_STREAM_PLAYBACK);

  exit (0);
}
```

The following is the output from device-info hw:0 on my system:

```
********** CAPTURE **********
max channels 2
min channels 2
min rate 44100 hz
max rate 192000 hz
```

```
min period time 83 usecs
max period time 11888617 usecs
min period size in frames 16
max period size in frames 524288
min periods per buffer 2
max periods per buffer 32
min buffer time 166 usecs
max buffer time 23777234 usecs
min buffer size in frames 32
max buffer size in frames 1048576
********** PLAYBACK **********
max channels 2
min channels 2
min rate 44100 hz
max rate 192000 hz
min period time 83 usecs
max period time 11888617 usecs
min period size in frames 16
max period size in frames 524288
min periods per buffer 2
max periods per buffer 32
min buffer time 166 usecs
max buffer time 23777234 usecs
min buffer size in frames 32
max buffer size in frames 1048576
```

This program works with any ALSA device, including the "plug" devices. The following output from device-info plughw:0 shows how the software wrapper can give a wider range of possible values:

```
********** CAPTURE **********
max channels 10000
min channels 1
min rate 4000 hz
max rate -1 hz
min period time 83 usecs
max period time 11888617 usecs
min period size in frames 0
max period size in frames -1
min periods per buffer 0
max periods per buffer -1
min buffer time 1 usecs
max buffer time -1 usecs
min buffer size in frames 1
max buffer size in frames -2
********** PLAYBACK **********
max channels 10000
min channels 1
min rate 4000 hz
max rate -1 hz
min period time 83 usecs
max period time 11888617 usecs
min period size in frames 0
```

```
max period size in frames -1
min periods per buffer 0
max periods per buffer -1
min buffer time 1 usecs
max buffer time -1 usecs
min buffer size in frames 1
max buffer size in frames -2
```

It can also be run with alias devices, such as device-info surround40.

ALSA Initialization

A line-by-line breakdown is at (http://soundprogramming.net/programming_apis/alsa_tutorial_1_initialization). It explains much of the common code in the programs that follow.

Capture Audio to a File

The following program is from Paul Davis's "A Tutorial on Using the ALSA Audio API" (http://equalarea.com/paul/alsa-audio.html):

```
/**
 * alsa_capture.c
 */

/* Copyright © 2002
 * Paul Davis
 * under the GPL license
 */

/**
 * Paul Davis
 * http://equalarea.com/paul/alsa-audio.html#howto
 */

/**
 * Jan Newmarch
 */

#include <stdio.h>
#include <stdlib.h>
#include <alsa/asoundlib.h>
#include <signal.h>

#define BUFSIZE 128
#define RATE 44100

FILE *fout = NULL;

/*
 * quit on ctrl-c
```

```
 */
void sigint(int sig) {
  if (fout != NULL) {
    fclose(fout);
  }
  exit(1);
}

main (int argc, char *argv[])
{
  int i;
  int err;
  short buf[BUFSIZE];
  snd_pcm_t *capture_handle;
  snd_pcm_hw_params_t *hw_params;
  snd_pcm_format_t rate = RATE;
  int nread;

  if (argc != 3) {
    fprintf(stderr, "Usage: %s cardname file\n", argv[0]);
    exit(1);
  }

  if ((fout = fopen(argv[2], "w")) == NULL) {
    fprintf(stderr, "Can't open %s for writing\n", argv[2]);
    exit(1);
  }

  signal(SIGINT, sigint);

  if ((err = snd_pcm_open (&capture_handle, argv[1], SND_PCM_STREAM_CAPTURE, 0)) < 0) {
    fprintf (stderr, "cannot open audio device %s (%s)\n",
             argv[1],
             snd_strerror (err));
    exit (1);
  }

  if ((err = snd_pcm_hw_params_malloc (&hw_params)) < 0) {
    fprintf (stderr, "cannot allocate hardware parameter structure (%s)\n",
             snd_strerror (err));
    exit (1);
  }

  if ((err = snd_pcm_hw_params_any (capture_handle, hw_params)) < 0) {
    fprintf (stderr, "cannot initialize hardware parameter structure (%s)\n",
             snd_strerror (err));
    exit (1);
  }

  if ((err = snd_pcm_hw_params_set_access (capture_handle, hw_params, SND_PCM_ACCESS_RW_
  INTERLEAVED)) < 0) {
    fprintf (stderr, "cannot set access type (%s)\n",
```

```
                    snd_strerror (err));
    exit (1);
}

if ((err = snd_pcm_hw_params_set_format (capture_handle, hw_params, SND_PCM_FORMAT_S16_
LE)) < 0) {
  fprintf (stderr, "cannot set sample format (%s)\n",
                snd_strerror (err));
  exit (1);
}

if ((err = snd_pcm_hw_params_set_rate_near (capture_handle, hw_params, &rate, 0)) < 0) {
  fprintf (stderr, "cannot set sample rate (%s)\n",
                snd_strerror (err));
  exit (1);
}
fprintf(stderr, "rate set to %d\n", rate);

if ((err = snd_pcm_hw_params_set_channels (capture_handle, hw_params, 2)) < 0) {
  fprintf (stderr, "cannot set channel count (%s)\n",
                snd_strerror (err));
  exit (1);
}

if ((err = snd_pcm_hw_params (capture_handle, hw_params)) < 0) {
  fprintf (stderr, "cannot set parameters (%s)\n",
                snd_strerror (err));
  exit (1);
}

snd_pcm_hw_params_free (hw_params);

/*
if ((err = snd_pcm_prepare (capture_handle)) < 0) {
  fprintf (stderr, "cannot prepare audio interface for use (%s)\n",
                snd_strerror (err));
  exit (1);
}
*/

while (1) {
  if ((nread = snd_pcm_readi (capture_handle, buf, BUFSIZE)) < 0) {
    fprintf (stderr, "read from audio interface failed (%s)\n",
                snd_strerror (err));
    /* recover */
    snd_pcm_prepare(capture_handle);
  } else {
    fwrite(buf, sizeof(short), nread, fout);
  }
}
```

```
  snd_pcm_close (capture_handle);
  exit(0);
}
```

Playback Audio from a File

To capture or play audio, a device must first be opened as in previous examples. A configuration space is then created, and the space is narrowed by setting values on the various parameters. The access type determines whether the samples are interleaved or not. The format determines the size of samples and whether they are little- or big-endian. All of these will return an error if the requested value cannot be set.

Some parameters need care when setting them. For example, there is a range of possible values for the sampling rate, but not all of these may be supported. A particular rate may be requested using snd_pcm_hw_params_set_rate. But if a requested rate is not possible, then an error will be returned. There are several ways of avoiding this.

- Try a number of rates until you get one that is supported.

- Test whether a rate is supported with snd_pcm_hw_params_test_rate.

- Request ALSA to give the nearest supported rate with snd_pcm_hw_params_set_rate_near. The actual rate chosen is set in the rate parameter.

- Instead of a hardware device such as hw:0, use a plug device such as plughw:0, which will support many more values by resampling.

Finally, once parameters are set for the configuration space, the restricted space is installed onto the device by snd_pcm_hw_params.

The calls on PCM devices will cause state changes to take place in the device. After opening, the device is in the state SND_PCM_STATE_OPEN. After setting the hardware configuration, the device is in the state SND_PCM_STATE_PREPARE. Applications can use the snd_pcm_start call to write or read data. The state may drop to SND_PCM_STATE_XRUN if an overrun or underrun occurs, and then a call to snd_pcm_prepare is needed to restore it to SND_PCM_STATE_PREPARE.

The call to readi reads interlaced data.

The following program is from Paul Davis's "A Tutorial on Using the ALSA Audio API" (http://equalarea.com/paul/alsa-audio.html):

```
/**
 * alsa_playback.c
 */


/*
 * Copyright © 2002
 * Paul Davis
 * under the GPL license
 */


/**
 * Paul Davis
 * http://equalarea.com/paul/alsa-audio.html#howto
 */


/**
 * Jan Newmarch
 */
```

```c
#include <stdio.h>
#include <stdlib.h>
#include <alsa/asoundlib.h>

main (int argc, char *argv[])
{
  int i;
  int err;
  int buf[128];
  snd_pcm_t *playback_handle;
  snd_pcm_hw_params_t *hw_params;
  FILE *fin;
  size_t nread;
  unsigned int rate = 44100;

  if (argc != 3) {
    fprintf(stderr, "Usage: %s card file\n", argv[0]);
    exit(1);
  }

  if ((err = snd_pcm_open (&playback_handle, argv[1], SND_PCM_STREAM_PLAYBACK, 0)) < 0) {
    fprintf (stderr, "cannot open audio device %s (%s)\n",
             argv[1],
             snd_strerror (err));
    exit (1);
  }

  if ((err = snd_pcm_hw_params_malloc (&hw_params)) < 0) {
    fprintf (stderr, "cannot allocate hardware parameter structure (%s)\n",
             snd_strerror (err));
    exit (1);
  }

  if ((err = snd_pcm_hw_params_any (playback_handle, hw_params)) < 0) {
    fprintf (stderr, "cannot initialize hardware parameter structure (%s)\n",
             snd_strerror (err));
    exit (1);
  }

  if ((err = snd_pcm_hw_params_set_access (playback_handle, hw_params, SND_PCM_ACCESS_RW_
INTERLEAVED)) < 0) {
    fprintf (stderr, "cannot set access type (%s)\n",
             snd_strerror (err));
    exit (1);
  }

  if ((err = snd_pcm_hw_params_set_format (playback_handle, hw_params, SND_PCM_FORMAT_S16_
LE)) < 0) {
    fprintf (stderr, "cannot set sample format (%s)\n",
             snd_strerror (err));
    exit (1);
  }
```

```
  if ((err = snd_pcm_hw_params_set_rate_near (playback_handle, hw_params, &rate, 0)) < 0) {
    fprintf (stderr, "cannot set sample rate (%s)\n",
             snd_strerror (err));
    exit (1);
  }
printf("Rate set to %d\n", rate);

  if ((err = snd_pcm_hw_params_set_channels (playback_handle, hw_params, 2)) < 0) {
    fprintf (stderr, "cannot set channel count (%s)\n",
             snd_strerror (err));
    exit (1);
  }

  if ((err = snd_pcm_hw_params (playback_handle, hw_params)) < 0) {
    fprintf (stderr, "cannot set parameters (%s)\n",
             snd_strerror (err));
    exit (1);
  }

snd_pcm_hw_params_free (hw_params);

/*
if ((err = snd_pcm_prepare (playback_handle)) < 0) {
  fprintf (stderr, "cannot prepare audio interface for use (%s)\n",
           snd_strerror (err));
  exit (1);
}
*/

  if ((fin = fopen(argv[2], "r")) == NULL) {
      fprintf(stderr, "Can't open %s for reading\n", argv[2]);
      exit(1);
  }

while ((nread = fread(buf, sizeof(int), 128, fin)) > 0) {
  //printf("writing\n");
  if ((err = snd_pcm_writei w(playback_handle, buf, nread)) != nread) {
    fprintf (stderr, "write to audio interface failed (%s)\n",
             snd_strerror (err));
    snd_pcm_prepare(playback_handle);
  }
}alsa_capture.c

snd_pcm_drain(playback_handle);
snd_pcm_close (playback_handle);
exit (0);
}
```

Check that the microphone is enabled using alsamixer. Record by doing the following:

```
alsa_capture hw:0 tmp.s16
```

Play back by doing the following:

```
sox -c 2 -r 44100 tmp.s16 tmp.wav
mplayer tmp.wav
```

or by using the next program:

```
alsa_playback hw:0 tmp.s16
```

Using Interrupts

The previous programs relied on ALSA to manage the devices. The call snd_pcm_writei will block until all frames are played or put into the playback ring buffer. This will be adequate for many uses. If you want to get finer control, then it is possible to set thresholds for how many frames a device can handle and then wait for that threshold to be reached. ALSA will cause a kernel interrupt to be generated when the threshold is reached, at which point the wait will terminate and the program can continue.

A program illustrating this is given in "A Tutorial on Using the ALSA Audio API" (http://equalarea.com/paul/alsa-audio.html).

Managing Latency

In the ALSA source distribution is a program /test/latency.c. This can be run with various parameters to test the latency of your system. *Warning: turn your volume way down low or the feedback might fry your speakers!* For example, on a low setting, the following gave a latency of only 0.93ms:

```
latency -m 128 -M 128
```

The "poor" latency test of the following gave a latency of 92.9ms.

```
latency -m 8192 -M 8192 -t 1 -p
```

Getting low latency is a combination of several things. For best results, a real-time Linux kernel tuned for latency is one prerequisite. For this, see the "Low latency howto" (www.alsa-project.org/main/index.php/Low_latency_howto). In ALSA itself, programmatically you need to set the internal buffer and period sizes using snd_pcm_hw_params_set_buffer_size_near and snd_pcm_hw_params_set_period_size_near, as is done in the latency.c program where low latency is gained by setting the buffer to 128 bytes and higher latency is gained by setting it to 8,192 bytes.

Playback of Captured Sound

Playback of captured sound involves two handles, possibly for different cards. The direct method of just combining two of these in a loop doesn't unfortunately work.

```
while (1) {
    int nread;
    if ((nread = snd_pcm_readi (capture_handle, buf, BUF_SIZE)) != BUF_SIZE) {
      fprintf (stderr, "read from audio interface failed (%s)\n",
               snd_strerror (nread));
      snd_pcm_prepare(capture_handle);
```

```
        continue;
      }

    printf("copying %d\n", nread);

    if ((err = snd_pcm_writei (playback_handle, buf, nread)) != nread) {
      if (err < 0) {
        fprintf (stderr, "write to audio interface failed (%s)\n",
                      snd_strerror (err));
      } else {
        fprintf (stderr, "write to audio interface failed after %d frames\n", err);
      }
      snd_pcm_prepare(playback_handle);
    }
}
```

On my computer it threw up a variety of errors, including broken pipe, device not ready, and device nonexistent.

There are many issues that must be addressed to play back captured sound directly. The first issue is that each sound card has its own timing clock. These clocks must be synchronized. This is difficult to maintain for consumer-grade cards as their clocks apparently are low quality and will drift or be erratic. Nevertheless, ALSA will attempt to synchronize clocks with the function snd_pcm_link, which takes two card handles as parameters.

The next issue is that finer control must be exercised over the buffers and how often ALSA will fill these buffers. This is controlled with two parameters: buffer size and period size (or buffer time and period time). The period size/time controls how often interrupts occur to fill the buffer. Typically, the period size (time) is set to half that of the buffer size (time). Relevant functions are snd_pcm_hw_params_set_buffer_size_near and snd_pcm_hw_params_set_period_size_near. Corresponding get functions can used to discover what values were actually set.

In addition to hardware parameters, ALSA can also set software parameters. The distinction between the two is not clear to me, but anyway, a "start threshold" and a "available minimum" have to be set as software parameters. I have managed to get working results by setting both of these to the period size, using snd_pcm_sw_params_set_start_threshold and snd_pcm_sw_params_set_avail_min. Setting software parameters is similar to setting hardware parameters: first a data structure is initialized with snd_pcm_sw_params_current, then the software space is restricted with setter calls, and finally the data is set into the card with snd_pcm_sw_params.

ALSA needs to keep the output as full as possible. Otherwise, it will generate a "write error." I have no idea why, but it seems to work only if two buffers are written to the playback device before attempts are made to read and copy from the capture device. Sometimes one buffer will do, but no more than two. To avoid extraneous unwanted noise at the beginning of playback, two buffers of silence work well.

The resultant program is playback-capture.c, as shown here:

```
/**
 * Jan Newmarch
 */

#define PERIOD_SIZE 1024
#define BUF_SIZE (PERIOD_SIZE * 2)

#include <stdio.h>
#include <stdlib.h>
#include <alsa/asoundlib.h>
```

```c
void print_pcm_state(snd_pcm_t *handle, char *name) {
  switch (snd_pcm_state(handle)) {
  case SND_PCM_STATE_OPEN:
    printf("state open %s\n", name);
    break;

  case SND_PCM_STATE_SETUP:
    printf("state setup %s\n", name);
    break;

  case SND_PCM_STATE_PREPARED:
    printf("state prepare %s\n", name);
    break;

  case SND_PCM_STATE_RUNNING:
    printf("state running %s\n", name);
    break;

  case SND_PCM_STATE_XRUN:
    printf("state xrun %s\n", name);
    break;

  default:
    printf("state other %s\n", name);
    break;

  }
}

int setparams(snd_pcm_t *handle, char *name) {
  snd_pcm_hw_params_t *hw_params;
  int err;

  if ((err = snd_pcm_hw_params_malloc (&hw_params)) < 0) {
    fprintf (stderr, "cannot allocate hardware parameter structure (%s)\n",
             snd_strerror (err));
    exit (1);
  }

  if ((err = snd_pcm_hw_params_any (handle, hw_params)) < 0) {
    fprintf (stderr, "cannot initialize hardware parameter structure (%s)\n",
             snd_strerror (err));
    exit (1);
  }

  if ((err = snd_pcm_hw_params_set_access (handle, hw_params, SND_PCM_ACCESS_RW_
INTERLEAVED)) < 0) {
    fprintf (stderr, "cannot set access type (%s)\n",
             snd_strerror (err));
    exit (1);
  }
```

```
if ((err = snd_pcm_hw_params_set_format (handle, hw_params, SND_PCM_FORMAT_S16_LE)) < 0) {
  fprintf (stderr, "cannot set sample format (%s)\n",
           snd_strerror (err));
  exit (1);
}

unsigned int rate = 48000;
if ((err = snd_pcm_hw_params_set_rate_near (handle, hw_params, &rate, 0)) < 0) {
  fprintf (stderr, "cannot set sample rate (%s)\n",
           snd_strerror (err));
  exit (1);
}
printf("Rate for %s is %d\n", name, rate);

if ((err = snd_pcm_hw_params_set_channels (handle, hw_params, 2)) < 0) {
  fprintf (stderr, "cannot set channel count (%s)\n",
           snd_strerror (err));
  exit (1);
}

snd_pcm_uframes_t buffersize = BUF_SIZE;
if ((err = snd_pcm_hw_params_set_buffer_size_near(handle, hw_params, &buffersize)) < 0) {
  printf("Unable to set buffer size %li: %s\n", BUF_SIZE, snd_strerror(err));
  exit (1);;
}

snd_pcm_uframes_t periodsize = PERIOD_SIZE;
fprintf(stderr, "period size now %d\n", periodsize);
if ((err = snd_pcm_hw_params_set_period_size_near(handle, hw_params, &periodsize, 0)) < 0)
{
  printf("Unable to set period size %li: %s\n", periodsize, snd_strerror(err));
  exit (1);
}

if ((err = snd_pcm_hw_params (handle, hw_params)) < 0) {
  fprintf (stderr, "cannot set parameters (%s)\n",
           snd_strerror (err));
  exit (1);
}

snd_pcm_uframes_t p_psize;
snd_pcm_hw_params_get_period_size(hw_params, &p_psize, NULL);
fprintf(stderr, "period size %d\n", p_psize);

snd_pcm_hw_params_get_buffer_size(hw_params, &p_psize);
fprintf(stderr, "buffer size %d\n", p_psize);

snd_pcm_hw_params_free (hw_params);

if ((err = snd_pcm_prepare (handle)) < 0) {
  fprintf (stderr, "cannot prepare audio interface for use (%s)\n",
           snd_strerror (err));
```

```
      exit (1);
    }

    return 0;
}

int set_sw_params(snd_pcm_t *handle, char *name) {
    snd_pcm_sw_params_t *swparams;
    int err;

    snd_pcm_sw_params_alloca(&swparams);

    err = snd_pcm_sw_params_current(handle, swparams);
    if (err < 0) {
      fprintf(stderr, "Broken configuration for this PCM: no configurations available\n");
      exit(1);
    }

    err = snd_pcm_sw_params_set_start_threshold(handle, swparams, PERIOD_SIZE);
    if (err < 0) {
      printf("Unable to set start threshold: %s\n", snd_strerror(err));
      return err;
    }
    err = snd_pcm_sw_params_set_avail_min(handle, swparams, PERIOD_SIZE);
    if (err < 0) {
      printf("Unable to set avail min: %s\n", snd_strerror(err));
      return err;
    }

    if (snd_pcm_sw_params(handle, swparams) < 0) {
      fprintf(stderr, "unable to install sw params:\n");
      exit(1);
    }

    return 0;
}

/************* some code from latency.c ***************/

main (int argc, char *argv[])
{
    int i;
    int err;
    int buf[BUF_SIZE];
    snd_pcm_t *playback_handle;
    snd_pcm_t *capture_handle;
    snd_pcm_hw_params_t *hw_params;
    FILE *fin;
    size_t nread;
    snd_pcm_format_t format = SND_PCM_FORMAT_S16_LE;
    if (argc != 3) {
      fprintf(stderr, "Usage: %s in-card out-card\n", argv[0]);
```

```
    exit(1);
}

/**** Out card *******/
if ((err = snd_pcm_open (&playback_handle, argv[2], SND_PCM_STREAM_PLAYBACK, 0)) < 0) {
  fprintf (stderr, "cannot open audio device %s (%s)\n",
            argv[2],
            snd_strerror (err));
  exit (1);
}

setparams(playback_handle, "playback");
set_sw_params(playback_handle, "playback");

/*********** In card **********/

if ((err = snd_pcm_open (&capture_handle, argv[1], SND_PCM_STREAM_CAPTURE, 0)) < 0) {
  fprintf (stderr, "cannot open audio device %s (%s)\n",
            argv[1],
            snd_strerror (err));
  exit (1);
}

setparams(capture_handle, "capture");
set_sw_params(capture_handle, "capture");

if ((err = snd_pcm_link(capture_handle, playback_handle)) < 0) {
  printf("Streams link error: %s\n", snd_strerror(err));
  exit(0);
}

if ((err = snd_pcm_prepare (playback_handle)) < 0) {
  fprintf (stderr, "cannot prepare playback audio interface for use (%s)\n",
            snd_strerror (err));
  exit (1);
}

/*************** stuff something into the playback buffer ***************/
if (snd_pcm_format_set_silence(format, buf, 2*BUF_SIZE) < 0) {
  fprintf(stderr, "silence error\n");
  exit(1);
}

int n = 0;
while (n++ < 2) {
  if (snd_pcm_writei (playback_handle, buf, BUF_SIZE) < 0) {
    fprintf(stderr, "write error\n");
    exit(1);
  }
}
```

```
/************ COPY ************/
while (1) {
  int nread;
  if ((nread = snd_pcm_readi (capture_handle, buf, BUF_SIZE)) != BUF_SIZE) {
    if (nread < 0) {
      fprintf (stderr, "read from audio interface failed (%s)\n",
               snd_strerror (nread));
    } else {
      fprintf (stderr, "read from audio interface failed after %d frames\n", nread);
    }
    snd_pcm_prepare(capture_handle);
    continue;
  }

  if ((err = snd_pcm_writei (playback_handle, buf, nread)) != nread) {
    if (err < 0) {
      fprintf (stderr, "write to audio interface failed (%s)\n",
               snd_strerror (err));
    } else {
      fprintf (stderr, "write to audio interface failed after %d frames\n", err);
    }
    snd_pcm_prepare(playback_handle);
  }
}

snd_pcm_drain(playback_handle);
snd_pcm_close (playback_handle);
exit (0);
}
```

Mixing Audio

If more than one application wants to write to a sound card, only one is allowed to do so or the signals must be mixed together. Some sound cards allow hardware mixing, but some do not. In this case, the mixing must be done in software, and ALSA has mechanisms to do this.

Mixing Using dmix

ALSA contains a plug-in called dmix that is enabled by default. This performs mixing of multiple audio input signals into an output signal in software. A description of this is given in "The Dmix Howto" (http://alsa. opensrc.org/Dmix). Basically, each application that wants to write audio to ALSA should use the plug-in plug:dmix instead of a hardware device such as hw:0. For example, the alsa_playback program discussed earlier can be called multiple times and have the ALSA inputs mixed together as follows:

```
alsa_playback plug:dmix tmp1.s16 &
alsa_playback plug:dmix tmp2.s16 &
alsa_playback plug:dmix tmp3.s16
```

Mixing Using PulseAudio

PulseAudio isn't covered until the next chapter, because it is generally considered to be a sound server, acting in the layer *above* ALSA. However, there is also an ALSA plug-in module whereby PulseAudio can appear as a plug-in device *below* ALSA! So, ALSA can write output to the PulseAudio plug-in, which can process it using the full capabilities of PulseAudio, which then feeds it back down into ALSA for rendering on a hardware device.

One of these capabilities is that PulseAudio contains a mixer. So, two (or more) applications can send audio to the PulseAudio plug-in, which will then mix the signals and send them back to ALSA.

The PulseAudio plug-in can appear as the PCM device `pulse` or `default`. So, the following three outputs will be mixed by PulseAudio and rendered by ALSA:

```
alsa_playback default tmp1.s16 &
alsa_playback pulse tmp2.s16 &
alsa_playback default tmp3.s16
```

Simple Mixer API: Volume Control

ALSA has a separate API for the mixer module. In fact, there are two: the asynchronous Mixer interface (`www.alsa-project.org/alsa-doc/alsa-lib/group___mixer.html`) and the simple Mixer interface (`www.alsa-project.org/alsa-doc/alsa-lib/group___simple_mixer.html`). I will cover just the simple interface.

The ALSA mixer does not have a great deal of functionality apart from mixing. Basically, it can get and set volumes on channels or globally. Setting the volume is illustrated by the following program, based on a function at `http://stackoverflow.com/questions/6787318/set-alsa-master-volume-from-c-code`:

```
#include <alsa/asoundlib.h>
#include <alsa/mixer.h>
#include <stdlib.h>

int main(int argc, char **argv) {

    snd_mixer_t *mixer;
    snd_mixer_selem_id_t *ident;
    snd_mixer_elem_t *elem;
    long min, max;
    long old_volume, volume;

    snd_mixer_open(&mixer, 0);
    snd_mixer_attach(mixer, "default");
    snd_mixer_selem_register(mixer, NULL, NULL);
    snd_mixer_load(mixer);

    snd_mixer_selem_id_alloca(&ident);
    snd_mixer_selem_id_set_index(ident, 0);
    snd_mixer_selem_id_set_name(ident, "Master");
    elem = snd_mixer_find_selem(mixer, ident);
    snd_mixer_selem_get_playback_volume_range(elem, &min, &max);
    snd_mixer_selem_get_playback_volume(elem, 0, &old_volume);
    printf("Min %ld max %ld current volume %ld\n", min, max, old_volume);
```

```
if (argc < 2) {
    fprintf(stderr, "Usage: %s volume (%ld - %ld)\n", argv[0], min, max);
    exit(1);
}
volume = atol(argv[1]);
snd_mixer_selem_set_playback_volume_all(elem, volume);
printf("Volume reset to %ld\n", volume);

exit(0);
}
```

Writing an ALSA Device Driver

If you need to write a device driver for a new sound card, see "Writing an ALSA Driver" (www.alsa-project.org/~tiwai/writing-an-alsa-driver.pdf) by Takashi Iwai.

Conclusion

ALSA is currently the lowest level of the audio stacks for Linux that is included in the kernel. It supplies device drivers with a standard API to access the different sound devices and cards. There are a variety of user-level tools to access and manipulate the devices, built using this API.

This chapter looked at the user-level tools and at building your own tools using the API. There was a pointer to building device drivers.

CHAPTER 6

PulseAudio

PulseAudio is a sound server, sitting above device drivers such as ALSA or OSS. It offers more capabilities than device drivers. PulseAudio is designed for consumer audio and makes it easy to use sound on desktops, laptops, and mobile devices. Multiple sources of sound can all play to the PulseAudio server, which will mix them together and play them. Low latency is not a design goal, so it is unsuitable for professional audio.

Resources

Here are some resources:

- PulseAudio home page (`www.freedesktop.org/wiki/Software/PulseAudio`)

- "PulseAudio and Jack" (`http://0pointer.de/blog/projects/when-pa-and-when-not.html`) by Lennart Poettering

- "Pro Audio is Easy, Consumer Audio is Hard" (`http://lac.linuxaudio.org/2010/recordings/day1_1400_Pro_Audio_is_Easy_Consumer_Audio_is_Hard.ogv`), a 60-minute talk by Lennart Poettering

- PulseAudio API documentation (`http://freedesktop.org/software/pulseaudio/doxygen/index.html`)

Starting, Stopping, and Pausing PulseAudio

If you have a current Linux system, PulseAudio is probably running. Test this by running the following from the command line:

```
ps agx | grep pulse
```

If you see a line like `/usr/bin/pulseaudio --start --log-target=syslog`, then it is running already. If it isn't running and you have it installed, then start it by using this:

```
pulseaudio --start
```

Stopping PulseAudio isn't so easy. Carla Schroder shows how at `www.linuxplanet.com/linuxplanet/tutorials/7130/2`. The basic problem is that PulseAudio is set to respawn itself after it is killed. You have to turn that off by editing `/etc/pulse/client.conf`, changing `autospawn = yes` to `autospawn = no`, and setting `daemon-binary` to `/bin/true`. Then you can kill the process, remove it from the startup files, and so on.

© Jan Newmarch 2017
J. Newmarch, *Linux Sound Programming*, DOI 10.1007/978-1-4842-2496-0_6

If you want to run another sound system (such as Jack) for a short while, you may just want to pause PulseAudio. You do this by using pasuspender. This takes a command (after --) and will pause access by the PulseAudio server to the audio devices until the subcommand has finished. For example, the following will run the Jack server, with PulseAudio getting out of the way until it has finished:

```
pasuspender -- jackd
```

User Space Tools

PulseAudio has a range of user-level tools in addition to a programming API. These tools give information about the PulseAudio system and allow a variety of controls. The Gnome project also has a control center that is PulseAudio-aware. This section considers these tools.

paman

This shows you information about the PulseAudio server, its devices, and its clients. Figures 6-1 to 6-3 show the type of information it gives.

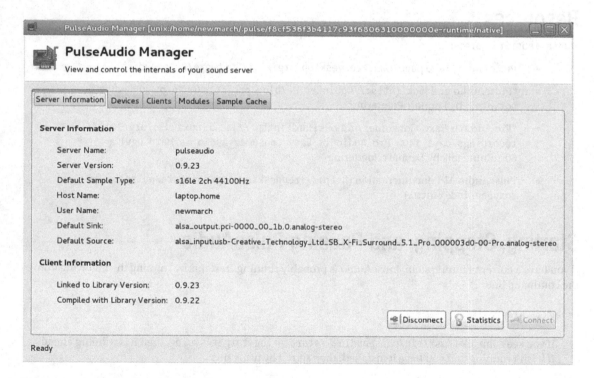

Figure 6-1. Pulse Audio Manager server information

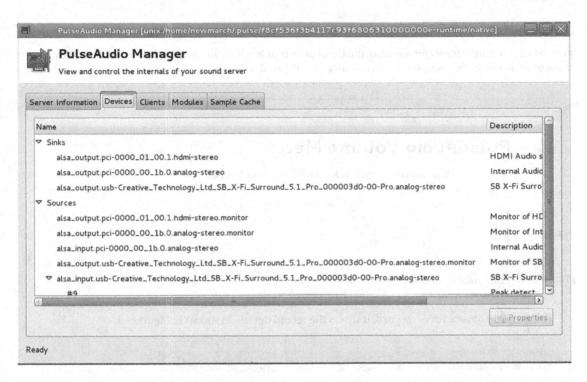

Figure 6-2. *Pulse Audio Manager device information*

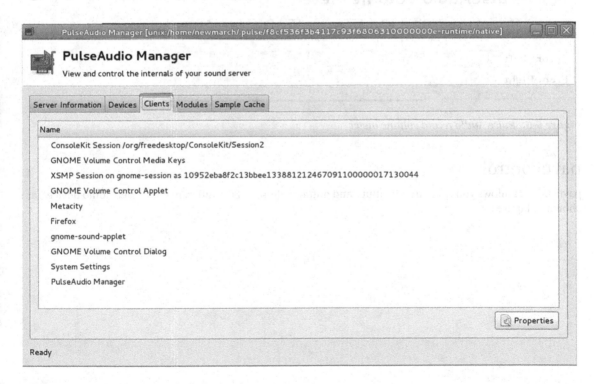

Figure 6-3. *Pulse Audio Manager client information*

pavumeter

pavumeter is a simple meter for showing the input or output levels of the default devices. When run by pavumeter, it shows the playback device, as shown in Figure 6-4.

Figure 6-4. *Pulse Audio playback volume meter*

If it is run by pavumeter --record, it shows the record device, as shown in Figure 6-5.

Figure 6-5. *Pulse Audio record volume meter*

pavucontrol

pavucontrol allows you to control the input and output volumes of the different connected audio devices, as shown in Figure 6-6.

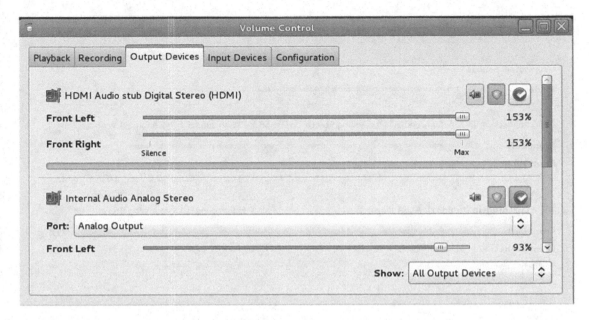

Figure 6-6. *Pulse Audio pavucontrol output devices*

With these tabs, pavucontrol is a device-level mixer, able to control the overall volume to individual devices.

One of the special advantages of PulseAudio is that it can perform application-level mixing. If two audio sources write to the same PulseAudio device, the audio will be mixed to the output device. pavucontrol can show the multiple applications using the Playback tab, showing all applications or all streams currently being mixed. Each stream can have its channel volumes individually controlled.

For example, karaoke on the cheap can be done by setting the straight-through module for the microphone to speaker with the following:

```
pactl load-module module-loopback latency_msec=1
```

The karaoke file is played by a karaoke player such as kmid through timidity. Here's an example:

```
kmid nightsin.kar
```

While these two are running, relative volumes can be controlled with the use of pavucontrol, as in Figure 6-7.

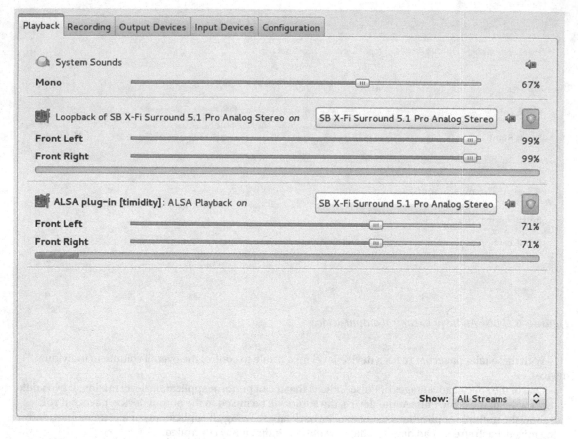

Figure 6-7. Pulse Audio pavucontrol multiple devices

Gnome Control Center (Sound)

The command gnome-control-center sound allows full view and control of the attached sound devices, including selection of the default input and output devices. It looks like Figure 6-8.

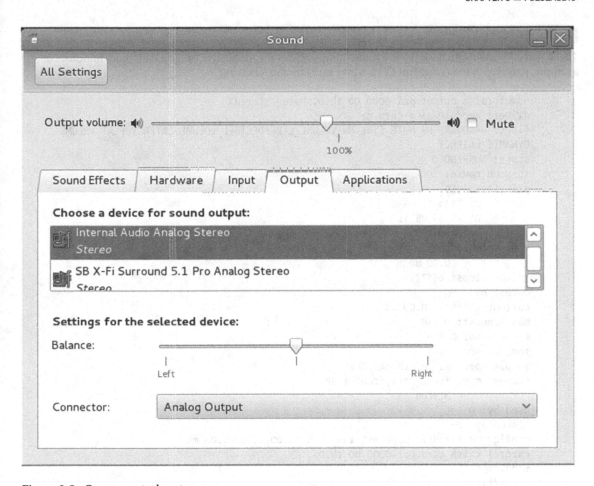

Figure 6-8. Gnome control center

parec/paplay/pacat

parec, paplay, and pacatare are command-line tools to record and play back sound files. They are all symbolic links to the same code, just differently named links. The default format is PCM s16. There are many options, but they don't always do quite what you want them to do. For example, to play from the default record device to the default playback device with minimum latency, use the following:

```
pacat -r --latency-msec=1 | pacat -p --latency-msec=1
```

This actually has a latency of about 50ms.

pactl/pacmd

These two commands do basically the same thing. pacmd is the interactive version with more options. For example, pacmd with the command list-sinks includes the following:

```
name: <alsa_output.pci-0000_00_1b.0.analog-stereo>
driver: <module-alsa-card.c>
flags: HARDWARE HW_MUTE_CTRL HW_VOLUME_CTRL DECIBEL_VOLUME LATENCY FLAT_VOLUME
DYNAMIC_LATENCY
state: SUSPENDED
suspend cause: IDLE
priority: 9959
volume: 0:  93% 1:  93%
        0: -1.88 dB 1: -1.88 dB
        balance 0.00
base volume: 100%
            0.00 dB
volume steps: 65537
muted: no
current latency: 0.00 ms
max request: 0 KiB
max rewind: 0 KiB
monitor source: 1
sample spec: s16le 2ch 44100Hz
channel map: front-left,front-right
            Stereo
used by: 0
linked by: 0
configured latency: 0.00 ms; range is 16.00 .. 2000.00 ms
card: 1 <alsa_card.pci-0000_00_1b.0>
module: 5
properties:
        alsa.resolution_bits = "16"
        device.api = "alsa"
        device.class = "sound"
        alsa.class = "generic"
        alsa.subclass = "generic-mix"
        alsa.name = "STAC92xx Analog"
        alsa.id = "STAC92xx Analog"
        alsa.subdevice = "0"
        alsa.subdevice_name = "subdevice #0"
        alsa.device = "0"
        alsa.card = "0"
        alsa.card_name = "HDA Intel PCH"
        alsa.long_card_name = "HDA Intel PCH at 0xe6e60000 irq 47"
        alsa.driver_name = "snd_hda_intel"
        device.bus_path = "pci-0000:00:1b.0"
        sysfs.path = "/devices/pci0000:00/0000:00:1b.0/sound/card0"
        device.bus = "pci"
        device.vendor.id = "8086"
        device.vendor.name = "Intel Corporation"
```

```
            device.product.id = "1c20"
            device.product.name = "6 Series/C200 Series Chipset Family High Definition
            Audio Controller"
            device.form_factor = "internal"
            device.string = "front:0"
            device.buffering.buffer_size = "352800"
            device.buffering.fragment_size = "176400"
            device.access_mode = "mmap+timer"
            device.profile.name = "analog-stereo"
            device.profile.description = "Analog Stereo"
            device.description = "Internal Audio Analog Stereo"
            alsa.mixer_name = "IDT 92HD90BXX"
            alsa.components = "HDA:111d76e7,10280494,00100102"
            module-udev-detect.discovered = "1"
            device.icon_name = "audio-card-pci"
    ports:
            analog-output: Analog Output (priority 9900)
            analog-output-headphones: Analog Headphones (priority 9000)
    active port: <analog-output>
```

Device Names

PulseAudio uses its own naming conventions. The names of source devices (such as microphones) can be found using code from the PulseAudio FAQ (`www.freedesktop.org/wiki/Software/PulseAudio/FAQ#How_do_I_record_stuff.3F`).

```
pactl list | grep -A2 'Source #' | grep 'Name: .*\.monitor$' | cut -d" " -f2
```

On my system, this produces the following:

```
alsa_output.pci-0000_01_00.1.hdmi-stereo.monitor
alsa_output.pci-0000_00_1b.0.analog-stereo.monitor
alsa_input.pci-0000_00_1b.0.analog-stereo
```

Similarly, the output devices are found with the following:

```
pactl list | grep -A2 'Sink #' | grep 'Name: .*\.monitor$' | cut -d" " -f2
```

This gives the following:

```
alsa_output.pci-0000_01_00.1.hdmi-stereo
alsa_output.pci-0000_00_1b.0.analog-stereo
```

Loopback Module

Using `pactl`, you can load the module `module-loopback` with this:

```
pactl load-module module-loopback latency_msec=1
```

When the module is loaded, sound is internally routed from the input device to the output device. The latency is effectively zero.

If you load this module into, say, your laptop, be careful about unplugging speakers, microphones, and so on. The internal speaker and microphone are close enough to set up a feedback loop. Unload module number N with this:

```
pactl unload-module N
```

(If you have forgotten the module number, just running pactl will list all modules so you can identify the loopback module.)

PulseAudio and ALSA

Output from pacmd shows that PulseAudio uses ALSA. The relationship is deeper: the default ALSA device is hw:0, but PulseAudio overrides that. In /etc/asound.conf is a hook to load /etc/alsa/pulse-default. conf, which contains the following:

```
pcm.!default {
    type pulse
    hint {
        description "Default"
    }
}
```

This replaces the default device with a PulseAudio module.

Opening the default ALSA device will actually call into PulseAudio, which will then call back into ALSA with the devices it chooses.

Programming with PulseAudio

The source for PulseAudio and its documentation is PulseAudio 2.0 (http://freedesktop.org/software/pulseaudio/doxygen/index.html). There are two ways of programming with PulseAudio: the simple API and the asynchronous API. Both are described in the following sections.

Simple API

PulseAudio has a "simple" API and a far more complex asynchronous API. The simple API may be good enough for your needs.

The simple API has a small set of functions, shown here:

```
pa_simple * pa_simple_new (const char *server, const char *name, pa_stream_direction_t dir,
const char *dev, const char *stream_name, const pa_sample_spec *ss, const pa_channel_map
*map, const pa_buffer_attr *attr, int *error)
        Create a new connection to the server.
void    pa_simple_free (pa_simple *s)
        Close and free the connection to the server.
int     pa_simple_write (pa_simple *s, const void *data, size_t bytes, int *error)
        Write some data to the server.
int     pa_simple_drain (pa_simple *s, int *error)
```

```
       Wait until all data already written is played by the daemon.
int    pa_simple_read (pa_simple *s, void *data, size_t bytes, int *error)
       Read some data from the server.
pa_usec_t pa_simple_get_latency (pa_simple *s, int *error)
       Return the playback latency.
int    pa_simple_flush (pa_simple *s, int *error)
       Flush the playback buffer.
```

Play a File

The program shown next to play from a file to the default output device is from the PulseAudio site. The basic structure is as follows:

1. Create a new playback stream (pa_simple_new).

2. Read blocks from the file (read)...

3. ...Write them to the stream (pa_simple_write).

4. Finish by flushing the stream (pa_simple_drain).

The program is pacat-simple.c. Rather weirdly, it does a dup2 to map the open file descriptor onto stdin and then reads from stdin. This isn't necessary. Why not just read from the original file descriptor?

```
/***
 *    This file is part of PulseAudio.
 *
 *    PulseAudio is free software; you can redistribute it and/or modify
 *    it under the terms of the GNU Lesser General Public License as published
 *    by the Free Software Foundation; either version 2.1 of the License,
 *    or (at your option) any later version.
 *
 *    PulseAudio is distributed in the hope that it will be useful, but
 *    WITHOUT ANY WARRANTY; without even the implied warranty of
 *    MERCHANTABILITY or FITNESS FOR A PARTICULAR PURPOSE. See the GNU
 *    General Public License for more details.
 *
 *    You should have received a copy of the GNU Lesser General Public License
 *    along with PulseAudio; if not, write to the Free Software
 *    Foundation, Inc., 59 Temple Place, Suite 330, Boston, MA 02111-1307
 *    USA.
 ****/

#ifdef HAVE_CONFIG_H
#include <config.h>
#endif

#include <stdio.h>
#include <unistd.h>
#include <string.h>
#include <errno.h>
#include <fcntl.h>
```

```c
#include <pulse/simple.h>
#include <pulse/error.h>

#define BUFSIZE 1024

int main(int argc, char*argv[]) {

    // set to NULL for default output device
    char *device = "alsa_output.pci-0000_00_1b.0.analog-stereo";

    /* The Sample format to use */
    static const pa_sample_spec ss = {
        .format = PA_SAMPLE_S16LE,
        .rate = 44100,
        .channels = 2
    };

    pa_simple *s = NULL;
    int ret = 1;
    int error;

    /* replace STDIN with the specified file if needed */
    if (argc > 1) {
        int fd;

        if ((fd = open(argv[1], O_RDONLY)) < 0) {
            fprintf(stderr, __FILE__": open() failed: %s\n", strerror(errno));
            goto finish;
        }

        if (dup2(fd, STDIN_FILENO) < 0) {
            fprintf(stderr, __FILE__": dup2() failed: %s\n", strerror(errno));
            goto finish;
        }

        close(fd);
    }

    /* Create a new playback stream */
    if (!(s = pa_simple_new(NULL, argv[0], PA_STREAM_PLAYBACK, device, "playback", &ss,
NULL, NULL, &error))) {
        fprintf(stderr, __FILE__": pa_simple_new() failed: %s\n", pa_strerror(error));
        goto finish;
    }

    for (;;) {
        uint8_t buf[BUFSIZE];
        ssize_t r;

#if 1
        pa_usec_t latency;
```

```
        if ((latency = pa_simple_get_latency(s, &error)) == (pa_usec_t) -1) {
            fprintf(stderr, __FILE__": pa_simple_get_latency() failed: %s\n", pa_
            strerror(error));
            goto finish;
        }

        fprintf(stderr, "%0.0f usec    \r", (float)latency);
#endif

        /* Read some data ... */
        if ((r = read(STDIN_FILENO, buf, sizeof(buf))) <= 0) {
            if (r == 0) /* EOF */
                break;

            fprintf(stderr, __FILE__": read() failed: %s\n", strerror(errno));
            goto finish;
        }

        /* ... and play it */
        if (pa_simple_write(s, buf, (size_t) r, &error) < 0) {
            fprintf(stderr, __FILE__": pa_simple_write() failed: %s\n", pa_strerror(error));
            goto finish;
        }
    }

    /* Make sure that every single sample was played */
    if (pa_simple_drain(s, &error) < 0) {
        fprintf(stderr, __FILE__": pa_simple_drain() failed: %s\n", pa_strerror(error));
        goto finish;
    }

    ret = 0;

finish:

    if (s)
        pa_simple_free(s);

    return ret;
}
```

Record to a File

The program shown next to record to a file from the default input device is from the PulseAudio site. It's called parec-simple.c. The basic structure is as follows:

1. Create a new recording stream (pa_simple_new).

2. Read blocks from the stream (pa_simple_read)...

3. ...Write them to the output (write).

4. Finish by releasing the stream (pa_simple_free).

Note that you need to tell PulseAudio the format to write the data, using a pa_sample_spec. Here I chose two-channel, 44100Hz, and PCM 16-bit little-endian format.

```
/***
   This file is part of PulseAudio.

   PulseAudio is free software; you can redistribute it and/or modify
   it under the terms of the GNU Lesser General Public License as published
   by the Free Software Foundation; either version 2.1 of the License,
   or (at your option) any later version.

   PulseAudio is distributed in the hope that it will be useful, but
   WITHOUT ANY WARRANTY; without even the implied warranty of
   MERCHANTABILITY or FITNESS FOR A PARTICULAR PURPOSE. See the GNU
   General Public License for more details.

   You should have received a copy of the GNU Lesser General Public License
   along with PulseAudio; if not, write to the Free Software
   Foundation, Inc., 59 Temple Place, Suite 330, Boston, MA 02111-1307
   USA.
***/

#ifdef HAVE_CONFIG_H
#include <config.h>
#endif

#include <stdio.h>
#include <unistd.h>
#include <string.h>
#include <errno.h>

#include <pulse/simple.h>
#include <pulse/error.h>

#define BUFSIZE 1024

/* A simple routine calling UNIX write() in a loop */
static ssize_t loop_write(int fd, const void*data, size_t size) {
    ssize_t ret = 0;

    while (size > 0) {
        ssize_t r;

        if ((r = write(fd, data, size)) < 0)
            return r;

        if (r == 0)
            break;
```

```
        ret += r;
        data = (const uint8_t*) data + r;
        size -= (size_t) r;
    }

    return ret;
}

int main(int argc, char*argv[]) {
    /* The sample type to use */
    static const pa_sample_spec ss = {
        .format = PA_SAMPLE_S16LE,
        .rate = 44100,
        .channels = 2
    };
    pa_simple *s = NULL;
    int ret = 1;
    int error;

    /* Create the recording stream */
    if (!(s = pa_simple_new(NULL, argv[0], PA_STREAM_RECORD, NULL, "record", &ss, NULL,
NULL, &error))) {
        fprintf(stderr, __FILE__": pa_simple_new() failed: %s\n", pa_strerror(error));
        goto finish;
    }

    for (;;) {
        uint8_t buf[BUFSIZE];

        /* Record some data ... */
        if (pa_simple_read(s, buf, sizeof(buf), &error) < 0) {
            fprintf(stderr, __FILE__": pa_simple_read() failed: %s\n", pa_strerror(error));
            goto finish;
        }

        /* And write it to STDOUT */
        if (loop_write(STDOUT_FILENO, buf, sizeof(buf)) != sizeof(buf)) {
            fprintf(stderr, __FILE__": write() failed: %s\n", strerror(errno));
            goto finish;
        }
    }

    ret = 0;

finish:

    if (s)
        pa_simple_free(s);

    return ret;
}
```

The output from this is a PCM s16 file. You can convert it to another format using sox (for example, sox -c 2 -r 44100 tmp.s16 tmp.wav), or you can import it as raw data into Audacity and play it directly.

How good are these for real-time audio? The first program can show the latency (change #if 0 to #if 1). This code can also be copied into the second one. The results are not good.

- Recording has a latency of 11ms on my laptop.

- Playback has a latency of 130ms.

Play from Source to Sink

You can combine the two programs to copy from the microphone to the speaker using a record and a playback stream. The program is pa-mic-2-speaker-simple.c, shown here:

```
#ifdef HAVE_CONFIG_H
#include <config.h>
#endif

#include <stdio.h>
#include <unistd.h>
#include <string.h>
#include <errno.h>
#include <fcntl.h>

#include <pulse/simple.h>
#include <pulse/error.h>

#define BUFSIZE 32

int main(int argc, char*argv[]) {

    /* The Sample format to use */
    static const pa_sample_spec ss = {
        .format = PA_SAMPLE_S16LE,
        .rate = 44100,
        .channels = 2
    };

    pa_simple *s_in, *s_out = NULL;
    int ret = 1;
    int error;

    /* Create a new playback stream */
    if (!(s_out = pa_simple_new(NULL, argv[0], PA_STREAM_PLAYBACK, NULL, "playback", &ss,
    NULL, NULL, &error))) {
        fprintf(stderr, __FILE__": pa_simple_new() failed: %s\n", pa_strerror(error));
        goto finish;
    }
```

```
        if (!(s_in = pa_simple_new(NULL, argv[0], PA_STREAM_RECORD, NULL, "record", &ss, NULL,
    NULL, &error))) {
            fprintf(stderr, __FILE__": pa_simple_new() failed: %s\n", pa_strerror(error));
            goto finish;
        }

    for (;;) {
        uint8_t buf[BUFSIZE];
        ssize_t r;

#if 1

        pa_usec_t latency;

        if ((latency = pa_simple_get_latency(s_in, &error)) == (pa_usec_t) -1) {
            fprintf(stderr, __FILE__": pa_simple_get_latency() failed: %s\n", pa_
            strerror(error));
            goto finish;
        }

        fprintf(stderr, "In: %0.0f usec    \r\n", (float)latency);

        if ((latency = pa_simple_get_latency(s_out, &error)) == (pa_usec_t) -1) {
            fprintf(stderr, __FILE__": pa_simple_get_latency() failed: %s\n", pa_
            strerror(error));
            goto finish;
        }

        fprintf(stderr, "Out: %0.0f usec    \r\n", (float)latency);
#endif

        if (pa_simple_read(s_in, buf, sizeof(buf), &error) < 0) {

            fprintf(stderr, __FILE__": read() failed: %s\n", strerror(errno));
            goto finish;
        }

        /* ... and play it */
        if (pa_simple_write(s_out, buf, sizeof(buf), &error) < 0) {
            fprintf(stderr, __FILE__": pa_simple_write() failed: %s\n", pa_strerror(error));
            goto finish;
        }
    }

    /* Make sure that every single sample was played */
    if (pa_simple_drain(s_out, &error) < 0) {
        fprintf(stderr, __FILE__": pa_simple_drain() failed: %s\n", pa_strerror(error));
        goto finish;
    }

    ret = 0;
```

```
finish:

    if (s_in)
        pa_simple_free(s_in);
    if (s_out)
        pa_simple_free(s_out);

    return ret;
}
```

Try running this and you will discover that the latency is noticeable and unsatisfactory.

Asynchronous API

The simple API is, well, simple. By contrast, the asynchronous API is large and complex. There are also few examples of using this API.

Nearly all interaction with this API is asynchronous. A call is made to the PulseAudio server, and when the response is ready, a library invokes a callback function that you will have passed to it when making the library call. This avoids the need for user code to either block or make polling calls.

The essential structure is as follows:

1. Create a PulseAudio main loop (synchronous: pa_mainloop_new).

2. Get the mainloop API object, which is a table of mainloop functions (synchronous: pa_mainloop_get_api).

3. Get a context object to talk to the PulseAudio server (synchronous: pa_context_new).

4. Establish a connection to the PulseAudio server. This is asynchronous: pa_context_connect.

5. Register a callback for context state changes from the server: pa_context_set_state_callback.

6. Commence the event-processing loop (pa_mainloop_run).

7. Within the context state callback, determine what state has changed. For example, the connection has been established.

8. Within this callback, set up, record, or playback streams.

9. Establish further callbacks for these streams.

10. Within the stream callbacks, do more processing, such as saving a recording stream to file.

Steps 1–7 will be common to most applications. The context state callback will be called in response to changes in the server. These are state changes such as PA_CONTEXT_CONNECTIN, PA_CONTEXT_SETTING_NAME, and so on. The change of relevance to most applications will be PA_CONTEXT_READY. This signifies that the application can make requests of the server in its steady state.

In step 8, the application will set its own behavior. This is done by setting up further callback functions for various operations, such as listing devices or playing audio.

List of Devices

The function pa_context_get_sink_info_list will set up a callback function to list source devices with the following:

pa_context_get_sink_info_list(c, sinklist_cb, NULL)

where c is the context, sinklist_cb is the application's callback, and NULL is user data passed to the callback.

The callback is called as follows:

void sinklist_cb(pa_context *c, const pa_sink_info *i, int eol, void *userdata)

The parameter eol can take three values: negative means a failure of some kind, zero means a valid entry for pa_sink_info, and positive means that there are no more valid entries in the list.

The structure pa_sink_info is defined as follows:

```
struct {
    const char *  name;
    uint32_t        index;
    const char *  description;
    pa_sample_spec          sample_spec;
    pa_channel_map          channel_map;
    uint32_t        owner_module;
    pa_cvolume    volume;
    int    mute;
    uint32_t        monitor_source;
    const char *  monitor_source_name;
    pa_usec_t     latency;
    const char *  driver;
    pa_sink_flags_t         flags;
    pa_proplist *           proplist;
    pa_usec_t     configured_latency;
    pa_volume_t    base_volume;
    pa_sink_state_t         state;
    uint32_t        n_volume_steps;
    uint32_t        card;
    uint32_t        n_ports;
    pa_sink_port_info **  ports;
    pa_sink_port_info *   active_port;
    uint8_t        n_formats;
    pa_format_info **       formats;
} pa_sink_info
```

Further information about this structure is maintained in the Doxygen "pa_sink_info Struct Reference" (http://freedesktop.org/software/pulseaudio/doxygen/structpa__sink__info.html).

For information, the major fields are name and description. The index is an opaque index into some data structure and is used in many PulseAudio functions. The proplist is a map of general information that may contain interesting information. This can be retrieved by iterating through the map.

There are similar callback and data structures for input devices.

A program to list input and output devices current when the application connects to the server is palist_devices.c:

```
/**
 * palist_devices.c
 * Jan Newmarch
 */

#include <stdio.h>
#include <string.h>
#include <pulse/pulseaudio.h>

#define _(x) x

// quit when this reaches 2
int no_more_sources_or_sinks = 0;

int ret;

pa_context *context;

void show_error(char *s) {
    fprintf(stderr, "%s\n", s);
}

void print_properties(pa_proplist *props) {
    void *state = NULL;

    printf("  Properties are: \n");
    while (1) {
        char *key;
        if ((key = pa_proplist_iterate(props, &state)) == NULL) {
            return;
        }
        char *value = pa_proplist_gets(props, key);
        printf("   key: %s, value: %s\n", key, value);
    }
}

/**
 * print information about a sink
 */
void sinklist_cb(pa_context *c, const pa_sink_info *i, int eol, void *userdata) {

    // If eol is set to a positive number, you're at the end of the list
    if (eol > 0) {
        printf("**No more sinks\n");
        no_more_sources_or_sinks++;
        if (no_more_sources_or_sinks == 2)
            exit(0);
        return;
    }
```

```c
        printf("Sink: name %s, description %s\n", i->name, i->description);
        print_properties(i->proplist);
}

/**
 * print information about a source
 */
void sourcelist_cb(pa_context *c, const pa_source_info *i, int eol, void *userdata) {
    if (eol > 0) {
        printf("**No more sources\n");
        no_more_sources_or_sinks++;
        if (no_more_sources_or_sinks == 2)
            exit(0);
        return;
    }

    printf("Source: name %s, description %s\n", i->name, i->description);
    print_properties(i->proplist);
}

void context_state_cb(pa_context *c, void *userdata) {

    switch (pa_context_get_state(c)) {
    case PA_CONTEXT_UNCONNECTED:
    case PA_CONTEXT_CONNECTING:
    case PA_CONTEXT_AUTHORIZING:
    case PA_CONTEXT_SETTING_NAME:
        break;

    case PA_CONTEXT_READY: {
        pa_operation *o;

        // set up a callback to tell us about source devices
        if (!(o = pa_context_get_source_info_list(c,
                                          sourcelist_cb,
                                          NULL
                                          ))) {
            show_error(_("pa_context_subscribe() failed"));
            return;
        }
        pa_operation_unref(o);

        // set up a callback to tell us about sink devices
        if (!(o = pa_context_get_sink_info_list(c,
                                          sinklist_cb,
                                          NULL
                                          ))) {
            show_error(_("pa_context_subscribe() failed"));
            return;
        }
```

```
            pa_operation_unref(o);

            break;
    }

    case PA_CONTEXT_FAILED:
    case PA_CONTEXT_TERMINATED:
    default:
        return;
    }
}

int main(int argc, char *argv[]) {

    // Define our pulse audio loop and connection variables
    pa_mainloop *pa_ml;
    pa_mainloop_api *pa_mlapi;

    // Create a mainloop API and connection to the default server
    pa_ml = pa_mainloop_new();
    pa_mlapi = pa_mainloop_get_api(pa_ml);
    context = pa_context_new(pa_mlapi, "Device list");

    // This function connects to the pulse server
    pa_context_connect(context, NULL, 0, NULL);

    // This function defines a callback so the server will tell us its state.
    pa_context_set_state_callback(context, context_state_cb, NULL);

    if (pa_mainloop_run(pa_ml, &ret) < 0) {
        printf("pa_mainloop_run() failed.");
        exit(1);
    }
}
```

On my laptop, this gives the following (elided):

```
Source: name alsa_output.pci-0000_01_00.1.hdmi-stereo.monitor, description Monitor of HDMI
Audio stub Digital Stereo (HDMI)
  Properties are:
  key: device.description, value: Monitor of HDMI Audio stub Digital Stereo (HDMI)
  key: device.class, value: monitor
  key: alsa.card, value: 1
  key: alsa.card_name, value: HDA NVidia
  key: alsa.long_card_name, value: HDA NVidia at 0xe5080000 irq 17
  key: alsa.driver_name, value: snd_hda_intel
  key: device.bus_path, value: pci-0000:01:00.1
  key: sysfs.path, value: /devices/pci0000:00/0000:00:01.0/0000:01:00.1/sound/card1
  key: device.bus, value: pci
```

```
  key: device.vendor.id, value: 10de
  key: device.vendor.name, value: nVidia Corporation
  key: device.product.id, value: 0e08
  key: device.product.name, value: HDMI Audio stub
  key: device.string, value: 1
  key: module-udev-detect.discovered, value: 1
  key: device.icon_name, value: audio-card-pci
Source: name alsa_output.pci-0000_00_1b.0.analog-stereo.monitor, description Monitor of
Internal Audio Analog Stereo
  Properties are:
  ...
Source: name alsa_input.pci-0000_00_1b.0.analog-stereo, description Internal Audio Analog
Stereo
  Properties are:
  ...
Source: name alsa_output.usb-Creative_Technology_Ltd_SB_X-Fi_Surround_5.1_Pro_000003d0-00-
Pro.analog-stereo.monitor, description Monitor of SB X-Fi Surround 5.1 Pro Analog Stereo
  Properties are:
  ...
Source: name alsa_input.usb-Creative_Technology_Ltd_SB_X-Fi_Surround_5.1_Pro_000003d0-00-
Pro.analog-stereo, description SB X-Fi Surround 5.1 Pro Analog Stereo
  Properties are:
  ...
**No more sources
Sink: name alsa_output.pci-0000_01_00.1.hdmi-stereo, description HDMI Audio stub Digital
Stereo (HDMI)
  Properties are:
  key: alsa.resolution_bits, value: 16
  key: device.api, value: alsa
  key: device.class, value: sound
  key: alsa.class, value: generic
  key: alsa.subclass, value: generic-mix
  key: alsa.name, value: HDMI 0
  key: alsa.id, value: HDMI 0
  key: alsa.subdevice, value: 0
  key: alsa.subdevice_name, value: subdevice #0
  key: alsa.device, value: 3
  key: alsa.card, value: 1
  key: alsa.card_name, value: HDA NVidia
  key: alsa.long_card_name, value: HDA NVidia at 0xe5080000 irq 17
  key: alsa.driver_name, value: snd_hda_intel
  key: device.bus_path, value: pci-0000:01:00.1
  key: sysfs.path, value: /devices/pci0000:00/0000:00:01.0/0000:01:00.1/sound/card1
  key: device.bus, value: pci
  key: device.vendor.id, value: 10de
  key: device.vendor.name, value: nVidia Corporation
  key: device.product.id, value: 0e08
  key: device.product.name, value: HDMI Audio stub
  key: device.string, value: hdmi:1
```

```
    key: device.buffering.buffer_size, value: 352768
    key: device.buffering.fragment_size, value: 176384
    key: device.access_mode, value: mmap+timer
    key: device.profile.name, value: hdmi-stereo
    key: device.profile.description, value: Digital Stereo (HDMI)
    key: device.description, value: HDMI Audio stub Digital Stereo (HDMI)
    key: alsa.mixer_name, value: Nvidia GPU 1c HDMI/DP
    key: alsa.components, value: HDA:10de001c,10281494,00100100
    key: module-udev-detect.discovered, value: 1
    key: device.icon_name, value: audio-card-pci
Sink: name alsa_output.pci-0000_00_1b.0.analog-stereo, description Internal Audio Analog
Stereo
    Properties are:
    ...
Sink: name alsa_output.usb-Creative_Technology_Ltd_SB_X-Fi_Surround_5.1_Pro_000003d0-00-Pro.
analog-stereo, description SB X-Fi Surround 5.1 Pro Analog Stereo
    Properties are:
    ...
**No more sinks
```

An alternative program with the same effect is PulseAudio: An Async Example To Get Device Lists (www.ypass.net/blog/2009/10/pulseaudio-an-async-example-to-get-device-lists) by Igor Brezac and Eric Connell. It doesn't follow quite as complex a route as the previous, as it only queries the server for its devices. However, it uses its own state machine to track where in the callback process it is!

Monitoring Ongoing Changes: New Sources and Sinks

The previous program listed the source and sink devices registered with PulseAudio at the time a connection to the server was established. However, when a new device is connected or an existing device is disconnected, PulseAudio registers a changes in the context, and this can also be monitored by callbacks.

The key to doing this is to *subscribe* to context changes with pa_context_subscribe. This takes a context, a mask of subscription events, and user data. Possible values of the mask are described at http://freedesktop.org/software/pulseaudio/doxygen/def_8h.html#ad4e7f11f879e8c77ae5289145ecf6947 and include PA_SUBSCRIPTION_MASK_SINK for changes in sinks and PA_SUBSCRIPTION_MASK_SINK_INPUT for sink input events.

Setting the callback function to monitor these changes is a bit odd. The function pa_context_subscribe takes a callback function of type pa_context_success_cb, but this doesn't contain information about what caused the callback. Instead, it is better to first call pa_context_set_subscribe_callback. This takes a callback function of type pa_context_subscribe_cb_t, which *does* get passed such information. Then use NULL for the callback in pa_context_subscribe!

Within a pa_context_subscribe_cb_t subscription callback, the cause of the callback can be examined and appropriate code called. If a new subscription to a sink is found, then information about the sink can be found with pa_context_get_sink_info_by_index, which takes another callback! After chasing through all these callbacks, you can eventually get information about new devices.

Note that the callback function used by pa_context_get_sink_info_list and the callback function used by pa_context_get_sink_info_by_index are the same. The callback is called once per sink device regardless of whether it is a singleton or one of a list of devices.

A program to list devices on connection and also to list changes as devices are connected or disconnected is palist_devices_ongoing.c:

```
/**
 * palist_clients.c
 * Jan Newmarch
 */

/***
    This file is based on pacat.c and pavuctl.c,  part of PulseAudio.

    pacat.c:
    Copyright 2004-2006 Lennart Poettering
    Copyright 2006 Pierre Ossman <ossman@cendio.se> for Cendio AB

    PulseAudio is free software; you can redistribute it and/or modify
    it under the terms of the GNU Lesser General Public License as published
    by the Free Software Foundation; either version 2.1 of the License,
    or (at your option) any later version.

    PulseAudio is distributed in the hope that it will be useful, but
    WITHOUT ANY WARRANTY; without even the implied warranty of
    MERCHANTABILITY or FITNESS FOR A PARTICULAR PURPOSE. See the GNU
    General Public License for more details.

    You should have received a copy of the GNU Lesser General Public License
    along with PulseAudio; if not, write to the Free Software
    Foundation, Inc., 59 Temple Place, Suite 330, Boston, MA 02111-1307
    USA.
***/

#include <stdio.h>
#include <string.h>
#include <pulse/pulseaudio.h>

#define _(x) x

int ret;

pa_context *context;

void show_error(char *s) {
    fprintf(stderr, "%s\n", s);
}

void print_properties(pa_proplist *props) {
    void *state = NULL;

    printf("  Properties are: \n");
    while (1) {
        char *key;
        if ((key = pa_proplist_iterate(props, &state)) == NULL) {
            return;
        }
```

85

```
            char *value = pa_proplist_gets(props, key);
            printf("    key: %s, value: %s\n", key, value);
    }
}


/**
 * print information about a sink
 */
void sink_cb(pa_context *c, const pa_sink_info *i, int eol, void *userdata) {

    // If eol is set to a positive number, you're at the end of the list
    if (eol > 0) {
        return;
    }

    printf("Sink: name %s, description %s\n", i->name, i->description);
    // print_properties(i->proplist);
}

/**
 * print information about a source
 */
void source_cb(pa_context *c, const pa_source_info *i, int eol, void *userdata) {
    if (eol > 0) {
        return;
    }

    printf("Source: name %s, description %s\n", i->name, i->description);
    // print_properties(i->proplist);
}

void subscribe_cb(pa_context *c, pa_subscription_event_type_t t, uint32_t index, void
*userdata) {

    switch (t & PA_SUBSCRIPTION_EVENT_FACILITY_MASK) {

    case PA_SUBSCRIPTION_EVENT_SINK:
        if ((t & PA_SUBSCRIPTION_EVENT_TYPE_MASK) == PA_SUBSCRIPTION_EVENT_REMOVE)
            printf("Removing sink index %d\n", index);
        else {
            pa_operation *o;
            if (!(o = pa_context_get_sink_info_by_index(c, index, sink_cb, NULL))) {
                show_error(_("pa_context_get_sink_info_by_index() failed"));
                return;
            }
            pa_operation_unref(o);
        }
        break;
```

```
    case PA_SUBSCRIPTION_EVENT_SOURCE:
        if ((t & PA_SUBSCRIPTION_EVENT_TYPE_MASK) == PA_SUBSCRIPTION_EVENT_REMOVE)
            printf("Removing source index %d\n", index);
        else {
            pa_operation *o;
            if (!(o = pa_context_get_source_info_by_index(c, index, source_cb, NULL))) {
                show_error(_("pa_context_get_source_info_by_index() failed"));
                return;
            }
            pa_operation_unref(o);
        }
        break;
    }
}

void context_state_cb(pa_context *c, void *userdata) {

    switch (pa_context_get_state(c)) {
    case PA_CONTEXT_UNCONNECTED:
    case PA_CONTEXT_CONNECTING:
    case PA_CONTEXT_AUTHORIZING:
    case PA_CONTEXT_SETTING_NAME:
        break;

    case PA_CONTEXT_READY: {
        pa_operation *o;

        if (!(o = pa_context_get_source_info_list(c,
                                                  source_cb,
                                                  NULL
                                                  ))) {
            show_error(_("pa_context_subscribe() failed"));
            return;
        }
        pa_operation_unref(o);

        if (!(o = pa_context_get_sink_info_list(c,
                                                sink_cb,
                                                NULL
                                                ))) {
            show_error(_("pa_context_subscribe() failed"));
            return;
        }
```

```
        pa_operation_unref(o);

        pa_context_set_subscribe_callback(c, subscribe_cb, NULL);

        if (!(o = pa_context_subscribe(c, (pa_subscription_mask_t)
                                (PA_SUBSCRIPTION_MASK_SINK|
                                 PA_SUBSCRIPTION_MASK_SOURCE), NULL, NULL))) {
            show_error(_("pa_context_subscribe() failed"));
            return;
        }
        pa_operation_unref(o);

        break;
    }

    case PA_CONTEXT_FAILED:
    case PA_CONTEXT_TERMINATED:
    default:
        return;
    }
}

int main(int argc, char *argv[]) {

    // Define our pulse audio loop and connection variables
    pa_mainloop *pa_ml;
    pa_mainloop_api *pa_mlapi;
    pa_operation *pa_op;
    pa_time_event *time_event;

    // Create a mainloop API and connection to the default server
    pa_ml = pa_mainloop_new();
    pa_mlapi = pa_mainloop_get_api(pa_ml);
    context = pa_context_new(pa_mlapi, "Device list");

    // This function connects to the pulse server
    pa_context_connect(context, NULL, 0, NULL);

    // This function defines a callback so the server will tell us its state.
    pa_context_set_state_callback(context, context_state_cb, NULL);

    if (pa_mainloop_run(pa_ml, &ret) < 0) {
        printf("pa_mainloop_run() failed.");
        exit(1);
    }
}
```

Record a Stream

If you download the source for PulseAudio from FreeDesktop.org (www.freedesktop.org/wiki/Software/ PulseAudio/Download), you will find a program called pacat.c in the utils directory. This program uses some of the private APIs and will not compile using the public libraries. It also has all the bells and whistles that you would expect from a production program. I've taken this and stripped out the complexities so that you can find your way into this API. The file is parec.c.

```
/**

 * parec.c
 * Jan Newmarch
 */

/***
  This file is based on pacat.c,  part of PulseAudio.

  pacat.c:
  Copyright 2004-2006 Lennart Poettering
  Copyright 2006 Pierre Ossman <ossman@cendio.se> for Cendio AB

  PulseAudio is free software; you can redistribute it and/or modify
  it under the terms of the GNU Lesser General Public License as published
  by the Free Software Foundation; either version 2.1 of the License,
  or (at your option) any later version.

  PulseAudio is distributed in the hope that it will be useful, but
  WITHOUT ANY WARRANTY; without even the implied warranty of
  MERCHANTABILITY or FITNESS FOR A PARTICULAR PURPOSE. See the GNU
  General Public License for more details.

  You should have received a copy of the GNU Lesser General Public License
  along with PulseAudio; if not, write to the Free Software
  Foundation, Inc., 59 Temple Place, Suite 330, Boston, MA 02111-1307
  USA.
***/

#include <stdio.h>
#include <string.h>
#include <pulse/pulseaudio.h>

#define CLEAR_LINE "\n"
#define _(x) x

// From pulsecore/macro.h
#define pa_memzero(x,l) (memset((x), 0, (l)))
#define pa_zero(x) (pa_memzero(&(x), sizeof(x)))

int fdout;
char *fname = "tmp.s16";
```

```c
int verbose = 1;
int ret;

pa_context *context;

static pa_sample_spec sample_spec = {
  .format = PA_SAMPLE_S16LE,
  .rate = 44100,
  .channels = 2
};

static pa_stream *stream = NULL;

/* This is my builtin card. Use paman to find yours
   or set it to NULL to get the default device
*/
static char *device = "alsa_input.pci-0000_00_1b.0.analog-stereo";

static pa_stream_flags_t flags = 0;

void stream_state_callback(pa_stream *s, void *userdata) {
  assert(s);

  switch (pa_stream_get_state(s)) {
  case PA_STREAM_CREATING:
    // The stream has been created, so
    // let's open a file to record to
    printf("Creating stream\n");
    fdout = creat(fname,  0711);
    break;

  case PA_STREAM_TERMINATED:
    close(fdout);
    break;

  case PA_STREAM_READY:

    // Just for info: no functionality in this branch
    if (verbose) {
      const pa_buffer_attr *a;
      char cmt[PA_CHANNEL_MAP_SNPRINT_MAX], sst[PA_SAMPLE_SPEC_SNPRINT_MAX];

      printf("Stream successfully created.");

      if (!(a = pa_stream_get_buffer_attr(s)))
        printf("pa_stream_get_buffer_attr() failed: %s", pa_strerror(pa_context_errno
        (pa_stream_get_context(s)))));
      else {
        printf("Buffer metrics: maxlength=%u, fragsize=%u", a->maxlength, a->fragsize);

      }
```

```
      printf("Connected to device %s (%u, %ssuspended).",
             pa_stream_get_device_name(s),
             pa_stream_get_device_index(s),
             pa_stream_is_suspended(s) ? "" : "not ");
    }

    break;

  case PA_STREAM_FAILED:
  default:
    printf("Stream error: %s", pa_strerror(pa_context_errno(pa_stream_get_context(s))));
    exit(1);
  }
}

/********** Stream callbacks *************/

/* This is called whenever new data is available */
static void stream_read_callback(pa_stream *s, size_t length, void *userdata) {

  assert(s);
  assert(length > 0);

  // Copy the data from the server out to a file
  fprintf(stderr, "Can read %d\n", length);

  while (pa_stream_readable_size(s) > 0) {
    const void *data;
    size_t length;

    // peek actually creates and fills the data vbl
    if (pa_stream_peek(s, &data, &length) < 0) {
      fprintf(stderr, "Read failed\n");
      exit(1);
      return;
    }
    fprintf(stderr, "Writing %d\n", length);
    write(fdout, data, length);

    // swallow the data peeked at before
    pa_stream_drop(s);
  }
}

// This callback gets called when our context changes state.  We really only
// care about when it's ready or if it has failed
void state_cb(pa_context *c, void *userdata) {
  pa_context_state_t state;
  int *pa_ready = userdata;
```

```
    printf("State changed\n");
    state = pa_context_get_state(c);
    switch  (state) {
      // There are just here for reference
    case PA_CONTEXT_UNCONNECTED:
    case PA_CONTEXT_CONNECTING:
    case PA_CONTEXT_AUTHORIZING:
    case PA_CONTEXT_SETTING_NAME:
    default:
      break;
    case PA_CONTEXT_FAILED:
    case PA_CONTEXT_TERMINATED:
      *pa_ready = 2;
      break;
    case PA_CONTEXT_READY: {
      pa_buffer_attr buffer_attr;

      if (verbose)
        printf("Connection established.%s\n", CLEAR_LINE);

      if (!(stream = pa_stream_new(c, "JanCapture", &sample_spec, NULL))) {
        printf("pa_stream_new() failed: %s", pa_strerror(pa_context_errno(c)));
        exit(1);
      }

      // Watch for changes in the stream state to create the output file
      pa_stream_set_state_callback(stream, stream_state_callback, NULL);

      // Watch for changes in the stream's read state to write to the output file
      pa_stream_set_read_callback(stream, stream_read_callback, NULL);

      // Set properties of the record buffer
      pa_zero(buffer_attr);
      buffer_attr.maxlength = (uint32_t) -1;
      buffer_attr.prebuf = (uint32_t) -1;
      buffer_attr.fragsize = buffer_attr.tlength = (uint32_t) -1;
      buffer_attr.minreq = (uint32_t) -1;

      // and start recording
      if (pa_stream_connect_record(stream, device, &buffer_attr, flags) < 0) {
        printf("pa_stream_connect_record() failed: %s", pa_strerror(pa_context_errno(c)));
        exit(1);
      }
    }

      break;
    }
}

int main(int argc, char *argv[]) {
```

```
// Define our pulse audio loop and connection variables
pa_mainloop *pa_ml;
pa_mainloop_api *pa_mlapi;
pa_operation *pa_op;
pa_time_event *time_event;

// Create a mainloop API and connection to the default server
pa_ml = pa_mainloop_new();
pa_mlapi = pa_mainloop_get_api(pa_ml);
context = pa_context_new(pa_mlapi, "test");

// This function connects to the pulse server
pa_context_connect(context, NULL, 0, NULL);

// This function defines a callback so the server will tell us its state.
pa_context_set_state_callback(context, state_cb, NULL);

if (pa_mainloop_run(pa_ml, &ret) < 0) {
    printf("pa_mainloop_run() failed.");
    exit(1);
}
}
```

Play a File

Recording an input stream is done within a stream read callback with the call pa_stream_peek. Similarly, playing an output stream is done with a stream write callback with the call pa_stream_write.

In the following program, the callback is set within the PA_CONTEXT_READY branch of the context state change callback. The stream write callback is passed the number of bytes the consuming stream is prepared to receive, so read that number of bytes from the file and write them to the stream.

Care has to be taken at the end of file. There may be unplayed material in PulseAudio's output buffers. This needs to be drained before the program can exit. This is done by the function pa_stream_drain. On end-of-file, first set the stream write callback to null so that the output stream doesn't keep calling for more input and then drain the stream. A stream drain complete callback will be called on completion of this, so the program can then exit (or do something else).

In this program, I include many more callbacks than in earlier ones to show the range of features that can be monitored.

The program is pacat2.c.

```
/**
 * pacat2.c
 * Jan Newmarch
 */

/***
   This file is based on pacat.c, part of PulseAudio.

   pacat.c:
   Copyright 2004-2006 Lennart Poettering
   Copyright 2006 Pierre Ossman <ossman@cendio.se> for Cendio AB
```

```
#include <stdio.h>
#include <string.h>
#include <pulse/pulseaudio.h>
#include <sys/stat.h>
#include <sys/types.h>
#include <fcntl.h>
#include <errno.h>
#include <unistd.h>

// ???
#define CLEAR_LINE "\n"

// From pulsecore/macro.h JN
#define pa_memzero(x,l) (memset((x), 0, (l)))
#define pa_zero(x) (pa_memzero(&(x), sizeof(x)))

int verbose = 1;
int ret;

static pa_volume_t volume = PA_VOLUME_NORM;
static int volume_is_set = 0;

static int fdin;

static pa_sample_spec sample_spec = {
  .format = PA_SAMPLE_S16LE,
  .rate = 44100,
  .channels = 2
};

static pa_stream *stream = NULL;
static pa_channel_map channel_map;
static pa_proplist *proplist = NULL;
```

```
// Define our pulse audio loop and connection variables
static pa_mainloop *mainloop;
static pa_mainloop_api *mainloop_api;
static pa_operation *pa_op;
static pa_context *context = NULL;

static void *buffer = NULL;
static size_t buffer_length = 0, buffer_index = 0;

static pa_io_event* stdio_event = NULL;

// Get device name from e.g. paman
//static char *device = "alsa_output.pci-0000_00_1b.0.analog-stereo";
// Use default device
static char *device = NULL;

static pa_stream_flags_t flags = 0;

static size_t latency = 0, process_time = 0;
static int32_t latency_msec = 1, process_time_msec = 0;

static int raw = 1;

/* Connection draining complete */
static void context_drain_complete(pa_context*c, void *userdata) {
  pa_context_disconnect(c);
}

static void stream_drain_complete(pa_stream*s, int success, void *userdata) {
  pa_operation *o = NULL;

  if (!success) {
    printf("Failed to drain stream: %s", pa_strerror(pa_context_errno(context)));
    exit(1);
  }

  if (verbose)
    printf("Playback stream drained.");

  pa_stream_disconnect(stream);
  pa_stream_unref(stream);
  stream = NULL;

  if (!(o = pa_context_drain(context, context_drain_complete, NULL)))
    pa_context_disconnect(context);
  else {
    pa_operation_unref(o);
    if (verbose)
      printf("Draining connection to server.");
  }
}
```

95

```
/* Start draining */
static void start_drain(void) {
  printf("Draining\n");
  if (stream) {
    pa_operation *o;

    pa_stream_set_write_callback(stream, NULL, NULL);

    if (!(o = pa_stream_drain(stream, stream_drain_complete, NULL))) {
      //printf("pa_stream_drain(): %s", pa_strerror(pa_context_errno(context)));
      exit(1);
      return;
    }

    pa_operation_unref(o);
  } else
    exit(0);
}

/* Write some data to the stream */
static void do_stream_write(size_t length) {
  size_t l;
  assert(length);

  printf("do stream write: Writing %d to stream\n", length);

  if (!buffer || !buffer_length) {
    buffer = pa_xmalloc(length);
    buffer_length = length;
    buffer_index = 0;
    //printf("  return without writing\n");
    //return;

  }

  while (buffer_length > 0) {
    l = read(fdin, buffer + buffer_index, buffer_length);
    if (l <= 0) {
      start_drain();
      return;
    }
    if (pa_stream_write(stream, (uint8_t*) buffer + buffer_index, l, NULL, 0, PA_SEEK_
    RELATIVE) < 0) {
      printf("pa_stream_write() failed: %s", pa_strerror(pa_context_errno(context)));
      exit(1);
      return;
    }
    buffer_length -= l;
    buffer_index += l;
```

```
    if (!buffer_length) {
      pa_xfree(buffer);
      buffer = NULL;
      buffer_index = buffer_length = 0;
    }
  }
}

void stream_state_callback(pa_stream *s, void *userdata) {
  assert(s);

  switch (pa_stream_get_state(s)) {
  case PA_STREAM_CREATING:
    break;
  case PA_STREAM_TERMINATED:
    break;

  case PA_STREAM_READY:

    if (verbose) {
      const pa_buffer_attr *a;
      char cmt[PA_CHANNEL_MAP_SNPRINT_MAX], sst[PA_SAMPLE_SPEC_SNPRINT_MAX];

      printf("Stream successfully created.\n");

      if (!(a = pa_stream_get_buffer_attr(s)))
        printf("pa_stream_get_buffer_attr() failed: %s\n", pa_strerror(pa_context_errno(pa_
        stream_get_context(s))));
      else {
        printf("Buffer metrics: maxlength=%u, fragsize=%u\n", a->maxlength, a->fragsize);

      }
      /*
        printf("Using sample spec '%s', channel map '%s'.",
        pa_sample_spec_snprint(sst, sizeof(sst), pa_stream_get_sample_spec(s)),
        pa_channel_map_snprint(cmt, sizeof(cmt), pa_stream_get_channel_map(s)));
      */

      printf("Connected to device %s (%u, %ssuspended).\n",
            pa_stream_get_device_name(s),
            pa_stream_get_device_index(s),
            pa_stream_is_suspended(s) ? "" : "not ");
    }

    break;

  case PA_STREAM_FAILED:
  default:
    printf("Stream error: %s", pa_strerror(pa_context_errno(pa_stream_get_context(s))));
    exit(1); //quit(1);
  }
}
```

```
/*********** Stream callbacks *************/

static void stream_success(pa_stream *s, int succes, void *userdata) {
  printf("Succeded\n");
}

static void stream_suspended_callback(pa_stream *s, void *userdata) {
  assert(s);

  if (verbose) {
    if (pa_stream_is_suspended(s))
      fprintf(stderr, "Stream device suspended.%s \n", CLEAR_LINE);
    else
      fprintf(stderr, "Stream device resumed.%s \n", CLEAR_LINE);
  }
}

static void stream_underflow_callback(pa_stream *s, void *userdata) {
  assert(s);

  if (verbose)
    fprintf(stderr, "Stream underrun.%s \n",  CLEAR_LINE);
}

static void stream_overflow_callback(pa_stream *s, void *userdata) {
  assert(s);

  if (verbose)
    fprintf(stderr, "Stream overrun.%s \n", CLEAR_LINE);
}

static void stream_started_callback(pa_stream *s, void *userdata) {
  assert(s);

  if (verbose)
    fprintf(stderr, "Stream started.%s \n", CLEAR_LINE);
}

static void stream_moved_callback(pa_stream *s, void *userdata) {
  assert(s);

  if (verbose)
    fprintf(stderr, "Stream moved to device %s (%u, %ssuspended).%s \n", pa_stream_get_
    device_name(s), pa_stream_get_device_index(s), pa_stream_is_suspended(s) ? "" :
    "not ",  CLEAR_LINE);
}

static void stream_buffer_attr_callback(pa_stream *s, void *userdata) {
  assert(s);
```

```
  if (verbose)
    fprintf(stderr, "Stream buffer attributes changed.%s \n",  CLEAR_LINE);
}

static void stream_event_callback(pa_stream *s, const char *name, pa_proplist *pl, void
*userdata) {
  char *t;

  assert(s);
  assert(name);
  assert(pl);

  t = pa_proplist_to_string_sep(pl, ", ");
  fprintf(stderr, "Got event '%s', properties '%s'\n", name, t);
  pa_xfree(t);
}

/* This is called whenever new data may be written to the stream */
static void stream_write_callback(pa_stream *s, size_t length, void *userdata) {
  //assert(s);
  //assert(length > 0);

  printf("Stream write callback: Ready to write %d bytes\n", length);

  printf("  do stream write from stream write callback\n");
  do_stream_write(length);

 }

// This callback gets called when our context changes state.  We really only
// care about when it's ready or if it has failed
void state_cb(pa_context *c, void *userdata) {
  pa_context_state_t state;
  int *pa_ready = userdata;

  printf("State changed\n");
  state = pa_context_get_state(c);
  switch (state) {
    // There are just here for reference
  case PA_CONTEXT_UNCONNECTED:
  case PA_CONTEXT_CONNECTING:
  case PA_CONTEXT_AUTHORIZING:
  case PA_CONTEXT_SETTING_NAME:
  default:
    break;
  case PA_CONTEXT_FAILED:
  case PA_CONTEXT_TERMINATED:
    *pa_ready = 2;
    break;
  case PA_CONTEXT_READY: {
    pa_buffer_attr buffer_attr;
```

99

```
    if (verbose)
      printf("Connection established.%s\n", CLEAR_LINE);

    if (!(stream = pa_stream_new(c, "JanPlayback", &sample_spec, NULL))) {
      printf("pa_stream_new() failed: %s", pa_strerror(pa_context_errno(c)));
      exit(1); // goto fail;
    }

    pa_stream_set_state_callback(stream, stream_state_callback, NULL);

    pa_stream_set_write_callback(stream, stream_write_callback, NULL);

    //pa_stream_set_read_callback(stream, stream_read_callback, NULL);

    pa_stream_set_suspended_callback(stream, stream_suspended_callback, NULL);
    pa_stream_set_moved_callback(stream, stream_moved_callback, NULL);
    pa_stream_set_underflow_callback(stream, stream_underflow_callback, NULL);
    pa_stream_set_overflow_callback(stream, stream_overflow_callback, NULL);

    pa_stream_set_started_callback(stream, stream_started_callback, NULL);

    pa_stream_set_event_callback(stream, stream_event_callback, NULL);
    pa_stream_set_buffer_attr_callback(stream, stream_buffer_attr_callback, NULL);

    pa_zero(buffer_attr);
    buffer_attr.maxlength = (uint32_t) -1;
    buffer_attr.prebuf = (uint32_t) -1;

    pa_cvolume cv;

    if (pa_stream_connect_playback(stream, NULL, &buffer_attr, flags,
                                   NULL,
                                   NULL) < 0) {
      printf("pa_stream_connect_playback() failed: %s", pa_strerror(pa_context_errno(c)));
      exit(1); //goto fail;
    } else {
      printf("Set playback callback\n");
    }

    pa_stream_trigger(stream, stream_success, NULL);
  }

    break;
  }
}

int main(int argc, char *argv[]) {

  struct stat st;
  off_t size;
  ssize_t nread;
```

```
// We'll need these state variables to keep track of our requests
int state = 0;
int pa_ready = 0;

if (argc != 2) {
  fprintf(stderr, "Usage: %s file\n", argv[0]);
  exit(1);
}
// slurp the whole file into buffer
if ((fdin = open(argv[1], O_RDONLY)) == -1) {
  perror("open");
  exit(1);
}

// Create a mainloop API and connection to the default server
mainloop = pa_mainloop_new();
mainloop_api = pa_mainloop_get_api(mainloop);
context = pa_context_new(mainloop_api, "test");

// This function connects to the pulse server
pa_context_connect(context, NULL, 0, NULL);
printf("Connecting\n");

// This function defines a callback so the server will tell us it's state.
// Our callback will wait for the state to be ready.  The callback will
// modify the variable to 1 so we know when we have a connection and it's
// ready.
// If there's an error, the callback will set pa_ready to 2
pa_context_set_state_callback(context, state_cb, &pa_ready);

if (pa_mainloop_run(mainloop, &ret) < 0) {
  printf("pa_mainloop_run() failed.");
  exit(1); // goto quit
}

}
```

With the latency set to the default, the number of bytes that can be written on each callback is 65,470 bytes. This gives a minimum latency of 65,470 / 44,100s, or about 1500ms. With the latency and process time both set to 1ms, the buffer size is about 1440 bytes, for a latency of 32ms.

Play a File Using I/O Callbacks

Writing a file to an output stream is simple: read from a file into a buffer and keep emptying the buffer by writing to the stream. Reading from a file is straightforward: use the standard Unix read function. You request a read of a number of bytes, and the read function returns the number of bytes actually read. This was discussed in the previous section.

The program in the PulseAudio distribution uses a more complex system. It uses I/O-ready callbacks to pass some handling to an I/O callback. This makes use of two functions.

- `pa_stream_writable_size` tells how many bytes can be written to the stream.

- `pa_stream_write` writes a number of bytes to a stream.

The logic becomes as follows: fill a buffer by reading from the file, and at the same time write as many bytes as possible from the buffer to the stream, up to the limit of the buffer size or however many bytes the stream can take, whichever is smaller.

In PulseAudio this is done asynchronously, using callback functions. The two relevant functions are as follows:

- The function `pa_stream_set_write_callback()` registers a callback that will be called whenever the stream is ready to be written to. Registering the callback looks like this:

  ```
  pa_stream_set_write_callback(stream, stream_write_callback, NULL)
  ```

  The callback is passed the stream to write to (`s`) and the number of bytes that can be written (`length`).

  ```
  void stream_write_callback(pa_stream *s, size_t length, void *userdata)
  ```

- A callback to read from files is registered by one of the functions kept in the `mainloop_api` table. The registering function is `io_new` and is passed a Unix file descriptor for the file and the callback function. Registering the callback looks like this:

  ```
  mainloop_api->io_new(mainloop_api,
                       fdin,
                       PA_IO_EVENT_INPUT,
                       stdin_callback, NULL))
  ```

  The callback is passed the file descriptor (`fd`) to read from.

  ```
  void stdin_callback(pa_mainloop_api *mainloop_api, pa_io_event *stdio_event,
                      int fd, pa_io_event_flags_t f, void *userdata)
  ```

■ **Note** The PulseAudio code does a `dup2` from the source file's descriptor to `STDIN_FILENO`, which matches the name of the function. I can't see the point of that, and their code uses `fd` anyway.

When should these callbacks be registered? The stream write callback can be registered at any time after the stream has been created, which is done by `pa_stream_new`. For the `stdin` callback, I could only get it to work properly by registering it once the stream was ready, that is, in the `PA_STREAM_READY` branch of the stream state callback function.

So, after all that, what is the logic of the program?

- In the `stdin` callback:
  - If the buffer has stuff in it, then just return. There's no point in adding any more.
  - If the buffer is empty, then query the stream to see how much can be written to it.
  - If the stream says no more, then just read something into the buffer and return.
  - If the stream can be written to, then read from the file into the buffer and write it to the stream.
- In the stream write callback:
  - If the buffer is nonempty, write its contents to the stream.

The program to play from a file currently looks like `pacat.c`.

```
/***
This file is based on pacat.c,  part of PulseAudio.

pacat.c:
Copyright 2004-2006 Lennart Poettering
Copyright 2006 Pierre Ossman <ossman@cendio.se> for Cendio AB

PulseAudio is free software; you can redistribute it and/or modify
it under the terms of the GNU Lesser General Public License as published
by the Free Software Foundation; either version 2.1 of the License,
or (at your option) any later version.

PulseAudio is distributed in the hope that it will be useful, but
WITHOUT ANY WARRANTY; without even the implied warranty of
MERCHANTABILITY or FITNESS FOR A PARTICULAR PURPOSE. See the GNU
General Public License for more details.

You should have received a copy of the GNU Lesser General Public License
along with PulseAudio; if not, write to the Free Software
Foundation, Inc., 59 Temple Place, Suite 330, Boston, MA 02111-1307
USA.
***/

#include <stdio.h>
#include <string.h>
#include <pulse/pulseaudio.h>
#include <sys/stat.h>
#include <sys/types.h>
#include <fcntl.h>
#include <errno.h>
#include <unistd.h>
```

```c
#define CLEAR_LINE "\n"

// From pulsecore/macro.h JN
#define pa_memzero(x,l) (memset((x), 0, (l)))
#define pa_zero(x) (pa_memzero(&(x), sizeof(x)))

int verbose = 1;
int ret;

static pa_volume_t volume = PA_VOLUME_NORM;
static int volume_is_set = 0;

static int fdin;.

static pa_sample_spec sample_spec = {
  .format = PA_SAMPLE_S16LE,
  .rate = 44100,
  .channels = 2
};

static pa_stream *stream = NULL;
static pa_channel_map channel_map;
static pa_proplist *proplist = NULL;

// Define our pulse audio loop and connection variables
static pa_mainloop *mainloop;
static pa_mainloop_api *mainloop_api;
static pa_operation *pa_op;
static pa_context *context = NULL;

static void *buffer = NULL;
static size_t buffer_length = 0, buffer_index = 0;

static pa_io_event* stdio_event = NULL;

static char *device = "alsa_output.pci-0000_00_1b.0.analog-stereo";

static pa_stream_flags_t flags = 0;

static size_t latency = 0, process_time = 0;
static int32_t latency_msec = 0, process_time_msec = 0;

static int raw = 1;

/* Write some data to the stream */
static void do_stream_write(size_t length) {
  size_t l;
  assert(length);
```

```
printf("do stream write: Writing %d to stream\n", length);

if (!buffer || !buffer_length) {
    printf("  return without writing\n");
    return;.
}

l = length;
if (l > buffer_length)
    l = buffer_length;
printf("  writing %d\n", l);
if (pa_stream_write(stream, (uint8_t*) buffer + buffer_index, l, NULL, 0, PA_SEEK_
RELATIVE) < 0) {
    printf("pa_stream_write() failed: %s", pa_strerror(pa_context_errno(context)));
    exit(1);
    return;
}

buffer_length -= l;
buffer_index += l;

if (!buffer_length) {
    pa_xfree(buffer);
    buffer = NULL;
    buffer_index = buffer_length = 0;
}

}

/* Connection draining complete */
static void context_drain_complete(pa_context*c, void *userdata) {
    pa_context_disconnect(c);
}

static void stream_drain_complete(pa_stream*s, int success, void *userdata) {
    pa_operation *o = NULL;

    if (!success) {
        printf("Failed to drain stream: %s", pa_strerror(pa_context_errno(context)));
        exit(1);
    }

    if (verbose)
        printf("Playback stream drained.");

    pa_stream_disconnect(stream);
    pa_stream_unref(stream);
    stream = NULL;
```

```
  if (!(o = pa_context_drain(context, context_drain_complete, NULL)))
    pa_context_disconnect(context);.
  else {
    pa_operation_unref(o);
    if (verbose)
      printf("Draining connection to server.");
  }
}

/* Start draining */
static void start_drain(void) {
  printf("Draining\n");
  if (stream) {
    pa_operation *o;

    pa_stream_set_write_callback(stream, NULL, NULL);

    if (!(o = pa_stream_drain(stream, stream_drain_complete, NULL))) {
      //printf("pa_stream_drain(): %s", pa_strerror(pa_context_errno(context)));
      exit(1);
      return;
    }

    pa_operation_unref(o);
  } else
    exit(0);
}

/* New data on STDIN **/
static void stdin_callback(pa_mainloop_api *mainloop_api, pa_io_event *stdio_event, int fd,
pa_io_event_flags_t f, void *userdata) {
  size_t l, w = 0;
  ssize_t r;

  printf("In stdin callback\n");
  //pa_assert(a == mainloop_api);
  // pa_assert(e);
  // pa_assert(stdio_event == e);

  if (buffer) {
    mainloop_api->io_enable(stdio_event, PA_IO_EVENT_NULL);
    printf("  Buffer isn't null\n");.
    return;
  }

  if (!stream || pa_stream_get_state(stream) != PA_STREAM_READY || !(l = w = pa_stream_
  writable_size(stream)))
    l = 4096;

  buffer = pa_xmalloc(l);
```

```
  if ((r = read(fd, buffer, 1)) <= 0) {
    if (r == 0) {
      it (verbose)
        printf("Got EOF.\n");

      start_drain();

    } else {
      printf("read() failed: %s\n", strerror(errno));
      exit(1);
    }

    mainloop_api->io_free(stdio_event);
    stdio_event = NULL;
    return;
  }
  printf("  Read %d\n", r);

  buffer_length = (uint32_t) r;
  buffer_index = 0;

  if (w) {
    printf("  do stream write from stdin callback\n");
    do_stream_write(w);
  }
}

void stream_state_callback(pa_stream *s, void *userdata) {
  assert(s);

  switch (pa_stream_get_state(s)) {
  case PA_STREAM_CREATING:.
    break;
  case PA_STREAM_TERMINATED:
    break;

  case PA_STREAM_READY:


    if (verbose) {
      const pa_buffer_attr *a;
      char cmt[PA_CHANNEL_MAP_SNPRINT_MAX], sst[PA_SAMPLE_SPEC_SNPRINT_MAX];

      printf("Stream successfully created.\n");

      if (!(a = pa_stream_get_buffer_attr(s)))
        printf("pa_stream_get_buffer_attr() failed: %s\n", pa_strerror(pa_context_errno(pa_
        stream_get_context(s))));
      else {
```

```
        printf("Buffer metrics: maxlength=%u, fragsize=%u\n", a->maxlength, a->fragsize);

    }
    /*
      printf("Using sample spec '%s', channel map '%s'.",
      pa_sample_spec_snprint(sst, sizeof(sst), pa_stream_get_sample_spec(s)),
      pa_channel_map_snprint(cmt, sizeof(cmt), pa_stream_get_channel_map(s)));.
    */

    printf("Connected to device %s (%u, %ssuspended).\n",
            pa_stream_get_device_name(s),
            pa_stream_get_device_index(s),
            pa_stream_is_suspended(s) ? "" : "not ");
    }

    // TRY HERE???

    if (!(stdio_event = mainloop_api->io_new(mainloop_api,
                                         fdin, // STDIN_FILENO,
                                         PA_IO_EVENT_INPUT,
                                         stdin_callback, NULL))) {
      printf("io_new() failed.");
      exit(1);
    }

    break;

  case PA_STREAM_FAILED:
  default:
    printf("Stream error: %s", pa_strerror(pa_context_errno(pa_stream_get_context(s))));
    exit(1); //quit(1);
  }
}

/*********** Stream callbacks *************/

static void stream_read_callback(pa_stream *s, size_t length, void *userdata) {
  printf("Raedy to read\n");
}

static void stream_success(pa_stream *s, int succes, void *userdata) {
  printf("Succeded\n").;
}

static void stream_suspended_callback(pa_stream *s, void *userdata) {
  assert(s);

  if (verbose) {
    if (pa_stream_is_suspended(s))
      fprintf(stderr, "Stream device suspended.%s \n", CLEAR_LINE);
    else
```

```
      fprintf(stderr, "Stream device resumed.%s \n", CLEAR_LINE);
  }
}

static void stream_underflow_callback(pa_stream *s, void *userdata) {
  assert(s);

  if (verbose)
    fprintf(stderr, "Stream underrun.%s \n",  CLEAR_LINE);
}

static void stream_overflow_callback(pa_stream *s, void *userdata) {
  assert(s);

  if (verbose)
    fprintf(stderr, "Stream overrun.%s \n", CLEAR_LINE);
}

static void stream_started_callback(pa_stream *s, void *userdata) {
  assert(s);

  if (verbose)
    fprintf(stderr, "Stream started.%s \n", CLEAR_LINE);
}

static void stream_moved_callback(pa_stream *s, void *userdata) {
  assert(s);.

  if (verbose)
    fprintf(stderr, "Stream moved to device %s (%u, %ssuspended).%s \n", pa_stream_get_
    device_name(s), pa_stream_get_device_index(s), pa_stream_is_suspended(s) ? "" :
    "not ",  CLEAR_LINE);
}

static void stream_buffer_attr_callback(pa_stream *s, void *userdata) {
  assert(s);

  if (verbose)
    fprintf(stderr, "Stream buffer attributes changed.%s \n",  CLEAR_LINE);
}

static void stream_event_callback(pa_stream *s, const char *name, pa_proplist *pl, void
*userdata) {
  char *t;

  assert(s);
  assert(name);
  assert(pl);
```

```
  t = pa_proplist_to_string_sep(pl, ", ");
  fprintf(stderr, "Got event '%s', properties '%s'\n", name, t);
  pa_xfree(t);
}

/* This is called whenever new data may be written to the stream */
static void stream_write_callback(pa_stream *s, size_t length, void *userdata) {
  //assert(s);.
  //assert(length > 0);

  printf("Stream write callback: Ready to write %d bytes\n", length);

  if (raw) {
    // assert(!sndfile);

    if (stdio_event)
      mainloop_api->io_enable(stdio_event, PA_IO_EVENT_INPUT);

    if (!buffer)
      return;
    printf("  do stream write from stream write callback\n");
    do_stream_write(length);

  }
}

// This callback gets called when our context changes state.  We really only
// care about when it's ready or if it has failed
void state_cb(pa_context *c, void *userdata) {
  pa_context_state_t state;
  int *pa_ready = userdata;

  printf("State changed\n");
  state = pa_context_get_state(c);
  switch   (state) {
    // There are just here for reference
  case PA_CONTEXT_UNCONNECTED:
  case PA_CONTEXT_CONNECTING:
  case PA_CONTEXT_AUTHORIZING:
  case PA_CONTEXT_SETTING_NAME:
  default:
    break;
  case PA_CONTEXT_FAILED:
  case PA_CONTEXT_TERMINATED:
    *pa_ready = 2;
    break;
  case PA_CONTEXT_READY: {
    pa_buffer_attr buffer_attr;

    if (verbose)
      printf("Connection established.%s\n", CLEAR_LINE);
```

```
  if (!(stream = pa_stream_new(c, "JanPlayback", &sample_spec, NULL))) {
    printf("pa_stream_new() failed: %s", pa_strerror(pa_context_errno(c)));
    exit(1); // goto fail;.
  }

  pa_stream_set_state_callback(stream, stream_state_callback, NULL);

  pa_stream_set_write_callback(stream, stream_write_callback, NULL);

  pa_stream_set_read_callback(stream, stream_read_callback, NULL);

  pa_stream_set_suspended_callback(stream, stream_suspended_callback, NULL);
  pa_stream_set_moved_callback(stream, stream_moved_callback, NULL);
  pa_stream_set_underflow_callback(stream, stream_underflow_callback, NULL);
  pa_stream_set_overflow_callback(stream, stream_overflow_callback, NULL);

  pa_stream_set_started_callback(stream, stream_started_callback, NULL);

  pa_stream_set_event_callback(stream, stream_event_callback, NULL);
  pa_stream_set_buffer_attr_callback(stream, stream_buffer_attr_callback, NULL);

  pa_zero(buffer_attr);
  buffer_attr.maxlength = (uint32_t) -1;
  buffer_attr.prebuf = (uint32_t) -1;

  buffer_attr.fragsize = buffer_attr.tlength = (uint32_t) -1;
  buffer_attr.minreq = (uint32_t) -1;

  pa_cvolume cv;

  if (pa_stream_connect_playback(stream, NULL, &buffer_attr, flags,
                                 NULL,
                                 NULL) < 0) {
    printf("pa_stream_connect_playback() failed: %s", pa_strerror(pa_context_errno(c)));.
    exit(1); //goto fail;
  } else {
    printf("Set playback callback\n");
  }

  pa_stream_trigger(stream, stream_success, NULL);
  }


    break;
  }
}
int main(int argc, char *argv[]) {

  struct stat st;
  off_t size;
  ssize_t nread;
```

```
// We'll need these state variables to keep track of our requests
int state = 0;
int pa_ready = 0;

if (argc != 2) {
  fprintf(stderr, "Usage: %s file\n", argv[0]);
  exit(1);
}
// slurp the whole file into buffer
if ((fdin = open(argv[1],  O_RDONLY)) == -1) {
  perror("open");
  exit(1);
}

// Create a mainloop API and connection to the default server
mainloop = pa_mainloop_new();
mainloop_api = pa_mainloop_get_api(mainloop);
context = pa_context_new(mainloop_api, "test");

// This function connects to the pulse server
pa_context_connect(context, NULL, 0, NULL);
printf("Connecting\n");

// This function defines a callback so the server will tell us it's state.
// Our callback will wait for the state to be ready.  The callback will
// modify the variable to 1 so we know when we have a connection and it's
// ready.
// If there's an error, the callback will set pa_ready to 2
pa_context_set_state_callback(context, state_cb, &pa_ready);.

if (pa_mainloop_run(mainloop, &ret) < 0) {
  printf("pa_mainloop_run() failed.");
  exit(1); // goto quit
}
}
```

Controlling Latency

Managing latency is described at www.freedesktop.org/wiki/Software/PulseAudio/Documentation/ Developer/Clients/LactencyControl.

In your code you then have to do the following when calling pa_stream_connect_playback() resp. pa_stream_connect_record():

- Pass PA_STREAM_ADJUST_LATENCY in the flags parameter. Only if this flag is set will PA reconfigure the low-level device's buffer size and adjust it to the latency you specify.

- Pass a pa_buffer_attr struct in the buffer_attr parameter. In the fields of this struct, make sure to initialize every single field to (uint32_t) -1, with the exception of tlength (for playback) resp. fragsize (for recording). Initialize those to the latency you want to achieve. Use pa_usec_to_bytes(&ss, ...) to convert the latency from a time unit to bytes.

The extra code is as follows:

```
// Set properties of the record buffer
pa_zero(buffer_attr);
buffer_attr.maxlength = (uint32_t) -1;
buffer_attr.prebuf = (uint32_t) -1;

if (latency_msec > 0) {
    buffer_attr.fragsize = buffer_attr.tlength = pa_usec_to_bytes(latency_msec * PA_USEC_
    PER_MSEC, &sample_spec);
    flags |= PA_STREAM_ADJUST_LATENCY;
} else if (latency > 0) {
    buffer_attr.fragsize = buffer_attr.tlength = (uint32_t) latency;
    flags |= PA_STREAM_ADJUST_LATENCY;
} else
    buffer_attr.fragsize = buffer_attr.tlength = (uint32_t) -1;

if (process_time_msec > 0) {
    buffer_attr.minreq = pa_usec_to_bytes(process_time_msec * PA_USEC_PER_MSEC,
    &sample_spec);
} else if (process_time > 0)
    buffer_attr.minreq = (uint32_t) process_time;
else
    buffer_attr.minreq = (uint32_t) -1;
```

PulseAudio also has mechanisms to estimate the latency of the devices. It uses information from timing events. A timer event callback has to be declared, as follows:

```
pa_context_rttime_new(context, pa_rtclock_now() + TIME_EVENT_USEC, time_event_callback,
NULL))
```

The timer event callback is a "single shot" callback. It installs a stream update timer callback and sets up another timer callback.

```
void time_event_callback(pa_mainloop_api *m,
                         pa_time_event *e, const struct timeval *t,
                         void *userdata) {
    if (stream && pa_stream_get_state(stream) == PA_STREAM_READY) {
        pa_operation *o;
        if (!(o = pa_stream_update_timing_info(stream, stream_update_timing_callback,
        NULL)))
            1; //pa_log(_("pa_stream_update_timing_info() failed: %s"), pa_strerror
            (pa_context_errno(context)));
        else
            pa_operation_unref(o);
    }

    pa_context_rttime_restart(context, e, pa_rtclock_now() + TIME_EVENT_USEC);
```

The stream update timer callback can then estimate the latency.

```
void stream_update_timing_callback(pa_stream *s, int success, void *userdata) {
    pa_usec_t l, usec;
    int negative = 0;

    // pa_assert(s);

    fprintf(stderr, "Update timing\n");

    if (!success ||
        pa_stream_get_time(s, &usec) < 0 ||
        pa_stream_get_latency(s, &l, &negative) < 0) {
        fprintf(stderr, "Failed to get latency\n");
        return;
    }

    fprintf(stderr, _("Time: %0.3f sec; Latency: %0.0f usec."),
            (float) usec / 1000000,
            (float) l * (negative?-1.0f:1.0f));
    fprintf(stderr, "            \r");
}
```

With latency left to PulseAudio by setting fragsize and tlength to -1, I got the following:

```
Time: 0.850 sec; Latency: 850365 usec.
Time: 0.900 sec; Latency: 900446 usec.
Time: 0.951 sec; Latency: 950548 usec.
Time: 1.001 sec; Latency: 1000940 usec.
Time: 1.051 sec; Latency: 50801 usec.
Time: 1.101 sec; Latency: 100934 usec.
Time: 1.151 sec; Latency: 151007 usec.
Time: 1.201 sec; Latency: 201019 usec.
Time: 1.251 sec; Latency: 251150 usec.
Time: 1.301 sec; Latency: 301160 usec.
Time: 1.351 sec; Latency: 351218 usec.
Time: 1.401 sec; Latency: 401329 usec.
Time: 1.451 sec; Latency: 451400 usec.
Time: 1.501 sec; Latency: 501465 usec.
Time: 1.551 sec; Latency: 551587 usec.
Time: 1.602 sec; Latency: 601594 usec.
```

With them set to 1ms, I got the following:

```
Time: 1.599 sec; Latency: 939 usec.
Time: 1.649 sec; Latency: 1105 usec.
Time: 1.699 sec; Latency: -158 usec.
Time: 1.750 sec; Latency: 1020 usec.
Time: 1.800 sec; Latency: 397 usec.
Time: 1.850 sec; Latency: -52 usec.
Time: 1.900 sec; Latency: 1827 usec.
```

```
Time: 1.950 sec; Latency: 529 usec.
Time: 2.000 sec; Latency: -90 usec.
Time: 2.050 sec; Latency: 997 usec.
Time: 2.100 sec; Latency: 436 usec.
Time: 2.150 sec; Latency: 866 usec.
Time: 2.200 sec; Latency: 406 usec.
Time: 2.251 sec; Latency: 1461 usec.
Time: 2.301 sec; Latency: 107 usec.
Time: 2.351 sec; Latency: 1257 usec.
```

The program to do all this is parec-latency.c.

```c
/* parec-latency.c */

#include <stdio.h>
#include <string.h>
#include <pulse/pulseaudio.h>

#define CLEAR_LINE "\n"
#define _(x) x

#define TIME_EVENT_USEC 50000

// From pulsecore/macro.h
#define pa_memzero(x,l) (memset((x), 0, (1)))
#define pa_zero(x) (pa_memzero(&(x), sizeof(x)))

int fdout;
char *fname = "tmp.pcm";

int verbose = 1;
int ret;

pa_context *context;

static pa_sample_spec sample_spec = {
  .format = PA_SAMPLE_S16LE,
  .rate = 44100,
  .channels = 2
};

static pa_stream *stream = NULL;

/* This is my builtin card. Use paman to find yours
   or set it to NULL to get the default device
*/
static char *device = "alsa_input.pci-0000_00_1b.0.analog-stereo";

static pa_stream_flags_t flags = 0;
```

```c
static size_t latency = 0, process_time = 0;
static int32_t latency_msec = 0, process_time_msec = 0;

void stream_state_callback(pa_stream *s, void *userdata) {
  assert(s);

  switch (pa_stream_get_state(s)) {
  case PA_STREAM_CREATING:
    // The stream has been created, so
    // let's open a file to record to
    printf("Creating stream\n");
    fdout = creat(fname,  0711);
    break;

  case PA_STREAM_TERMINATED:
    close(fdout);
    break;

  case PA_STREAM_READY:

    // Just for info: no functionality in this branch
    if (verbose) {
      const pa_buffer_attr *a;
      char cmt[PA_CHANNEL_MAP_SNPRINT_MAX], sst[PA_SAMPLE_SPEC_SNPRINT_MAX];

      printf("Stream successfully created.");

      if (!(a = pa_stream_get_buffer_attr(s)))
        printf("pa_stream_get_buffer_attr() failed: %s", pa_strerror(pa_context_errno(pa_
stream_get_context(s))));
      else {
        printf("Buffer metrics: maxlength=%u, fragsize=%u", a->maxlength, a->fragsize);

      }

      printf("Connected to device %s (%u, %ssuspended).",
             pa_stream_get_device_name(s),
             pa_stream_get_device_index(s),
             pa_stream_is_suspended(s) ? "" : "not ");
    }

    break;

  case PA_STREAM_FAILED:
  default:
    printf("Stream error: %s", pa_strerror(pa_context_errno(pa_stream_get_context(s))));
    exit(1);
  }
}
```

```
/* Show the current latency */
static void stream_update_timing_callback(pa_stream *s, int success, void *userdata) {
    pa_usec_t l, usec;
    int negative = 0;

    // pa_assert(s);

    fprintf(stderr, "Update timing\n");

    if (!success ||
        pa_stream_get_time(s, &usec) < 0 ||
        pa_stream_get_latency(s, &l, &negative) < 0) {
        // pa_log(_("Failed to get latency"));
        //pa_log(_("Failed to get latency: %s"), pa_strerror(pa_context_errno(context)));
        // quit(1);
        return;
    }

    fprintf(stderr, _("Time: %0.3f sec; Latency: %0.0f usec.\n"),
            (float) usec / 1000000,
            (float) l * (negative?-1.0f:1.0f));
    //fprintf(stderr, "          \r");
}

static void time_event_callback(pa_mainloop_api *m,
                                pa_time_event *e, const struct timeval *t,
                                void *userdata) {
    if (stream && pa_stream_get_state(stream) == PA_STREAM_READY) {
        pa_operation *o;
        if (!(o = pa_stream_update_timing_info(stream, stream_update_timing_callback,
        NULL)))
            1; //pa_log(_("pa_stream_update_timing_info() failed: %s"), pa_strerror(pa_
            context_errno(context)));
        else
            pa_operation_unref(o);
    }

    pa_context_rttime_restart(context, e, pa_rtclock_now() + TIME_EVENT_USEC);
}

void get_latency(pa_stream *s) {
  pa_usec_t latency;
  int neg;
  pa_timing_info *timing_info;

  timing_info = pa_stream_get_timing_info(s);

  if (pa_stream_get_latency(s, &latency, &neg) != 0) {
    fprintf(stderr, __FILE__": pa_stream_get_latency() failed\n");
    return;
  }
```

```
    fprintf(stderr, "%0.0f usec    \r", (float)latency);
}

/*********** Stream callbacks *************/

/* This is called whenever new data is available */
static void stream_read_callback(pa_stream *s, size_t length, void *userdata) {

  assert(s);
  assert(length > 0);

  // Copy the data from the server out to a file
  //fprintf(stderr, "Can read %d\n", length);

  while (pa_stream_readable_size(s) > 0) {
    const void *data;
    size_t length;

    //get_latency(s);

    // peek actually creates and fills the data vbl
    if (pa_stream_peek(s, &data, &length) < 0) {
      fprintf(stderr, "Read failed\n");
      exit(1);
      return;
    }
    fprintf(stderr, "Writing %d\n", length);
    write(fdout, data, length);

    // swallow the data peeked at before
    pa_stream_drop(s);
  }
}

// This callback gets called when our context changes state.  We really only
// care about when it's ready or if it has failed
void state_cb(pa_context *c, void *userdata) {
  pa_context_state_t state;
  int *pa_ready = userdata;

  printf("State changed\n");
  state = pa_context_get_state(c);
  switch  (state) {
    // There are just here for reference
  case PA_CONTEXT_UNCONNECTED:
  case PA_CONTEXT_CONNECTING:
  case PA_CONTEXT_AUTHORIZING:
  case PA_CONTEXT_SETTING_NAME:
  default:
    break;
  case PA_CONTEXT_FAILED:
```

```
case PA_CONTEXT_TERMINATED:
  *pa_ready = 2;
  break;
case PA_CONTEXT_READY: {
  pa_buffer_attr buffer_attr;

  if (verbose)
    printf("Connection established.%s\n", CLEAR_LINE);

  if (!(stream = pa_stream_new(c, "JanCapture", &sample_spec, NULL))) {
    printf("pa_stream_new() failed: %s", pa_strerror(pa_context_errno(c)));
    exit(1);
  }

  // Watch for changes in the stream state to create the output file
  pa_stream_set_state_callback(stream, stream_state_callback, NULL);

  // Watch for changes in the stream's read state to write to the output file
  pa_stream_set_read_callback(stream, stream_read_callback, NULL);

  // timing info
  pa_stream_update_timing_info(stream, stream_update_timing_callback, NULL);

  // Set properties of the record buffer
  pa_zero(buffer_attr);
  buffer_attr.maxlength = (uint32_t) -1;
  buffer_attr.prebuf = (uint32_t) -1;

  if (latency_msec > 0) {
    buffer_attr.fragsize = buffer_attr.tlength = pa_usec_to_bytes(latency_msec * PA_USEC_
    PER_MSEC, &sample_spec);
    flags |= PA_STREAM_ADJUST_LATENCY;
  } else if (latency > 0) {
    buffer_attr.fragsize = buffer_attr.tlength = (uint32_t) latency;
    flags |= PA_STREAM_ADJUST_LATENCY;
  } else
    buffer_attr.fragsize = buffer_attr.tlength = (uint32_t) -1;

  if (process_time_msec > 0) {
    buffer_attr.minreq = pa_usec_to_bytes(process_time_msec * PA_USEC_PER_MSEC,
    &sample_spec);
  } else if (process_time > 0)
    buffer_attr.minreq = (uint32_t) process_time;
  else
    buffer_attr.minreq = (uint32_t) -1;

  flags |= PA_STREAM_INTERPOLATE_TIMING;

  get_latency(stream);

  // and start recording
```

```
    if (pa_stream_connect_record(stream, device, &buffer_attr, flags) < 0) {
      printf("pa_stream_connect_record() failed: %s", pa_strerror(pa_context_errno(c)));
      exit(1);
    }
  }

    break;
  }
}

int main(int argc, char *argv[]) {

  // Define our pulse audio loop and connection variables
  pa_mainloop *pa_ml;
  pa_mainloop_api *pa_mlapi;
  pa_operation *pa_op;
  pa_time_event *time_event;

  // Create a mainloop API and connection to the default server
  pa_ml = pa_mainloop_new();
  pa_mlapi = pa_mainloop_get_api(pa_ml);
  context = pa_context_new(pa_mlapi, "test");

  // This function connects to the pulse server
  pa_context_connect(context, NULL, 0, NULL);

  // This function defines a callback so the server will tell us its state.
  pa_context_set_state_callback(context, state_cb, NULL);

  if (!(time_event = pa_context_rttime_new(context, pa_rtclock_now() + TIME_EVENT_USEC,
time_event_callback, NULL))) {
    //pa_log(_("pa_context_rttime_new() failed."));
    //goto quit;
  }

  if (pa_mainloop_run(pa_ml, &ret) < 0) {
    printf("pa_mainloop_run() failed.");
    exit(1);
  }
}
```

Play Microphone to Speaker

Combining what you have so far, you get pa-mic-2-speaker.c.

```
/*
 * Copy from microphone to speaker
 * pa-mic-2-speaker.c
 */
```

```c
#include <stdio.h>
#include <string.h>
#include <pulse/pulseaudio.h>

#define CLEAR_LINE "\n"
#define BUFF_LEN 4096

// From pulsecore/macro.h
#define pa_memzero(x,l) (memset((x), 0, (l)))
#define pa_zero(x) (pa_memzero(&(x), sizeof(x)))

static void *buffer = NULL;
static size_t buffer_length = 0, buffer_index = 0;

int verbose = 1;
int ret;

static pa_sample_spec sample_spec = {
  .format = PA_SAMPLE_S16LE,
  .rate = 44100,
  .channels = 2
};

static pa_stream *istream = NULL,
                 *ostream = NULL;

// This is my builtin card. Use paman to find yours
//static char *device = "alsa_input.pci-0000_00_1b.0.analog-stereo";
static char *idevice = NULL;
static char *odevice = NULL;

static pa_stream_flags_t flags = 0;

static size_t latency = 0, process_time = 0;
static int32_t latency_msec = 1, process_time_msec = 0;

void stream_state_callback(pa_stream *s, void *userdata) {
  assert(s);

  switch (pa_stream_get_state(s)) {
  case PA_STREAM_CREATING:
    // The stream has been created, so
    // let's open a file to record to
    printf("Creating stream\n");
    // fdout = creat(fname,  0711);
    buffer = pa_xmalloc(BUFF_LEN);
    buffer_length = BUFF_LEN;
    buffer_index = 0;
    break;
```

```c
  case PA_STREAM_TERMINATED:
    // close(fdout);
    break;

  case PA_STREAM_READY:

    // Just for info: no functionality in this branch
    if (verbose) {
      const pa_buffer_attr *a;
      char cmt[PA_CHANNEL_MAP_SNPRINT_MAX], sst[PA_SAMPLE_SPEC_SNPRINT_MAX];

      printf("Stream successfully created.");

      if (!(a = pa_stream_get_buffer_attr(s)))
        printf("pa_stream_get_buffer_attr() failed: %s", pa_strerror(pa_context_errno(pa_
        stream_get_context(s))));
      else {
        printf("Buffer metrics: maxlength=%u, fragsize=%u", a->maxlength, a->fragsize);

      }

      printf("Connected to device %s (%u, %ssuspended).",
              pa_stream_get_device_name(s),
              pa_stream_get_device_index(s),
              pa_stream_is_suspended(s) ? "" : "not ");
    }

    break;

  case PA_STREAM_FAILED:
  default:
    printf("Stream error: %s", pa_strerror(pa_context_errno(pa_stream_get_context(s))));
    exit(1);
  }
}

/*********** Stream callbacks **************/

/* This is called whenever new data is available */
static void stream_read_callback(pa_stream *s, size_t length, void *userdata) {

  assert(s);
  assert(length > 0);

  // Copy the data from the server out to a file
  fprintf(stderr, "Can read %d\n", length);

  while (pa_stream_readable_size(s) > 0) {
    const void *data;
    size_t length, lout;
```

```
    // peek actually creates and fills the data vbl
    if (pa_stream_peek(s, &data, &length) < 0) {
      fprintf(stderr, "Read failed\n");
      exit(1);
      return;
    }

    fprintf(stderr, "read %d\n", length);
    lout =  pa_stream_writable_size(ostream);
    fprintf(stderr, "Writable: %d\n", lout);
    if (lout == 0) {
      fprintf(stderr, "can't write, zero writable\n");
      return;
    }
    if (lout < length) {
      fprintf(stderr, "Truncating read\n");
      length = lout;
  }

  if (pa_stream_write(ostream, (uint8_t*) data, length, NULL, 0, PA_SEEK_RELATIVE) < 0) {
    fprintf(stderr, "pa_stream_write() failed\n");
    exit(1);
    return;
  }

    // STICK OUR CODE HERE TO WRITE OUT
    //fprintf(stderr, "Writing %d\n", length);
    //write(fdout, data, length);

    // swallow the data peeked at before
    pa_stream_drop(s);
  }
}

/* This is called whenever new data may be written to the stream */
// We don't actually write anything this time
static void stream_write_callback(pa_stream *s, size_t length, void *userdata) {
  //assert(s);
  //assert(length > 0);

  printf("Stream write callback: Ready to write %d bytes\n", length);
 }

// This callback gets called when our context changes state.  We really only
// care about when it's ready or if it has failed
void state_cb(pa_context *c, void *userdata) {
  pa_context_state_t state;
  int *pa_ready = userdata;

  printf("State changed\n");
  state = pa_context_get_state(c);
```

```
switch  (state) {
  // There are just here for reference
case PA_CONTEXT_UNCONNECTED:
case PA_CONTEXT_CONNECTING:
case PA_CONTEXT_AUTHORIZING:
case PA_CONTEXT_SETTING_NAME:
default:
  break;
case PA_CONTEXT_FAILED:
case PA_CONTEXT_TERMINATED:
  *pa_ready = 2;
  break;
case PA_CONTEXT_READY: {
  pa_buffer_attr buffer_attr;

  if (verbose)
    printf("Connection established.%s\n", CLEAR_LINE);

  if (!(istream = pa_stream_new(c, "JanCapture", &sample_spec, NULL))) {
    printf("pa_stream_new() failed: %s", pa_strerror(pa_context_errno(c)));
    exit(1);
  }

  if (!(ostream = pa_stream_new(c, "JanPlayback", &sample_spec, NULL))) {
    printf("pa_stream_new() failed: %s", pa_strerror(pa_context_errno(c)));
    exit(1);
  }

  // Watch for changes in the stream state to create the output file
  pa_stream_set_state_callback(istream, stream_state_callback, NULL);

  // Watch for changes in the stream's read state to write to the output file
  pa_stream_set_read_callback(istream, stream_read_callback, NULL);

  pa_stream_set_write_callback(ostream, stream_write_callback, NULL);

  // Set properties of the record buffer
  pa_zero(buffer_attr);
  buffer_attr.maxlength = (uint32_t) -1;
  buffer_attr.prebuf = (uint32_t) -1;

  if (latency_msec > 0) {
    buffer_attr.fragsize = buffer_attr.tlength = pa_usec_to_bytes(latency_msec * PA_USEC_
    PER_MSEC, &sample_spec);
    flags |= PA_STREAM_ADJUST_LATENCY;
  } else if (latency > 0) {
    buffer_attr.fragsize = buffer_attr.tlength = (uint32_t) latency;
    flags |= PA_STREAM_ADJUST_LATENCY;
  } else
    buffer_attr.fragsize = buffer_attr.tlength = (uint32_t) -1;
```

```
    if (process_time_msec > 0) {
      buffer_attr.minreq = pa_usec_to_bytes(process_time_msec * PA_USEC_PER_MSEC, &sample_
      spec);
    } else if (process_time > 0)
      buffer_attr.minreq = (uint32_t) process_time;
    else
      buffer_attr.minreq = (uint32_t) -1;

    // and start recording
    if (pa_stream_connect_record(istream, idevice, &buffer_attr, flags) < 0) {
      printf("pa_stream_connect_record() failed: %s", pa_strerror(pa_context_errno(c)));
      exit(1);
    }

    if (pa_stream_connect_playback(ostream, odevice, &buffer_attr, flags,
                                   NULL,
                                   NULL) < 0) {
      printf("pa_stream_connect_playback() failed: %s", pa_strerror(pa_context_errno(c)));
      exit(1); //goto fail;
    } else {
      printf("Set playback callback\n");
    }

  }

  break;
  }
}

int main(int argc, char *argv[]) {

  // Define our pulse audio loop and connection variables
  pa_mainloop *pa_ml;
  pa_mainloop_api *pa_mlapi;
  pa_operation *pa_op;
  pa_context *pa_ctx;

  // Create a mainloop API and connection to the default server
  pa_ml = pa_mainloop_new();
  pa_mlapi = pa_mainloop_get_api(pa_ml);
  pa_ctx = pa_context_new(pa_mlapi, "test");

  // This function connects to the pulse server
  pa_context_connect(pa_ctx, NULL, 0, NULL);

  // This function defines a callback so the server will tell us its state.
  pa_context_set_state_callback(pa_ctx, state_cb, NULL);

  if (pa_mainloop_run(pa_ml, &ret) < 0) {
    printf("pa_mainloop_run() failed.");
    exit(1);
  }
}
```

When the latency is set to 1ms for everything, the actual latency is about 16ms to 28ms. I couldn't detect it.

Setting the Volume on Devices

Each device can have its input or output volume controlled by PulseAudio. The principal called-for sinks are pa_context_set_sink_volume_by_name and pa_context_set_sink_volume_by_index, with similar calls for sources.

These calls make use of a structure called pa_cvolume. This structure can be manipulated using calls such as the following:

- pa_cvolume_init

- pa_cvolume_set

- pa_cvolume_mute

In the following program, you set the volume on a particular device by reading integer values from stdin and using these to set the value. Such a loop should probably best take place in a separate thread to the PulseAudio framework. Rather than introducing application threading here, I make use of an alternative set of PulseAudio calls that set up a separate thread for the PulseAudio main loop. These calls are as follows:

- pa_threaded_mainloop instead of pa_mainloop

- pa_threaded_mainloop_get_api instead of pa_mainloop_get_api

- pa_threaded_mainloop_start instead of pa_mainloop_start

The threaded calls allow you to start PulseAudio in its own thread and leave the current thread for reading volume values. This gives the relatively simple program pavolume.c.

```
/**
 * pavolume.c
 * Jan Newmarch
 */

#include <stdio.h>
#include <string.h>
#include <pulse/pulseaudio.h>

#define _(x) x

char *device = "alsa_output.pci-0000_00_1b.0.analog-stereo";

int ret;

pa_context *context;

void show_error(char *s) {
    fprintf(stderr, "%s\n", s);
}

void volume_cb(pa_context *c, int success, void *userdata) {
    if (success)
        printf("Volume set\n");
```

```
    else
        printf("Volume not set\n");
}

void context_state_cb(pa_context *c, void *userdata) {

    switch (pa_context_get_state(c)) {
    case PA_CONTEXT_UNCONNECTED:
    case PA_CONTEXT_CONNECTING:
    case PA_CONTEXT_AUTHORIZING:
    case PA_CONTEXT_SETTING_NAME:
        break;

    case PA_CONTEXT_READY: {
        pa_operation *o;

        break;
    }

    case PA_CONTEXT_FAILED:
    case PA_CONTEXT_TERMINATED:
    default:
        return;
    }
}

int main(int argc, char *argv[]) {
    long volume = 0;
    char buf[128];
    struct pa_cvolume v;

    // Define our pulse audio loop and connection variables
    pa_threaded_mainloop *pa_ml;
    pa_mainloop_api *pa_mlapi;

    // Create a mainloop API and connection to the default server
    //pa_ml = pa_mainloop_new();
    pa_ml = pa_threaded_mainloop_new();
    pa_mlapi = pa_threaded_mainloop_get_api(pa_ml);
    context = pa_context_new(pa_mlapi, "Voulme control");

    // This function connects to the pulse server
    pa_context_connect(context, NULL, 0, NULL);

    // This function defines a callback so the server will tell us its state.
    pa_context_set_state_callback(context, context_state_cb, NULL);

    pa_threaded_mainloop_start(pa_ml);
    printf("Enter volume for device %s\n");
```

```
    pa_cvolume_init(&v);
    while (1) {
        puts("Enter an integer 0-65536\n");
        fgets(buf, 128, stdin);
        volume = atoi(buf);
        pa_cvolume_set(&v, 2, volume);
        pa_context_set_sink_volume_by_name(context,
                                           device,
                                           &v,
                                           volume_cb,
                                           NULL
                                           );
    }
}
```

Listing Clients

PulseAudio is a server that talks to devices at the bottom layer and to clients at the top layer. The clients are producers and consumers of audio. One of the roles of PulseAudio is to mix signals from different source clients to shared output devices. To do this, PulseAudio keeps track of registrations by clients and can make these available to other clients with suitable callbacks.

The program palist_clients.c is similar to the program palist_devices.c. The principal difference is that when the context changes state to PA_CONTEXT_READY, the application subscribes to PA_SUBSCRIPTION_MASK_CLIENT instead of (PA_SUBSCRIPTION_MASK_SINK|PA_SUBSCRIPTION_MASK_SOURCE), and the subscription callback asks for pa_context_get_client_info instead of pa_context_get_source_info.

The program palist_clients.c is as follows:

```
/**
 * palist_clients.c
 * Jan Newmarch
 */

#include <stdio.h>
#include <string.h>
#include <pulse/pulseaudio.h>

#define CLEAR_LINE "\n"
#define _(x) x

// From pulsecore/macro.h
//#define pa_memzero(x,l) (memset((x), 0, (l)))
//#define pa_zero(x) (pa_memzero(&(x), sizeof(x)))

int ret;

pa_context *context;

void show_error(char *s) {
    /* stub */
}
```

```
void print_properties(pa_proplist *props) {
    void *state = NULL;

    printf("  Properties are: \n");
    while (1) {
        char *key;
        if ((key = pa_proplist_iterate(props, &state)) == NULL) {
            return;
        }
        char *value = pa_proplist_gets(props, key);
        printf("   key %s, value %s\n", key, value);
    }
}

void add_client_cb(pa_context *context, const pa_client_info *i, int eol, void *userdata) {

    if (eol < 0) {
        if (pa_context_errno(context) == PA_ERR_NOENTITY)
            return;

        show_error(_("Client callback failure"));
        return;
    }

    if (eol > 0) {
        return;
    }

    printf("Found a new client index %d name %s eol %d\n", i->index, i->name, eol);
    print_properties(i->proplist);
}

void remove_client_cb(pa_context *context, const pa_client_info *i, int eol, void *userdata)
{

    if (eol < 0) {
        if (pa_context_errno(context) == PA_ERR_NOENTITY)
            return;

        show_error(_("Client callback failure"));
        return;
    }

    if (eol > 0) {
        return;
    }

    printf("Removing a client index %d name %s\n", i->index, i->name);
    print_properties(i->proplist);
}
```

```
void subscribe_cb(pa_context *c, pa_subscription_event_type_t t, uint32_t index, void
*userdata) {

    switch (t & PA_SUBSCRIPTION_EVENT_FACILITY_MASK) {

    case PA_SUBSCRIPTION_EVENT_CLIENT:
        if ((t & PA_SUBSCRIPTION_EVENT_TYPE_MASK) == PA_SUBSCRIPTION_EVENT_REMOVE) {
            printf("Remove event at index %d\n", index);
            pa_operation *o;
            if (!(o = pa_context_get_client_info(c, index, remove_client_cb, NULL))) {
                show_error(_("pa_context_get_client_info() failed"));
                return;
            }
            pa_operation_unref(o);

        } else {
            pa_operation *o;
            if (!(o = pa_context_get_client_info(c, index, add_client_cb, NULL))) {
                show_error(_("pa_context_get_client_info() failed"));
                return;
            }
            pa_operation_unref(o);
        }
        break;
    }
}

void context_state_cb(pa_context *c, void *userdata) {

    switch (pa_context_get_state(c)) {
    case PA_CONTEXT_UNCONNECTED:
    case PA_CONTEXT_CONNECTING:
    case PA_CONTEXT_AUTHORIZING:
    case PA_CONTEXT_SETTING_NAME:
        break;

    case PA_CONTEXT_READY: {
        pa_operation *o;

        pa_context_set_subscribe_callback(c, subscribe_cb, NULL);

        if (!(o = pa_context_subscribe(c, (pa_subscription_mask_t)
                                    (PA_SUBSCRIPTION_MASK_CLIENT), NULL, NULL))) {
            show_error(_("pa_context_subscribe() failed"));
            return;
        }
        pa_operation_unref(o);
```

```
        if (!(o = pa_context_get_client_info_list(context,
                                           add_client_cb,
                                           NULL
        ) )) {
            show_error(_("pa_context_subscribe() failed"));
            return;
        }
        pa_operation_unref(o);

        break;
    }

    case PA_CONTEXT_FAILED:
        return;

    case PA_CONTEXT_TERMINATED:
    default:
        return;
    }
}

void stream_state_callback(pa_stream *s, void *userdata) {
    assert(s);

    switch (pa_stream_get_state(s)) {
    case PA_STREAM_CREATING:
        break;

    case PA_STREAM_TERMINATED:
        break;

    case PA_STREAM_READY:

        break;

    case PA_STREAM_FAILED:
    default:
        printf("Stream error: %s", pa_strerror(pa_context_errno(pa_stream_get_context(s))));
        exit(1);
    }
}

int main(int argc, char *argv[]) {

    // Define our pulse audio loop and connection variables
    pa_mainloop *pa_ml;
    pa_mainloop_api *pa_mlapi;
    pa_operation *pa_op;
    pa_time_event *time_event;
```

```
    // Create a mainloop API and connection to the default server
    pa_ml = pa_mainloop_new();
    pa_mlapi = pa_mainloop_get_api(pa_ml);
    context = pa_context_new(pa_mlapi, "test");


    // This function connects to the pulse server
    pa_context_connect(context, NULL, 0, NULL);

    // This function defines a callback so the server will tell us its state.
    //pa_context_set_state_callback(context, state_cb, NULL);
    pa_context_set_state_callback(context, context_state_cb, NULL);

    if (pa_mainloop_run(pa_ml, &ret) < 0) {
        printf("pa_mainloop_run() failed.");
        exit(1);
    }
}
```

The output on my system is as follows (elided):

```
Found a new client index 0 name ConsoleKit Session /org/freedesktop/ConsoleKit/Session2 eol 0
  Properties are:
   key application.name, value ConsoleKit Session /org/freedesktop/ConsoleKit/Session2
   key console-kit.session, value /org/freedesktop/ConsoleKit/Session2
Found a new client index 4 name XSMP Session on gnome-session as
1057eba7239ba1ec3d1363598095985901000000018790044 eol 0
  Properties are:
   key application.name, value XSMP Session on gnome-session as
1057eba7239ba1ec3d1363598095985901000000018790044
   key xsmp.vendor, value gnome-session
   key xsmp.client.id, value 1057eba7239ba1ec3d1363598095985901000000018790044
Found a new client index 5 name GNOME Volume Control Media Keys eol 0
  Properties are:
   ...
Found a new client index 7 name GNOME Volume Control Applet eol 0
  Properties are:
   ...
Found a new client index 53 name Metacity eol 0
  Properties are:
   ...
Found a new client index 54 name Firefox eol 0
  Properties are:
   ...
Found a new client index 248 name PulseAudio Volume Control eol 0
  Properties are:
   ...
Found a new client index 341 name test eol 0
  Properties are:
   ...
```

Listing Client Sources and Sinks

Clients can act as sources; programs such as MPlayer and VLC do just that, sending streams to PulseAudio. Other clients can act as sinks. The clients themselves are monitored by the previous program. To monitor their activity, you set the mask on pa_subscribe_callback to (PA_SUBSCRIPTION_MASK_CLIENT | PA_SUBSCRIPTION_MASK_SINK_INPUT | PA_SUBSCRIPTION_MASK_SOURCE_OUTPUT). Within the subscription callback you make calls to pa_context_get_sink_input_info within the PA_SUBSCRIPTION_EVENT_SINK_INPUT branch and do the same for the source output.

The sink input callback is passed the structure pa_sink_input_info. This contains the familiar name and index fields but also has an integer field called client. This links the sink input back to the index of the client responsible for the sink. In the following program, you list all the clients as well so that these links can followed visually. Programmatically, PulseAudio makes you keep much information (such as what clients have what indices) yourself; this is ignored here.

The program to list clients and monitor changes in their input and output streams is pamonitor_clients.c.

```
/**
 * pamonitor_clients.c
 * Jan Newmarch
 */

#include <stdio.h>
#include <string.h>
#include <pulse/pulseaudio.h>

#define CLEAR_LINE "\n"
#define _(x) x

// From pulsecore/macro.h
#define pa_memzero(x,l) (memset((x), 0, (l)))
#define pa_zero(x) (pa_memzero(&(x), sizeof(x)))

int ret;

pa_context *context;

void show_error(char *s) {
    /* stub */
}

void add_client_cb(pa_context *context, const pa_client_info *i, int eol, void *userdata) {

    if (eol < 0) {
        if (pa_context_errno(context) == PA_ERR_NOENTITY)
            return;

        show_error(_("Client callback failure"));
        return;
    }
```

```
    if (eol > 0) {
        return;
    }

    printf("Found a new client index %d name %s eol %d\n", i->index, i->name, eol);
}

void remove_client_cb(pa_context *context, const pa_client_info *i, int eol, void *userdata)
{

    if (eol < 0) {
        if (pa_context_errno(context) == PA_ERR_NOENTITY)
            return;

        show_error(_("Client callback failure"));
        return;
    }

    if (eol > 0) {
        return;
    }

    printf("Removing a client index %d name %s\n", i->index, i->name);
}

void sink_input_cb(pa_context *c, const pa_sink_input_info *i, int eol, void *userdata) {
    if (eol < 0) {
        if (pa_context_errno(context) == PA_ERR_NOENTITY)
            return;

        show_error(_("Sink input callback failure"));
        return;
    }

    if (eol > 0) {
        return;
    }
    printf("Sink input found index %d name %s for client %d\n", i->index, i->name,
i->client);
}

void source_output_cb(pa_context *c, const pa_source_output_info *i, int eol, void
*userdata) {
    if (eol < 0) {
        if (pa_context_errno(context) == PA_ERR_NOENTITY)
            return;

        show_error(_("Source output callback failure"));
        return;
    }
```

```
    if (eol > 0) {
        return;
    }
    printf("Source output found index %d name %s for client %d\n", i->index, i->name,
i->client);
}

void subscribe_cb(pa_context *c, pa_subscription_event_type_t t, uint32_t index, void
*userdata) {

    switch (t & PA_SUBSCRIPTION_EVENT_FACILITY_MASK) {

    case PA_SUBSCRIPTION_EVENT_CLIENT:
        if ((t & PA_SUBSCRIPTION_EVENT_TYPE_MASK) == PA_SUBSCRIPTION_EVENT_REMOVE) {
            printf("Remove event at index %d\n", index);
            pa_operation *o;
            if (!(o = pa_context_get_client_info(c, index, remove_client_cb, NULL))) {
                show_error(_("pa_context_get_client_info() failed"));
                return;
            }
            pa_operation_unref(o);

        } else {
            pa_operation *o;
            if (!(o = pa_context_get_client_info(c, index, add_client_cb, NULL))) {
                show_error(_("pa_context_get_client_info() failed"));
                return;
            }
            pa_operation_unref(o);
        }
        break;

    case PA_SUBSCRIPTION_EVENT_SINK_INPUT:
        if ((t & PA_SUBSCRIPTION_EVENT_TYPE_MASK) == PA_SUBSCRIPTION_EVENT_REMOVE)
            printf("Removing sink input %d\n", index);
        else {
            pa_operation *o;
            if (!(o = pa_context_get_sink_input_info(context, index, sink_input_cb, NULL))) {
                show_error(_("pa_context_get_sink_input_info() failed"));
                return;
            }
            pa_operation_unref(o);
        }
        break;

    case PA_SUBSCRIPTION_EVENT_SOURCE_OUTPUT:
        if ((t & PA_SUBSCRIPTION_EVENT_TYPE_MASK) == PA_SUBSCRIPTION_EVENT_REMOVE)
            printf("Removing source output %d\n", index);
        else {
            pa_operation *o;
```

```
                    if (!(o = pa_context_get_source_output_info(context, index, source_output_cb,
                NULL))) {
                        show_error(_("pa_context_get_sink_input_info() failed"));
                        return;
                    }
                    pa_operation_unref(o);
            }
            break;
    }
}

void context_state_cb(pa_context *c, void *userdata) {

    switch (pa_context_get_state(c)) {
    case PA_CONTEXT_UNCONNECTED:
    case PA_CONTEXT_CONNECTING:
    case PA_CONTEXT_AUTHORIZING:
    case PA_CONTEXT_SETTING_NAME:
        break;

    case PA_CONTEXT_READY: {
        pa_operation *o;

        pa_context_set_subscribe_callback(c, subscribe_cb, NULL);

        if (!(o = pa_context_subscribe(c, (pa_subscription_mask_t)
                                    (PA_SUBSCRIPTION_MASK_CLIENT |
                                     PA_SUBSCRIPTION_MASK_SINK_INPUT |
                                     PA_SUBSCRIPTION_MASK_SOURCE_OUTPUT), NULL, NULL))) {
            show_error(_("pa_context_subscribe() failed"));
            return;
        }
        pa_operation_unref(o);

        if (!(o = pa_context_get_client_info_list(context,
                                            add_client_cb,
                                            NULL
        ) )) {
            show_error(_("pa_context_subscribe() failed"));
            return;
        }
        pa_operation_unref(o);

        break;
    }

    case PA_CONTEXT_FAILED:
        return;
```

```
    case PA_CONTEXT_TERMINATED:
    default:
        // Gtk::Main::quit();
        return;
    }
}

void stream_state_callback(pa_stream *s, void *userdata) {
    assert(s);

    switch (pa_stream_get_state(s)) {
    case PA_STREAM_CREATING:
        break;

    case PA_STREAM_TERMINATED:
        break;

    case PA_STREAM_READY:
        break;

    case PA_STREAM_FAILED:
    default:
        printf("Stream error: %s", pa_strerror(pa_context_errno(pa_stream_get_context(s))));
        exit(1);
    }
}

int main(int argc, char *argv[]) {

    // Define our pulse audio loop and connection variables
    pa_mainloop *pa_ml;
    pa_mainloop_api *pa_mlapi;
    pa_operation *pa_op;
    pa_time_event *time_event;

    // Create a mainloop API and connection to the default server
    pa_ml = pa_mainloop_new();
    pa_mlapi = pa_mainloop_get_api(pa_ml);
    context = pa_context_new(pa_mlapi, "test");

    // This function connects to the pulse server
    pa_context_connect(context, NULL, 0, NULL);

    // This function defines a callback so the server will tell us its state.
    //pa_context_set_state_callback(context, state_cb, NULL);
    pa_context_set_state_callback(context, context_state_cb, NULL);

    if (pa_mainloop_run(pa_ml, &ret) < 0) {
        printf("pa_mainloop_run() failed.");
        exit(1);
    }
}
```

The output on my system is as follows:

```
Found a new client index 0 name ConsoleKit Session /org/freedesktop/ConsoleKit/Session2 eol 0
Found a new client index 4 name XSMP Session on gnome-session as
1057eba7239ba1ec3d1363598095985901000000018790044 eol 0
Found a new client index 5 name GNOME Volume Control Media Keys eol 0
Found a new client index 7 name GNOME Volume Control Applet eol 0
Found a new client index 53 name Metacity eol 0
Found a new client index 54 name Firefox eol 0
Found a new client index 248 name PulseAudio Volume Control eol 0
Found a new client index 342 name test eol 0
```

Controlling the Volume of a Sink Client

One of the significant features of PulseAudio is that not only can it mix streams to a device, but it can also control the volume of each stream. This is in addition to the volume control of each device. In pavucontrol you can see this on the Playback tab, where the volume of playback clients can be adjusted.

Programmatically this is done by calling pa_context_set_sink_input_volume with parameters that are the index of the sink input and the volume. In the following program, I follow what I did in the pavolume_client.c program where I set PulseAudio to run in a separate thread and input values for the volume in the main thread. A slight difference is that you have to wait for a client to start up a sink input, which you do by sleeping until the sink input callback assigns a nonzero value to the sink_index variable. Crude, yes. In a program such as pavucontrol, the GUI runs in separate threads anyway, and you do not need to resort to such simple tricks.

The program is pavolume_sink.c. If you play a file using, for example, MPlayer, then its volume can be adjusted by this program.

```c
/**
 * pavolume_sink.c
 * Jan Newmarch
 */

#include <stdio.h>
#include <string.h>
#include <pulse/pulseaudio.h>

#define CLEAR_LINE "\n"
#define _(x) x

int ret;

// sink we will control volume on when it is non-zero
int sink_index = 0;
int sink_num_channels;

pa_context *context;

void show_error(char *s) {
    /* stub */
}
```

```
void sink_input_cb(pa_context *c, const pa_sink_input_info *i, int eol, void *userdata) {
    if (eol < 0) {
        if (pa_context_errno(context) == PA_ERR_NOENTITY)
            return;

        show_error(_("Sink input callback failure"));
        return;
    }

    if (eol > 0) {
        return;
    }
    printf("Sink input found index %d name %s for client %d\n", i->index, i->name,
    i->client);
    sink_num_channels = i->channel_map.channels;
    sink_index = i->index;
}

void volume_cb(pa_context *c, int success, void *userdata) {
    if (success)
        printf("Volume set\n");
    else
        printf("Volume not set\n");
}

void subscribe_cb(pa_context *c, pa_subscription_event_type_t t, uint32_t index, void
*userdata) {

    switch (t & PA_SUBSCRIPTION_EVENT_FACILITY_MASK) {

    case PA_SUBSCRIPTION_EVENT_SINK_INPUT:
        if ((t & PA_SUBSCRIPTION_EVENT_TYPE_MASK) == PA_SUBSCRIPTION_EVENT_REMOVE)
            printf("Removing sink input %d\n", index);
        else {
            pa_operation *o;
            if (!(o = pa_context_get_sink_input_info(context, index, sink_input_cb, NULL))) {
                show_error(_("pa_context_get_sink_input_info() failed"));
                return;
            }
            pa_operation_unref(o);
        }
        break;
    }
}

void context_state_cb(pa_context *c, void *userdata) {

    switch (pa_context_get_state(c)) {
    case PA_CONTEXT_UNCONNECTED:
    case PA_CONTEXT_CONNECTING:
    case PA_CONTEXT_AUTHORIZING:
```

```
    case PA_CONTEXT_SETTING_NAME:
        break;

    case PA_CONTEXT_READY: {
        pa_operation *o;

        pa_context_set_subscribe_callback(c, subscribe_cb, NULL);

        if (!(o = pa_context_subscribe(c, (pa_subscription_mask_t)
                                    (PA_SUBSCRIPTION_MASK_SINK_INPUT), NULL, NULL))) {
            show_error(_("pa_context_subscribe() failed"));
            return;
        }
        break;
    }

    case PA_CONTEXT_FAILED:
        return;

    case PA_CONTEXT_TERMINATED:
    default:
        // Gtk::Main::quit();
        return;
    }
}

void stream_state_callback(pa_stream *s, void *userdata) {
    assert(s);

    switch (pa_stream_get_state(s)) {
    case PA_STREAM_CREATING:
        break;

    case PA_STREAM_TERMINATED:
        break;

    case PA_STREAM_READY:
        break;

    case PA_STREAM_FAILED:
    default:
        printf("Stream error: %s", pa_strerror(pa_context_errno(pa_stream_get_context(s))));
        exit(1);
    }
}

int main(int argc, char *argv[]) {

    // Define our pulse audio loop and connection variables
    pa_threaded_mainloop *pa_ml;
    pa_mainloop_api *pa_mlapi;
    pa_operation *pa_op;
```

```
pa_time_event *time_event;
long volume = 0;
char buf[128];
struct pa_cvolume v;

// Create a mainloop API and connection to the default server
pa_ml = pa_threaded_mainloop_new();
pa_mlapi = pa_threaded_mainloop_get_api(pa_ml);
context = pa_context_new(pa_mlapi, "test");

// This function connects to the pulse server
pa_context_connect(context, NULL, 0, NULL);

// This function defines a callback so the server will tell us its state.
//pa_context_set_state_callback(context, state_cb, NULL);
pa_context_set_state_callback(context, context_state_cb, NULL);

pa_threaded_mainloop_start(pa_ml);

/* wait till there is a sink */
while (sink_index == 0) {
    sleep(1);
}

printf("Enter volume for sink %d\n", sink_index);
pa_cvolume_init(&v);
while (1) {
    puts("Enter an integer 0-65536");
    fgets(buf, 128, stdin);
    volume = atoi(buf);
    pa_cvolume_set(&v, sink_num_channels, volume);
    pa_context_set_sink_input_volume(context,
                                     sink_index,
                                     &v,
                                     volume_cb,
                                     NULL
                                     );

}
}
```

Conclusion

This chapter looked at PulseAudio. This is currently the standard sound system for consumer Linux. There are a number of utilities for exploring PulseAudio. There are two APIs: the simple API and the asynchronous API. The chapter looked at playing and recording using these APIs. Some other aspects of PulseAudio were also examined.

Latency is not a goal, and it is not designed for real-time audio. However, you can request that the latency be made small, and if PulseAudio can do it, it will give you reasonable performance. However, PulseAudio makes no guarantees about latency, so if a maximum latency is critical, then PulseAudio may not be suitable.

PulseAudio is currently built on top of ALSA and usually interacts by making itself the default ALSA plug-in.

CHAPTER 7

■■■

Jack

The role of a sound server in Linux is to take inputs from a number of sources and route them to a number of sinks. Several audio servers are available in Linux, with the primary ones being PulseAudio and Jack. They are designed for different roles: PulseAudio is intended for consumer audio systems, while Jack is designed for professional audio. Lennart Poettering at `http://0pointer.de/blog/projects/when-pa-and-when-not.html` draws up a table of differences. The main one is that Jack is intended for environments in which low latency is critical, with Jack introducing less than 5ms latency into an audio chain, while PulseAudio can introduce up to 2-second delays. Other differences are that PulseAudio can run on low-quality systems including mobile phones, while Jack is usually run on high-quality audio equipment. The article "Knowing Jack" gives a gentle introduction to Jack. This chapter looks at tools built specifically for Jack, how applications use Jack, and finally programming with Jack.

Resources

Here are some resources:

- The Jack API (`http://jackaudio.org/files/docs/html/index.html`)

- "Knowing Jack" (`http://linux-sound.org/knowing-jack.html`)

- ArchLinux Pro Audio (`https://wiki.archlinux.org/index.php/Pro_Audio`)

- Gentoo Jack (`http://gentoo-en.vfose.ru/wiki/JACK`)

- Paul Davis talk on Jack architecture (`http://lac.linuxaudio.org/2003/zkm/recordings/paul_davis-jack.ogg`)

- "Knowing Jack" (`www.linux-magazine.com/content/download/63041/486886/version/1/file/JACK_Audio_Server.pdf`) by Dave Phillips in Linux Magazine

- Writing Audio Applications with JACK (`http://dis-dot-dat.net/index.cgi?item=/jacktuts/starting/`)

Starting Jack

Jack is available in the repositories of most distros. You want to install Jack2 rather than Jack1. For programming, you will also need the libjack2 dev package, which may get installed along with the Jack2 package.

The Jack server is jackd. It has one required parameter, which is a sound back end such as ALSA. The minimal command is as follows:

```
jackd -dalsa
```

Following the option -dalsa ALSA options can appear. On one of my computers aplay -l shows card 0 has devices 3, 7, and 8, and I needed to specify one of these:

```
jackd -dalsa -d hw:0,3
```

If you are using a normal Linux distro such as Fedora or Ubuntu, this will quite likely fail if the PulseAudio system is running. This may need to be stopped, or at least paused, while you run Jack. See the previous chapter for stopping PulseAudio. To pause it, I usually run this in a terminal window:

```
pasuspender cat
```

This will pause PulseAudio until cat terminates, which it will do when you enter Ctrl-D.

jackd will try to start using the Linux real-time scheduler. If you want to run without it, use the following option:

```
jackd --no-realtime -dalsa
```

If you want to run with the real-time scheduler, there are several ways.

- Run the server from the root user.

```
sudo jackd -dalsa
```

- Add a user to the audio and jackuser groups, as follows:

```
useradd -G audio newmarch
useradd -G jackuser newmarch
```

(You will need to log out and back in before this takes effect.)

Note that if you run the server as the root user, then you will not be able to connect to it from clients that are not in the jackuser group.

No apparent systemd or upstart scripts exist for Jack, but there are instructions for starting Jack at boot time at http://gentoo-en.vfose.ru/wiki/JACK#Starting_JACK_at_boot_time. The following instructions are excerpted from that, which is under a GPL license (last modified in 2012):

```
#!/sbin/runscript
# This programm will be used by init in order to launch jackd with the privileges
# and id of the user defined into /etc/conf.d/jackd

depend() {
        need alsasound
}

start() {
        if ! test -f "${JACKDHOME}/.jackdrc"; then
                eerror "You must start and configure jackd before launch it. Sorry."
```

```
                eerror "You can use qjackctl for that."
                return 1
        else JACKDOPTS=$(cat "${JACKDHOME}/.jackdrc"|sed -e 's\/usr/bin/jackd \\')
        fi

        if [ -e /var/run/jackd.pid ]; then
                rm /var/run/jackd.pid
        fi

        ebegin "Starting JACK Daemon"
        env HOME="${JACKDHOME}" start-stop-daemon --start \
                --quiet --background \
                --make-pidfile --pidfile /var/run/jackd.pid \
                -c ${JACKDUSER} \
                -x /usr/bin/jackd -- ${JACKDOPTS} >${LOG}

        sleep 2
        if ! pgrep -u ${JACKDUSER} jackd > /dev/null; then
                eerror "JACK daemon can't be started! Check logfile: ${LOG}"
        fi
        eend $?
}

stop() {
        ebegin "Stopping JACK daemon -- please wait"
        start-stop-daemon --stop --pidfile /var/run/jackd.pid &>/dev/null
        eend $?
}

restart() {
        svc_stop
        while `pgrep -u ${JACKDUSER} jackd >/dev/null`; do
                sleep 1
        done
        svc_start
}
```

File: /etc/conf.d/jackd:

```
# owner of jackd process (Must be an existing user.)
JACKDUSER="dom"

# .jackdrc location for that user (Must be existing, JACKDUSER can use
# qjackctl in order to create it.)
JACKDHOME="/home/${JACKDUSER}"

# logfile (/dev/null for nowhere)
LOG=/var/log/jackd.log
```

Create and save those 2 files. Don't forget to adjust JACKDUSER to the wanted user name (the same as yours I guess; [Author: Yes, that is what the Gentoo instructions say!]). We need to make /etc/init.d/jackd executable:

```
# chmod +x /etc/init.d/jackd
```

Adding the script into the default run-level:

```
# rc-update add jackd default
```

Before restarting your system or starting this script, you must be sure that jackd is configured for $JACKUSER or jackd will fail. This is because the script will read /home/${USER}/.jackdrc. If this file doesn't exist, the easiest way to create it is to run QJackCtl as explained above.

Note on Realtime: Due to a limitation in the implementation of start-stop-daemon, it is not possible to start jackd in realtime mode as a non-root user by this method if using pam_limits. start-stop-daemon does not implement support for pam_sessions, meaning that changes to limits.conf have no effect in this context.

User Tools

There is really only one tool that you need to use with Jack: qjackctl. This gives a graphical view of which Jack applications are playing and allows you to link inputs and outputs.

A simple tutorial on using qjackctl is HowToQjackCtlConnections (https://help.ubuntu.com/community/HowToQjackCtlConnections). It is actually amazingly simple to use: click a source and link it to a destination by clicking the destination. A line will be shown linking them. That's all you have to do. Many Jack applications will do this for you, so you just observe the results. Illustrations of this are given later in the chapter.

Applications Using Jack

There are many pieces of software using Jack, described in "Applications using JACK" (http://jackaudio.org/applications).

mplayer

To run mplayer using Jack, add the option -ao jack.

```
mplayer -ao jack 54154.mp3
```

mplayer used in this way will connect to the Jack system output device. To output to another Jack application such as jack-rack, append the output application to the audio output command.

```
mplayer -ao jack:port=jack_rack 54154.mp3
```

VLC

VLC will play to Jack output if the Jack module (https://wiki.videolan.org/Documentation:Modules/jack/) is included. This is available as a downloadable Debian package called vlc-plugin-jack. You can check whether you have it by seeing if jack is listed as a module in vlc --list shows ALSA but not Jack.

Play a file using Jack by doing the following:

```
vlc --aout jack 54154.mp3
```

You should be able to connect to a particular Jack application using the option --jack-connect-regex <string>.

TiMidity

TiMidity is a MIDI player discussed in Chapter 21. It can play to Jack output devices with this:

```
timidity -Oj 54154.mid
```

Jack-Supplied Programs

Jack comes with a large number of clients.

jack_alias	jack_midisine
jack_bufsize	jack_monitor_client
jack_connect	jack_multiple_metro
jack_control	jack_net_master
jack_cpu	jack_net_slave
jack_cpu_load	jack_netsource
jackd	jack_rec
jackdbus	jack_samplerate
jack_disconnect	jack_server_control
jack_evmon	jack_session_notify
jack_freewheel	jack_showtime
jack_iodelay	jack_simple_client
jack_latent_client	jack_simple_session_client
jack_load	jack_test
jack_lsp	jack_thru
jack_metro	jack_transport
jack_midi_dump	jack_unload
jack_midi_latency_test	jack_wait
jack_midiseq	jack_zombie

For many of these, the source code is available in the Jack source code distribution, and there is a man page for each one.

Running, say, jack_thru connects the system capture ports to the jack_thru input ports and the jack_thru output ports to the system playback ports. You can then do things such as disconnect ports using client:port for the port name as follows:

```
jack_disconnect jack_thru:output_1 system:playback_1
```

These command-line tools allow you to do the same kind of actions as qjackctl.

Other Jack Programs

The page Applications using JACK (http://jackaudio.org/applications) lists many applications using Jack.

The page Jack MIDI Apps (http://apps.linuxaudio.org/apps/categories/jack_midi) at linuxaudio.org lists many MIDI applications using Jack.

Using a Different Sound Card

The default ALSA device for Jack will be hw:0. If you want to use a different sound card, then you can specify this when starting Jack, as follows:

```
jackd -dalsa -dhw:0
```

I have a USB Sound Blaster card, which requires some extra parameters.

```
jackd -dalsa -dhw:2 -r 48000 -S
```

This doesn't work great; I get a regular "ticking" sound.
Without the -S (16-bit) flag, I just get this cryptic line:

```
ALSA: cannot set hardware parameters for playback
```

Alternatively, I can run this:

```
jackd -dalsa -dplughw:2 -r 48000
```

When I start it this way, Jack advises against using ALSA plug devices, but it works best so far.

How Can I Use Multiple Sound Cards with Jack?

Jack is intended for professional audio use. In such a system there will generally be only a single digital sample "clock." In this "ideal" Jack world, there would not be multiple independent sound cards each with their own clock. I'm just going to talk about this ideal world. If you need to run Jack in a situation where there is more than one sound card, then see "How can I use multiple soundcards with JACK?" (http://jackaudio.org/multiple_devices).

Mixing Audio

If two output ports from two different sources are connected to the same input port, then Jack will mix them for you. This allows you to sing along to your favorite MP3 file with no effort.

1. Connect the microphone capture ports to the playback ports. Avoid setting up a feedback loop between your laptop's microphone and speakers by, for example, plugging in headphones.

2. Start a player such as mplayer,which will also connect to the playback ports with something like the following:

   ```
   mplayer -ao jack <MP3 file >
   ```

3. Start singing.

Of course, there is no volume control on each source. You can insert a mixer such as jack_mixer (http://home.gna.org/jackmixer/), maybe in your distro too, and then use that to control the volume of each source, as shown in the qjackctl screen in Figure 7-1.

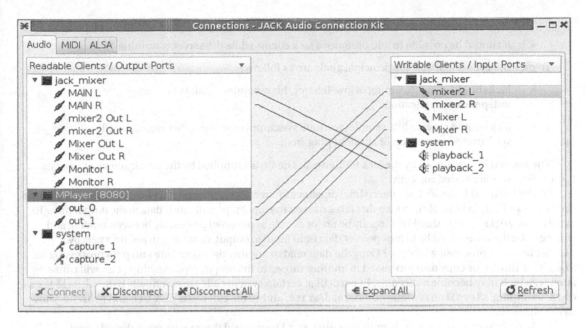

Figure 7-1. *qjackctl showing a mixer of mplayer and system*

Writing Audio Applications with Jack

The design of Jack is discussed at the JACK Audio Connection Kit (http://lac.linuxaudio.org/2003/zkm/slides/paul_davis-jack/title.html) by its primary author Paul Davis. The goals are as follows:

- Jack should allow streaming of low-latency, high-bandwidth data between independent applications.

- Although not a requirement, Jack should support any streaming data type, not just audio.

- In an active Jack setup, there will be one server and one or more Jack plug-ins. It will be possible to run multiple Jack servers, but each server will form an independent Jack setup. Jack will not define any interfaces between Jack servers.

- Applications connected using Jack may have their own graphical interfaces. Jack will not make any specifications as to different GUI toolkits or libraries. As a consequence of this requirement, different parts of a running Jack setup may be spread across multiple processes.

- Jack should provide full, sample-accurate synchronization (in other words, totally synchronous execution of all client plug-ins).

- To represent audio data, Jack should use 32-bit IEEE floats, normalized to value range [-1,1].

- Only noninterleaved audio streams will be supported.

- One Jack client may consume or produce multiple data streams.

- The Jack API should be specified in ANSI C. There are no restrictions on how servers and clients are to be implemented.

- It should be possible to connect already running applications.

- It should be possible to add or remove Jack clients while the server is running.

To pick the eyes out of this, the principal goals are as follows:

- Jack should allow streaming of low-latency, high-bandwidth data between independent applications.

- Jack should provide full, sample-accurate synchronization (in other words, totally synchronous execution of all client plug-ins).

The second is guaranteed by the Jack framework. The first is supplied by the Jack framework, as long as the applications are coded correctly.

Under the hood Jack uses fast Linux (Unix) pipelines to stream data from one application to another. Within each Jack application is a real-time loop that takes data off the input pipe and sends data to the output pipe. To avoid latency delays, there should essentially be no (or as little as possible) processing between reading and writing data; the ideal would be to pass pointer data from input to output, or at most to just do a memcpy.

So, how can processing be done? Copy the data read to another data structure and pass processing off to another thread, or copy data processed in another thread to the output pipe. Anything else will cause latency, which may become noticeable. In particular, certain system calls are essentially banned: malloc can cause swapping; sleep is an obvious no-no; read/write, and so on, can cause disk I/O; and pthread_cond_wait will...wait.

Jack applications are inherently multithreaded. In a Linux world this means Posix threads, and fortunately there is the book *PThreads Primer* (http://www8.cs.umu.se/kurser/TDBC64/VT03/pthreads/pthread-primer.pdf) by Bil Lewis and Daniel J. Berg to tell you all about Posix threads!

These are the mechanisms to set up a Jack application:

1. Open a connection to a Jack server: jack_client_open.

2. Examine the status of the connection and bailout if needed.

3. Install a process callback handler to manage I/O: jack_set_process_callback.

4. Install a shutdown callback: jack_on_shutdown.

5. Register input and output ports with the Jack server: jack_port_register. Note that each port carries only a mono channel, so for stereo you will get two input ports. This does *not* as yet link them to the pipelines.

6. Activate the ports. In other words, tell Jack to start its processing thread: jack_activate.

7. Connect the ports to the pipelines: jack_connect.

8. Sit there in some way. For a text client, just sleep in a loop. A GUI client might have a GUI processing loop.

Compiling

The following examples need to be linked to various libraries. These are the jack, sndfile, pthread, and math libraries. The appropriate flags are as follows:

```
INCLUDES = $(shell pkg-config --cflags jack sndfile)
LDLIBS =  $(shell pkg-config --libs jack sndfile) -lpthread -lm
```

Port Information

Jack uses ports that carry mono 32-bit data. Each port has a name as a string and properties such as input and output. Once a connection to a Jack server has been made, queries for ports known to the server can be made using jack_get_ports. If the arguments are NULL or zero, then all ports are returned, or patterns can be used to restrict the port names returned. Once a port name is found, it can be turned into a jack_port_t, and its properties can be queried.

A program to do this is listports.c, shown here:

```c
/** @file listports.c
 *
 * @brief This client delays one channel by 4096 framse.
 */

#include <stdio.h>
#include <errno.h>
#include <stdlib.h>
#include <string.h>
#include <math.h>
#include <signal.h>
#ifndef WIN32
#include <unistd.h>
#endif
#include <jack/jack.h>

jack_client_t *client;

void print_port_info(char *name) {
    printf("Port name is %s\n", name);
    jack_port_t *port = jack_port_by_name (client, name);
    if (port == NULL) {
        printf("No port by name %s\n", name);
        return;
    }
    printf("  Type is %s\n", jack_port_type(port));

    int flags = jack_port_flags(port);
    if (flags & JackPortIsInput)
        printf("  Is an input port\n");
    else
        printf("  Is an output port\n");
    char **connections = jack_port_get_connections(port);
    char **c = connections;
    printf("  Connected to:\n");
    while ((c != NULL) && (*c != NULL)) {
        printf("    %s\n", *c++);
    }
    if (connections != NULL)
        jack_free(connections);
}
```

```c
int
main ( int argc, char *argv[] )
{
    int i;
    const char **ports;
    const char *client_name;
    const char *server_name = NULL;
    jack_options_t options = JackNullOption;
    jack_status_t status;

    if ( argc >= 2 )        /* client name specified? */
    {
        client_name = argv[1];
        if ( argc >= 3 )    /* server name specified? */
        {
            server_name = argv[2];
            options |= JackServerName;
        }
    }
    else                /* use basename of argv[0] */
    {
        client_name = strrchr ( argv[0], '/' );
        if ( client_name == 0 )
        {
            client_name = argv[0];
        }
        else
        {
            client_name++;
        }
    }

    /* open a client connection to the JACK server */

    client = jack_client_open ( client_name, options, &status, server_name );
    if ( client == NULL )
    {
        fprintf ( stderr, "jack_client_open() failed, "
                  "status = 0x%2.0x\n", status );
        if ( status & JackServerFailed )
        {
            fprintf ( stderr, "Unable to connect to JACK server\n" );
        }
        exit ( 1 );
    }
    if ( status & JackServerStarted )
    {
        fprintf ( stderr, "JACK server started\n" );
    }
    if ( status & JackNameNotUnique )
    {
        client_name = jack_get_client_name ( client );
```

```
        fprintf ( stderr, "unique name `%s' assigned\n", client_name );
    }

    if ( jack_activate ( client ) )
    {
        fprintf ( stderr, "cannot activate client" );
        exit ( 1 );
    }

     ports = jack_get_ports ( client, NULL, NULL, 0 );
    if ( ports == NULL )
    {
        fprintf ( stderr, "no ports\n" );
        exit ( 1 );
    }
    char **p = ports;
    while (*p != NULL)
        print_port_info(*p++);
    jack_free(ports);

    jack_client_close ( client );
    exit ( 0 );
}
```

Copy Input to Output

The Jack source code distribution has an example clients subdirectory. Included in this subdirectory is the client thru_client.c, which just copies input to output. The processing heart of this example is the function process. This function takes a number of frames available on both input and output as parameters and the function loops through the (stereo) channels, gets corresponding input and output buffers (for input and output pipelines), and copies data from input to corresponding output.

The code is as follows:

```
/** @file thru_client.c
 *
 * @brief This simple through client demonstrates the basic features of JACK
 * as they would be used by many applications.
 */

#include <stdio.h>
#include <errno.h>
#include <stdlib.h>
#include <string.h>
#include <math.h>
#include <signal.h>
#ifndef WIN32
#include <unistd.h>
#endif
#include <jack/jack.h>

jack_port_t **input_ports;
```

```
jack_port_t **output_ports;
jack_client_t *client;

static void signal_handler ( int sig )
{
    jack_client_close ( client );
    fprintf ( stderr, "signal received, exiting ...\n" );
    exit ( 0 );
}

/**
 * The process callback for this JACK application is called in a
 * special realtime thread once for each audio cycle.
 *
 * This client follows a simple rule: when the JACK transport is
 * running, copy the input port to the output.  When it stops, exit.
 */

int
process ( jack_nframes_t nframes, void *arg )
{
    int i;
    jack_default_audio_sample_t *in, *out;
    for ( i = 0; i < 2; i++ )
    {
        in = jack_port_get_buffer ( input_ports[i], nframes );
        out = jack_port_get_buffer ( output_ports[i], nframes );
        memcpy ( out, in, nframes * sizeof ( jack_default_audio_sample_t ) );
    }
    return 0;
}

/**
 * JACK calls this shutdown_callback if the server ever shuts down or
 * decides to disconnect the client.
 */
void
jack_shutdown ( void *arg )
{
    free ( input_ports );
    free ( output_ports );
    exit ( 1 );
}

int
main ( int argc, char *argv[] )
{
    int i;
    const char **ports;
    const char *client_name;
    const char *server_name = NULL;
    jack_options_t options = JackNullOption;
```

```
jack_status_t status;

if ( argc >= 2 )        /* client name specified? */
{
    client_name = argv[1];
    if ( argc >= 3 )    /* server name specified? */
    {
        server_name = argv[2];
        options |= JackServerName;
    }
}
else                /* use basename of argv[0] */
{
    client_name = strrchr ( argv[0], '/' );
    if ( client_name == 0 )
    {
        client_name = argv[0];
    }
    else
    {
        client_name++;
    }
}

/* open a client connection to the JACK server */

client = jack_client_open ( client_name, options, &status, server_name );
if ( client == NULL )
{
    fprintf ( stderr, "jack_client_open() failed, "
            "status = 0x%2.0x\n", status );
    if ( status & JackServerFailed )
    {
        fprintf ( stderr, "Unable to connect to JACK server\n" );
    }
    exit ( 1 );
}
if ( status & JackServerStarted )
{
    fprintf ( stderr, "JACK server started\n" );
}
if ( status & JackNameNotUnique )
{
    client_name = jack_get_client_name ( client );
    fprintf ( stderr, "unique name `%s' assigned\n", client_name );
}

/* tell the JACK server to call `process()' whenever
   there is work to be done.
*/

jack_set_process_callback ( client, process, 0 );
```

```
/* tell the JACK server to call `jack_shutdown()' if
   it ever shuts down, either entirely, or if it
   just decides to stop calling us.
*/

jack_on_shutdown ( client, jack_shutdown, 0 );

/* create two ports pairs*/
input_ports = ( jack_port_t** ) calloc ( 2, sizeof ( jack_port_t* ) );
output_ports = ( jack_port_t** ) calloc ( 2, sizeof ( jack_port_t* ) );

char port_name[16];
for ( i = 0; i < 2; i++ )
{
    sprintf ( port_name, "input_%d", i + 1 );
    input_ports[i] = jack_port_register ( client, port_name, JACK_DEFAULT_AUDIO_TYPE,
    JackPortIsInput, 0 );
    sprintf ( port_name, "output_%d", i + 1 );
    output_ports[i] = jack_port_register ( client, port_name, JACK_DEFAULT_AUDIO_TYPE,
    JackPortIsOutput, 0 );
    if ( ( input_ports[i] == NULL ) || ( output_ports[i] == NULL ) )
    {
        fprintf ( stderr, "no more JACK ports available\n" );
        exit ( 1 );
    }
}

/* Tell the JACK server that we are ready to roll.  Our
 * process() callback will start running now. */

if ( jack_activate ( client ) )
{
    fprintf ( stderr, "cannot activate client" );
    exit ( 1 );
}

/* Connect the ports.  You can't do this before the client is
 * activated, because we can't make connections to clients
 * that aren't running.  Note the confusing (but necessary)
 * orientation of the driver backend ports: playback ports are
 * "input" to the backend, and capture ports are "output" from
 * it.
 */

ports = jack_get_ports ( client, NULL, NULL, JackPortIsPhysical|JackPortIsOutput );
if ( ports == NULL )
{
    fprintf ( stderr, "no physical capture ports\n" );
    exit ( 1 );
}

for ( i = 0; i < 2; i++ )
```

```
        if ( jack_connect ( client, ports[i], jack_port_name ( input_ports[i] ) ) )
            fprintf ( stderr, "cannot connect input ports\n" );

    free ( ports );

    ports = jack_get_ports ( client, NULL, NULL, JackPortIsPhysical|JackPortIsInput );
    if ( ports == NULL )
    {
        fprintf ( stderr, "no physical playback ports\n" );
        exit ( 1 );
    }

    for ( i = 0; i < 2; i++ )
        if ( jack_connect ( client, jack_port_name ( output_ports[i] ), ports[i] ) )
            fprintf ( stderr, "cannot connect input ports\n" );

    free ( ports );

    /* install a signal handler to properly quits jack client */
#ifdef WIN32
    signal ( SIGINT, signal_handler );
    signal ( SIGABRT, signal_handler );
    signal ( SIGTERM, signal_handler );
#else
    signal ( SIGQUIT, signal_handler );
    signal ( SIGTERM, signal_handler );
    signal ( SIGHUP, signal_handler );
    signal ( SIGINT, signal_handler );
#endif

    /* keep running until the transport stops */

    while (1)
    {
#ifdef WIN32
        Sleep ( 1000 );
#else
        sleep ( 1 );
#endif
    }

    jack_client_close ( client );
    exit ( 0 );
}
```

Delaying Audio

While this book is not about audio effects, you can easily introduce one effect—latency—by just delaying sounds. Now this—and any time-consuming actions—are against the spirit (and implementation!) of Jack, so it can be done only in cooperation with the Jack model.

The simplest idea is just to throw in sleep commands at the right places. This would assume that calls to the process callback happen asynchronously, but they don't—they happen synchronously within the Jack processing thread. Activities that cost time aren't allowed. If you try it, you will end up with lots of xruns at best and seizures of Jack at worst.

In this case, the solution is straightforward: keep a buffer in which previous inputs are kept, and read older entries out of this buffer when output is requested. A "big enough" wrap-around array will do this, where old entries are read out and new entries read in.

The following program, delay.c, will copy the left channel in real time but delay the left channel by 4,096 samples:

```
/** @file delay.c
 *
 * @brief This client delays one channel by 4096 framse.
 */

#include <stdio.h>
#include <errno.h>
#include <stdlib.h>
#include <string.h>
#include <math.h>
#include <signal.h>
#ifndef WIN32
#include <unistd.h>
#endif
#include <jack/jack.h>

jack_port_t **input_ports;
jack_port_t **output_ports;
jack_client_t *client;

#define SIZE 8192
#define DELAY 4096
jack_default_audio_sample_t buffer[SIZE];
int idx, delay_idx;

static void signal_handler ( int sig )
{
    jack_client_close ( client );
    fprintf ( stderr, "signal received, exiting ...\n" );
    exit ( 0 );
}

static void copy2out( jack_default_audio_sample_t *out,
                      jack_nframes_t nframes) {
    if (delay_idx + nframes < SIZE) {
        memcpy(out, buffer + delay_idx,
                nframes * sizeof ( jack_default_audio_sample_t ) );
    } else {
        int frames_to_end = SIZE - delay_idx;
        int overflow = delay_idx + nframes - SIZE;
        memcpy(out, buffer + delay_idx,
                frames_to_end * sizeof ( jack_default_audio_sample_t ) );
```

```
        memcpy(out, buffer, overflow * sizeof(jack_default_audio_sample_t));
    }
    delay_idx = (delay_idx + nframes) % SIZE;
}

static void copy2buffer( jack_default_audio_sample_t *in,
                         jack_nframes_t nframes) {
    if (idx + nframes < SIZE) {
        memcpy(buffer + idx, in,
                nframes * sizeof ( jack_default_audio_sample_t ) );
    } else {
        int frames_to_end = SIZE - idx;
        int overflow = idx + nframes - SIZE;
        memcpy(buffer + idx, in,
                frames_to_end * sizeof ( jack_default_audio_sample_t ) );
        memcpy(buffer, in, overflow * sizeof(jack_default_audio_sample_t));
    }
    idx = (idx + nframes) % SIZE;
}

/**
 * The process callback for this JACK application is called in a
 * special realtime thread once for each audio cycle.
 *
 * This client follows a simple rule: when the JACK transport is
 * running, copy the input port to the output.  When it stops, exit.
 */

int
process ( jack_nframes_t nframes, void *arg )
{
    int i;
    jack_default_audio_sample_t *in, *out;

    in = jack_port_get_buffer ( input_ports[0], nframes );
    out = jack_port_get_buffer ( output_ports[0], nframes );
    memcpy ( out, in, nframes * sizeof ( jack_default_audio_sample_t ) );

    in = jack_port_get_buffer ( input_ports[1], nframes );
    out = jack_port_get_buffer ( output_ports[1], nframes );
    copy2out(out, nframes);
    copy2buffer(in, nframes);

    return 0;
}

/**
 * JACK calls this shutdown_callback if the server ever shuts down or
 * decides to disconnect the client.
 */
void
jack_shutdown ( void *arg )
```

```
{
    free ( input_ports );
    free ( output_ports );
    exit ( 1 );
}

int
main ( int argc, char *argv[] )
{
    int i;
    const char **ports;
    const char *client_name;
    const char *server_name = NULL;
    jack_options_t options = JackNullOption;
    jack_status_t status;

    if ( argc >= 2 )        /* client name specified? */
    {
        client_name = argv[1];
        if ( argc >= 3 )    /* server name specified? */
        {
            server_name = argv[2];
            options |= JackServerName;
        }
    }
    else                /* use basename of argv[0] */
    {
        client_name = strrchr ( argv[0], '/' );
        if ( client_name == 0 )
        {
            client_name = argv[0];
        }
        else
        {
            client_name++;
        }
    }

    /* open a client connection to the JACK server */

    client = jack_client_open ( client_name, options, &status, server_name );
    if ( client == NULL )
    {
        fprintf ( stderr, "jack_client_open() failed, "
                    "status = 0x%2.0x\n", status );
        if ( status & JackServerFailed )
        {
            fprintf ( stderr, "Unable to connect to JACK server\n" );
        }
        exit ( 1 );
    }
    if ( status & JackServerStarted )
```

```
{
    fprintf ( stderr, "JACK server started\n" );
}
if ( status & JackNameNotUnique )
{
    client_name = jack_get_client_name ( client );
    fprintf ( stderr, "unique name `%s' assigned\n", client_name );
}

/* tell the JACK server to call `process()' whenever
   there is work to be done.
*/

jack_set_process_callback ( client, process, 0 );

/* tell the JACK server to call `jack_shutdown()' if
   it ever shuts down, either entirely, or if it
   just decides to stop calling us.
*/

jack_on_shutdown ( client, jack_shutdown, 0 );

/* create two ports pairs*/
input_ports = ( jack_port_t** ) calloc ( 2, sizeof ( jack_port_t* ) );
output_ports = ( jack_port_t** ) calloc ( 2, sizeof ( jack_port_t* ) );

char port_name[16];
for ( i = 0; i < 2; i++ )
{
    sprintf ( port_name, "input_%d", i + 1 );
    input_ports[i] = jack_port_register ( client, port_name, JACK_DEFAULT_AUDIO_TYPE,
    JackPortIsInput, 0 );
    sprintf ( port_name, "output_%d", i + 1 );
    output_ports[i] = jack_port_register ( client, port_name, JACK_DEFAULT_AUDIO_TYPE,
    JackPortIsOutput, 0 );
    if ( ( input_ports[i] == NULL ) || ( output_ports[i] == NULL ) )
    {
        fprintf ( stderr, "no more JACK ports available\n" );
        exit ( 1 );
    }
}

bzero(buffer, SIZE * sizeof ( jack_default_audio_sample_t ));
delay_idx = 0;
idx = DELAY;

/* Tell the JACK server that we are ready to roll.  Our
 * process() callback will start running now. */

if ( jack_activate ( client ) )
{
```

161

```
        fprintf ( stderr, "cannot activate client" );
        exit ( 1 );
    }

    /* Connect the ports.  You can't do this before the client is
     * activated, because we can't make connections to clients
     * that aren't running.  Note the confusing (but necessary)
     * orientation of the driver backend ports: playback ports are
     * "input" to the backend, and capture ports are "output" from
     * it.
     */

    ports = jack_get_ports ( client, NULL, NULL, JackPortIsPhysical|JackPortIsOutput );
    if ( ports == NULL )
    {
        fprintf ( stderr, "no physical capture ports\n" );
        exit ( 1 );
    }

    for ( i = 0; i < 2; i++ )
        if ( jack_connect ( client, ports[i], jack_port_name ( input_ports[i] ) ) )
            fprintf ( stderr, "cannot connect input ports\n" );

    free ( ports );

    ports = jack_get_ports ( client, NULL, NULL, JackPortIsPhysical|JackPortIsInput );
    if ( ports == NULL )
    {
        fprintf ( stderr, "no physical playback ports\n" );
        exit ( 1 );
    }

    for ( i = 0; i < 2; i++ )
        if ( jack_connect ( client, jack_port_name ( output_ports[i] ), ports[i] ) )
            fprintf ( stderr, "cannot connect input ports\n" );

    free ( ports );

    /* install a signal handler to properly quits jack client */
#ifdef WIN32
    signal ( SIGINT, signal_handler );
    signal ( SIGABRT, signal_handler );
    signal ( SIGTERM, signal_handler );
#else
    signal ( SIGQUIT, signal_handler );
    signal ( SIGTERM, signal_handler );
    signal ( SIGHUP, signal_handler );
    signal ( SIGINT, signal_handler );
#endif

    /* keep running until the transport stops */
```

```
    while (1)
    {
#ifdef WIN32
        Sleep ( 1000 );
#else
        sleep ( 1 );
#endif
    }

    jack_client_close ( client );
    exit ( 0 );
}
```

Audacity with Jack

Audacity is Jack-aware. You can use it to capture and display Jack streams. But that doesn't mean that for the user it plays in a *nice* way! With a running Jack system, starting Audacity registers it with Jack, but there are no input or output ports. These show up only when you start a record session with Audacity. It then establishes its own links within Jack.

For example, with thru_client as the only client within Jack, qjackctl shows the connections, as shown in Figure 7-2.

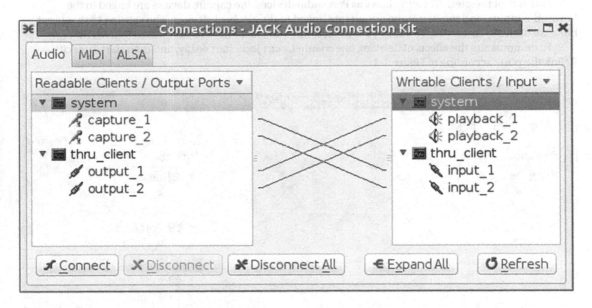

Figure 7-2. *Qjackctl showing thru_client*

In this figure, the capture devices are connected to the thru_client inputs, and the thru_client outputs are connected to the playback outputs.

Just starting Audacity but not recording anything makes no changes to this connection graph.

But when Audacity starts recording with thru_client already running, qjackctl shows the links established, as in Figure 7-3.

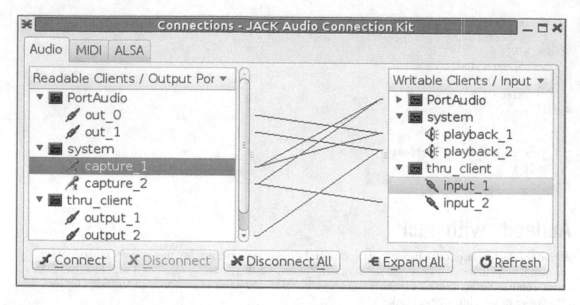

Figure 7-3. *Qjackctl with thru_client and Audacity*

This is a lot messier: Audacity shows as PortAudio devices, the capture devices are linked to the PortAudio inputs, and the PortAudio outputs are linked to the playback devices. The existing `thru_client` links are basically discarded. To set up your desired situation, these have to be relinked as needed.

To demonstrate the effects of delaying one channel, start Jack, start `delay`, and then start Audacity. Relink the ports according to Figure 7-4.

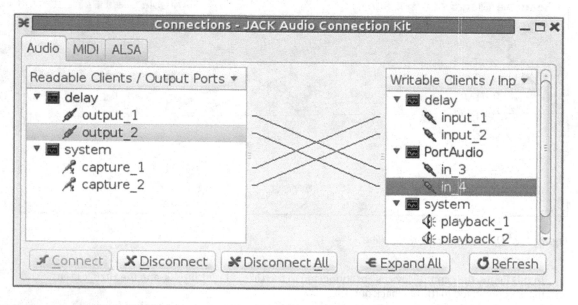

Figure 7-4. *Qjackctl wih delay*

That is, capture ports are linked to delay input ports, delay output ports are linked to PortAudio (Audacity) input ports, and PortAudio output ports are linked to playback ports.

The waveforms captured by Audacity clearly show the delay on the left channel compared to the right (Figure 7-5).

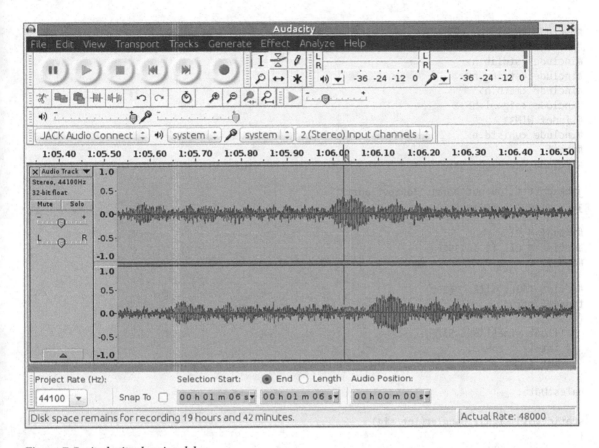

Figure 7-5. *Audacity showing delay*

Play a Sine Wave

The copy example does not show the detail of what is in the buffers: the contents are from jack_default_audio_sample_t. What these are is described in the macro JACK_DEFAULT_AUDIO_TYPE with the default value "32 bit float mono audio."

To do anything more than simply pass audio through, you need to handle the data in this format. The example program simple_client.c fills an array with 32-bit floating point sine curve values. On each call to process, it copies data from the sine curve array into the output buffers. The increment into the sine curve array is different for the left and right channels to give a different note on each channel.

Note that the calculation of the sine curve array is *not* done within the process function. That would be too slow and would cause latency.

The program is as follows:

```
/** @file simple_client.c
 *
 * @brief This simple client demonstrates the basic features of JACK
 * as they would be used by many applications.
 */

#include <stdio.h>
#include <errno.h>
#include <stdlib.h>
#include <string.h>
#include <math.h>
#include <signal.h>
#ifndef WIN32
#include <unistd.h>
#endif
#include <jack/jack.h>

jack_port_t *output_port1, *output_port2;
jack_client_t *client;

#ifndef M_PI
#define M_PI  (3.14159265)
#endif

#define TABLE_SIZE   (200)
typedef struct
{
    float sine[TABLE_SIZE];
    int left_phase;
    int right_phase;
}
paTestData;

static void signal_handler(int sig)
{
        jack_client_close(client);
        fprintf(stderr, "signal received, exiting ...\n");
        exit(0);
}

/**
 * The process callback for this JACK application is called in a
 * special realtime thread once for each audio cycle.
 *
 * This client follows a simple rule: when the JACK transport is
 * running, copy the input port to the output.  When it stops, exit.
 */

int
process (jack_nframes_t nframes, void *arg)
{
        jack_default_audio_sample_t *out1, *out2;
        paTestData *data = (paTestData*)arg;
```

```
        int i;

        out1 = (jack_default_audio_sample_t*)jack_port_get_buffer (output_port1, nframes);
        out2 = (jack_default_audio_sample_t*)jack_port_get_buffer (output_port2, nframes);

        for( i=0; i<nframes; i++ )
    {
        out1[i] = data->sine[data->left_phase];   /* left */
        out2[i] = data->sine[data->right_phase];   /* right */
        data->left_phase += 1;
        if( data->left_phase >= TABLE_SIZE ) data->left_phase -= TABLE_SIZE;
        data->right_phase += 3; /* higher pitch so we can distinguish left and right. */
        if( data->right_phase >= TABLE_SIZE ) data->right_phase -= TABLE_SIZE;
    }

        return 0;
}

/**
 * JACK calls this shutdown_callback if the server ever shuts down or
 * decides to disconnect the client.
 */
void
jack_shutdown (void *arg)
{
        exit (1);
}

int
main (int argc, char *argv[])
{
        const char **ports;
        const char *client_name;
        const char *server_name = NULL;
        jack_options_t options = JackNullOption;
        jack_status_t status;
        paTestData data;
        int i;

        if (argc >= 2) {                    /* client name specified? */
                client_name = argv[1];
                if (argc >= 3) {            /* server name specified? */
                        server_name = argv[2];
            int my_option = JackNullOption | JackServerName;
                        options = (jack_options_t)my_option;
                }
        } else {                            /* use basename of argv[0] */
                client_name = strrchr(argv[0], '/');
                if (client_name == 0) {
                        client_name = argv[0];
                } else {
                        client_name++;
```

```
            }
        }

    for( i=0; i<TABLE_SIZE; i++ )
{
    data.sine[i] = 0.2 * (float) sin( ((double)i/(double)TABLE_SIZE) * M_PI * 2. );
}
data.left_phase = data.right_phase = 0;

    /* open a client connection to the JACK server */

    client = jack_client_open (client_name, options, &status, server_name);
    if (client == NULL) {
            fprintf (stderr, "jack_client_open() failed, "
                    "status = 0x%2.0x\n", status);
            if (status & JackServerFailed) {
                    fprintf (stderr, "Unable to connect to JACK server\n");
            }
            exit (1);
    }
    if (status & JackServerStarted) {
            fprintf (stderr, "JACK server started\n");
    }
    if (status & JackNameNotUnique) {
            client_name = jack_get_client_name(client);
            fprintf (stderr, "unique name `%s' assigned\n", client_name);
    }

    /* tell the JACK server to call `process()' whenever
       there is work to be done.
    */

    jack_set_process_callback (client, process, &data);

    /* tell the JACK server to call `jack_shutdown()' if
       it ever shuts down, either entirely, or if it
       just decides to stop calling us.
    */

    jack_on_shutdown (client, jack_shutdown, 0);

    /* create two ports */

    output_port1 = jack_port_register (client, "output1",
                                JACK_DEFAULT_AUDIO_TYPE,
                                JackPortIsOutput, 0);

    output_port2 = jack_port_register (client, "output2",
                                JACK_DEFAULT_AUDIO_TYPE,
                                JackPortIsOutput, 0);

    if ((output_port1 == NULL) || (output_port2 == NULL)) {
```

```
                fprintf(stderr, "no more JACK ports available\n");
                exit (1);
        }

        /* Tell the JACK server that we are ready to roll.  Our
         * process() callback will start running now. */

        if (jack_activate (client)) {
                fprintf (stderr, "cannot activate client");
                exit (1);
        }

        /* Connect the ports.  You can't do this before the client is
         * activated, because we can't make connections to clients
         * that aren't running.  Note the confusing (but necessary)
         * orientation of the driver backend ports: playback ports are
         * "input" to the backend, and capture ports are "output" from
         * it.
         */

        ports = jack_get_ports (client, NULL, NULL,
                                JackPortIsPhysical|JackPortIsInput);
        if (ports == NULL) {
                fprintf(stderr, "no physical playback ports\n");
                exit (1);
        }

        if (jack_connect (client, jack_port_name (output_port1), ports[0])) {
                fprintf (stderr, "cannot connect output ports\n");
        }

        if (jack_connect (client, jack_port_name (output_port2), ports[1])) {
                fprintf (stderr, "cannot connect output ports\n");
        }

        free (ports);

    /* install a signal handler to properly quits jack client */
#ifdef WIN32
        signal(SIGINT, signal_handler);
    signal(SIGABRT, signal_handler);
        signal(SIGTERM, signal_handler);
#else
        signal(SIGQUIT, signal_handler);
        signal(SIGTERM, signal_handler);
        signal(SIGHUP, signal_handler);
        signal(SIGINT, signal_handler);
#endif

        /* keep running until the Ctrl+C */

        while (1) {
```

```
        #ifdef WIN32
                Sleep(1000);
        #else
                sleep (1);
        #endif
        }

        jack_client_close (client);
        exit (0);
}
```

Saving Input to Disk

Disk I/O cannot be performed within the Jack processing loop; it is just too slow. Saving input to a file requires use of a separate thread to manage disk I/O and pass control between the Jack and disk threads.

The program capture_client.c from the examples does this.

```
/*

    Copyright (C) 2001 Paul Davis
    Copyright (C) 2003 Jack O'Quin

    This program is free software; you can redistribute it and/or modify
    it under the terms of the GNU General Public License as published by
    the Free Software Foundation; either version 2 of the License, or
    (at your option) any later version.

    This program is distributed in the hope that it will be useful,
    but WITHOUT ANY WARRANTY; without even the implied warranty of
    MERCHANTABILITY or FITNESS FOR A PARTICULAR PURPOSE.  See the
    GNU General Public License for more details.

    You should have received a copy of the GNU General Public License
    along with this program; if not, write to the Free Software
    Foundation, Inc., 675 Mass Ave, Cambridge, MA 02139, USA.

    * 2002/08/23 - modify for libsndfile 1.0.0 <andy@alsaplayer.org>
    * 2003/05/26 - use ringbuffers - joq
*/

#include <stdio.h>
#include <stdlib.h>
#include <string.h>
#include <errno.h>
#include <unistd.h>
#include <sndfile.h>
#include <pthread.h>
#include <signal.h>
#include <getopt.h>
#include <jack/jack.h>
#include <jack/ringbuffer.h>
```

```
typedef struct _thread_info {
    pthread_t thread_id;
    SNDFILE *sf;
    jack_nframes_t duration;
    jack_nframes_t rb_size;
    jack_client_t *client;
    unsigned int channels;
    int bitdepth;
    char *path;
    volatile int can_capture;
    volatile int can_process;
    volatile int status;
} jack_thread_info_t;

/* JACK data */
unsigned int nports;
jack_port_t **ports;
jack_default_audio_sample_t **in;
jack_nframes_t nframes;
const size_t sample_size = sizeof(jack_default_audio_sample_t);

/* Synchronization between process thread and disk thread. */
#define DEFAULT_RB_SIZE 16384           /* ringbuffer size in frames */
jack_ringbuffer_t *rb;
pthread_mutex_t disk_thread_lock = PTHREAD_MUTEX_INITIALIZER;
pthread_cond_t   data_ready = PTHREAD_COND_INITIALIZER;
long overruns = 0;
jack_client_t *client;

static void signal_handler(int sig)
{
        jack_client_close(client);
        fprintf(stderr, "signal received, exiting ...\n");
        exit(0);
}

static void *
disk_thread (void *arg)
{
        jack_thread_info_t *info = (jack_thread_info_t *) arg;
        static jack_nframes_t total_captured = 0;
        jack_nframes_t samples_per_frame = info->channels;
        size_t bytes_per_frame = samples_per_frame * sample_size;
        void *framebuf = malloc (bytes_per_frame);

        pthread_setcanceltype (PTHREAD_CANCEL_ASYNCHRONOUS, NULL);
        pthread_mutex_lock (&disk_thread_lock);

        info->status = 0;

        while (1) {
```

```
                    /* Write the data one frame at a time.  This is
                     * inefficient, but makes things simpler. */
                    while (info->can_capture &&
                            (jack_ringbuffer_read_space (rb) >= bytes_per_frame)) {

                            jack_ringbuffer_read (rb, framebuf, bytes_per_frame);

                            if (sf_writef_float (info->sf, framebuf, 1) != 1) {
                                    char errstr[256];
                                    sf_error_str (0, errstr, sizeof (errstr) - 1);
                                    fprintf (stderr,
                                            "cannot write sndfile (%s)\n",
                                            errstr);
                                    info->status = EIO; /* write failed */
                                    goto done;
                            }

                            if (++total_captured >= info->duration) {
                                    printf ("disk thread finished\n");
                                    goto done;
                            }
                    }

                    /* wait until process() signals more data */
                    pthread_cond_wait (&data_ready, &disk_thread_lock);
            }

 done:
            pthread_mutex_unlock (&disk_thread_lock);
            free (framebuf);
            return 0;
}

static int
process (jack_nframes_t nframes, void *arg)
{
            int chn;
            size_t i;
            jack_thread_info_t *info = (jack_thread_info_t *) arg;

            /* Do nothing until we're ready to begin. */
            if ((!info->can_process) || (!info->can_capture))
                    return 0;

            for (chn = 0; chn < nports; chn++)
                    in[chn] = jack_port_get_buffer (ports[chn], nframes);

            /* Sndfile requires interleaved data.  It is simpler here to
             * just queue interleaved samples to a single ringbuffer. */
            for (i = 0; i < nframes; i++) {
                    for (chn = 0; chn < nports; chn++) {
```

```
                    if (jack_ringbuffer_write (rb, (void *) (in[chn]+i),
                                        sample_size)
                        < sample_size)
                            overruns++;
                }
        }

        /* Tell the disk thread there is work to do.  If it is already
         * running, the lock will not be available.  We can't wait
         * here in the process() thread, but we don't need to signal
         * in that case, because the disk thread will read all the
         * data queued before waiting again. */
        if (pthread_mutex_trylock (&disk_thread_lock) == 0) {
            pthread_cond_signal (&data_ready);
            pthread_mutex_unlock (&disk_thread_lock);
        }

        return 0;
}

static void
jack_shutdown (void *arg)
{
        fprintf(stderr, "JACK shut down, exiting ...\n");
        exit(1);
}

static void
setup_disk_thread (jack_thread_info_t *info)
{
        SF_INFO sf_info;
        int short_mask;

        sf_info.samplerate = jack_get_sample_rate (info->client);
        sf_info.channels = info->channels;

        switch (info->bitdepth) {
                case 8: short_mask = SF_FORMAT_PCM_U8;
                        break;
                case 16: short_mask = SF_FORMAT_PCM_16;
                        break;
                case 24: short_mask = SF_FORMAT_PCM_24;
                        break;
                case 32: short_mask = SF_FORMAT_PCM_32;
                        break;
                default: short_mask = SF_FORMAT_PCM_16;
                        break;
        }
        sf_info.format = SF_FORMAT_WAV|short_mask;

        if ((info->sf = sf_open (info->path, SFM_WRITE, &sf_info)) == NULL) {
                char errstr[256];
                sf_error_str (0, errstr, sizeof (errstr) - 1);
```

```
                    fprintf (stderr, "cannot open sndfile \"%s\" for output (%s)\n", info->path,
                    errstr);
                    jack_client_close (info->client);
                    exit (1);
        }

        info->duration *= sf_info.samplerate;
        info->can_capture = 0;

        pthread_create (&info->thread_id, NULL, disk_thread, info);
}

static void
run_disk_thread (jack_thread_info_t *info)
{
        info->can_capture = 1;
        pthread_join (info->thread_id, NULL);
        sf_close (info->sf);
        if (overruns > 0) {
                fprintf (stderr,
                            "jackrec failed with %ld overruns.\n", overruns);
                fprintf (stderr, " try a bigger buffer than -B %"
                            PRIu32 ".\n", info->rb_size);
                info->status = EPIPE;
        }
}

static void
setup_ports (int sources, char *source_names[], jack_thread_info_t *info)
{
        unsigned int i;
        size_t in_size;

        /* Allocate data structures that depend on the number of ports. */
        nports = sources;
        ports = (jack_port_t **) malloc (sizeof (jack_port_t *) * nports);
        in_size =  nports * sizeof (jack_default_audio_sample_t *);
        in = (jack_default_audio_sample_t **) malloc (in_size);
        rb = jack_ringbuffer_create (nports * sample_size * info->rb_size);

        /* When JACK is running realtime, jack_activate() will have
         * called mlockall() to lock our pages into memory.  But, we
         * still need to touch any newly allocated pages before
         * process() starts using them.  Otherwise, a page fault could
         * create a delay that would force JACK to shut us down. */
        memset(in, 0, in_size);
        memset(rb->buf, 0, rb->size);

        for (i = 0; i < nports; i++) {
                char name[64];

                sprintf (name, "input%d", i+1);
```

```
                if ((ports[i] = jack_port_register (info->client, name, JACK_DEFAULT_AUDIO_
            TYPE, JackPortIsInput, 0)) == 0) {
                        fprintf (stderr, "cannot register input port \"%s\"!\n", name);
                        jack_client_close (info->client);
                        exit (1);
                }
        }

        for (i = 0; i < nports; i++) {
                if (jack_connect (info->client, source_names[i], jack_port_name (ports[i])))
{
                        fprintf (stderr, "cannot connect input port %s to %s\n", jack_port_
                        name (ports[i]), source_names[i]);
                        jack_client_close (info->client);
                        exit (1);
                }
        }

        info->can_process = 1;          /* process() can start, now */
}
int
main (int argc, char *argv[])
{
    jack_thread_info_t thread_info;
        int c;
        int longopt_index = 0;
        extern int optind, opterr;
        int show_usage = 0;
        char *optstring = "d:f:b:B:h";
        struct option long_options[] = {
                { "help", 0, 0, 'h' },
                { "duration", 1, 0, 'd' },
                { "file", 1, 0, 'f' },
                { "bitdepth", 1, 0, 'b' },
                { "bufsize", 1, 0, 'B' },
                { 0, 0, 0, 0 }
        };

        memset (&thread_info, 0, sizeof (thread_info));
        thread_info.rb_size = DEFAULT_RB_SIZE;
        opterr = 0;

        while ((c = getopt_long (argc, argv, optstring, long_options, &longopt_index))
        != -1) {
                switch (c) {
                case 1:
                        /* getopt signals end of '-' options */
                        break;

                case 'h':
                        show_usage++;
                        break;
```

```
                case 'd':
                        thread_info.duration = atoi (optarg);
                        break;
                case 'f':
                        thread_info.path = optarg;
                        break;
                case 'b':
                        thread_info.bitdepth = atoi (optarg);
                        break;
                case 'B':
                        thread_info.rb_size = atoi (optarg);
                        break;
                default:
                        fprintf (stderr, "error\n");
                        show_usage++;
                        break;
                }
        }

        if (show_usage || thread_info.path == NULL || optind == argc) {
                fprintf (stderr, "usage: jackrec -f filename [ -d second ] [ -b bitdepth ]
                [ -B bufsize ] port1 [ port2 ... ]\n");
                exit (1);
        }

        if ((client = jack_client_open ("jackrec", JackNullOption, NULL)) == 0) {
                fprintf (stderr, "JACK server not running?\n");
                exit (1);
        }

        thread_info.client = client;
        thread_info.channels = argc - optind;
        thread_info.can_process = 0;

        setup_disk_thread (&thread_info);

        jack_set_process_callback (client, process, &thread_info);
        jack_on_shutdown (client, jack_shutdown, &thread_info);

        if (jack_activate (client)) {
                fprintf (stderr, "cannot activate client");
        }

        setup_ports (argc - optind, &argv[optind], &thread_info);

    /* install a signal handler to properly quits jack client */
    signal(SIGQUIT, signal_handler);
    signal(SIGTERM, signal_handler);
    signal(SIGHUP, signal_handler);
    signal(SIGINT, signal_handler);
```

```
    run_disk_thread (&thread_info);

    jack_client_close (client);

    jack_ringbuffer_free (rb);

    exit (0);
}
```

Interacting with ALSA Devices

Jack will eventually get its input from, and send its output to, devices. Currently, they are most likely to be ALSA devices. Consequently, there must be a bridge between Jack processing and ALSA input and output. This will involve all the complexity of ALSA programming.

Fortunately, there are Jack clients that do this. The Jack framework will talk to these, as specified when starting the Jack server.

```
jackd -dalsa
```

So, you don't need to worry about that interface. For the brave and curious, the Jack source has a directory of examples, which includes the files `alsa_in.c` and `alsa_out.c`. They contains comments from the author such as "`// Alsa stuff… i dont want to touch this bullshit in the next years.... please…`", giving you fair warning that it's not easy and not necessary for general Jack programming.

Conclusion

This chapter covered using Jack from a user viewpoint and also looked at programming Jack clients.

Interfacing with ALSA Devices

Conclusion

CHAPTER 8

■ ■ ■

Session Management

A complex sound system may consist of multiple sound sources, multiple filters, and multiple outputs. If they have to be set up fresh each time they are used, then there can be errors, wasted time, and so on. Session management attempts to solve these problems.

Resources

Here are some resources:

- "A brief survey of Linux audio session managers" by Dave Phillips (`http://lwn.net/Articles/533594/`)

- "Session Management Overview" (`http://wiki.linuxaudio.org/wiki/session_management`) contains links to many resources

- JACK-AUDIO-CONNECTION-KIT, Session API for clients (`http://jackaudio.org/files/docs/html/group__SessionClientFunctions.html`)

- LADI Session Handler (`http://ladish.org/`)

- Non Session Management API (`http://non.tuxfamily.org/nsm/API.html`)

Session Management Issues

Whenever there are multiple modules linked in some way, there can be a need to manage the modules and their linkages. These needs arise quite quickly in the Jack environment, which is designed for multiple linkages. It doesn't take a complex arrangement of Jack modules for management to become tedious. For example, consider the mixer session of the previous chapter in Figure 8-1.

© Jan Newmarch 2017
J. Newmarch, *Linux Sound Programming*, DOI 10.1007/978-1-4842-2496-0_8

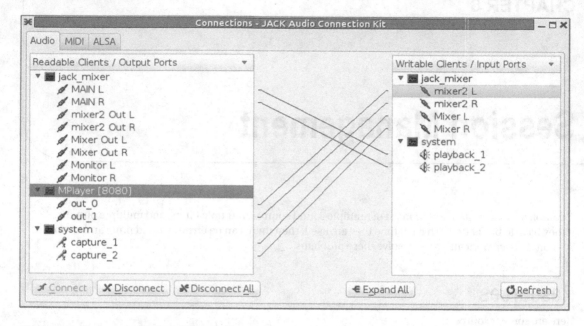

Figure 8-1. Jack connecting multiple applications

Setting this up from the beginning requires the following:

1. Start jackd and qjackctl.

2. Start jack_mixer.

3. Open two new sets of input ports on the mixer.

4. Connect the MAIN mixer output ports to the playback ports.

5. Connect the microphone ports to one set of mixer input ports.

6. Start mplayer, which automatically connects to the playback ports.

7. Disconnect the mplayer output ports from the playback ports and reconnect them to the other set of mixer input ports.

You don't want to do this every time you play a song!

The LADISH session manager identifies different levels of control of applications by session managers (http://ladish.org/wiki/levels). Removing the explicit references to particular managers and frameworks, the levels are as follows:

- *Level 0*: An application is not linked to a session-handling library. The user has to save application projects manually or rely on autosave support from the application.

- *Level 1*: An application is not linked to a session-handling library. The application saves when particular messages or signals are received.

- *Level 2*: An application is linked to a session management library. It has limited interaction with the session handler because of limitations in the session manager.

- *Level 3*: An application is linked to a sophisticated session manager. It has full interaction with the session handler.

As Dave Phillips points out, "The use of these levels is an attempt to sort and regulate the various possible conditions for any Linux audio application. Those conditions include the degree of JACK compliance, any WINE or DOS requirements, network operation, the multiplicity of existing APIs, and so forth."

The current batch of session management frameworks used for Linux audio includes

- LASH

- Jack session management

- LADISH

- Non-session manager

- Chino

The existence of multiple managers means that most applications will support the protocols of only one or at most a few. If you choose a particular manager, then you will be restricted to the applications you can run under its control.

jack_connect

The programs jack_connect and jack_disconnect can be used to reconfigure connections between clients. For example, the MIDI player TiMidity will connect its output ports to the first available Jack input ports, which are generally the system ports connected to the sound card. If you want to connect TiMidity to, say, jack-rack, then its output ports have to be first disconnected and then connected to the correct ones. On the other hand, jack-rack does not connect to anything by default so may need to be connected to the system ports. This is done with the following:

```
jack_disconnect TiMidity:port_1 system:playback_1
jack_disconnect TiMidity:port_2 system:playback_2

jack_connect TiMidity:port_1 jack_rack:in_1
jack_connect TiMidity:port_2 jack_rack:in_2

jack_connect jack_rack:out_1 system:playback_1
jack_connect jack_rack:out_2 system:playback_2
```

LASH

This was the earliest successful session manager for Linux audio but has since fallen out of use. It does not seem to be in the Ubuntu repositories anymore.

One of the applications requiring LASH is jack_mixer. Even worse, it uses the Python LASH module from the python-lash.2.7.4-0ubuntu package. The only copy I can find requires a version of Python less than 2.7, and the installed version of Python is 2.7.4. This is an application that currently will not benefit from current session management tools. While it might run as Level 1 with LASH, it can run only at Level 0 with other session managers.

So, there are Jack applications that require LASH for session management, but no such support seems to exist anymore.

Jack Sessions

You can find a list of Jack session-aware applications as of 2016 at http://wiki.linuxaudio.org/apps/categories/jack_session.

qjackctl has a session manager that will allow you to save and restore sessions. You save a session by clicking the Session button and then choosing a session name and directory. qjackctl stores the session information as an XML file in whatever directory you save it in. For the previous session, this looks like the following:

```
<!DOCTYPE qjackctlSession>
<session name="session2">
 <client name="jack_mixer">
  <port type="out" name="MAIN L">
   <connect port="playback_1" client="system"/>
  </port>
  <port type="out" name="MAIN R">
   <connect port="playback_2" client="system"/>
  </port>
  <port type="in" name="midi in"/>
  <port type="out" name="Monitor L"/>
  <port type="out" name="Monitor R"/>
  <port type="in" name="Mixer L">
   <connect port="capture_1" client="system"/>
  </port>
  <port type="in" name="Mixer R">
   <connect port="capture_2" client="system"/>
  </port>
  <port type="out" name="Mixer Out L"/>
  <port type="out" name="Mixer Out R"/>
  <port type="in" name="mixer2 L">
   <connect port="out_0" client="MPlayer [8955]"/>
  </port>
  <port type="in" name="mixer2 R">
   <connect port="out_1" client="MPlayer [8955]"/>
  </port>
  <port type="out" name="mixer2 Out L"/>
  <port type="out" name="mixer2 Out R"/>
 </client>
 <client name="system">
  <port type="out" name="capture_1">
   <connect port="Mixer L" client="jack_mixer"/>
  </port>
  <port type="out" name="capture_2">
   <connect port="Mixer R" client="jack_mixer"/>
  </port>
  <port type="in" name="playback_1">
   <connect port="MAIN L" client="jack_mixer"/>
  </port>
  <port type="in" name="playback_2">
   <connect port="MAIN R" client="jack_mixer"/>
  </port>
 </client>
 <client name="MPlayer [8955]">
  <port type="out" name="out_0">
   <connect port="mixer2 L" client="jack_mixer"/>
  </port>
```

```
  <port type="out" name="out_1">
    <connect port="mixer2 R" client="jack_mixer"/>
  </port>
 </client>
</session>
```

On loading the session, it looks like Figure 8-2.

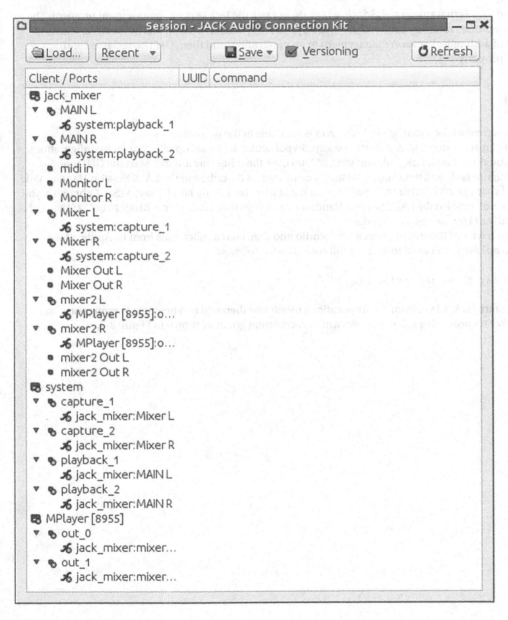

Figure 8-2. *qjackctl showing Jack session*

As you can see, there are many red Xs. Restoring a session doesn't start these particular applications. If you restart jack_mixer by hand, then it establishes the links between its MAIN output ports and system playback ports, and several of the red Xs disappear. But it doesn't create the extra ports that were created earlier. You need to repeat the work of creating new input ports with the right names; then qjackctl does reestablish the connections, and more red Xs disappear.

If you run mplayer again, it just establishes its own default connections to the playback ports and has to be remapped by hand. It doesn't even seem to meet Level 0, as qjackctl doesn't remap its connections automatically.

The issue here is that mplayer and jack_mixer do not talk the Jack session management protocol. The session manager does reset any connections made by some applications, but not all of them. An example is given later of adding Jack session management to an application, and then it will be restarted and reconnected properly.

LADISH

LADISH is designed as the successor to LASH and is available in the repositories.

LADISH can start, stop and configure sessions. In particular, it can set up different Jack configurations. This means you do not start Jack and then start LADISH; it's the other way around: start the GUI tool gladish, configure Jack, and then start a session. The process is described in the LADI Session Handler Wiki (http://ladish.org/wiki/tutorial). Follow it, in particular connecting Jack to, say, ALSA. Otherwise, you will get no sound! See also the LADI Session Handler (www.penguinproducer.com/Blog/2011/12/the-ladi-session-handler/) by the Penguin Producer.

Once you have LADISH set up, start a new Studio and then start applications from its Applications menu. To run mplayer, you need to give the full command as follows:

```
mplayer -ao jack 54154.mp3
```

You can start jack_mixer from the Applications menu and then add two new sets of input ports, as in Chapter 7. After reconnecting them, you end with a connection graph as shown in Figure 8-3.

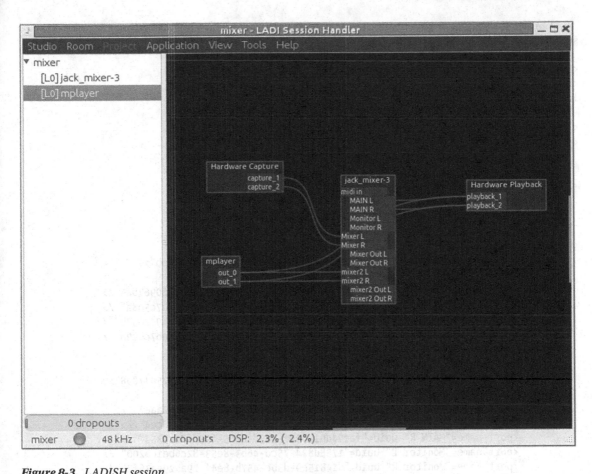

Figure 8-3. *LADISH session*

Connection graphs are stored as XML files in $HOME/.ladish. For example, the graph in Figure 8-3 is stored as follows:

```
<?xml version="1.0"?>
<!--
ladish Studio configuration.
-->
<!-- Sun Sep 29 10:49:54 2013 -->
<studio>
  <jack>
    <conf>
      <parameter path="/engine/driver">alsa</parameter>
      <parameter path="/engine/client-timeout">500</parameter>
      <parameter path="/engine/port-max">64</parameter>
    </conf>
    <clients>
      <client name="system" uuid="5ef937c6-46f7-45cd-8441-8ff6e2aee4eb">
        <ports>
          <port name="capture_1" uuid="9432f206-44c3-45cb-8024-3ba7160962bc" />
          <port name="capture_2" uuid="3c9acf5c-c91d-4692-add2-e3defb7c508a" />
          <port name="playback_1" uuid="95c68011-dab9-401c-8904-b3d149e20570" />
          <port name="playback_2" uuid="5b8e9215-3ff4-4973-8c0b-1eb5ab7ccc9b" />
        </ports>
      </client>
      <client name="jack_mixer-3" uuid="4538833e-d7e7-47d0-8a43-67ee25d17898">
        <ports>
          <port name="midi in" uuid="17d04191-f59d-4d16-970c-55030162aae7" />
          <port name="MAIN L" uuid="9d986401-c303-4f35-89b7-a32e10120ce4" />
          <port name="MAIN R" uuid="fae94d01-00ef-449d-8e05-f95df84c5357" />
          <port name="Monitor L" uuid="1758d824-75cd-46b3-8e53-82c6be1ca200" />
          <port name="Monitor R" uuid="d14815e9-d3bc-457b-8e4f-29ad29ea36f7" />
          <port name="Mixer L" uuid="07d388ed-d00a-4ee0-92aa-3ae79200e11e" />
          <port name="Mixer R" uuid="d1eb3400-75ce-422d-b9b8-b7e670f95428" />
          <port name="Mixer Out L" uuid="fad2a77e-6146-4919-856f-b6f7befdb84d" />
          <port name="Mixer Out R" uuid="920c5d12-9f62-46aa-b191-52bfbb94065d" />
          <port name="mixer2 L" uuid="c2b96996-9cd1-41dd-a750-192bb5717438" />
          <port name="mixer2 R" uuid="3de52738-d7e8-4733-bf08-3ea2b6372a4c" />
          <port name="mixer2 Out L" uuid="4e08eba4-a0c1-4e76-9dff-c14f76d5328e" />
          <port name="mixer2 Out R" uuid="9d2f79a5-e2d0-484b-b094-98ef7a4f61a7" />
        </ports>
      </client>
      <client name="mplayer" uuid="66e0d45f-2e21-4fbf-ac34-5d3658ee018a">
        <ports>
          <port name="out_0" uuid="83152a6e-e6f6-4357-93ce-020ba58b7d00" />
          <port name="out_1" uuid="55a05594-174d-48a5-805b-96d2c9e77cf1" />
        </ports>
      </client>
    </clients>
  </jack>
  <clients>
    <client name="Hardware Capture" uuid="47c1cd18-7b21-4389-bec4-6e0658e1d6b1"
    naming="app">
```

```
<ports>
  <port name="capture_1" uuid="9432f206-44c3-45cb-8024-3ba7160962bc" type="audio"
  direction="output" />
  <port name="capture_2" uuid="3c9acf5c-c91d-4692-add2-e3defb7c508a" type="audio"
  direction="output" />
</ports>
<dict>
  <key name="http://ladish.org/ns/canvas/x">1364.000000</key>
  <key name="http://ladish.org/ns/canvas/y">1083.000000</key>
</dict>
</client>
<client name="Hardware Playback" uuid="b2a0bb06-28d8-4bfe-956e-eb24378f9629"
naming="app">
  <ports>
    <port name="playback_1" uuid="95c68011-dab9-401c-8904-b3d149e20570" type="audio"
    direction="input" />
    <port name="playback_2" uuid="5b8e9215-3ff4-4973-8c0b-1eb5ab7ccc9b" type="audio"
    direction="input" />
  </ports>
  <dict>
    <key name="http://ladish.org/ns/canvas/x">1745.000000</key>
    <key name="http://ladish.org/ns/canvas/y">1112.000000</key>
  </dict>
</client>
<client name="jack_mixer-3" uuid="4b198f0f-5a77-4486-9f54-f7ec044d9bf2" naming="app"
app="98729282-8b18-4bcf-b929-41bc53f2b4ed">
  <ports>
    <port name="midi in" uuid="17d04191-f59d-4d16-970c-55030162aae7" type="midi"
    direction="input" />
    <port name="MAIN L" uuid="9d986401-c303-4f35-89b7-a32e10120ce4" type="audio"
    direction="output" />
    <port name="MAIN R" uuid="fae94d01-00ef-449d-8e05-f95df84c5357" type="audio"
    direction="output" />
    <port name="Monitor L" uuid="1758d824-75cd-46b3-8e53-82c6be1ca200" type="audio"
    direction="output" />
    <port name="Monitor R" uuid="d14815e9-d3bc-457b-8e4f-29ad29ea36f7" type="audio"
    direction="output" />
    <port name="Mixer L" uuid="07d388ed-d00a-4ee0-92aa-3ae79200e11e" type="audio"
    direction="input" />
    <port name="Mixer R" uuid="d1eb3400-75ce-422d-b9b8-b7e670f95428" type="audio"
    direction="input" />
    <port name="Mixer Out L" uuid="fad2a77e-6146-4919-856f-b6f7befdb84d" type="audio"
    direction="output" />
    <port name="Mixer Out R" uuid="920c5d12-9f62-46aa-b191-52bfbb94065d" type="audio"
    direction="output" />
    <port name="mixer2 L" uuid="c2b96996-9cd1-41dd-a750-192bb5717438" type="audio"
    direction="input" />
    <port name="mixer2 R" uuid="3de52738-d7e8-4733-bf08-3ea2b6372a4c" type="audio"
    direction="input" />
    <port name="mixer2 Out L" uuid="4e08eba4-a0c1-4e76-9dff-c14f76d5328e" type="audio"
    direction="output" />
```

```
      <port name="mixer2 Out R" uuid="9d2f79a5-e2d0-484b-b094-98ef7a4f61a7" type="audio"
      direction="output" />
    </ports>
    <dict>
      <key name="http://ladish.org/ns/canvas/x">1560.000000</key>
      <key name="http://ladish.org/ns/canvas/y">1104.000000</key>
    </dict>
  </client>
  <client name="mplayer" uuid="2f15cfec-7f6d-41b4-80e8-e1ae80c3be9e" naming="app"
app="7a9be17b-eb40-4be3-a9dc-82f36bbceeeb">
    <ports>
      <port name="out_0" uuid="83152a6e-e6f6-4357-93ce-020ba58b7d00" type="audio"
      direction="output" />
      <port name="out_1" uuid="55a05594-174d-48a5-805b-96d2c9e77cf1" type="audio"
      direction="output" />
    </ports>
    <dict>
      <key name="http://ladish.org/ns/canvas/x">1350.000000</key>
      <key name="http://ladish.org/ns/canvas/y">1229.000000</key>
    </dict>
  </client>
 </clients>
 <connections>
  <connection port1="9432f206-44c3-45cb-8024-3ba7160962bc" port2="07d388ed-d00a-4ee0-92aa-
3ae79200e11e" />
  <connection port1="3c9acf5c-c91d-4692-add2-e3defb7c508a" port2="d1eb3400-75ce-422d-b9b8-
b7e670f95428" />
  <connection port1="fad2a77e-6146-4919-856f-b6f7befdb84d" port2="95c68011-dab9-401c-8904-
b3d149e20570" />
  <connection port1="920c5d12-9f62-46aa-b191-52bfbb94065d" port2="5b8e9215-3ff4-4973-8c0b-
1eb5ab7ccc9b" />
  <connection port1="83152a6e-e6f6-4357-93ce-020ba58b7d00" port2="c2b96996-9cd1-41dd-a750-
192bb5717438" />
  <connection port1="55a05594-174d-48a5-805b-96d2c9e77cf1" port2="3de52738-d7e8-4733-bf08-
3ea2b6372a4c" />
 </connections>
 <applications>
  <application name="jack_mixer-3" uuid="98729282-8b18-4bcf-b929-41bc53f2b4ed"
  terminal="false" level="0" autorun="true">jack_mixer</application>
  <application name="mplayer" uuid="7a9be17b-eb40-4be3-a9dc-82f36bbceeeb" terminal="true"
  level="0" autorun="true">mplayer -ao jack %2Fhome%2Fhttpd%2Fhtml%2FLinuxSound%2FKaraoke%
  2FSubtitles%2Fsongs%2F54154.mp3</application>
 </applications>
</studio>
```

The full command to restart mplayer is stored in this file, as are all the connections made.

On stopping and restarting a session, mplayer is started with the same MP3 file but has the default connections. It ignores the connections of the LADISH session. Similarly, jack_mixer is restarted, but the additional ports have to be re-created by hand. This is not a LADISH-aware application, so it runs at Level 0. However, once created, the LADISH reconnections are made.

You can find a list of LADISH-aware applications at http://wiki.linuxaudio.org/apps/all/ladish.

From the user's viewpoint, the differences between these session managers are as follows:

- Jack applications can be started in any manner and will be picked up by the Jack session manager. However, any specific command-line parameters will be lost.

- Applications need to be started by the LADISH session manager in order to be managed by it. However, it can record command-line parameters and restart the application using them.

From a developer's viewpoint, the difference between these session managers is as follows:

- Jack session–aware applications can be started in any manner and will encode the command line required to restart them in the program.

Jack Session API

Applications that can be managed by Jack sessions (JS) may be Jack session–aware at Level 1 or Jack session-unaware. For the unaware ones, the best that can be done is for the session manager to maybe start and stop them. For the Jack session–aware applications, they must be set up to do the following:

- Register with a Jack session manager

- Respond to messages from the Jack session manager

- Be startable with session information

The response to a Jack session message will generally do the following:

- Save the application's state into a file, where the directory is given by the session manager.

- Reply to the session manager with a command that can be used to restart the application, with enough information that it can restore its state (typically the name of the file in which it stored its state information).

Jack session–aware clients identify themselves to the session manager by a unique universal identifier (UUID). It doesn't seem to matter what this is or how it is generated. The client application just makes it up as long as it is an integer represented as a string. This is passed to the session manager when registering but should also be passed back to the client when it is restarted by the session manager. This is done by a command-line argument to the application, and the format of the command line is also up to the client.

A simple case might be two options (-u for UUID and -f for saved state file). This would be parsed using getopt as follows:

```
int main(int argc, char **argv) {
  int c;
  char *file = NULL;
  char *uuid = "13";
  while ((c = getopt (argc, argv, "f:u:")) != -1)
    switch (c) {
      case 'u':
        uuid = optarg;
        break;
      case 'f':
        file = optarg;
        break;
      ...
```

```
    }
  }
  ...
}
```

The application could then restore its state using the information it has previously stored in the state file and then register again with a session manager with the following:

```
jack_client *client;
client = jack_client_open("myapp", JackSessionID, NULL, uuid);
jack_set_session_callback(client, session_callback, NULL);
```

The callback function session_callback is invoked whenever the session manager needs to communicate with the application. It takes a jack_session_event and whatever was passed as the last argument to jack_set_session_callback.

The job of the callback is then to save state information, pass information back to the session manager, and perhaps exit.

```
int session_callback(jack_session_event_t *ev) {
  char filename[256];
  char command[256];

  snprintf(filename, sizeof(filename), "%smyfile.state", ev->session_dir);
  snprintf(command,  sizeof(command),
          "my_app -u %s -f ${SESSION_DIR}myfile.state", ev->client_uuid);
  your_save_function(filename);
  ev->command_line = strdup(command);
  jack_session_reply(jack_client, ev);
  if(ev->type == JackSessionSaveAndQuit)
      quit();
  jack_session_event_free(ev);
  return 0;
}
```

trac suggests (http://trac.jackaudio.org/wiki/WalkThrough/Dev/JackSession) that if this is run in a multithreaded environment such as GTK, it should be run when other threads are idle, for example, with g_idel_add.

I can illustrate this with the delay program from Chapter 7. Adding the extra code gives a revised delay.c. I have enclosed the extra code with #ifdef JACK_SESSION for ease in seeing the changes.

```
/** @file delay.c
 *
 * @brief This client delays one channel by 4096 framse.
 */

#define JACK_SESSION

#include <stdio.h>
#include <errno.h>
#include <stdlib.h>
#include <string.h>
#include <math.h>
```

```
#include <signal.h>
#ifndef WIN32
#include <unistd.h>
#endif
#include <jack/jack.h>

#ifdef JACK_SESSION
#include <jack/session.h>
#endif

jack_port_t **input_ports;
jack_port_t **output_ports;
jack_client_t *client;

#define SIZE 8192
#define DELAY 4096
jack_default_audio_sample_t buffer[SIZE];
int idx, delay_idx;

static void signal_handler ( int sig )
{
    jack_client_close ( client );
    fprintf ( stderr, "signal received, exiting ...\n" );
    exit ( 0 );
}

static void copy2out( jack_default_audio_sample_t *out,
                      jack_nframes_t nframes) {
    if (delay_idx + nframes < SIZE) {
        memcpy(out, buffer + delay_idx,
               nframes * sizeof ( jack_default_audio_sample_t ) );
    } else {
        int frames_to_end = SIZE - delay_idx;
        int overflow = delay_idx + nframes - SIZE;
        memcpy(out, buffer + delay_idx,
               frames_to_end * sizeof ( jack_default_audio_sample_t ) );
        memcpy(out, buffer, overflow * sizeof(jack_default_audio_sample_t));
    }
    delay_idx = (delay_idx + nframes) % SIZE;
}

static void copy2buffer( jack_default_audio_sample_t *in,
                         jack_nframes_t nframes) {
    if (idx + nframes < SIZE) {
        memcpy(buffer + idx, in,
               nframes * sizeof ( jack_default_audio_sample_t ) );
    } else {
        int frames_to_end = SIZE - idx;
        int overflow = idx + nframes - SIZE;
        memcpy(buffer + idx, in,
               frames_to_end * sizeof ( jack_default_audio_sample_t ) );
        memcpy(buffer, in, overflow * sizeof(jack_default_audio_sample_t));
```

```
    }
    idx = (idx + nframes) % SIZE;
}

/**
 * The process callback for this JACK application is called in a
 * special realtime thread once for each audio cycle.
 *
 * This client follows a simple rule: when the JACK transport is
 * running, copy the input port to the output.  When it stops, exit.
 */

int
process ( jack_nframes_t nframes, void *arg )
{
    int i;
    jack_default_audio_sample_t *in, *out;

    in = jack_port_get_buffer ( input_ports[0], nframes );
    out = jack_port_get_buffer ( output_ports[0], nframes );
    memcpy ( out, in, nframes * sizeof ( jack_default_audio_sample_t ) );

    in = jack_port_get_buffer ( input_ports[1], nframes );
    out = jack_port_get_buffer ( output_ports[1], nframes );
    copy2out(out, nframes);
    copy2buffer(in, nframes);

    return 0;
}

/**
 * JACK calls this shutdown_callback if the server ever shuts down or
 * decides to disconnect the client.
 */
void
jack_shutdown ( void *arg ) {
    free ( input_ports );
    free ( output_ports );
    exit ( 1 );
}

#ifdef JACK_SESSION
/*
 * Callback function for JS
 */
void session_callback(jack_session_event_t *ev, void *args) {
    char command[256];

    snprintf(command,  sizeof(command),
            "/home/httpd/html/LinuxSound/Sampled/SessionManagement/delay -u %s",
            ev->client_uuid);
    ev->flags = JackSessionNeedTerminal;
```

```
    ev->command_line = strdup(command);
    jack_session_reply(client, ev);

    if(ev->type == JackSessionSaveAndQuit)
        jack_shutdown(NULL);

    jack_session_event_free(ev);
}
#endif

int main ( int argc, char *argv[] ) {
    int i;
    const char **ports;
    const char *client_name;
    const char *server_name = NULL;
    jack_status_t status;

#ifdef JACK_SESSION
    /*
     * Extra code for JS
     */
    int c;
    char *uuid = "13";
    while ((c = getopt (argc, argv, "u:")) != -1)
        switch (c) {
        case 'u':
            uuid = optarg;
            break;
        }
    printf("UUID is %s\n", uuid);
#endif

    client_name = strrchr ( argv[0], '/' );
    if ( client_name == 0 ) {
        client_name = argv[0];
    }
    else {
        client_name++;
    }

    /* open a client connection to the JACK server */
    /* Changed args for JS */

#ifdef JACK_SESSION
    client = jack_client_open ( client_name, JackSessionID, &status, uuid);
#else
    client = jack_client_open ( client_name, JackNullOption, &status);
#endif
    if ( client == NULL )
        {
            fprintf ( stderr, "jack_client_open() failed, "
                     "status = 0x%2.0x\n", status );
```

```
                    if ( status & JackServerFailed )
                        {
                            fprintf ( stderr, "Unable to connect to JACK server\n" );
                        }
                    exit ( 1 );
                }
        if ( status & JackServerStarted )
            {
                fprintf ( stderr, "JACK server started\n" );
            }
        if ( status & JackNameNotUnique )
            {
                client_name = jack_get_client_name ( client );
                fprintf ( stderr, "unique name `%s' assigned\n", client_name );
            }

#ifdef JACK_SESSION
    /* Set callback function for JS
    */
    jack_set_session_callback(client, session_callback, NULL);
#endif

    /* tell the JACK server to call `process()' whenever
        there is work to be done.
    */
    jack_set_process_callback ( client, process, 0 );

    /* tell the JACK server to call `jack_shutdown()' if
        it ever shuts down, either entirely, or if it
        just decides to stop calling us.
    */

    jack_on_shutdown ( client, jack_shutdown, 0 );

    /* create two ports pairs*/
    input_ports = ( jack_port_t** ) calloc ( 2, sizeof ( jack_port_t* ) );
    output_ports = ( jack_port_t** ) calloc ( 2, sizeof ( jack_port_t* ) );

    char port_name[16];
    for ( i = 0; i < 2; i++ )
        {
            sprintf ( port_name, "input_%d", i + 1 );
            input_ports[i] = jack_port_register ( client, port_name, JACK_DEFAULT_AUDIO_
            TYPE, JackPortIsInput, 0 );
            sprintf ( port_name, "output_%d", i + 1 );
            output_ports[i] = jack_port_register ( client, port_name, JACK_DEFAULT_AUDIO_
            TYPE, JackPortIsOutput, 0 );
            if ( ( input_ports[i] == NULL ) || ( output_ports[i] == NULL ) )
                {
                    fprintf ( stderr, "no more JACK ports available\n" );
                    exit ( 1 );
```

```
            }
    }

bzero(buffer, SIZE * sizeof ( jack_default_audio_sample_t ));
delay_idx = 0;
idx = DELAY;

/* Tell the JACK server that we are ready to roll.  Our
 * process() callback will start running now. */

if ( jack_activate ( client ) )
    {
        fprintf ( stderr, "cannot activate client" );
        exit ( 1 );
    }

/* Connect the ports.  You can't do this before the client is
 * activated, because we can't make connections to clients
 * that aren't running.  Note the confusing (but necessary)
 * orientation of the driver backend ports: playback ports are
 * "input" to the backend, and capture ports are "output" from
 * it.
 */

ports = jack_get_ports ( client, NULL, NULL, JackPortIsPhysical|JackPortIsOutput );
if ( ports == NULL )
    {
        fprintf ( stderr, "no physical capture ports\n" );
        exit ( 1 );
    }

for ( i = 0; i < 2; i++ )
    if ( jack_connect ( client, ports[i], jack_port_name ( input_ports[i] ) ) )
        fprintf ( stderr, "cannot connect input ports\n" );

free ( ports );

ports = jack_get_ports ( client, NULL, NULL, JackPortIsPhysical|JackPortIsInput );
if ( ports == NULL )
    {
        fprintf ( stderr, "no physical playback ports\n" );
        exit ( 1 );
    }

for ( i = 0; i < 2; i++ )
    if ( jack_connect ( client, jack_port_name ( output_ports[i] ), ports[i] ) )
        fprintf ( stderr, "cannot connect input ports\n" );

free ( ports );

/* install a signal handler to properly quits jack client */
```

```
#ifdef WIN32
    signal ( SIGINT, signal_handler );
    signal ( SIGABRT, signal_handler );
    signal ( SIGTERM, signal_handler );
#else
    signal ( SIGQUIT, signal_handler );
    signal ( SIGTERM, signal_handler );
    signal ( SIGHUP, signal_handler );
    signal ( SIGINT, signal_handler );
#endif

    /* keep running until the transport stops */

    while (1)
        {
#ifdef WIN32
            Sleep ( 1000 );
#else
            sleep ( 1 );
#endif
        }

    jack_client_close ( client );
    exit ( 0 );
}
```

LADISH API

If an application is Jack session–aware, then the LADISH GUI tool gladish can manage the application as a Level 1 application. In other words, gladish can manage Jack session and LADISH clients equally. In that sense, there is no need to additionally add LADISH awareness to an application unless you prefer the LADISH way of managing sessions.

For how to build LADISH-aware apps at Level 1, see http://ladish.org/wiki/code_examples. For LADI Session Handler, see http://ladish.org/.

Conclusion

This chapter looked at some of the session management systems. The set of session managers covered is not exhaustive. Visit http://lwn.net/Articles/533594/ for a list of several more, such as the Non Session Manager and Chino. However, the situation is not particularly satisfactory, and there is substantial room for improvement.

CHAPTER 9

■ ■ ■

Java Sound

This chapter covers the essentials of programming sampled data using the Java Sound API. The chapter assumes a good working knowledge of Java. Java Sound has been around since the early days of Java. It deals with both sampled and MIDI data, and it is a comprehensive system.

Resources

Many resources are available for Java Sound.

- The Java Platform Standard Edition 7 API Specification (http://docs.oracle.com/javase/7/docs/api/) is the reference point for all the standard Java APIs, including javax.sound.sampled.

- The "Trail: Sound" tutorial at Java Tutorials (http://docs.oracle.com/javase/tutorial/sound/index.html) gives a good overview of both the sampled and MIDI packages.

- The FAQ about audio programming at Java Sound Resources (www.jsresources.org/faq_audio.html) answers many questions about Java Sound.

- The Sound Group (http://openjdk.java.net/groups/sound/) consists of developers designing, implementing, and maintaining various OpenJDK sound components. It's your hook into finding out more about the ongoing development of Java Sound in the open source community.

Key Java Sound Classes

These are the key classes:

- The AudioSystem class is the entry point for all sampled audio classes.

- The AudioFormat class specifies information about the format, such as sampling rate.

- The AudioInputStream class supplies an input stream from the target line of a mixer.

- The Mixer class represents an audio device.

- The SourceDataLine class represents an input line to a device.

- The TargetDataLine class represents an output line from a device.

© Jan Newmarch 2017
J. Newmarch, *Linux Sound Programming*, DOI 10.1007/978-1-4842-2496-0_9

Information About Devices

Each device is represented by a Mixer object. Ask the AudioSystem for a list of these. Each mixer has a set of target (output) lines and source (input lines). Query each mixer about these separately. The following program is called DeviceInfo.java:

```java
import javax.sound.sampled.*;

public class DeviceInfo {

    public static void main(String[] args) throws Exception {

        Mixer.Info[] minfoSet = AudioSystem.getMixerInfo();
        System.out.println("Mixers:");
        for (Mixer.Info minfo: minfoSet) {
            System.out.println("    " + minfo.toString());

            Mixer m = AudioSystem.getMixer(minfo);
            System.out.println("    Mixer: " + m.toString());
            System.out.println("      Source lines");
            Line.Info[] slines = m.getSourceLineInfo();
            for (Line.Info s: slines) {
                System.out.println("        " + s.toString());
            }

            Line.Info[] tlines = m.getTargetLineInfo();
            System.out.println("      Target lines");
            for (Line.Info t: tlines) {
                System.out.println("        " + t.toString());
            }
        }
    }
}
```

The following is part of the output on my system:

```
Mixers:
    PulseAudio Mixer, version 0.02
      Source lines
        interface SourceDataLine supporting 42 audio formats, and buffers of
        0 to 1000000 bytes
        interface Clip supporting 42 audio formats, and buffers of 0 to 1000000 bytes
      Target lines
        interface TargetDataLine supporting 42 audio formats, and buffers of
        0 to 1000000 bytes
    default [default], version 1.0.24
      Source lines
        interface SourceDataLine supporting 512 audio formats, and buffers of at
        least 32 bytes
        interface Clip supporting 512 audio formats, and buffers of at least 32 bytes
      Target lines
```

```
      interface TargetDataLine supporting 512 audio formats, and buffers of at
      least 32 bytes
PCH [plughw:0,0], version 1.0.24
   Source lines
      interface SourceDataLine supporting 24 audio formats, and buffers of at
      least 32 bytes
      interface Clip supporting 24 audio formats, and buffers of at least 32 bytes
   Target lines
      interface TargetDataLine supporting 24 audio formats, and buffers of at
      least 32 bytes
NVidia [plughw:1,3], version 1.0.24
   Source lines
      interface SourceDataLine supporting 96 audio formats, and buffers of at
      least 32 bytes
      interface Clip supporting 96 audio formats, and buffers of at least 32 bytes
   Target lines
NVidia [plughw:1,7], version 1.0.24
   Source lines
      interface SourceDataLine supporting 96 audio formats, and buffers of at
      least 32 bytes
      interface Clip supporting 96 audio formats, and buffers of at least 32 bytes
   Target lines
NVidia [plughw:1,8], version 1.0.24
   Source lines
      interface SourceDataLine supporting 96 audio formats, and buffers of at
      least 32 bytes
      interface Clip supporting 96 audio formats, and buffers of at least 32 bytes
   Target lines
```

This shows both PulseAudio and ALSA mixers. Further queries could show what the supported formats are, for example.

Playing Audio from a File

To play from a file, appropriate objects must be created for reading from the file and for writing to the output device. These are as follows:

- An AudioInputStream is requested from the AudioSystem. It is created with the filename as a parameter.

- A source data line is created for the output. The nomenclature may be confusing: the program produces *output*, but this is *input* to the data line. So, the data line must be a source for the output device. The creation of a data line is a multistep process.

  - First create an AudioFormat object to specify parameters for the data line.

  - Create a DataLine.Info for a source data line with the audion format.

  - Request a source data line from the AudioSystem that will handle the DataLine. Info.

Following these steps, data can then be read from the input stream and written to the data line. Figure 9-1 shows the UML class diagram for the relevant classes.

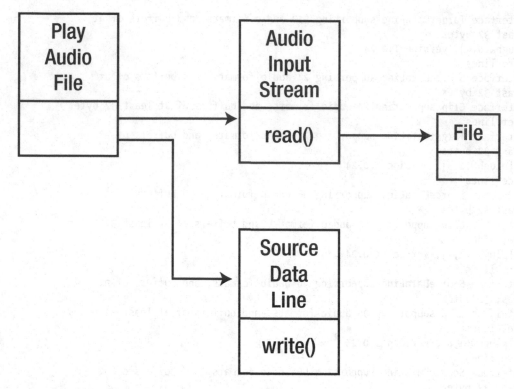

Figure 9-1. *Class diagram for playing audio from a file*

```
import java.io.File;
import java.io.IOException;

import javax.sound.sampled.AudioFormat;
import javax.sound.sampled.AudioInputStream;
import javax.sound.sampled.AudioSystem;
import javax.sound.sampled.DataLine;
import javax.sound.sampled.FloatControl;
import javax.sound.sampled.LineUnavailableException;
import javax.sound.sampled.SourceDataLine;

public class PlayAudioFile {
    /** Plays audio from given file names. */
    public static void main(String [] args) {
        // Check for given sound file names.
        if (args.length < 1) {
            System.out.println("Usage: java Play <sound file names>*");
            System.exit(0);
        }

        // Process arguments.
        for (int i = 0; i < args.length; i++)
            playAudioFile(args[i]);
```

```java
        // Must exit explicitly since audio creates non-daemon threads.
        System.exit(0);
    } // main

    public static void playAudioFile(String fileName) {
        File soundFile = new File(fileName);

        try {
            // Create a stream from the given file.
            // Throws IOException or UnsupportedAudioFileException
            AudioInputStream audioInputStream = AudioSystem.getAudioInputStream(soundFile);
            // AudioSystem.getAudioInputStream(inputStream); // alternate audio stream from
            inputstream
            playAudioStream(audioInputStream);
        } catch (Exception e) {
            System.out.println("Problem with file " + fileName + ":");
            e.printStackTrace();
        }
    } // playAudioFile

    /** Plays audio from the given audio input stream. */
    public static void playAudioStream(AudioInputStream audioInputStream) {
        // Audio format provides information like sample rate, size, channels.
        AudioFormat audioFormat = audioInputStream.getFormat();
        System.out.println("Play input audio format=" + audioFormat);

        // Open a data line to play our type of sampled audio.
        // Use SourceDataLine for play and TargetDataLine for record.
        DataLine.Info info = new DataLine.Info(SourceDataLine.class, audioFormat);
        if (!AudioSystem.isLineSupported(info)) {
            System.out.println("Play.playAudioStream does not handle this type of audio on
            this system.");
            return;
        }

        try {
            // Create a SourceDataLine for play back (throws LineUnavailableException).
            SourceDataLine dataLine = (SourceDataLine) AudioSystem.getLine(info);
            // System.out.println("SourceDataLine class=" + dataLine.getClass());

            // The line acquires system resources (throws LineAvailableException).
            dataLine.open(audioFormat);

            // Adjust the volume on the output line.
            if(dataLine.isControlSupported(FloatControl.Type.MASTER_GAIN)) {
                FloatControl volume = (FloatControl) dataLine.getControl(FloatControl.Type.
                MASTER_GAIN);
                volume.setValue(6.0F);
            }

            // Allows the line to move data in and out to a port.
            dataLine.start();
```

```
        // Create a buffer for moving data from the audio stream to the line.
        int bufferSize = (int) audioFormat.getSampleRate() * audioFormat.getFrameSize();
        byte [] buffer = new byte[ bufferSize ];

        // Move the data until done or there is an error.
        try {
            int bytesRead = 0;
            while (bytesRead >= 0) {
                bytesRead = audioInputStream.read(buffer, 0, buffer.length);
                if (bytesRead >= 0) {
                    // System.out.println("Play.playAudioStream bytes read=" + bytesRead +
                    // ", frame size=" + audioFormat.getFrameSize() + ", frames read=" +
                    bytesRead / audioFormat.getFrameSize());
                    // Odd sized sounds throw an exception if we don't write the same
                    amount.
                    int framesWritten = dataLine.write(buffer, 0, bytesRead);
                }
            } // while
        } catch (IOException e) {
            e.printStackTrace();
        }

        System.out.println("Play.playAudioStream draining line.");
        // Continues data line I/O until its buffer is drained.
        dataLine.drain();

        System.out.println("Play.playAudioStream closing line.");
        // Closes the data line, freeing any resources such as the audio device.
        dataLine.close();
    } catch (LineUnavailableException e) {
        e.printStackTrace();
    }
    } // playAudioStream
} // PlayAudioFile
```

Recording Audio to a File

Most of the work to do this is in preparation of an audio input stream. Once that is done, the method write of AudioSystem will copy input from the audio input stream to the output file.

To prepare the audio input stream, follow these steps:

1.   Create an AudioFormat object describing the parameters of the input.

2.   The microphone *produces* audio. So, it needs a TargetDataLine. So, create a DataLine.Info for a target data line.

3.   Ask the AudioSystem for a line satisfying the information.

4.   Wrap the line in an AudioInputStream.

The output is just a Java File.

Then use the AudioSystem function write() to copy the stream to the file. Figure 9-2 shows the UML class diagram.

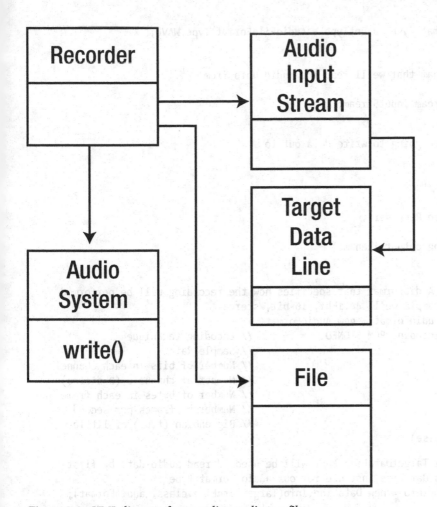

Figure 9-2. *UML diagram for recording audio to a file*

The program is as follows:

```java
import javax.sound.sampled.*;
import java.io.File;

/**
 * Sample audio recorder
 */
public class Recorder extends Thread
{
    /**
     * The TargetDataLine that we'll use to read data from
     */
    private TargetDataLine line;

    /**
     * The audio format type that we'll encode the audio data with
     */
```

```java
private AudioFileFormat.Type targetType = AudioFileFormat.Type.WAVE;

/**
 * The AudioInputStream that we'll read the audio data from
 */
private AudioInputStream inputStream;

/**
 * The file that we're going to write data out to
 */
private File file;

/**
 * Creates a new Audio Recorder
 */
public Recorder(String outputFilename)
{
    try {
        // Create an AudioFormat that specifies how the recording will be performed
        // In this example we'll 44.1Khz, 16-bit, stereo
        AudioFormat audioFormat = new AudioFormat(
        AudioFormat.Encoding.PCM_SIGNED,           // Encoding technique
        44100.0F,                                  // Sample Rate
        16,                                        // Number of bits in each channel
        2,                                         // Number of channels (2=stereo)
        4,                                         // Number of bytes in each frame
        44100.0F,                                  // Number of frames per second
        false);                                    // Big-endian (true) or little-
        // endian (false)

        // Create our TargetDataLine that will be used to read audio data by first
        // creating a DataLine instance for our audio format type
        DataLine.Info info = new DataLine.Info(TargetDataLine.class, audioFormat);

        // Next we ask the AudioSystem to retrieve a line that matches the
        // DataLine Info
        this.line = (TargetDataLine)AudioSystem.getLine(info);

        // Open the TargetDataLine with the specified format
        this.line.open(audioFormat);

        // Create an AudioInputStream that we can use to read from the line
        this.inputStream = new AudioInputStream(this.line);

        // Create the output file
        this.file = new File(outputFilename);
    }
    catch(Exception e) {
        e.printStackTrace();
    }
}
```

```java
    public void startRecording() {
        // Start the TargetDataLine
        this.line.start();

        // Start our thread
        start();
    }

    public void stopRecording() {
        // Stop and close the TargetDataLine
        this.line.stop();
        this.line.close();
    }

    public void run() {
        try {
            // Ask the AudioSystem class to write audio data from the audio input stream
            // to our file in the specified data type (PCM 44.1Khz, 16-bit, stereo)
            AudioSystem.write(this.inputStream, this.targetType, this.file);
        }
        catch(Exception e) {
            e.printStackTrace();
        }
    }

    public static void main(String[] args) {
        if (args.length == 0) {
            System.out.println("Usage: Recorder <filename>");
            System.exit(0);
        }

        try {
            // Create a recorder that writes WAVE data to the specified filename
            Recorder r = new Recorder(args[0]);
            System.out.println("Press ENTER to start recording");
            System.in.read();

            // Start the recorder
            r.startRecording();

            System.out.println("Press ENTER to stop recording");
            System.in.read();

            // Stop the recorder
            r.stopRecording();

            System.out.println("Recording complete");
        }
        catch(Exception e) {
            e.printStackTrace();
        }
    }

}
```

Play Microphone to Speaker

This is a combination of the previous two programs. An AudioInputStream is prepared for reading from the microphone. A SourceDataLine is prepared for writing to the speaker. The data is copied from the first to the second by reading from the audio input stream and writing to the source data line. Figure 9-3 shows the UML class diagram.

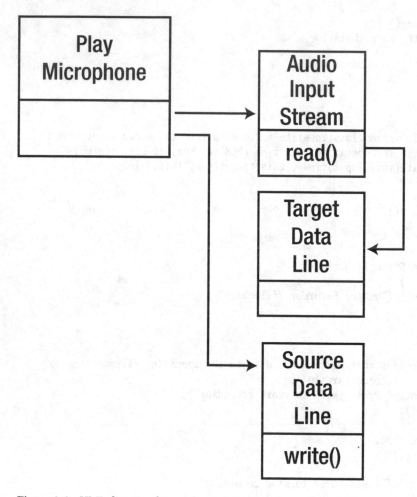

Figure 9-3. *UML diagram for sending microphone input to a speaker*

The program is as follows:

```
import java.io.File;
import java.io.IOException;

import javax.sound.sampled.AudioFormat;
import javax.sound.sampled.AudioInputStream;
import javax.sound.sampled.AudioSystem;
```

```java
import javax.sound.sampled.DataLine;
import javax.sound.sampled.Line;
import javax.sound.sampled.Line.Info;
import javax.sound.sampled.TargetDataLine;
import javax.sound.sampled.FloatControl;
import javax.sound.sampled.LineUnavailableException;
import javax.sound.sampled.SourceDataLine;

public class PlayMicrophone {
    private static final int FRAMES_PER_BUFFER = 1024;

    public static void main(String[] args) throws Exception {
        new PlayMicrophone().playAudio();
    }

    private void out(String strMessage)
    {
        System.out.println(strMessage);
    }

    //This method creates and returns an
    // AudioFormat object for a given set of format
    // parameters.  If these parameters don't work
    // well for you, try some of the other
    // allowable parameter values, which are shown
    // in comments following the declarations.
    private  AudioFormat getAudioFormat(){
        float sampleRate = 44100.0F;    //8000,11025,16000,22050,44100
        int sampleSizeInBits = 16;      //8,16
        int channels = 1;               //1,2
        boolean signed = true;          //true,false
        boolean bigEndian = false;      //true,false
        return new AudioFormat(samplcRate,
                               sampleSizeInBits,
                               channels,
                               signed,
                               bigEndian);
    }//end getAudioFormat

    public void playAudio() throws Exception {
        AudioFormat audioFormat;
        TargetDataLine targetDataLine;

        audioFormat = getAudioFormat();
        DataLine.Info dataLineInfo =
            new DataLine.Info(
                              TargetDataLine.class,
                              audioFormat);
        targetDataLine = (TargetDataLine)
            AudioSystem.getLine(dataLineInfo);
```

```
        /*
        Line.Info lines[] = AudioSystem.getTargetLineInfo(dataLineInfo);
        for (int n = 0; n < lines.length; n++) {
            System.out.println("Target " + lines[n].toString() + " " + lines[n].
            getLineClass());
        }
        targetDataLine = (TargetDataLine)
            AudioSystem.getLine(lines[0]);
        */

        targetDataLine.open(audioFormat,
                            audioFormat.getFrameSize() * FRAMES_PER_BUFFER);
        targetDataLine.start();

        playAudioStream(new AudioInputStream(targetDataLine));

        /*
        File soundFile = new File( fileName );

        try {
            // Create a stream from the given file.
            // Throws IOException or UnsupportedAudioFileException
            AudioInputStream audioInputStream = AudioSystem.getAudioInputStream( soundFile );
            // AudioSystem.getAudioInputStream( inputStream ); // alternate audio stream
            from inputstream
            playAudioStream( audioInputStream );
        } catch ( Exception e ) {
            System.out.println( "Problem with file " + fileName + ":" );
            e.printStackTrace();
        }
        */
    } // playAudioFile

    /** Plays audio from the given audio input stream. */
    public void playAudioStream( AudioInputStream audioInputStream ) {
        // Audio format provides information like sample rate, size, channels.
        AudioFormat audioFormat = audioInputStream.getFormat();
        System.out.println( "Play input audio format=" + audioFormat );

        // Open a data line to play our type of sampled audio.
        // Use SourceDataLine for play and TargetDataLine for record.
        DataLine.Info info = new DataLine.Info( SourceDataLine.class, audioFormat );

        Line.Info lines[] = AudioSystem.getSourceLineInfo(info);
        for (int n = 0; n < lines.length; n++) {
            System.out.println("Source " + lines[n].toString() + " " + lines[n].
            getLineClass());
        }

        if ( !AudioSystem.isLineSupported( info ) ) {
            System.out.println( "Play.playAudioStream does not handle this type of audio on
            this system." );
```

```
        return;
    }

    try {
        // Create a SourceDataLine for play back (throws LineUnavailableException).
        SourceDataLine dataLine = (SourceDataLine) AudioSystem.getLine( info );
        // System.out.println( "SourceDataLine class=" + dataLine.getClass() );

        // The line acquires system resources (throws LineAvailableException).
        dataLine.open( audioFormat,
                       audioFormat.getFrameSize() * FRAMES_PER_BUFFER);

        // Adjust the volume on the output line.
        if( dataLine.isControlSupported( FloatControl.Type.MASTER_GAIN ) ) {
            FloatControl volume = (FloatControl) dataLine.getControl( FloatControl.Type.
            MASTER_GAIN );
            volume.setValue( 6.0F );
        }

        // Allows the line to move data in and out to a port.
        dataLine.start();

        // Create a buffer for moving data from the audio stream to the line.
        int bufferSize = (int) audioFormat.getSampleRate() * audioFormat.getFrameSize();
        bufferSize = audioFormat.getFrameSize() * FRAMES_PER_BUFFER;
        System.out.println("Buffer size: " + bufferSize);
        byte [] buffer = new byte[ bufferSize ];

        // Move the data until done or there is an error.
        try {
            int bytesRead = 0;
            while ( bytesRead >= 0 ) {
                bytesRead = audioInputStream.read( buffer, 0, buffer.length );
                if ( bytesRead >= 0 ) {
                    System.out.println( "Play.playAudioStream bytes read=" + bytesRead +
                    ", frame size=" + audioFormat.getFrameSize() + ", frames read=" +
                    bytesRead / audioFormat.getFrameSize() );
                    // Odd sized sounds throw an exception if we don't write the same
                    amount.
                    int framesWritten = dataLine.write( buffer, 0, bytesRead );
                }
            } // while
        } catch ( IOException e ) {
            e.printStackTrace();
        }

        System.out.println( "Play.playAudioStream draining line." );
        // Continues data line I/O until its buffer is drained.
        dataLine.drain();
```

```
                System.out.println( "Play.playAudioStream closing line." );
                // Closes the data line, freeing any resources such as the audio device.
                dataLine.close();
        } catch ( LineUnavailableException e ) {
                e.printStackTrace();
        }
    } // playAudioStream

}
```

Where Does JavaSound Get Its Devices From?

The first program in this chapter showed a list of mixer devices and their attributes. How does Java get this information? This section covers JDK 1.8, and OpenJDK will probably be similar. You will need the Java source from Oracle to track through this. Alternatively, move on.

The file jre/lib/resources.jar contains a list of resources used by the JRE runtime. This is a zip file and contains the file META-INF/services/javax.sound.sampled.spi.MixerProvider. On my system, the contents of this file are as follows:

```
# last mixer is default mixer
com.sun.media.sound.PortMixerProvider
com.sun.media.sound.DirectAudioDeviceProvider
```

The class com.sun.media.sound.PortMixerProvider is in the file java/media/src/share/native/com/sun/media/sound/PortMixerProvider.java on my system. It extends MixerProvider and implements methods such as Mixer.Info[] getMixerInfo. This class stores the device information.

The bulk of the work done by this class is actually performed by native methods in the C file java/media/src/share/native/com/sun/media/sound/PortMixerProvider.c, which implements the two methods nGetNumDevices and nNewPortMixerInfo used by the PortMixerProvider class. Unfortunately, there's not much joy to be found in this C file, as it just makes calls to the C functions PORT_GetPortMixerCount and PORT_GetPortMixerDescription.

There are three files containing these functions.

```
java/media/src/windows/native/com/sun/media/sound/PLATFORM_API_WinOS_Ports.c
java/media/src/solaris/native/com/sun/media/sound/PLATFORM_API_SolarisOS_Ports.c
java/media/src/solaris/native/com/sun/media/sound/PLATFORM_API_LinuxOS_ALSA_Ports.c
```

In the file PLATFORM_API_LinuxOS_ALSA_Ports.c, you will see the function calls to ALSA as described in Chapter 5. These calls fill in information about the ALSA devices for use by JavaSound.

Conclusion

The Java Sound API is well-documented. I have shown four simple programs here, but more complex ones are possible. The link to the underlying sound system was briefly discussed.

CHAPTER 10

■ ■ ■

GStreamer

GStreamer is a library of components that can be hooked together in complex pipelines. It can be used for filtering, converting formats, and mixing. It can handle both audio and video formats, but this chapter covers only audio. It looks at the user-level mechanisms for using GStreamer and also the programming model for linking GStreamer components. A reference is given for writing new components.

Resources

Here are some resources:

- Multipurpose multimedia processing with GStreamer (www.ibm.com/developerworks/aix/library/au-gstreamer.html?ca=dgr-lnxw07GStreamer) by Maciej Katafiasz

- GStreamer plug-in reference (http://gstreamer.freedesktop.org/documentation/)

- "GStreamer Writer's Guide" for plug-ins (1.9.90) (https://gstreamer.freedesktop.org/data/doc/gstreamer/head/pwg/html/index.html)

Overview

GStreamer uses a pipeline model to connect *elements*, which are sources, filters, and sinks. Figure 10-1 shows the model.

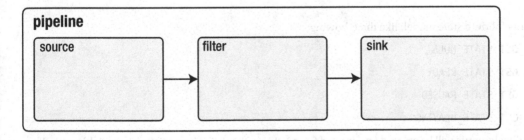

Figure 10-1. GStreamer pipeline model

Each element has zero or more *pads*, which can be source pads producing data or sink pads consuming data, as shown in Figure 10-2.

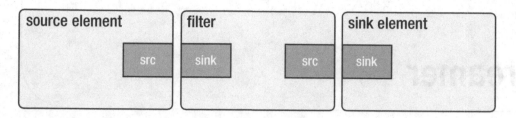

Figure 10-2. *GStreamer source and sink pads*

Pads can be static or may be dynamically created or destroyed in response to events. For example, to process a container file such as MP4, the element has to read enough of the file before it can work out the format of the contained object, such as an H.264 video. Once that is done, it can create a source pad for the next stage to consume the data.

GStreamer is not restricted to linear pipelines like command languages such as bash. A demuxer, for example, may need to separate audio from video and process each separately, as in Figure 10-3.

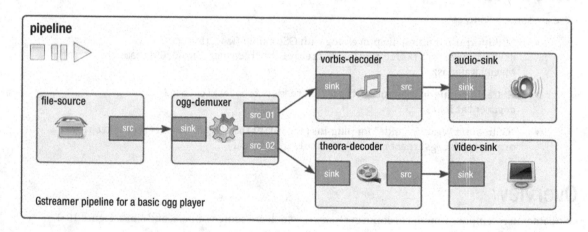

Figure 10-3. *Complex GStreamer pipeline*

Elements follow a state model, like the following:

- GST_STATE_NULL
- GST_STATE_READY
- GST_STATE_PAUSED
- GST_STATE_PLAYING

Generally elements will be created and moved from NULL to PLAYING. Finer control is available with the other states.

Elements can also generate *events* that contain information on the state of the data stream. Events are generally handled internally but may be watched, such as events signaling the end of a data stream or the format of a data stream.

A *plug-in* is a loadable block of code. Generally a plug-in contains the implementation of a single element, but it may contain more.

Each pad has an associated list of *capabilities*. Each capability is a statement about what the pad can handle. This includes information about data types (for example, audio/raw), format (S32LE, U32LE, S16LE, U16LE, and so on), data rate (for example, 1-2147483647 bits per second), and so on. When a source pad is linked to a sink pad, these capabilities are used to determine how the elements will communicate.

Command-Line Processing

There are three levels of dealing with GStreamer: by using the command line, by writing C programs (or Python, Perl, C++, and so on) to link elements, or by writing new elements. This section covers command-line tools.

gst-inspect

The command gst-inspect (on my Ubuntu system, gst-inspect-1.0) with no arguments shows the list of plug-ins, their elements, and a brief description. A brief extract is as follows:

```
...
audiomixer:  liveadder: AudioMixer
audioparsers:  aacparse: AAC audio stream parser
audioparsers:  ac3parse: AC3 audio stream parser
audioparsers:  amrparse: AMR audio stream parser
audioparsers:  dcaparse: DTS Coherent Acoustics audio stream parser
audioparsers:  flacparse: FLAC audio parser
audioparsers:  mpegaudioparse: MPEG1 Audio Parser
audioparsers:  sbcparse: SBC audio parser
audioparsers:  wavpackparse: Wavpack audio stream parser
audiorate:  audiorate: Audio rate adjuster
...
```

This shows that the plug-in audioparsers contains a number of elements such as aacparse, which is an "AAC audio stream parser."

When run with a plug-in as an argument, gst-inspect shows a little more detail about the plug-in.

```
$gst-inspect-1.0 audioparsers
Plugin Details:
  Name                  audioparsers
  Description           Parsers for various audio formats
  Filename              /usr/lib/x86_64-linux-gnu/gstreamer-1.0/libgstaudioparsers.so
  Version               1.8.1
  License               LGPL
  Source module         gst-plugins-good
  Source release date   2016-04-20
  Binary package        GStreamer Good Plugins (Ubuntu)
  Origin URL            https://launchpad.net/distros/ubuntu/+source/gst-plugins-good1.0

  aacparse: AAC audio stream parser
  amrparse: AMR audio stream parser
  ac3parse: AC3 audio stream parser
```

213

```
dcaparse: DTS Coherent Acoustics audio stream parser
flacparse: FLAC audio parser
mpegaudioparse: MPEG1 Audio Parser
sbcparse: SBC audio parser
wavpackparse: Wavpack audio stream parser

8 features:
+-- 8 elements
```

In particular, note that it is from the module gst-plugins-good. Plug-ins are categorized as to stability, licenses, and so on.

When run with the element as an argument, gst-inspect shows a lot of information about the element.

```
$gst-inspect-1.0 aacparse
Factory Details:
  Rank                     primary + 1 (257)
  Long-name                AAC audio stream parser
  Klass                    Codec/Parser/Audio
  Description              Advanced Audio Coding parser
  Author                   Stefan Kost <stefan.kost@nokia.com>

Plugin Details:
  Name                     audioparsers
  Description              Parsers for various audio formats
  Filename                 /usr/lib/x86_64-linux-gnu/gstreamer-1.0/libgstaudioparsers.so
  Version                  1.8.1
  License                  LGPL
  Source module            gst-plugins-good
  Source release date      2016-04-20
  Binary package           GStreamer Good Plugins (Ubuntu)
  Origin URL               https://launchpad.net/distros/ubuntu/+source/gst-plugins-good1.0

GObject
 +----GInitiallyUnowned
       +----GstObject
             +----GstElement
                   +----GstBaseParse
                         +----GstAacParse

Pad Templates:
  SINK template: 'sink'
    Availability: Always
    Capabilities:
      audio/mpeg
            mpegversion: { 2, 4 }

  SRC template: 'src'
    Availability: Always
    Capabilities:
      audio/mpeg
                framed: true
```

```
        mpegversion: { 2, 4 }
        stream-format: { raw, adts, adif, loas }

Element Flags:
  no flags set

Element Implementation:
  Has change_state() function: gst_base_parse_change_state

Element has no clocking capabilities.
Element has no URI handling capabilities.

Pads:
  SINK: 'sink'
    Pad Template: 'sink'
  SRC: 'src'
    Pad Template: 'src'

Element Properties:
  name                : The name of the object
                        flags: readable, writable
                        String. Default: "aacparse0"
  parent              : The parent of the object
                        flags: readable, writable
                        Object of type "GstObject"
  disable-passthrough : Force processing (disables passthrough)
                        flags: readable, writable
                        Boolean. Default: false
```

This shows that it can take audio/mpeg version 2 or 4 and convert the data into audio/mpeg version 2 or 4 in a variety of formats.

gst-discoverer

The command gst-discoverer (on my system gst-discoverer-1.0) can be used to give information about resources such as files or URIs. On an audio file called audio_01.ogg, it gives the following information:

```
$gst-discoverer-1.0 enigma/audio_01.ogg
Analyzing file:enigma/audio_01.ogg
Done discovering file:enigma/audio_01.ogg

Topology:
  container: Ogg
    audio: Vorbis

Properties:
  Duration: 0:02:03.586666666
  Seekable: yes
  Tags:
      encoder: Xiph.Org libVorbis I 20020717
      encoder version: 0
```

```
audio codec: Vorbis
nominal bitrate: 112001
bitrate: 112001
container format: Ogg
```

gst-device-monitor

This command can give a lot of information about the devices on your system:

```
$gst-device-monitor-1.0
Probing devices...

Device found:

        name  : Monitor of Built-in Audio Digital Stereo (HDMI)
        class : Audio/Source
        caps  : audio/x-raw, format=(string){ S16LE, S16BE, F32LE, F32BE, S32LE, S32BE,
                S24LE, S24BE, S24_32LE, S24_32BE, U8 }, layout=(string)interleaved,
                rate=(int)[ 1, 2147483647 ], channels=(int)[ 1, 32 ];
                audio/x-alaw, rate=(int)[ 1, 2147483647 ], channels=(int)[ 1, 32 ];
                audio/x-mulaw, rate=(int)[ 1, 2147483647 ], channels=(int)[ 1, 32 ];
        properties:
                device.description = "Monitor\ of\ Built-in\ Audio\ Digital\ Stereo\
                \(HDMI\)"
                device.class = monitor
                alsa.card = 0
                alsa.card_name = "HDA\ Intel\ HDMI"
                alsa.long_card_name = "HDA\ Intel\ HDMI\ at\ 0xf7214000\ irq\ 52"
                alsa.driver_name = snd_hda_intel
                device.bus_path = pci-0000:00:03.0
                sysfs.path = /devices/pci0000:00/0000:00:03.0/sound/card0
                device.bus = pci
                device.vendor.id = 8086
                device.vendor.name = "Intel\ Corporation"
                device.product.id = 160c
                device.product.name = "Broadwell-U\ Audio\ Controller"
                device.form_factor = internal
                device.string = 0
                module-udev-detect.discovered = 1
                device.icon_name = audio-card-pci
...
```

That is plenty of information about the audio capabilities of my HDMI monitor, and it is followed by other information about the audio and video capabilities of my other devices.

gst-play

This program is a one-stop shop to play all sorts of media files and URIs, as follows:

```
$gst-play-1.0 enigma/audio_01.ogg
```

gst-launch

The gst-launch program allows you to build a pipeline of commands to process media data. The format is as follows:

```
gst-launch <elmt> [<args>] ! <elmt> [<args>] ! ...
```

For example, to play a WAV file through ALSA, use the following:

```
$gst-launch-1.0 filesrc location=enigma/audio_01.wav ! wavparse ! alsasink
```

The hardest part of using GStreamer pipelines appears to be in choosing the appropriate plug-ins. This looks like a bit of a fine art; see the GStreamer cheat sheet at http://wiki.oz9aec.net/index.php/Gstreamer_cheat_sheet for help.

For example, Ogg files are a container format, usually containing Vorbis audio streams and Theora video streams (although they can contain other data formats). They play either the audio or the video or both, and the streams have to be extracted from the container using a demultiplexer, decoded, and then played. There are a variety of ways of just playing the audio, including these three:

```
$gst-launch-1.0 filesrc location=enigma/audio_01.ogg ! oggdemux ! vorbisdec !
audioconvert ! alsasink

$gst-launch-1.0 filesrc location=enigma/audio_01.ogg ! oggdemux ! vorbisdec !
autoaudiosink

$gst-launch-1.0 uridecodebin uri=file:enigma/audio_01.ogg ! audioconvert ! autoaudiosink
```

The syntax of GStreamer pipelines allows a pipeline to be split into multiple pipes, for example to manage both the audio and video streams. This is covered in the online documentation of GStreamer.

C Programming

The same pipeline principles hold as for gst-launch, but of course at the C programming level there is far more plumbing to look after. The following program from the GStreamer SDK Basic tutorials at http://docs.gstreamer.com/display/GstSDK/Basic+tutorials does the same as the last of the gst-launch examples ($gst-launch-1.0 uridecodebin uri=... ! audioconvert ! autoaudiosink).

The GStreamer elements are created by calls such as this:

```
data.source = gst_element_factory_make ("uridecodebin", "source");
```

The pipeline is built with this:

```
data.pipeline = gst_pipeline_new ("test-pipeline")
gst_bin_add_many (GST_BIN (data.pipeline), data.source, data.convert , data.sink, NULL);
```

Eventually all the elements have to be linked. Right now, convert and sink can be linked with the following:

```
gst_element_link (data.convert, data.sink)
```

The URI to play is set with the following:

```
g_object_set (data.source, "uri", "http://docs.gstreamer.com/media/sintel_trailer-480p.
webm", NULL);
```

The data source is a container; in my previous example it was an Ogg container, and here it's a web media URL. This will not create a source pad on the data source element until enough of the data has been read to determine the data format and parameters. Consequently, the C program has to add an event handler for pad-added, which it does with this:

```
g_signal_connect (data.source, "pad-added", G_CALLBACK (pad_added_handler), &data);
```

When a pad is added to the source, the pad_added_handler will be called. This does much type checking and getting the new pad but finally does the key step of linking the source and convert elements.

```
gst_pad_link (new_pad, sink_pad)
```

Then the application starts playing by changing the state to PLAYING and waits for normal termination (GST_MESSAGE_EOS) or other messages.

```
gst_element_set_state (data.pipeline, GST_STATE_PLAYING);
bus = gst_element_get_bus (data.pipeline);
msg = gst_bus_timed_pop_filtered (bus, GST_CLOCK_TIME_NONE,
        GST_MESSAGE_STATE_CHANGED | GST_MESSAGE_ERROR | GST_MESSAGE_EOS);
```

The last section of code does cleanup. The complete program is as follows:

```
#include <gst/gst.h>

/* Structure to contain all our information, so we can pass it to callbacks */
typedef struct _CustomData {
  GstElement *pipeline;
  GstElement *source;
  GstElement *convert;
  GstElement *sink;
} CustomData;

/* Handler for the pad-added signal */
static void pad_added_handler (GstElement *src, GstPad *pad, CustomData *data);

int main(int argc, char *argv[]) {
  CustomData data;
  GstBus *bus;
  GstMessage *msg;
  GstStateChangeReturn ret;
  gboolean terminate = FALSE;

  /* Initialize GStreamer */
  gst_init (&argc, &argv);

  /* Create the elements */
  data.source = gst_element_factory_make ("uridecodebin", "source");
```

```
data.convert = gst_element_factory_make ("audioconvert", "convert");
data.sink = gst_element_factory_make ("autoaudiosink", "sink");

/* Create the empty pipeline */
data.pipeline = gst_pipeline_new ("test-pipeline");

if (!data.pipeline || !data.source || !data.convert || !data.sink) {
  g_printerr ("Not all elements could be created.\n");
  return -1;
}

/* Build the pipeline. Note that we are NOT linking the source at this
 * point. We will do it later. */
gst_bin_add_many (GST_BIN (data.pipeline), data.source, data.convert , data.sink, NULL);
if (!gst_element_link (data.convert, data.sink)) {
  g_printerr ("Elements could not be linked.\n");
  gst_object_unref (data.pipeline);
  return -1;
}

/* Set the URI to play */
g_object_set (data.source, "uri", "http://docs.gstreamer.com/media/sintel_trailer-480p.
webm", NULL);

/* Connect to the pad-added signal */
g_signal_connect (data.source, "pad-added", G_CALLBACK (pad_added_handler), &data);

/* Start playing */
ret = gst_element_set_state (data.pipeline, GST_STATE_PLAYING);
if (ret == GST_STATE_CHANGE_FAILURE) {
  g_printerr ("Unable to set the pipeline to the playing state.\n");
  gst_object_unref (data.pipeline);
  return -1;
}

/* Listen to the bus */
bus = gst_element_get_bus (data.pipeline);
do {
  msg = gst_bus_timed_pop_filtered (bus, GST_CLOCK_TIME_NONE,
      GST_MESSAGE_STATE_CHANGED | GST_MESSAGE_ERROR | GST_MESSAGE_EOS);

  /* Parse message */
  if (msg != NULL) {
    GError *err;
    gchar *debug_info;

    switch (GST_MESSAGE_TYPE (msg)) {
      case GST_MESSAGE_ERROR:
        gst_message_parse_error (msg, &err, &debug_info);
        g_printerr ("Error received from element %s: %s\n", GST_OBJECT_NAME (msg->src),
        err->message);
```

```
            g_printerr ("Debugging information: %s\n", debug_info ? debug_info : "none");
            g_clear_error (&err);
            g_free (debug_info);
            terminate = TRUE;
            break;
        case GST_MESSAGE_EOS:
            g_print ("End-Of-Stream reached.\n");
            terminate = TRUE;
            break;
        case GST_MESSAGE_STATE_CHANGED:
            /* We are only interested in state-changed messages from the pipeline */
            if (GST_MESSAGE_SRC (msg) == GST_OBJECT (data.pipeline)) {
              GstState old_state, new_state, pending_state;
              gst_message_parse_state_changed (msg, &old_state, &new_state, &pending_state);
              g_print ("Pipeline state changed from %s to %s:\n",
                  gst_element_state_get_name (old_state), gst_element_state_get_name (new_
                  state));
            }
            break;
        default:
            /* We should not reach here */
            g_printerr ("Unexpected message received.\n");
            break;
      }
      gst_message_unref (msg);
    }
  } while (!terminate);

  /* Free resources */
  gst_object_unref (bus);
  gst_element_set_state (data.pipeline, GST_STATE_NULL);
  gst_object_unref (data.pipeline);
  return 0;
}

/* This function will be called by the pad-added signal */
static void pad_added_handler (GstElement *src, GstPad *new_pad, CustomData *data) {
  GstPad *sink_pad = gst_element_get_static_pad (data->convert, "sink");
  GstPadLinkReturn ret;
  GstCaps *new_pad_caps = NULL;
  GstStructure *new_pad_struct = NULL;
  const gchar *new_pad_type = NULL;

  g_print ("Received new pad '%s' from '%s':\n", GST_PAD_NAME (new_pad), GST_ELEMENT_NAME
(src));

  /* If our converter is already linked, we have nothing to do here */
  if (gst_pad_is_linked (sink_pad)) {
    g_print ("  We are already linked. Ignoring.\n");
    goto exit;
  }
```

```
/* Check the new pad's type */
new_pad_caps = gst_pad_get_caps (new_pad);
new_pad_struct = gst_caps_get_structure (new_pad_caps, 0);
new_pad_type = gst_structure_get_name (new_pad_struct);
if (!g_str_has_prefix (new_pad_type, "audio/x-raw")) {
  g_print ("  It has type '%s' which is not raw audio. Ignoring.\n", new_pad_type);
  goto exit;
}

/* Attempt the link */
ret = gst_pad_link (new_pad, sink_pad);
if (GST_PAD_LINK_FAILED (ret)) {
  g_print ("  Type is '%s' but link failed.\n", new_pad_type);
} else {
  g_print ("  Link succeeded (type '%s').\n", new_pad_type);
}

exit:
  /* Unreference the new pad's caps, if we got them */
  if (new_pad_caps != NULL)
    gst_caps_unref (new_pad_caps);

  /* Unreference the sink pad */
  gst_object_unref (sink_pad);
}
```

Writing Plug-ins

Writing new GStreamer plug-ins is a nontrivial task. The document "GStreamer Writer's Guide" at https://gstreamer.freedesktop.org/data/doc/gstreamer/head/pwg/html/index.html gives extensive advice on this.

Conclusion

This chapter looked at using GStreamer both from the command line and from an example C program. There is a huge list of available plug-ins that will meet the many needs of audio/visual developers. I have only touched the surface of GStreamer, and it has many other features, including integration with the GTK toolkit.

CHAPTER 11

libao

According to the libao documentation (www.xiph.org/ao/doc/overview.html), "libao is designed to make it easy to do simple audio output using various audio devices and libraries. For this reason, complex audio control features are missing and will probably never be added. However, if you just want to be able to open whatever audio device is available and play sound, libao should be just fine."

Resources

Check out the following:

- libao documentation (www.xiph.org/ao/doc/)

libao

libao is an extremely minimal library; it basically just plays audio data. It does not decode any of the standard file formats: no WAV, MP3, Vorbis, and so on, support. You have to configure the format parameters of bits, channels, rates, and byte formats and then send the appropriate data to the device. Its primary use is to output PCM data and can be used once a codec has been decoded or to play simple sounds like sine waves.

The following is a simple example from the libao site to play a sine tone for one second:

```
/*
 *
 * ao_example.c
 *
 *     Written by Stan Seibert - July 2001
 *
 * Legal Terms:
 *
 *     This source file is released into the public domain.  It is
 *     distributed without any warranty; without even the implied
 *     warranty * of merchantability or fitness for a particular
 *     purpose.
 *
 * Function:
 *
 *     This program opens the default driver and plays a 440 Hz tone for
 *     one second.
 *
```

© Jan Newmarch 2017
J. Newmarch, *Linux Sound Programming*, DOI 10.1007/978-1-4842-2496-0_11

```
 * Compilation command line (for Linux systems):
 *
 *      gcc -lao -ldl -lm -o ao_example ao_example.c
 *
 */


#include <stdio.h>
#include <ao/ao.h>
#include <math.h>

#define BUF_SIZE 4096

int main(int argc, char **argv)
{
        ao_device *device;
        ao_sample_format format;
        int default_driver;
        char *buffer;
        int buf_size;
        int sample;
        float freq = 440.0;
        int i;

        /* -- Initialize -- */

        fprintf(stderr, "libao example program\n");

        ao_initialize();

        /* -- Setup for default driver -- */

        default_driver = ao_default_driver_id();

        memset(&format, 0, sizeof(format));
        format.bits = 16;
        format.channels = 2;
        format.rate = 44100;
        format.byte_format = AO_FMT_LITTLE;

        /* -- Open driver -- */
        device = ao_open_live(default_driver, &format, NULL /* no options */);
        if (device == NULL) {
                fprintf(stderr, "Error opening device.\n");
                return 1;
        }

        /* -- Play some stuff -- */
        buf_size = format.bits/8 * format.channels * format.rate;
        buffer = calloc(buf_size,
                        sizeof(char));
```

```
    for (i = 0; i < format.rate; i++) {
        sample = (int)(0.75 * 32768.0 *
                sin(2 * M_PI * freq * ((float) i/format.rate)));

        /* Put the same stuff in left and right channel */
        buffer[4*i] = buffer[4*i+2] = sample & 0xff;
        buffer[4*i+1] = buffer[4*i+3] = (sample >> 8) & 0xff;
    }
    ao_play(device, buffer, buf_size);

    /* -- Close and shutdown -- */
    ao_close(device);

    ao_shutdown();

  return (0);
}
```

Conclusion

libao is not complex; it is a basic library to play sounds to whatever device is available. It will suit cases where you have the sound in a known PCM format.

CHAPTER 12

FFmpeg/Libav

According to "A FFmpeg Tutorial for Beginners" (http://keycorner.org/pub/text/doc/ffmpegtutorial.htm), FFmpeg is a complete, cross-platform command-line tool capable of recording, converting, and streaming digital audio and video in various formats. It can be used to do most multimedia tasks quickly and easily, such as audio compression, audio/video format conversion, extracting images from a video, and more.

FFmpeg consists of a set of command-line tools and a set of libraries that can be used for transforming audio (and video) files from one format to another. It can work both on containers and on codecs. It is not designed for playing or recording audio; it's more a general-purpose conversion tool.

Resources

- FFmpeg home page (http://ffmpeg.org/)
- FFmpeg documentation (http://ffmpeg.org/ffmpeg.html)
- Libav home page (https://libav.org/)
- An FFmpeg and SDL tutorial (http://dranger.com/ffmpeg/) with updated code at https://github.com/chelyaev/ffmpeg-tutorial

The FFmpeg/Libav Controversy

FFmpeg was started in 2000 to provide libraries and programs for handling multimedia data. However, over the years there were a number of disputes between the developers, leading to a fork in 2011 to the Libav project. The two projects have continued since then, pretty much in parallel and often borrowing from each other. However, the situation has remained acrimonious, and there appears little possibility of resolution.

This is unfortunate for developers. While programs are generally portable between the two systems, there are sometimes differences in the APIs and in behavior. There is also the issue of distro support. For many years Debian and derivatives supported only Libav and omitted FFmpeg. This has changed, and both are supported now. See "Why Debian returned to FFmpeg" (https://lwn.net/Articles/650816/) for a discussion of some of the issues.

© Jan Newmarch 2017
J. Newmarch, *Linux Sound Programming*, DOI 10.1007/978-1-4842-2496-0_12

FFmpeg Command-Line Tools

The principal FFmpeg tool is ffmpeg itself. The simplest use is as a converter from one format to another, as follows:

```
ffmpeg -i file.ogg file.mp3
```

This will convert an Ogg container of Vorbis codec data to an MPEG container of MP2 codec data. The Libav equivalent is avconv, which runs similarly.

```
avconv -i file.ogg file.mp3
```

Internally, ffmpeg uses a pipeline of modules, as in Figure 12-1.

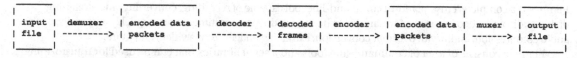

Figure 12-1. *FFmpeg/Libav pipeline (Source:* http://ffmpeg.org/ffmpeg.html*)*

The muxer/demuxer and decoder/encoder can all be set using options if the defaults are not appropriate.

The following are other commands:

- ffprobe gives information about a file.

- ffplay is a simple media player.

- ffserver is a media server.

Programming

There are a number of libraries that can be used for FFmpeg/Libav programming. Libav builds the following libraries:

- libavcodec

- libavdevice

- libavfilter

- libavformat

- libavresample

- libavutil

FFmepg builds the following:

- libavcodec

- libavdevice

- libavfilter

- libavformat

- libavresample
- libavutil
- libpostproc
- libswresample
- libswscale

The extra libraries in FFmpeg are for video postprocessing and scaling.

Using either of these systems is not a straightforward process. The Libav site states, "Libav has always been a very experimental and developer-driven project. It is a key component in many multimedia projects and has new features added constantly. To provide a stable foundation, major releases are cut every four to six months and maintained across at least two years."

The FFmpeg site states, "FFmpeg has always been a very experimental and developer-driven project. It is a key component in many multimedia projects and has new features added constantly. Development branch snapshots work really well 99 percent of the time, so people are not afraid to use them."

My experience has been that this "experimental" nature of both projects has led to an unstable core API, regularly obsoleting and replacing key functions. For example, the function avcodec_decode_audio in libavcodec version 56 is now up to version 4: avcodec_decode_audio4. And even that version is now deprecated in the upstream versions of FFmpeg and Libav (version 57) in favor of functions such as avcodec_send_packet that do not exist in version 56. This is in addition to having two projects with the same goals and generally identical APIs but not always. For example, FFmpeg has swr_alloc_set_opts, while Libav uses av_opt_set_int. In addition, the audiovisual codecs and containers themselves are continually evolving.

The result of this is that many example programs on the Internet no longer compile, use deprecated APIs, or belong to the "other" system. This is not to detract from two systems with superb achievements, but I just wish it wasn't so messy.

Decoding an MP3 File

The following program decodes an MP3 file into a raw PCM file. This is about as simple a task as one can do with FFmpeg/Libav, but it is unfortunately not straightforward. First, you have to note that you want to deal with a *codec*, not a file *containing* a codec. This is not an FFmpeg/Libav issue but a general one.

Files with the extension .mpg or .mp3 may contain a number of different formats. If I run the command file on a number of files that I have, I get different results.

```
BST.mp3: MPEG ADTS, layer III, v1, 128 kbps, 44.1 kHz, Stereo
Beethoven_Fr_Elise.mp3: MPEG ADTS, layer III, v1, 128 kbps, 44.1 kHz, Stereo
Angel-no-vocal.mp3: Audio file with ID3 version 2.3.0
01DooWackaDoo.mp3: Audio file with ID3 version 2.3.0, \
    contains: MPEG ADTS, layer III, v1, 224 kbps, 44.1 kHz, JntStereo
```

The first two files just contain a single codec and can be managed by the following program. The third and fourth files are container files, containing MPEG+ID3 data. These need to be managed using the avformat functions such as av_read_frame[1].

The program is basically a standard example in the FFmpeg/Libav source distributions. It is based on ffmpeg-3.2/doc/examples/decoding_encoding.c in the FFmpeg source and is based on libav-12/doc/examples/avcodec.c in the Libav source. One may note in passing that both programs use avcodec_decode_audio4, which is deprecated in both these upstream versions, and neither has examples of the replacement function avcodec_send_packet.

---

[1]Examples of av_read_frame are given in Chapter 15 and 21.

A more serious issue is that, increasingly, MP3 files use a *planar* format. In this, different channels are in different *planes*. The FFmpeg/Libav function avcodec_decode_audio4 handles this correctly by placing each plane in a separate data array, but when it is output as PCM data, the planes have to be interleaved. This is not done in the examples and may result in incorrect PCM data (lots of clicking noises, followed by half-speed audio).

The relevant FFmpeg functions are as follows:

- av_register_all: Register all the possible muxers, demuxers, and protocols.

- avformat_open_input: Open the input stream.

- av_find_stream_info: Extract stream information.

- av_init_packet: Set default values in a packet.

- avcodec_find_decoder: Find a suitable decoder.

- avcodec_alloc_context3: Set default values for the primary data structure.

- avcodec_open2: Open the decoder.

- fread: The FFmpeg processing loop reads a buffer at a time from the data stream.

- avcodec_decode_audio4: This decodes audio frames into raw audio data.

The rest of the code interleaves the data streams to output to a PCM file. The resultant file can be played with the following:

```
aplay -c 2 -r 44100 /tmp/test.sw -f S16_LE
```

The program is as follows:

```
/*
 * copyright (c) 2001 Fabrice Bellard
 *
 * This file is part of Libav.
 *
 * Libav is free software; you can redistribute it and/or
 * modify it under the terms of the GNU Lesser General Public
 * License as published by the Free Software Foundation; either
 * version 2.1 of the License, or (at your option) any later version.
 *
 * Libav is distributed in the hope that it will be useful,
 * but WITHOUT ANY WARRANTY; without even the implied warranty of
 * MERCHANTABILITY or FITNESS FOR A PARTICULAR PURPOSE.  See the GNU
 * Lesser General Public License for more details.
 *
 * You should have received a copy of the GNU Lesser General Public
 * License along with Libav; if not, write to the Free Software
 * Foundation, Inc., 51 Franklin Street, Fifth Floor, Boston, MA 02110-1301 USA
 */

// From http://code.haskell.org/~thielema/audiovideo-example/cbits/
// Adapted to version version 2.8.6-1ubuntu2 by Jan Newmarch
```

```
/**
 * @file
 * libavcodec API use example.
 *
 * @example libavcodec/api-example.c
 * Note that this library only handles codecs (mpeg, mpeg4, etc...),
 * not file formats (avi, vob, etc...). See library 'libavformat' for the
 * format handling
 */

#include <stdlib.h>
#include <stdio.h>
#include <string.h>

#ifdef HAVE_AV_CONFIG_H
#undef HAVE_AV_CONFIG_H
#endif

#include "libavcodec/avcodec.h"
#include <libavformat/avformat.h>

#define INBUF_SIZE 4096
#define AUDIO_INBUF_SIZE 20480
#define AUDIO_REFILL_THRESH 4096

void die(char *s) {
    fputs(s, stderr);
    exit(1);
}

/*
 * Audio decoding.
 */
static void audio_decode_example(AVFormatContext* container,
                            const char *outfilename, const char *filename)
{
    AVCodec *codec;
    AVCodecContext *context = NULL;
    int len;
    FILE *f, *outfile;
    uint8_t inbuf[AUDIO_INBUF_SIZE + FF_INPUT_BUFFER_PADDING_SIZE];
    AVPacket avpkt;
    AVFrame *decoded_frame = NULL;
    int num_streams = 0;
    int sample_size = 0;

    av_init_packet(&avpkt);

    printf("Audio decoding\n");
```

```
int stream_id = -1;

// To find the first audio stream. This process may not be necessary
// if you can gurarantee that the container contains only the desired
// audio stream
int i;
for (i = 0; i < container->nb_streams; i++) {
    if (container->streams[i]->codec->codec_type == AVMEDIA_TYPE_AUDIO) {
        stream_id = i;
        break;
    }
}

/* find the appropriate audio decoder */
AVCodecContext* codec_context = container->streams[stream_id]->codec;
codec = avcodec_find_decoder(codec_context->codec_id);
if (!codec) {
    fprintf(stderr, "codec not found\n");
    exit(1);
}

context = avcodec_alloc_context3(codec);;

/* open it */
if (avcodec_open2(context, codec, NULL) < 0) {
    fprintf(stderr, "could not open codec\n");
    exit(1);
}

f = fopen(filename, "rb");
if (!f) {
    fprintf(stderr, "could not open %s\n", filename);
    exit(1);
}
outfile = fopen(outfilename, "wb");
if (!outfile) {
    av_free(context);
    exit(1);
}

/* decode until eof */
avpkt.data = inbuf;
avpkt.size = fread(inbuf, 1, AUDIO_INBUF_SIZE, f);

while (avpkt.size > 0) {
    int got_frame = 0;

    if (!decoded_frame) {
        if (!(decoded_frame = av_frame_alloc())) {
            fprintf(stderr, "out of memory\n");
            exit(1);
        }
```

```
    } else {
        av_frame_unref(decoded_frame);
    }
    printf("Stream idx %d\n", avpkt.stream_index);

    len = avcodec_decode_audio4(context, decoded_frame, &got_frame, &avpkt);
    if (len < 0) {
        fprintf(stderr, "Error while decoding\n");
        exit(1);
    }
    if (got_frame) {
        printf("Decoded frame nb_samples %d, format %d\n",
                decoded_frame->nb_samples,
                decoded_frame->format);
        if (decoded_frame->data[1] != NULL)
            printf("Data[1] not null\n");
        else
            printf("Data[1] is null\n");
        /* if a frame has been decoded, output it */
        int data_size = av_samples_get_buffer_size(NULL, context->channels,
                                                    decoded_frame->nb_samples,
                                                    context->sample_fmt, 1);
        // first time: count the number of  planar streams
        if (num_streams == 0) {
            while (num_streams < AV_NUM_DATA_POINTERS &&
                    decoded_frame->data[num_streams] != NULL)
                num_streams++;
            printf("Number of streams %d\n", num_streams);
        }

        // first time: set sample_size from 0 to e.g 2 for 16-bit data
        if (sample_size == 0) {
            sample_size =
                data_size / (num_streams * decoded_frame->nb_samples);
        }

        int m, n;
        for (n = 0; n < decoded_frame->nb_samples; n++) {
            // interleave the samples from the planar streams
            for (m = 0; m < num_streams; m++) {
                fwrite(&decoded_frame->data[m][n*sample_size],
                        1, sample_size, outfile);
            }
        }
    }
    avpkt.size -= len;
    avpkt.data += len;
    if (avpkt.size < AUDIO_REFILL_THRESH) {
        /* Refill the input buffer, to avoid trying to decode
         * incomplete frames. Instead of this, one could also use
         * a parser, or use a proper container format through
```

```
                   * libavformat. */
              memmove(inbuf, avpkt.data, avpkt.size);
              avpkt.data = inbuf;
              len = fread(avpkt.data + avpkt.size, 1,
                          AUDIO_INBUF_SIZE - avpkt.size, f);
              if (len > 0)
                  avpkt.size += len;
        }
    }

    fclose(outfile);
    fclose(f);

    avcodec_close(context);
    av_free(context);
    av_free(decoded_frame);
}

int main(int argc, char **argv)
{
    const char *filename = "Beethoven_Fr_Elise.mp3";
    AVFormatContext *pFormatCtx = NULL;

    if (argc == 2) {
        filename = argv[1];
    }

    // Register all formats and codecs
    av_register_all();
    if(avformat_open_input(&pFormatCtx, filename, NULL, NULL)!=0) {
        fprintf(stderr, "Can't get format of file %s\n", filename);
        return -1; // Couldn't open file
    }
    // Retrieve stream information
    if(avformat_find_stream_info(pFormatCtx, NULL)<0)
        return -1; // Couldn't find stream information
    av_dump_format(pFormatCtx, 0, filename, 0);
    printf("Num streams %d\n", pFormatCtx->nb_streams);
    printf("Bit rate %d\n", pFormatCtx->bit_rate);
    audio_decode_example(pFormatCtx, "/tmp/test.sw", filename);

    return 0;
}
```

Conclusion

This chapter briefly considered FFmpeg/Libav, looking at the libavcodec library. There is considerably more complexity to FFmpeg and Libav, and they can do far more complex transformations. In addition, they can do video processing and this is illustrated in Chapter 15.

## CHAPTER 13

OpenMAX IL

OpenMAX is an open standard for audio and video from the Khronos Group that is designed for low-capability devices. Vendors of cards are expected to produce implementations. There is little by way of general Linux implementations, but Broadcom has implemented one of the specifications (OpenMAX IL), and its chip is used in the Raspberry Pi. Other Khronos specifications (OpenMAX AL and OpenSL ES) have been implemented in Android devices, accessible by the Native Development Kit (NDK), but these are not intended for direct use; they're intended for use only through Java APIs. They are not discussed in this book. This chapter discusses only OpenMAX IL.

Resources

Here are some resources:

- The OpenMAX Integration Layer (IL) standard (http://elinux.org/images/e/e0/ The_OpenMAX_Integration_Layer_standard.pdf), from eLinux.

- The Khronos home page (www.khronos.org/) gives the specifications for free download; they are quite well done and readable.

- LIM OpenMAX Implementation (http://limoa.sourceforge.net/) is a Linux implementation. The download of 1.0 is OK from lim-omx-1.0.tar.gz (http:// sourceforge.net/projects/limoa/files/1.0/lim-omx-1.0.tar.gz/download).

- The OpenMAX IL Bellagio package (http://omxil.sourceforge.net/) source, DEB package, and RPM are available.

- Texas Instruments OpenMax Development Guide (http://processors.wiki. ti.com/index.php/OpenMax_Development_Guide).

- OpenMAX (Open Media Acceleration) (www.cnx-software.com/2011/11/11/ openmax-open-media-acceleration/).

© Jan Newmarch 2017
J. Newmarch, *Linux Sound Programming*, DOI 10.1007/978-1-4842-2496-0_13

Quotes

Here are some quotes:

- According to jamesh, "OpenMAX is a complete and utter nightmare to use…" (`www.raspberrypi.org/forums/viewtopic.php?t=5621`).

- According to dom (`www.raspberrypi.org/forums/memberlist.php?mode=viewprofile&u=754`), "I have written a fair bit of [OpenMAX] client code and find it very hard. You have to get an awful lot right before you get anything useful out. Just lots of OMX_ErrorInvalidState and OMX_ErrorBadParameter messages if you are lucky. Nothing happening at all if you are not…."

- According to Twinkletoes (`www.raspberrypi.org/forums/viewtopic.php?t=6577`), "I'm from a DirectShow background, and I thought that was badly documented… then I met [OpenMAX]. Lots of ppts saying lovely things about it, but no documentation or code examples I can find."

OpenMAX IL Concepts

The OpenMAX IL API is quite distinct from that of OpenMAX AL. The basic concept is of a *component*, which is an audio/video (or other) processing unit of some type, such as a volume control, a mixer, or an output device. Each component has zero or more input and output *ports*, and each port can have one or more *buffers* that carry data.

OpenMAX IL is typically meant for use by an A/V framework of some kind, such as OpenMAX AL. In addition to OpenMAX AL, there is currently a GStreamer plug-in that uses OpenMAX IL underneath. But one can also build stand-alone applications where direct calls are made into the OpenMAX IL API. Collectively, these are all known as *IL clients*.

The OpenMAX IL API is difficult to work with directly. Error messages are frequently quite useless, threads will block without explanation until everything is *exactly* right, and silently blocking doesn't give you any clues about what isn't right. In addition, the examples I have to work with don't follow the specification exactly correctly, which can lead to much wasted time.

OpenMAX IL components use buffers to carry data. A component will usually process data from an input buffer and place it on an output buffer. This processing is not visible to the API, so it allows vendors to implement components in hardware or software, built on top of other A/V components, and so on. OpenMAX IL gives mechanisms for setting and getting parameters of components, for calling standard functions on the components, or for getting data in and out of components.

While some of the OpenMAX IL calls are synchronous, those that require possibly substantial amounts of processing are asynchronous, communicating the results through callback functions. This leads naturally to a multithreaded processing model, although OpenMAX IL does not visibly use any thread libraries and should be agnostic to how an IL client uses threads. The Bellagio examples use pthreads, while the Broadcom examples for the Raspberry Pi use Broadcom's VideoCore OS (vcos) threads (`https://github.com/raspberrypi/userland/blob/master/interface/vcos/vcos_semaphore.h`).

There are two mechanisms for getting data into and out of components. The first is where the IL client makes calls on the component. All components are required to support this mechanism. The second is where a *tunnel* is set up between two components for data to flow along a shared buffer. A component is not required to support this mechanism.

OpenMAX IL Components

OpenMAX IL in 1.1.2 lists a number of standard components, including (for audio) a decoder, an encoder, a mixer, a reader, a renderer, a writer, a capturer, and a processor. An IL client gets such a component by calling OMX_GetHandle(), passing in the name of the component. This is a problem: the components do not have a standard name.

The 1.1.2 specification says, "Since components are requested by name, a naming convention is defined. OpenMAX IL component names are zero-terminated strings with the following format: OMX.<vendor_name>.<vendor_specified_convention>, for example, OMX.CompanyABC.MP3Decoder. productXYZ. No standardization among component names is dictated across different vendors."

At this point, you have to look at the currently available implementations as this lack of standardization causes differences even on the most basic programs.

Implementations

The following are the implementations.

Raspberry Pi

The Raspberry Pi has a Broadcom graphics processing unit (GPU), and Broadcom supports OpenMAX IL. The include files needed to build applications are in /opt/vc/include/IL, /opt/vc/include, and /opt/vc/include/interface/vcos/pthreads. The libraries that need to be linked are in the /opt/vc/lib directory and are openmaxil and bcm_host.

The Broadcom libraries need additional code to be called as well as standard OpenMAX IL functions. In addition, there are a number of (legal) extensions to OpenMAX IL that are not found in the specification or in other implementations. These are described in /opt/vc/include/IL/OMX_Broadcom.h. For these reasons I define RASPBERRY_PI to allow these to be dealt with.

The compile line for listcomponents.c, for example, is as follows:

```
cc -g -DRASPBERRY_PI -I /opt/vc/include/IL -I /opt/vc/include \
    -I /opt/vc/include/interface/vcos/pthreads \
    -o listcomponents listcomponents.c \
    -L /opt/vc/lib -l openmaxil -l bcm_host
```

The Broadcom implementation is closed source. It appears to be a thin wrapper around its GPU API, and Broadcom will not release any details of that API. This means you cannot extend the set of components, or the codecs supported, since there are no details of how to build new components. While the set of components is reasonable, currently there is no support for codecs other than PCM, and there is no support of non-GPU hardware such as USB sound cards.

OtherCrashOverride (www.raspberrypi.org/phpBB3/viewtopic.php?f=70&t=33101&p=287590 #p287590) says he has managed to get the Broadcom components running under the LIM implementation, but I haven't confirmed that yet.

The implementation on the Raspberry Pi is very weak as far as audio is concerned because all audio decoding is expected to be done in software, and it can only play PCM data. Video is more impressive and is discussed in my book *Raspberry Pi GPU Audio Video Programming*.

Bellagio

The Bellagio library does not require additional code or have any extensions. There are a few minor bugs, so I define BELLAGIO to handle them. I built from source but didn't install, so the includes and libraries are in a funny place. My compile line is as follows:

```
cc  -g -DBELLAGIO -I ../libomxil-bellagio-0.9.3/include/ \
    -o listcomponents listcomponents.c \
    -L ../libomxil-bellagio-0.9.3/src/.libs -l omxil-bellagio
```

This is the line at run time:

```
export LD_LIBRARY_PATH=../libomxil-bellagio-0.9.3/src/.libs/
./listcomponents
```

The Bellagio code is open source.

LIM

Downloading the 1.1 version was a hassle because the 1.1 download uses a Git repo that has disappeared (as of November 2016). Instead, you have to run the following:

```
git clone git://limoa.git.sourceforge.net/gitroot/limoa/limoi-components
git clone git://limoa.git.sourceforge.net/gitroot/limoa/limoi-core
git clone git://limoa.git.sourceforge.net/gitroot/limoa/limoi-plugins
git clone git://limoa.git.sourceforge.net/gitroot/limoa/limutil
git clone git://limoa.git.sourceforge.net/gitroot/limoa/manifest
```

You have to copy the root.mk file in the build to a top-level folder containing all the code and rename it Makefile. The root.readme file has build instructions. Thanks to OtherCrashOverride (www.raspberrypi.org/phpBB3/viewtopic.php?f=70&t=33101&p=286516#p286516) for these instructions.

Building the library had some minor hiccups. I had to comment out a couple of lines from one video file as it referred to nonexistent structure fields and had to remove -Werrors from one Makefile.am as otherwise a warning about an unused variable would abort the compile.

The library build puts files in a new directory in my HOME. I have found some minor bugs in the implementation so far. My compile line is as follows:

```
cc -g -DLIM -I ../../lim-omx-1.1/LIM/limoi-core/include/ \
   -o listcomponents listcomponents.c \
   -L /home/newmarch/osm-build/lib/ -l limoa -l limoi-core
```

Here is the line at runtime:

```
export LD_LIBRARY_PATH=/home/newmarch/osm-build/lib/
./listcomponents
```

The LIM code is open source.

Hardware-Supported Versions

You can find a list of hardware-supported versions at OpenMAX IL Conformant Products (`www.khronos.org/conformance/adopters/conformant-products#openmaxil`).

Implementations of Components

The Bellagio library (you need the source package to see these files) lists in its README only two audio components.

- OMX audio volume control
- OMX audio mixer component

Their names (from the example test files) are `OMX.st.volume.component` and `OMX.st.audio.mixer`, respectively. The company behind Bellagio is STMicroelectronics (`www.st.com/internet/com/home/home.jsp`), which explains the `st`.

The Broadcom OpenMAX IL implementation used on the Raspberry Pi is much better documented. If you download the firmware-master file for the Raspberry Pi, it lists the IL components in the documentation/ilcomponents directory. This lists the components audio_capture, audio_decode, audio_encode, audio_lowpower, audio_mixer, audio_processor, audio_render, and audio_splitter.

Many of the OpenMAX IL function calls in the Broadcom examples are buried in Broadcom convenience functions as follows:

```
ilclient_create_component(st->client, &st->audio_render,
                "audio_render",
                ILCLIENT_ENABLE_INPUT_BUFFERS | ILCLIENT_DISABLE_ALL_PORTS);
```

This wraps around `OMX_GetHandle()`. But at least `ilclient.h` states, "Component names as provided are automatically prefixed with `OMX.broadcom.` before passing to the IL core." So, you can conclude that the real names are, for example, `OMX.broadcom.audio_render`, and so on.

There is a simple way of programmatically getting the supported components. First initialize the OpenMAX system with `OMX_init()` and then make calls to `OMX_ComponentNameEnum()`. For successive index values, it returns a unique name each time, until it finally returns an error value of `OMX_ErrorNoMore`.

Each component may support a number of *roles*. These are given by `OMX_GetRolesOfComponent`. The 1.1 specification lists classes of audio components and associated roles in Section 8.6, "Standard Audio Components." The LIM library matches these, while Bellagio and Broadcom do not.

The following program is `listcomponents.c`:

```
#include <stdio.h>
#include <stdlib.h>

#include <OMX_Core.h>

#ifdef RASPBERRY_PI
#include <bcm_host.h>
#endif

OMX_ERRORTYPE err;

//extern OMX_COMPONENTREGISTERTYPE OMX_ComponentRegistered[];
```

```
void listroles(char *name) {
    int n;
    OMX_U32 numRoles;
    OMX_U8 *roles[32];

    /* get the number of roles by passing in a NULL roles param */
    err = OMX_GetRolesOfComponent(name, &numRoles, NULL);
    if (err != OMX_ErrorNone) {
        fprintf(stderr, "Getting roles failed\n", 0);
        exit(1);
    }
    printf("  Num roles is %d\n", numRoles);
    if (numRoles > 32) {
        printf("Too many roles to list\n");
        return;
    }

    /* now get the roles */
    for (n = 0; n < numRoles; n++) {
        roles[n] = malloc(OMX_MAX_STRINGNAME_SIZE);
    }
    err = OMX_GetRolesOfComponent(name, &numRoles, roles);
    if (err != OMX_ErrorNone) {
        fprintf(stderr, "Getting roles failed\n", 0);
        exit(1);
    }
    for (n = 0; n < numRoles; n++) {
        printf("    role: %s\n", roles[n]);
        free(roles[n]);
    }

    /* This is in version 1.2
    for (i = 0; OMX_ErrorNoMore != err; i++) {
        err = OMX_RoleOfComponentEnum(role, name, i);
        if (OMX_ErrorNone == err) {
            printf("  Role of omponent is %s\n", role);
        }
    }
    */
}

int main(int argc, char** argv) {

    int i;
    unsigned char name[OMX_MAX_STRINGNAME_SIZE];

# ifdef RASPBERRY_PI
    bcm_host_init();
# endif

    err = OMX_Init();
```

```
    if (err != OMX_ErrorNone) {
        fprintf(stderr, "OMX_Init() failed\n", 0);
        exit(1);
    }

    err = OMX_ErrorNone;
    for (i = 0; OMX_ErrorNoMore != err; i++) {
        err = OMX_ComponentNameEnum(name, OMX_MAX_STRINGNAME_SIZE, i);
        if (OMX_ErrorNone == err) {
            printf("Component is %s\n", name);
            listroles(name);
        }
    }
    printf("No more components\n");

    /*
    i= 0 ;
    while (1) {
        printf("Component %s\n", OMX_ComponentRegistered[i++]);
    }
    */
    exit(0);
}
```

The output from the Bellagio library is as follows:

```
Component is OMX.st.clocksrc
  Num roles is 1
    role: clocksrc
Component is OMX.st.clocksrc
  Num roles is 1
    role: clocksrc
Component is OMX.st.video.scheduler
  Num roles is 1
    role: video.scheduler
Component is OMX.st.video.scheduler
  Num roles is 1
    role: video.scheduler
Component is OMX.st.volume.component
  Num roles is 1
    role: volume.component
Component is OMX.st.volume.component
  Num roles is 1
    role: volume.component
Component is OMX.st.audio.mixer
  Num roles is 1
    role: audio.mixer
Component is OMX.st.audio.mixer
  Num roles is 1
    role: audio.mixer
```

```
Component is OMX.st.clocksrc
  Num roles is 1
    role: clocksrc
Component is OMX.st.clocksrc
  Num roles is 1
    role: clocksrc
Component is OMX.st.video.scheduler
  Num roles is 1
    role: video.scheduler
Component is OMX.st.video.scheduler
  Num roles is 1
    role: video.scheduler
Component is OMX.st.volume.component
  Num roles is 1
    role: volume.component
Component is OMX.st.volume.component
  Num roles is 1
    role: volume.component
Component is OMX.st.audio.mixer
  Num roles is 1
    role: audio.mixer
Component is OMX.st.audio.mixer
  Num roles is 1
    role: audio.mixer
No more components
```

This is not quite correct. The OpenMAX IL specification says that each component must appear once only, and not be repeated.

The Raspberry Pi reports a large number of components but does not define a role for any of them.

```
Component is OMX.broadcom.audio_capture
  Num roles is 0
Component is OMX.broadcom.audio_decode
  Num roles is 0
Component is OMX.broadcom.audio_encode
  Num roles is 0
Component is OMX.broadcom.audio_render
  Num roles is 0
Component is OMX.broadcom.audio_mixer
  Num roles is 0
Component is OMX.broadcom.audio_splitter
  Num roles is 0
Component is OMX.broadcom.audio_processor
  Num roles is 0
Component is OMX.broadcom.camera
  Num roles is 0
Component is OMX.broadcom.clock
  Num roles is 0
Component is OMX.broadcom.coverage
  Num roles is 0
Component is OMX.broadcom.egl_render
  Num roles is 0
```

```
Component is OMX.broadcom.image_fx
  Num roles is 0
Component is OMX.broadcom.image_decode
  Num roles is 0
Component is OMX.broadcom.image_encode
  Num roles is 0
Component is OMX.broadcom.image_read
  Num roles is 0
Component is OMX.broadcom.image_write
  Num roles is 0
Component is OMX.broadcom.read_media
  Num roles is 0
Component is OMX.broadcom.resize
  Num roles is 0
Component is OMX.broadcom.source
  Num roles is 0
Component is OMX.broadcom.text_scheduler
  Num roles is 0
Component is OMX.broadcom.transition
  Num roles is 0
Component is OMX.broadcom.video_decode
  Num roles is 0
Component is OMX.broadcom.video_encode
  Num roles is 0
Component is OMX.broadcom.video_render
  Num roles is 0
Component is OMX.broadcom.video_scheduler
  Num roles is 0
Component is OMX.broadcom.video_splitter
  Num roles is 0
Component is OMX.broadcom.visualisation
  Num roles is 0
Component is OMX.broadcom.write_media
  Num roles is 0
Component is OMX.broadcom.write_still
  Num roles is 0
No more components
```

The output from LIM is as follows:

```
Component is OMX.limoi.alsa_sink
  Num roles is 1
    role: audio_renderer.pcm
Component is OMX.limoi.clock
  Num roles is 1
    role: clock.binary
Component is OMX.limoi.ffmpeg.decode.audio
  Num roles is 8
    role: audio_decoder.aac
    role: audio_decoder.adpcm
    role: audio_decoder.amr
```

```
      role: audio_decoder.mp3
      role: audio_decoder.ogg
      role: audio_decoder.pcm
      role: audio_decoder.ra
      role: audio_decoder.wma
Component is OMX.limoi.ffmpeg.decode.video
   Num roles is 7
      role: video_decoder.avc
      role: video_decoder.h263
      role: video_decoder.mjpeg
      role: video_decoder.mpeg2
      role: video_decoder.mpeg4
      role: video_decoder.rv
      role: video_decoder.wmv
Component is OMX.limoi.ffmpeg.demux
   Num roles is 1
      role: container_demuxer.all
Component is OMX.limoi.ffmpeg.encode.audio
   Num roles is 2
      role: audio_encoder.aac
      role: audio_encoder.mp3
Component is OMX.limoi.ffmpeg.encode.video
   Num roles is 2
      role: video_encoder.h263
      role: video_encoder.mpeg4
Component is OMX.limoi.ffmpeg.mux
   Num roles is 1
      role: container_muxer.all
Component is OMX.limoi.ogg_dec
   Num roles is 1
      role: audio_decoder_with_framing.ogg
Component is OMX.limoi.sdl.renderer.video
   Num roles is 1
      role: iv_renderer.yuv.overlay
Component is OMX.limoi.video_scheduler
   Num roles is 1
      role: video_scheduler.binary
No more components
```

Getting Information About an IL Component

You will next look at how to get information about the OpenMAX IL system and any component that you use. All IL clients must initialize OpenMAX IL by calling OMX_Init(). Nearly all functions return error values, and the style used by Bellagio is as follows:

```
err = OMX_Init();
if(err != OMX_ErrorNone) {
    fprintf(stderr, "OMX_Init() failed\n", 0);
    exit(1);
}
```

This looks like a reasonable style to me, so I follow it in the sequel.

The next requirement is to get a handle to a component. This requires the vendor's name for the component, which can be found using the listcomponents.c program shown earlier. The function OMX_GetHandle takes some parameters, including a set of callback functions. These are needed to track the behavior of the application but are not needed for the example in this section. This code shows how to get a handle to the Bellagio Volume component:

```
OMX_HANDLETYPE handle;
OMX_CALLBACKTYPE callbacks;
OMX_ERRORTYPE err;

err = OMX_GetHandle(&handle, "OMX.st.volume.component", NULL /*appPriv */, &callbacks);
if(err != OMX_ErrorNone) {
    fprintf(stderr, "OMX_GetHandle failed\n", 0);
    exit(1);
}
```

The component has ports, and the ports have channels. Getting and setting information about these is done by the functions OMX_GetParameter(), OMX_SetParameter(), OMX_GetConfig(), and OMX_GetConfig(). The ...Parameter calls are made before the component is "loaded," and the ...Config calls are made after it is loaded.

C is not an OO language, and this is an ordinary function call (well, actually it's a macro). In an OO language it would be a method of an object taking another object as a parameter, as in component.method(object). In OpenMAX IL the Get/Set function takes the calling "object" as the first parameter (the component, an indicator of what type of "object" the method's parameter is), an index into possible "object" types, and a structure for the parameter object. The index values are related to structures in Table 4-2 of the 1.1 specification.

The calls take a (pointer to a) structure for filling in or extracting values. The structures are all normalized so that they share common fields such as the size of the structure. In Bellagio examples, this is done with a macro setHeader(). The structure passed in to get port information is usually a generic structure of type OMX_PORT_PARAM_TYPE. Some fields can be accessed directly, some need a typecast to a more specialized type, and some are buried down in unions and have to be extracted.

Ports are labeled by integer indices. There are different ports for different functions, such as audio, image, video, and other. To get information about the starting value for audio ports, use the following:

```
setHeader(&param, sizeof(OMX_PORT_PARAM_TYPE));
err = OMX_GetParameter(handle, OMX_IndexParamAudioInit, &param);
if(err != OMX_ErrorNone){
    fprintf(stderr, "Error in getting OMX_PORT_PARAM_TYPE parameter\n", 0);
    exit(1);
}
printf("Audio ports start on %d\n",
        ((OMX_PORT_PARAM_TYPE)param).nStartPortNumber);
printf("There are %d open ports\n",
        ((OMX_PORT_PARAM_TYPE)param).nPorts);
```

The macro setHeader just fills in header information such as version numbers and the size of the data structure.

Particular ports may now be queried about their capabilities. You can query for the type of the port (audio or otherwise), the direction (input or output), and information about the MIME type supported.

```
OMX_PARAM_PORTDEFINITIONTYPE sPortDef;

setHeader(&sPortDef, sizeof(OMX_PARAM_PORTDEFINITIONTYPE));
sPortDef.nPortIndex = 0;
err = OMX_GetParameter(handle, OMX_IndexParamPortDefinition, &sPortDef);
if(err != OMX_ErrorNone){
    fprintf(stderr, "Error in getting OMX_PORT_PARAM_TYPE parameter\n", 0);
  exit(1);
}
if (sPortDef.eDomain == OMX_PortDomainAudio) {
    printf("Is an audio port\n");
} else {
    printf("Is other device port\n");
}

if (sPortDef.eDir == OMX_DirInput) {
    printf("Port is an input port\n");
} else {
    printf("Port is an output port\n");
}

/* the Audio Port info is buried in a union format.audio within the struct */
printf("Port min buffers %d,  mimetype %s, encoding %d\n",
        sPortDef.nBufferCountMin,
        sPortDef.format.audio.cMIMEType,
        sPortDef.format.audio.eEncoding);
```

The Bellagio library returns "raw/audio" for the MIME type supported by its volume control component. This is not a valid MIME type as listed by IANA MIME Media Types (www.iana.org/assignments/media-types), though. The value returned from the encoding is zero, corresponding to OMX_AUDIO_CodingUnused, which also does not seem to be correct.

If you try the same program on the Raspberry Pi component audio_render and on the LIM component OMX.limoi.alsa_sink, you get NULL for the MIME type but an encoding value of 2, which is OMX_AUDIO_CodingPCM. PCM has a MIME type of audio/L16, so NULL seems inappropriate.

An OpenMAX IL library allows a port to be queried for the data types it supports. This is done by querying for an OMX_AUDIO_PARAM_PORTFORMATTYPE object using the index OMX_IndexParamAudioPortFormat. According to the specification, for each index from zero upward, a call to GetParameter() should return an encoding such as OMX_AUDIO_CodingPCM or OMX_AUDIO_CodingMp3 until there are no more supported formats, on which it returns OMX_ErrorNoMore.

The Bellagio code returns a value of OMX_AUDIO_CodingUnused, which is not correct. The LIM code does not set a value at all, so you just get garbage. The Broadcom implementation works OK, but as will be discussed returns values that are not actually supported. So, there is limited value in this call.

The following code tests this:

```
void getSupportedAudioFormats(int indentLevel, int portNumber) {
    OMX_AUDIO_PARAM_PORTFORMATTYPE sAudioPortFormat;

    setHeader(&sAudioPortFormat, sizeof(OMX_AUDIO_PARAM_PORTFORMATTYPE));
    sAudioPortFormat.nIndex = 0;
    sAudioPortFormat.nPortIndex = portNumber;
```

```
    printf("Supported audio formats are:\n");
    for(;;) {
        err = OMX_GetParameter(handle, OMX_IndexParamAudioPortFormat, &sAudioPortFormat);
        if (err == OMX_ErrorNoMore) {
            printf("No more formats supported\n");
            return;
        }

        /* This shouldn't occur, but does with Broadcom library */
        if (sAudioPortFormat.eEncoding == OMX_AUDIO_CodingUnused) {
            printf("No coding format returned\n");
            return;
        }

        switch (sAudioPortFormat.eEncoding) {
        case OMX_AUDIO_CodingPCM:
            printf("Supported encoding is PCM\n");
            break;
        case OMX_AUDIO_CodingVORBIS:
            printf("Supported encoding is Ogg Vorbis\n");
            break;
        case OMX_AUDIO_CodingMP3:
            printf("Supported encoding is MP3\n");
            break;
#ifdef RASPBERRY_PI
        case OMX_AUDIO_CodingFLAC:
            printf("Supported encoding is FLAC\n");
            break;
        case OMX_AUDIO_CodingDDP:
            printf("Supported encoding is DDP\n");
            break;
        case OMX_AUDIO_CodingDTS:
            printf("Supported encoding is DTS\n");
            break;
        case OMX_AUDIO_CodingWMAPRO:
            printf("Supported encoding is WMAPRO\n");
            break;
#endif
        case OMX_AUDIO_CodingAAC:
            printf("Supported encoding is AAC\n");
            break;
        case OMX_AUDIO_CodingWMA:
            printf("Supported encoding is WMA\n");
            break;
        case OMX_AUDIO_CodingRA:
            printf("Supported encoding is RA\n");
            break;
        case OMX_AUDIO_CodingAMR:
            printf("Supported encoding is AMR\n");
            break;
```

```
            case OMX_AUDIO_CodingEVRC:
                printf("Supported encoding is EVRC\n");
                break;
            case OMX_AUDIO_CodingG726:
                printf("Supported encoding is G726\n");
                break;
            case OMX_AUDIO_CodingMIDI:
                printf("Supported encoding is MIDI\n");
                break;
            case OMX_AUDIO_CodingATRAC3:
                printf("Supported encoding is ATRAC3\n");
                break;
            case OMX_AUDIO_CodingATRACX:
                printf("Supported encoding is ATRACX\n");
                break;
            case OMX_AUDIO_CodingATRACAAL:
                printf("Supported encoding is ATRACAAL\n");
                break;
            default:
                printf("Supported encoding is %d\n",
                        sAudioPortFormat.eEncoding);
            }
            sAudioPortFormat.nIndex++;
    }
}
```

Note that the code contains enum values such as OMX_AUDIO_CodingATRAC3, which are specific to the Broadcom library. These are legal values according to an OpenMAX IL extension mechanism but of course are not portable values.

The Bellagio library incorrectly returns OMX_AUDIO_CodingUnused for every index value.

The Broadcom library can return lots of values. For example, for the audio_decode component, it returns the following:

```
Supported audio formats are:
Supported encoding is MP3
Supported encoding is PCM
Supported encoding is AAC
Supported encoding is WMA
Supported encoding is Ogg Vorbis
Supported encoding is RA
Supported encoding is AMR
Supported encoding is EVRC
Supported encoding is G726
Supported encoding is FLAC
Supported encoding is DDP
Supported encoding is DTS
Supported encoding is WMAPRO
Supported encoding is ATRAC3
Supported encoding is ATRACX
Supported encoding is ATRACAAL
Supported encoding is MIDI
No more formats supported
```

Regrettably, none of these is actually supported except for PCM. The following is according to jamesh in "OMX_AllocateBuffer fails for audio decoder component":

> *The way it works is that the component passes back success for all the codecs it can potentially support (i.e., all the codecs we've ever had going). That is then constrained by what codecs are actually installed. It would be better to run time detect which codecs are present, but that code has never been written since it's never been required. It's also unlikely ever to be done as Broadcom no longer support audio codecs in this way—they have moved off the Videocore to the host CPU since they are now powerful enough to handle any audio decoding task.*

That's kind of sad, really.

Putting all the bits together gives the program info.c, shown here:

```
/**
   Based on code
   Copyright (C) 2007-2009 STMicroelectronics
   Copyright (C) 2007-2009 Nokia Corporation and/or its subsidiary(-ies).
   under the LGPL
*/

#include <stdio.h>
#include <stdlib.h>
#include <fcntl.h>
#include <string.h>
#include <pthread.h>
#include <unistd.h>
#include <sys/stat.h>

#include <OMX_Core.h>
#include <OMX_Component.h>
#include <OMX_Types.h>
#include <OMX_Audio.h>

#ifdef RASPBERRY_PI
#include <bcm_host.h>
#endif

OMX_ERRORTYPE err;
OMX_HANDLETYPE handle;
OMX_VERSIONTYPE specVersion, compVersion;

OMX_CALLBACKTYPE callbacks;

#define indent {int n = 0; while (n++ < indentLevel*2) putchar(' ');}

static void setHeader(OMX_PTR header, OMX_U32 size) {
    /* header->nVersion */
    OMX_VERSIONTYPE* ver = (OMX_VERSIONTYPE*)(header + sizeof(OMX_U32));
    /* header->nSize */
```

```
    *((OMX_U32*)header) = size;

    /* for 1.2
        ver->s.nVersionMajor = OMX_VERSION_MAJOR;
        ver->s.nVersionMinor = OMX_VERSION_MINOR;
        ver->s.nRevision = OMX_VERSION_REVISION;
        ver->s.nStep = OMX_VERSION_STEP;
    */
    ver->s.nVersionMajor = specVersion.s.nVersionMajor;
    ver->s.nVersionMinor = specVersion.s.nVersionMinor;
    ver->s.nRevision = specVersion.s.nRevision;
    ver->s.nStep = specVersion.s.nStep;
}

void printState() {
    OMX_STATETYPE state;
    err = OMX_GetState(handle, &state);
    if (err != OMX_ErrorNone) {
        fprintf(stderr, "Error on getting state\n");
        exit(1);
    }
    switch (state) {
    case OMX_StateLoaded: fprintf(stderr, "StateLoaded\n"); break;
    case OMX_StateIdle: fprintf(stderr, "StateIdle\n"); break;
    case OMX_StateExecuting: fprintf(stderr, "StateExecuting\n"); break;
    case OMX_StatePause: fprintf(stderr, "StatePause\n"); break;
    case OMX_StateWaitForResources: fprintf(stderr, "StateWiat\n"); break;
    default:  fprintf(stderr, "State unknown\n"); break;
    }
}

OMX_ERRORTYPE setEncoding(int portNumber, OMX_AUDIO_CODINGTYPE encoding) {
    OMX_PARAM_PORTDEFINITIONTYPE sPortDef;

    setHeader(&sPortDef, sizeof(OMX_PARAM_PORTDEFINITIONTYPE));
    sPortDef.nPortIndex = portNumber;
    sPortDef.nPortIndex = portNumber;
    err = OMX_GetParameter(handle, OMX_IndexParamPortDefinition, &sPortDef);
    if(err != OMX_ErrorNone){
        fprintf(stderr, "Error in getting OMX_PORT_DEFINITION_TYPE parameter\n",
0);
        exit(1);
    }

    sPortDef.format.audio.eEncoding = encoding;
    sPortDef.nBufferCountActual = sPortDef.nBufferCountMin;

    err = OMX_SetParameter(handle, OMX_IndexParamPortDefinition, &sPortDef);
    return err;
}
```

```
void getPCMInformation(int indentLevel, int portNumber) {
    /* assert: PCM is a supported mode */
    OMX_AUDIO_PARAM_PCMMODETYPE sPCMMode;

    /* set it into PCM format before asking for PCM info */
    if (setEncoding(portNumber, OMX_AUDIO_CodingPCM) != OMX_ErrorNone) {
        fprintf(stderr, "Error in setting coding to PCM\n");
        return;
    }

    setHeader(&sPCMMode, sizeof(OMX_AUDIO_PARAM_PCMMODETYPE));
    sPCMMode.nPortIndex = portNumber;
    err = OMX_GetParameter(handle, OMX_IndexParamAudioPcm, &sPCMMode);
    if(err != OMX_ErrorNone){
        indent printf("PCM mode unsupported\n");
    } else {
        indent printf("  PCM default sampling rate %d\n", sPCMMode.nSamplingRate);
        indent printf("  PCM default bits per sample %d\n", sPCMMode.nBitPerSample);
        indent printf("  PCM default number of channels %d\n", sPCMMode.nChannels);
    }

    /*
    setHeader(&sAudioPortFormat, sizeof(OMX_AUDIO_PARAM_PORTFORMATTYPE));
    sAudioPortFormat.nIndex = 0;
    sAudioPortFormat.nPortIndex = portNumber;
    */

}
void getMP3Information(int indentLevel, int portNumber) {
    /* assert: MP3 is a supported mode */
    OMX_AUDIO_PARAM_MP3TYPE sMP3Mode;

    /* set it into MP3 format before asking for MP3 info */
    if (setEncoding(portNumber, OMX_AUDIO_CodingMP3) != OMX_ErrorNone) {
        fprintf(stderr, "Error in setting coding to MP3\n");
        return;
    }

    setHeader(&sMP3Mode, sizeof(OMX_AUDIO_PARAM_MP3TYPE));
    sMP3Mode.nPortIndex = portNumber;
    err = OMX_GetParameter(handle, OMX_IndexParamAudioMp3, &sMP3Mode);
    if(err != OMX_ErrorNone){
        indent printf("MP3 mode unsupported\n");
    } else {
        indent printf("  MP3 default sampling rate %d\n", sMP3Mode.nSampleRate);
        indent printf("  MP3 default bits per sample %d\n", sMP3Mode.nBitRate);
        indent printf("  MP3 default number of channels %d\n", sMP3Mode.nChannels);
    }
}
```

```
void getSupportedAudioFormats(int indentLevel, int portNumber) {
    OMX_AUDIO_PARAM_PORTFORMATTYPE sAudioPortFormat;

    setHeader(&sAudioPortFormat, sizeof(OMX_AUDIO_PARAM_PORTFORMATTYPE));
    sAudioPortFormat.nIndex = 0;
    sAudioPortFormat.nPortIndex = portNumber;

#ifdef LIM
    printf("LIM doesn't set audio formats properly\n");
    return;
#endif

    indent printf("Supported audio formats are:\n");
    for(;;) {
        err = OMX_GetParameter(handle, OMX_IndexParamAudioPortFormat, &sAudioPortFormat);
        if (err == OMX_ErrorNoMore) {
            indent printf("No more formats supported\n");
            return;
        }

        /* This shouldn't occur, but does with Broadcom library */
        if (sAudioPortFormat.eEncoding == OMX_AUDIO_CodingUnused) {
            indent printf("No coding format returned\n");
            return;
        }

        switch (sAudioPortFormat.eEncoding) {
        case OMX_AUDIO_CodingPCM:
            indent printf("Supported encoding is PCM\n");
            getPCMInformation(indentLevel+1, portNumber);
            break;
        case OMX_AUDIO_CodingVORBIS:
            indent printf("Supported encoding is Ogg Vorbis\n");
            break;
        case OMX_AUDIO_CodingMP3:
            indent printf("Supported encoding is MP3\n");
            getMP3Information(indentLevel+1, portNumber);
            break;
#ifdef RASPBERRY_PI
        case OMX_AUDIO_CodingFLAC:
            indent printf("Supported encoding is FLAC\n");
            break;
        case OMX_AUDIO_CodingDDP:
            indent printf("Supported encoding is DDP\n");
            break;
        case OMX_AUDIO_CodingDTS:
            indent printf("Supported encoding is DTS\n");
            break;
        case OMX_AUDIO_CodingWMAPRO:
            indent printf("Supported encoding is WMAPRO\n");
            break;
        case OMX_AUDIO_CodingATRAC3:
```

```
                indent printf("Supported encoding is ATRAC3\n");
                break;
            case OMX_AUDIO_CodingATRACX:
                indent printf("Supported encoding is ATRACX\n");
                break;
            case OMX_AUDIO_CodingATRACAAL:
                indent printf("Supported encoding is ATRACAAL\n");
                break;
#endif
            case OMX_AUDIO_CodingAAC:
                indent printf("Supported encoding is AAC\n");
                break;
            case OMX_AUDIO_CodingWMA:
                indent printf("Supported encoding is WMA\n");
                break;
            case OMX_AUDIO_CodingRA:
                indent printf("Supported encoding is RA\n");
                break;
            case OMX_AUDIO_CodingAMR:
                indent printf("Supported encoding is AMR\n");
                break;
            case OMX_AUDIO_CodingEVRC:
                indent printf("Supported encoding is EVRC\n");
                break;
            case OMX_AUDIO_CodingG726:
                indent printf("Supported encoding is G726\n");
                break;
            case OMX_AUDIO_CodingMIDI:
                indent printf("Supported encoding is MIDI\n");
                break;

            /*
            case OMX_AUDIO_Coding:
                indent printf("Supported encoding is \n");
                break;
            */
            default:
                indent printf("Supported encoding is not PCM or MP3 or Vorbis, is 0x%X\n",
                    sAudioPortFormat.eEncoding);
        }
        sAudioPortFormat.nIndex++;
    }
}

void getAudioPortInformation(int indentLevel, int nPort, OMX_PARAM_PORTDEFINITIONTYPE
sPortDef) {
    indent printf("Port %d requires %d buffers\n", nPort, sPortDef.nBufferCountMin);
    indent printf("Port %d has min buffer size %d bytes\n", nPort, sPortDef.nBufferSize);

    if (sPortDef.eDir == OMX_DirInput) {
        indent printf("Port %d is an input port\n", nPort);
    } else {
```

```
            indent printf("Port %d is an output port\n",  nPort);
        }
    switch (sPortDef.eDomain) {
    case OMX_PortDomainAudio:
        indent printf("Port %d is an audio port\n", nPort);
        indent printf("Port mimetype %s\n",
                sPortDef.format.audio.cMIMEType);

        switch (sPortDef.format.audio.eEncoding) {
        case OMX_AUDIO_CodingPCM:
            indent printf("Port encoding is PCM\n");
            break;
        case OMX_AUDIO_CodingVORBIS:
            indent printf("Port encoding is Ogg Vorbis\n");
            break;
        case OMX_AUDIO_CodingMP3:
            indent printf("Port encoding is MP3\n");
            break;
        default:
            indent printf("Port encoding is not PCM or MP3 or Vorbis, is %d\n",
                    sPortDef.format.audio.eEncoding);
        }
        getSupportedAudioFormats(indentLevel+1, nPort);

        break;
        /* could put other port types here */
    default:
        indent printf("Port %d is not an audio port\n",  nPort);
    }
}

void getAllAudioPortsInformation(int indentLevel) {
    OMX_PORT_PARAM_TYPE param;
    OMX_PARAM_PORTDEFINITIONTYPE sPortDef;

    int startPortNumber;
    int nPorts;
    int n;

    setHeader(&param, sizeof(OMX_PORT_PARAM_TYPE));

    err = OMX_GetParameter(handle, OMX_IndexParamAudioInit, &param);
    if(err != OMX_ErrorNone){
        fprintf(stderr, "Error in getting audio OMX_PORT_PARAM_TYPE parameter\n", 0);
        return;
    }
    indent printf("Audio ports:\n");
    indentLevel++;

    startPortNumber = param.nStartPortNumber;
    nPorts = param.nPorts;
```

```
    if (nPorts == 0) {
        indent printf("No ports of this type\n");
        return;
    }

    indent printf("Ports start on %d\n", startPortNumber);
    indent printf("There are %d open ports\n", nPorts);

    for (n = 0; n < nPorts; n++) {
        setHeader(&sPortDef, sizeof(OMX_PARAM_PORTDEFINITIONTYPE));
        sPortDef.nPortIndex = startPortNumber + n;
        err = OMX_GetParameter(handle, OMX_IndexParamPortDefinition, &sPortDef);
        if(err != OMX_ErrorNone){
            fprintf(stderr, "Error in getting OMX_PORT_DEFINITION_TYPE parameter\n", 0);
            exit(1);
        }
        getAudioPortInformation(indentLevel+1, startPortNumber + n, sPortDef);
    }
}

void getAllVideoPortsInformation(int indentLevel) {
    OMX_PORT_PARAM_TYPE param;
    int startPortNumber;
    int nPorts;
    int n;

    setHeader(&param, sizeof(OMX_PORT_PARAM_TYPE));

    err = OMX_GetParameter(handle, OMX_IndexParamVideoInit, &param);
    if(err != OMX_ErrorNone){
        fprintf(stderr, "Error in getting video OMX_PORT_PARAM_TYPE parameter\n", 0);
        return;
    }
    printf("Video ports:\n");
    indentLevel++;

    startPortNumber = param.nStartPortNumber;
    nPorts = param.nPorts;
    if (nPorts == 0) {
        indent printf("No ports of this type\n");
        return;
    }

    indent printf("Ports start on %d\n", startPortNumber);
    indent printf("There are %d open ports\n", nPorts);
}

void getAllImagePortsInformation(int indentLevel) {
    OMX_PORT_PARAM_TYPE param;
    int startPortNumber;
    int nPorts;
    int n;
```

```
    setHeader(&param, sizeof(OMX_PORT_PARAM_TYPE));

    err = OMX_GetParameter(handle, OMX_IndexParamVideoInit, &param);
    if(err != OMX_ErrorNone){
        fprintf(stderr, "Error in getting image OMX_PORT_PARAM_TYPE parameter\n", 0);
        return;
    }
    printf("Image ports:\n");
    indentLevel++;

    startPortNumber = param.nStartPortNumber;
    nPorts = param.nPorts;
    if (nPorts == 0) {
        indent printf("No ports of this type\n");
        return;
    }

    indent printf("Ports start on %d\n", startPortNumber);
    indent printf("There are %d open ports\n", nPorts);
}

void getAllOtherPortsInformation(int indentLevel) {
    OMX_PORT_PARAM_TYPE param;
    int startPortNumber;
    int nPorts;
    int n;

    setHeader(&param, sizeof(OMX_PORT_PARAM_TYPE));

    err = OMX_GetParameter(handle, OMX_IndexParamVideoInit, &param);
    if(err != OMX_ErrorNone){
        fprintf(stderr, "Error in getting other OMX_PORT_PARAM_TYPE parameter\n", 0);
        exit(1);
    }
    printf("Other ports:\n");
    indentLevel++;

    startPortNumber = param.nStartPortNumber;
    nPorts = param.nPorts;
    if (nPorts == 0) {
        indent printf("No ports of this type\n");
        return;
    }

    indent printf("Ports start on %d\n", startPortNumber);
    indent printf("There are %d open ports\n", nPorts);
}

int main(int argc, char** argv) {

    OMX_PORT_PARAM_TYPE param;
```

```
    OMX_PARAM_PORTDEFINITIONTYPE sPortDef;
    OMX_AUDIO_PORTDEFINITIONTYPE sAudioPortDef;
    OMX_AUDIO_PARAM_PORTFORMATTYPE sAudioPortFormat;
    OMX_AUDIO_PARAM_PCMMODETYPE sPCMMode;

#ifdef RASPBERRY_PI
    char *componentName = "OMX.broadcom.audio_mixer";
#endif
#ifdef LIM
    char *componentName = "OMX.limoi.alsa_sink";
#else
    char *componentName = "OMX.st.volume.component";
#endif
    unsigned char name[128]; /* spec says 128 is max name length */
    OMX_UUIDTYPE uid;
    int startPortNumber;
    int nPorts;
    int n;

    /* ovveride component name by command line argument */
    if (argc == 2) {
        componentName = argv[1];
    }

# ifdef RASPBERRY_PI
    bcm_host_init();
# endif

    err = OMX_Init();
    if(err != OMX_ErrorNone) {
        fprintf(stderr, "OMX_Init() failed\n", 0);
        exit(1);
    }
    /** Ask the core for a handle to the volume control component
     */
    err = OMX_GetHandle(&handle, componentName, NULL /*app private data */, &callbacks);
    if (err != OMX_ErrorNone) {
        fprintf(stderr, "OMX_GetHandle failed\n", 0);
        exit(1);
    }
    err = OMX_GetComponentVersion(handle, name, &compVersion, &specVersion, &uid);
    if (err != OMX_ErrorNone) {
        fprintf(stderr, "OMX_GetComponentVersion failed\n", 0);
        exit(1);
    }
    printf("Component name: %s version %d.%d, Spec version %d.%d\n",
            name, compVersion.s.nVersionMajor,
            compVersion.s.nVersionMinor,
            specVersion.s.nVersionMajor,
            specVersion.s.nVersionMinor);
```

```
    /** Get  ports information */
    getAllAudioPortsInformation(0);
    getAllVideoPortsInformation(0);
    getAllImagePortsInformation(0);
    getAllOtherPortsInformation(0);

    exit(0);
}
```

The Makefile for the Bellagio version is as follows:

```
INCLUDES=-I ../libomxil-bellagio-0.9.3/include/
LIBS=-L ../libomxil-bellagio-0.9.3/src/.libs -l omxil-bellagio
CFLAGS = -g

info: info.c
        cc $(FLAGS) $(INCLUDES) -o info info.c $(LIBS)
```

The output using the Bellagio implementation is as follows:

```
Component name: OMX.st.volume.component version 1.1, Spec version 1.1
Audio ports:
  Ports start on 0
  There are 2 open ports
    Port 0 requires 2 buffers
    Port 0 is an input port
    Port 0 is an audio port
    Port mimetype raw/audio
    Port encoding is not PCM or MP3 or Vorbis, is 0
      Supported audio formats are:
      No coding format returned
    Port 1 requires 2 buffers
    Port 1 is an output port
    Port 1 is an audio port
    Port mimetype raw/audio
    Port encoding is not PCM or MP3 or Vorbis, is 0
      Supported audio formats are:
      No coding format returned
Video ports:
  No ports of this type
Image ports:
  No ports of this type
Other ports:
  No ports of this type
```

The Makefile for the Raspberry Pi is as follows:

```
INCLUDES=-I /opt/vc/include/IL -I /opt/vc/include -I /opt/vc/include/interface/vcos/pthreads
CFLAGS=-g -DRASPBERRY_PI
LIBS=-L /opt/vc/lib -l openmaxil -l bcm_host
```

```
info: info.c
        cc $(CFLAGS) $(INCLUDES) -o info info.c $(LIBS)
```

The output on the Raspberry Pi for the audio_render component is as follows:

```
Audio ports:
  Ports start on 100
  There are 1 open ports
    Port 100 requires 1 buffers
    Port 100 is an input port
    Port 100 is an audio port
    Port mimetype (null)
    Port encoding is PCM
      Supported audio formats are:
      Supported encoding is PCM
          PCM default sampling rate 44100
          PCM default bits per sample 16
          PCM default number of channels 2
      Supported encoding is DDP
      No more formats supported
Video ports:
  No ports of this type
Image ports:
  No ports of this type
Other ports:
  No ports of this type
```

The Makefile for LIM is as follows:

```
INCLUDES=-I ../../lim-omx-1.1/LIM/limoi-core/include/
#LIBS=-L ../../lim-omx-1.1/LIM/limoi-base/src/.libs -l limoi-base
LIBS = -L /home/newmarch/osm-build/lib/ -l limoa -l limoi-core
CFLAGS = -g -DLIM

info: info.c
        cc $(CFLAGS) $(INCLUDES) -o info info.c $(LIBS)
```

The output on LIM for the alsa_sink component is as follows:

```
Component name: OMX.limoi.alsa_sink version 0.0, Spec version 1.1
Audio ports:
  Ports start on 0
  There are 1 open ports
    Port 0 requires 2 buffers
    Port 0 is an input port
    Port 0 is an audio port
    Port mimetype (null)
    Port encoding is PCM
LIM doesn't set audio formats properly
Error in getting video OMX_PORT_PARAM_TYPE parameter
Error in getting image OMX_PORT_PARAM_TYPE parameter
Error in getting other OMX_PORT_PARAM_TYPE parameter
```

The LIM implementation throws errors when the component does not support a mode (here an audio component does not support video, image, or other). This is against the 1.1 specification, which says the following:

```
"All standard components shall support the following parameters:
 o OMX_IndexParamPortDefinition
 o OMX_IndexParamCompBufferSupplier
 o OMX_IndexParamAudioInit
 o OMX_IndexParamImageInit
 o OMX_IndexParamVideoInit
 o OMX_IndexParamOtherInit"
```

I suppose you could argue that an `alsa_sink` component isn't a standard one, so it is allowed. Well, OK…

Playing PCM Audio Files

Playing audio to an output device requires the use of an `audio_render` device. This is one of the standard devices in the 1.1 specification and is included in the Broadcom Raspberry Pi library but not in the Bellagio library. LIM has a component `alsa_sink`, which plays the same role.

The structure of a program to play audio is as follows:

1. Initialize the library and audio render component.

2. Continually fill input buffers and ask the component to empty the buffers.

3. Capture events from the component saying that a buffer has been emptied in order to schedule refilling the buffer and requesting it to be emptied.

4. Clean up on completion.

Note that the Raspberry Pi audio render component will *only* play PCM data and that the LIM `alsa_sink` component only plays back at 44,100Hz.

State

Initializing the component is a multistep process that depends on the state of the component. Components are created in the `Loaded` state. They transition from one state to another through `OMX_SendCommand(handle, OMX_CommandStateSet, <next state>, <param>)`. The next state from `Loaded` should be `Idle` and from there to `Executing`. There are other states that you need not be concerned about.

Requests to change state are asynchronous. The send command returns immediately (well, within 5 milliseconds). When the actual change of state occurs, an event handler callback function is called.

Threads

Some commands require a component to be in a particular state. Requests to put a component into a state are asynchronous. So, a request can be made by a client, but then the client might have to wait until the state change has occurred. This is best done by the client suspending operation of its thread until woken up by the state change occurring in the event handler.

Linux/Unix has standardized on the Posix pthreads library for managing multiple threads. For our purposes, you use two parts from this library: the ability to place a *mutex* around critical sections and the ability to suspend/wake up threads based on *conditions*. Pthreads are covered in many places, with a short and good tutorial by Blaise Barney called "POSIX Threads Programming" (https://computing.llnl.gov/tutorials/pthreads/#Misc).

The functions and data you use are as follows:

```
pthread_mutex_t mutex;
OMX_STATETYPE currentState = OMX_StateLoaded;
pthread_cond_t stateCond;

void waitFor(OMX_STATETYPE state) {
    pthread_mutex_lock(&mutex);
    while (currentState != state)
        pthread_cond_wait(&stateCond, &mutex);
    fprintf(stderr, "Wait successfully completed\n");
    pthread_mutex_unlock(&mutex);
}

void wakeUp(OMX_STATETYPE newState) {
    pthread_mutex_lock(&mutex);
    currentState = newState;
    pthread_cond_signal(&stateCond);
    pthread_mutex_unlock(&mutex);
}
pthread_mutex_t empty_mutex;
int emptyState = 0;
OMX_BUFFERHEADERTYPE* pEmptyBuffer;
pthread_cond_t emptyStateCond;

void waitForEmpty() {
    pthread_mutex_lock(&empty_mutex);
    while (emptyState == 1)
        pthread_cond_wait(&emptyStateCond, &empty_mutex);
    emptyState = 1;
    pthread_mutex_unlock(&empty_mutex);
}

void wakeUpEmpty(OMX_BUFFERHEADERTYPE* pBuffer) {
    pthread_mutex_lock(&empty_mutex);
    emptyState = 0;
    pEmptyBuffer = pBuffer;
    pthread_cond_signal(&emptyStateCond);
    pthread_mutex_unlock(&empty_mutex);
}

void mutex_init() {
    int n = pthread_mutex_init(&mutex, NULL);
    if ( n != 0) {
        fprintf(stderr, "Can't init state mutex\n");
    }
```

```
    n = pthread_mutex_init(&empty_mutex, NULL);
    if ( n != 0) {
        fprintf(stderr, "Can't init empty mutex\n");
    }
}
```

Hungarian Notation in OpenMAX IL

Hungarian notation was invented by Charles Simonyi to add type or functional information to variable, structure, and field names. A form was heavily used in the Microsoft Windows SDK. A simplified form is used in OpenMAX IL by prefixing variables, fields, and so on, as follows:

- n prefixes a number of some kind.

- p prefixes a pointer.

- s prefixes a structure or a string.

- c prefixes a callback function.

The value of such conventions is highly debatable.

Callbacks

Two types of callback functions are relevant to this example: event callbacks that occur on changes of state and some other events, and empty buffer callbacks that occur when a component has emptied an input buffer. These are registered with the following:

```
OMX_CALLBACKTYPE callbacks  = { .EventHandler = cEventHandler,
            .EmptyBufferDone = cEmptyBufferDone,
};
err = OMX_GetHandle(&handle, componentName, NULL /*app private data */, &callbacks);
```

Component Resources

Each component has a number of ports that have to be configured. The ports are some of the component's *resources*. Each port starts off as enabled but may be set to disabled with OMX_SendCommand(handle, OMX_CommandPortDisable, <port number>, NULL).

Enabled ports can have *buffers* allocated for the transfer of data into and out of the component. This can be done in two ways: OMX_AllocateBuffer asks the component to perform the allocation for the client, while with OMX_UseBuffer the client hands a buffer to the component. As there may be buffer memory alignment issues, I prefer to let the component do the allocation.

Here is a tricky part. To allocate or use buffers on a component, a request must be made to transition from Loaded state to Idle. So, a call to OMX_SendCommand(handle, OMX_CommandStateSet, OMX_StateIdle, <param>) must be made before buffers are allocated. *But* the transition to Idle will not take place until each port is either disabled or all buffers for it are allocated.

This last step cost me nearly a week of head scratching. The audio_render component has two ports: an input audio port and a time update port. While I had configured the audio port correctly, I had not disabled the time port because I didn't realize it had one. Consequently, the transition to Idle never took place. The following is the code to handle this:

```
setHeader(&param, sizeof(OMX_PORT_PARAM_TYPF));
err = OMX_GetParameter(handle, OMX_IndexParamOtherInit, &param);
if(err != OMX_ErrorNone){
    fprintf(stderr, "Error in getting OMX_PORT_PARAM_TYPE parameter\n", 0);
    exit(1);
}
startPortNumber = ((OMX_PORT_PARAM_TYPE)param).nStartPortNumber;
nPorts = ((OMX_PORT_PARAM_TYPE)param).nPorts;
printf("Other has %d ports\n", nPorts);
/* and disable it */
err = OMX_SendCommand(handle, OMX_CommandPortDisable, startPortNumber, NULL);
if (err != OMX_ErrorNone) {
    fprintf(stderr, "Error on setting port to disabled\n");
    exit(1);
}
```

Here is how to set parameters for the audio port:

```
/** Get audio port information */
setHeader(&param, sizeof(OMX_PORT_PARAM_TYPE));
err = OMX_GetParameter(handle, OMX_IndexParamAudioInit, &param);
if(err != OMX_ErrorNone){
    fprintf(stderr, "Error in getting OMX_PORT_PARAM_TYPE parameter\n", 0);
    exit(1);
}
startPortNumber = ((OMX_PORT_PARAM_TYPE)param).nStartPortNumber;
nPorts = ((OMX_PORT_PARAM_TYPE)param).nPorts;
if (nPorts > 1) {
    fprintf(stderr, "Render device has more than one port\n");
    exit(1);
}

setHeader(&sPortDef, sizeof(OMX_PARAM_PORTDEFINITIONTYPE));
sPortDef.nPortIndex = startPortNumber;
err = OMX_GetParameter(handle, OMX_IndexParamPortDefinition, &sPortDef);
if(err != OMX_ErrorNone){
    fprintf(stderr, "Error in getting OMX_PORT_DEFINITION_TYPE parameter\n", 0);
    exit(1);
}
if (sPortDef.eDomain != OMX_PortDomainAudio) {
    fprintf(stderr, "Port %d is not an audio port\n", startPortNumber);
    exit(1);
}

if (sPortDef.eDir != OMX_DirInput) {
    fprintf(stderr, "Port is not an input port\n");
    exit(1);
}
if (sPortDef.format.audio.eEncoding == OMX_AUDIO_CodingPCM) {
    printf("Port encoding is PCM\n");
}   else {
```

```
        printf("Port has unknown encoding\n");
    }

    /* create minimum number of buffers for the port */
    nBuffers = sPortDef.nBufferCountActual = sPortDef.nBufferCountMin;
    printf("Number of bufers is %d\n", nBuffers);
    err = OMX_SetParameter(handle, OMX_IndexParamPortDefinition, &sPortDef);
    if(err != OMX_ErrorNone){
        fprintf(stderr, "Error in setting OMX_PORT_PARAM_TYPE parameter\n", 0);
        exit(1);
    }

    /* call to put state into idle before allocating buffers */
    err = OMX_SendCommand(handle, OMX_CommandStateSet, OMX_StateIdle, NULL);
    if (err != OMX_ErrorNone) {
        fprintf(stderr, "Error on setting state to idle\n");
        exit(1);
    }

    err = OMX_SendCommand(handle, OMX_CommandPortEnable, startPortNumber, NULL);
    if (err != OMX_ErrorNone) {
        fprintf(stderr, "Error on setting port to enabled\n");
        exit(1);
    }

    nBufferSize = sPortDef.nBufferSize;
    printf("%d buffers of size is %d\n", nBuffers, nBufferSize);

    inBuffers = malloc(nBuffers * sizeof(OMX_BUFFERHEADERTYPE *));
    if (inBuffers == NULL) {
        fprintf(stderr, "Can't allocate buffers\n");
        exit(1);
    }
    for (n = 0; n < nBuffers; n++) {
        err = OMX_AllocateBuffer(handle, inBuffers+n, startPortNumber, NULL,
                            nBufferSize);
        if (err != OMX_ErrorNone) {
            fprintf(stderr, "Error on AllocateBuffer in 1%i\n", err);
            exit(1);
        }

    }

    waitFor(OMX_StateIdle);
    /* try setting the encoding to PCM mode */
    setHeader(&sPCMMode, sizeof(OMX_AUDIO_PARAM_PCMMODETYPE));
    sPCMMode.nPortIndex = startPortNumber;
    err = OMX_GetParameter(handle, OMX_IndexParamAudioPcm, &sPCMMode);
    if(err != OMX_ErrorNone){
        printf("PCM mode unsupported\n");
        exit(1);
```

```
    } else {
        printf("PCM mode supported\n");
        printf("PCM sampling rate %d\n", sPCMMode.nSamplingRate);
        printf("PCM nChannels %d\n", sPCMMode.nChannels);
    }
```

Setting the Output Device

OpenMAX has a standard audio render component. But what device does it render to? The built-in sound card? A USB sound card? That is not a part of OpenMAX IL; there isn't even a way to list the audio devices, only the audio components.

OpenMAX has an extension mechanism that can be used by an OpenMAX implementor to answer questions like this. The Broadcom core implementation has extension types OMX_CONFIG_BRCMAUDIODESTINATIONTYPE (and OMX_CONFIG_BRCMAUDIOSOURCETYPE) that can be used to set the audio destination (source) device. Here is code to do this:

```
void setOutputDevice(const char *name) {
    int32_t success = -1;
    OMX_CONFIG_BRCMAUDIODESTINATIONTYPE arDest;

    if (name && strlen(name) < sizeof(arDest.sName)) {
        setHeader(&arDest, sizeof(OMX_CONFIG_BRCMAUDIODESTINATIONTYPE));
        strcpy((char *)arDest.sName, name);

        err = OMX_SetParameter(handle, OMX_IndexConfigBrcmAudioDestination, &arDest);
        if (err != OMX_ErrorNone) {
            fprintf(stderr, "Error on setting audio destination\n");
            exit(1);
        }
    }
}
```

Here is where it descends into murkiness again. The header file <IL/OMX_Broadcom.h> states that the default value of sName is "local" but doesn't give any other values. The Raspberry Pi forums say that this refers to the 3.5mm analog audio out and that HDMI is chosen by using the value "hdmi." No other values are documented, and it seems that the Broadcom OpenMAX IL does not support any other audio devices. In particular, USB audio devices are not supported by the current Broadcom OpenMAX IL components for either input or output. So, you can't use OpenMAX IL for, say, audio capture on the Raspberry Pi since it has no Broadcom-supported audio input.

Main Loop

Playing the audio file once all the ports are set up consists of filling buffers, waiting for them to empty, and then refilling them until the data is finished. There are two possible styles.

- Fill the buffers once in the main loop and then continue to fill and empty them in the empty buffer callbacks.

- In the main loop, fill and empty the buffers continually, waiting between each fill for the buffer to empty.

The Bellagio example uses the first technique. However, the 1.2 specification says that "...the IL client shall not call IL core or component functions from within an IL callback context," so this is not a good technique. The Raspberry Pi examples use the second technique but use a nonstandard call to find the latency and delay for that time. It is better to just set up more pthreads conditions and block on those.

This leads to a main loop that looks like this:

```
emptyState = 1;
for (;;) {
    int data_read = read(fd, inBuffers[0]->pBuffer, nBufferSize);
    inBuffers[0]->nFilledLen = data_read;
    inBuffers[0]->nOffset = 0;
    filesize -= data_read;
    if (data_read <= 0) {
        fprintf(stderr, "In the %s no more input data available\n", __func__);
        inBuffers[0]->nFilledLen=0;
        inBuffers[0]->nFlags = OMX_BUFFERFLAG_EOS;
        bEOS=OMX_TRUE;
        err = OMX_EmptyThisBuffer(handle, inBuffers[0]);
        break;
    }
    if(!bEOS) {
        fprintf(stderr, "Emptying again buffer %p %d bytes, %d to go\n", inBuffers[0],
        data_read, filesize);
        err = OMX_EmptyThisBuffer(handle, inBuffers[0]);
    }else {
        fprintf(stderr, "In %s Dropping Empty This buffer to Audio Dec\n", __func__);
    }
    waitForEmpty();
    printf("Waited for empty\n");
}

printf("Buffers emptied\n");
```

Complete Program

The complete program is as follows:

```
/**
   Based on code
   Copyright (C) 2007-2009 STMicroelectronics
   Copyright (C) 2007-2009 Nokia Corporation and/or its subsidiary(-ies).
   under the LGPL
*/

#include <stdio.h>
#include <stdlib.h>
#include <fcntl.h>
#include <string.h>
#include <pthread.h>
#include <unistd.h>
```

```c
#include <sys/stat.h>
#include <pthread.h>

#include <OMX_Core.h>
#include <OMX_Component.h>
#include <OMX_Types.h>
#include <OMX_Audio.h>

#ifdef RASPBERRY_PI
#include <bcm_host.h>
#include <IL/OMX_Broadcom.h>
#endif

OMX_ERRORTYPE err;
OMX_HANDLETYPE handle;
OMX_VERSIONTYPE specVersion, compVersion;

int fd = 0;
unsigned int filesize;
static OMX_BOOL bEOS=OMX_FALSE;

OMX_U32 nBufferSize;
int nBuffers;

pthread_mutex_t mutex;
OMX_STATETYPE currentState = OMX_StateLoaded;
pthread_cond_t stateCond;

void waitFor(OMX_STATETYPE state) {
    pthread_mutex_lock(&mutex);
    while (currentState != state)
        pthread_cond_wait(&stateCond, &mutex);
    pthread_mutex_unlock(&mutex);
}

void wakeUp(OMX_STATETYPE newState) {
    pthread_mutex_lock(&mutex);
    currentState = newState;
    pthread_cond_signal(&stateCond);
    pthread_mutex_unlock(&mutex);
}

pthread_mutex_t empty_mutex;
int emptyState = 0;
OMX_BUFFERHEADERTYPE* pEmptyBuffer;
pthread_cond_t emptyStateCond;

void waitForEmpty() {
    pthread_mutex_lock(&empty_mutex);
    while (emptyState == 1)
        pthread_cond_wait(&emptyStateCond, &empty_mutex);
```

```
    emptyState = 1;
    pthread_mutex_unlock(&empty_mutex);
}

void wakeUpEmpty(OMX_BUFFERHEADERTYPE* pBuffer) {
    pthread_mutex_lock(&empty_mutex);
    emptyState = 0;
    pEmptyBuffer = pBuffer;
    pthread_cond_signal(&emptyStateCond);
    pthread_mutex_unlock(&empty_mutex);
}

void mutex_init() {
    int n = pthread_mutex_init(&mutex, NULL);
    if ( n != 0) {
        fprintf(stderr, "Can't init state mutex\n");
    }
    n = pthread_mutex_init(&empty_mutex, NULL);
    if ( n != 0) {
        fprintf(stderr, "Can't init empty mutex\n");
    }
}

static void display_help() {
    fprintf(stderr, "Usage: render input_file");
}

/** Gets the file descriptor's size
 * @return the size of the file. If size cannot be computed
 * (i.e. stdin, zero is returned)
 */
static int getFileSize(int fd) {

    struct stat input_file_stat;
    int err;

    /* Obtain input file length */
    err = fstat(fd, &input_file_stat);
    if(err){
        fprintf(stderr, "fstat failed",0);
        exit(-1);
    }
    return input_file_stat.st_size;
}

OMX_ERRORTYPE cEventHandler(
                        OMX_HANDLETYPE hComponent,
                        OMX_PTR pAppData,
                        OMX_EVENTTYPE eEvent,
                        OMX_U32 Data1,
                        OMX_U32 Data2,
                        OMX_PTR pEventData) {
```

```
    fprintf(stderr, "Hi there, I am in the %s callback\n", __func__);
    if(eEvent == OMX_EventCmdComplete) {
        if (Data1 == OMX_CommandStateSet) {
            fprintf(stderr, "Component State changed in ", 0);
            switch ((int)Data2) {
            case OMX_StateInvalid:
                fprintf(stderr, "OMX_StateInvalid\n", 0);
                break;
            case OMX_StateLoaded:
                fprintf(stderr, "OMX_StateLoaded\n", 0);
                break;
            case OMX_StateIdle:
                fprintf(stderr, "OMX_StateIdle\n",0);
                break;
            case OMX_StateExecuting:
                fprintf(stderr, "OMX_StateExecuting\n",0);
                break;
            case OMX_StatePause:
                fprintf(stderr, "OMX_StatePause\n",0);
                break;
            case OMX_StateWaitForResources:
                fprintf(stderr, "OMX_StateWaitForResources\n",0);
                break;
            }
            wakeUp((int) Data2);
        } else  if (Data1 == OMX_CommandPortEnable){

        } else if (Data1 == OMX_CommandPortDisable){

        }
    } else if(eEvent == OMX_EventBufferFlag) {
        if((int)Data2 == OMX_BUFFERFLAG_EOS) {

        }
    } else {
        fprintf(stderr, "Param1 is %i\n", (int)Data1);
        fprintf(stderr, "Param2 is %i\n", (int)Data2);
    }

    return OMX_ErrorNone;
}

OMX_ERRORTYPE cEmptyBufferDone(
                            OMX_HANDLETYPE hComponent,
                            OMX_PTR pAppData,
                            OMX_BUFFERHEADERTYPE* pBuffer) {

    fprintf(stderr, "Hi there, I am in the %s callback.\n", __func__);
    if (bEOS) {
        fprintf(stderr, "Buffers emptied, exiting\n");
    }
```

```
        wakeUpEmpty(pBuffer);
        fprintf(stderr, "Exiting callback\n");

        return OMX_ErrorNone;
    }

    OMX_CALLBACKTYPE callbacks  = { .EventHandler = cEventHandler,
                                    .EmptyBufferDone = cEmptyBufferDone,
    };

    void printState() {
        OMX_STATETYPE state;
        err = OMX_GetState(handle, &state);
        if (err != OMX_ErrorNone) {
            fprintf(stderr, "Error on getting state\n");
            exit(1);
        }
        switch (state) {
        case OMX_StateLoaded: fprintf(stderr, "StateLoaded\n"); break;
        case OMX_StateIdle: fprintf(stderr, "StateIdle\n"); break;
        case OMX_StateExecuting: fprintf(stderr, "StateExecuting\n"); break;
        case OMX_StatePause: fprintf(stderr, "StatePause\n"); break;
        case OMX_StateWaitForResources: fprintf(stderr, "StateWiat\n"); break;
        default:  fprintf(stderr, "State unknown\n"); break;
        }
    }

    static void setHeader(OMX_PTR header, OMX_U32 size) {
        /* header->nVersion */
        OMX_VERSIONTYPE* ver = (OMX_VERSIONTYPE*)(header + sizeof(OMX_U32));
        /* header->nSize */
        *((OMX_U32*)header) = size;

        /* for 1.2
            ver->s.nVersionMajor = OMX_VERSION_MAJOR;
            ver->s.nVersionMinor = OMX_VERSION_MINOR;
            ver->s.nRevision = OMX_VERSION_REVISION;
            ver->s.nStep = OMX_VERSION_STEP;
        */
        ver->s.nVersionMajor = specVersion.s.nVersionMajor;
        ver->s.nVersionMinor = specVersion.s.nVersionMinor;
        ver->s.nRevision = specVersion.s.nRevision;
        ver->s.nStep = specVersion.s.nStep;
    }

    /**
     * Disable unwanted ports, or we can't transition to Idle state
     */
    void disablePort(OMX_INDEXTYPE paramType) {
        OMX_PORT_PARAM_TYPE param;
        int nPorts;
```

```
    int startPortNumber;
    int n;

    setHeader(&param, sizeof(OMX_PORT_PARAM_TYPE));
    err = OMX_GetParameter(handle, paramType, &param);
    if(err != OMX_ErrorNone){
        fprintf(stderr, "Error in getting OMX_PORT_PARAM_TYPE parameter\n", 0);
        exit(1);
    }
    startPortNumber = ((OMX_PORT_PARAM_TYPE)param).nStartPortNumber;
    nPorts = ((OMX_PORT_PARAM_TYPE)param).nPorts;
    if (nPorts > 0) {
        fprintf(stderr, "Other has %d ports\n", nPorts);
        /* and disable it */
        for (n = 0; n < nPorts; n++) {
            err = OMX_SendCommand(handle, OMX_CommandPortDisable, n + startPortNumber, NULL);
            if (err != OMX_ErrorNone) {
                fprintf(stderr, "Error on setting port to disabled\n");
                exit(1);
            }
        }
    }
}

#ifdef RASPBERRY_PI
/* For the RPi name can be "hdmi" or "local" */
void setOutputDevice(const char *name) {
    int32_t success = -1;
    OMX_CONFIG_BRCMAUDIODESTINATIONTYPE arDest;

    if (name && strlen(name) < sizeof(arDest.sName)) {
        setHeader(&arDest, sizeof(OMX_CONFIG_BRCMAUDIODESTINATIONTYPE));
        strcpy((char *)arDest.sName, name);

        err = OMX_SetParameter(handle, OMX_IndexConfigBrcmAudioDestination, &arDest);
        if (err != OMX_ErrorNone) {
            fprintf(stderr, "Error on setting audio destination\n");
            exit(1);
        }
    }
}
#endif

void setPCMMode(int startPortNumber) {
    OMX_AUDIO_PARAM_PCMMODETYPE sPCMMode;

    setHeader(&sPCMMode, sizeof(OMX_AUDIO_PARAM_PCMMODETYPE));
    sPCMMode.nPortIndex = startPortNumber;
    sPCMMode.nSamplingRate = 48000;
    sPCMMode.nChannels;
```

271

```
        err = OMX_SetParameter(handle, OMX_IndexParamAudioPcm, &sPCMMode);
        if(err != OMX_ErrorNone){
            fprintf(stderr, "PCM mode unsupported\n");
            return;
        } else {
            fprintf(stderr, "PCM mode supported\n");
            fprintf(stderr, "PCM sampling rate %d\n", sPCMMode.nSamplingRate);
            fprintf(stderr, "PCM nChannels %d\n", sPCMMode.nChannels);
        }
}

int main(int argc, char** argv) {

    OMX_PORT_PARAM_TYPE param;
    OMX_PARAM_PORTDEFINITIONTYPE sPortDef;
    OMX_AUDIO_PORTDEFINITIONTYPE sAudioPortDef;
    OMX_AUDIO_PARAM_PORTFORMATTYPE sAudioPortFormat;
    OMX_AUDIO_PARAM_PCMMODETYPE sPCMMode;
    OMX_BUFFERHEADERTYPE **inBuffers;

#ifdef RASPBERRY_PI
    char *componentName = "OMX.broadcom.audio_render";
#endif
#ifdef LIM
    char *componentName = "OMX.limoi.alsa_sink";
#endif
    unsigned char name[OMX_MAX_STRINGNAME_SIZE];
    OMX_UUIDTYPE uid;
    int startPortNumber;
    int nPorts;
    int n;

# ifdef RASPBERRY_PI
    bcm_host_init();
# endif

    fprintf(stderr, "Thread id is %p\n", pthread_self());
    if(argc < 2){
        display_help();
        exit(1);
    }

    fd = open(argv[1], O_RDONLY);
    if(fd < 0){
        perror("Error opening input file\n");
        exit(1);
    }
    filesize = getFileSize(fd);

    err = OMX_Init();
    if(err != OMX_ErrorNone) {
        fprintf(stderr, "OMX_Init() failed\n", 0);
```

```
    exit(1);
}
/** Ask the core for a handle to the audio render component
 */
err = OMX_GetHandle(&handle, componentName, NULL /*app private data */, &callbacks);
if(err != OMX_ErrorNone) {
    fprintf(stderr, "OMX_GetHandle failed\n", 0);
    exit(1);
}
err = OMX_GetComponentVersion(handle, name, &compVersion, &specVersion, &uid);
if(err != OMX_ErrorNone) {
    fprintf(stderr, "OMX_GetComponentVersion failed\n", 0);
    exit(1);
}


/** disable other ports */
disablePort(OMX_IndexParamOtherInit);

/** Get audio port information */
setHeader(&param, sizeof(OMX_PORT_PARAM_TYPE));
err = OMX_GetParameter(handle, OMX_IndexParamAudioInit, &param);
if(err != OMX_ErrorNone){
    fprintf(stderr, "Error in getting OMX_PORT_PARAM_TYPE parameter\n", 0);
    exit(1);
}
startPortNumber = ((OMX_PORT_PARAM_TYPE)param).nStartPortNumber;
nPorts = ((OMX_PORT_PARAM_TYPE)param).nPorts;
if (nPorts > 1) {
    fprintf(stderr, "Render device has more than one port\n");
    exit(1);
}

/* Get and check port information */
setHeader(&sPortDef, sizeof(OMX_PARAM_PORTDEFINITIONTYPE));
sPortDef.nPortIndex = startPortNumber;
err = OMX_GetParameter(handle, OMX_IndexParamPortDefinition, &sPortDef);
if(err != OMX_ErrorNone){
    fprintf(stderr, "Error in getting OMX_PORT_DEFINITION_TYPE parameter\n", 0);
    exit(1);
}
if (sPortDef.eDomain != OMX_PortDomainAudio) {
    fprintf(stderr, "Port %d is not an audio port\n", startPortNumber);
    exit(1);
}

if (sPortDef.eDir != OMX_DirInput) {
    fprintf(stderr, "Port is not an input port\n");
    exit(1);
}
if (sPortDef.format.audio.eEncoding == OMX_AUDIO_CodingPCM) {
    fprintf(stderr, "Port encoding is PCM\n");
```

```
}   else {
    fprintf(stderr, "Port has unknown encoding\n");
}

/* Create minimum number of buffers for the port */
nBuffers = sPortDef.nBufferCountActual = sPortDef.nBufferCountMin;
fprintf(stderr, "Number of bufers is %d\n", nBuffers);
err = OMX_SetParameter(handle, OMX_IndexParamPortDefinition, &sPortDef);
if(err != OMX_ErrorNone){
    fprintf(stderr, "Error in setting OMX_PORT_PARAM_TYPE parameter\n", 0);
    exit(1);
}
if (sPortDef.bEnabled) {
    fprintf(stderr, "Port is enabled\n");
} else {
    fprintf(stderr, "Port is not enabled\n");
}

/* call to put state into idle before allocating buffers */
err = OMX_SendCommand(handle, OMX_CommandStateSet, OMX_StateIdle, NULL);
if (err != OMX_ErrorNone) {
    fprintf(stderr, "Error on setting state to idle\n");
    exit(1);
}

err = OMX_SendCommand(handle, OMX_CommandPortEnable, startPortNumber, NULL);
if (err != OMX_ErrorNone) {
    fprintf(stderr, "Error on setting port to enabled\n");
    exit(1);
}

/* Configure buffers for the port */
nBufferSize = sPortDef.nBufferSize;
fprintf(stderr, "%d buffers of size is %d\n", nBuffers, nBufferSize);

inBuffers = malloc(nBuffers * sizeof(OMX_BUFFERHEADERTYPE *));
if (inBuffers == NULL) {
    fprintf(stderr, "Can't allocate buffers\n");
    exit(1);
}

for (n = 0; n < nBuffers; n++) {
    err = OMX_AllocateBuffer(handle, inBuffers+n, startPortNumber, NULL,
                             nBufferSize);
    if (err != OMX_ErrorNone) {
        fprintf(stderr, "Error on AllocateBuffer in 1%i\n", err);
        exit(1);
    }
}
/* Make sure we've reached Idle state */
waitFor(OMX_StateIdle);
```

```
    /* Now try to switch to Executing state */
    err = OMX_SendCommand(handle, OMX_CommandStateSet, OMX_StateExecuting, NULL);
    if(err != OMX_ErrorNone){
        exit(1);
    }


    /* One buffer is the minimum for Broadcom component, so use that */
    pEmptyBuffer = inBuffers[0];
    emptyState = 1;
    /* Fill and empty buffer */
    for (;;) {
        int data_read = read(fd, pEmptyBuffer->pBuffer, nBufferSize);
        pEmptyBuffer->nFilledLen = data_read;
        pEmptyBuffer->nOffset = 0;
        filesize -= data_read;
        if (data_read <= 0) {
            fprintf(stderr, "In the %s no more input data available\n", __func__);
            pEmptyBuffer->nFilledLen=0;
            pEmptyBuffer->nFlags = OMX_BUFFERFLAG_EOS;
            bEOS=OMX_TRUE;
        }
        fprintf(stderr, "Emptying again buffer %p %d bytes, %d to go\n", pEmptyBuffer, data_
        read, filesize);
        err = OMX_EmptyThisBuffer(handle, pEmptyBuffer);
        waitForEmpty();
        fprintf(stderr, "Waited for empty\n");
        if (bEOS) {
            fprintf(stderr, "Exiting loop\n");
            break;
        }
    }
    fprintf(stderr, "Buffers emptied\n");
    exit(0);
}
```

Conclusion

The Khronos Group has produced specifications for audio and video in low-capability systems. These are currently used by Android and by the Raspberry Pi. This chapter has given an introductory overview of these specifications and some example programs. The LIM package has not been updated since 2012, while Bellagio hasn't been updated since 2011, so they do not appear to be actively maintained. The RPi, on the other hand, is thriving, and OpenMAX programming using the GPU is covered in detail in my book *Raspberry Pi GPU Audio Video Programming*.

CHAPTER 14

LADSPA

Linux Audio Plug-Ins (LADSPA) is a set of plug-ins that can be used by applications to add effects such as delays and filters. It was designed with simplicity in mind so is capable of only a limited number of effects. Nevertheless, these can be quite wide-ranging and are sufficient for a large variety of applications.

Resources

Here are some resources:

- "Linux Audio Plug-Ins: A Look Into LADSPA" (`www.linuxdevcenter.com/pub/a/linux/2001/02/02/ladspa.html`) by Dave Phillips

- Linux Audio Developer's Simple Plug-in API (`www.ladspa.org/`)

User-Level Tools

LADSPA plug-ins live in a directory defaulting to `/usr/lib/ladspa`. This can be controlled by the environment variable `LADSPA_PATH`. This directory will contain a set of `.so` files as LADSPA plug-ins.

Each plug-in contains information about itself, and you can inspect the set of plug-ins by running the command-line tool `listplugins`. By installing just LADPSA, the default plug-ins are as follows:

```
/usr/lib/ladspa/amp.so:
        Mono Amplifier (1048/amp_mono)
        Stereo Amplifier (1049/amp_stereo)
/usr/lib/ladspa/delay.so:
        Simple Delay Line (1043/delay_5s)
/usr/lib/ladspa/filter.so:
        Simple Low Pass Filter (1041/lpf)
        Simple High Pass Filter (1042/hpf)
/usr/lib/ladspa/sine.so:
        Sine Oscillator (Freq:audio, Amp:audio) (1044/sine_faaa)
        Sine Oscillator (Freq:audio, Amp:control) (1045/sine_faac)
        Sine Oscillator (Freq:control, Amp:audio) (1046/sine_fcaa)
        Sine Oscillator (Freq:control, Amp:control) (1047/sine_fcac)
/usr/lib/ladspa/noise.so:
        White Noise Source (1050/noise_white)
```

© Jan Newmarch 2017
J. Newmarch, *Linux Sound Programming*, DOI 10.1007/978-1-4842-2496-0_14

You can find more detailed information about each plug-in from the tool analyseplugin. For example, here's the information for the amp plug-in:

```
$analyseplugin amp

Plugin Name: "Mono Amplifier"
Plugin Label: "amp_mono"
Plugin Unique ID: 1048
Maker: "Richard Furse (LADSPA example plugins)"
Copyright: "None"
Must Run Real-Time: No
Has activate() Function: No
Has deactivate() Function: No
Has run_adding() Function: No
Environment: Normal or Hard Real-Time
Ports:   "Gain" input, control, 0 to ..., default 1, logarithmic
         "Input" input, audio
         "Output" output, audio

Plugin Name: "Stereo Amplifier"
Plugin Label: "amp_stereo"
Plugin Unique ID: 1049
Maker: "Richard Furse (LADSPA example plugins)"
Copyright: "None"
Must Run Real-Time: No
Has activate() Function: No
Has deactivate() Function: No
Has run_adding() Function: No
Environment: Normal or Hard Real-Time
Ports:   "Gain" input, control, 0 to ..., default 1, logarithmic
         "Input (Left)" input, audio
         "Output (Left)" output, audio
         "Input (Right)" input, audio
         "Output (Right)" output, audio
```

A simple test of each plug-in can be performed using applyplugin. When run with no arguments, it gives a usage message.

```
$applyplugin
Usage:  applyplugin [flags] <input Wave file> <output Wave file>
        <LADSPA plugin file name> <plugin label> <Control1> <Control2>...
        [<LADSPA plugin file name> <plugin label> <Control1> <Control2>...]...
Flags:  -s<seconds>  Add seconds of silence after end of input file.
```

This takes an input and an output WAV file as first and second parameters. The next ones are the names of the .so file and the plug-in label chosen. This is followed by values of the controls. For the amp plug-in, the file name is amp.so, the stereo plug-in is amp_stereo, and there is only one control for gain as a value between 0 and 1. To halve the volume of a file containing stereo WAV data, use this:

```
applyplugin 54154.wav tmp.wav amp.so amp_stereo 0.5
```

The Type LADSPA_Descriptor

Communication between an application and a LADSPA plug-in takes place through a data structure of type LADSPA_Descriptor. This has fields that contain all the information that is shown by listplugins and analyseplugins. In addition, it contains fields that control memory layout, whether or not it supports hard real time, and so on.

unsigned long UniqueID

> Each plug-in must have a unique ID within the LADSPA system.

const char * Label

> This is the label used to refer to the plug-in within the LADSPA system.

const char * Name

> This is the "user-friendly" name of the plug-in. For example, the amp file (shown later) contains two plug-ins. The mono amplifier has ID 1048, label amp_mono, and name Mono Amplifier, while the stereo amplifier has ID 1049, label amp_stereo, and name Stereo Amplifier.

const char * Maker, * Copyright

> This should be obvious.

unsigned long PortCount

> This indicates the number of ports (input *and* output) present on the plug-in.

const LADSPA_PortDescriptor * PortDescriptors

> This member indicates an array of port descriptors. Valid indices vary from 0 to PortCount-1.

const char * const * PortNames

> This member indicates an array of null-terminated strings describing ports. For example, the mono amplifier has two input ports and one output port labeled Gain, Input, and Output. The Input port has port descriptor (LADSPA_PORT_INPUT | LADSPA_PORT_AUDIO), while the Output port has port descriptor (LADSPA_PORT_OUTPUT | LADSPA_PORT_AUDIO)

LADSPA_PortRangeHint * PortRangeHints

> This is an array of type LADSPA_PortRangeHint, one element for each port. This allows the plug-in to pass information such as whether it has a value that is bounded above or below, and, if so, what that bound is, whether it should be treated as a Boolean value, and so on. These hints could be used by, say, a GUI to give a visual control display for the plug-in.

Additionally, it contains fields that are function pointers, which are called by the LADSPA runtime to initialize the plug-in, handle data, and clean up. These fields are as follows:

instantiate

> This takes the sample rate as a parameter. It is responsible for general instantiation of the plug-in, setting local parameters, allocating memory, and so on. It returns a pointer to a plug-in-specific data structure containing all the information relating to that plug-in. This pointer will be passed as the first parameter to the other functions so that they can retrieve information for this plug-in.

connect_port

> This takes three parameters, the second and third being the port number and the address on which data will be readable/writable, respectively. The plug-in is expected to read/write data from the LADSPA runtime using this address only for each port. It will be called before run or run_adding.

activate/deactivate

> These may be called to reinitialize the plug-in state. They may be NULL.

run

> This function is where all the plug-in's real work is done. Its second parameter is the number of samples that are ready to read/write.

cleanup

> This is obvious.

Other function fields are normally set to NULL.

Loading a Plug-in

An application can load a plug-in by calling loadLADSPAPluginLibrary with one parameter, which is the name of the plug-in file. Note that there is no LADSPA library. LADPSA supplies a header file called ladspa.h, and the distribution may include a file load.c, which implements loadLADSPAPluginLibrary (it searches the directories in the LADSPA_PATH).

When a plug-in is loaded by dlopen, the function _init is called with no parameters. This may be used to set up the plug-in and build, for example, the LADSPA_Descriptor.

A DLL must have an entry point that you can hook into. For LADSPA, each plug-in must define a function LADSPA_Descriptor * ladspa_descriptor(unsigned long Index). The values for indices 0, 1, ... are the LADSPA_Descriptor values for each of the plug-ins included in the file.

A Mono Amplifier Client

The analyseplugin amp command showed that the amp plug-in contains two plug-in modules: a mono and a stereo plug-in. The mono plug-in has a plug-in label of amp_mono, which will correspond to the field Label of a LADSPA_Descriptor.

Using this plug-in means you have to load the plug-in file, get a handle to the ladspa_descriptor structure, and then look through the descriptors, checking the labels until it finds the amp_mono plug-in.

Loading a plug-in file is done through functions in the load.c program included in the LADSPA package. The relevant code is as follows:

```
char *pcPluginFilename = "amp.so";
void *pvPluginHandle = loadLADSPAPluginLibrary(pcPluginFilename);
dlerror();

pfDescriptorFunction
    = (LADSPA_Descriptor_Function)dlsym(pvPluginHandle, "ladspa_descriptor");
if (!pfDescriptorFunction) {
    const char * pcError = dlerror();
```

```
    if (pcError)
        fprintf(stderr,
                "Unable to find ladspa_descriptor() function in plugin file "
                "\"%s\": %s.\n"
                "Are you sure this is a LADSPA plugin file?\n",
                pcPluginFilename,
                pcError);
    return 1;
}
```

Once it's loaded, search for the amp_mono plug-in:

```
char *pcPluginLabel = "amp_mono";
for (lPluginIndex = 0;; lPluginIndex++) {
    psDescriptor = pfDescriptorFunction(lPluginIndex);
    if (!psDescriptor)
        break;
    if (pcPluginLabel != NULL) {
        if (strcmp(pcPluginLabel, psDescriptor->Label) != 0)
            continue;
    }
    // got mono_amp
```

You know there are three ports—control, input, and output—so you look through the list of ports to assign indices and connect the relevant arrays to the plug-in descriptor.

Hidden in here is a critical part: not only do you set up the inputs and outputs of the plug-in, but also the *control* mechanism. The analyseplugin report shows that there is a Gain port with a control. This needs to be fed in. The control port only needs the address of a float value, which is the amount of amplification that will occur. This is done with the following code:

```
    handle = psDescriptor->instantiate(psDescriptor, SAMPLE_RATE);
    if (handle == NULL) {
        fprintf(stderr, "Can't instantiate plugin %s\n", pcPluginLabel);
        exit(1);
    }

    // get ports
    int lPortIndex;
    printf("Num ports %lu\n", psDescriptor->PortCount);
    for (lPortIndex = 0;
         lPortIndex < psDescriptor->PortCount;
         lPortIndex++) {
        if (LADSPA_IS_PORT_INPUT
            (psDescriptor->PortDescriptors[lPortIndex])
            && LADSPA_IS_PORT_AUDIO
            (psDescriptor->PortDescriptors[lPortIndex])) {
            printf("input %d\n", lPortIndex);
            lInputPortIndex = lPortIndex;

            psDescriptor->connect_port(handle,
                                       lInputPortIndex, pInBuffer);
```

```
        } else if (LADSPA_IS_PORT_OUTPUT
                    (psDescriptor->PortDescriptors[lPortIndex])
                    && LADSPA_IS_PORT_AUDIO
                    (psDescriptor->PortDescriptors[lPortIndex])) {
            printf("output %d\n", lPortIndex);
            lOutputPortIndex = lPortIndex;

            psDescriptor->connect_port(handle,
                                        lOutputPortIndex, pOutBuffer);
        }

        if (LADSPA_IS_PORT_CONTROL
            (psDescriptor->PortDescriptors[lPortIndex])) {
            printf("control %d\n", lPortIndex);
            LADSPA_Data control = 0.5f; // here is where we say to halve the volume
            psDescriptor->connect_port(handle,
                                        lPortIndex, &control);
        }
    }
    // we've got what we wanted
```

The run_plugin function then just loops, reading samples from the input file, applying the plug-in's run function, and writing to the output file.

```
void run_plugin() {
    sf_count_t numread;

    open_files();

    // it's NULL for the amp plugin
    if (psDescriptor->activate != NULL)
        psDescriptor->activate(handle);

    while ((numread = fill_input_buffer()) > 0) {
        printf("Num read %d\n", numread);
        psDescriptor->run(handle, numread);
        empty_output_buffer(numread);
    }
}
```

I've used the libsndfile library to simplify reading and writing files in whatever format they are in, using fill_input_buffer and empty_output_buffer.

The complete program is called mono_amp.c, shown here:

```
#include <stdlib.h>
#include <stdio.h>
#include <ladspa.h>
#include <dlfcn.h>
#include <sndfile.h>
```

```c
#include "utils.h"

const LADSPA_Descriptor * psDescriptor;
LADSPA_Descriptor_Function pfDescriptorFunction;
LADSPA_Handle handle;

// choose the mono plugin from the amp file
char *pcPluginFilename = "amp.so";
char *pcPluginLabel = "amp_mono";

long lInputPortIndex = -1;
long lOutputPortIndex = -1;

SNDFILE* pInFile;
SNDFILE* pOutFile;

// for the amplifier, the sample rate doesn't really matter
#define SAMPLE_RATE 44100

// the buffer size isn't really important either
#define BUF_SIZE 2048
LADSPA_Data pInBuffer[BUF_SIZE];
LADSPA_Data pOutBuffer[BUF_SIZE];

// How much we are amplifying the sound by
LADSPA_Data control = 0.5f;

char *pInFilePath = "/home/local/antialize-wkhtmltopdf-7cb5810/scripts/static-build/linux-
local/qts/demos/mobile/quickhit/plugins/LevelTemplate/sound/enableship.wav";
char *pOutFilePath = "tmp.wav";

void open_files() {
    // using libsndfile functions for easy read/write
    SF_INFO sfinfo;

    sfinfo.format = 0;
    pInFile = sf_open(pInFilePath, SFM_READ, &sfinfo);
    if (pInFile == NULL) {
        perror("can't open input file");
        exit(1);
    }

    pOutFile = sf_open(pOutFilePath, SFM_WRITE, &sfinfo);
    if (pOutFile == NULL) {
        perror("can't open output file");
        exit(1);
    }
}

sf_count_t fill_input_buffer() {
    return sf_read_float(pInFile, pInBuffer, BUF_SIZE);
}
```

```
void empty_output_buffer(sf_count_t numread) {
    sf_write_float(pOutFile, pOutBuffer, numread);
}

void run_plugin() {
    sf_count_t numread;

    open_files();

    // it's NULL for the amp plugin
    if (psDescriptor->activate != NULL)
        psDescriptor->activate(handle);

    while ((numread = fill_input_buffer()) > 0) {
        printf("Num read %d\n", numread);
        psDescriptor->run(handle, numread);
        empty_output_buffer(numread);
    }
}

int main(int argc, char *argv[]) {
    int lPluginIndex;

    void *pvPluginHandle = loadLADSPAPluginLibrary(pcPluginFilename);
    dlerror();

    pfDescriptorFunction
        = (LADSPA_Descriptor_Function)dlsym(pvPluginHandle, "ladspa_descriptor");
    if (!pfDescriptorFunction) {
        const char * pcError = dlerror();
        if (pcError)
            fprintf(stderr,
                "Unable to find ladspa_descriptor() function in plugin file "
                "\"%s\": %s.\n"
                "Are you sure this is a LADSPA plugin file?\n",
                pcPluginFilename,
                pcError);
        return 1;
    }

    for (lPluginIndex = 0;; lPluginIndex++) {
        psDescriptor = pfDescriptorFunction(lPluginIndex);
        if (!psDescriptor)
            break;
        if (pcPluginLabel != NULL) {
            if (strcmp(pcPluginLabel, psDescriptor->Label) != 0)
                continue;
        }
        // got mono_amp

        handle = psDescriptor->instantiate(psDescriptor, SAMPLE_RATE);
```

```
    if (handle == NULL) {
        fprintf(stderr, "Can't instantiate plugin %s\n", pcPluginLabel);
        exit(1);
    }

    // get ports
    int lPortIndex;
    printf("Num ports %lu\n", psDescriptor->PortCount);
    for (lPortIndex = 0;
         lPortIndex < psDescriptor->PortCount;
         lPortIndex++) {
        if (LADSPA_IS_PORT_INPUT
            (psDescriptor->PortDescriptors[lPortIndex])
            && LADSPA_IS_PORT_AUDIO
            (psDescriptor->PortDescriptors[lPortIndex])) {
            printf("input %d\n", lPortIndex);
            lInputPortIndex = lPortIndex;

            psDescriptor->connect_port(handle,
                                    lInputPortIndex, pInBuffer);
        } else if (LADSPA_IS_PORT_OUTPUT
                (psDescriptor->PortDescriptors[lPortIndex])
                && LADSPA_IS_PORT_AUDIO
                (psDescriptor->PortDescriptors[lPortIndex])) {
            printf("output %d\n", lPortIndex);
            lOutputPortIndex = lPortIndex;

            psDescriptor->connect_port(handle,
                                    lOutputPortIndex, pOutBuffer);
        }

        if (LADSPA_IS_PORT_CONTROL
            (psDescriptor->PortDescriptors[lPortIndex])) {
            printf("control %d\n", lPortIndex);
            psDescriptor->connect_port(handle,
                                    lPortIndex, &control);
        }
    }
    // we've got what we wanted, get out of this loop
    break;
}

if ((psDescriptor == NULL) ||
    (lInputPortIndex == -1) ||
    (lOutputPortIndex == -1)) {
    fprintf(stderr, "Can't find plugin information\n");
    exit(1);
}

run_plugin();

exit(0);
}
```

It is run just by calling mono_amp, with no arguments because the input and output files are hard-coded into the program.

A Stereo Amplifer with GUI

The amp file contains a stereo amplifier as well as a mono amplifier. This causes several differences for managing the plug-in. There are now two input ports and two output ports but still only one control port for the amplification factor. You need an array of input ports and an array of output ports. This just adds a little complexity.

The major difference is in handling the streams: libsndfile returns *frames* of sound, with the two channels of a stereo signal interleaved. These have to be split out into separate channels for each input port, and then the two output ports have to interleaved back together.

Adding a GUI such as GTK is fairly straightforward. The following code just shows a slider to control the volume. The GUI code and the LADSPA code must obviously run in different (POSIX) threads. There is really only one tricky point: the control value is not supposed to change during execution of the run function. This could be protected by locks, but in this case that is too heavyweight: just keep a copy of the control as modified by the slider and bring that across before each call to run.

The code is written to use GTK v3 and is as follows:

```
#include <gtk/gtk.h>


#include <stdlib.h>
#include <stdio.h>
#include <ladspa.h>
#include <dlfcn.h>
#include <sndfile.h>

#include "utils.h"

gint count = 0;
char buf[5];

pthread_t ladspa_thread;

const LADSPA_Descriptor * psDescriptor;
LADSPA_Descriptor_Function pfDescriptorFunction;
LADSPA_Handle handle;

// choose the mono plugin from the amp file
char *pcPluginFilename = "amp.so";
char *pcPluginLabel = "amp_stereo";

long lInputPortIndex = -1;
long lOutputPortIndex = -1;

int inBufferIndex = 0;
int outBufferIndex = 0;

SNDFILE* pInFile;
SNDFILE* pOutFile;
```

```
// for the amplifier, the sample rate doesn't really matter
#define SAMPLE_RATE 44100

// the buffer size isn't really important either
#define BUF_SIZE 2048
LADSPA_Data pInStereoBuffer[2*BUF_SIZE];
LADSPA_Data pOutStereoBuffer[2*BUF_SIZE];
LADSPA_Data pInBuffer[2][BUF_SIZE];
LADSPA_Data pOutBuffer[2][BUF_SIZE];

// How much we are amplifying the sound by
// We aren't allowed to change the control values
// during execution of run(). We could put a lock
// around run() or simpler, change the value of
// control only outside of run()
LADSPA_Data control;
LADSPA_Data pre_control = 0.2f;

char *pInFilePath = "/home/newmarch/Music/karaoke/nights/nightsinwhite-0.wav";
char *pOutFilePath = "tmp.wav";

void open_files() {
    // using libsndfile functions for easy read/write
    SF_INFO sfinfo;

    sfinfo.format = 0;
    pInFile = sf_open(pInFilePath, SFM_READ, &sfinfo);
    if (pInFile == NULL) {
        perror("can't open input file");
        exit(1);
    }

    pOutFile = sf_open(pOutFilePath, SFM_WRITE, &sfinfo);
    if (pOutFile == NULL) {
        perror("can't open output file");
        exit(1);
    }
}

sf_count_t fill_input_buffer() {
    int numread = sf_read_float(pInFile, pInStereoBuffer, 2*BUF_SIZE);

    // split frames into samples for each channel
    int n;
    for (n = 0; n < numread; n += 2) {
        pInBuffer[0][n/2] = pInStereoBuffer[n];
        pInBuffer[1][n/2] = pInStereoBuffer[n+1];
    }
    return numread/2;
}
```

```
void empty_output_buffer(sf_count_t numread) {
    // combine output samples back into frames
    int n;
    for (n = 0; n < 2*numread; n += 2) {
        pOutStereoBuffer[n] = pOutBuffer[0][n/2];
        pOutStereoBuffer[n+1] = pOutBuffer[1][n/2];
    }

    sf_write_float(pOutFile, pOutStereoBuffer, 2*numread);
}

gpointer run_plugin(gpointer args) {
    sf_count_t numread;

    // it's NULL for the amp plugin
    if (psDescriptor->activate != NULL)
        psDescriptor->activate(handle);

    while ((numread = fill_input_buffer()) > 0) {
        // reset control outside of run()
        control = pre_control;

        psDescriptor->run(handle, numread);
        empty_output_buffer(numread);
        usleep(1000);
    }
    printf("Plugin finished!\n");
}

void setup_ladspa() {
    int lPluginIndex;

    void *pvPluginHandle = loadLADSPAPluginLibrary(pcPluginFilename);
    dlerror();

    pfDescriptorFunction
        = (LADSPA_Descriptor_Function)dlsym(pvPluginHandle, "ladspa_descriptor");
    if (!pfDescriptorFunction) {
        const char * pcError = dlerror();
        if (pcError)
            fprintf(stderr,
                    "Unable to find ladspa_descriptor() function in plugin file "
                    "\"%s\": %s.\n"
                    "Are you sure this is a LADSPA plugin file?\n",
                    pcPluginFilename,
                    pcError);
        exit(1);
    }

    for (lPluginIndex = 0;; lPluginIndex++) {
        psDescriptor = pfDescriptorFunction(lPluginIndex);
```

```
    if (!psDescriptor)
        break;
    if (pcPluginLabel != NULL) {
        if (strcmp(pcPluginLabel, psDescriptor->Label) != 0)
            continue;
    }
    // got stero_amp

    handle = psDescriptor->instantiate(psDescriptor, SAMPLE_RATE);
    if (handle == NULL) {
        fprintf(stderr, "Can't instantiate plugin %s\n", pcPluginLabel);
        exit(1);
    }

    // get ports
    int lPortIndex;
    printf("Num ports %lu\n", psDescriptor->PortCount);
    for (lPortIndex = 0;
         lPortIndex < psDescriptor->PortCount;
         lPortIndex++) {
        if (LADSPA_IS_PORT_AUDIO
            (psDescriptor->PortDescriptors[lPortIndex])) {
            if (LADSPA_IS_PORT_INPUT
                (psDescriptor->PortDescriptors[lPortIndex])) {
                printf("input %d\n", lPortIndex);
                lInputPortIndex = lPortIndex;

                psDescriptor->connect_port(handle,
                                        lInputPortIndex, pInBuffer[inBufferIndex++]);
            } else if (LADSPA_IS_PORT_OUTPUT
                    (psDescriptor->PortDescriptors[lPortIndex])) {
                printf("output %d\n", lPortIndex);
                lOutputPortIndex = lPortIndex;

                psDescriptor->connect_port(handle,
                                        lOutputPortIndex, pOutBuffer[outBufferIndex++]);
            }
        }

        if (LADSPA_IS_PORT_CONTROL
            (psDescriptor->PortDescriptors[lPortIndex])) {
            printf("control %d\n", lPortIndex);
            psDescriptor->connect_port(handle,
                                    lPortIndex, &control);
        }
    }
    // we've got what we wanted, get out of this loop
    break;
}
```

```
    if ((psDescriptor == NULL) ||
        (lInputPortIndex == -1) ||
        (lOutputPortIndex == -1)) {
        fprintf(stderr, "Can't find plugin information\n");
        exit(1);
    }

    open_files();

    pthread_create(&ladspa_thread, NULL, run_plugin, NULL);
}

void slider_change(GtkAdjustment *adj,  gpointer data)
{
    count++;

    pre_control = gtk_adjustment_get_value(adj);
    //gtk_label_set_text(GTK_LABEL(label), buf);
}

int main(int argc, char** argv) {

    //GtkWidget *label;
    GtkWidget *window;
    GtkWidget *frame;
    GtkWidget *slider;
    GtkAdjustment *adjustment;

    setup_ladspa();

    gtk_init(&argc, &argv);

    window = gtk_window_new(GTK_WINDOW_TOPLEVEL);
    gtk_window_set_position(GTK_WINDOW(window), GTK_WIN_POS_CENTER);
    gtk_window_set_default_size(GTK_WINDOW(window), 250, 80);
    gtk_window_set_title(GTK_WINDOW(window), "Volume");

    frame = gtk_fixed_new();
    gtk_container_add(GTK_CONTAINER(window), frame);

    adjustment = gtk_adjustment_new(1.0,
                                    0.0,
                                    2.0,
                                    0.1,
                                    1.0,
                                    0.0);
    slider = gtk_scale_new(GTK_ORIENTATION_HORIZONTAL,
                           adjustment);
    gtk_widget_set_size_request(slider, 240, 5);
    gtk_fixed_put(GTK_FIXED(frame), slider, 5, 20);
```

```
//label = gtk_label_new("0");
//gtk_fixed_put(GTK_FIXED(frame), label, 190, 58);

gtk_widget_show_all(window);

g_signal_connect(window, "destroy",
                 G_CALLBACK (gtk_main_quit), NULL);

g_signal_connect(adjustment, "value-changed",
                 G_CALLBACK(slider_change), NULL);

gtk_main();

return 0;
}
```

It is run just by calling stereo_amp, no arguments.

The amp Program

The program you have been calling in the last two sections is the amp program, which is in the file ladspa_sdk/src/plugins/amp.c in the LADSPA source code. This is worth examining if you want to write a LADSPA plug-in yourself or want to see what is involved. There are several critical functions.

- The function _init() is called by the DLL loader. Its role is primarily to set up a LADSPA_Descriptor for each plug-in component. This is long-winded. It includes all the information printable by analyseplugin such as the following:

  ```
  g_psMonoDescriptor->Name = strdup("Mono Amplifier");
  ```

- It also contains internal function pointers such as the function to run when the mono amplifier needs to do some work.

  ```
  g_psMonoDescriptor->run = runMonoAmplifier;
  ```

- The function _fini() is called to clean up all data when the plug-in is unloaded.

The meat of the plug-in is what to do to samples as they are processed. The input samples are contained in one buffer, the output samples are contained in another, and for the mono amplifier each input sample needs to be multiplied by the gain factor to give an output sample. The code is as follows:

```
void
runMonoAmplifier(LADSPA_Handle Instance,
                 unsigned long SampleCount) {

  LADSPA_Data * pfInput;
  LADSPA_Data * pfOutput;
  LADSPA_Data fGain;
  Amplifier * psAmplifier;
  unsigned long lSampleIndex;
```

```
    psAmplifier = (Amplifier *)Instance;

    pfInput = psAmplifier->m_pfInputBuffer1;
    pfOutput = psAmplifier->m_pfOutputBuffer1;
    fGain = *(psAmplifier->m_pfControlValue);

    for (lSampleIndex = 0; lSampleIndex *lt; SampleCount; lSampleIndex++)
      *(pfOutput++) = *(pfInput++) * fGain;
}
```

Conclusion

LADSPA is a commonly used framework for audio effects plug-ins. This chapter covered some command-line tools and also the programming model.

■ ■ ■

## CHAPTER 15

Displaying Video with Overlays Using Gtk and FFmpeg

This chapter has nothing to do with sound. Videos often accompany audio. Karaoke oftens overlays the video with lyrics. Building an application to include video as well as audio takes you into the realm of graphical user interfaces (GUIs). This is a complex area in its own right and deserves (and has!) many books, including my own from many years back on the X Window System and Motif. This diversion chapter is about programming the video side of this, using FFmpeg, Gtk, Cairo, and Pango. I assume that you are familiar with the concepts of widgets, events, event handlers, and so on, that underlie all current GUI frameworks.

Motif lost its status as a major GUI for Linux/Unix systems a long time ago. There are many alternatives now, including Gtk (the Gimp toolkit), tcl/Tk, Java Swing, KDE, XFCE, and so on. Each has its own adherents, domains of use, quirks, idiosyncrasies, and so on. No single GUI will satisfy everyone.

In this chapter, I deal with Gtk. The reasons are threefold.

- It has a C library. It also has a Python library, which is nice, and I might use it one day. Most important, It Is *not* C++ based. C++ is one of my least favorite languages. I once came across a quote (source lost) that "C++ is a laboratory experiment that escaped," and I completely agree with that assessment.

- It has good support for i18n (internationalization). I want to be able to play Chinese karaoke files, so this is important to me.

- It is not Java-based. Don't get me wrong, I really like Java and have been programming in it for years. The MIDI API is pretty good, and of course everything else such as i18n is great. But for MIDI it is a CPU hog and is unusable on low-powered devices such as the Raspberry Pi, and generally the audio/video API has not progressed in years.

Nevertheless, as I struggled to get my head around Gtk version 2.0 versus 3.0, Cairo, Pango, Glib, and so on, I thought it might have been easier just to fix the Java MIDI engine! This was not a pleasant experience, as the sequel will show.

FFmpeg

To play MPEG files, OGV files, or similar, you need a decoder. The main contenders seem to be GStreamer and FFmpeg. For no particular reason, I chose FFmpeg.

© Jan Newmarch 2017
J. Newmarch, *Linux Sound Programming*, DOI 10.1007/978-1-4842-2496-0_15

The following program reads from a video file and stores the first five frames to disk. It is taken directly from "An FFmpeg and SDL Tutorial" (http://dranger.com/ffmpeg/) by Stephen Dranger. The program is play_video.c, shown here:

```
// tutorial01.c
// Code based on a tutorial by Martin Bohme (boehme@inb.uni-luebeckREMOVETHIS.de)
// Tested on Gentoo, CVS version 5/01/07 compiled with GCC 4.1.1
// With updates from https://github.com/chelyaev/ffmpeg-tutorial
// Updates tested on:
// LAVC 54.59.100, LAVF 54.29.104, LSWS 2.1.101
// on GCC 4.7.2 in Debian February 2015

#include <libavcodec/avcodec.h>
#include <libavformat/avformat.h>
#include <libswscale/swscale.h>

/* Requires
    libavcodec-dev
    libavformat-dev
    libswscale
*/

void SaveFrame(AVFrame *pFrame, int width, int height, int iFrame) {
    FILE *pFile;
    char szFilename[32];
    int  y;

    // Open file
    sprintf(szFilename, "frame%d.ppm", iFrame);
    pFile=fopen(szFilename, "wb");
    if(pFile==NULL)
        return;

    // Write header
    fprintf(pFile, "P6\n%d %d\n255\n", width, height);

    // Write pixel data
    for(y=0; y<height; y++)
        fwrite(pFrame->data[0]+y*pFrame->linesize[0], 1, width*3, pFile);

    // Close file
    fclose(pFile);
}

main(int argc, char **argv) {
    AVFormatContext *pFormatCtx = NULL;
    int i, videoStream;
    AVCodecContext *pCodecCtx = NULL;
    AVCodec *pCodec = NULL;
    AVFrame *pFrame = NULL;
    AVFrame *pFrameRGB = NULL;
    AVPacket packet;
```

```
int frameFinished;
int numBytes;
uint8_t *buffer = NULL;

AVDictionary *optionsDict = NULL;
struct SwsContext *sws_ctx = NULL;

if(argc < 2) {
    printf("Please provide a movie file\n");
    return -1;
}
// Register all formats and codecs
av_register_all();

// Open video file
if(avformat_open_input(&pFormatCtx, argv[1], NULL, NULL)!=0)
    return -1; // Couldn't open file

// Retrieve stream information
if(avformat_find_stream_info(pFormatCtx, NULL)<0)
    return -1; // Couldn't find stream information

// Dump information about file onto standard error
av_dump_format(pFormatCtx, 0, argv[1], 0);

// Find the first video stream
videoStream=-1;
for(i=0; i<pFormatCtx->nb_streams; i++)
    if(pFormatCtx->streams[i]->codec->codec_type==AVMEDIA_TYPE_VIDEO) {
        videoStream=i;
        break;
    }
if(videoStream==-1)
    return -1; // Didn't find a video stream

// Get a pointer to the codec context for the video stream
pCodecCtx=pFormatCtx->streams[videoStream]->codec;

// Find the decoder for the video stream
pCodec=avcodec_find_decoder(pCodecCtx->codec_id);
if(pCodec==NULL) {
    fprintf(stderr, "Unsupported codec!\n");
    return -1; // Codec not found
}
// Open codec
if(avcodec_open2(pCodecCtx, pCodec, &optionsDict)<0)
    return -1; // Could not open codec

// Allocate video frame
pFrame=avcodec_alloc_frame();

// Allocate an AVFrame structure
```

```
pFrameRGB=avcodec_alloc_frame();
if(pFrameRGB==NULL)
    return -1;

// Determine required buffer size and allocate buffer
numBytes=avpicture_get_size(PIX_FMT_RGB24, pCodecCtx->width,
                            pCodecCtx->height);
buffer=(uint8_t *)av_malloc(numBytes*sizeof(uint8_t));

sws_ctx =
    sws_getContext
    (
     pCodecCtx->width,
     pCodecCtx->height,
     pCodecCtx->pix_fmt,
     pCodecCtx->width,
     pCodecCtx->height,
     PIX_FMT_RGB24,
     SWS_BILINEAR,
     NULL,
     NULL,
     NULL
    );

// Assign appropriate parts of buffer to image planes in pFrameRGB
// Note that pFrameRGB is an AVFrame, but AVFrame is a superset
// of AVPicture
avpicture_fill((AVPicture *)pFrameRGB, buffer, PIX_FMT_RGB24,
               pCodecCtx->width, pCodecCtx->height);

// Read frames and save first five frames to disk
i=0;
while(av_read_frame(pFormatCtx, &packet)>=0) {
    // Is this a packet from the video stream?
    if(packet.stream_index==videoStream) {
        // Decode video frame
        avcodec_decode_video2(pCodecCtx, pFrame, &frameFinished,
                              &packet);

        // Did we get a video frame?
        if(frameFinished) {
            // Convert the image from its native format to RGB
            sws_scale
                (
                 sws_ctx,
                 (uint8_t const * const *)pFrame->data,
                 pFrame->linesize,
                 0,
                 pCodecCtx->height,
                 pFrameRGB->data,
                 pFrameRGB->linesize
                );
```

```
            printf("Read frame\n");
            // Save the frame to disk
            if(++i<=5)
                SaveFrame(pFrameRGB, pCodecCtx->width, pCodecCtx->height,
                            i);
            else
                break;
        }
    }

    // Free the packet that was allocated by av_read_frame
    av_free_packet(&packet);
}

// Free the RGB image
av_free(buffer);
av_free(pFrameRGB);

// Free the YUV frame
av_free(pFrame);

// Close the codec
avcodec_close(pCodecCtx);

// Close the video file
avformat_close_input(&pFormatCtx);

return 0;

}
```

Basic Gtk

Gtk is a fairly standard GUI toolkit. Simple programs are described in many tutorials such as "First programs in GTK+" (http://zetcode.com/tutorials/gtktutorial/firstprograms/). Refer to such tutorials for the basics of Gtk programming.

I include the following example without explanation; it uses three child widgets, two buttons, and one label. The label will hold an integer number. The buttons will increase or decrease this number.

```
#include <gtk/gtk.h>

gint count = 0;
char buf[5];

void increase(GtkWidget *widget, gpointer label)
{
    count++;

    sprintf(buf, "%d", count);
    gtk_label_set_text(GTK_LABEL(label), buf);
}
```

```
void decrease(GtkWidget *widget, gpointer label)
{
    count--;

    sprintf(buf, "%d", count);
    gtk_label_set_text(GTK_LABEL(label), buf);
}

int main(int argc, char** argv) {

    GtkWidget *label;
    GtkWidget *window;
    GtkWidget *frame;
    GtkWidget *plus;
    GtkWidget *minus;

    gtk_init(&argc, &argv);

    window = gtk_window_new(GTK_WINDOW_TOPLEVEL);
    gtk_window_set_position(GTK_WINDOW(window), GTK_WIN_POS_CENTER);
    gtk_window_set_default_size(GTK_WINDOW(window), 250, 180);
    gtk_window_set_title(GTK_WINDOW(window), "+-");

    frame = gtk_fixed_new();
    gtk_container_add(GTK_CONTAINER(window), frame);

    plus = gtk_button_new_with_label("+");
    gtk_widget_set_size_request(plus, 80, 35);
    gtk_fixed_put(GTK_FIXED(frame), plus, 50, 20);

    minus = gtk_button_new_with_label("-");
    gtk_widget_set_size_request(minus, 80, 35);
    gtk_fixed_put(GTK_FIXED(frame), minus, 50, 80);

    label = gtk_label_new("0");
    gtk_fixed_put(GTK_FIXED(frame), label, 190, 58);

    gtk_widget_show_all(window);

    g_signal_connect(window, "destroy",
    G_CALLBACK (gtk_main_quit), NULL);

    g_signal_connect(plus, "clicked",
    G_CALLBACK(increase), label);

    g_signal_connect(minus, "clicked",
    G_CALLBACK(decrease), label);

    gtk_main();

    return 0;
}
```

Gtk, like every other GUI toolkit, has a large number of widgets. These are listed in the GTK+ 3 Reference Manual (https://developer.gnome.org/gtk3/3.0/). This includes the widget GtkImage (https://developer.gnome.org/gtk3/3.0/GtkImage.html). As would be expected from the name, it can take a set of pixels from somewhere and build them into an image that can be displayed.

The following example shows an image loaded from a file:

```
#include <gtk/gtk.h>

int main( int argc, char *argv[])
{
    GtkWidget *window, *image;

    gtk_init(&argc, &argv);

    window = gtk_window_new(GTK_WINDOW_TOPLEVEL);

    image = gtk_image_new_from_file("jan-small.png");
    gtk_container_add(GTK_CONTAINER(window), image);

    g_signal_connect(G_OBJECT(window), "destroy", G_CALLBACK(gtk_main_quit), NULL);
    gtk_widget_show(image);
    gtk_widget_show(window);
    gtk_main();

    return 0;
}
```

Versions of Gtk

Gtk currently (as of November 2016) has major versions 2 and 3. The macro GTK_MAJOR_VERSION can be used to detect version 2 or 3. However, Gtk also depends on a number of other libraries, and it can get confusing working out which documentation pages you should be looking at. Here is a list of the principal libraries and their primary API pages:

Gtk 3 (https://developer.gnome.org/gtk3/3.0/)

- Gdk 3 (https://developer.gnome.org/gdk3/stable/)

- Cairo 1 (http://cairographics.org/manual/)

- Pango 1 (https://developer.gnome.org/pango/stable/)

- Gdk Pixbuf 2 (https://developer.gnome.org/gdk-pixbuf/unstable/)

- Glib 2 (https://developer.gnome.org/glib/)

- Freetype 2 (www.freetype.org/freetype2/docs/reference/ft2-toc.html)

Gtk 2

- Gdk 2 (https://developer.gnome.org/gdk2/2.24/)

- Cairo 1 (http://cairographics.org/manual/)

- Pango 1 (https://developer.gnome.org/pango/stable/)

- Glib 2 (https://developer.gnome.org/glib/)
- Freetype 2 (www.freetype.org/freetype2/docs/reference/ft2-toc.html)

Displaying the Video Using Gtk

Say you want to take the images produced by FFmpeg as AVFrames and display them in a GtkImage. You don't want to use code that reads from a file because reading and writing files at 30 frames per second would be ludicrous. Instead, you want some in-memory representation of the frames to load into the GtkImage.

Here is where you hit the first snag: the suitable in-memory representation changed in an incompatable way between Gtk 2.0 and Gtk 3.0. I'm only going to talk in the language of the X Window System since I don't know about other underlying systems such as Microsoft Windows.

See "Migrating from GTK+ 2.x to GTK+ 3" (https://developer.gnome.org/gtk3/3.5/gtk-migrating-2-to-3.html) for a description of some of the changes between these versions.

Pixmaps

The X Window System architecture model is a client-server model that has clients (applications) talking to servers (devices with graphic displays and input devices). At the lowest level (Xlib), a client will send basic requests such as "draw a line from here to there" to the server. The server will draw the line using information on the server side such as current line thickness, color, and so on.

If you want to keep an array of pixels to represent an image, then this array is usually kept on the X Window server in a *pixmap*. Pixmaps can be created and modified by applications by sending messages across the wire from the client to the server. Even a simple modification such as changing the value of a single pixel involves a network round-trip, and this can obviously become expensive if done often.

Pixbufs

Pixbufs are client-side equivalents of pixmaps. They can be manipulated by the client without round-trips to the X Window server. This reduces time and network overheads in manipulating them. However, it means that information that would have been kept on the server now has to be built and maintained on the client application side.

X, Wayland, and Mir

The X Window System is nearly 30 years old. During that time it has evolved to meet changes in hardware and in software requirements, while still maintaining backward compatibility.

Significant changes have occurred in hardware during this 30 years: multicore systems are now prevalent, and GPUs have brought changes in processing video. And generally the amount of memory (cache and RAM) means that memory is no longer such an issue.

At the same time, the software side has evolved. It is now common to make use of a "compositing window manager" such as Compiz so that you can have effects such as wobbly windows. This is not good for the X Window model: requests from the application go to the X server, but then a requested image has to be passed to the compositing window manager, which will perform its effects and then send images back to the X server. This is big increase in network traffic, in which the X server is now just playing the role of display rather than compositor.

Application libraries have now evolved so that much of the work that was formerly done by the X server can now be done on the application side by libraries such as Cairo, Pixman, Freetype, Fontconfig, and Pango.

All of these changes have led to proposals for new back-end servers, which live cooperatively in this evolved world. This has been sparked by the development of Wayland (http://wayland.freedesktop.org/) but is a bit messed up by Ubuntu forking this to develop Mir (https://wiki.ubuntu.com/Mir/). Don't buy into the arguments. Just Google for *mir and wayland*.

In a simplistic sense, what it means here is that in the future pixmaps are out while pixbufs are in.

Gtk 3.0

With Gtk 3.0, pixmaps no longer exist. You only have pixbufs in the data structure GdkPixbuf. To display the FFmpeg-decoded video, you pick up after the image has been transcoded to the picture_RGB, translate it into a GdkPixbuf, and create the GtkImage.

```
pixbuf = gdk_pixbuf_new_from_data(picture_RGB->data[0], GDK_COLORSPACE_RGB,
                                  0, 8, width, height,
                                  picture_RGB->linesize[0],
                                  pixmap_destroy_notify,
                                  NULL);
gtk_image_set_from_pixbuf((GtkImage*) image, pixbuf);
```

Gtk 2.0

Gtk 2.0 still has pixmaps in the structure GdkPixmap. In theory, it should be possible to have code similar to the Gtk 3.0 code using the function GdkPixmap *gdk_pixmap_create_from_data(GdkDrawable *drawable, const gchar *data, gint width, gint height, gint depth, const GdkColor *fg, const GdkColor *bg), which is documented in the GDK 2 Reference Manual in "Bitmaps and Pixmaps" (https://developer.gnome.org/gdk/unstable/gdk-Bitmaps-and-Pixmaps.html#gdk-pixmap-create-from-data), and then call void gtk_image_set_from_pixmap(GtkImage *image, GdkPixmap *pixmap, GdkBitmap *mask), documented in the Gtk 2.6 reference manual at GtkImage (www.gtk.org/api/2.6/gtk/GtkImage.html#gtk-image-set-from-pixmap).

The only problem is that I couldn't get the function gdk_pixmap_create_from_data to work. No matter what argument I tried for the drawable, the call always barfed on either its type or its value. For example, a documented value is NULL, but this always caused an assertion error ("should not be NULL").

So, what does work? Well, all I could find was a bit of a mess of both pixmaps *and* pixbufs: create a pixbuf filled with video data, create a pixmap, write the pixbuf data into the pixmap, and then fill the image with the pixmap data.

```
pixbuf = gdk_pixbuf_new_from_data(picture_RGB->data[0], GDK_COLORSPACE_RGB,
                                  0, 8, width, height,
                                  picture_RGB->linesize[0],
                                  pixmap_destroy_notify,
                                  NULL);
pixmap = gdk_pixmap_new(window->window, width, height, -1);
gdk_draw_pixbuf((GdkDrawable *) pixmap, NULL,
                pixbuf,
                0, 0, 0, 0, wifth, height,
                GDK_RGB_DITHER_NORMAL, 0, 0);

gtk_image_set_from_pixmap((GtkImage*) image, pixmap, NULL);
```

Threads and Gtk

The video will need to play in its own thread. Gtk will set up a GUI processing loop in its thread. Since this is Linux, you will use Posix pthreads. The video thread will need to be started explicitly with the following:

```
pthread_t tid;
pthread_create(&tid, NULL, play_background, NULL);
```

Here the function play_background calls the FFmpeg code to decode the video file. Note that the thread should not be started until the application has been realized, or it will attempt to draw into nonexistent windows.

The Gtk thread will be started by the call to the following:

```
gtk_main();
```

That's straightforward enough. But now you have to handle the video thread making calls into the GUI thread in order to draw the image. The best document I have found on this is "Is GTK+ thread safe? How do I write multi-threaded GTK+ applications?" (https://developer.gnome.org/gtk-faq/stable/x481.html). Basically it states that code that can affect the Gtk thread should be enclosed with a gdk_threads_enter() … gdk_threads_leave() pair.

That's OK for Gtk 2.0. What about Gtk 3.0? Ooops! Those calls are now deprecated. So, what are you supposed to do? So far (as of July 2013), all that seems to exist are developer dialogues such as at https://mail.gnome.org/archives/gtk-devel-list/2012-August/msg00020.html, which states:

> *"We have never done a great job of explaining when gdk_threads_enter/leave are required, it seems. As a consequence, a good number of the critical sections I've seen marked throughout my jhbuild checkout are unnecessary. If your application doesn't call gdk_threads_init or gdk_threads_set_lock_functions, there's no need to use enter/leave. Libraries are a different story, of course."*

The actual solution is in a different direction, and the solution is shown in https://developer.gnome.org/gdk3/stable/gdk3-Threads.html: Gtk is not thread-safe. Calls within the Gtk thread are safe, but most Gtk calls made from different threads are not. If you need to make a Gtk call from another thread, make a call to gdk_threads_add_idle() to a function that will run in the Gtk thread. Data relevant to that delayed call may be passed as another argument to gdk_threads_add_idle().

For the rest of this chapter, you will only consider Gtk 3 and not Gtk 2.

The Code

Finally, it's time to see the code to play a video in a Gtk application that works with Gtk 3.0. It is gtk_play_video.c. I will break it into pieces.

The function that plays the video runs as a background thread. It reads frames and creates a pixbuf, using Gtk 3. It is as follows:

```
static gboolean draw_image(gpointer user_data) {
    GdkPixbuf *pixbuf = (GdkPixbuf *) user_data;

    gtk_image_set_from_pixbuf((GtkImage *) image, pixbuf);
    gtk_widget_queue_draw(image);
    g_object_unref(pixbuf);
```

```
    return G_SOURCE_REMOVE;
}
 static gpointer play_background(gpointer args) {

  int i;
  AVPacket packet;
  int frameFinished;
  AVFrame *pFrame = NULL;

  /* initialize packet, set data to NULL, let the demuxer fill it */
  /* http://ffmpeg.org/doxygen/trunk/doc_2examples_2demuxing_8c-example.html#a80 */
  av_init_packet(&packet);
  packet.data = NULL;
  packet.size = 0;

  int bytesDecoded;
  GdkPixbuf *pixbuf;
  AVFrame *picture_RGB;
  char *buffer;

  pFrame=avcodec_alloc_frame();

  i=0;
  picture_RGB = avcodec_alloc_frame();
  buffer = malloc (avpicture_get_size(PIX_FMT_RGB24, WIDTH, HEIGHT));
  avpicture_fill((AVPicture *)picture_RGB, buffer, PIX_FMT_RGB24, WIDTH, HEIGHT);

  while(av_read_frame(pFormatCtx, &packet)>=0) {
      if(packet.stream_index==videoStream) {
          usleep(33670);   // 29.7 frames per second
          // Decode video frame
          avcodec_decode_video2(pCodecCtx, pFrame, &frameFinished,
                              &packet);

          int width = pCodecCtx->width;
          int height = pCodecCtx->height;

          sws_ctx = sws_getContext(width, height, pCodecCtx->pix_fmt, width, height,
                            PIX_FMT_RGB24, SWS_BICUBIC, NULL, NULL, NULL);

          if (frameFinished) {

              sws_scale(sws_ctx,  (uint8_t const * const *) pFrame->data, pFrame-
              >linesize, 0, height,
                          picture_RGB->data, picture_RGB->linesize);

              printf("old width %d new width %d\n",  pCodecCtx->width, picture_RGB-
              >width);
              pixbuf = gdk_pixbuf_new_from_data(picture_RGB->data[0], GDK_COLORSPACE_RGB,
                                    0, 8, width, height,
                                    picture_RGB->linesize[0], pixmap_destroy_
                                    notify,
                                    NULL);
```

303

```
                    gdk_threads_add_idle(draw_image, pixbuf);

                    gtk_image_set_from_pixbuf((GtkImage*) image, pixbuf);

                }
                sws_freeContext(sws_ctx);
            }
            av_free_packet(&packet);
            g_thread_yield();
        }

        printf("Video over!\n");
        exit(0);
}
```

This function is set to run when in its own thread and when there is a window for it to be drawn in.

```
/* Called when the windows are realized
 */
static void realize_cb (GtkWidget *widget, gpointer data) {
    /* start the video playing in its own thread */
    GThread *tid;
    tid = g_thread_new("video",
                       play_background,
                       NULL);
}
```

The main function is responsible for initializing the FFmpeg environment for reading the video and then setting up a Gtk window for it to draw. It is as follows:

```
int main(int argc, char** argv)
{

    int i;

    /* FFMpeg stuff */

    AVFrame *pFrame = NULL;
    AVPacket packet;

    AVDictionary *optionsDict = NULL;

    av_register_all();

    if(avformat_open_input(&pFormatCtx, "/home/httpd/html/ComputersComputing/simpson.mpg",
    NULL, NULL)!=0)
        return -1; // Couldn't open file

    // Retrieve stream information
    if(avformat_find_stream_info(pFormatCtx, NULL)<0)
        return -1; // Couldn't find stream information
```

```
// Dump information about file onto standard error
av_dump_format(pFormatCtx, 0, argv[1], 0);

// Find the first video stream
videoStream=-1;
for(i=0; i<pFormatCtx->nb_streams; i++)
    if(pFormatCtx->streams[i]->codec->codec_type==AVMEDIA_TYPE_VIDEO) {
        videoStream=i;
        break;
    }
if(videoStream==-1)
    return -1; // Didn't find a video stream

for(i=0; i<pFormatCtx->nb_streams; i++)
    if(pFormatCtx->streams[i]->codec->codec_type==AVMEDIA_TYPE_AUDIO) {
        printf("Found an audio stream too\n");
        break;
    }

// Get a pointer to the codec context for the video stream
pCodecCtx=pFormatCtx->streams[videoStream]->codec;

// Find the decoder for the video stream
pCodec=avcodec_find_decoder(pCodecCtx->codec_id);
if(pCodec==NULL) {
    fprintf(stderr, "Unsupported codec!\n");
    return -1; // Codec not found
}

// Open codec
if(avcodec_open2(pCodecCtx, pCodec, &optionsDict)<0)
    return -1; // Could not open codec

width =  pCodecCtx->width;
height =  pCodecCtx->height;

sws_ctx =
    sws_getContext
    (
    pCodecCtx->width,
    pCodecCtx->height,
    pCodecCtx->pix_fmt,
    pCodecCtx->width,
    pCodecCtx->height,
    PIX_FMT_YUV420P,
    SWS_BILINEAR,
    NULL,
    NULL,
    NULL
    );

/* GTK stuff now */
```

```
    gtk_init (&argc, &argv);

    window = gtk_window_new (GTK_WINDOW_TOPLEVEL);

    /* When the window is given the "delete-event" signal (this is given
     * by the window manager, usually by the "close" option, or on the
     * titlebar), we ask it to call the delete_event () function
     * as defined above. The data passed to the callback
     * function is NULL and is ignored in the callback function. */
    g_signal_connect (window, "delete-event",
                      G_CALLBACK (delete_event), NULL);

    /* Here we connect the "destroy" event to a signal handler.
     * This event occurs when we call gtk_widget_destroy() on the window,
     * or if we return FALSE in the "delete-event" callback. */
    g_signal_connect (window, "destroy",
                      G_CALLBACK (destroy), NULL);

    g_signal_connect (window, "realize", G_CALLBACK (realize_cb), NULL);

    /* Sets the border width of the window. */
    gtk_container_set_border_width (GTK_CONTAINER (window), 10);

    image = gtk_image_new();
    gtk_widget_show (image);

    /* This packs the button into the window (a gtk container). */
    gtk_container_add (GTK_CONTAINER (window), image);

    /* and the window */
    gtk_widget_show (window);

    /* All GTK applications must have a gtk_main(). Control ends here
     * and waits for an event to occur (like a key press or
     * mouse event). */
    gtk_main ();

    return 0;
}
```

Overlaying an Image on Top of an Image

It is common in a movie on TV to see a fixed image layered on top of the video. Subtitles can be an example of dynamic images but may be text overlaid instead. This section just considers one image on top of another.

In Gtk 2.0 it is surprisingly easy: draw one pixbuf into a pixmap and then draw the overlay pixbuf into the same pixmap.

```
pixmap = gdk_pixmap_new(window->window, 720, 480, -1);

gdk_draw_pixbuf((GdkDrawable *) pixmap, NULL,
                pixbuf,
```

```
                0, 0, 0, 0, 720, 480,
                GDK_RGB_DITHER_NORMAL, 0, 0);

// overlay another pixbuf
gdk_draw_pixbuf((GdkDrawable *) pixmap, NULL,
                overlay_pixbuf,
                0, 0, 0, 0, overlay_width, overlay_height,
                GDK_RGB_DITHER_NORMAL, 0, 0);

gtk_image_set_from_pixmap((GtkImage*) image, pixmap, NULL);

gtk_widget_queue_draw(image);
```

Gtk 3.0 does not seem so straightforward as pixmaps have disappeared. Various pages suggest using Cairo surfaces instead, and later sections will look at that. But "The GdkPixbuf Structure" (https://developer.gnome.org/gdk-pixbuf/unstable/gdk-pixbuf-The-GdkPixbuf-Structure.html) suggests that as long as you get the data types aligned, you can just write the pixels of the second image into the pixbuf data of the first. The page (although old) called "Gdk-pixbuf" (http://openbooks.sourceforge.net/books/wga/graphics-gdk-pixbuf.html) is a useful tutorial on Gdk pixbufs. One of the details you have to get right is the *rowstride* of each image: the two-dimensional image is stored as a linear array of bytes, and the rowstride tells how many bytes make up a row. Typically there are 3 or 4 bytes per pixel (for RGB or RGB+alpha), and these also need to be matched between the images.

The Gtk 3 overlay function is as follows:

```
static void overlay(GdkPixbuf *pixbuf, GdkPixbuf *overlay_pixbuf,
                    int height_offset, int width_offset) {
    int overlay_width, overlay_height, overlay_rowstride, overlay_n_channels;
    guchar *overlay_pixels, *overlay_p;
    guchar red, green, blue, alpha;
    int m, n;
    int rowstride, n_channels, width, height;
    guchar *pixels, *p;

    if (overlay_pixbuf == NULL) {
        return;
    }

    /* get stuff out of overlay pixbuf */
    overlay_n_channels = gdk_pixbuf_get_n_channels (overlay_pixbuf);
    n_channels =  gdk_pixbuf_get_n_channels(pixbuf);
    printf("Overlay has %d channels, destination has %d channels\n",
        overlay_n_channels, n_channels);
    overlay_width = gdk_pixbuf_get_width (overlay_pixbuf);
    overlay_height = gdk_pixbuf_get_height (overlay_pixbuf);

    overlay_rowstride = gdk_pixbuf_get_rowstride (overlay_pixbuf);
    overlay_pixels = gdk_pixbuf_get_pixels (overlay_pixbuf);

    rowstride = gdk_pixbuf_get_rowstride (pixbuf);
    width = gdk_pixbuf_get_width (pixbuf);
    pixels = gdk_pixbuf_get_pixels (pixbuf);
```

```
        printf("Overlay: width %d str8ide %d\n", overlay_width, overlay_rowstride);
        printf("Dest: width  str8ide %d\n", rowstride);

        for (m = 0; m < overlay_width; m++) {
            for (n = 0; n < overlay_height; n++) {
                overlay_p = overlay_pixels + n * overlay_rowstride + m * overlay_n_channels;
                red = overlay_p[0];
                green = overlay_p[1];
                blue = overlay_p[2];
                if (overlay_n_channels == 4)
                    alpha = overlay_p[3];
                else
                    alpha = 0;

                p = pixels + (n+height_offset) * rowstride + (m+width_offset) * n_channels;
                p[0] = red;
                p[1] = green;
                p[2] = blue;
                if (n_channels == 4)
                    p[3] = alpha;
            }
        }
    }
```

Alpha Channel

An overlay image may have some "transparent" parts in it. You don't want such parts to be overlaid onto the underlying image. But such parts will need to have a value in the array of pixels. Even zero is a value: black! Some images will have another byte per pixel allocated as the *alpha channel*. This has a value to show how transparent the pixel is. A value of 255 means not transparent at all, and a value of zero means totally transparent.

The simplest way of combining a transparent pixel with the underlying pixel is simply to not do so: leave the underlying pixel untouched. More complex algorithms are pointed to by the Wikipedia "Alpha compositing" (http://en.wikipedia.org/wiki/Alpha_compositing) page.

Converting an image that doesn't have an alpha channel to one that does can be done using the function gdk_pixbuf_add_alpha. This can also be used to set the value of the alpha channel by matching against a color. For example, the following should set the alpha value to 0 for any white pixels and to 255 for all others:

```
pixbuf = gdk_pixbuf_add_alpha(pixbuf, TRUE, 255, 255, 255);
```

Unfortunately, it seems to want to leave an "edge" of pixels, which should be marked as transparent.

With alpha marking in place, a simple test can be used in the overlay function as to whether or not to perform the overlay.

```
if (alpha < 128) {
    continue;
}
```

It's not worth giving a complete program just for a couple of changed lines. It is gtk_play_video_overlay_alpha.c.

Using Cairo to Draw on an Image

With the disappearance of pixmaps from Gtk 3.0, Cairo is now the only real way of assembling multiple components into an image. You can find general Cairo information http://cairographics.org/documentation/, a tutorial at http://zetcode.com/gfx/cairo/, and information about overlaying onto images at http://zetcode.com/gfx/cairo/cairoimages/.

Cairo takes sources and a destination. The sources can be changed and frequently are from an image source to a color source, and so on. The destination is where the drawn stuff ends up.

Destinations can be in memory or at a variety of back ends. You want an in-memory destination so that you can extract a pixbuf from it, with all operations done on the client side. You create a destination as a *surface* of type cairo_surface_t and set it into a *Cairo context* of type cairo_t with the following:

```
cairo_surface_t *surface = cairo_image_surface_create (CAIRO_FORMAT_ARGB32,
                                                        width, height);
cairo_t *cr = cairo_create(surface);
```

The Cairo context cr is then used to set sources, perform drawing, and so on. At the end of this, you will extract a pixmap from the surface.

The first step is to set the source to the pixbuf for each frame of the video and to paint this to the destination with the following:

```
gdk_cairo_set_source_pixbuf(cr, pixbuf, 0, 0);
cairo_paint (cr);
```

You can overlay another image on top of this by changing the source to the overlay image and painting that:

```
gdk_cairo_set_source_pixbuf(cr, overlay_pixbuf, 300, 200);
cairo_paint (cr);
```

Note that Cairo will do any alpha blending that is required if the overlay has "transparent" pixels.

To draw the text, you need to reset the source to an RGB surface, set all the parameters for the text, and draw the text into the destination. This is done with the following:

```
// white text
cairo_set_source_rgb(cr, 1.0, 1.0, 1.0);
// this is a standard font for Cairo
cairo_select_font_face (cr, "cairo:serif",
                        CAIRO_FONT_SLANT_NORMAL,
                        CAIRO_FONT_WEIGHT_BOLD);
cairo_set_font_size (cr, 20);
cairo_move_to(cr, 10.0, 50.0);
cairo_show_text (cr, "hello");
```

Finally, you want to extract the final image from the destination and set it into the GdkImage for display. Here there is another difference between Gtk 2.0 and Gtk 3.0: Gtk 3.0 has a function gdk_pixbuf_get_from_surface that will return a GdkPixbuf; Gtk 2.0 has no such function. You will look at the Gtk 3.0 version here.

```
pixbuf = gdk_pixbuf_get_from_surface(surface,
                                     0,
                                     0,
                                     width,
                                     height);
```

309

```
gdk_threads_add_idle(draw_image, pixbuf);
```

The revised function to play the video using Cairo is as follows:

```
static gboolean draw_image(gpointer user_data) {
    GdkPixbuf *pixbuf = (GdkPixbuf *) user_data;

    gtk_image_set_from_pixbuf((GtkImage *) image, pixbuf);
    gtk_widget_queue_draw(image);
    g_object_unref(pixbuf);

    return G_SOURCE_REMOVE;
}

static void *play_background(void *args) {

    int i;
    AVPacket packet;
    int frameFinished;
    AVFrame *pFrame = NULL;

    int bytesDecoded;
    GdkPixbuf *pixbuf;
    GdkPixbuf *overlay_pixbuf;
    AVFrame *picture_RGB;
    char *buffer;

    GError *error = NULL;
    overlay_pixbuf = gdk_pixbuf_new_from_file(OVERLAY_IMAGE, &error);
    if (!overlay_pixbuf) {
        fprintf(stderr, "%s\n", error->message);
        g_error_free(error);
        exit(1);
    }

    // add an alpha layer for a white background
    overlay_pixbuf = gdk_pixbuf_add_alpha(overlay_pixbuf, TRUE, 255, 255, 255);

    int overlay_width = gdk_pixbuf_get_width(overlay_pixbuf);
    int overlay_height =  gdk_pixbuf_get_height(overlay_pixbuf);

    pFrame=avcodec_alloc_frame();

    i=0;
    picture_RGB = avcodec_alloc_frame();
    buffer = malloc (avpicture_get_size(PIX_FMT_RGB24, 720, 576));
    avpicture_fill((AVPicture *)picture_RGB, buffer, PIX_FMT_RGB24, 720, 576);

    while(av_read_frame(pFormatCtx, &packet)>=0) {
        if(packet.stream_index==videoStream) {
            usleep(33670);  // 29.7 frames per second
```

```
// Decode video frame
avcodec_decode_video2(pCodecCtx, pFrame, &frameFinished,
                      &packet);

int width = pCodecCtx->width;
int height = pCodecCtx->height;

sws_ctx = sws_getContext(width, height, pCodecCtx->pix_fmt, width, height,
                         PIX_FMT_RGB24, SWS_BICUBIC, NULL, NULL, NULL);

if (frameFinished) {
    printf("Frame %d\n", i++);

    sws_scale(sws_ctx,  (uint8_t const * const *) pFrame->data, pFrame-
>linesize, 0, height, picture_RGB->data, picture_RGB->linesize);

    printf("old width %d new width %d\n",  pCodecCtx->width, picture_RGB-
>width);
    pixbuf = gdk_pixbuf_new_from_data(picture_RGB->data[0], GDK_COLORSPACE_RGB,
                                      0, 8, width, height,
                                      picture_RGB->linesize[0], pixmap_destroy_
                                      notify,
                                      NULL);
    // Create the destination surface
    cairo_surface_t *surface = cairo_image_surface_create (CAIRO_FORMAT_ARGB32,
                                                  width, height);
    cairo_t *cr = cairo_create(surface);

    // draw the background image
    gdk_cairo_set_source_pixbuf(cr, pixbuf, 0, 0);
    cairo_paint (cr);

    // overlay an image on top
    // alpha blending will be done by Cairo
    gdk_cairo_set_source_pixbuf(cr, overlay_pixbuf, 300, 200);
    cairo_paint (cr);

    // draw some white text on top
    cairo_set_source_rgb(cr, 1.0, 1.0, 1.0);
    // this is a standard font for Cairo
    cairo_select_font_face (cr, "cairo:serif",
                            CAIRO_FONT_SLANT_NORMAL,
                            CAIRO_FONT_WEIGHT_BOLD);
    cairo_set_font_size (cr, 20);
    cairo_move_to(cr, 10.0, 50.0);
    cairo_show_text (cr, "hello");

    pixbuf = gdk_pixbuf_get_from_surface(surface,
                                         0,
                                         0,
                                         width,
                                         height);
```

```
                gdk_threads_add_idle(draw_image, pixbuf);

                sws_freeContext(sws_ctx);
                cairo_surface_destroy(surface);
                cairo_destroy(cr);


            }
        }
        av_free_packet(&packet);
    }

    printf("Video over!\n");
    exit(0);
}
```

Drawing Text Using Pango

While Cairo can draw any form of text, the functions such as `cairo_show_text` do not have much flexibility. Drawing in, say, multiple colors will involve much work. Pango is a library for handling all aspects of text. There is a Pango Reference Manual at https://developer.gnome.org/pango/stable/. A good tutorial is at www.ibm.com/developerworks/library/l-u-pango2/.

The simplest way of coloring text (and some other effects) is to create the text marked up with HTML such as this:

```
gchar *markup_text = "<span foreground=\"red\">hello </span><span
foreground=\"black\">world</span>";
```

This has "hello" in red and "world" in black. This is then parsed into the text "red black" and a set of attribute markups.

```
gchar *markup_text = "<span foreground=\"red\">hello </span><span
foreground=\"black\">world</span>";
PangoAttrList *attrs;
gchar *text;

pango_parse_markup (markup_text, -1,0, &attrs, &text, NULL, NULL);
```

This can be rendered into a Cairo context by creating a `PangoLayout` from the Cairo context, laying out the text with its attributes in the Pango layout and then showing this layout in the Cairo context.

```
PangoLayout *layout;
PangoFontDescription *desc;

cairo_move_to(cr, 300.0, 50.0);
layout = pango_cairo_create_layout (cr);
pango_layout_set_text (layout, text, -1);
pango_layout_set_attributes(layout, attrs);
pango_cairo_update_layout (cr, layout);
pango_cairo_show_layout (cr, layout);
```

(Yes, there is a lot of jumping around between libraries in all of this!)

As before, once all content has been drawn into the Cairo context, it can be extracted as a pixbuf from the Cairo surface destination, set into the GtkImage, and added to the Gtk event queue.

The revised function to draw the video using Pango is as follows:

```
static gboolean draw_image(gpointer user_data) {
    GdkPixbuf *pixbuf = (GdkPixbuf *) user_data;

    gtk_image_set_from_pixbuf((GtkImage *) image, pixbuf);
    gtk_widget_queue_draw(image);
    g_object_unref(pixbuf);

    return G_SOURCE_REMOVE;
}

static void *play_background(void *args) {

    int i;
    AVPacket packet;
    int frameFinished;
    AVFrame *pFrame = NULL;

    /* initialize packet, set data to NULL, let the demuxer fill it */
    /* http://ffmpeg.org/doxygen/trunk/doc_2examples_2demuxing_8c-example.html#a80 */
    av_init_packet(&packet);
    packet.data = NULL;
    packet.size = 0;

    int bytesDecoded;
    GdkPixbuf *pixbuf;
    GdkPixbuf *overlay_pixbuf;
    AVFrame *picture_RGB;
    char *buffer;

    // Pango marked up text, half red, half black
    gchar *markup_text = "<span foreground=\"red\">hello</span><span
foreground=\"black\">world</span>";
    PangoAttrList *attrs;
    gchar *text;

    pango_parse_markup (markup_text, -1,0, &attrs, &text, NULL, NULL);

    GError *error = NULL;
    overlay_pixbuf = gdk_pixbuf_new_from_file(OVERLAY_IMAGE, &error);
    if (!overlay_pixbuf) {
        fprintf(stderr, "%s\n", error->message);
        g_error_free(error);
        exit(1);
    }
```

```
    // add an alpha layer for a white background
    overlay_pixbuf = gdk_pixbuf_add_alpha(overlay_pixbuf, TRUE, 255, 255, 255);

    int overlay_width = gdk_pixbuf_get_width(overlay_pixbuf);
    int overlay_height = gdk_pixbuf_get_height(overlay_pixbuf);

    pFrame=avcodec_alloc_frame();

    i=0;
    picture_RGB = avcodec_alloc_frame();
    buffer = malloc (avpicture_get_size(PIX_FMT_RGB24, 720, 576));
    avpicture_fill((AVPicture *)picture_RGB, buffer, PIX_FMT_RGB24, 720, 576);

    while(av_read_frame(pFormatCtx, &packet)>=0) {
        if(packet.stream_index==videoStream) {
            usleep(33670);  // 29.7 frames per second
            // Decode video frame
            avcodec_decode_video2(pCodecCtx, pFrame, &frameFinished,
                                    &packet);

            int width = pCodecCtx->width;
            int height = pCodecCtx->height;

            sws_ctx = sws_getContext(width, height, pCodecCtx->pix_fmt, width, height,
                                    PIX_FMT_RGB24, SWS_BICUBIC, NULL, NULL, NULL);

            if (frameFinished) {
                printf("Frame %d\n", i++);

                sws_scale(sws_ctx, (uint8_t const * const *) pFrame->data, pFrame-
                >linesize, 0, height,
                            picture_RGB->data, picture_RGB->linesize);

                printf("old width %d new width %d\n", pCodecCtx->width, picture_RGB-
                >width);
                pixbuf = gdk_pixbuf_new_from_data(picture_RGB->data[0], GDK_COLORSPACE_RGB,
                                    0, 8, width, height,
                                    picture_RGB->linesize[0], pixmap_destroy_
                                    notify,
                                    NULL);

                // Create the destination surface
                cairo_surface_t *surface = cairo_image_surface_create (CAIRO_FORMAT_ARGB32,
                                                            width, height);
                cairo_t *cr = cairo_create(surface);

                // draw the background image
                gdk_cairo_set_source_pixbuf(cr, pixbuf, 0, 0);
                cairo_paint (cr);

                // overlay an image on top
```

```c
                // alpha blending will be done by Cairo
                gdk_cairo_set_source_pixbuf(cr, overlay_pixbuf, 300, 200);
                cairo_paint (cr);

                // draw some white text on top
                cairo_set_source_rgb(cr, 1.0, 1.0, 1.0);
                // this is a standard font for Cairo
                cairo_select_font_face (cr, "cairo:serif",
                                        CAIRO_FONT_SLANT_NORMAL,
                                        CAIRO_FONT_WEIGHT_BOLD);
                cairo_set_font_size (cr, 20);
                cairo_move_to(cr, 10.0, 50.0);
                cairo_show_text (cr, "hello");

                // draw Pango text
                PangoLayout *layout;
                PangoFontDescription *desc;

                cairo_move_to(cr, 300.0, 50.0);
                layout = pango_cairo_create_layout (cr);
                pango_layout_set_text (layout, text, -1);
                pango_layout_set_attributes(layout, attrs);
                pango_cairo_update_layout (cr, layout);
                pango_cairo_show_layout (cr, layout);

                pixbuf = gdk_pixbuf_get_from_surface(surface,
                                                     0,
                                                     0,
                                                     width,
                                                     height);

                gdk_threads_add_idle(draw_image, pixbuf);

                sws_freeContext(sws_ctx);
                g_object_unref(layout);
                cairo_surface_destroy(surface);
                cairo_destroy(cr);

            }
        }
        av_free_packet(&packet);
    }

    printf("Video over!\n");
    exit(0);
}
```

Conclusion

Getting to grips with some aspects of the Gtk toolkit is not trivial. You will use some of this material in later chapters, which is why it has been pulled out of the sound sections of this book and placed in its own chapter. Those not interested in Linux sound may nevertheless find it useful.

CHAPTER 16

MIDI

MIDI is the electronic equivalent of sheet music. It is basically a set of instructions to tell MIDI players which notes to play, how loud, which instruments to use, what effects to employ, and when to stop playing notes.

MIDI comes in two forms: a "wire" format, in which MIDI commands are sent across a stream and expected to be handled when received, and a file format, in which the MIDI commands are stored in a file and are read and played from the file.

MIDI was invented so that musical instruments could communicate and so that one instrument could control another. It has been heavily used in electronic music but is generally applicable to any electronic instruments. Computers can of course be considered as MIDI instruments with the right software.

Resources

Here are some resources:

- *Introduction to Computer Music: Volume One*; Chapter 3, "MIDI" (www.indiana. edu/~emusic/etext/MIDI/chapter3_MIDI.shtml)

- MIDI Manufacturers Association: Tutorials (www.midi.org/aboutmidi/tutorials. php)

- Ted's Linux MIDI Guide (http://tedfelix.com/linux/linux-midi.html)

- Standard MIDI-File Format Spec. 1.1 (www.cs.cmu.edu/~music/cmsip/readings/ Standard-MIDI-file-format-updated.pdf)

Components of a MIDI System

A MIDI system can be a single instrument, both generating and consuming MIDI events. What are commonly called *synthesizers* typically have a keyboard and multiple controls to generate the MIDI events and also have the hardware to produce sounds from these controls.

Synthesizer

A synthesizer in the abstract is a consumer of MIDI events and a producer of sound, through loudspeakers or headphones. A synthesizer may do this in hardware but may also do it in software using tables known as *sound fonts*. There are many sound fonts, and they are discussed in the next chapter.

Sequencers

Synthesizers react in real time to MIDI events. The most important of these are events to play notes. Now sheet music uses notes of different kinds (crochets, quavers, and so on) to signal duration. MIDI instead uses NOTE ON and NOTE OFF events.

These note events can't be sent to the synthesizer all at once, or it would attempt to play them all at once. If the MIDI events are generated by a person at a keyboard, say, then they control how they are sent.

In this book, you will be looking at the case where the MIDI events are stored in a file. Consequently, the file reader must control the timing at which events are sent to a synthesizer. It is the role of the sequencer to send events to a synthesizer at appropriate times.

Other Components

A minimal system will consist of a sequencer (either a human or a component) sending MIDI at the correct times to a synthesizer. There may be other components, though, including drum machines, devices to produce sound effects such as reverb or delay, or samplers that have previously recorded or digitized audio and can play them back.

MIDI Events

There are several categories of MIDI event. The main ones for our purposes are the program change events, note events, and meta events.

Program Change Events

Instruments or "voices" are associated with channels. The establishment between voices and channels is typically done at the beginning of play but can be changed by program change events.

Note Events

Note events are either NOTE ON or NOTE OFF. They include a channel to select the instrument to play. They have a number that represents the note. There are 128 of these, from 0 to 127, and they correspond to the notes C0 (8.175Hz) to G10 (12543.854Hz). These values can be changed, for example, for microtonal music, but that is out of the scope of this book. A note event also contains a velocity, which gives the volume of the note.

Meta Events

There are a set of meta events that give information about the MIDI system playing. These include copyright notices and the sequence or track name but most importantly for karaoke are Lyric and Text events.

These meta events are not sent on the wire. A synthesizer won't know what to do with a copyright notice, say. Meta events are contained in MIDI files and may be interpreted by whatever is reading from the file.

This leads to a difference in behavior in sequencers, which you will come across when you look at karaoke systems: some sequencers make meta information available such as the Java sequencer. Others do not, such as fluidsynth.

Conclusion

MIDI systems have been around since the early 1980s. In that sense, they are "old" technology, and replacement proposals are often made. Nevertheless, MIDI has remained a persistent electronic format. This chapter looked at the components of a MIDI system and gave an abstract view of the MIDI messages.

CHAPTER 17

User-Level Tools for MIDI

This chapter gives an overview of the principal tools used for playing MIDI files. It does not include MIDI editors, MIDI producers, and so on.

Resources

Check out this resource:

- Ted's Linux MIDI Guide (http://tedfelix.com/linux/linux-midi.html)

Sound Fonts

The tools described in this chapter each include a software synthesizer, which produces audio as PCM data from the MIDI data fed to it. The MIDI data contains information about the instrument playing each note, and of course, every instrument sounds different. So, the synthesizer must make use of mapping information from MIDI notes + instrument into PCM data.

The mapping is usually done using *sound font* files. There are various formats for this. The primary one is the .sf2 format (http://connect.creativelabs.com/developer/SoundFont/Forms/AllItems.aspx/). Some synthesizers (such as TiMidity) can also use Gravis UltraSound patches, which are recorded real instruments.

Many sound font files have been created. See, for example, "Links to SoundFonts and other similar files" (www.synthfont.com/links_to_soundfonts.html) (although many of the links are broken).

- A common sound font is from FluidSynth, named /usr/share/sounds/sf2/ FluidR3_GM.sf2. This file is nearly 150Mb. Sound fonts are not small!

- Java Sound has a sound font called soundbank-emg.sf2. This is considerably smaller at 1.9Mb!

- Another popular sound font is at GeneralUser_GS_1.44-MuseScore (www. schristiancollins.com/soundfonts/GeneralUser_GS_1.44-MuseScore.zip) by S. Christian Collins. This is not so large, at 31Mb.

- You can find a small sound font by Tim Brechbill; it's 6Mb (linked from http:// musescore.org/en/handbook/soundfont)

- You can find a list of sound fonts at the "TiMidity++ Configuration File Package v2004/8/3" page (http://timidity.s11.xrea.com/files/readme_cfgp.htm)

© Jan Newmarch 2017
J. Newmarch, *Linux Sound Programming*, DOI 10.1007/978-1-4842-2496-0_17

Possibly surprisingly, using different sound fonts doesn't seem to make much difference to CPU usage. For FluidSynth, they all use about 60 percent to 70 percent CPU on one song. They do, of course, sound different.

TiMidity

TiMidity is a "software sound renderer (MIDI sequencer and MOD player)". Its home page is Maemo.org (http://maemo.org/packages/view/timidity/).

Timidity can be used to play MIDI files by giving them on the command line, like so:

```
timidity rehab.mid
```

The default sound fonts used by TiMidity are Gravis UltraSound patches, from the /usr/share/midi/ freepats/ directory. These sound fonts are missing many instruments so should be replaced by another such as the FluidSynth fonts. The settings are made in the configurations file /etc/timidity/timidity.cfg.

TiMidity as a Server

TiMidity can also be run as an ALSA server listening on a port (see "Using MIDI with UNIX" at http://wiki.winehq.org/MIDI).

```
timidity -iAD -B2,8 -Os1l -s 44100
```

The -iAD option runs it as a daemon process in the background as an ALSA sequencer client. The -B2,8 option selects the number of buffer fragments. The -Os1l option selects ALSA output as PCM. The -s option is the sample size. (For the Raspberry Pi, I found that -B0,12 worked better than -B2,8.)

In this mode, ALSA can send messages to it. The command

```
aconnect -0
```

will show output such as the following:

```
client 14: 'Midi Through' [type=kernel]
0 'Midi Through Port-0'
laptop:/home/httpd/html/LinuxSound/MIDI/Python/pyPortMidi-0.0.3$aconnect -o
client 14: 'Midi Through' [type=kernel]
0 'Midi Through Port-0'
client 128: 'TiMidity' [type=user]
0 'TiMidity port 0 '
1 'TiMidity port 1 '
2 'TiMidity port 2 '
3 'TiMidity port 3 '
```

The Midi Through port is not useful, but the TiMidity ports are. MIDI files can then be played by an ALSA sequencer, as follows:

```
aplaymidi -p128:0 rehab.mid
```

Setting TiMidity Output Device

You can change the default output for TiMidity using the -O option. The TiMidity help (`timidity -h`) shows, for example, the following:

```
Available output modes (-O, --output-mode option):
  -Os         ALSA pcm device
  -Ow         RIFF WAVE file
  -Or         Raw waveform data
  -Ou         Sun audio file
  -Oa         AIFF file
  -Ol         List MIDI event
  -Om         Write MIDI file
  -OM         MOD -> MIDI file conversion
```

For some of these modes, the device name can also be set, using the -o option. For example, to play a file using the hw:2 ALSA device, use this:

```
timidity -Os -o hw:2 ...
```

TiMidity and Jack

TiMidity can be run with Jack output using the -Oj option. In a user-based environment such as Ubuntu, you may need to stop or pause PulseAudio, start the Jack server, and then run TiMidity. PulseAudio may be paused with the following, for example, in one terminal:

```
pasuspender cat
```

In another, start the Jack daemon using ALSA input and output.

```
jackd -dalsa
```

In a third terminal, run TiMidity.

```
timidity -Oj 54154.mid
```

The links may be shown graphically by also running qjackctl.

GStreamer

GStreamer allows you to build "pipelines" that can be played using gst-launch. It can play MIDI files with this, for example:

```
gst-launch filesrc location="rehab.mid" ! decodebin ! alsasink
```

fluidsynth

fluidsynth is a command-line MIDI player. It runs under ALSA with a command line, as shown here:

```
fluidsynth -a alsa -l <sound font> <files...>
```

The sound font is set explicitly on the command line, so it can be set to another sound font. qsynth is a GUI interface to fluidsynth.
You can use fluidsynth to convert MIDI files to WAV files with this:

```
fluidsynth -F out.wav /usr/share/sounds/sf2/FluidR3_GM.sf2 myfile.mid
```

fluidsynth as a Server

fluidsynth can be run as a server in the same way as TiMidity. Use this:

```
fluidsynth --server --audio-driver=alsa /usr/share/sounds/sf2/FluidR3_GM.sf2
```

Then a connect -o will show the ports, and it can be played to with the following:

```
amidi -p 128:0 <midi-file>
```

Rosegarden

Rosegarden is a well-rounded audio and MIDI sequencer, score editor, and general-purpose music composition and editing environment. Its home page is at www.rosegardenmusic.com/. It is not a stand-alone synthsesizer; it uses fluidsynth, for example.

WildMIDI

The aim of this sequencer/synthesizer is to be *small*. It succeeds at this.

Comparison

On playing the same song with the different systems, I observed the following CPU patterns:
TiMidity + PulseAudio (with GUS or SF2 sound fonts)

> 12 to 20 percent CPU

fluidsynth + PulseAudio

> 65 to 72 percent CPU

WildMIDI

> 6 percent CPU

Java Sound

> 52 to 60 percent

GStreamer

> 15 to 20 percent CPU

VLC

VLC is a general-purpose media player. There is a VLC module (`https://wiki.videolan.org/Midi`) to handle MIDI files using `fluidsynth`. To get this working on a Debian system, you first need to install the `vlc-plugin-fluidsynth` package. Then in Advanced Options of VLC, choose Codecs-Audio Codecs-FluidSynth. You will need to set the sound font, for example, to `/usr/share/sounds/sf2/FluidR3_GM.sf2`.

Conclusion

This chapter looked at a variety of user-level tools for manipulating MIDI. It has primarily included players, but there are also a large number of MIDI editors, producers, and so on.

CHAPTER 18

MIDI Java Sound

Java Sound has a well-developed MIDI system, with cleanly separated components such as sequencers and synthesizers, and it allows hooks for meta events as well as ordinary MIDI events. This chapter considers programming using the MIDI API.

Resources

Many resources are available for Java Sound.

- The Java Platform Standard Edition 7 API Specification (http://docs.oracle.com/javase/7/docs/api/) is the reference point for all the standard Java APIs, including javax.sound.sampled.

- The "Trail: Sound" tutorial at Java Tutorials (http://docs.oracle.com/javase/tutorial/sound/index.html) gives a good overview of both the sampled and MIDI packages.

- The Audio Programming FAQ at Java Sound Resources (www.jsresources.org/faq_audio.html) answers many questions about Java Sound.

- The Java Sound Programmer Guide (http://docs.oracle.com/javase/7/docs/technotes/guides/sound/programmer_guide/contents.html) is a full book from Oracle (formerly Sun MicroSystems) about Java Sound.

- The Sound Group (http://openjdk.java.net/groups/sound/) consists of developers designing, implementing, and maintaining the various OpenJDK sound components. It's your hook into finding out more about the ongoing development of Java Sound in the open source community.

- Check out the Gervill software sound synthesizer source (https://java.net/projects/gervill/sources/Mercurial/show).

Key Java Sound MIDI Classes

Java Sound relies on a set of classes for its MIDI support. These are standard in Java. The following are the principal classes:

- The MidiSystem class is the entry point for all MIDI classes.

- A MidiDevice includes synthesizers, sequencers, MIDI input ports, and MIDI output ports.

© Jan Newmarch 2017
J. Newmarch, *Linux Sound Programming*, DOI 10.1007/978-1-4842-2496-0_18

- A Transmitter sends MidiEvent objects to a Receiver. A Transmitter is the *source* of MIDI events, and a Receiver is a *consumer* of events.

- A Sequencer is a device for capturing and playing back sequences of MIDI events. It has transmitters, because it typically sends the MIDI messages stored in the sequence to another device, such as a synthesizer or MIDI output port. It also has receivers because it can capture MIDI messages and store them in a sequence. (http://docs.oracle.com/javase/7/docs/technotes/guides/sound/programmer_ guide/chapter8.html#118852).

- A Synthesizer is a device for generating sound. It's the only object in the javax. sound.midi package that produces audio data (http://docs.oracle.com/javase/7/ docs/technotes/guides/sound/programmer_guide/chapter8.html#118852).

Device Information

Device information is found by querying MidiSystem for its list of DeviceInfo objects. Each information object contains fields such as Name and Vendor. You can find the actual device using this information object with MidiSystem.getMidiDevice(info). The device can then be queried for its receivers and transmitters and its type as sequencer or synthesizer.

One annoying part is that you cannot get a list of all the device's transmitters and receivers, only those that are *open*. You can ask for the default transmitter and receiver, which will implicitly open them. So, you can see that the list may be empty before asking for the default, but it will be nonempty afterward if there is a default! If there are no defaults, a MidiUnavailableException exception will be thrown.

The program is as follows:

```java
import javax.sound.midi.*;
import java.util.*;

public class DeviceInfo {

    public static void main(String[] args) throws Exception {
        MidiDevice.Info[] devices;

        /*
        MidiDevice.Info[] info = p.getDeviceInfo();
        for (int m = 0; m < info.length; m++) {
            System.out.println(info[m].toString());
        }
        */

        System.out.println("MIDI devices:");
        devices = MidiSystem.getMidiDeviceInfo();
        for (MidiDevice.Info info: devices) {
            System.out.println("    Name: " + info.toString() +
                            ", Decription: " +
                            info.getDescription() +
                            ", Vendor: " +
                            info.getVendor());
            MidiDevice device = MidiSystem.getMidiDevice(info);
            if (! device.isOpen()) {
                device.open();
```

```
        }
        if (device instanceof Sequencer) {
            System.out.println("         Device is a sequencer");
        }
        if (device instanceof Synthesizer) {
            System.out.println("         Device is a synthesizer");
        }
        System.out.println("         Open receivers:");
        List<Receiver> receivers = device.getReceivers();
        for (Receiver r: receivers) {
            System.out.println("                  " + r.toString());
        }
        try {
            System.out.println("\n         Default receiver: " +
                               device.getReceiver().toString());

            System.out.println("\n         Open receivers now:");
            receivers = device.getReceivers();
            for (Receiver r: receivers) {
                System.out.println("                  " + r.toString());
            }
        } catch(MidiUnavailableException e) {
            System.out.println("         No default receiver");
        }

        System.out.println("\n         Open transmitters:");
        List<Transmitter> transmitters = device.getTransmitters();
        for (Transmitter t: transmitters) {
            System.out.println("                  " + t.toString());
        }
        try {
            System.out.println("\n         Default transmitter: " +
                               device.getTransmitter().toString());

            System.out.println("\n         Open transmitters now:");
            transmitters = device.getTransmitters();
            for (Transmitter t: transmitters) {
                System.out.println("                  " + t.toString());
            }
        } catch(MidiUnavailableException e) {
            System.out.println("         No default transmitter");
        }
        device.close();
}

Sequencer sequencer = MidiSystem.getSequencer();
System.out.println("Default system sequencer is " +
                   sequencer.getDeviceInfo().toString() +
                   " (" + sequencer.getClass() + ")");

Synthesizer synthesizer = MidiSystem.getSynthesizer();
System.out.println("Default system synthesizer is " +
```

```
                              synthesizer.getDeviceInfo().toString() +
                         " (" + synthesizer.getClass() + ")");

    }
}
```

The output on my system is as follows:

```
MIDI devices:
    Name: Gervill, Decription: Software MIDI Synthesizer, Vendor: OpenJDK
        Device is a synthesizer
        Open receivers:

        Default receiver: com.sun.media.sound.SoftReceiver@72f2a824

        Open receivers now:
            com.sun.media.sound.SoftReceiver@72f2a824

        Open transmitters:
        No default transmitter
    Name: Real Time Sequencer, Decription: Software sequencer, Vendor: Oracle Corporation
        Device is a sequencer
        Open receivers:

        Default receiver: com.sun.media.sound.RealTimeSequencer$SequencerReceiver@c23c5ff

        Open receivers now:
            com.sun.media.sound.RealTimeSequencer$SequencerReceiver@c23c5ff

        Open transmitters:
        Default transmitter: com.sun.media.sound.RealTimeSequencer$SequencerTransmitter@4e1
3aa4e

        Open transmitters now:
            com.sun.media.sound.RealTimeSequencer$SequencerTransmitter@4e13aa4e
Default system sequencer is Real Time Sequencer
Default system synthesizer is Gervill
```

Dumping a MIDI File

These two programs from jsresources.org dump a MIDI file to the console. The MidiSystem creates a Sequence from a file. Each track of the sequence is looped through, and each event within each track is examined. While it would be possible to print *in situ*, each event is passed to a Receiver object, which in this case is DumpReceiver. That object could do anything but in this case just prints the event to stdout.

The DumpSequence.java program reads a MIDI file given as a command-line argument and dumps a listing of its contents in readable form to standard output. It first gets a Sequence and prints out information about the sequence and then gets each track in turn, printing out the contents of the track.

```
/*
 *      DumpSequence.java
 *
```

```
 *      This file is part of jsresources.org
 */

/*
 * Copyright (c) 1999, 2000 by Matthias Pfisterer
 * All rights reserved.
 *
 * Redistribution and use in source and binary forms, with or without
 * modification, are permitted provided that the following conditions
 * are met:
 *
 * - Redistributions of source code must retain the above copyright notice,
 *   this list of conditions and the following disclaimer.
 * - Redistributions in binary form must reproduce the above copyright
 *   notice, this list of conditions and the following disclaimer in the
 *   documentation and/or other materials provided with the distribution.
 *
 * THIS SOFTWARE IS PROVIDED BY THE COPYRIGHT HOLDERS AND CONTRIBUTORS
 * "AS IS" AND ANY EXPRESS OR IMPLIED WARRANTIES, INCLUDING, BUT NOT
 * LIMITED TO, THE IMPLIED WARRANTIES OF MERCHANTABILITY AND FITNESS
 * FOR A PARTICULAR PURPOSE ARE DISCLAIMED. IN NO EVENT SHALL THE
 * COPYRIGHT OWNER OR CONTRIBUTORS BE LIABLE FOR ANY DIRECT, INDIRECT,
 * INCIDENTAL, SPECIAL, EXEMPLARY, OR CONSEQUENTIAL DAMAGES
 * (INCLUDING, BUT NOT LIMITED TO, PROCUREMENT OF SUBSTITUTE GOODS OR
 * SERVICES; LOSS OF USE, DATA, OR PROFITS; OR BUSINESS INTERRUPTION)
 * HOWEVER CAUSED AND ON ANY THEORY OF LIABILITY, WHETHER IN CONTRACT,
 * STRICT LIABILITY, OR TORT (INCLUDING NEGLIGENCE OR OTHERWISE)
 * ARISING IN ANY WAY OUT OF THE USE OF THIS SOFTWARE, EVEN IF ADVISED
 * OF THE POSSIBILITY OF SUCH DAMAGE.
 */

import java.io.File;
import java.io.IOException;

import javax.sound.midi.MidiSystem;
import javax.sound.midi.InvalidMidiDataException;
import javax.sound.midi.Sequence;
import javax.sound.midi.Track;
import javax.sound.midi.MidiEvent;
import javax.sound.midi.MidiMessage;
import javax.sound.midi.ShortMessage;
import javax.sound.midi.MetaMessage;
import javax.sound.midi.SysexMessage;
import javax.sound.midi.Receiver;

public class DumpSequence
{
    private static String[]    sm_astrKeyNames = {"C", "C#", "D", "D#", "E", "F", "F#", "G",
"G#", "A", "A#", "B"};

    private static Receiver    sm_receiver = new DumpReceiver(System.out, true);
```

```java
public static void main(String[] args) {
    /*
     *      We check that there is exactly one command-line
     *      argument. If not, we display the usage message and
     *      exit.
     */
    if (args.length != 1) {
        out("DumpSequence: usage:");
        out("\tjava DumpSequence <midifile>");
        System.exit(1);
    }
    /*
     *      Now, that we're shure there is an argument, we take it as
     *      the filename of the soundfile we want to play.
     */
    String  strFilename = args[0];
    File    midiFile = new File(strFilename);

    /*
     *      We try to get a Sequence object, which the content
     *      of the MIDI file.
     */
    Sequence        sequence = null;
    try {
        sequence = MidiSystem.getSequence(midiFile);
    } catch (InvalidMidiDataException e) {
        e.printStackTrace();
        System.exit(1);
    } catch (IOException e) {
        e.printStackTrace();
        System.exit(1);
    }

    /*
     *          And now, we output the data.
     */
    if (sequence == null) {
        out("Cannot retrieve Sequence.");
    } else {
        out("---------------------------------------------------------------------------");
        out("File: " + strFilename);
        out("---------------------------------------------------------------------------");
        out("Length: " + sequence.getTickLength() + " ticks");
        out("Duration: " + sequence.getMicrosecondLength() + " microseconds");
        out("---------------------------------------------------------------------------");
        float       fDivisionType = sequence.getDivisionType();
        String      strDivisionType = null;
        if (fDivisionType == Sequence.PPQ) {
            strDivisionType = "PPQ";
        } else if (fDivisionType == Sequence.SMPTE_24) {
            strDivisionType = "SMPTE, 24 frames per second";
        } else if (fDivisionType == Sequence.SMPTE_25) {
```

```
                strDivisionType = "SMPTE, 25 frames per second";
        } else if (fDivisionType == Sequence.SMPTE_30DROP) {
                strDivisionType = "SMPTE, 29.97 frames per second";
        } else if (fDivisionType == Sequence.SMPTE_30) {
                strDivisionType = "SMPTE, 30 frames per second";
        }

        out("DivisionType: " + strDivisionType);

        String      strResolutionType = null;
        if (sequence.getDivisionType() == Sequence.PPQ) {
            strResolutionType = " ticks per beat";
        } else {
            strResolutionType = " ticks per frame";
        }
        out("Resolution: " + sequence.getResolution() + strResolutionType);
        out("-------------------------------------------------------------------------");
        Track[]    tracks = sequence.getTracks();
        for (int nTrack = 0; nTrack < tracks.length; nTrack++) {
            out("Track " + nTrack + ":");
            out("-----------------------");
            Track          track = tracks[nTrack];
            for (int nEvent = 0; nEvent < track.size(); nEvent++) {
                MidiEvent  event = track.get(nEvent);
                output(event);
            }
            out("-------------------------------------------------------------------------");
        }
    }
}

public static void output(MidiEvent event) {
    MidiMessage     message = event.getMessage();
    long            lTicks = event.getTick();
    sm_receiver.send(message, lTicks);
}

private static void out(String strMessage) {
    System.out.println(strMessage);
}
}
/*** DumpSequence.java ***/
```

There are several sites with legal, free MIDI files. The file http://files.mididb.com/amy-winehouse/rehab.mid gives the result.

```
-------------------------------------------------------------------------
File: rehab.mid
-------------------------------------------------------------------------
Length: 251475 ticks
Duration: 216788738 microseconds
-------------------------------------------------------------------------
```

```
DivisionType: PPQ
Resolution: 480 ticks per beat
--------------------------------------------------------------------------------
Track 0:
----------------------
tick 0: Time Signature: 4/4, MIDI clocks per metronome tick: 24, 1/32 per 24 MIDI clocks: 8
tick 0: Key Signature: C major
tick 0: SMTPE Offset: 32:0:0.0.0
tick 0: Set Tempo: 145.0 bpm
tick 0: End of Track
--------------------------------------------------------------------------------
Track 1:
----------------------
tick 0: Sequence/Track Name: amy winehouse - rehab
tick 0: Instrument Name: GM Device
tick 40: Sysex message: F0 7E 7F 09 01 F7
tick 40: End of Track
--------------------------------------------------------------------------------
Track 2:
----------------------
tick 0: MIDI Channel Prefix: 1
tick 0: Sequence/Track Name: amy winehouse - rehab
tick 0: Instrument Name: GM Device  2
tick 480: [B1 79 00] channel 2: control change 121 value: 0
tick 485: [B1 0A 40] channel 2: control change 10 value: 64
tick 490: [B1 5D 14] channel 2: control change 93 value: 20
tick 495: [B1 5B 00] channel 2: control change 91 value: 0
tick 500: [B1 0B 7F] channel 2: control change 11 value: 127
tick 505: [B1 07 69] channel 2: control change 7 value: 105
tick 510: [E1 00 40] channel 2: pitch wheel change 8192
tick 515: [B1 00 00] channel 2: control change 0 value: 0
tick 520: [C1 22] channel 2: program change 34
...
```

Playing a MIDI File

To play a MIDI file, you create a Sequence from a File, using the MidiSystem. You also create a Sequencer from the MidiSystem and pass it the sequence. The sequencer will output MIDI messages through its Transmitter. This completes the setup of the MIDI event generation side of the system.

The play side is constructed by getting a Synthesizer from the MidiSystem. The Receiver is found from the synthesizer and is given to the transmitter of MIDI events. Play commences by calling start() on the sequencer, which reads from the file and passes MIDI events to its transmitter. These are passed to the synthesizer's receiver and played. Figure 18-1 shows the UML class diagram for the relevant classes.

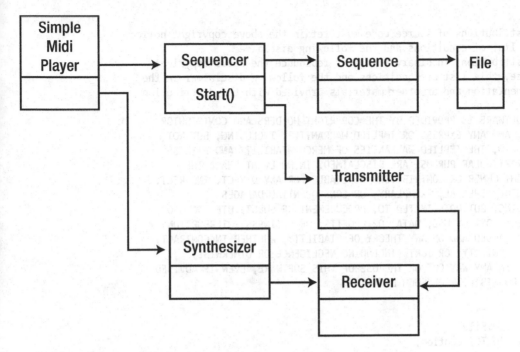

Figure 18-1. *Class diagram for the SimpleMidiPlayer*

This code is from playing an audio file (easy). The original is heavily commented, but I have removed much of it for print book. The logic is that you load a sequence from a file, get the default sequencer, and set the sequence into the sequencer. Sequencers are not necessarily synthesizers, but the default sequencer usually is. If not, you get the default synthesizer and then hook up the sequencer's transmitter to the synthesizer's receiver. Then the MIDI file is played by calling start() on the sequencer.

```
/*
 *       SimpleMidiPlayer.java
 *
 *       This file is part of jsresources.org
 */


/*
 * Copyright (c) 1999 - 2001 by Matthias Pfisterer
 * All rights reserved.
 *
 * Redistribution and use in source and binary forms, with or without
 * modification, are permitted provided that the following conditions
 * are met:
```

```
 *
 * - Redistributions of source code must retain the above copyright notice,
 *   this list of conditions and the following disclaimer.
 * - Redistributions in binary form must reproduce the above copyright
 *   notice, this list of conditions and the following disclaimer in the
 *   documentation and/or other materials provided with the distribution.
 *
 * THIS SOFTWARE IS PROVIDED BY THE COPYRIGHT HOLDERS AND CONTRIBUTORS
 * "AS IS" AND ANY EXPRESS OR IMPLIED WARRANTIES, INCLUDING, BUT NOT
 * LIMITED TO, THE IMPLIED WARRANTIES OF MERCHANTABILITY AND FITNESS
 * FOR A PARTICULAR PURPOSE ARE DISCLAIMED. IN NO EVENT SHALL THE
 * COPYRIGHT OWNER OR CONTRIBUTORS BE LIABLE FOR ANY DIRECT, INDIRECT,
 * INCIDENTAL, SPECIAL, EXEMPLARY, OR CONSEQUENTIAL DAMAGES
 * (INCLUDING, BUT NOT LIMITED TO, PROCUREMENT OF SUBSTITUTE GOODS OR
 * SERVICES; LOSS OF USE, DATA, OR PROFITS; OR BUSINESS INTERRUPTION)
 * HOWEVER CAUSED AND ON ANY THEORY OF LIABILITY, WHETHER IN CONTRACT,
 * STRICT LIABILITY, OR TORT (INCLUDING NEGLIGENCE OR OTHERWISE)
 * ARISING IN ANY WAY OUT OF THE USE OF THIS SOFTWARE, EVEN IF ADVISED
 * OF THE POSSIBILITY OF SUCH DAMAGE.
 */

import java.io.File;
import java.io.IOException;

import javax.sound.midi.InvalidMidiDataException;
import javax.sound.midi.MidiSystem;
import javax.sound.midi.MidiUnavailableException;
import javax.sound.midi.MetaEventListener;
import javax.sound.midi.MetaMessage;
import javax.sound.midi.Sequence;
import javax.sound.midi.Sequencer;
import javax.sound.midi.Synthesizer;
import javax.sound.midi.Receiver;
import javax.sound.midi.Transmitter;
import javax.sound.midi.MidiChannel;
import javax.sound.midi.ShortMessage;

public class SimpleMidiPlayer {

    private static Sequencer sm_sequencer = null;
    private static Synthesizer sm_synthesizer = null;

    public static void main(String[]args) {

        if (args.length == 0 || args[0].equals("-h")) {
            printUsageAndExit();
        }

        String strFilename = args[0];
        File midiFile = new File(strFilename);
```

```
/*
 *      We read in the MIDI file to a Sequence object.
 */
Sequence sequence = null;
try {
    sequence = MidiSystem.getSequence(midiFile);
}
catch(InvalidMidiDataException e) {
    e.printStackTrace();
    System.exit(1);
}
catch(IOException e) {
    e.printStackTrace();
    System.exit(1);
}

/*
 *      Now, we need a Sequencer to play the sequence.
 *      Here, we simply request the default sequencer.
 *      With an argument of false, it does not create
 *      a default syntesizer.
 */
try {
    sm_sequencer = MidiSystem.getSequencer(false);
}
catch(MidiUnavailableException e) {
    e.printStackTrace();
    System.exit(1);
}
if (sm_sequencer == null) {
    out("SimpleMidiPlayer.main(): can't get a Sequencer");
    System.exit(1);
}

try {
    sm_sequencer.open();
}
catch(MidiUnavailableException e) {
    e.printStackTrace();
    System.exit(1);
}

/*
 *      Next step is to tell the Sequencer which
 *      Sequence it has to play.
 */
try {
    sm_sequencer.setSequence(sequence);
}
catch(InvalidMidiDataException e) {
    e.printStackTrace();
```

```
            System.exit(1);
        }

        Receiver synthReceiver = null;
        if (!(sm_sequencer instanceof Synthesizer)) {
            /*
             *      We try to get the default synthesizer, open()
             *      it and chain it to the sequencer with a
             *      Transmitter-Receiver pair.
             */
            try {
                sm_synthesizer = MidiSystem.getSynthesizer();
                sm_synthesizer.open();
                synthReceiver = sm_synthesizer.getReceiver();
                Transmitter seqTransmitter = sm_sequencer.getTransmitter();
                seqTransmitter.setReceiver(synthReceiver);
            }
            catch(MidiUnavailableException e) {
                e.printStackTrace();
            }
        }

        /*
         *      Now, we can start playing
         */
        sm_sequencer.start();

        try {
            Thread.sleep(5000);
        }
        catch(InterruptedException e) {
            e.printStackTrace();
        }
    }

    private static void printUsageAndExit() {
        out("SimpleMidiPlayer: usage:");
        out("\tjava SimpleMidiPlayer <midifile>");
        System.exit(1);
    }

    private static void out(String strMessage) {
        System.out.println(strMessage);
    }
}
```

Playing a file to an external MIDI synthesizer

I have an Edirol Studio Canvas SD-20 synthesizer that I bought for a few hundred Australian dollars. This plugs into a PC through a USB port. ALSA recognizes this with the following:

```
$ amidi -l
Dir Device     Name
IO  hw:2,0,0   SD-20 Part A
IO  hw:2,0,1   SD-20 Part B
I   hw:2,0,2   SD-20 MIDI
```

The MidiDevice.Info device information lists hw:2,0,0 twice, once for input and once for output, and is similar for the other values. The device information can be identified by the toString method, which returns values such as "SD20 [hw:2,0,0]". From the device information, the device can be found like before using MidiSystem.getMidiDevice(info). The input and output devices can be distinguished by the number of maxOutputReceivers it supports: zero means none, while any other value (including –1!) means it has a MIDI receiver. Selecting an external receiver is done with code to replace the previous setting of the synthesizer with this:

```
            Receiver        synthReceiver = null;
            MidiDevice.Info[] devices;
            devices = MidiSystem.getMidiDeviceInfo();

            for (MidiDevice.Info info: devices) {
                System.out.println("    Name: " + info.toString() +
                                   ", Decription: " +
                                   info.getDescription() +
                                   ", Vendor: " +
                                   info.getVendor());
                if (info.toString().equals("SD20 [hw:2,0,0]")) {
                    MidiDevice device = MidiSystem.getMidiDevice(info);
                    if (device.getMaxReceivers() != 0) {
                        try {
                            device.open();
                            System.out.println("  max receivers: " + device.
                            getMaxReceivers());
                            receiver = device.getReceiver();
                            System.out.println("Found a receiver");
                            break;
                        } catch(Exception e) {}
                    }
                }
            }

        if (receiver == null) {
    System.out.println("Receiver is null");
    System.exit(1);
        }
        try {
    Transmitter seqTransmitter = sm_sequencer.getTransmitter();
    seqTransmitter.setReceiver(receiver);
        }
    catch(MidiUnavailableException e) {
        e.printStackTrace();
        }

        /*
         *     Now, we can start playing as before
         */
```

Changing the Soundbank

The soundbank is a set of "sounds" encoded in some way that are used to generate the music played. The default sound synthesizer for Java is the Gervill synthesizer, and it looks for its default soundbank in $HOME/.gervill/ soundbank-emg.sf2. This default soundbank is tiny; it's only 1.9MB in size. And it sounds, well, poor quality.

DaWicked1 in "Better Java-midi instrument sounds for Linux" (www.minecraftforum.net/forums/ mapping-and-modding/mapping-and-modding-tutorials/1571330-better-java-midi-instrument-sounds-for-linux) offers two methods to improve this: the simpler way is to replace the sound font with a better one such as the FluidSynth font, using the default name.

The second method is programmatic and probably better as it allows more flexibility and choice at runtime.

Changing Pitch and Speed

Changing the speed of playback of a MIDI file means changing the rate that MIDI messages are sent from the sequencer. The Java sequencers have methods to control this such as setTempoFactor. The sequencer will respond to this method by sending the messages at a different rate.

Changing the pitch of the notes can be done by altering the pitch of the NOTE_ON and NOTE_OFF messages. This has to be done not just for future notes but also for notes currently playing. Fortunately, there is a MIDI command called Pitch Bend, which can be sent to a synthesizer to change the pitch of all currently playing and future notes. A Pitch Bend value of 0x2000 corresponds to no pitch change; values up to 0x4000 are increases in pitch, and below are decreases in pitch. There are many sites giving complex formulae for this, but the simplest seems to be MIDI Pitch Bend Range (www.ultimatemetal.com/forum/threads/ midi-pitch-bend-range.680677/), which states that a change of pitch by 683 is roughly a semitone. So, you change the pitch value and send a new Pitch Bend event to the receiver.

You look for input from the user of ←, ↑, →, ↓ (Esc-[A, and so on). These then call the appropriate method. The program illustrating this is an adaptation of the SimpleMidiPlayer given earlier in the chapter and is called AdjustableMidiPlayer.java. In the main body, you replace the call to sleep with the following:

```
BufferedReader br = new BufferedReader(new
                                InputStreamReader(System.in));
String str = null;
System.out.println("Enter lines of text.");
System.out.println("Enter 'stop' to quit.");
do {
    try {
        str = br.readLine();
        if (str.length() >= 2) {
            byte[] bytes = str.getBytes();
            if (bytes[0] == 27 && bytes[1] == 91) {
                if (bytes[2] == 65) {
                    // up
                    increasePitch();
                } else if (bytes[2] == 66) {
                    // down
                    decreasePitch();
                } else if (bytes[2] == 67) {
                    //right
                    faster();
                } else if (bytes[2] == 68) {
                    //left
```

```
                        slower();
                }
            }
        }
        } catch(java.io.IOException e) {
        }
    } while(!str.equals("stop"));
}
```

where the new functions are given by

```
    private void increasePitch() {
        // 683 from www.ultimatemetal.com/forum/threads/midi-pitch-bend-range.680677/
        pitch += 683;
        for (int n = 0; n < 16; n++) {
            try {
                MidiMessage msg =
                    new ShortMessage(ShortMessage.PITCH_BEND,
                            n,
                            pitch & 0x7F, pitch >> 7);
                synthReceiver.send(msg, 0);
            } catch (Exception e) {
            }
        }
    }

    private void decreasePitch() {
        // 683 from www.ultimatemetal.com/forum/threads/midi-pitch-bend-range.680677/
        pitch -= 683;
        for (int n = 0; n < 16; n++) {
            try {
                MidiMessage msg =
                    new ShortMessage(ShortMessage.PITCH_BEND,
                            n,
                            pitch & 0x7F, pitch >> 7);
                synthReceiver.send(msg, 0);
            } catch (Exception e) {
            }
        }
    }

    float speed = 1.0f;

    private void faster() {
        speed *= 1.2f;
        sm_sequencer.setTempoFactor(speed);
    }

    private void slower() {
        speed /= 1.2f;
        sm_sequencer.setTempoFactor(speed);
    }
```

Using TiMidity Instead of the Default Gervill Synthesizer

The soft synth TiMidity can be run as a back-end synthesizer using the ALSA sequencer with the following:

```
$timidity -iA -B2,8 -Os -EFreverb=0

Opening sequencer port: 128:0 128:1 128:2 128:3
```

(It's similar for FluidSynth.) This is opened on ports 128:0, and so on.

Unfortunately, this is not directly visible to Java Sound, which expects either the default Gervill synthesizer or a raw MIDI synthesizer such as a hardware synthesizer. As discussed in Chapter 19, you can fix this by using ALSA raw MIDI ports.

You add raw MIDI ports with the following:

```
modprobe snd-seq snd-virmidi
```

This will bring virtual devices both into the ALSA raw MIDI and into the ALSA sequencer spaces:

```
$amidi -l
Dir Device    Name
IO  hw:3,0    Virtual Raw MIDI (16 subdevices)
IO  hw:3,1    Virtual Raw MIDI (16 subdevices)
IO  hw:3,2    Virtual Raw MIDI (16 subdevices)
IO  hw:3,3    Virtual Raw MIDI (16 subdevices)

$aplaymidi -l
 Port   Client name              Port name
 14:0   Midi Through             Midi Through Port-0
 28:0   Virtual Raw MIDI 3-0     VirMIDI 3-0
 29:0   Virtual Raw MIDI 3-1     VirMIDI 3-1
 30:0   Virtual Raw MIDI 3-2     VirMIDI 3-2
 31:0   Virtual Raw MIDI 3-3     VirMIDI 3-3
```

Virtual raw MIDI port 3-0 can then be connected to TiMidity port 0 with the following:

```
aconnect 28:0 128:0
```

The final step in playing to TiMidity is to change one line of AdaptableMidiPlayer.java from this:

```
if (info.toString().equals("SD20 [hw:2,0,0]")) {
```

to this:

```
if (info.toString().equals("VirMIDI [hw:3,0,0]")) {
```

Conclusion

This chapter built a number of programs using the MIDI API and discussed how to use external hardware synthesizers and soft synthesizers such as TiMidity.

CHAPTER 19

MIDI ALSA

ALSA offers some support for MIDI devices via a sequencer API. Clients can send MIDI events to the sequencer, and it will play them according to the timing of the events. Other clients can then receive these sequenced events and, for example, synthesize them.

Resources

Here are some resources:

- 'ALSA Sequencer" (www.alsa-project.org/~frank/alsa-sequencer/index.html), a design document.

- "ALSA Programming HOWTO" (www.suse.de/~mana/alsa090_howto.html) includes writing a sequencer client, a MIDI router, combining PCM and MIDI (miniFMsynth), and scheduling MIDI events (miniArp).

- MIDI Sequencer API (http://alsa-project.org/alsa-doc/alsa-lib/group___sequencer.html).

- Sequencer interface (http://alsa-project.org/alsa-doc/alsa-lib/seq.html).

- ALSA Sequencer System (www.alsa-project.org/~tiwai/lk2k/lk2k.html) is an in-depth view of the sequencer system by Takashi Iwai.

ALSA Sequencer Clients

ALSA supplies a sequencer that can receive MIDI events from one set of clients and play them according to the timing information in the events to other clients. The clients that can send such events are file readers such as aplaymidi or other sequencers. Clients can also read events as they should be played. Possible consuming clients include splitters, routers, or soft synthesizers such as TiMidity.

TiMidity can be run as an ALSA sequencer client, which will consume MIDI events and synthesize them, according to http://linux-audio.com/TiMidity-howto.html.

```
timidity -iA -B2,8 -Os -EFreverb=0
```

© Jan Newmarch 2017
J. Newmarch, *Linux Sound Programming*, DOI 10.1007/978-1-4842-2496-0_19

On my computer, this produced the following:

```
Requested buffer size 2048, fragment size 1024
ALSA pcm 'default' set buffer size 2048, period size 680 bytes
TiMidity starting in ALSA server mode
Opening sequencer port: 129:0 129:1 129:2 129:3
```

Then it sat there waiting for a connection to be made.

FluidSynth can also be used as a server (see Ted's Linux MIDI Guide at http://tedfelix.com/linux/linux-midi.html).

```
fluidsynth --server --audio-driver=alsa -C0 -R1 -l /usr/share/soundfonts/FluidR3_GM.sf2
```

The ALSA sequencer sends MIDI "wire" events. This does not include MIDI file events such as text or lyric meta events. This makes it pretty useless for a karaoke player. It is possible to modify the file reader aplaymid to send meta events to, say, a listener (like the Java MetaEventListener), but as these come from the file reader rather than the sequencer, they generally arrive well before the time they will get sequenced to be played. Pity.

Programs such as pykaraoke make use of the ALSA sequencer. However, to get the timing of the lyrics right, it includes a MIDI file parser and basically acts as a second sequencer just to extract and display the text/lyric events.

aconnect

The program aconnect can be used to list sequencer servers and clients such as sequencers. I have set two clients running: TiMidity and seqdemo (discussed later). This command

```
aconnect -o
```

shows the following:

```
client 14: 'Midi Through' [type=kernel]
    0 'Midi Through Port-0'
client 128: 'TiMidity' [type=user]
    0 'TiMidity port 0 '
    1 'TiMidity port 1 '
    2 'TiMidity port 2 '
    3 'TiMidity port 3 '
client 129: 'ALSA Sequencer Demo' [type=user]
    0 'ALSA Sequencer Demo'
```

When run with the -i option, it produces the following:

```
$aconnect -i
client 0: 'System' [type=kernel]
    0 'Timer           '
    1 'Announce        '
client 14: 'Midi Through' [type=kernel]
    0 'Midi Through Port-0'
```

The program aconnect can establish a connection between input and output clients with the following:

```
aconnect in out
```

344

seqdemo

The program seqdemo.c from Matthias Nagorni's "ALSA Programming HOWTO" is a basic sequencer client. It opens a MIDI sound sequencer client and then sits in a polling loop, printing information about the MIDI event received. It gives a simple introduction to the ALSA MIDI API.

The code for seqdemo.c is as follows:

```
/* seqdemo.c by Matthias Nagorni */

#include <stdio.h>
#include <stdlib.h>
#include <unistd.h>
#include <alsa/asoundlib.h>

snd_seq_t *open_seq();
void midi_action(snd_seq_t *seq_handle);

snd_seq_t *open_seq() {

  snd_seq_t *seq_handle;
  int portid;

  if (snd_seq_open(&seq_handle, "default", SND_SEQ_OPEN_INPUT, 0) < 0) {
    fprintf(stderr, "Error opening ALSA sequencer.\n");
    exit(1);
  }
  snd_seq_set_client_name(seq_handle, "ALSA Sequencer Demo");
  if ((portid = snd_seq_create_simple_port(seq_handle, "ALSA Sequencer Demo",
            SND_SEQ_PORT_CAP_WRITE|SND_SEQ_PORT_CAP_SUBS_WRITE,
            SND_SEQ_PORT_TYPE_APPLICATION)) < 0) {
    fprintf(stderr, "Error creating sequencer port.\n");
    exit(1);
  }
  return(seq_handle);
}

void midi_action(snd_seq_t *seq_handle) {

  snd_seq_event_t *ev;

  do {
    snd_seq_event_input(seq_handle, &ev);
    switch (ev->type) {
      case SND_SEQ_EVENT_CONTROLLER:
        fprintf(stderr, "Control event on Channel %2d: %5d       \r",
                ev->data.control.channel, ev->data.control.value);
        break;
      case SND_SEQ_EVENT_PITCHBEND:
        fprintf(stderr, "Pitchbender event on Channel %2d: %5d   \r",
                ev->data.control.channel, ev->data.control.value);
        break;
```

345

```
      case SND_SEQ_EVENT_NOTEON:
        fprintf(stderr, "Note On event on Channel %2d: %5d         \r",
                ev->data.control.channel, ev->data.note.note);
        break;
      case SND_SEQ_EVENT_NOTEOFF:
        fprintf(stderr, "Note Off event on Channel %2d: %5d        \r",
                ev->data.control.channel, ev->data.note.note);
        break;            ALSA Programming HOWTO
    }
    snd_seq_free_event(ev);
  } while (snd_seq_event_input_pending(seq_handle, 0) > 0);
}

int main(int argc, char *argv[]) {

  snd_seq_t *seq_handle;c
  int npfd;
  struct pollfd *pfd;

  seq_handle = open_seq();
  npfd = snd_seq_poll_descriptors_count(seq_handle, POLLIN);
  pfd = (struct pollfd *)alloca(npfd * sizeof(struct pollfd));
  snd_seq_poll_descriptors(seq_handle, pfd, npfd, POLLIN);
  while (1) {
    if (poll(pfd, npfd, 100000) > 0) {
      midi_action(seq_handle);
    }
  }
}
```

aplaymidi

The program aplaymidi will play to a back-end MIDI synthesizer such as TiMidity. It requires a port name, which can be found with the following:

```
aplaymidi -l
```

The output will look like this:

```
Port    Client name              Port name
14:0    Midi Through             Midi Through Port-0
128:0   TiMidity                 TiMidity port 0
128:1   TiMidity                 TiMidity port 1
128:2   TiMidity                 TiMidity port 2
128:3   TiMidity                 TiMidity port 3
131:0   aseqdump                 aseqdump
```

The port numbers are the same as those used by aconnect. These are not the ALSA device names (hw:0, and so on) but are special to the ALSA sequencer API.

It can then play a MIDI file to one of these ports as follows:

```
aplaymidi -p 128:0 54154.mid
```

The code can be found at SourceArchive.com (http://alsa-utils.sourcearchive.com/documentation/1.0.8/aplaymidi_8c-source.html).

Raw MIDI Ports

According to the RawMidi interface (www.alsa-project.org/alsa-doc/alsa-lib/rawmidi.html), the RawMidi interface "is designed to write or read raw (unchanged) MIDI data over the MIDI line without any timestamps defined in interface."

Raw MIDI Physical Devices

The raw MIDI interface is typically used to manage hardware MIDI devices. For example, if I plug in an Edirol SD-20 synthesizer to a USB port, it shows under amidi as follows:

```
$amidi -l
Dir Device     Name
IO  hw:2,0,0   SD-20 Part A
IO  hw:2,0,1   SD-20 Part B
I   hw:2,0,2   SD-20 MIDI
```

These names use the same pattern as the ALSA playback and record devices of hw: . . . .

Raw MIDI Virtual Devices

The Linux kernel module snd_virmidi can create virtual raw MIDI devices. First add the modules (see https://wiki.allegro.cc/index.php?title=Using_TiMidity%2B%2B_with_ALSA_raw_MIDI and AlsaMidiOverview [http://alsa.opensrc.org/AlsaMidiOverview).

```
modprobe snd-seq snd-virmidi
```

This will bring virtual devices both into the ALSA raw MIDI and into the ALSA sequencer spaces:

```
$amidi -l
Dir Device     Name
IO  hw:3,0     Virtual Raw MIDI (16 subdevices)
IO  hw:3,1     Virtual Raw MIDI (16 subdevices)
IO  hw:3,2     Virtual Raw MIDI (16 subdevices)
IO  hw:3,3     Virtual Raw MIDI (16 subdevices)

$aplaymidi -l
 Port   Client name                  Port name
 14:0   Midi Through                 Midi Through Port-0
 28:0   Virtual Raw MIDI 3-0         VirMIDI 3-0
 29:0   Virtual Raw MIDI 3-1         VirMIDI 3-1
 30:0   Virtual Raw MIDI 3-2         VirMIDI 3-2
 31:0   Virtual Raw MIDI 3-3         VirMIDI 3-3
```

Mapping MIDI Clients into MIDI Raw Space

Some programs/APIs use the ALSA sequencer space; others use the ALSA raw MIDI space. Virtual ports allow a client using one space to use a client from a different space.

For example, TiMidity can be run as a sequencer client with the following:

```
timidity -iA -B2,8 -Os -EFreverb=0
```

This only shows in the sequencer space, not in the raw MIDI space, and shows to aconnect -o as follows:

```
$aconnect -o
client 14: 'Midi Through' [type=kernel]
    0 'Midi Through Port-0'
client 28: 'Virtual Raw MIDI 3-0' [type=kernel]
    0 'VirMIDI 3-0     '
client 29: 'Virtual Raw MIDI 3-1' [type=kernel]
    0 'VirMIDI 3-1     '
client 30: 'Virtual Raw MIDI 3-2' [type=kernel]
    0 'VirMIDI 3-2     '
client 31: 'Virtual Raw MIDI 3-3' [type=kernel]
    0 'VirMIDI 3-3     '
client 128: 'TiMidity' [type=user]
    0 'TiMidity port 0 '
    1 'TiMidity port 1 '
    2 'TiMidity port 2 '
    3 'TiMidity port 3 '
```

aconnect -i shows the virtual ports as follows:

```
$aconnect -i
client 0: 'System' [type=kernel]
    0 'Timer           '
    1 'Announce        '
client 14: 'Midi Through' [type=kernel]
    0 'Midi Through Port-0'
client 28: 'Virtual Raw MIDI 3-0' [type=kernel]
    0 'VirMIDI 3-0     '
client 29: 'Virtual Raw MIDI 3-1' [type=kernel]
    0 'VirMIDI 3-1     '
client 30: 'Virtual Raw MIDI 3-2' [type=kernel]
    0 'VirMIDI 3-2     '
client 31: 'Virtual Raw MIDI 3-3' [type=kernel]
    0 'VirMIDI 3-3     '
```

Virtual Raw MIDI 3-0 can then be connected to TiMidity port 0 with the following:

```
aconnect 28:0 128:0
```

Clients can then send MIDI messages to the raw MIDI device hw:3,0 and TiMidity will synthesize them. I used this in the previous chapter by showing how to replace the default Java synthesizer with TiMidity.

Turning Off All Notes

If you have something playing out to a device or soft synth, then if that something gets interrupted, it may not finish playing cleanly. For example, it may have started a NOTE ON on some channel but because of the interrupt will not have sent a note off. The synthesizer will continue to play the note.

To stop it playing, use amidi to send "raw" MIDI commands. The hexadecimal sequence 00 B0 7B 00 will send "all notes off on channel 0." Similarly, the command 00 B1 7B 00 will send "all notes off on channel 1," and there are only 16 possible channels.

The relevant commands for a raw device on port hw:1,0 are as follows:

```
amidi -p hw:1,0 -S "00 B0 7B 00"
...
```

Conclusion

This chapter briefly discussed the MIDI models available under ALSA. While there is a substantial programming API behind this, you have mainly used the commands amidi, aplaymidi, and aconnect, and see the API using the seqdemo.c program.

CHAPTER 20

■ ■ ■

FluidSynth

FluidSynth is an application for playing MIDI files and a library for MIDI applications.

Resources

Here are some resources:

- FluidSynth home page (http://sourceforge.net/apps/trac/fluidsynth/)

- FluidSynth download page (http://sourceforge.net/projects/fluidsynth/)

- FluidSynth 1.1 developer documentation (http://fluidsynth.sourceforge.net/api/)

- Sourcearchive.com fluidsynth documentation
  (http://fluidsynth.sourcearchive.com/documentation/1.1.5-1/main.html)

Players

fluidsynth is a command-line MIDI player. It runs under ALSA with a command line, like so:

```
fluidsynth -a alsa -l <soundfont> <files...>
```

A commonly used sound font is /usr/share/sounds/sf2/FluidR3_GM.sf2.
Qsynth is a GUI interface to fluidsynth. It looks like Figure 20-1.

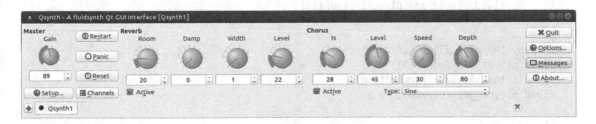

Figure 20-1. *Qsynth*

© Jan Newmarch 2017
J. Newmarch, *Linux Sound Programming*, DOI 10.1007/978-1-4842-2496-0_20

Play MIDI Files

The FluidSynth API consists of the following:

- A sequencer created using new_fluid_player

- A synthesizer created using new_fluid_synth

- An audio player created using new_fluid_audio_driver, which runs in a separate thread

- A "settings" object that can be used to control many features of the other components, created by new_fluid_settings and modified by calls such as fluid_settings_setstr

A typical program to play a sequence of MIDI files using ALSA follows. It creates the various objects, sets the audio player to use ALSA, and then adds each sound font and MIDI file to the player. The call to fluid_player_play then plays each MIDI file in turn.

```
#include <fluidsynth.h>
#include <fluid_midi.h>

int main(int argc, char** argv)
{
    int i;
    fluid_settings_t* settings;
    fluid_synth_t* synth;
    fluid_player_t* player;
    fluid_audio_driver_t* adriver;

    settings = new_fluid_settings();
    fluid_settings_setstr(settings, "audio.driver", "alsa");
    synth = new_fluid_synth(settings);
    player = new_fluid_player(synth);

    adriver = new_fluid_audio_driver(settings, synth);
    /* process command line arguments */
    for (i = 1; i < argc; i++) {
        if (fluid_is_soundfont(argv[i])) {
            fluid_synth_sfload(synth, argv[1], 1);
        } else {
            fluid_player_add(player, argv[i]);
        }
    }
    /* play the midi files, if any */
    fluid_player_play(player);
    /* wait for playback termination */
    fluid_player_join(player);
```

```
    /* cleanup */
    delete_fluid_audio_driver(adriver);
    delete_fluid_player(player);
    delete_fluid_synth(synth);
    delete_fluid_settings(settings);
    return 0;
}
```

Python

pyFluidSynth is a Python binding to FluidSynth that allows you to send MIDI commands to FluidSynth.

Conclusion

This chapter has briefly discussed the programming model and API for FluidSynth.

## CHAPTER 21

TiMidity

TiMidity is designed as a stand-alone application. To add to this, you should build a new "interface." It can also be subverted to act as though it is a library that can be called. This chapter explains both ways.

TiMidity Design

TiMidity is designed as a stand-alone application. When it's built, you get a single executable but do not get a library of functions that can be called, unlike FluidSynth, for example.

What you *can* do with TiMidity is to add different interfaces. For example, there are ncurses, Xaw, and dumb interfaces that can be invoked at runtime with the following, for example:

```
timidity -in ...
timidity -ia ...
timidity -id ...
```

There are also others with more specialized uses such as WRD, emacs, ALSA, and remote interfaces. For example, the Xaw interface looks like Figure 21-1.

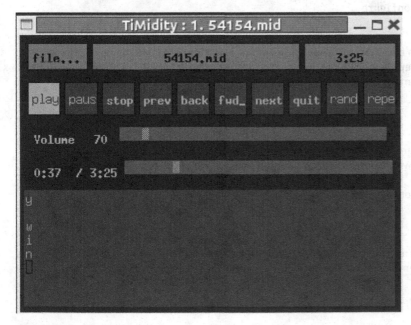

Figure 21-1. TiMidity with Xaw interface

© Jan Newmarch 2017

J. Newmarch, *Linux Sound Programming*, DOI 10.1007/978-1-4842-2496-0_21

The idea seems to be that if you want something extra, perhaps you should build a custom interface and drive it from TiMidity.

That doesn't always suit me, as I would prefer to be able to embed TiMidity into my own applications in a simple way. The rest of this chapter looks at both ways.

- Turning TiMidity into a library and including it in your own code
- Building your own interface

Turning TiMidity into a Library

TiMidity is not designed as a library, so you have to convince it otherwise. That isn't hard; you just have to mess around with the build system.

Managed Environments Hook

A system whereby the application is in control doesn't work so well in a managed environment such as Windows (or probably the many more recent ones such as Android). In such environments you can't call TiMidity's main but rather the main function belonging to the framework. This in turn will call an appropriate function in the application.

To make use of such hooks, you need to download the source code of TiMidity, either from a package manager or from the TiMidity++ site (http://timidity.sourceforge.net/).

For TiMidity, the variations on the main function are in the file timidity/timidity.c. Controlled by various defines, you can have main or win_main. One of the more interesting defines is ANOTHER_MAIN. If this is defined, none of the versions of the main function is compiled, and you end with main-free object modules.

If you build TiMidity from the top-level source directory in the following way, it will produce an error that the main function is not defined:

```
CFLAGS="-DANOTHER_MAIN" ./configure
make
```

That's the hook you need to take TiMidity from being a stand-alone application to being able to be called as a library from another application. Note that you *cannot* just remove timidity/timidity.c from the build. That file contains too many other critical functions!

Building the Library

To build TiMidity as a static library, remove the main function as shown earlier and attempt to build TiMidity. I found I needed to also specify which output system I wanted to use, such as ALSA.

```
CFLAGS="-DANOTHER_MAIN" ./configure --enable-audio=alsa
nake clean
make
```

This builds several .ar files and lots of object .o modules but fails to build the final timidity executable as (of course) there is no main function. It also leaves a bunch of unlinked files in the timidity subdirectory.

You can collect all the object modules into an archive file by running this from the top of the TiMidity source directory:

```
ar cru  libtimidity.a */*.o
ranlib libtimidity.a
```

Since you will have to build TiMidity from the source, check that it is working in normal mode before you try to build this alternative library version. That way, you can find out that you need, say, the libasound-dev library in order to use ALSA, before you get mixed up in this other stuff!

Library Entry Points

TiMidity built with ANOTHER_MAIN exposes these public entry points:

```
void timidity_start_initialize(void);
int timidity_pre_load_configuration(void);
int timidity_post_load_configuration(void);
void timidity_init_player(void);
int timidity_play_main(int nfiles, char **files);
int got_a_configuration;
```

They do not seem to be defined in any convenient header file.

A Minimal Application

The real TiMidity application is coded to work on many different operating systems with many different versions of libraries. Most of those dependencies are taken care of in building the object files and library, as shown earlier.

A minimal application just wraps your own main around the library entry points in my_main.c.

```
#include <stdio.h>

extern void timidity_start_initialize(void);
extern int timidity_pre_load_configuration(void);
extern int timidity_post_load_configuration(void);
extern void timidity_init_player(void);
extern int timidity_play_main(int nfiles, char **files);
extern int got_a_configuration;

int main(int argc, char **argv)
{
    int err, main_ret;

    timidity_start_initialize();

    if ((err = timidity_pre_load_configuration()) != 0)
        return err;
```

```
    err += timidity_post_load_configuration();

    if (err) {
        printf("couldn't load configuration file\n");
        exit(1);
    }

    timidity_init_player();

    main_ret = timidity_play_main(argc, argv);

    return main_ret;
}
```

The `compile` command needs to bring in the TiMidity library and any other required library and is for an ALSA application.

```
my_timidity: my_main.o
        gcc -g -o my_timidity my_main.o libtimidity.a  -lasound -lm
```

Playing a Background Video to a MIDI File

As a more complex example, let's look at playing a video file while also playing a MIDI file. Assume that the video file has no audio component and there is no attempt to perform any synchronization between the two streams—that is an extra order of complexity!

To play a video file, you can use the FFmpeg library to decode a video stream into video frames. You then need to display the frames in some kind of GUI object, and there are many toolkits for doing this. I've chosen the Gtk toolkit as it underlies Gnome, is in C, supports many other things such as i18n, and so on. I've based my code on "An ffmpeg and SDL Tutorial" (http://dranger.com/ffmpeg/) by Stephen Dranger, which uses the SDL toolkit for display.

This runs the video and the MIDI in separate threads using the `pthreads` package. I've cheated a bit by hard-coding the names of the files and fixing the size of the video frames. It was a real bummer getting it to work under Gtk 3.0 as that has removed pixmaps and it took too, too long to find out what was going on.

I've split the code into two files, one to play the video using Gtk and the other to play the TiMidity library and invoke the video. The video-playing file is `video_code.c`. The code is omitted here as it is essentially the code described in Chapter 15.

The file `video_player.c` sets up the TiMidity environment, calls the video to play in the background, and then calls `play_midi`. It is as follows:

```
#include <string.h>
#include <pthread.h>
#include <stdio.h>
#include <stdlib.h>

void timidity_start_initialize(void);
int timidity_pre_load_configuration(void);
int timidity_post_load_configuration(void);
void timidity_init_player(void);
```

```
void *init_gtk(void *args);
void init_ffmpeg();

#define MIDI_FILE "54154.mid"

static void *play_midi(void *args) {
    char *argv[1];
    argv[0] = MIDI_FILE;
    int argc = 1;

    timidity_play_main(argc, argv);

    printf("Audio finished\n");
    exit(0);
}

int main(int argc, char** argv)
{

    int i;

    /* Timidity stuff */
    int err;

    timidity_start_initialize();
    if ((err = timidity_pre_load_configuration()) == 0) {
        err = timidity_post_load_configuration();
    }
    if (err) {
        printf("couldn't load configuration file\n");
        exit(1);
    }

    timidity_init_player();

    init_ffmpeg();
    pthread_t tid_gtk;
    pthread_create(&tid_gtk, NULL, init_gtk, NULL);

    play_midi(NULL);
    return 0;
}
```

Building a New Interface

The previous section played the MIDI and also a background video essentially as separate applications, as separate noninteracting threads. TiMidity allows a greater integration of a user interface that can be added dynamically to TiMidity.

Shared Objects

You can build your own interfaces and add them to TiMidity without changing or recompiling TiMidity. Such interfaces are built as dynamically loadable shared libraries and are loaded when TiMidity starts.

You have to be a little careful with compile and link flags to build these libraries (see "Building shared objects in Linux" at http://stackoverflow.com/questions/7252550/loadable-bash-builtin). To build the shared object if_my_interface.so from my_interface.c, I use the following:

```
gcc  -fPIC $(CFLAGS) -c -o my_interface.o my_interface.c
gcc -shared -o if_my_interface.so my_interface.o
```

TiMidity will only load files that begin with if_. They can reside in any directory, with the default being something like /usr/lib/timidity or /usr/local/lib/timidity (see the "supported dynamic load interfaces" directory from timidity -h).

The default directory to load dynamic modules can be overridden with the option -d, as follows:

```
timidity -d. -im --trace 54154.mid
```

Entry Point

Each interface must have a unique function that can be called by the dynamic loader. Recall that interfaces are selected with the command-line option -i, such as timidity -iT ..., to choose the VT100 interface. Your interface must have a single ASCII letter identifier that isn't used by any other interface, say m for "my interface." The loader will then look for a function, as shown next, where the m in the function name is the identifier:

```
ControlMode *interface_m_loader(void)
```

This function is simple: it just returns the address of a structure of type ControlMode that is defined elsewhere in the interface's code.

```
ControlMode *interface_m_loader(void)
{
    return &ctl;
}
```

ControlMode

The ControlMode structure is as follows:

```
typedef struct {
  char *id_name, id_character;
  char *id_short_name;
  int verbosity, trace_playing, opened;

  int32 flags;

  int  (*open)(int using_stdin, int using_stdout);
  void (*close)(void);
  int (*pass_playing_list)(int number_of_files, char *list_of_files[]);
  int  (*read)(int32 *valp);
  int  (*write)(char *buf, int32 size);
  int  (*cmsg)(int type, int verbosity_level, char *fmt, ...);
  void (*event)(CtlEvent *ev);  /* Control events */
} ControlMode;
```

This defines information about the interface and a set of functions that are called by TiMidity in response to events and actions within TiMidity. For example, for "my interface" this structure is as follows:

```
ControlMode ctl=
    {
        "my interface", 'm',
        "my iface",
        1,          /* verbosity */
        0,          /* trace playing */
        0,          /* opened */
        0,          /* flags */
        ctl_open,
        ctl_close,
        pass_playing_list,
        ctl_read,
        NULL,       /* write */
        cmsg,
        ctl_event
    };
```

Some of these fields are obvious, but some are less so.

open

This is called to set which files are used for I/O.

close

This is called to close them.

pass_playing_list

This function is passed a list of files to play. The most likely action is to walk through this list, calling play_midi_file on each.

read

I'm not sure what this is for yet.

write

I'm not sure what this is for yet.

cmsg

This is called with information messages.

event

This is the major function for handling MIDI control events. Typically it will be a big switch for each type of control event.

Include Files

This is messy. A typical interface will need to know some of the constants and functions used by TiMidity. While these are organized logically for TiMidity, they are not organized conveniently for a new interface. So, you have to keep pulling in extra includes, which point to other externals, which require more includes, and so on. These may be in different directories such timidity and utils, so you have to point to many different include directories.

Note that you will need the TiMidity source code to get these include files; you can download them from SourceForge TiMidity++ (http://sourceforge.net/projects/timidity/?source=dlp).

My Simple Interface

This basically does the same as the "dumb" interface built into TiMidity. It is loaded from the current directory and invoked with the following:

```
timidity -im -d. 54154.mid
```

The code is in one file, my_interface.c.

There are two major functions in the following code, and the rest has been elided. The important functions are ctl_event and ctl_lyric. The function ctl_event handles events generated by TiMidity. For this interface, you just want to print lyrics as they play, so when a CTLE_LYRIC event occurs, call ctl_lyric. The ctl_lyric function looks up the lyric using the TiMidity function event2string and prints it to the output, printing newlines if needed according to the lyric text. The interface file is as follows:

```
/*
  my_interface.c
*/

#ifdef HAVE_CONFIG_H
#include "config.h"
#endif /* HAVE_CONFIG_H */
#include <stdio.h>
#include <stdlib.h>
#include <stdarg.h>
```

```c
#ifndef NO_STRING_H
#include <string.h>
#else
#include <strings.h>
#endif

#include "support.h"
#include "timidity.h"
#include "output.h"
#include "controls.h"
#include "instrum.h"
#include "playmidi.h"
#include "readmidi.h"

static int ctl_open(int using_stdin, int using_stdout);
static void ctl_close(void);
static int ctl_read(int32 *valp);
static int cmsg(int type, int verbosity_level, char *fmt, ...);
static void ctl_total_time(long tt);
static void ctl_file_name(char *name);
static void ctl_current_time(int ct);
static void ctl_lyric(int lyricid);
static void ctl_event(CtlEvent *e);
static int pass_playing_list(int number_of_files, char *list_of_files[]);

#define ctl karaoke_control_mode

ControlMode ctl=
    {
        "my interface", 'm',
        "my iface",
        1,              /* verbosity */
        0,              /* trace playing */
        0,              /* opened */
        0,              /* flags */
        ctl_open,
        ctl_close,
        pass_playing_list,
        ctl_read,
        NULL,           /* write */
        cmsg,
        ctl_event
    };

static FILE *outfp;
int karaoke_error_count;
static char *current_file;
struct midi_file_info *current_file_info;
```

```
static int pass_playing_list(int number_of_files, char *list_of_files[]) {
    int n;

    for (n = 0; n < number_of_files; n++) {
        printf("Playing list %s\n", list_of_files[n]);

        current_file = list_of_files[n];

        play_midi_file( list_of_files[n]);
    }
    return 0;
}

/*ARGSUSED*/
static int ctl_open(int using_stdin, int using_stdout)
{
    // sets output channel and prints info about the file

}

static void ctl_close(void)
{
    // close error channel

}

/*ARGSUSED*/
static int ctl_read(int32 *valp)
{
    return RC_NONE;
}

static int cmsg(int type, int verbosity_level, char *fmt, ...)
{
    // prints an error message

    return 0;
}

static void ctl_total_time(long tt)
{
    // counts playing time

}

static void ctl_file_name(char *name)
{
    // prints playing status

}
```

```
static void ctl_current_time(int secs)
{
    // keeps track of current time

}

static void ctl_lyric(int lyricid)
{
    char *lyric;

    current_file_info = get_midi_file_info(current_file, 1);

    lyric = event2string(lyricid);
    if(lyric != NULL)
        {
            if(lyric[0] == ME_KARAOKE_LYRIC)
                {
                    if(lyric[1] == '/' || lyric[1] == '\\')
                        {
                            fprintf(outfp, "\n%s", lyric + 2);
                            fflush(outfp);
                        }
                    else if(lyric[1] == '@')
                        {
                            if(lyric[2] == 'L')
                                fprintf(outfp, "\nLanguage: %s\n", lyric + 3);
                            else if(lyric[2] == 'T')
                                fprintf(outfp, "Title: %s\n", lyric + 3);
                            else
                                fprintf(outfp, "%s\n", lyric + 1);
                        }
                    else
                        {
                            fputs(lyric + 1, outfp);
                            fflush(outfp);
                        }
                }
            else
                {
                    if(lyric[0] == ME_CHORUS_TEXT || lyric[0] == ME_INSERT_TEXT)
                        fprintf(outfp, "\r");
                    fputs(lyric + 1, outfp);
                    fflush(outfp);
                }
        }
}
```

```
static void ctl_event(CtlEvent *e)
{
    switch(e->type)
        {
        case CTLE_NOW_LOADING:
            ctl_file_name((char *)e->v1);
            break;
        case CTLE_LOADING_DONE:
            // MIDI file is loaded, about to play
            current_file_info = get_midi_file_info(current_file, 1);
            if (current_file_info != NULL) {
                printf("file info not NULL\n");
            } else {
                printf("File info is NULL\n");
            }
            break;
        case CTLE_PLAY_START:

            ctl_total_time(e->v1);
            break;
        case CTLE_CURRENT_TIME:
            ctl_current_time((int)e->v1);
            break;
#ifndef CFG_FOR_SF
        case CTLE_LYRIC:
            ctl_lyric((int)e->v1);
            break;
#endif
        }
}

/*
 * interface_<id>_loader();
 */
ControlMode *interface_m_loader(void)
{
    return &ctl;
}
```

It is compiled to the interface file if_my_interface.so with the following:

```
gcc  -fPIC -c -o my_interface.o my_interface.c
gcc -shared  -o if_my_interface.so my_interface.o
```

Running My Simple Interface

When I tried to run the interface using the standard package TiMidity v2.13.2-40.1, it crashed in a memory-free call. The code is stripped, so tracking down why is not easy, and I haven't bothered to do so yet—I'm not sure what libraries, versions of code, and so on, the package distro was compiled against.

I had built my own copy of TiMidity from source. This worked fine. Note that when you build TiMidity from source, you need to specify that it can load dynamic modules, for example, with the following:

```
congfigure --enable-audio=alsa --enable-vt100 --enable-debug –enable-dynamic
```

With the source built in a sub-directory TiMidity++-2.14.0, playing using this interface is done by

```
TiMidity++-2.14.0/timidity/timidity -d. -im 54154.mid
```

Playing a Background Video to a MIDI File

You can take the code from playing a video given earlier and put it as the "back end" of a TiMidity system as a "video" interface. Essentially all that needs to be done is to change `ctl_open` from the simple interface to call the Gtk code to play the video and change the identity of the interface.

The new "video" interface is `video_player_interface.c`. The only essential change is to `ctl_open`, which now reads as follows:

```
extern void init_gtk(void *args);


/*ARGSUSED*/
static int ctl_open(int using_stdin, int using_stdout)
{

    outfp=stdout;
    ctl.opened=1;

    init_ffmpeg();

    /* start Gtk in its own thread */
    pthread_t tid_gtk;
    pthread_create(&tid_gtk, NULL, init_gtk, NULL);

    return 0;
}

if_video_player.so
```

The build command is as follows:

```
CFLAGS = -ITiMidity++-2.14.0/timidity -ITiMidity++-2.14.0 -ITiMidity++-2.14.0/utils  $(shell
pkg-config --cflags gtk+-3.0 libavformat libavcodec libswscale libavutil )

LIBS3 =  $(shell pkg-config --libs gtk+-3.0 libavformat libavcodec libswscale libavutil )

video_code.o: video_code.c
        gcc  -fPIC $(CFLAGS) -c -o video_code.o video_code.c

if_video_player.so: video_player_interface.c video_code.o
        gcc  -fPIC $(CFLAGS) -c -o video_player_interface.o video_player_interface.c
        gcc -shared -o if_video_player.so video_player_interface.o video_code.o \
        $(LIBS3)
```

It is run with the following:

```
TiMidity++-2.14.0/timidity/timidity -d. -iv
 54154.mid
```

Conclusion

TiMidity is not designed for use by other applications. Either you add a new interface or work around the TiMidity design to produce a library. This chapter has shown both mechanisms and illustrated them with simple and more complex examples.

CHAPTER 22

Overview of Karaoke Systems

This chapter gives a quick summary of the successive chapters.

The whole purpose of this book—from my point of view—is to document what is going on in Linux sound in my path to building a Linux karaoke system. This chapter looks at various explorations I have made using the material of previous chapters.

First, what are my goals?

- Be able to play KAR files (one of the possible karaoke file formats)

- Show the lyrics at least one line at a time, highlighting the characters when they should be sung

- For Chinese songs, show the Pinyin (English) form of the lyrics as well as the Chinese characters

- Play a movie in the background

- Display the melody in some form

- Show the notes actually sung against the melody

- Score the results in some way

Nothing I have yet done gets anywhere near these goals. Let me pick out the highlights of my explorations so far:

- The simplest "off-the-shelf" system is PyKaraoke, with kmid a close follower. These play KAR files and highlight the lyrics but no more.

- The simplest way to add microphone input to such a system is to use an external mixer. These can also do reverb and other effects.

- Jack and PulseAudio can trivially be used to add microphone input as play-through, but effects take more work.

- Java is really cool for nearly everything—except latency ruins it in the end.

- FluidSynth can be hacked to give hooks to hang Karaoke from. But it is CPU intensive and doesn't leave room for much other processing.

- TiMidity is a stand-alone system with configurable back ends. It can be configured to give a crude karaoke system. But it can be hacked to make it into a library, which gives it more potential. It is not as CPU intensive as FluidSynth.

© Jan Newmarch 2017
J. Newmarch, *Linux Sound Programming*, DOI 10.1007/978-1-4842-2496-0_22

- Playing a background movie can be done using FFmpeg and a GUI such as Gtk. Gtk also has the mechanisms for overlaying highlighted lyrics on top of the video, but Gtk 2 and Gtk 3 differ in the mechanism.

- TiMidity can be combined with FFmpeg and Gtk to display highlighted lyrics against a movie background.

- Scoring is still out of sight right now, although the Java library TarsosDSP can give lots of information.

The following chapters cover these topics:

User-level tools

> Karaoke is an "audience participation" sound system, in which the soundtrack and usually the melody are played along with a moving display of the lyrics. This chapter considers the features, formats, and user-level tools for playing karaoke.

Decoding the DKD files on the Songken Karaoke DVD

> This chapter is about getting the information off my Songken Karaoke DVD so that I can start writing programs to play the songs. It is not directly involved in playing sound under Linux and is given as an appendix.

Java Sound

> Java Sound has no direct support for karaoke. This chapter looks at how to combine the Java Sound libraries with other libraries such as Swing to give a karaoke player for MIDI files.

Subtitles

> Many karaoke systems use subtitles imposed over a movie of some kind. This chapter looks at how to do this with Linux systems. There are limited choices, but it is possible.

FluidSynth

> FluidSynth is an application for playing MIDI files and a library for MIDI applications. It does not have the hooks for playing karaoke files. This chapter discusses an extension to FluidSynth, which adds appropriate hooks and then uses these to build a variety of karaoke systems.

TiMidity

> TiMidity is designed as a stand-alone application with a particular kind of extensibility. Out of the box it can sort of play karaoke but not well. This chapter looks at how to work with TiMidity to build a karaoke system.

CHAPTER 23

■ ■ ■

Karaoke User-Level Tools

Karaoke is an "audience participation" sound system, in which the soundtrack and usually the melody are played along with a moving display of the lyrics. Within this, there can be variations or different features.

- The lyrics can be shown all at once, while the music plays in sequence.
- The lyrics can be highlighted in synchronization with the melody line.
- The melody line maybe will always play or can be switched off.
- Some players will also include a vocalist singing the song.
- Some players with vocals will turn off the vocals when someone is singing.
- Some players will give a graphical display of the notes of the melody.
- Some players will give a graphical display of the melody and also show the notes the singers are singing.
- Some players will produce scores based on some evaluation of the singer's accuracy. The basis of such scoring is usually not known.
- Some players allow you to change the playback speed and the playback pitch.
- Most players will accept two microphones and can have reverb effects added to the singer's voices.
- Many players will allow you to select songs in advance to build a dynamic playlist.

Karaoke is popular in Asia and has a following in European countries. Karaoke systems are believed to have originated in Asia, although the history according to Wikipedia (http://en.wikipedia.org/wiki/Karaoke) is a little muddy.

There are various file formats for karaoke described at www.karawin.fr/defenst.php. This chapter considers the features, formats, and user-level tools for playing karaoke.

Video CD Systems

Video CDs are an older form of video storage on an optical disc. The resolution is fairly low, typically 352×240 pixels, with a frame rate of 25 frames per second. Although they were used by a few movies, they have been supplanted for movies by DVDs. However, they were used extensively at one stage for karaoke discs.

The cheaper CD/DVD players from Asia often have microphone inputs and can be used as karaoke players with VCD discs. Typically files are simple movies in AVI or MPEG format, so you can just sing along. While the lyrics are usually displayed, highlighted in time to the melody, there are no advanced features such as scoring or a display of the melody.

If you have VCD discs, they can be mounted as IC9660 files on your computer, but on a Linux system you cannot directly extract the files. Players such as VLC, MPlayer, and Totem can play files from them.

You need to use something like vcdimager to extract files from a VCD disc. This may be in your package system, or you can download it from the GNU developer site (www.gnu.org/software/vcdimager/) and build it from source. The video files can then be extracted as MPEG or AVI files with the following:

```
vcdxrip --cdrom-device=/dev/cdrom --rip
```

(On my system I had to replace /dev/cdrom with /dev/sr1 as I could not extract from the default DVD player. I found out what device it was by running mount and then unmounted it with umount.)

CD+G Discs

According to Wikipedia's "CD+G" page (https://en.wikipedia.org/wiki/CD%2BG), "CD+G (also known as CD+Graphics) is an extension of the compact disc standard that can present low-resolution graphics alongside the audio data on the disc when played on a compatible device. CD+G discs are often used for karaoke machines, which utilize this functionality to present onscreen lyrics for the song contained on the disc."

Each song is composed of two files: an audio file and a video file containing the lyrics (and maybe some background scenes).

There are many discs that you can buy using this format. You can't play them directly on your computer. Rhythmbox will play the audio but not the video. VLC and Totem don't like them.

Ripping the files onto your computer for storage on your hard disk is not so straightforward. The audio discs do not have a file system in the normal sense. For example, you cannot mount them using the Unix mount command; they are not even in ISO format. Instead, you need to use a program like cdrdao to rip the files to a binary file and then work on that.

```
$ cdrdao read-cd --driver generic-mmc-raw --device /dev/cdroms/cdrom0 --read-subchan rw_raw mycd.toc
```

The previous code creates a data file and a table of contents file.

The format of the CDG files has not apparently been publically released but is described by Jim Bumgardner (back in 1995!) at "CD+G Revealed: Playing back Karaoke tracks in Software" (http://jbum.com/cdg_revealed.html).

Programs such as Sound Juicer will extract the audio tracks but leave the video behind.

MP3+G Files

MP3+G files are CD+G files adapted for use on a normal PC. They consist of an MP3 file containing the audio and a CDG file containing the lyrics. Frequently they are zipped together.

Many sites selling CD+G files also sell MP3+G files. Various sites give instructions on how to create your own MP3+G files. There are not many free sites.

The program cgdrip.py from cdgtools-0.3.2 can rip CD+G files from an audio disc and convert them to a pair of MP3+G files. The instructions from the (Python) source code are as follows:

```
# To start using cdgrip immediately, try the following from the
# command-line (replacing the --device option by the path to your
# CD device):
#
```

```
#   $ cdrdao read-cd --driver generic-mmc-raw --device /dev/cdroms/cdrom0 --read-subchan
    rw_raw mycd.toc
#   $ python cdgrip.py --with-cddb --delete-bin-toc mycd.toc
#
# You may need to use a different --driver option or --read-subchan mode
# to cdrdao depending on your CD device. For more in depth details, see
# the usage instructions below.
```

Buying CD+G or MP3+G Files

There are many sites selling CD+G and MP3+G songs. Just do a Google search. However, the average price per song is about $3, and if you want to build up a large collection, that can become expensive. Some sites will give discounts for larger volume purchases, but even at $30 for 100 songs, the expense can be high.

Sites with very large collections come and go. At the time of writing, aceume.com offers 14,000 English songs for US 399. But you could buy their AK3C Android All-in-one Cloud Karaoke Player with 21,000 English songs and 35,000 Chinese songs included for US 600. That makes the economics of building your own karaoke player become shakier. I will ignore that issue here—it's your choice!

Converting MP3+G to Video Files

The tool ffmpeg can merge the audio and video to a single video file with the following, for example:

```
ffmpeg -i Track1.cdg -i Track1.mp3 -y Track1.avi
```

Use the following to create an AVI file containing both video and audio:

```
avconv -i Track1.cdg -i Track1.mp3 test.avi
avconv -i test.avi -c:v libx264 -c:a copy outputfile.mp4
```

This can be played by VLC, MPlayer, Rhythmbox, and so on.

There is a program called cdg2video. It is last dated February 2011, and changes in the FFmpeg internals means that it no longer compiles. Even if you fix the obvious changes, there are a huge number of complaints from the C compiler about the use of deprecated FFmpeg functions.

MPEG-4 Files

It is becoming common to have karaoke systems using MPEG-4 video players. These embed all of the information into a video. There is no scoring system with players of these files.

Some rate them as much higher sound quality; see http://boards.straightdope.com/sdmb/showthread.php?t=83441, for example. I suggest it is more an issue with the synthesizer used than the format. Certainly high-end synthesizer manufacturers such as Yamaha would not agree!

MPEG-4 files are certainly larger than the corresponding MIDI files, and you will need a substantial disk to hold many of them.

There are many sites selling MP4 songs. Just do a Google search. However, the average price per song is about $3, and if you want to build up a large collection, that can become very expensive.

At the time of writing, there doesn't seem to be a site selling large volumes of MPEG-4 songs. However, there have been in the past and may be in the future.

Karaoke Machines

There are many karaoke machines that come with a DVD. In most cases, the songs are stored as MIDI files, with the song track in one MIDI file and the lyrics in another. Some more recent systems will use WMA files for the soundtrack, and this allows one track to have a vocal supplied and the other without the vocal. Such systems will usually include a scoring mechanism, although the basis for the scoring is not made explicit. The most recent ones are hard-disk-based, usually with MP4 files. They do not seem to have a scoring system. The suppliers of these systems change regularly, even if the systems themselves are only re-badged. I own systems by Malata and Sonken, but they were purchased many years ago. I'm not convinced that more recent models are necessarily improvements.

The two systems I own show different characteristics. The Sonken MD-388[1] plays songs from multiple languages, such as Chinese, Korean, English, and so on. My wife is Chinese, but I cannot read Chinese characters. There is an Anglicized script called *PinYin*, and the Sonken shows both the Chinese characters and the PinYin, so I can sing along too. It looks like Figure 23-1.

Figure 23-1. *Screen dump of Sonken player*

---

[1]This is no longer sold by Sonken. However, there are similar models sold under different brand names.

The Malata MDVD-6619[2] does not show the PinYin when playing Chinese songs. But it does show the notes you are supposed to be singing and the notes you are actually singing. Figure 23-2 shows that I am way off-key.

Figure 23-2. *Screen dump of Malata player*

MIDI Players

Karaoke files in MIDI format can be found from several sites, usually ending in .kar. Any MIDI player such as TiMidity can play such files. However, they do not always show the lyrics synchronized to the melody.

Finding MIDI Files

There are several sites on the Web offering files in MIDI format.

- MIDIZone (www.free-midi.org/)
- midiworld (www.midiworld.com/)
- CoolMIDI (www.cool-midi.com/)
- ElectroFresh (http://electrofresh.com/)

---

[2]Newer models are sold in China but currently with a very limited English repertoire.

- Freemidi (http://freemidi.org/)

- Karaoke Version (www.karaoke-version.com/)—for example, "House of the Rising Sun" melody on track 4

- MIDaoke (www.midaoke.com/)—for example, Pink Floyd's "Wish You Were Here" melody on track 2

- Home Musician (http://karaoke.homemusician.net/)—for example, the Eagles' "Hotel California" has the melody labeled "Melody" on Clarinet on track 4

KAR File Format

There is no formal standard for karaoke MIDI files. There is a widely accepted industry format called the MIDI Karaoke Type 1 file format.

The following is from MIDI karaoke FAQ (http://gnese.free.fr/Projects/KaraokeTime/Fichiers/karfaq.html):

> *What is the MIDI Karaoke Type 1 (.KAR) file format?* A MIDI karaoke file is a standard MIDI file type 1 that contains a separate track with lyrics of the song entered as text events. Load one of the MIDI karaoke files into a sequencer to examine the contents of the tracks of the file. The first track contains text events that are used to make the file recognizable as the MIDI karaoke file. The @KMIDI KARAOKE FILE text event is used for that purpose. The optional text event @V0100 denotes the format version number. Anything starting with @I is any information you want to include in the file.
>
> The second track contains the text meta events for the lyrics of the song. The first event is @LENGL. It identifies the language of the song, in this case, English. The next couple of events start with @T, which identifies the title of the songs. You can have up to three events like these. The first event should contain the title of the song. Some programs (such as Soft Karaoke) read this event to get the name of the song to be displayed in the File Open dialog box. The second event usually contains the performer or author of the song. The third event can contain any copyright information or anything else.
>
> The rest of the second track contains the words of the song. Each event is the syllable that is supposed to be sung at the time of the event. If the text starts with \, it means to clear the screen and show the words at the top of the screen. If the text starts with /, it means to go to the next line.
>
> Important note: There can be only three lines per screen in a .kar file for Soft Karaoke to play the file correctly. In other words, there can be only two forward slashes beginning each line in a line of lyrics. The next line has to start with a back slash.

There are several weaknesses in this format, listed here:

- The list of possible languages is not specified, only English.

- The encoding of text is not specified (for example, Unicode UTF-8).

- There is no means of identifying the channel carrying the melody.

PyKaraoke

PyKaraoke is a dedicated karaoke player written in Python, using a variety of libraries such as Pygame and WxPython. It plays the song and shows where in the lyrics you are. A screen dump of "Smoke Gets in Your Eyes" (www.midikaraoke.com/cgi-bin/songdir/jump.cgi?ID=1280) looks like Figure 23-3.

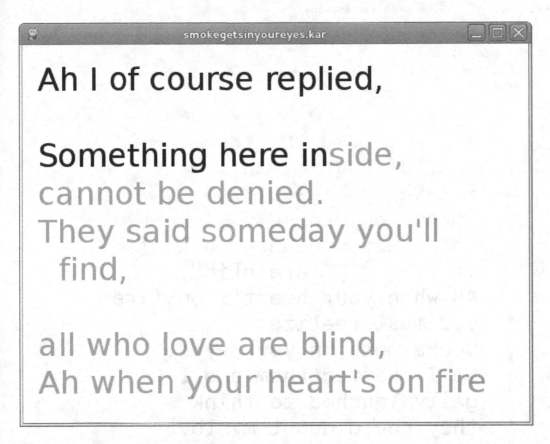

Figure 23-3. *Screen dump of PyKaraoke*

PyKaraoke plays the soundtrack and displays the lyrics. It does not act as a proper karaoke system by also playing the singer's input. But PyKaraoke uses the PulseAudio system, so you can simultaneously play other programs. In particular, you can have PyKaraoke running in one window, while pa-mic-2-speaker is running in another. PulseAudio will mix the two output streams and play both sources together. Of course, there will no scoring possible in such a system without extra work.

kmid[3]

kmid is a KDE-based karaoke player. It plays the song and shows where in the lyrics you are. A screen dump of "Smoke Gets in Your Eyes" looks like Figure 23-4.

---

[3]kmid seems to have disappeared from current KDE versions. This is a real shame since it was very good.

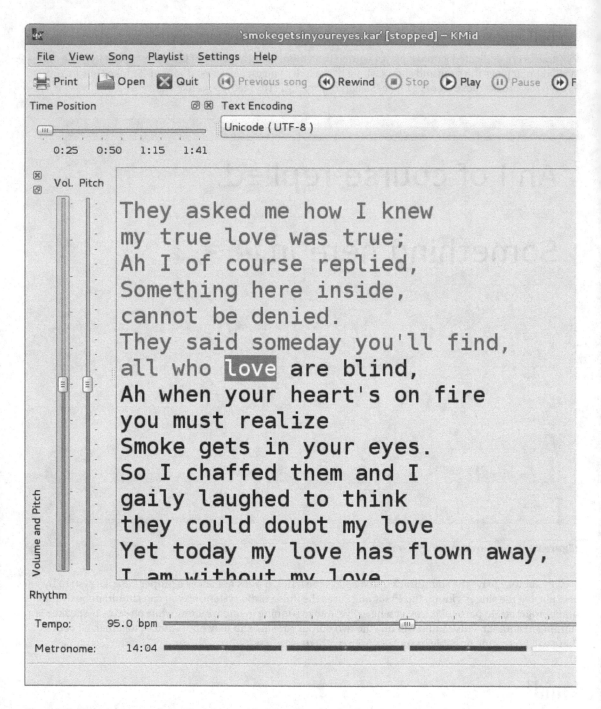

Figure 23-4. kmid *screen dump.* kmid *uses either TiMidity or FluidSynth as a MIDI back end.*

kmid plays the soundtrack and displays the lyrics. It does not act as a proper karaoke system by also playing the singer's input. But kmid can use the PulseAudio system, so you can simultaneously play other programs. In particular, you can have kmid running in one window, while pa-mic-2-speaker is running in another. PulseAudio will mix the two output streams and play both sources together. Of course, there will no scoring possible in such a system without extra work.

Microphone Inputs and Reverb Effects

Nearly all PCs and laptops have a sound card to play audio. While nearly all of these also have a microphone input, some do not. For example, my Dell laptop does not, the Raspberry Pi does not, and many Android TV media boxes do not.

Those computers without microphone inputs often have USB ports. They will usually accept USB sound cards, and if the USB has a microphone input, then that is recognized.

If you want to support two or more microphones, then you will need the corresponding number of sound cards or a mixer device. I have seen the Behringer MX-400 MicroMix, a four-channel compact low-noise mixer, for $20, or you can find circuit diagrams on electronics sites (Google *circuit diagram for audio mixer*).

Reverb is an effect that gives a fuller "body" to the voice by adding (artificial) echoes with different delays. Behringer also makes the MIX800 MiniMix, which can mix two microphones with reverb effects and also has a pass-through for line input (so you can play the music and control the microphones). (I have no links to Behringer.) A similar unit is the UNIFY K9 Reverb Computer Karaoke Mixer.

DVD players from China often have dual microphone inputs with mix and reverb capabilities. Given that they can cost as little as $13. Admittedly, for 1,000 units, it shows that mixing and reverb should not be too costly. My guess is that they use something like the Mitsubishi M65845AFP (www.datasheetcatalog.org/datasheet/MitsubishiElectricCorporation/mXuuvys.pdf), "DIGITAL ECHO WITH MICROPHONE MIXING CIRCUIT." The data sheet shows a number of possible configurations, for those who like to build their own.

Conclusion

There are a variety of karaoke systems, using VCD discs or dedicated systems. MIDI format karaoke files can be played using ordinary MIDI software, and there are a couple of Linux karaoke players.

CHAPTER 24

■ ■ ■

MP3+G

This chapter explores using karaoke files in MP3+G format. Files are pulled off a server to a (small) computer attached to a display device (my TV). Files are chosen using a Java Swing application running on Linux or Windows.

In Chapter 23, I discussed the MP3+G format for karaoke. Each "song" consists of two files: an MP3 file for the audio and a low-quality CDG file for the video (mainly the lyrics). Often these two files are zipped together.

Files can be extracted from CDG karaoke discs by using `cdrdao` and `cdgrip.py`. They can be played by VLC when given the MP3 file as an argument. It will pick up the CDG file from the same directory.

Many people will have built up a sizeable collection of MP3+G songs. In this chapter, you will consider how to list and play them, along with keeping lists of favorite songs. The chapter looks at a Java application to perform this and is really just standard Swing programming. There are no special audio or karaoke features considered in this chapter.

I keep my files on a server. I can access them in many ways on the other computers in the house: Samba shares, HTTP downloads, SSH file system (`sshfs`), and so on. Some mechanisms are less portable than others; for example, `sshfs` is not a standard Windows application, and SMB/Samba is not a standard Android client. So, after getting everything working using `sshfs` (a no-brainer under standard Linux), I then converted the applications to HTTP access. This has its own wrinkles.

The environment looks like Figure 24-1.

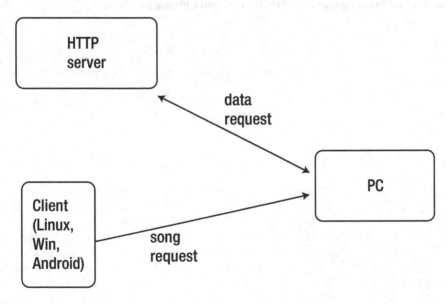

Figure 24-1. *Client requesting songs on an HTTP server to play on PC*

© Jan Newmarch 2017
J. Newmarch, *Linux Sound Programming*, DOI 10.1007/978-1-4842-2496-0_24

The Java client application for Linux and Windows looks like Figure 24-2.

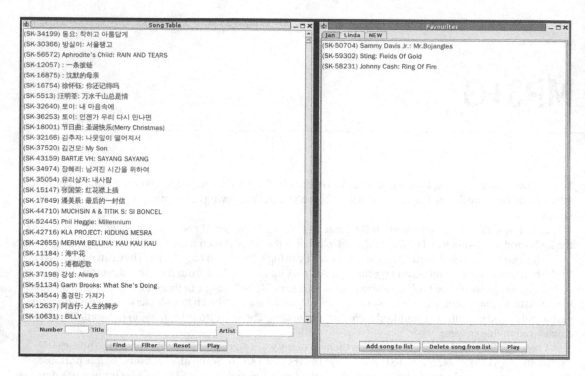

Figure 24-2. *User interface on client*

This shows the main window of songs and on its right the favorites window for two people, Jan and Linda. The application handles multiple languages; English, Korean, and Chinese are shown.

Filters can be applied to the main song list. For example, filtering on the singer Sting gives Figure 24-3.

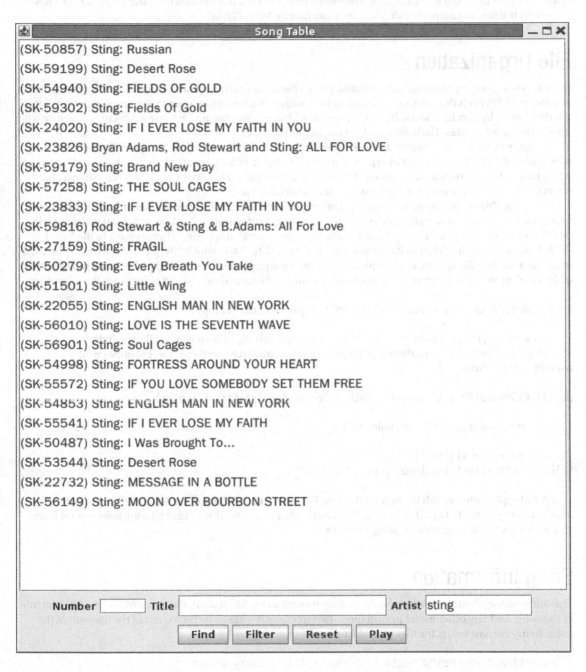

Figure 24-3. Songs by Sting

When Play is clicked, information about the selection is sent to the media player, currently a CubieBoard2 connected to my HiFi/TV. The media computer fetches the files from the HTTP server. Files are played on the media computer using VLC as it can handle MP3+G files.

File Organization

If MP3+G songs are ripped from CDG karaoke discs, then a natural organization would be to store the files in directories, with each directory corresponding to one disc. You could give even more structure by grouping the directories by common artist, by style of music, and so on. You can just assume a directory structure with music files as leaf nodes. These files are kept on the HTTP server.

I currently have a large number of these files on my server. Information about these files needs to be supplied to the clients. After a bit of experimentation, a Vector of SongInformation is created and serialized using Java's object serialization methods. The serialized file is also kept on the HTTP server. When a client starts up, it gets this file from the HTTP server and deserializes it.

Building this vector means walking the directory tree on the HTTP server and recording information as it goes. The Java code to walk directory trees is fairly straightforward. It is a little tedious if you want it to be OS independent, but Java 1.7 introduced mechanisms to make this easier. These belong to the New I/O (NIO.2) system. The first class of importance is java.nio.file.Path, which "[is] an object that may be used to locate a file in a file system. It will typically represent a system-dependent file path." A string representing a file location in, say, a Linux or a Windows file system can be turned into a Path object with the following:

```
Path startingDir = FileSystems.getDefault().getPath(dirString);
```

Traversing a file system from a given path is done by walking a file tree and calling a node "visitor" at each point. The visitor is a subclass of SimpleFileVisitor<Path>, and only for leaf nodes would you override the method.

```
public FileVisitResult visitFile(Path file, BasicFileAttributes attr)
```

The traversal is done with the following:

```
Visitor pf = new Visitor();
Files.walkFileTree(startingDir, pf);
```

A full explanation of this is given on the Java Tutorials site in "Walking the File Tree" (http://docs.oracle.com/javase/tutorial/essential/io/walk.html). You use this to load all song information from disc into a vector of song paths in SongTable.java.

Song Information

The information about each song should include its path in the file system, the name of the artist(s), the title of the song, and any other useful information. This information has to be pulled out of the file path of the song. In my current setup, the files look like this:

```
/server/KARAOKE/Sonken/SK-50154 - Crosby, Stills - Carry On.mp3
```

Each song has a reasonably unique identifier (SK-50154), a unique path, and an artist and title. Reasonably straightforward pattern matching code can extract these parts, as shown here:

```
Path file = ...
String fname = file.getFileName().toString();
if (fname.endsWith(".zip") ||
    fname.endsWith(".mp3")) {
    String root = fname.substring(0, fname.length()-4);
    String parts[] = root.split(" - ", 3);
    if (parts.length != 3)
        return;

        String index = parts[0];
        String artist = parts[1];
        String title = parts[2];

        SongInformation info = new SongInformation(file,
                                        index,
                                        title,
                                        artist);
```

(The patterns produced by cdrip.py are not quite the same, but the code is easily changed.)

The SongInformation class captures this information and also includes methods for pattern matching of a string against the various fields. For example, to check whether a title matches, use this:

```
public boolean titleMatch(String pattern) {
    return title.matches("(?i).*" + pattern + ".*");
}
```

This gives a case-independent match using Java regular expression support. See "Java Regex Tutorial" (www.vogella.com/articles/JavaRegularExpressions/article.html) by Lars Vogel for more details.

The following is the complete SongInformation file:

```
import java.nio.file.Path;
import java.io.Serializable;

public class SongInformation implements Serializable {

    // Public fields of each song record

    public String path;

    public String index;

    /**
     * song title in Unicode
     */
    public String title;
```

```java
    /**
     * artist in Unicode
     */
    public String artist;

    public SongInformation(Path path,
                           String index,
                           String title,
                           String artist) {
        this.path = path.toString();
        this.index = index;
        this.title = title;
        this.artist = artist;
    }

    public String toString() {
        return "(" + index + ") " + artist + ": " + title;
    }

    public boolean titleMatch(String pattern) {
        return title.matches("(?i).*" + pattern + ".*");
    }

    public boolean artistMatch(String pattern) {
        return artist.matches("(?i).*" + pattern + ".*");
    }

    public boolean numberMatch(String pattern) {
        return index.equals(pattern);
    }
}
```

Song Table

The SongTable builds up a vector of SongInformation objects by traversing the file tree.

If there are many songs (say, in the thousands), this can lead to a slow startup time. To reduce this, once a table is loaded, it is saved to disk as a persistent object by writing it to an ObjectOutputStream. The next time the program is started, an attempt is made to read it back from this using an ObjectInputStream. Note that you do *not* use the Java Persistence API (http://en.wikibooks.org/wiki/Java_Persistence/What_is_Java_persistence%3F). Designed for J2EE, it is too heavyweight for our purposes here.

The SongTable also includes code to build smaller song tables based on matches between patterns and the title (or artist or number). It can search for matches between a pattern and a song and build a new table based on the matches. It contains a pointer to the original table for restoration later. This allows searches for patterns to use the same data structure.

The code for SongTable is as follows:

```java
import java.util.Vector;
import java.io.FileInputStream;
import java.io.*;
import java.nio.charset.Charset;
import java.nio.file.Files;
import java.nio.file.Path;
import java.nio.file.Paths;
import java.nio.file.SimpleFileVisitor;
import java.nio.file.FileVisitResult;
import java.nio.file.FileSystems;
import java.nio.file.attribute.*;

class Visitor
    extends SimpleFileVisitor<Path> {

    private Vector<SongInformation> songs;

    public Visitor(Vector<SongInformation> songs) {
        this.songs = songs;
    }

    @Override
    public FileVisitResult visitFile(Path file,
                                BasicFileAttributes attr) {
        if (attr.isRegularFile()) {
            String fname = file.getFileName().toString();
            //System.out.println("Regular file " + fname);
            if (fname.endsWith(".zip") ||
                fname.endsWith(".mp3") ||
                fname.endsWith(".kar")) {
                String root = fname.substring(0, fname.length()-4);
                //System.err.println(" root " + root);
                String parts[] = root.split(" - ", 3);
                if (parts.length != 3)
                    return java.nio.file.FileVisitResult.CONTINUE;

                String index = parts[0];
                String artist = parts[1];
                String title = parts[2];

                SongInformation info = new SongInformation(file,
                                                    index,
                                                    title,
                                                    artist);
                songs.add(info);
            }
        }

        return java.nio.file.FileVisitResult.CONTINUE;
    }
}
```

```java
public class SongTable {

    private static final String SONG_INFO_ROOT = "/server/KARAOKE/KARAOKE/";

    private static Vector<SongInformation> allSongs;

    public Vector<SongInformation> songs =
        new Vector<SongInformation>  ();

    public static long[] langCount = new long[0x23];

    public SongTable(Vector<SongInformation> songs) {
        this.songs = songs;
    }

    public SongTable(String[] args) throws java.io.IOException,
                                     java.io.FileNotFoundException {
        if (args.length >= 1) {
            System.err.println("Loading from " + args[0]);
            loadTableFromSource(args[0]);
            saveTableToStore();
        } else {
            loadTableFromStore();
        }
    }

    private boolean loadTableFromStore() {
        try {
            File storeFile = new File("/server/KARAOKE/SongStore");
            FileInputStream in = new FileInputStream(storeFile);
            ObjectInputStream is = new ObjectInputStream(in);
            songs = (Vector<SongInformation>) is.readObject();
            in.close();
        } catch(Exception e) {
            System.err.println("Can't load store file " + e.toString());
            return false;
        }
        return true;
    }

    private void saveTableToStore() {
        try {
            File storeFile = new File("/server/KARAOKE/SongStore");
            FileOutputStream out = new FileOutputStream(storeFile);
            ObjectOutputStream os = new ObjectOutputStream(out);
            os.writeObject(songs);
            os.flush();
            out.close();
        } catch(Exception e) {
            System.err.println("Can't save store file " + e.toString());
        }
    }
```

```
private void loadTableFromSource(String dir) throws java.io.IOException,
                          java.io.FileNotFoundException {

    Path startingDir = FileSystems.getDefault().getPath(dir);
    Visitor pf = new Visitor(songs);
    Files.walkFileTree(startingDir, pf);
}

public java.util.Iterator<SongInformation> iterator() {
    return songs.iterator();
}

public SongTable titleMatches( String pattern) {
    Vector<SongInformation> matchSongs =
        new Vector<SongInformation> ();

    for (SongInformation song: songs) {
        if (song.titleMatch(pattern)) {
            matchSongs.add(song);
        }
    }
    return new SongTable(matchSongs);
}

public SongTable artistMatches( String pattern) {
    Vector<SongInformation> matchSongs =
        new Vector<SongInformation> ();

    for (SongInformation song: songs) {
        if (song.artistMatch(pattern)) {
            matchSongs.add(song);
        }
    }
    return new SongTable(matchSongs);
}

public SongTable numberMatches( String pattern) {
    Vector<SongInformation> matchSongs =
        new Vector<SongInformation> ();

    for (SongInformation song: songs) {
        if (song.numberMatch(pattern)) {
            matchSongs.add(song);
        }
    }
    return new SongTable(matchSongs);
}
```

```
    public String toString() {
        StringBuffer buf = new StringBuffer();
        for (SongInformation song: songs) {
            buf.append(song.toString() + "\n");
        }
        return buf.toString();
    }

    public static void main(String[] args) {
        // for testing
        SongTable songs = null;
        try {
            songs = new SongTable(new String[] {SONG_INFO_ROOT});
        } catch(Exception e) {
            System.err.println(e.toString());
            System.exit(1);
        }

        System.out.println(songs.artistMatches("Tom Jones").toString());

        System.exit(0);
    }
}
```

Favorites

I've built this system for my home environment system, and I have a regular group of friends visit. We each have our favorite songs to sing, so we have made up lists on scraps of paper that get lost, have wine spilled on them, and so on. So, this system includes a favorites list of songs.

Each favorites list is essentially just another SongTable. But I have put a JList around the table to display it. The JList uses a DefaultListModel, and the constructor loads a song table into this list by iterating through the table and adding elements.

```
        int n = 0;
        java.util.Iterator<SongInformation> iter = favouriteSongs.iterator();
        while(iter.hasNext()) {
            model.add(n++, iter.next());
        }
```

Other Swing code adds three buttons along the bottom:

- Add song to list

- Delete song from list

- Play song

Adding a song to the list means taking the selected item from the main song table and adding it to this table. The main table is passed into the constructor and just kept for the purpose of getting its selection. The selected object is added to both the Swing JList and to the favorites SongTable.

Playing a song is done in a simple way: the full path to the song is written to standard output, newline terminated. Another program in a pipeline can then pick this up; this is covered later in the chapter.

Favorites aren't much good if they don't persist from one day to the next! So, the same object storage method as before is used as with the full song table. Each favorites file is saved on each change to the server.

The following is the code for Favourites:

```java
import java.awt.*;
import java.awt.event.*;
import javax.swing.event.*;
import javax.swing.*;
import javax.swing.SwingUtilities;
import java.util.regex.*;
import java.io.*;
import java.nio.file.FileSystems;
import java.nio.file.*;

public class Favourites extends JPanel {
    private DefaultListModel model = new DefaultListModel();
    private JList list;

    // whose favoutites these are
    private String user;

    // songs in this favourites list
    private final SongTable favouriteSongs;

    // pointer back to main song table list
    private final SongTableSwing songTable;

    // This font displays Asian and European characters.
    // It should be in your distro.
    // Fonts displaying all Unicode are zysong.ttf and Cyberbit.ttf
    // See http://unicode.org/resources/fonts.html
    private Font font = new Font("WenQuanYi Zen Hei", Font.PLAIN, 16);

    private int findIndex = -1;

    public Favourites(final SongTableSwing songTable,
                      final SongTable favouriteSongs,
                      String user) {
        this.songTable = songTable;
        this.favouriteSongs = favouriteSongs;
        this.user = user;

        if (font == null) {
            System.err.println("Can't find font");
        }

        int n = 0;
        java.util.Iterator<SongInformation> iter = favouriteSongs.iterator();
        while(iter.hasNext()) {
            model.add(n++, iter.next());
        }
```

```
        BorderLayout mgr = new BorderLayout();

        list = new JList(model);
        list.setFont(font);
        JScrollPane scrollPane = new JScrollPane(list);

        setLayout(mgr);
        add(scrollPane, BorderLayout.CENTER);

        JPanel bottomPanel = new JPanel();
        bottomPanel.setLayout(new GridLayout(2, 1));
        add(bottomPanel, BorderLayout.SOUTH);

        JPanel searchPanel = new JPanel();
        bottomPanel.add(searchPanel);
        searchPanel.setLayout(new FlowLayout());

        JPanel buttonPanel = new JPanel();
        bottomPanel.add(buttonPanel);
        buttonPanel.setLayout(new FlowLayout());

        JButton addSong = new JButton("Add song to list");
        JButton deleteSong = new JButton("Delete song from list");
        JButton play = new JButton("Play");

        buttonPanel.add(addSong);
        buttonPanel.add(deleteSong);
        buttonPanel.add(play);

        play.addActionListener(new ActionListener() {
                public void actionPerformed(ActionEvent e) {
                    playSong();
                }
            });

        deleteSong.addActionListener(new ActionListener() {
                public void actionPerformed(ActionEvent e) {
                    SongInformation song = (SongInformation) list.getSelectedValue();
                    model.removeElement(song);
                    favouriteSongs.songs.remove(song);
                    saveToStore();
                }
            });

        addSong.addActionListener(new ActionListener() {
                public void actionPerformed(ActionEvent e) {
                    SongInformation song = songTable.getSelection();
                    model.addElement(song);
                    favouriteSongs.songs.add(song);
                    saveToStore();
                }
            });
    }
```

```
    private void saveToStore() {
        try {
            File storeFile = new File("/server/KARAOKE/favourites/" + user);
            FileOutputStream out = new FileOutputStream(storeFile);
            ObjectOutputStream os = new ObjectOutputStream(out);
            os.writeObject(favouriteSongs.songs);
            os.flush();
            out.close();
        } catch(Exception e) {
            System.err.println("Can't save favourites file " + e.toString());
        }
    }

    /**
     * "play" a song by printing its file path to standard out.
     * Can be used in a pipeline this way
     */
    public void playSong() {
        SongInformation song = (SongInformation) list.getSelectedValue();
        if (song == null) {
            return;
        }
        System.out.println(song.path.toString());
    }

    class SongInformationRenderer extends JLabel implements ListCellRenderer {

        public Component getListCellRendererComponent(
                                              JList list,
                                              Object value,
                                              int index,
                                              boolean isSelected,
                                              boolean cellHasFocus) {
            setText(value.toString());
            return this;
        }
    }
}
```

All Favorites

There's nothing special here. It just loads the tables for each person and builds a Favourites object that it places in a JTabbedPane. It also adds a New tab for adding more users.

The code for AllFavourites is as follows:

```
import java.awt.*;
import java.awt.event.*;
import javax.swing.*;
import java.util.Vector;
import java.nio.file.*;
import java.io.*;
```

```java
public class AllFavourites extends JTabbedPane {
    private SongTableSwing songTable;

    public AllFavourites(SongTableSwing songTable) {
        this.songTable = songTable;

        loadFavourites();

        NewPanel newP = new NewPanel(this);
        addTab("NEW", null, newP);
    }

    private void loadFavourites() {
        String userHome = System.getProperty("user.home");
        Path favouritesPath = FileSystems.getDefault().getPath("/server/KARAOKE/favourites");
        try {
            DirectoryStream<Path> stream =
                Files.newDirectoryStream(favouritesPath);
            for (Path entry: stream) {
                int nelmts = entry.getNameCount();
                Path last = entry.subpath(nelmts-1, nelmts);
                System.err.println("Favourite: " + last.toString());
                File storeFile = entry.toFile();

                FileInputStream in = new FileInputStream(storeFile);
                ObjectInputStream is = new ObjectInputStream(in);
                Vector<SongInformation> favouriteSongs =
                    (Vector<SongInformation>) is.readObject();
                in.close();
                for (SongInformation s: favouriteSongs) {
                    System.err.println("Fav: " + s.toString());
                }

                SongTable favouriteSongsTable = new SongTable(favouriteSongs);
                Favourites f = new Favourites(songTable,
                                              favouriteSongsTable,
                                              last.toString());
                addTab(last.toString(), null, f, last.toString());
                System.err.println("Loaded favs " + last.toString());
            }
        } catch(Exception e) {
            System.err.println(e.toString());
        }
    }

    class NewPanel extends JPanel {
        private JTabbedPane pane;

        public NewPanel(final JTabbedPane pane) {
            this.pane = pane;
```

```
        setLayout(new FlowLayout());
        JLabel nameLabel = new JLabel("Name of new person");
        final JTextField nameField = new JTextField(10);
        add(nameLabel);
        add(nameField);

        nameField.addActionListener(new ActionListener(){
                public void actionPerformed(ActionEvent e){
                    String name = nameField.getText();

                    SongTable songs = new SongTable(new Vector<SongInformation>());
                    Favourites favs = new Favourites(songTable, songs, name);

                    pane.addTab(name, null, favs);
                }});


    }
  }
}
```

Swing Song Table

This is mainly code to get the different song tables loaded and to buld the Swing interface. It also filters the showing table based on the patterns matched. The originally loaded table is kept for restoration and patching matching. The code for SongTableSwing is as follows:

```java
import java.awt.*;
import java.awt.event.*;
import javax.swing.event.*;
import javax.swing.*;
import javax.swing.SwingUtilities;
import java.util.regex.*;
import java.io.*;

public class SongTableSwing extends JPanel {
    private DefaultListModel model = new DefaultListModel();
    private JList list;
    private static SongTable allSongs;

    private JTextField numberField;
    private JTextField langField;
    private JTextField titleField;
    private JTextField artistField;

    // This font displays Asian and European characters.
    // It should be in your distro.
    // Fonts displaying all Unicode are zysong.ttf and Cyberbit.ttf
    // See http://unicode.org/resources/fonts.html
    private Font font = new Font("WenQuanYi Zen Hei", Font.PLAIN, 16);
    // font = new Font("Bitstream Cyberbit", Font.PLAIN, 16);
```

```java
private int findIndex = -1;

/**
 * Describe <code>main</code> method here.
 *
 * @param args a <code>String</code> value
 */
public static final void main(final String[] args) {
    if (args.length >= 1 &&
        args[0].startsWith("-h")) {
        System.err.println("Usage: java SongTableSwing [song directory]");
        System.exit(0);
    }

    allSongs = null;
    try {
        allSongs = new SongTable(args);
    } catch(Exception e) {
        System.err.println(e.toString());
        System.exit(1);
    }

    JFrame frame = new JFrame();
    frame.setTitle("Song Table");
    frame.setSize(700, 800);
    frame.setDefaultCloseOperation(JFrame.EXIT_ON_CLOSE);

    SongTableSwing panel = new SongTableSwing(allSongs);
    frame.getContentPane().add(panel);

    frame.setVisible(true);

    JFrame favourites = new JFrame();
    favourites.setTitle("Favourites");
    favourites.setSize(600, 800);
    favourites.setDefaultCloseOperation(JFrame.EXIT_ON_CLOSE);

    AllFavourites lists = new AllFavourites(panel);
    favourites.getContentPane().add(lists);

    favourites.setVisible(true);

}

public SongTableSwing(SongTable songs) {

    if (font == null) {
        System.err.println("Can't fnd font");
    }
```

```
int n = 0;
java.util.Iterator<SongInformation> iter = songs.iterator();
while(iter.hasNext()) {
    model.add(n++, iter.next());
    // model.add(n++, iter.next().toString());
}

BorderLayout mgr = new BorderLayout();

list = new JList(model);
// list = new JList(songs);
list.setFont(font);
JScrollPane scrollPane = new JScrollPane(list);

// Support DnD
list.setDragEnabled(true);

setLayout(mgr);
add(scrollPane, BorderLayout.CENTER);

JPanel bottomPanel = new JPanel();
bottomPanel.setLayout(new GridLayout(2, 1));
add(bottomPanel, BorderLayout.SOUTH);

JPanel searchPanel = new JPanel();
bottomPanel.add(searchPanel);
searchPanel.setLayout(new FlowLayout());

JLabel numberLabel = new JLabel("Number");
numberField = new JTextField(5);

JLabel langLabel = new JLabel("Language");
langField = new JTextField(8);

JLabel titleLabel = new JLabel("Title");
titleField = new JTextField(20);
titleField.setFont(font);

JLabel artistLabel = new JLabel("Artist");
artistField = new JTextField(10);
artistField.setFont(font);

searchPanel.add(numberLabel);
searchPanel.add(numberField);
searchPanel.add(titleLabel);
searchPanel.add(titleField);
searchPanel.add(artistLabel);
searchPanel.add(artistField);
```

```java
titleField.getDocument().addDocumentListener(new DocumentListener() {
        public void changedUpdate(DocumentEvent e) {
            // rest find to -1 to restart any find searches
            findIndex = -1;
            // System.out.println("reset find index");
        }
        public void insertUpdate(DocumentEvent e) {
            findIndex = -1;
            // System.out.println("reset insert find index");
        }
        public void removeUpdate(DocumentEvent e) {
            findIndex = -1;
            // System.out.println("reset remove find index");
        }
    }
    );
artistField.getDocument().addDocumentListener(new DocumentListener() {
        public void changedUpdate(DocumentEvent e) {
            // rest find to -1 to restart any find searches
            findIndex = -1;
            // System.out.println("reset insert find index");
        }
        public void insertUpdate(DocumentEvent e) {
            findIndex = -1;
            // System.out.println("reset insert find index");
        }
        public void removeUpdate(DocumentEvent e) {
            findIndex = -1;
            // System.out.println("reset insert find index");
        }
    }
    );

titleField.addActionListener(new ActionListener(){
        public void actionPerformed(ActionEvent e){
            filterSongs();
        }});
artistField.addActionListener(new ActionListener(){
        public void actionPerformed(ActionEvent e){
            filterSongs();
        }});

JPanel buttonPanel = new JPanel();
bottomPanel.add(buttonPanel);
buttonPanel.setLayout(new FlowLayout());

JButton find = new JButton("Find");
JButton filter = new JButton("Filter");
JButton reset = new JButton("Reset");
JButton play = new JButton("Play");
```

```
        buttonPanel.add(find);
        buttonPanel.add(filter);
        buttonPanel.add(reset);
        buttonPanel.add(play);

        find.addActionListener(new ActionListener() {
            public void actionPerformed(ActionEvent e) {
                findSong();
            }
        });

        filter.addActionListener(new ActionListener() {
            public void actionPerformed(ActionEvent e) {
                filterSongs();
            }
        });

        reset.addActionListener(new ActionListener() {
            public void actionPerformed(ActionEvent e) {
                resetSongs();
            }
        });

        play.addActionListener(new ActionListener() {
            public void actionPerformed(ActionEvent e) {
                playSong();
            }
        });

    }

public void findSong() {
    String number = numberField.getText();
    String language = langField.getText();
    String title = titleField.getText();
    String artist = artistField.getText();

    if (number.length() != 0) {
        return;
    }

    for (int n = findIndex + 1; n < model.getSize(); n++) {
        SongInformation info = (SongInformation) model.getElementAt(n);

        if ((title.length() != 0) && (artist.length() != 0)) {
            if (info.titleMatch(title) && info.artistMatch(artist)) {
                findIndex = n;
                list.setSelectedIndex(n);
                list.ensureIndexIsVisible(n);
                break;
            }
        }
```

```
            } else {
                if ((title.length() != 0) && info.titleMatch(title)) {
                    findIndex = n;
                    list.setSelectedIndex(n);
                    list.ensureIndexIsVisible(n);
                    break;
                } else if ((artist.length() != 0) && info.artistMatch(artist)) {
                    findIndex = n;
                    list.setSelectedIndex(n);
                    list.ensureIndexIsVisible(n);
                    break;

                }
            }

        }
    }

    public void filterSongs() {
        String title = titleField.getText();
        String artist = artistField.getText();
        String number = numberField.getText();
        SongTable filteredSongs = allSongs;

        if (allSongs == null) {
            return;
        }

        if (title.length() != 0) {
            filteredSongs = filteredSongs.titleMatches(title);
        }
        if (artist.length() != 0) {
            filteredSongs = filteredSongs.artistMatches(artist);
        }
        if (number.length() != 0) {
            filteredSongs = filteredSongs.numberMatches(number);
        }

        model.clear();
        int n = 0;
        java.util.Iterator<SongInformation> iter = filteredSongs.iterator();
        while(iter.hasNext()) {
            model.add(n++, iter.next());
        }
    }
```

```java
    public void resetSongs() {
        artistField.setText("");
        titleField.setText("");
        model.clear();
        int n = 0;
        java.util.Iterator<SongInformation> iter = allSongs.iterator();
        while(iter.hasNext()) {
            model.add(n++, iter.next());
        }
    }
    /**
     * "play" a song by printing its file path to standard out.
     * Can be used in a pipeline this way
     */
    public void playSong() {
        SongInformation song = (SongInformation) list.getSelectedValue();
        if (song == null) {
            return;
        }
        System.out.println(song.path);
    }

    public SongInformation getSelection() {
        return (SongInformation) (list.getSelectedValue());
    }

    class SongInformationRenderer extends JLabel implements ListCellRenderer {

        public Component getListCellRendererComponent(
                                            JList list,
                                            Object value,
                                            int index,
                                            boolean isSelected,
                                            boolean cellHasFocus) {
            setText(value.toString());
            return this;
        }
    }
}
```

Playing Songs

Whenever a song is "played," its file path is written to standard output. This makes it suitable for use in a bash shell pipeline such as the following:

```bash
#!/bin/bash

VLC_OPTS="--play-and-exit --fullscreen"
```

```
java  SongTableSwing |
while read line
do
        if expr match "$line" ".*mp3"
        then
                vlc $VLC_OPTS "$line"
        elif expr match "$line" ".*zip"
        then
                rm -f /tmp/karaoke/*
                unzip -d /tmp/karaoke "$line"
                vlc $VLC_OPTS /tmp/karaoke/*.mp3
        fi
done
```

VLC

VLC is an immensely flexible media player. It relies on a large set of plug-ins to enhance its basic core functionality. You saw in an earlier chapter that if a directory contains both an MP3 file and a CDG file with the same base name, then by asking it to play the MP3 file, it will also show the CDG video.

Common expectations of karaoke players are that you can adjust the speed and pitch. Currently VLC cannot adjust pitch, but it does have a plug-in to adjust speed (while keeping the pitch unchanged). This plug-in can be accessed by the Lua interface to VLC. Once it's set up, you can send commands such as the following across standard input from the process that started VLC (such as a command-line shell):

```
rate 1.04
```

This will change the speed and leave the pitch unchanged.

Setting up VLC to accept Lua commands from stdin can be done with the following command options:

```
vlc -I luaintf --lua-intf cli ...
```

Note that this takes away the standard GUI controls (menus, and so on) and controls VLC from stdin only.

Currently, it is not simple to add pitch control to VLC. Take a deep breath.

- Turn off PulseAudio and start Jack.

- Run jack-rack and install the TAP_pitch filter.

- Run VLC with Jack output.

- Using qjackctl, hook VLC to output through jack-rack, which outputs to a system.

- Control pitch through the jack-rack GUI.

Playing Songs Across the Network

I actually want to play songs from my server disk to a Raspberry Pi or CubieBoard connected to my TV and control the play from a netbook sitting on my lap. This is a distributed system.

Mounting server files on a computer is simple: you can use NFS, Samba, and so on. I am currently using sshfs as follows:

```
sshfs -o idmap=user -o rw -o allow_other newmarch@192.168.1.101:/home/httpd/html /server
```

For remote access/control, I replace the run command of the last section by a TCP client/server. On the client, controlling the player, I have this:

```
java SongTableSwing | client 192.168.1.7
```

On the (Raspberry Pi/CubieBoard) server, I run this:

```
#!/bin/bash
set -x
VLC_OPTS="--play-and-exit -f"

server |
while read line
do
        if expr match "$line" ".*mp3"
        then
                vlc $VLC_OPTS "$line"
        elif expr match "$line" ".*zip"
        then
                rm -f /tmp/karaoke/*
                unzip -d /tmp/karaoke "$line"
                vlc $VLC_OPTS /tmp/karaoke/*.mp3
        fi
done
```

The client/server files are just standard TCP files. The client reads a newline-terminated string from standard input and writes it to the server, and the server prints the same line to standard output. Here is client.c:

```
#include <stdio.h>
#include <sys/types.h>
#include <sys/socket.h>
#include <netinet/in.h>
#include <stdlib.h>
#include <string.h>

#define SIZE 1024
char buf[SIZE];
#define PORT 13000
int main(int argc, char *argv[]) {
    int sockfd;
    int nread;
    struct sockaddr_in serv_addr;
    if (argc != 2) {
        fprintf(stderr, "usage: %s IPaddr\n", argv[0]);
        exit(1);
    }
```

```
        while (fgets(buf, SIZE , stdin) != NULL) {
            /* create endpoint */
            if ((sockfd = socket(AF_INET, SOCK_STREAM, 0)) < 0) {
                perror(NULL); exit(2);
            }
            /* connect to server */
            serv_addr.sin_family = AF_INET;
            serv_addr.sin_addr.s_addr = inet_addr(argv[1]);
            serv_addr.sin_port = htons(PORT);

            while (connect(sockfd,
                            (struct sockaddr *) &serv_addr,
                            sizeof(serv_addr)) < 0) {
                /* allow for timesouts etc */
                perror(NULL);
                sleep(1);
            }

            printf("%s", buf);
            nread = strlen(buf);
            /* transfer data and quit */
            write(sockfd, buf, nread);
            close(sockfd);
        }
}
```

Here is server.c:

```
#include <stdio.h>
#include <sys/types.h>
#include <sys/socket.h>
#include <netinet/in.h>
#include <stdlib.h>
#include <signal.h>

#define SIZE 1024
char buf[SIZE];
#define TIME_PORT 13000

int sockfd, client_sockfd;

void intHandler(int dummy) {
    close(client_sockfd);
    close(sockfd);
    exit(1);
}

int main(int argc, char *argv[]) {
    int sockfd, client_sockfd;
    int nread, len;
    struct sockaddr_in serv_addr, client_addr;
    time_t t;
```

```
    signal(SIGINT, intHandler);

    /* create endpoint */
    if ((sockfd = socket(AF_INET, SOCK_STREAM, 0)) < 0) {
        perror(NULL); exit(2);
    }
    /* bind address */
    serv_addr.sin_family = AF_INET;
    serv_addr.sin_addr.s_addr = htonl(INADDR_ANY);
    serv_addr.sin_port = htons(TIME_PORT);
    if (bind(sockfd,
            (struct sockaddr *) &serv_addr,
            sizeof(serv_addr)) < 0) {
        perror(NULL); exit(3);
    }
    /* specify queue */
    listen(sockfd, 5);
    for (;;) {
        len = sizeof(client_addr);
        client_sockfd = accept(sockfd,
                                (struct sockaddr *) &client_addr,
                                &len);
        if (client_sockfd == -1) {
            perror(NULL); continue;
        }
        while ((nread = read(client_sockfd, buf, SIZE-1)) > 0) {
            buf[nread] = '\0';
            fputs(buf, stdout);
            fflush(stdout);
        }
        close(client_sockfd);
    }
}
```

Conclusion

This chapter showed how to build a player for MP3+G files.

CHAPTER 25

■ ■ ■

Karaoke Applications Using Java Sound

Java has no library support for karaoke. That is too application specific. In this chapter, I give you code for a karaoke player that can play KAR files. The player will show two lines of the lyrics to be played, with words already played being highlighted in red. Along the top, it shows a simple piano keyboard with the notes that are played in channel 1 of the MIDI file. In the middle, it shows the melody line, with a vertical line in the middle to show the currently playing note.

The player looks like Figure 25-1.

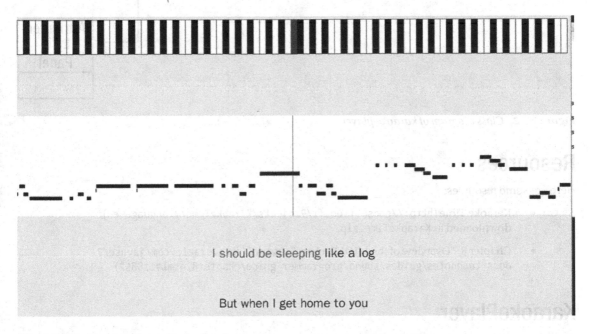

Figure 25-1. *User interface of karaoke player*

© Jan Newmarch 2017

J. Newmarch, *Linux Sound Programming*, DOI 10.1007/978-1-4842-2496-0_25

Figure 25-2 shows the UML diagram.

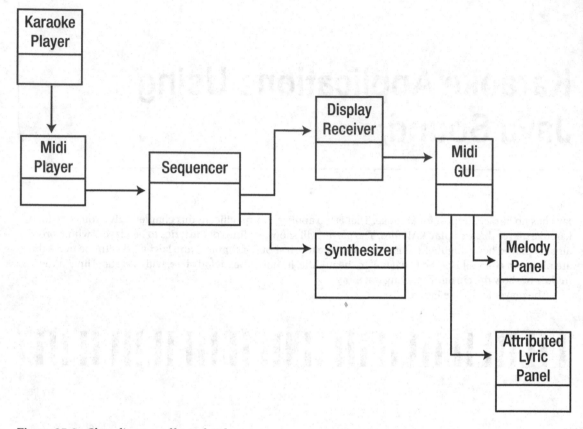

Figure 25-2. *Class diagram of karaoke player*

Resources

Here are some resources:

- Karaoke Time (http://gnese.free.fr/Projects/KaraokeTime/?language=en), downloaded as KaraokeTime.zip.

- Chapter 8, "Overview of the MIDI Package" (http://docs.oracle.com/javase/7/docs/technotes/guides/sound/programmer_guide/chapter8.html#118852)

KaraokePlayer

The KaraokePlayer class extracts the file name of the karaoke file and creates a MidiPlayer to handle the file.

```
/*
 * KaraokePlayer.java
 *
 */
```

```
import javax.swing.*;

public class KaraokePlayer {

    public static void main(String[] args) throws Exception {
        if (args.length != 1) {
            System.err.println("KaraokePlayer: usage: " +
                                "KaraokePlayer <midifile>");
            System.exit(1);
        }
        String  strFilename = args[0];

        MidiPlayer midiPlayer = new MidiPlayer();
        midiPlayer.playMidiFile(strFilename);
    }
}
```

MidiPlayer

The MidiPlayer class creates a Sequence from the file. Sequence information is required at many places, so rather than pass the sequence in parameters, it is stored in a singleton (static) object, a SequenceInformation. This makes the sequence effectively a global object to the system.

The player then gets the default sequencer and transmits MIDI events to two receiver objects: the default synthesizer to play the events and a DisplayReceiver to manage all the GUI handling. The Sequencer method getTransmitter() is misnamed: each time it is called, it returns a *new* transmitter, each time playing the same events to the respective receivers.

The following is from the Java SE documentation, specifically, Chapter 10, "Transmitting and Receiving MIDI Messages" (http://docs.oracle.com/javase/7/docs/technotes/guides/sound/programmer_guide/chapter10.html):

> This code [in their example] introduces a dual invocation of the MidiDevice. getTransmitter method, assigning the results to inPortTrans1 and inPortTrans2. As mentioned earlier, a device can own multiple transmitters and receivers. Each time MidiDevice.getTransmitter() is invoked for a given device, another transmitter is returned, until no more are available, at which time an exception will be thrown.

That way, the sequencer can send to two receivers.

Receivers do not get MetaMessages. These contain information such as text or lyric events. The DisplayReceiver is registered as a MetaEventListener so that it can manage these events as well as other events.

The MidiPlayer is as follows:

```
import javax.sound.midi.MidiSystem;
import javax.sound.midi.InvalidMidiDataException;
import javax.sound.midi.Sequence;
import javax.sound.midi.Receiver;
import javax.sound.midi.Sequencer;
import javax.sound.midi.Transmitter;
import javax.sound.midi.MidiChannel;
import javax.sound.midi.MidiDevice;
import javax.sound.midi.Synthesizer;
```

```java
import javax.sound.midi.ShortMessage;
import javax.sound.midi.SysexMessage;

import java.io.File;
import java.io.IOException;

public class MidiPlayer {

    private DisplayReceiver receiver;

    public  void playMidiFile(String strFilename) throws Exception {
        File    midiFile = new File(strFilename);

        /*
         *      We try to get a Sequence object, loaded with the content
         *      of the MIDI file.
         */
        Sequence         sequence = null;
        try {
            sequence = MidiSystem.getSequence(midiFile);
        }
        catch (InvalidMidiDataException e) {
            e.printStackTrace();
            System.exit(1);
        }
        catch (IOException e) {
            e.printStackTrace();
            System.exit(1);
        }

        if (sequence == null) {
            out("Cannot retrieve Sequence.");
        } else {
            SequenceInformation.setSequence(sequence);
            playMidi(sequence);
        }
    }

    public  void playMidi(Sequence sequence) throws Exception {

        Sequencer sequencer = MidiSystem.getSequencer(true);
        sequencer.open();
        sequencer.setSequence(sequence);

        receiver = new DisplayReceiver(sequencer);
        sequencer.getTransmitter().setReceiver(receiver);
        sequencer.addMetaEventListener(receiver);

        if (sequencer instanceof Synthesizer) {
            Debug.println("Sequencer is also a synthesizer");
        } else {
```

```
    Debug.println("Sequencer is not a synthesizer");
}
//sequencer.start();

/*
Synthesizer synthesizer = MidiSystem.getSynthesizer();
synthesizer.open();

if (synthesizer.getDefaultSoundbank() == null) {
    // then you know that java sound is using the hardware soundbank
    Debug.println("Synthesizer using h/w soundbank");
} else Debug.println("Synthesizer using s/w soundbank");

Receiver synthReceiver = synthesizer.getReceiver();
Transmitter seqTransmitter = sequencer.getTransmitter();
seqTransmitter.setReceiver(synthReceiver);
MidiChannel[] channels = synthesizer.getChannels();
Debug.println("Num channels is " + channels.length);
*/
sequencer.start();

/* default synth doesn't support pitch bending
Synthesizer synthesizer = MidiSystem.getSynthesizer();
MidiChannel[] channels = synthesizer.getChannels();
for (int i = 0; i < channels.length; i++) {
    System.out.printf("Channel %d has bend %d\n", i, channels[i].getPitchBend());
    channels[i].setPitchBend(16000);
    System.out.printf("Channel %d now has bend %d\n", i, channels[i].getPitchBend());
}
*/

/* set volume - doesn't work */
/*KaraokeUML
for (int i = 0; i < channels.length; i++) {
    channels[i].controlChange(7, 0);
}
*/
/*
System.out.println("Turning notes off");
for (int i = 0; i < channels.length; i++) {
    channels[i].allNotesOff();
    channels[i].allSoundOff();
}
*/

/* set volume - doesn't work either */
/*
try {
    Thread.sleep(5000);
} catch (InterruptedException e) {
    // TODO Auto-generated catch block
    e.printStackTrace();
}
```

```
            if (synthReceiver == MidiSystem.getReceiver())
                System.out.println("Reciver is default");
            else
                System.out.println("Reciver is not default");
            System.out.println("Receiver is " + synthReceiver.toString());
            //synthReceiver = MidiSystem.getReceiver();
            System.out.println("Receiver is now " + synthReceiver.toString());
            ShortMessage volMessage = new ShortMessage();
            int midiVolume = 1;
            for (Receiver rec: synthesizer.getReceivers()) {
                System.out.println("Setting vol on recveiver " + rec.toString());
            for (int i = 0; i < channels.length; i++) {
                try {
                    // volMessage.setMessage(ShortMessage.CONTROL_CHANGE, i, 123, midiVolume);
                    volMessage.setMessage(ShortMessage.CONTROL_CHANGE, i, 7, midiVolume);
                } catch (InvalidMidiDataException e) {
                    e.printStackTrace();
                }
            }
                synthReceiver.send(volMessage, -1);
                rec.send(volMessage, -1);
            }
            }
            System.out.println("Changed midi volume");
            */
            /* master volume control using sysex */
            /* http://www.blitter.com/~russtopia/MIDI/~jglatt/tech/midispec/mastrvol.htm */
            /*
            SysexMessage sysexMessage = new SysexMessage();
            /* volume values from http://www.bandtrax.com.au/sysex.htm */
            /* default volume 0x7F * 128 + 0x7F from */
            /*
            byte[] data = {(byte) 0xF0, (byte) 0x7F, (byte) 0x7F, (byte) 0x04,
                           (byte) 0x01, (byte) 0x0, (byte) 0x7F, (byte) 0xF7};
            sysexMessage.setMessage(data, data.length);
            synthReceiver.send(sysexMessage, -1);
            for (Receiver rec: synthesizer.getReceivers()) {
                System.out.println("Setting vol on recveiver " + rec.toString());
                rec.send(sysexMessage, -1);
            }
            */
    }

    public DisplayReceiver getReceiver() {
        return receiver;
    }

    private static void out(String strMessage)
    {
        System.out.println(strMessage);
    }
}
```

DisplayReceiver

The DisplayReceiver collects both ShortMessages as a Receiver and MetaMessages as a MetaEventListener. These are needed to see both the notes and the lyrics.

The DisplayReceiver decodes the notes and text sent to it. In turn, it passes these to a MidiGUI to show them. This class is as follows:

```
/**
 * DisplayReceiver
 *
 * Acts as a Midi receiver to the default Java Midi sequencer.
 * It collects Midi events and Midi meta messages from the sequencer.
 * these are handed to a UI object for display.
 *
 * The current UI object is a MidiGUI but could be replaced.
 */

import javax.sound.midi.*;
import javax.swing.SwingUtilities;

public class DisplayReceiver implements Receiver,
                                        MetaEventListener {
    private MidiGUI gui;KaraokeUML
    private Sequencer sequencer;
    private int melodyChannel = SequenceInformation.getMelodyChannel();

    public DisplayReceiver(Sequencer sequencer) {
        this.sequencer = sequencer;
        gui = new MidiGUI(sequencer);
    }

    public void close() {
    }

    /**
     * Called by a Transmitter to receive events
     * as a Receiver
     */
    public void send(MidiMessage msg, long timeStamp) {
        // Note on/off messages come from the midi player
        // but not meta messages

        if (msg instanceof ShortMessage) {
            ShortMessage smsg = (ShortMessage) msg;

            String strMessage = "Channel " + smsg.getChannel() + " ";

            switch (smsg.getCommand())
                {
                case Constants.MIDI_NOTE_OFF:
                    strMessage += "note Off " +
```

413

```
                    getKeyName(smsg.getData1()) + " " + timeStamp;
                break;

            case Constants.MIDI_NOTE_ON:
                strMessage += "note On " +
                    getKeyName(smsg.getData1()) + " " + timeStamp;
                break;
            }
        Debug.println(strMessage);
        if (smsg.getChannel() == melodyChannel) {
            gui.setNote(timeStamp, smsg.getCommand(), smsg.getData1());
        }

    }
}

public void meta(MetaMessage msg) {
    Debug.println("Reciever got a meta message");
    if (((MetaMessage) msg).getType() == Constants.MIDI_TEXT_TYPE) {
        setLyric((MetaMessage) msg);
    } else if (((MetaMessage) msg).getType() == Constants.MIDI_END_OF_TRACK)  {
        System.exit(0);
    }
}

public void setLyric(MetaMessage message) {
    byte[] data = message.getData();
    String str = new String(data);
    Debug.println("Lyric +\"" + str + "\" at " + sequencer.getTickPosition());
    gui.setLyric(str);

}

private static String[] keyNames = {"C", "C#", "D", "D#", "E", "F", "F#", "G", "G#",
 "A", "A#", "B"};

public static String getKeyName(int keyNumber) {
    if (keyNumber > 127) {
        return "illegal value";
    } else {
        int note = keyNumber % 12;
        int octave = keyNumber / 12;
        return keyNames[note] + (octave - 1);
    }
}

}
```

MidiGUI

The MidiGUI is called with two methods: setLyric() and setNote(). The GUI consists of three main areas: an area to give a "piano" view of the melody as it is played (pianoPanel), an area to show the complete set of melody notes (melodyPanel), and a set of Panels to show the lyrics. setNote() is fairly straightforward in that it just calls drawNote() in the pianoPanel. setLyric() is considerably more complex.

Most karaoke players show a couple of lines of text for the lyrics. As lyrics are played, typically the text will change color to match. When the end of a line is reached, focus will switch to the next line, and the previous line will be replaced with another line of lyrics.

Each line must hold a line of lyrics. The line must be able to react to lyrics as they are played. This is handled by an AttributedTextPanel, shown later. The main task is to feed changes in lyrics through to the selected panel so that it can display them in the correct colors.

The other principal task for the MidiGUI here is to switch focus between AttributedTextPanels when the end of line is detected and to update the next line of text. The new lines of text can't come from the lyrics as they are played but must instead be constructed from the sequence containing all the notes and lyrics. The convenience class SequenceInformation (shown later) takes a Sequence object and has a method to extract an array of LyricLine objects. Each panel displaying a line is given a line from this array.

```java
import javax.swing.*;
import java.awt.*;
import java.awt.event.*;
import javax.sound.midi.*;
import java.util.Vector;
import java.util.Map;
import java.io.*;

public class MidiGUI extends JFrame {
    //private GridLayout mgr = new GridLayout(3,1);
    private BorderLayout mgr = new BorderLayout();

    private PianoPanel pianoPanel;
    private MelodyPanel melodyPanel;

    private AttributedLyricPanel lyric1;
    private AttributedLyricPanel lyric2;
    private AttributedLyricPanel[] lyricLinePanels;
    private int whichLyricPanel = 0;

    private JPanel lyricsPanel = new JPanel();

    private Sequencer sequencer;
    private Sequence sequence;
    private Vector<LyricLine> lyricLines;

    private int lyricLine = -1;

    private boolean inLyricHeader = true;
    private Vector<DurationNote> melodyNotes;

    private Map<Character, String> pinyinMap;
```

415

```
    private int language;

    public MidiGUI(final Sequencer sequencer) {
        this.sequencer = sequencer;
        sequence = sequencer.getSequence();

        // get lyrics and notes from Sequence Info
        lyricLines = SequenceInformation.getLyrics();
        melodyNotes = SequenceInformation.getMelodyNotes();
        language = SequenceInformation.getLanguage();

        pianoPanel = new PianoPanel(sequencer);
        melodyPanel = new MelodyPanel(sequencer);

        pinyinMap = CharsetEncoding.loadPinyinMap();
        lyric1 = new AttributedLyricPanel(pinyinMap);
        lyric2 = new AttributedLyricPanel(pinyinMap);
        lyricLinePanels = new AttributedLyricPanel[] {
            lyric1, lyric2};

        Debug.println("Lyrics ");

        for (LyricLine line: lyricLines) {
            Debug.println(line.line + " " + line.startTick + " " + line.endTick +
                        " num notes " + line.notes.size());
        }

        getContentPane().setLayout(mgr);
        /*
        getContentPane().add(pianoPanel);
        getContentPane().add(melodyPanel);

        getContentPane().add(lyricsPanel);
        */
        getContentPane().add(pianoPanel, BorderLayout.PAGE_START);
        getContentPane().add(melodyPanel,  BorderLayout.CENTER);

        getContentPane().add(lyricsPanel,  BorderLayout.PAGE_END);

        lyricsPanel.setLayout(new GridLayout(2, 1));
        lyricsPanel.add(lyric1);
        lyricsPanel.add(lyric2);
        setLanguage(language);

        setText(lyricLinePanels[whichLyricPanel], lyricLines.elementAt(0).line);

        Debug.println("First lyric line: " + lyricLines.elementAt(0).line);
        if (lyricLine < lyricLines.size() - 1) {
            setText(lyricLinePanels[(whichLyricPanel+1) % 2], lyricLines.elementAt(1).line);
            Debug.println("Second lyric line: " + lyricLines.elementAt(1).line);
        }
```

```java
        // handle window closing
        setDefaultCloseOperation(JFrame.DO_NOTHING_ON_CLOSE);
        addWindowListener(new WindowAdapter() {
                public void windowClosing(WindowEvent e) {
                    sequencer.stop();
                    System.exit(0);
                }
            });

        // handle resize events
        addComponentListener(new ComponentAdapter() {
                public void componentResized(ComponentEvent e) {
                    Debug.printf("Component has resized to width %d, height %d\n",
                                    getWidth(), getHeight());
                    // force resize of children - especially the middle MelodyPanel
                    e.getComponent().validate();
                }
                public void componentShown(ComponentEvent e) {
                    Debug.printf("Component is visible with width %d, height %d\n",
                                    getWidth(), getHeight());
                }
            });

        setSize(1600, 900);
        setVisible(true);
    }

    public void setLanguage(int lang) {
        lyric1.setLanguage(lang);
        lyric2.setLanguage(lang);
    }

    /**
     * A lyric starts with a header section
     * We have to skip over that, but can pick useful
     * data out of it
     */

    /**
     * header format is
     *   \@Llanguage code
     *   \@Ttitle
     *   \@Tsinger
     */

    public void setLyric(String txt) {
        Debug.println("Setting lyric to " + txt);
        if (inLyricHeader) {
            if (txt.startsWith("@")) {
                Debug.println("Header: " + txt);
                return;
```

417

```java
        } else {
            inLyricHeader = false;
        }
    }

    if ((lyricLine == -1) && (txt.charAt(0) == '\\')) {
        lyricLine = 0;
        colourLyric(lyricLinePanels[whichLyricPanel], txt.substring(1));
        // lyricLinePanels[whichLyricPanel].colourLyric(txt.substring(1));
        return;
    }

    if (txt.equals("\r\n") || (txt.charAt(0) == '/') || (txt.charAt(0) == '\\')) {
        if (lyricLine < lyricLines.size() -1)
            Debug.println("Setting next lyric line to \"" +
                        lyricLines.elementAt(lyricLine + 1).line + "\"");

        final int thisPanel = whichLyricPanel;
        whichLyricPanel = (whichLyricPanel + 1) % 2;

        Debug.println("Setting new lyric line at tick " +
                    sequencer.getTickPosition());

        lyricLine++;

        // if it's a \ r /, the rest of the txt should be the next  word to
        // be coloured

        if ((txt.charAt(0) == '/') || (txt.charAt(0) == '\\')) {
            Debug.println("Colouring newline of " + txt);
            colourLyric(lyricLinePanels[whichLyricPanel], txt.substring(1));
        }

        // Update the current line of text to show the one after next
        // But delay the update until 0.25 seconds after the next line
        // starts playing, to preserve visual continuity
        if (lyricLine + 1 < lyricLines.size()) {
            /*
              long startNextLineTick = lyricLines.elementAt(lyricLine).startTick;
              long delayForTicks = startNextLineTick - sequencer.getTickPosition();
              Debug.println("Next  current "  + startNextLineTick + " " + sequencer.
                            getTickPosition());
              float microSecsPerQNote = sequencer.getTempoInMPQ();
              float delayInMicroSecs = microSecsPerQNote * delayForTicks / 24 + 250000L;
            */

            final Vector<DurationNote> notes = lyricLines.elementAt(lyricLine).notes;

            final int nextLineForPanel = lyricLine + 1;

            if (lyricLines.size() >= nextLineForPanel) {
```

```
                   Timer timer = new Timer((int) 1000,
                                   new ActionListener() {
                                      public void actionPerformed(ActionEvent e) {
                                          if (nextLineForPanel >= lyricLines.size()) {
                                              return;
                                          }
                                          setText(lyricLinePanels[t
                                            hisPanel], lyricLines.
                                            elementAt(nextLineForPanel).line);
                                          //lyricLinePanels[thisPanel].
                                              setText(lyricLines.
                                              elementAt(nextLineForPanel).line);
                                      }
                                   });
                   timer.setRepeats(false);
                   timer.start();
               } else {
                   // no more lines
               }
           }
       } else {
           Debug.println("Playing lyric " + txt);
           colourLyric(lyricLinePanels[whichLyricPanel], txt);
           //lyricLinePanels[whichLyricPanel].colourLyric(txt);
       }
}

/**
 * colour the lyric of a panel.
 * called by one thread, makes changes in GUI thread
 */
private void colourLyric(final AttributedLyricPanel p, final String txt) {
    SwingUtilities.invokeLater(new Runnable() {
            public void run() {
                Debug.print("Colouring lyric \"" + txt + "\"");
                if (p == lyric1) Debug.println(" on panel 1");
                else Debug.println(" on panel 2");
                p.colourLyric(txt);
            }
        }
    );
}

/**
 * set the lyric of a panel.
 * called by one thread, makes changes in GUI thread
 */
private void setText(final AttributedLyricPanel p, final String txt) {
    SwingUtilities.invokeLater(new Runnable() {
            public void run() {
```

```
                    Debug.println("Setting text \"" + txt + "\"");
                    if (p == lyric1) Debug.println(" on panel 1");
                    else Debug.println(" on panel 2");
                    p.setText(txt);
                }
            }
        );
    }

    public void setNote(long timeStamp, int onOff, int note) {
        Debug.printf("Setting note in gui to %d\n", note);

        if (onOff == Constants.MIDI_NOTE_OFF) {
            pianoPanel.drawNoteOff(note);
        } else if (onOff == Constants.MIDI_NOTE_ON) {
            pianoPanel.drawNoteOn(note);
        }
    }
}
```

AttributedLyricPanel

The panel to display a line of lyrics must be able to show text in two colors: the lyrics already played and the lyrics yet to be played. The Java AttributedText class is useful for this, as the text can be marked with different attributes such as colors. This is wrapped in an AttributedTextPanel, shown later.

One minor wrinkle concerns language. Chinese has both the character form and a Romanized form called PinYin. Chinese speakers can read the character form. People like me can understand only the PinYin form. So if the language is Chinese, then the AttributedTextPanel shows the PinYin alongside the Chinese characters. The language identity should be passed to the AttributedLyricPanel as well.

The AttributedLyricPanel is as follows:

```
import javax.swing.*;
import java.awt.*;
import java.awt.font.*;
import java.text.*;
import java.util.Map;

public class AttributedLyricPanel extends JPanel {

    private final int PINYIN_Y = 40;
    private final int TEXT_Y = 90;

    private String text;
    private AttributedString attrText;
    private int coloured = 0;
    private Font font = new Font(Constants.CHINESE_FONT, Font.PLAIN, 36);
    private Font smallFont = new Font(Constants.CHINESE_FONT, Font.PLAIN, 24);
    private Color red = Color.RED;
    private int language;
    private String pinyinTxt = null;
```

```java
private Map<Character, String> pinyinMap = null;

public AttributedLyricPanel(Map<Character, String> pinyinMap) {
    this.pinyinMap = pinyinMap;
}

public Dimension getPreferredSize() {
    return new Dimension(1000, TEXT_Y + 20);
}

public void setLanguage(int lang) {
    language = lang;
    Debug.printf("Lang in panel is %X\n", lang);
}

public boolean isChinese() {
    switch (language) {
    case SongInformation.CHINESE1:
    case SongInformation.CHINESE2:
    case SongInformation.CHINESE8:
    case SongInformation.CHINESE131:
    case SongInformation.TAIWANESE3:
    case SongInformation.TAIWANESE7:
    case SongInformation.CANTONESE:
        return true;
    }
    return false;
}

public void setText(String txt) {
    coloured = 0;
    text = txt;
    Debug.println("set text " + text);
    attrText = new AttributedString(text);
    if (text.length() == 0) {
        return;
    }
    attrText.addAttribute(TextAttribute.FONT, font, 0, text.length());

    if (isChinese()) {
        pinyinTxt = "";
        for (int n = 0; n < txt.length(); n++) {
            char ch = txt.charAt(n);
            String pinyin = pinyinMap.get(ch);
            if (pinyin != null) {
                pinyinTxt += pinyin + " ";
            } else {
                Debug.printf("No pinyin map for character \"%c\"\n", ch);
            }
        }
    }
```

```java
        repaint();
    }

    public void colourLyric(String txt) {
        coloured += txt.length();
        if (coloured != 0) {
            repaint();
        }
    }

    /**
     * Draw the string with the first part in red, rest in green.
     * String is centred
     */

    @Override
    public void paintComponent(Graphics g) {
        if ((text.length() == 0) || (coloured > text.length())) {
            return;
        }
        g.setFont(font);
        FontMetrics metrics = g.getFontMetrics();
        int strWidth = metrics.stringWidth(text);
        int panelWidth = getWidth();
        int offset = (panelWidth - strWidth) / 2;

        if (coloured != 0) {
            try {
                attrText.addAttribute(TextAttribute.FOREGROUND, red, 0, coloured);
            } catch(Exception e) {
                System.out.println(attrText.toString() + " " + e.toString());
            }
        }
        g.clearRect(0, 0, getWidth(), getHeight());
        try {
            g.drawString(attrText.getIterator(), offset, TEXT_Y);
        } catch (Exception e) {
            System.err.println("Attr Str exception on " + text);
        }
        // Draw the Pinyin if it's not zero
        if (pinyinTxt != null && pinyinTxt.length() != 0) {
            g.setFont(smallFont);
            metrics = g.getFontMetrics();
            strWidth = metrics.stringWidth(pinyinTxt);
            offset = (panelWidth - strWidth) / 2;

            g.drawString(pinyinTxt, offset, PINYIN_Y);
            g.setFont(font);
        }
    }
}
```

PianoPanel

The PianoPanel shows a piano-like keyboard. As a note is turned on, it colors the note in blue and returns to normal any previously playing note. When a note is turned off, the note reverts to its normal color (black or white).

Coloring notes is called by setNote as none on/note off messages come from the sequencer. The PianoPanel is as follows:

```java
import java.util.Vector;
import javax.swing.*;
import java.awt.*;
import javax.sound.midi.*;

public class PianoPanel extends JPanel {

    private final int HEIGHT = 100;
    private final int HEIGHT_OFFSET = 10;

    long timeStamp;
    private Vector<DurationNote> notes;
    private Vector<DurationNote> sungNotes;
    private int lastNoteDrawn = -1;
    private Sequencer sequencer;
    private Sequence sequence;
    private int maxNote;
    private int minNote;

    private Vector<DurationNote> unresolvedNotes = new Vector<DurationNote> ();

    private int playingNote = -1;

    public PianoPanel(Sequencer sequencer) {

        maxNote = SequenceInformation.getMaxMelodyNote();
        minNote = SequenceInformation.getMinMelodyNote();
        Debug.println("Max: " + maxNote + " Min " + minNote);
    }

    public Dimension getPreferredSize() {
        return new Dimension(1000, 120);
    }

    public void drawNoteOff(int note) {
        if (note < minNote || note > maxNote) {
            return;
        }

        Debug.println("Note off played is " + note);
        if (note != playingNote) {
            // Sometimes "note off" followed immediately by "note on"
            // gets mixed up to "note on" followed by "note off".
```

423

```
                    // Ignore the "note off" since the next note has already
                    // been processed
                    Debug.println("Ignoring note off");
                    return;
                }
            playingNote = -1;
            repaint();
        }

        public void drawNoteOn(int note) {
            if (note < minNote || note > maxNote) {
                return;
            }

            Debug.println("Note on played is " + note);
            playingNote = note;
            repaint();

        }

        private void drawPiano(Graphics g, int width, int height) {
            int noteWidth = width / (Constants.MIDI_NOTE_C8 - Constants.MIDI_NOTE_A0);
            for (int noteNum =  Constants.MIDI_NOTE_A0; // A0
                 noteNum <=  Constants.MIDI_NOTE_C8; // C8
                 noteNum++) {

                drawNote(g, noteNum, noteWidth);
            }
        }

        private void drawNote(Graphics g, int noteNum, int width) {
            if (isWhite(noteNum)) {
                noteNum -= Constants.MIDI_NOTE_A0;
                g.setColor(Color.WHITE);
                g.fillRect(noteNum*width, HEIGHT_OFFSET, width, HEIGHT);
                g.setColor(Color.BLACK);
                g.drawRect(noteNum*width, HEIGHT_OFFSET, width, HEIGHT);
            } else {
                noteNum -= Constants.MIDI_NOTE_A0;
                g.setColor(Color.BLACK);
                g.fillRect(noteNum*width, HEIGHT_OFFSET, width, HEIGHT);
            }
            if (playingNote != -1) {
                g.setColor(Color.BLUE);
                g.fillRect((playingNote - Constants.MIDI_NOTE_A0) * width, HEIGHT_OFFSET, width, HEIGHT);
            }
        }
```

```java
    private boolean isWhite(int noteNum) {
        noteNum = noteNum % 12;
        switch (noteNum) {
        case 1:
        case 3:
        case 6:
        case 8:
        case 10:
        case 13:
            return false;
        default:
            return true;
        }
    }

    @Override
    public void paintComponent(Graphics g) {

        int ht = getHeight();
        int width = getWidth();

        drawPiano(g, width, ht);

    }
}
```

MelodyPanel

The MelodyPanel is a scrolling panel showing all the notes of the melody. The currently playing note is centered in the display. This is done by drawing all the notes into a BufferedImage and then copying across the relevant part every 50 milliseconds.

The MelodyPancl is as follows:

```java
import java.util.Vector;
import javax.swing.*;
import java.awt.*;
import java.awt.event.*;
import javax.sound.midi.*;
import java.awt.image.BufferedImage;
import java.io.*;
import javax.imageio.*;

public class MelodyPanel extends JPanel {

    private static int DBL_BUF_SCALE = 2;
    private static final int NOTE_HEIGHT = 10;
    private static final int SLEEP_MSECS = 5;
```

```java
    private long timeStamp;
    private Vector<DurationNote> notes;
    private Sequencer sequencer;
    private Sequence sequence;
    private int maxNote;
    private int minNote;
    private long tickLength = -1;
    private long currentTick = -1;
    private Image image = null;

    /**
     * The panel where the melody notes are shown in a
     * scrolling panel
     */
    public MelodyPanel(Sequencer sequencer) {

        maxNote = SequenceInformation.getMaxMelodyNote();
        minNote = SequenceInformation.getMinMelodyNote();
        Debug.println("Max: " + maxNote + " Min " + minNote);
        notes = SequenceInformation.getMelodyNotes();
        this.sequencer = sequencer;
        tickLength = sequencer.getTickLength() + 1000; // hack to make white space at end,
        plus fix bug

        //new TickPointer().start();
        // handle resize events
        addComponentListener(new ComponentAdapter() {
                public void componentResized(ComponentEvent e) {
                    Debug.printf("Component melody panel has resized to width %d, height %d\n",
                                        getWidth(), getHeight());
                }
                public void componentShown(ComponentEvent e) {
                    Debug.printf("Component malody panel is visible with width %d, height %d\n",
                                        getWidth(), getHeight());
                }
            });

    }

    /**
     * Redraw the melody image after each tick
     * to give a scrolling effect
     */
    private class TickPointer extends Thread {
        public void run() {
            while (true) {
                currentTick = sequencer.getTickPosition();
                MelodyPanel.this.repaint();
                /*
                SwingUtilities.invokeLater(
                                                new Runnable() {
```

```
                                    public void run() {
                                        synchronized(MelodyPanel.this) {
                                        MelodyPanel.this.repaint();
                                        }
                                    }
                                });
            */
            try {
                sleep(SLEEP_MSECS);
            } catch (Exception e) {
                // keep going
                e.printStackTrace();
            }
        }
    }
}


/**
 * Draw the melody into a buffer so we can just copy bits to the screen
 */
private void drawMelody(Graphics g, int front, int width, int height) {
    try {
    g.setColor(Color.WHITE);
    g.fillRect(0, 0, width, height);
    g.setColor(Color.BLACK);

    String title = SequenceInformation.getTitle();
    if (title != null) {
        //Font f = new Font("SanSerif", Font.ITALIC, 40);
        Font f = new Font(Constants.CHINESE_FONT, Font.ITALIC, 40);
        g.setFont(f);
        int strWidth = g.getFontMetrics().stringWidth(title);
        g.drawString(title, (front - strWidth/2), height/2);
        Debug.println("Drawn title " + title);
    }

    for (DurationNote note: notes) {
        long startNote = note.startTick;
        long endNote = note.endTick;
        int value = note.note;

        int ht = (value - minNote) * (height - NOTE_HEIGHT) / (maxNote - minNote) + NOTE_HEIGHT/2;
        // it's upside down
        ht = height - ht;

        long start = front + (int) (startNote * DBL_BUF_SCALE);
        long end = front + (int) (endNote * DBL_BUF_SCALE);
```

```
            drawNote(g, ht, start, end);
            //g.drawString(title, (int)start, (int)height/2);
        }
    } catch(Exception e) {
        System.err.println("Drawing melody error " + e.toString());
    }
}

/**
 * Draw a horizontal bar to represent a nore
 */
private void drawNote(Graphics g, int height, long start, long end) {
    Debug.printf("Drawing melody at start %d end %d height %d\n", start, end,  height -
    NOTE_HEIGHT/2);

    g.fillRect((int) start, height - NOTE_HEIGHT/2, (int) (end-start), NOTE_HEIGHT);
}

/**
 * Draw a vertical line in the middle of the screen to
 * represent where we are in the playing notes
 */
private void paintTick(Graphics g, long width, long height) {
    long x = (currentTick * width) / tickLength;
    g.drawLine((int) width/2, 0, (int) width/2, (int) height);
    //System.err.println("Painted tcik");
}

// leave space at the front of the image to draw title, etc
int front = 1000;

/**
 * First time, draw the melody notes into an off-screen buffer
 * After that, copy a segment of the buffer into the image,
 * with the centre of the image the current note
 */
@Override
public void paintComponent(Graphics g) {
    int ht = getHeight();
    int width = getWidth();
    //int front = width / 2;

    synchronized(this) {
    if (image == null) {
        /*
         * We want to stretch out the notes so that they appear nice and wide on the screen.
         * A DBL_BUF_SCALE of 2 does this okay. But then tickLength * DBL_BUF_SCALE may end
         * up larger than an int, and we can't make a BufferedImage wider than MAXINT.
         * So we may have to adjust DBL_BUF_SCALE.
         *
         * Yes, I know we ask Java to rescale images on the fly, but that costs in runtime.
         */
```

```java
            Debug.println("tick*DBLBUFSCALE " + tickLength * DBL_BUF_SCALE);

            if ((long) (tickLength * DBL_BUF_SCALE) > (long) Short.MAX_VALUE) {
                // DBL_BUF_SCALE = ((float)  Integer.MAX_VALUE) / ((float) tickLength);
                DBL_BUF_SCALE = 1;
                Debug.println("Adjusted DBL_BUF_SCALE to "+ DBL_BUF_SCALE);
            }

            Debug.println("DBL_BUF_SCALE is "+ DBL_BUF_SCALE);

            // draw melody into a buffered image
            Debug.printf("New buffered img width %d ht %d\n", tickLength, ht);
            image = new BufferedImage(front + (int) (tickLength * DBL_BUF_SCALE), ht,
                    BufferedImage.TYPE_INT_RGB);
            Graphics ig = image.getGraphics();
            drawMelody(ig, front, (int) (tickLength * DBL_BUF_SCALE), ht);
            new TickPointer().start();

            try {
                File outputfile = new File("saved.png");
                ImageIO.write((BufferedImage) image, "png", outputfile);
            } catch (Exception e) {
                System.err.println("Error in image write " + e.toString());
            }

        }
        //System.err.printf("Drawing img from %d ht %d width %d\n",
        //                  front + (int) (currentTick * DBL_BUF_SCALE - width/2), ht, width);

        boolean b = g.drawImage(image, 0, 0, width, ht,
                        front + (int) (currentTick * DBL_BUF_SCALE - width/2), 0,
                        front + (int) (currentTick * DBL_BUF_SCALE + width/2), ht,
                null);
        /*System.out.printf("Ht of BI %d, width %d\n", ((BufferedImage)image).getHeight(),
                    ((BufferedImage) image).getWidth());
        */

        //if (b) System.err.println("Drawn ok"); else System.err.println("NOt drawn ok");
        paintTick(g, width, ht);
        }
    }

}
```

SequenceInformation

The SequenceInformation class is a convenience class that is used by several other classes. It stores a copy of the sequence, the lyric lines, and the melody notes to show lyrics and melody by the user interface, as well as the song title, the maximum and minimum notes to set the scale of the notes display, and which channel the melody is on.

```java
public class SequenceInformation {

    private static Sequence sequence = null;
    private static Vector<LyricLine> lyricLines = null;
    private static Vector<DurationNote> melodyNotes = null;
    private static int lang = -1;
    private static String title = null;
    private static String performer = null;
    private static int maxNote;
    private static int minNote;

    private static int melodyChannel = -1;// no such channel
    ...
}
```

The methods of this class are as follows:

```java
public static void setSequence(Sequence seq)
public static long getTickLength()
public static int getMelodyChannel()
public static int getLanguage()
public static String getTitle()
public static String getPerformer()
public static Vector<LyricLine> getLyrics()
public static Vector<DurationNote> getMelodyNotes()
public static int getMaxMelodyNote()
public static int getMinMelodyNote()
```

The code to getLyrics() needs to walk through the tracks in the sequence looking for MetaMessages of type MIDI_TEXT_TYPE and then adding them to the current line or starting a new line on a line break. Along the way it picks up the metadata of performer and title from the start of the file.

```java
/*
 * Build a vector of lyric lines
 * Each line has a start and an end tick
 * and a string for the lyrics in that line
 */
public static Vector<LyricLine> getLyrics() {
    if (lyricLines != null) {
        return lyricLines;
    }
```

```
lyricLines = new Vector<LyricLine> ();
LyricLine nextLyricLine = new LyricLine();
StringBuffer buff = new StringBuffer();
long ticks = OL;

Track[] tracks = sequence.getTracks();
for (int nTrack = 0; nTrack < tracks.length; nTrack++) {
    for (int n = 0; n < tracks[nTrack].size(); n++) {
        MidiEvent evt = tracks[nTrack].get(n);
        MidiMessage msg = evt.getMessage();
        ticks = evt.getTick();

        if (msg instanceof MetaMessage) {
            Debug.println("Got a meta mesg in seq");
            if (((MetaMessage) msg).getType() == Constants.MIDI_TEXT_TYPE) {
                MetaMessage message = (MetaMessage) msg;

                byte[] data = message.getData();
                String str = new String(data);
                Debug.println("Got a text mesg in seq \"" + str + "\" " + ticks);

                if (ticks == 0) {
                    if (str.startsWith("@L")) {
                        lang = decodeLang(str.substring(2));
                    } else if (str.startsWith("@T")) {
                        if (title == null) {
                            title = str.substring(2);
                        } else {
                            performer = str.substring(2);
                        }
                    }
                }
                if (ticks > 0) {
                    //if (str.equals("\r") || str.equals("\n")) {
                    if ((data[0] == '/') || (data[0] == '\\')) {
                        if (buff.length() == 0) {
                            // blank line -  maybe at start of song
                            // fix start time from NO_TICK
                            nextLyricLine.startTick = ticks;
                        } else {
                            nextLyricLine.line = buff.toString();
                            nextLyricLine.endTick = ticks;
                            lyricLines.add(nextLyricLine);
                            buff.delete(0, buff.length());

                            nextLyricLine = new LyricLine();
                        }
                        buff.append(str.substring(1));
                    } else {
                        if (nextLyricLine.startTick == Constants.NO_TICK) {
```

```
                              nextLyricLine.startTick = ticks;
                          }
                          buff.append(str);
                      }
                  }
              }
          }
      }
      // save last line (but only once)
      if (buff.length() != 0) {
          nextLyricLine.line = buff.toString();
          nextLyricLine.endTick = ticks;
          lyricLines.add(nextLyricLine);
          buff.delete(0, buff.length());
      }
  }
  if (Debug.DEBUG) {
      dumpLyrics();
  }
  return lyricLines;
}
```

The code for getMelodyNotes() traverses the sequence looking for MIDI on/off notes in the melody channel. The code is a little bit messy because of some songs having "unclean" data: they may contain note values outside of the permissible range and sometimes overlap instead of one note finishing before the next starts. This code is as follows:

```
/*
 * gets a vector of lyric notes
 * side-effect: sets last tick
 */
public static Vector<DurationNote> getMelodyNotes() {
    if (melodyChannel == -1) {
        getMelodyChannel();
    }

    if (melodyNotes != null) {
        return melodyNotes;
    }

    melodyNotes = new Vector<DurationNote> ();
    Vector<DurationNote> unresolvedNotes = new Vector<DurationNote> ();

    Track[] tracks = sequence.getTracks();
    for (int nTrack = 0; nTrack < tracks.length; nTrack++) {
        for (int n = 0; n < tracks[nTrack].size(); n++) {
            MidiEvent evt = tracks[nTrack].get(n);
            MidiMessage msg = evt.getMessage();
            long ticks = evt.getTick();
```

```
            if (msg instanceof ShortMessage) {
                ShortMessage smsg= (ShortMessage) msg;
                if (smsg.getChannel() == melodyChannel) {
                    int note = smsg.getData1();
                    if (note < Constants.MIDI_NOTE_AO || note > Constants.MIDI_NOTE_C8)
{
                        continue;
                    }

                    if (smsg.getCommand() == Constants.MIDI_NOTE_ON) {
                        // note on
                        DurationNote dnote = new DurationNote(ticks, note);
                        melodyNotes.add(dnote);
                        unresolvedNotes.add(dnote);

                    } else if (smsg.getCommand() == Constants.MIDI_NOTE_OFF) {
                        // note off
                        for (int m = 0; m < unresolvedNotes.size(); m++) {
                            DurationNote dnote = unresolvedNotes.elementAt(m);
                            if (dnote.note == note) {
                                dnote.duration = ticks - dnote.startTick;
                                dnote.endTick = ticks;
                                unresolvedNotes.remove(m);
                            }
                        }

                    }

                }
            }
        }
    }
    return melodyNotes;
}
```

The last method of any complexity is getMelodyChannel(). MIDI messages do not distinguish which channel contains the melody. Most songs have the melody on channel 1, but not all. So, a heuristic has to be used: search for a channel where the first note to be played is pretty close to the first real lyric. This is not 100 percent reliable.

```
public static int getMelodyChannel() {
    boolean firstNoteSeen[] = {false, false, false, false, false, false, false, false,
                               false, false, false, false, false, false, false, false};
    boolean possibleChannel[] = {false, false, false, false, false, false, false, false,
                                 false, false, false, false, false, false, false, false};
    if (melodyChannel != -1) {
        return melodyChannel;
    }

    if (lyricLines == null) {
        lyricLines = getLyrics();
    }
```

```
        long startLyricTick = ((LyricLine) lyricLines.get(0)).startTick;
        Debug.printf("Lyrics start at %d\n", startLyricTick);

        Track[] tracks = sequence.getTracks();
        for (int nTrack = 0; nTrack < tracks.length; nTrack++) {
            Track track = tracks[nTrack];
            for (int nEvent = 0; nEvent < track.size(); nEvent++) {
                MidiEvent evt = track.get(nEvent);
                MidiMessage msg = evt.getMessage();
                if (msg instanceof ShortMessage) {
                    ShortMessage smsg= (ShortMessage) msg;
                    int channel = smsg.getChannel();
                    if (firstNoteSeen[channel]) {
                        continue;
                    }
                    if (smsg.getCommand() == Constants.MIDI_NOTE_ON) {
                        long tick = evt.getTick();
                        Debug.printf("First note on for channel %d at tick %d\n",
                                            channel, tick);
                        firstNoteSeen[channel] = true;
                        if (Math.abs(startLyricTick - tick) < 10) {
                            // close enough - we hope!
                            melodyChannel = channel;
                            possibleChannel[channel] = true;
                            Debug.printf("Possible melody channel is %d\n", channel);
                        }
                        if (tick > startLyricTick + 11) {
                            break;
                        }
                    }
                }
            }
        }

        return melodyChannel;
    }
```

The other methods are relatively straightforward and are omitted.

PinYin

For Chinese language files, one of my aims was to display the PinYin (Romanized form) of the Chinese hierographic characters. For this, I need to be able to rewrite any sequence of Chinese characters into their PinYin form. I couldn't find a list of characters and their corresponding characters. The closest is the Chinese-English Dictionary (www.mandarintools.com/worddict.html) from which you can download the dictionary as a text file. Typical lines in this file are as follows:

不賴 不赖 [bu4 lai4] /not bad/good/fine/

Each line has the traditional characters followed by the simplified characters, the PinYin in [...], and then English meanings.

I used the following shell script to make a list of character/PinYin pairs:

```
#!/bin/bash

# get pairs of character + pinyin by throwing away other stuff in the dictionary

awk '{print $2, $3}' cedict_ts.u8 | grep -v '[A-Z]' |
  grep -v '^.[^ ]' | sed -e 's/\[//' -e 's/\]//' -e 's/[0-9]$//' |
    sort | uniq -w 1 > pinyinmap.txt
```

to give lines such as the following:

```
好 hao
灼 shuo
如 ru
妃 fei
```

This can then be read into a Java Map, and then quick lookups can be done to translate Chinese to PinYin.

Karaoke Player with Sampling

The karaoke player described so far is functionally equivalent to kmidi and pykar. It plays KAR files, shows the notes, and scrolls through the lyrics. To sing along with it, you need to use an ALSA or PulseAudio player.

But Java can also play sampled sounds, as discussed in an earlier chapter. So, that code can be brought into the karaoke player to give a more complete solution. For MIDI, Java normally gives only a Gervill synthesizer, which is a software synthesizer that plays out through the PulseAudio default device. The actual output device is not accessible through Java and is controlled by the underlying PulseAudio output device. But for sampled media, the input devices can be controlled. So, in the following code, a selection box allows a choice of sampled input device and leaves the output device to the default.

```
/*
 * KaraokePlayer.java
 *
 */

import javax.swing.*;
import javax.sound.sampled.*;

public class KaraokePlayerSampled {

    public static void main(String[] args) throws Exception {
        if (args.length != 1) {
            System.err.println("KaraokePlayer: usage: " +
                            "KaraokePlayer <midifile>");
            System.exit(1);
        }
        String  strFilename = args[0];
```

```java
        Mixer.Info[] mixerInfo = AudioSystem.getMixerInfo();

        String[] possibleValues = new String[mixerInfo.length];
        for(int cnt = 0; cnt < mixerInfo.length; cnt++){
            possibleValues[cnt] = mixerInfo[cnt].getName();
        }
        Object selectedValue = JOptionPane.showInputDialog(null, "Choose mixer", "Input",
                                            JOptionPane.INFORMATION_MESSAGE, null,
                                            possibleValues, possibleValues[0]);

        System.out.println("Mixer string selected " + ((String)selectedValue));

        Mixer mixer = null;
        for(int cnt = 0; cnt < mixerInfo.length; cnt++){
            if (mixerInfo[cnt].getName().equals((String)selectedValue)) {
                mixer = AudioSystem.getMixer(mixerInfo[cnt]);
                System.out.println("Got a mixer");
                break;
            }
        }//end for loop

        MidiPlayer midiPlayer = new MidiPlayer();
        midiPlayer.playMidiFile(strFilename);

        SampledPlayer sampledPlayer = new SampledPlayer(/* midiPlayer.getReceiver(), */ mixer);
        sampledPlayer.playAudio();
    }
}
```

The code to play the sampled media is pretty much the same as you have seen before.

```java
import java.io.IOException;

import javax.sound.sampled.Line;
import javax.sound.sampled.Mixer;
import javax.sound.sampled.AudioFormat;
import javax.sound.sampled.AudioInputStream;
import javax.sound.sampled.AudioSystem;
import javax.sound.sampled.DataLine;
import javax.sound.sampled.TargetDataLine;
import javax.sound.sampled.FloatControl;
import javax.sound.sampled.LineUnavailableException;
import javax.sound.sampled.SourceDataLine;
import javax.sound.sampled.Control;

import javax.swing.*;

public class SampledPlayer {

    private DisplayReceiver receiver;
    private Mixer mixer;
```

```java
public SampledPlayer(/* DisplayReceiver receiver, */ Mixer mixer) {
    this.receiver = receiver;
    this.mixer = mixer;
}

//This method creates and returns an
// AudioFormat object for a given set of format
// parameters.  If these parameters don't work
// well for you, try some of the other
// allowable parameter values, which are shown
// in comments following the declarations.
private static AudioFormat getAudioFormat(){
    float sampleRate = 44100.0F;
    //8000,11025,16000,22050,44100
    int sampleSizeInBits = 16;
    //8,16
    int channels = 1;
    //1,2
    boolean signed = true;
    //true,false
    boolean bigEndian = false;
    //true,false
    return new AudioFormat(sampleRate,
                           sampleSizeInBits,
                           channels,
                           signed,
                           bigEndian);
}//end getAudioFormat

public  void playAudio() throws Exception {
    AudioFormat audioFormat;
    TargetDataLine targetDataLine;

    audioFormat = getAudioFormat();
    DataLine.Info dataLineInfo =
        new DataLine.Info(
                          TargetDataLine.class,
                          audioFormat);
    targetDataLine = (TargetDataLine)
        AudioSystem.getLine(dataLineInfo);

    targetDataLine.open(audioFormat,
                        audioFormat.getFrameSize() * Constants.FRAMES_PER_BUFFER);
    targetDataLine.start();

    /*
    for (Control control: targetDataLine.getControls()) {
        System.out.println("Target control: " + control.getType());
    }
    */

    playAudioStream(new AudioInputStream(targetDataLine), mixer);
} // playAudioFile
```

```java
    /** Plays audio from the given audio input stream. */
    public  void playAudioStream(AudioInputStream audioInputStream, Mixer mixer) {

        new AudioPlayer(audioInputStream, mixer).start();
    } // playAudioStream

    class AudioPlayer extends Thread {
        AudioInputStream audioInputStream;
        SourceDataLine dataLine;
        AudioFormat audioFormat;

        // YIN stuff
        // PitchProcessorWrapper ppw;

        AudioPlayer( AudioInputStream audioInputStream, Mixer mixer) {
            this.audioInputStream = audioInputStream;

            // Set to nearly max, like Midi sequencer does
            Thread curr = Thread.currentThread();
            Debug.println("Priority on sampled: " + curr.getPriority());
            int priority = Thread.NORM_PRIORITY
                + ((Thread.MAX_PRIORITY - Thread.NORM_PRIORITY) * 3) / 4;
            curr.setPriority(priority);
            Debug.println("Priority now on sampled: " + curr.getPriority());

            // Audio format provides information like sample rate, size, channels.
            audioFormat = audioInputStream.getFormat();
            Debug.println( "Play input audio format=" + audioFormat );

            // Open a data line to play our type of sampled audio.
            // Use SourceDataLine for play and TargetDataLine for record.

            if (mixer == null) {
                System.out.println("can't find a mixer");
            } else {
                Line.Info[] lines = mixer.getSourceLineInfo();
                if (lines.length >= 1) {
                    try {
                        dataLine = (SourceDataLine) AudioSystem.getLine(lines[0]);
                        System.out.println("Got a source line for " + mixer.toString());
                    } catch(Exception e) {
                    }
                } else {
                    System.out.println("no source lines for this mixer " + mixer.toString());
                }
            }

                for (Control control: mixer.getControls()) {
                    System.out.println("Mixer control: " + control.getType());
                }
```

```java
DataLine.Info info = null;
if (dataLine == null) {
    info = new DataLine.Info( SourceDataLine.class, audioFormat );
    if ( !AudioSystem.isLineSupported( info ) ) {
        System.out.println( "Play.playAudioStream does not handle this type of
         audio on this system." );
        return;
    }
}

try {
    // Create a SourceDataLine for play back (throws LineUnavailableException).
    if (dataLine == null) {
        dataLine = (SourceDataLine) AudioSystem.getLine( info );
    }
    Debug.println( "SourceDataLine class=" + dataLine.getClass() );

    // The line acquires system resources (throws LineAvailableException).
    dataLine.open( audioFormat,
                   audioFormat.getFrameSize() * Constants.FRAMES_PER_BUFFER);

    for (Control control: dataLine.getControls()) {
        System.out.println("Source control: " + control.getType());
    }
    // Adjust the volume on the output line.
    if( dataLine.isControlSupported( FloatControl.Type.VOLUME) ) {
        // if( dataLine.isControlSupported( FloatControl.Type.MASTER_GAIN ) ) {
        //FloatControl volume = (FloatControl) dataLine.getControl(
                                FloatControl.Type.MASTER_GAIN );
        FloatControl volume = (FloatControl) dataLine.getControl( FloatControl.
                              Type.VOLUME);
        System.out.println("Max vol " + volume.getMaximum());
        System.out.println("Min vol " + volume.getMinimum());
        System.out.println("Current vol " + volume.getValue());
        volume.setValue( 60000.0F );
        System.out.println("New vol " + volume.getValue());
    } else {
        System.out.println("Volume control not supported");
    }
    if (dataLine.isControlSupported( FloatControl.Type.REVERB_RETURN)) {
        System.out.println("reverb return supported");
    } else {
        System.out.println("reverb return not supported");
    }
    if (dataLine.isControlSupported( FloatControl.Type.REVERB_SEND)) {
        System.out.println("reverb send supported");
    } else {
        System.out.println("reverb send not supported");
    }

} catch ( LineUnavailableException e ) {
    e.printStackTrace();
}
```

439

```java
            // ppw = new PitchProcessorWrapper(audioInputStream, receiver);
        }

    public void run() {

            // Allows the line to move data in and out to a port.
            dataLine.start();

            // Create a buffer for moving data from the audio stream to the line.
            int bufferSize = (int) audioFormat.getSampleRate() * audioFormat.getFrameSize();
            bufferSize =  audioFormat.getFrameSize() * Constants.FRAMES_PER_BUFFER;
            Debug.println("Buffer size: " + bufferSize);
            byte [] buffer = new byte[bufferSize];

            try {
                int bytesRead = 0;
                while ( bytesRead >= 0 ) {
                    bytesRead = audioInputStream.read( buffer, 0, buffer.length );
                    if ( bytesRead >= 0 ) {
                        int framesWritten = dataLine.write( buffer, 0, bytesRead );
                        // ppw.write(buffer, bytesRead);
                    }
                } // while
            } catch ( IOException e ) {
                e.printStackTrace();
            }

            // Continues data line I/O until its buffer is drained.
            dataLine.drain();

            Debug.println( "Sampled player closing line." );
            // Closes the data line, freeing any resources such as the audio device.
            dataLine.close();
        }
    }

    // Turn into a GUI version or pick up from prefs
    public void listMixers() {
        try{
            Mixer.Info[] mixerInfo =
                AudioSystem.getMixerInfo();
            System.out.println("Available mixers:");
            for(int cnt = 0; cnt < mixerInfo.length;
                cnt++){
                System.out.println(mixerInfo[cnt].
                                getName());

                Mixer mixer = AudioSystem.getMixer(mixerInfo[cnt]);
                Line.Info[] sourceLines = mixer.getSourceLineInfo();
                for (Line.Info s: sourceLines) {
                    System.out.println("  Source line: " + s.toString());
```

```
            }
            Line.Info[] targetLines = mixer.getTargetLineInfo();
            for (Line.Info t: targetLines) {
                System.out.println("  Target line: " + t.toString());
            }

        }//end for loop
    } catch(Exception e) {
    }
    }
}
```

Comments on Device Choices

If the default devices are chosen, the input and output devices are the PulseAudio default devices. Normally these would both be the computer's sound card. However, the default devices can be changed using, for example, the PulseAudio volume control. These can set either the input device, the output device, or both. The dialogue can also be used to set the input device for sampled media.

This raises a number of possible scenarios:

- The default PulseAudio device selects the same device for input and output.

- The default PulseAudio device selects different devices for input and output.

- The default PulseAudio device is used for output, while the ALSA device is used for input, but the physical device is the same.

- The default PulseAudio device is used for output, while the ALSA device is used for input, and the physical devices are different.

Using different devices raises the problem of clock drift, where the devices have different clocks that are not synchronized. The worst case seems to be the second one, where over a three-minute song on my system I could hear a noticeable lag in playing the sampled audio, while the KAR file played happily. It also introduced a noticeable latency in playing the sampled audio.

Performance

The program top can give you a good idea of how much CPU is used by various processes. My current computer is a high-end Dell laptop with a quad-core Intel i7-2760QM CPU running at 2.4GHz. According to CPU Benchmarks (www.cpubenchmark.net/), the processor is in the "High End CPU Chart." On this computer, tested with various KAR files, PulseAudio takes about 30 percent of the CPU, while Java takes about 60 percent. On occasions these figures were exceeded. There is not much left for additional functionality!

In addition, while playing a MIDI file, sometimes the Java process hangs, resuming with up to 600 percent CPU usage (I don't know how top manages to record that). This makes it effectively unusable, and I am not sure where the problem lies.

Conclusion

Java Sound has no direct support for karaoke. This chapter looked at how to combine the Java Sound libraries with other libraries such as Swing to create a karaoke player for MIDI files. It requires a high-end computer to run these programs.

Subtitles and Closed Captions

Many karaoke systems use subtitles[1] imposed over a movie of some kind. Programs like kmid and my Java programs play lyrics on some sort of canvas object. This gives a pretty boring background. Video CDs or MPEG-4 files have a nicer background but have the lyrics hard-coded onto the background video, so there is little chance for manipulation of them. CD+G files keep the lyrics separate from the video, but there doesn't seem to be any way of playing them directly from Linux. They can be converted to MP3+G, and they can be played by VLC, which loads the MP3 file and picks up the corresponding .cdg file.

This chapter considers subtitles that can be created independently, combined with video and audio in some way, and then played. The current situation is not completely satisfactory.

Resources

Check out this resource:

- "Subtitling with Linux Tutorial" (http://sub.wordnerd.de/linux-subs.html)

Subtitle Formats

This chapter is concerned here with what are called *soft subtitles*, where the subtitles are stored in a separate file from the video or audio and are combined during rendering. The Wikipedia page "Subtitle (captioning)" (http://en.wikipedia.org/wiki/Subtitle_(captioning)) is a long article going into many issues about subtitling. It also contains a list of subtitle formats, but the one that seems to be of most use in this context is SubStation Alpha.

MPlayer

According to the MPlayer page "Subtitles and OSD" (www.mplayerhq.hu/DOCS/HTML/en/subosd.htm), the following are the formats recognized by MPlayer:

1. VOBsub

2. OGM

3. CC (closed caption)

---

[1]Rigorously, subtitles refer to what is spoken, while closed captions may include other sounds such as doors slamming. For karaoke, there is no need to distinguish them.

© Jan Newmarch 2017
J. Newmarch, *Linux Sound Programming*, DOI 10.1007/978-1-4842-2496-0_26

4. MicroDVD

5. SubRip

6. SubViewer

7. Sami

8. VPlayer

9. RT

10. SSA

11. PJS (Phoenix Japanimation Society)

12. MPsub

13. AQTitle

14. JACOsub

VLC

According to VLC (www.videolan.org/vlc/features.php?cat=sub), support under Linux includes the following subtitle formats:

1. DVD

2. Text files (MicroDVD, SubRIP, SubViewer, SSA1-5, SAMI, VPlayer)

3. Closed captions

4. Vobsub

5. Universal Subtitle Format (USF)

6. SVCD/CVD

7. DVB

8. OGM

9. CMML

10. Kate

If you play some sort of video file, say XYZ.mpg, and there is also a file with the same root name and appropriate extension such as XYZ.ass (the extension for SubStation Alpha), then VLC will automatically load the subtitles file and play it. If the subtitles file has a different name, then it can be loaded from the VLC menu Video ➤ Subtitles Track. However, this does not appear to be as reliable as sharing the name.

Gnome Subtitles

See "Gnome Subtitles 1.3 is out!" (http://gnome-subtitles.sourceforge.net/). Gnome supports Adobe Encore DVD, Advanced Sub Station, Alpha AQ, Title DKS Subtitle Format FAB Subtitler Karaoke Lyrics LRC Karaoke Lyrics VKT MacSUB MicroDVD MPlayer MPlayer 2 MPSub Panimator Phoenix Japanimation Society Power DivX Sofni SubCreator 1.x SubRip Sub Station Alpha SubViewer 1.0, SubViewer 2.0, and ViPlay Subtitle File.

SubStation Alpha

The SSA/ASS specification is at MooDub.free (http://moodub.free.fr/video/ass-specs.doc). It is brief and appears to contain some minor errors with respect to later specifications and implementations. For example, the time format is different. Or are the later ones all wrong?

SSA/ASS files can be used stand-alone. They can also be included in container formats such as Matroska files, discussed briefly in Chapter 3. When they are embedded into MKV files, some restrictions (www.matroska.org/technical/specs/subtitles/ssa.html) are made, such as the text being converted into UTF-8 Unicode.

ASS files are divided into several sections.

1. General information about the environment the subtitle file expects, such as the X and Y resolutions

2. Style information such as colors and fonts

3. Event information, which is where the subtitle text is given along with timing information and any special effects to be applied

Under normal circumstances you would not directly create such files using a text editor. Instead, the program Aegisub gives you a GUI environment in which to create the files. Essentially, you just enter the text lines, plus the start and end times for each line to be displayed.

Figure 26-1 shows a screen dump.

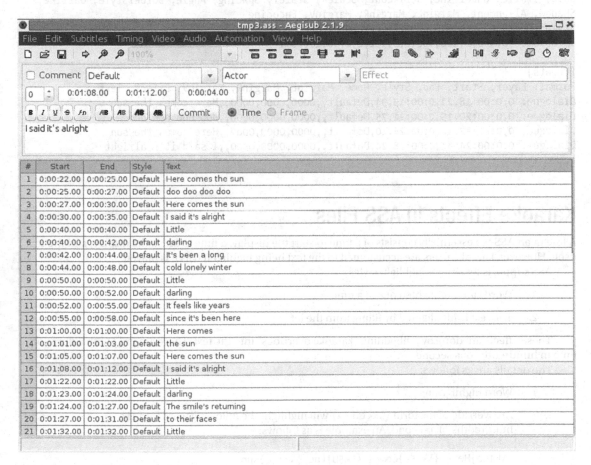

Figure 26-1. *Aegisub screenshot*

Many special effects are possible. The video on Bill Cresswell's blog (https://billcreswell. wordpress.com/tag/aegisub/) is an excellent example. Here is the direct YouTube link: www.youtube.com/ watch?v=OZOdgdglrAo.

For completeness, here is part of an ASS file I created:

```
[Script Info]
; Script generated by Aegisub 2.1.9
; http://www.aegisub.org/
Title: Default Aegisub file
ScriptType: v4.00+
WrapStyle: 0
PlayResX: 640
PlayResY: 480
ScaledBorderAndShadow: yes
Video Aspect Ratio: 0
Video Zoom: 6
Video Position: 0

[V4+ Styles]
Format: Name, Fontname, Fontsize, PrimaryColour, SecondaryColour, OutlineColour, BackColour,
Bold, Italic, Underline, StrikeOut, ScaleX, ScaleY, Spacing, Angle, BorderStyle, Outline,
Shadow, Alignment, MarginL, MarginR, MarginV, Encoding
Style: Default,Arial,20,&H00FFFFFF,&H00B4FCFC,&H00000008,
&H80000008,0,0,0,0,100,100,0,0,1,2,2,2,10,10,10,1

[Events]
Format: Layer, Start, End, Style, Name, MarginL, MarginR, MarginV, Effect, Text
Dialogue: 0,0:00:18.22,0:00:19.94,Default,,0000,0000,0000,,Here comes the sun
Dialogue: 0,0:00:20.19,0:00:21.75,Default,,0000,0000,0000,,doo doo doo doo
Dialogue: 0,0:00:22.16,0:00:24.20,Default,,0000,0000,0000,,Here comes the sun
Dialogue: 0,0:00:24.61,0:00:28.24,Default,,0000,0000,0000,,I said it's alright
...
```

Karaoke Effects in ASS Files

A line in an ASS file essentially consists of a time to start the display, a time to finish the display, and the text itself. However, karaoke users are accustomed to the text being highlighted as it is played.

ASS supports two major highlight styles.

1. Words are highlighted one at a time.

2. The text is highlighted by filling from the left.

These effects are done by embedding "karaoke overrides" into the text. These are in {} with a duration time in hundredths of a second.

The details are as follows:

1. Word highlighting

   An override of the form {\k<time>} will highlight the following word for time hundredths of a second. An example is as follows:

   {\k100}Here {\k150}comes {\k50}the {\k150}sun

2. Fill highlighting

An override of the form {\kf<time>} will progressively fill up the following word for time hundredths of a second. An example is as follows:

{\kf100}Here {\kf150}comes {\kf50}the {\kf150}sun

The three styles appear as follows:

3. Lines with no highlighting (see Figure 26-2)

Figure 26-2. Subtitles without highlighting

4. Word highlighting (see Figure 26-3)

Figure 26-3. *Subtitles with word highlighting*

5. Fill highlighting (see Figure 26-4)

Figure 26-4. *Subtitles with fill highlighting*

Multiline Karaoke

Ideally, a karaoke system should have a "look-ahead" mechanism whereby you can see the next line before having to sing it. This can be done by showing two lines of text with overlapping times at different heights. The algorithm is as follows:

```
When line N with markup is shown,
    show line N+1 without markup
After line N is finished, continue showing line N+1
When line N+1 is due to show,
    finish showing unmarked line N+1
    show line N+1 with markup
```

Here is the song "Here Comes the Sun" with lyrics:

```
Here comes the sun
doo doo doo doo
Here comes the sun
I said it's alright
```

The resultant ASS file should look like this:

```
Dialogue: 0,0:00:18.22,0:00:19.94,Default,,0000,0000,0100,,{\kf16}Here
{\kf46}comes {\kf43}the {\kf67}sun
Dialogue: 0,0:00:18.22,0:00:20.19,Default,,0000,0000,0000,,doo doo doo doo
Dialogue: 0,0:00:20.19,0:00:21.75,Default,,0000,0000,0000,,{\kf17}doo
{\kf25}doo {\kf21}doo {\kf92}doo
Dialogue: 0,0:00:20.19,0:00:22.16,Default,,0000,0000,0100,,Here comes the sun
Dialogue: 0,0:00:22.16,0:00:24.20,Default,,0000,0000,0100,,{\kf17}Here
{\kf46}comes {\kf43}the {\kf97}sun
Dialogue: 0,0:00:22.16,0:00:24.61,Default,,0000,0000,0000,,I said it's alright
```

Figure 26-5 shows what it looks like.

Figure 26-5. *Multiline subtitles*

libass

SubStation Alpha and its renderers appear to have been through a complex history. According to "The old and present: VSFilter" (http://blog.aegisub.org/2010/02/old-and-present-vsfilter.html), the ASS format was finalized in about 2004, and the renderer VSFilter was made open source at that time. However, around 2007 development of VSFilter ceased, and several forks were made. These introduced several extensions to the format, such as the blur tag by Aegisub. Some of these forks since merged, some were abandoned, and for some of these forks there is still code in the wild.

libass (http://code.google.com/p/libass/) is the main rendering library for Linux. An alternative, xy-vsfilter, claims to be faster, more reliable, and so on, but does not seem to have a Linux implementation. libass supports some of the later extensions. These seem to be the Aegisub 2008 extensions, according to "VSFilter hacks" (http://blog.aegisub.org/2008/07/vsfilter-hacks.html).

Converting KAR Files to MKV Files with ASS Subtitles

Follow these steps:

1. To pull out the lyrics from a KAR or MIDI file, use the Java DumpSequence given in Chapter 18, as follows, to get a dump of all events:

   ```
   java DumpSequence  song.kar  > song.dump
   ```

2. For line-only display, use the following Python script generated by Aegisub 2.1.9 to extract the lyrics and save them in ASS format:

   ```
   #!/usr/bin/python

   import fileinput
   import string
   import math

   TEXT_STR = "Dialogue: 0,%s,%s,Default,,0000,0000,0000,Karaoke,"

   textStr = TEXT_STR
   startTime = -1
   endTime = -1

   def printPreface():
       print '[Script Info]\r\n\
   ; Script generated by Aegisub 2.1.9\r\n\
   ; http://www.aegisub.org/\r\n\
   Title: Default Aegisub file\r\n\
   ScriptType: v4.00+\r\n\
   WrapStyle: 0\r\n\
   PlayResX: 640\r\n\
   PlayResY: 480\r\n\
   ScaledBorderAndShadow: yes\r\n\
   Video Aspect Ratio: 0\r\n\
   Video Zoom: 6\r\n\
   Video Position: 0\r\n\
   ```

```
\r\n\
[V4+ Styles]\r\n\
Format: Name, Fontname, Fontsize, PrimaryColour, SecondaryColour, OutlineColour,
BackColour, Bold, Italic, Underline, StrikeOut, ScaleX, ScaleY, Spacing, Angle,
BorderStyle, Outline, Shadow, Alignment, MarginL, MarginR, MarginV, Encoding\r\n\
Style: Default,Arial,36,&H00FFFFFF,&H0000000FF,&H00000000,
&H00000000,0,0,0,0,100,100,0,0,1,2,2,2,10,10,10,1\r\n\
\r\n\
[Events]\r\n\
Format: Layer, Start, End, Style, Name, MarginL, MarginR, MarginV, Effect, Text'

def timeFormat(s):
    global microSecondsPerTick

    tf = float(s)
    tf /= 62.6   #ticks per sec

    # This should be right , but is too slow
    #tf = (tf * microSecondsPerTick) / 1000000

    t = int(math.floor(tf))
    hundredths = round((tf-t)*100)
    secs = t % 60
    t /= 60
    mins = t % 60
    t /= 60
    hrs = t
    return "%01d:%02d:%02d.%02d" % (hrs, mins, secs, hundredths)

def doLyric(words):
    global textStr
    global startTime
    global endTime
    global TEXT_STR

    if words[1] == "0:":
        #print "skipping"
        return

    time = string.rstrip(words[1], ':')
    if startTime == -1:
        startTime = time
    #print words[1],
    if len(words) == 5:
        if words[4][0] == '\\' or words[4][0] == '/':
            #print "My name is %s and weight is %d kg!" % ('Zara', 21)
            #print startTime, endTime
            print textStr % (timeFormat(startTime), timeFormat(endTime)) + "\r\n",
            textStr = TEXT_STR + words[4][:1]
            startTime = -1
        else:
```

```
                textStr += words[4]
        else:
            textStr += ' '

        endTime = time

printPreface()

for line in fileinput.input():
    words = line.split()

    if len(words) >= 2:
        if words[0] == "Resolution:":
            ticksPerBeat = words[1]
        elif words[0] == "Length:":
            numTicks = int(words[1])
        elif words[0] == "Duration:":
            duration = int(words[1])
            microSecondsPerTick = duration/numTicks
            # print "Duration %d numTicks %d microSecondsPerTick %d" %
            (duration, numTicks, microSecondsPerTick)

    if len(words) >= 3 and words[2] == "Text":
        doLyric(words)
```

Here's an example:

```
python lyric2ass4kar.py song.dump > song.ass
```

3. For fill lyrics display, use the following Python script to extract the lyrics and save
    them in ASS format:

```
#!/usr/bin/python



import fileinput
import string
import math

TEXT_STR = "Dialogue: 0,%s,%s,Default,,0000,0000,0000,,"

textStr = "{\kf%d}"
plainTextStr = ""
startTime = -1
startWordTime = -1
endTime = -1
```

```python
        def printPreface():
            print '[Script Info]\r\n\
        ; Script generated by Aegisub 2.1.9\r\n\
        ; http://www.aegisub.org/\r\n\
        Title: Default Aegisub file\r\n\
        ScriptType: v4.00+\r\n\
        WrapStyle: 0\r\n\
        PlayResX: 640\r\n\
        PlayResY: 480\r\n\
        ScaledBorderAndShadow: yes\r\n\
        Video Aspect Ratio: 0\r\n\
        Video Zoom: 6\r\n\
        Video Position: 0\r\n\
        \r\n\
        [V4+ Styles]\r\n\
        Format: Name, Fontname, Fontsize, PrimaryColour, SecondaryColour, OutlineColour,
        BackColour, Bold, Italic, Underline, StrikeOut, ScaleX, ScaleY, Spacing, Angle,
        BorderStyle, Outline, Shadow, Alignment, MarginL, MarginR, MarginV, Encoding\r\n\
        Style: Default,Arial,36,&H00FFFFFF,&H000000FF,&H00000000,
        &H00000000,0,0,0,0,100,100,0,0,1,2,2,2,10,10,10,1\r\n\
        \r\n\
        [Events]\r\n\
        Format: Layer, Start, End, Style, Name, MarginL, MarginR, MarginV, Effect, Text'

        def timeFormat(s):
            global microSecondsPerTick

            tf = float(s)

            # frames per sec should be 60: 120 beats/min, 30 ticks per beat
            # but it is too slow on 54154
            tf /= 62.6   #ticks per sec

            # This should be right , but is too slow
            # tf = (tf * microSecondsPerTick) / 1000000

            t = int(math.floor(tf))
            hundredths = round((tf-t)*100)
            secs = t % 60
            t /= 60
            mins = t % 60
            t /= 60
            hrs = t
            return "%01d:%02d:%02d.%02d" % (hrs, mins, secs, hundredths)

        def durat(end, start):
            fend = float(end)
            fstart = float(start)
            d = (fend - fstart) / 62.9
            #print end, start, d
            return round(d*100)
```

```
    def doLyric(words):
        global textStr
        global plainTextStr
        global startTime
        global endTime
        global TEXT_STR
        global startWordTime
        global lineNum

        if words[1] == "0:":
            #print "skipping"
            return

        time = string.rstrip(words[1], ':')
        if startTime == -1:
            startTime = time
            startWordTime = time
            previousEndTime = time
        #print words[1],
        if len(words) == 5:
            if words[4][0] == '\\' or words[4][0] == '/':
                #print "My name is %s and weight is %d kg!" % ('Zara', 21)
                #print startTime, endTime
                dur = durat(time, startWordTime)
                textStr = textStr % (dur)
                if len(words[4]) == 1:
                    print TEXT_STR % (timeFormat(startTime),
                                        timeFormat(endTime)) + \
                                        textStr + "\r\n",

                # next word
                textStr = "{\kf%d}" + words[4][1:]
                startTime = -1
            else:
                textStr += words[4]
        else:
            # it's a space, gets lost by the split
            dur = durat(time, startWordTime)
            textStr = textStr % (dur) + " {\kf%d}"
            startWordTime = time

        endTime = time

printPreface()
# print "Dialogue: 0,0:00:18.22,0:00:19.94,Default,,0000,0000,0000,,{\k16}Here {\
k46}comes {\k43}the {\k67}sun"

for line in fileinput.input():
    words = line.split()
```

```
        if len(words) >= 2:
            if words[0] == "Resolution:":
                ticksPerBeat = words[1]
            elif words[0] == "Length:":
                numTicks = int(words[1])
            elif words[0] == "Duration:":
                duration = int(words[1])
                microSecondsPerTick = duration/numTicks
                # print "Duration %d numTicks %d microSecondsPerTick %d" % (duration,
                numTicks, microSecondsPerTick)

        if len(words) >= 3 and words[2] == "Text":
            doLyric(words)
```

Here's an example:

```
python lyric2karaokeass4kar.py song.dump > song.ass
```

4. For multiline lyrics display, use the following Python script to extract the lyrics
    and save them in ASS format:

```
#!/usr/bin/python

import fileinput
import string
import math

START_EVENTS = ["Dialogue: 0,%s,%s,Default,,0000,0000,0000,,",
                "Dialogue: 0,%s,%s,Default,,0000,0000,0100,,"]

TEXT_STR = "Dialogue: 0,%s,%s,Default,,0000,0000,0000,,"
TEXT_STR2 = "Dialogue: 0,%s,%s,Default,,0000,0000,0100,,"

textStr = "{\kf%d}"
plainTextStr = ""
startTime = -1
previousStartTime = -1
startWordTime = -1
endTime = -1
previousEndTime = -1
lineNum = 0

def printPreface():
    print '[Script Info]\r\n\
; Script generated by Aegisub 2.1.9\r\n\
; http://www.aegisub.org/\r\n\
Title: Default Aegisub file\r\n\
ScriptType: v4.00+\r\n\
WrapStyle: 0\r\n\
PlayResX: 640\r\n\
```

```
PlayResY: 480\r\n\
ScaledBorderAndShadow: yes\r\n\
Video Aspect Ratio: 0\r\n\
Video Zoom: 6\r\n\
Video Position: 0\r\n\
\r\n\
[V4+ Styles]\r\n\
Format: Name, Fontname, Fontsize, PrimaryColour, SecondaryColour, OutlineColour,
BackColour, Bold, Italic, Underline, StrikeOut, ScaleX, ScaleY, Spacing, Angle,
BorderStyle, Outline, Shadow, Alignment, MarginL, MarginR, MarginV, Encoding\r\n\
Style: Default,Arial,36,&H00FFFFFF,&H000000FF,&H00000000,
&H00000000,0,0,0,0,100,100,0,0,1,2,2,2,10,10,10,1\r\n\
\r\n\
[Events]\r\n\
Format: Layer, Start, End, Style, Name, MarginL, MarginR, MarginV, Effect, Text'

def timeFormat(s):
    global microSecondsPerTick

    tf = float(s)
    # print "factori is %f instead of %f" % ((1.0*microSecondsPerTick / 1000000),
    (1.0/62.9))
    # frames per sec should be 60: 120 beats/min, 30 ticks per beat
    # but it is too slow on 54154
    tf /= 62.6   #ticks per sec

    # This should be right , but is too slow
    # tf = (tf * microSecondsPerTick) / 1000000

    t = int(math.floor(tf))
    hundredths = round((tf-t)*100)
    secs = t % 60
    t /= 60#!/usr/bin/python

import fileinput
import string
import math

START_EVENTS = ["Dialogue: 0,%s,%s,Default,,0000,0000,0000,,",
                "Dialogue: 0,%s,%s,Default,,0000,0000,0100,,"]

TEXT_STR = "Dialogue: 0,%s,%s,Default,,0000,0000,0000,,"
TEXT_STR2 = "Dialogue: 0,%s,%s,Default,,0000,0000,0100,,"

textStr = "{\kf%d}"
plainTextStr = ""
startTime = -1
previousStartTime = -1
startWordTime = -1
endTime = -1
previousEndTime = -1
lineNum = 0
```

```python
def printPreface():
    print '[Script Info]\r\n\
; Script generated by Aegisub 2.1.9\r\n\
; http://www.aegisub.org/\r\n\
Title: Default Aegisub file\r\n\
ScriptType: v4.00+\r\n\
WrapStyle: 0\r\n\
PlayResX: 640\r\n\
PlayResY: 480\r\n\
ScaledBorderAndShadow: yes\r\n\
Video Aspect Ratio: 0\r\n\
Video Zoom: 6\r\n\
Video Position: 0\r\n\
\r\n\
[V4+ Styles]\r\n\
Format: Name, Fontname, Fontsize, PrimaryColour, SecondaryColour, OutlineColour, \
BackColour, Bold, Italic, Underline, StrikeOut, ScaleX, ScaleY, Spacing, Angle, \
BorderStyle, Outline, Shadow, Alignment, MarginL, MarginR, MarginV, Encoding\r\n\
Style: Default,Arial,36,&H00FFFFFF,&H000000FF,&H00000000,\
&H00000000,0,0,0,0,100,100,0,0,1,2,2,2,10,10,10,1\r\n\
\r\n\
[Events]\r\n\
Format: Layer, Start, End, Style, Name, MarginL, MarginR, MarginV, Effect, Text'

def timeFormat(s):
    global microSecondsPerTick

    tf = float(s)
    # print "factori is %f instead of %f" % ((1.0*microSecondsPerTick / 1000000), 
(1.0/62.9))
    # frames per sec should be 60: 120 beats/min, 30 ticks per beat
    # but it is too slow on 54154
    tf /= 62.6   #ticks per sec

    # This should be right , but is too slow
    # tf = (tf * microSecondsPerTick) / 1000000

    t = int(math.floor(tf))
    hundredths = round((tf-t)*100)
    secs = t % 60
    t /= 60
    mins = t % 60
    t /= 60
    hrs = t
    return "%01d:%02d:%02d.%02d" % (hrs, mins, secs, hundredths)

def durat(end, start):
    fend = float(end)
    fstart = float(start)
    d = (fend - fstart) / 62.9
    #print end, start, d
    return round(d*100)
```

```python
def doLyric(words):
    global textStr
    global plainTextStr
    global startTime
    global endTime
    global previousStartTime
    global previousEndTime
    global TEXT_STR
    global startWordTime
    global lineNum

    if words[1] == "0:":
        #print "skipping"
        return

    time = string.rstrip(words[1], ':')
    if startTime == -1:
        startTime = time
        startWordTime = time
        previousEndTime = time
    #print words[1],
    if len(words) == 5:
        if words[4][0] == '\\' or words[4][0] == '/':
            #print "My name is %s and weight is %d kg!" % ('Zara', 21)
            #print startTime, endTime
            dur = durat(time, startWordTime)
            textStr = textStr % (dur)

            if len(words[4]) == 1:

                if previousStartTime != -1:
                    print START_EVENTS[lineNum % 2] %
                    (timeFormat(previousStartTime),
                                                    timeFormat
                                                    (previousEndTime)) + \
                                                    plainTextStr + "\r\n",
                    print START_EVENTS[lineNum % 2] % (timeFormat(startTime),
                                                    timeFormat(endTime)) + \
                                                    textStr + "\r\n",

            # next word
            lineNum += 1
            #previousEndTime = time
            textStr = "{\kf%d}" + words[4][1:]
            plainTextStr = words[4][1:]
            previousStartTime = startTime
            startTime = -1
        else:
            textStr += words[4]
            plainTextStr += words[4]
    else:
```

```
            #print textStr
            #dur = duration(time, startWordTime)
            dur = durat(time, startWordTime)
            textStr = textStr % (dur) + " {\kf%d}"
            plainTextStr += ' '
            startWordTime = time

        endTime = time

    printPreface()
    # print "Dialogue: 0,0:00:18.22,0:00:19.94,Default,,0000,0000,0000,,
    {\k16}Here {\k46}comes {\k43}the {\k67}sun"

    for line in fileinput.input():
        words = line.split()

        if len(words) >= 2:
            if words[0] == "Resolution:":
                ticksPerBeat = words[1]
            elif words[0] == "Length:":
                numTicks = int(words[1])
            elif words[0] == "Duration:":
                duration = int(words[1])
                microSecondsPerTick = duration/numTicks
                # print "Duration %d numTicks %d microSecondsPerTick %d" %
                (duration, numTicks, microSecondsPerTick)

        if len(words) >= 3 and words[2] == "Text":
            doLyric(words)
        mins = t % 60
        t /= 60
        hrs = t
        return "%01d:%02d:%02d.%02d" % (hrs, mins, secs, hundredths)

    def durat(end, start):
        fend = float(end)
        fstart = float(start)
        d = (fend - fstart) / 62.9
        #print end, start, d
        return round(d*100)

    def doLyric(words):
        global textStr
        global plainTextStr
        global startTime
        global endTime
        global previousStartTime
        global previousEndTime
        global TEXT_STR
        global startWordTime
        global lineNum
```

```python
    if words[1] == "0:":
        #print "skipping"
        return

    time = string.rstrip(words[1], ':')
    if startTime == -1:
        startTime = time
        startWordTime = time
        previousEndTime = time
    #print words[1],
    if len(words) == 5:
        if words[4][0] == '\\' or words[4][0] == '/':
            #print "My name is %s and weight is %d kg!" % ('Zara', 21)
            #print startTime, endTime
            dur = durat(time, startWordTime)
            textStr = textStr % (dur)

            if len(words[4]) == 1:

                if previousStartTime != -1:
                    print START_EVENTS[lineNum % 2] %
                    (timeFormat(previousStartTime),
                                                      timeFormat
(previousEndTime)) + \
                                                      plainTextStr + "\r\n",
                print START_EVENTS[lineNum % 2] % (timeFormat(startTime),
                                                   timeFormat(endTime)) + \
                                                   textStr + "\r\n",

            # next word
            lineNum += 1
            #previousEndTime = time
            textStr = "{\kf%d}" + words[4][1:]
            plainTextStr = words[4][1:]
            previousStartTime = startTime
            startTime = -1
        else:
            textStr += words[4]
            plainTextStr += words[4]
    else:
        #print textStr
        #dur = duration(time, startWordTime)
        dur = durat(time, startWordTime)
        textStr = textStr % (dur) + " {\kf%d}"
        plainTextStr += ' '
        startWordTime = time

    endTime = time
```

```
printPreface()
# print "Dialogue: 0,0:00:18.22,0:00:19.94,Default,,0000,0000,0000,,
{\k16}Here {\k46}comes {\k43}the {\k67}sun"

for line in fileinput.input():
    words = line.split()

    if len(words) >= 2:
        if words[0] == "Resolution:":
            ticksPerBeat = words[1]
        elif words[0] == "Length:":
            numTicks = int(words[1])
        elif words[0] == "Duration:":
            duration = int(words[1])
            microSecondsPerTick = duration/numTicks
            # print "Duration %d numTicks %d microSecondsPerTick %d" %
            (duration, numTicks, microSecondsPerTick)

    if len(words) >= 3 and words[2] == "Text":
        doLyric(words)
```

Here is an example:

```
python lyric2karaokeass4kar.py song.dump > song.ass
```

5. Convert the MIDI sound file to a WAV file using fluidsynth.

```
fluidsynth -F song.wav /usr/share/sounds/sf2/FluidR3_GM.sf2 song.kar
```

6. Convert the WAV file to MP3.

```
lame song.wav song.mp3
```

7. Find a suitable video-only file for your background (I used one off my karaoke discs) and then merge them into an MKV file.

```
mkvmerge -o 54154.mkv 54154.mp3 54154.ass BACK01.MPG
```

The resultant MKV file can then be played as a stand-alone file by MPlayer.

```
mplayer song.mkv
```

It can also be played by VLC, but only with the ASS file present.

```
vlc song.mkv
```

Screen captures were shown earlier in the chapter, depending on the karaoke effect chosen.

Timing is, however, an issue. The default MIDI tempo is 120 beats per minute, and a common tick rate is 30 ticks per beat. This leads to a rate of 60 MIDI ticks per second. However, you are now playing MP3 files and ASS files, neither of which are MIDI files anymore and which are not necessarily synchronized. With a rate of 60 ticks per second in converting from MIDI to ASS, the lyrics run too slowly. Experimentally I have found 62.9 to be a reasonable rate for at least some files.

HTML5 Subtitles

HTML5 has support for video types, although exactly what video format is supported by which brower is variable. This includes support for subtitles and closed captions, using the HTML 5.1 track element. A search will turn up several detailed articles discussing this in more detail.

You need to prepare a file of timing and text instructions. The format shown in examples is as a .vtt file and can be as follows:

```
WEBVTT


1
00:00:01.000 --> 00:00:30.000  D:vertical A:start
This is the first line of text, displaying from 1-30 seconds

2
00:00:35.000 --> 00:00:50.000
And the second line of text
separated over two lines from 35 to 50 seconds
```

Here the first line is WEBVTT, and blocks of text are separated by blank lines. The format of VTT files is specified at "WebVTT: The Web Video Text Tracks Format" (http://dev.w3.org/html5/webvtt/).

The HTML then references the audio/video files and the subtitles file as follows:

```
<video  controls>
  <source src="output.webm" controls>
  <track src="54154.vtt" kind="subtitles" srclang="en" label="English" default />
  <!-- fallback for rubbish browsers -->
</video>
```

Figure 26-6 shows a screen capture.

Figure 26-6. *HTML5 subtitles*

There does not seem to be any mechanism for highlighting words progressively in a line. Possibly JavaScript may be able to do so, but after a cursory look, it doesn't seem likely. This makes it not yet suitable for karaoke.

Conclusion

This chapter discussed methods for overlaying subtitle text onto a changing video image. It is feasible, but there are only a few viable mechanisms.

CHAPTER 27

Karaoke FluidSynth

FluidSynth is an application for playing MIDI files and a library for MIDI applications. It does not have the hooks for playing karaoke files. This chapter discusses an extension to FluidSynth that adds appropriate hooks and then uses these to build a variety of karaoke systems.

Resources

Here are some resources:

- FluidSynth home page (`http://sourceforge.net/apps/trac/fluidsynth/`)

- FluidSynth download page (`http://sourceforge.net/projects/fluidsynth/`)

- FluidSynth 1.1 developer documentation (`http://fluidsynth.sourceforge.net/api/`)

- SourceArchive's fluidsynth documentation (`http://fluidsynth.sourcearchive.com/documentation/1.1.5-1/main.html`)

Players

`fluidsynth` is a command-line MIDI player. It runs under ALSA with the following command line:

```
fluidsynth -a alsa -l <soundfont> <files...>
```

Play MIDI Files

The FluidSynth API consists of the following:

- A sequencer created using `new_fluid_player`

- A synthesizer created using `new_fluid_synth`

- An audio player created using `new_fluid_audio_driver` that runs in a separate thread

© Jan Newmarch 2017
J. Newmarch, *Linux Sound Programming*, DOI 10.1007/978-1-4842-2496-0_27

- A "settings" object that can be used to control many features of the other components, created with new_fluid_settings and modified with calls such as fluid_settings_setstr

A typical program to play a sequence of MIDI files using ALSA follows. It creates the various objects, sets the audio player to use ALSA, and then adds each sound font and MIDI file to the player. The call to fluid_player_play then plays each MIDI file in turn. This program is just a repeat of the program shown in Chapter 20.

```c
#include <fluidsynth.h>
#include <fluid_midi.h>

int main(int argc, char** argv)
{
    int i;
    fluid_settings_t* settings;
    fluid_synth_t* synth;
    fluid_player_t* player;
    fluid_audio_driver_t* adriver;

    settings = new_fluid_settings();
    fluid_settings_setstr(settings, "audio.driver", "alsa");
    synth = new_fluid_synth(settings);
    player = new_fluid_player(synth);

    adriver = new_fluid_audio_driver(settings, synth);
    /* process command line arguments */
    for (i = 1; i < argc; i++) {
        if (fluid_is_soundfont(argv[i])) {
            fluid_synth_sfload(synth, argv[1], 1);
        } else {
            fluid_player_add(player, argv[i]);
        }
    }
    /* play the midi files, if any */
    fluid_player_play(player);
    /* wait for playback termination */
    fluid_player_join(player);
    /* cleanup */
    delete_fluid_audio_driver(adriver);
    delete_fluid_player(player);
    delete_fluid_synth(synth);
    delete_fluid_settings(settings);
    return 0;
}
```

Extending FluidSynth with Callbacks

Callbacks are functions registered with an application that are called when certain events occur. To build a karaoke player, you need to know the following:

- When a file is loaded so that you can extract all the lyrics from it for display at the right times

- When each meta lyric or text event occurs as output from a sequencer so that you can see what lyric is about to be sung

The first of these is fairly straightforward: FluidSynth has a function fluid_player_load that will load a file. You can change the code to add a suitable callback into that function that will give you access to the loaded MIDI file.

Getting lyric or text events out of a sequencer is not so easy, since they are never meant to appear! The MIDI specification allows these event types within a MIDI file, but they are not wire types so should never be sent from a sequencer to a synthesizer. The Java MIDI API makes them available by an out-of-band call to a meta event handler. FluidSynth just throws them away.

On the other hand, FluidSynth already has a callback to handle MIDI events sent from the sequencer to the synthesizer. It is the function fluid_synth_handle_midi_event and is set with the call fluid_player_ set_playback_callback. What you need to do is to first alter the existing FluidSynth code so that lyric and text events are passed through. Then insert a new playback callback that will intercept those events and do something with them while passing on all other events to the default handler. The default handler will ignore any such events anyway, so it does not need to be changed.

I have added one new function to FluidSynth, fluid_player_set_onload_callback, and added appropriate code to pass on some meta events. Then it is a matter of writing an onload callback to walk through the MIDI data from the parsed input file and writing a suitable MIDI event callback to handle the intercepted meta events while passing the rest through to the default handler.

These changes have been made to give a new source package fluidsynth-1.1.6-karaoke.tar.bz2. If you just want to work from a patch file, that is fluid.patch. The patch has been submitted to the FluidSynth maintainers.

To build from this package, do the same as you normally would.

```
tar jxf fluidsynth-1.1.6-karaoke.tar.bz2
cd fluidsynth-1.1.6
./configure
make clean
make
```

To get ALSA support, you will need to have installed the libasound2-dev package, like for Jack and other packages. You probably won't have many of them installed, so don't run make install or you will overwrite the normal fluidsynth package, which will probably have more features.

The previous program modified to just print out the lyric lines and the lyric events as they occur is karaoke_player.c, shown here:

```
#include <fluidsynth.h>
#include <fluid_midi.h>

/**
 * This MIDI event callback filters out the TEXT and LYRIC events
 * and passes the rest to the default event handler.
```

```
 * Here we just print the text of the event, more
 * complex handling can be done
 */
int event_callback(void *data, fluid_midi_event_t *event) {
    fluid_synth_t* synth = (fluid_synth_t*) data;
    int type = fluid_midi_event_get_type(event);
    int chan = fluid_midi_event_get_channel(event);
    if (synth == NULL) printf("Synth is null\n");
    switch(type) {
    case MIDI_TEXT:
        printf("Callback: Playing text event %s (length %d)\n",
                (char *) event->paramptr, event->param1);
        return  FLUID_OK;

    case MIDI_LYRIC:
        printf("Callback: Playing lyric event %d %s\n",
                event->param1, (char *) event->paramptr);
        return  FLUID_OK;
    }
    return fluid_synth_handle_midi_event( data, event);
}

/**
 * This is called whenever new data is loaded, such as a new file.
 * Here we extract the TEXT and LYRIC events and just print them
 * to stdout. They could e.g. be saved and displayed in a GUI
 * as the events are received by the event callback.
 */
int onload_callback(void *data, fluid_player_t *player) {
    printf("Load callback, tracks %d \n", player->ntracks);
    int n;
    for (n = 0; n < player->ntracks; n++) {
        fluid_track_t *track = player->track[n];
        printf("Track %d\n", n);
        fluid_midi_event_t *event = fluid_track_first_event(track);
        while (event != NULL) {
            switch (event->type) {
            case MIDI_TEXT:
            case MIDI_LYRIC:
                printf("Loaded event %s\n", (char *) event->paramptr);
            }
            event = fluid_track_next_event(track);
        }
    }
    return FLUID_OK;
}

int main(int argc, char** argv)
{
    int i;
    fluid_settings_t* settings;
```

```
fluid_synth_t* synth;
fluid_player_t* player;
fluid_audio_driver_t* adriver;
settings = new_fluid_settings();
fluid_settings_setstr(settings, "audio.driver", "alsa");
fluid_settings_setint(settings, "synth.polyphony", 64);
synth = new_fluid_synth(settings);
player = new_fluid_player(synth);

/* Set the MIDI event callback to our own functions rather than the system default */
fluid_player_set_playback_callback(player, event_callback, synth);

/* Add an onload callback so we can get information from new data before it plays */
fluid_player_set_onload_callback(player, onload_callback, NULL);

adriver = new_fluid_audio_driver(settings, synth);
/* process command line arguments */
for (i = 1; i < argc; i++) {
    if (fluid_is_soundfont(argv[i])) {
        fluid_synth_sfload(synth, argv[1], 1);
    } else {
        fluid_player_add(player, argv[i]);
    }
}
/* play the midi files, if any */
fluid_player_play(player);
/* wait for playback termination */
fluid_player_join(player);
/* cleanup */
delete_fluid_audio_driver(adriver);
delete_fluid_player(player);
delete_fluid_synth(synth);
delete_fluid_settings(settings);
return 0;
}
```

Assuming the new fluidsynth package is in an immediate subdirectory, to compile the program, you will need to pick up the local includes and libraries.

```
gcc -g -I fluidsynth-1.1.6/include/ -I fluidsynth-1.1.6/src/midi/ -I fluidsynth-1.1.6/src/
utils/ -c -o karaoke_player.o karaoke_player.c

gcc karaoke_player.o -Lfluidsynth-1.1.6/src/.libs -l fluidsynth -o karaoke_player
```

To run the program, you will also need to pick up the local library and the sound font file.

```
export LD_LIBRARY_PATH=./fluidsynth-1.1.6/src/.libs/
./karaoke_player /usr/share/soundfonts/FluidR3_GM.sf2 54154.mid
```

The output for a typical KAR file is as follows:

```
Load callback, tracks 1
Track 0
Loaded event #
Loaded event 0
Loaded event 0
Loaded event 0
Loaded event 1
Loaded event

...

Callback: Playing lyric event 2 #
Callback: Playing lyric event 2 0
Callback: Playing lyric event 2 0
Callback: Playing lyric event 2 0
Callback: Playing lyric event 2 1
Callback: Playing lyric event 3
```

Displaying and Coloring Text with Gtk

While there are many ways in which karaoke text can be displayed, a common pattern is to display two lines of text: the currently playing line and the next one. The current line is progressively highlighted and on completion is replaced by the next line.

In Chapter 25 you did that. But the Java libraries have not been polished and are distinctly slow and heavyweight. They also seem to be low priority on Oracle's development schedule for Java. So, here you will look at an alternative GUI and make use of the FluidSynth library. I chose the Gtk library for the reasons outlined in Chapter 15.

The first task is to build up an array of lyric lines as the file is loaded. You are asssuming KAR format files with up-front information as to the title, and so on, prefixed with @ and with newlines prefixed with \.

```
struct _lyric_t {
    gchar *lyric;
    long tick;
};
typedef struct _lyric_t lyric_t;

struct _lyric_lines_t {
    char *language;
    char *title;
    char *performer;
    GArray *lines; // array of GString *
};
typedef struct _lyric_lines_t lyric_lines_t;

GArray *lyrics;
lyric_lines_t lyric_lines;
```

```c
void build_lyric_lines() {
    int n;
    lyric_t *plyric;
    GString *line = g_string_new("");
    GArray *lines =  g_array_sized_new(FALSE, FALSE, sizeof(GString *), 64);

    lyric_lines.title = NULL;

    for (n = 0; n < lyrics->len; n++) {
        plyric = g_array_index(lyrics, lyric_t *, n);
        gchar *lyric = plyric->lyric;
        int tick = plyric->tick;

        if ((strlen(lyric) >= 2) && (lyric[0] == '@') && (lyric[1] == 'L')) {
            lyric_lines.language =  lyric + 2;
            continue;
        }

        if ((strlen(lyric) >= 2) && (lyric[0] == '@') && (lyric[1] == 'T')) {
            if (lyric_lines.title == NULL) {
                lyric_lines.title = lyric + 2;
            } else {
                lyric_lines.performer = lyric + 2;
            }
            continue;
        }

        if (lyric[0] == '@') {
            // some other stuff like @KMIDI KARAOKE FILE
            continue;
        }

        if ((lyric[0] == '/') || (lyric[0] == '\\')) {
            // start of a new line
            // add to lines
            g_array_append_val(lines, line);
            line = g_string_new(lyric + 1);
        } else {
            line = g_string_append(line, lyric);
        }
    }
    lyric_lines.lines = lines;

    printf("Title is %s, performer is %s, language is %s\n",
            lyric_lines.title, lyric_lines.performer, lyric_lines.language);
    for (n = 0; n < lines->len; n++) {
        printf("Line is %s\n", g_array_index(lines, GString *, n)->str);
    }
}
```

This is called from the onload callback.

```
int onload_callback(void *data, fluid_player_t *player) {
    long ticks = 0L;
    lyric_t *plyric;

    printf("Load callback, tracks %d \n", player->ntracks);
    int n;
    for (n = 0; n < player->ntracks; n++) {
        fluid_track_t *track = player->track[n];
        printf("Track %d\n", n);
        fluid_midi_event_t *event = fluid_track_first_event(track);
        while (event != NULL) {
            switch (fluid_midi_event_get_type (event)) {
            case MIDI_TEXT:
            case MIDI_LYRIC:
                /* there's no fluid_midi_event_get_sysex()
                   or fluid_midi_event_get_time() so we
                   have to look inside the opaque struct
                */
                ticks += event->dtime;
                printf("Loaded event %s for time %d\n",
                        event->paramptr,
                        ticks);
                plyric = g_new(lyric_t, 1);
                plyric->lyric = g_strdup(event->paramptr);
                plyric->tick = ticks;
                g_array_append_val(lyrics, plyric);
            }
            event = fluid_track_next_event(track);
        }
    }

    printf("Saved %d lyric events\n", lyrics->len);
    for (n = 0; n < lyrics->len; n++) {
        plyric = g_array_index(lyrics, lyric_t *, n);
        printf("Saved lyric %s at %d\n", plyric->lyric, plyric->tick);
    }

    build_lyric_lines();
}
```

The standard GUI part is to build an interface consisting of two labels, one above the other to hold lines of lyrics. This is just ordinary Gtk.

The final part is to handle lyric or text events from the sequencer. If the event is a \, then the current text in a label must be replaced with new text, after a small pause. Otherwise, the text in the label has to be progressively colored to indicate what is next to be played.

In Chapter 15, I discussed using Cairo to draw in pixbufs and using Pango to structure the text. The Gtk label understands Pango directly, so you just use Pango to format the text and display it in the label. This involves constructing an HTML string with the first part colored red and the rest in black. This can be set in the label, and there is no need to use Cairo.

The program is gtkkaraoke_player.c.

■ **Warning**   The following program crashes regularly when trying to copy a Pango attribute list in the Gtk code for sizing a label. Debugging shows that the Pango copy function is set to NULL somewhere in Gtk and shouldn't be. I have no fix as yet and haven't replicated the bug in a simple enough way to log a bug report.

```c
#include <fluidsynth.h>
#include <fluid_midi.h>
#include <string.h>

#include <gtk/gtk.h>

/* GString stuff from https://developer.gnome.org/glib/2.31/glib-Strings.html
   Memory alloc from https://developer.gnome.org/glib/2.30/glib-Memory-Allocation.html
   Packing demo from https://developer.gnome.org/gtk-tutorial/2.90/x386.html
   Thread stuff from https://developer.gnome.org/gtk-faq/stable/x481.html
   GArrays from http://www.gtk.org/api/2.6/glib/glib-Arrays.html
   Pango attributes from http://www.ibm.com/developerworks/library/l-u-pango2/
   Timeouts at http://www.gtk.org/tutorial1.2/gtk_tut-17.html
 */

struct _lyric_t {
    gchar *lyric;
    long tick;

};
typedef struct _lyric_t lyric_t;

struct _lyric_lines_t {
    char *language;
    char *title;
    char *performer;
    GArray *lines; // array of GString *
};
typedef struct _lyric_lines_t lyric_lines_t;

GArray *lyrics;

lyric_lines_t lyric_lines;

fluid_synth_t* synth;

GtkWidget *lyric_labels[2];

fluid_player_t* player;

int current_panel = -1;  // panel showing current lyric line
int current_line = 0;   // which line is the current lyric
```

```
gchar *current_lyric;    // currently playing lyric line
GString *front_of_lyric;  // part of lyric to be coloured red
GString *end_of_lyric;     // part of lyric to not be coloured

gchar *markup[] = {"<span foreground=\"red\">",
                   "</span><span foreground=\"black\">",
                   "</span>"};
gchar *markup_newline[] = {"<span foreground=\"black\">",
                   "</span>"};
GString *marked_up_label;

struct _reset_label_data {
    GtkLabel *label;
    gchar *text;
    PangoAttrList *attrs;
};

typedef struct _reset_label_data reset_label_data;

/**
 * redraw a label some time later
 */
gint reset_label_cb(gpointer data) {
    reset_label_data *rdata = ( reset_label_data *) data;

    if (rdata->label == NULL) {
        printf("Label is null, cant set its text \n");
        return FALSE;
    }

    printf("Resetting label callback to \"%s\"\n", rdata->text);

    gdk_threads_enter();

    gchar *str;
    str = g_strconcat(markup_newline[0], rdata->text, markup_newline[1], NULL);

    PangoAttrList *attrs;
    gchar *text;
    pango_parse_markup (str, -1,0, &attrs, &text, NULL, NULL);

    gtk_label_set_text(rdata->label, text);
    gtk_label_set_attributes(rdata->label, attrs);

    gdk_threads_leave();

    GtkAllocation* alloc = g_new(GtkAllocation, 1);
    gtk_widget_get_allocation((GtkWidget *) (rdata->label), alloc);
    printf("Set label text to \"%s\"\n", gtk_label_get_text(rdata->label));
    printf("Label has height %d width %d\n", alloc->height, alloc->width);
```

```
    printf("Set other label text to \"%s\"\n",
            gtk_label_get_text(rdata->label == lyric_labels[0] ?
                               lyric_labels[1] : lyric_labels[0]));
    gtk_widget_get_allocation((GtkWidget *) (rdata->label  == lyric_labels[0] ?
                               lyric_labels[1] : lyric_labels[0]), alloc);
    printf("Label has height %d width %d\n", alloc->height, alloc->width);

    return FALSE;
}

/**
 * This MIDI event callback filters out the TEXT and LYRIC events
 * and passes the rest to the default event handler.
 * Here we colour the text in a Gtk label
 */
int event_callback(void *data, fluid_midi_event_t *event) {
    fluid_synth_t* synth = (fluid_synth_t*) data;
    int type = fluid_midi_event_get_type(event);
    int chan = fluid_midi_event_get_channel(event);
    if (synth == NULL) printf("Synth is null\n");
    switch(type) {
    case MIDI_TEXT:
        printf("Callback: Playing text event %s (length %d)\n",
                (char *) event->paramptr, event->param1);

        if (((char *) event->paramptr)[0] == '\\') {
            // we've got a new line, change the label text on the NEXT panel
            int next_panel = current_panel; // really (current_panel+2)%2
            int next_line = current_line + 2;
            gchar *next_lyric;

            if (current_line + 2 >= lyric_lines.lines->len) {
                return FLUID_OK;
            }
            current_line += 1;
            current_panel = (current_panel + 1) % 2;

            // set up new line as current line
            char *lyric =  event->paramptr;

            // find the next line from lyric_lines array
            current_lyric = g_array_index(lyric_lines.lines, GString *, current_line)->str;

            // lyric is in 2 parts: front coloured, end uncoloured
            front_of_lyric = g_string_new(lyric+1); // lose \
            end_of_lyric = g_string_new(current_lyric);
            printf("New line. Setting front to %s end to \"%s\"\n", lyric+1, current_lyric);

            // update label for next line after this one
            char *str = g_array_index(lyric_lines.lines, GString *, next_line)->str;
            printf("Setting text in label %d to \"%s\"\n", next_panel, str);
```

```
        next_lyric = g_array_index(lyric_lines.lines, GString *, next_line)->str;

        gdk_threads_enter();

        // change the label after one second to avoid visual "jar"
        reset_label_data *label_data;
        label_data = g_new(reset_label_data, 1);
        label_data->label = (GtkLabel *) lyric_labels[next_panel];
        label_data->text = next_lyric;
        g_timeout_add(1000, reset_label_cb, label_data);

        // Dies if you try to flush at this point!
        // gdk_flush();

        gdk_threads_leave();
    } else {
        // change text colour as chars are played, using Pango attributes
        char *lyric =  event->paramptr;
        if ((front_of_lyric != NULL) && (lyric != NULL)) {
            // add the new lyric to the front of the existing coloured
            g_string_append(front_of_lyric, lyric);
            char *s = front_of_lyric->str;
            printf("Displaying \"%s\"\n", current_lyric);
            printf("  Colouring \"%s\"\n", s);
            printf("  Not colouring \"%s\"\n", current_lyric + strlen(s));

            // todo: avoid memory leak
            marked_up_label = g_string_new(markup[0]);
            g_string_append(marked_up_label, s);
            g_string_append(marked_up_label, markup[1]);
            g_string_append(marked_up_label, current_lyric + strlen(s));
            g_string_append(marked_up_label, markup[2]);
            printf("Marked up label \"%s\"\n", marked_up_label->str);

            /* Example from http://www.ibm.com/developerworks/library/l-u-pango2/
             */
            PangoAttrList *attrs;
            gchar *text;
            gdk_threads_enter();
            pango_parse_markup (marked_up_label->str, -1,0, &attrs, &text, NULL, NULL);
            printf("Marked up label parsed ok\n");
            gtk_label_set_text((GtkLabel *) lyric_labels[current_panel],
                               text);
            gtk_label_set_attributes(GTK_LABEL(lyric_labels[current_panel]), attrs);
            // Dies if you try to flush at this point!
            //gdk_flush();

            gdk_threads_leave();
        }
    }
    return  FLUID_OK;
```

```
    case MIDI_LYRIC:
        printf("Callback: Playing lyric event %d %s\n",
                event->param1, (char *) event->paramptr);
        return  FLUID_OK;

    case MIDI_EOT:
        printf("End of track\n");
        exit(0);
    }
    // default handler for all other events
    return fluid_synth_handle_midi_event( data, event);
}

/*
 * Build array of lyric lines from the MIDI file data
 */
void build_lyric_lines() {
    int n;
    lyric_t *plyric;
    GString *line = g_string_new("");
    GArray *lines =  g_array_sized_new(FALSE, FALSE, sizeof(GString *), 64);

    lyric_lines.title = NULL;

    for (n = 0; n < lyrics->len; n++) {
        plyric = g_array_index(lyrics, lyric_t *, n);
        gchar *lyric = plyric->lyric;
        int tick = plyric->tick;

        if ((strlen(lyric) >= 2) && (lyric[0] == '@') && (lyric[1] == 'L')) {
            lyric_lines.language =  lyric + 2;
            continue;
        }

        if ((strlen(lyric) >= 2) && (lyric[0] == '@') && (lyric[1] == 'T')) {
            if (lyric_lines.title == NULL) {
                lyric_lines.title = lyric + 2;
            } else {
                lyric_lines.performer = lyric + 2;
            }
            continue;
        }

        if (lyric[0] == '@') {
            // some other stuff like @KMIDI KARAOKE FILE
            continue;
        }
```

477

```
        if ((lyric[0] == '/') || (lyric[0] == '\\')) {
            // start of a new line
            // add to lines
            g_array_append_val(lines, line);
            line = g_string_new(lyric + 1);
        } else {
            line = g_string_append(line, lyric);
        }
    }
    lyric_lines.lines = lines;

    printf("Title is %s, performer is %s, language is %s\n",
            lyric_lines.title, lyric_lines.performer, lyric_lines.language);
    for (n = 0; n < lines->len; n++) {
        printf("Line is %s\n", g_array_index(lines, GString *, n)->str);
    }

}

/**
 * This is called whenever new data is loaded, such as a new file.
 * Here we extract the TEXT and LYRIC events and save them
 * into an array
 */
int onload_callback(void *data, fluid_player_t *player) {
    long ticks = 0L;
    lyric_t *plyric;

    printf("Load callback, tracks %d \n", player->ntracks);
    int n;
    for (n = 0; n < player->ntracks; n++) {
        fluid_track_t *track = player->track[n];
        printf("Track %d\n", n);
        fluid_midi_event_t *event = fluid_track_first_event(track);
        while (event != NULL) {
            switch (fluid_midi_event_get_type (event)) {
            case MIDI_TEXT:
            case MIDI_LYRIC:
                /* there's no fluid_midi_event_get_sysex()
                   or fluid_midi_event_get_time() so we
                   have to look inside the opaque struct
                */
                ticks += event->dtime;
                printf("Loaded event %s for time %ld\n",
                        (char *) event->paramptr,
                        ticks);
                plyric = g_new(lyric_t, 1);
                plyric->lyric = g_strdup(event->paramptr);
                plyric->tick = ticks;
                g_array_append_val(lyrics, plyric);
            }
```

```
                event = fluid_track_next_event(track);
        }
    }

    printf("Saved %d lyric events\n", lyrics->len);
    for (n = 0; n < lyrics->len; n++) {
        plyric = g_array_index(lyrics, lyric_t *, n);
        printf("Saved lyric %s at %ld\n", plyric->lyric, plyric->tick);
    }

    build_lyric_lines();

    // stick the first two lines into the labels so we can see
    // what is coming
    gdk_threads_enter();
    char *str = g_array_index(lyric_lines.lines, GString *, 1)->str;
    gtk_label_set_text((GtkLabel *) lyric_labels[0], str);
    str = g_array_index(lyric_lines.lines, GString *, 2)->str;
    gtk_label_set_text((GtkLabel *) lyric_labels[1], str);
    // gdk_flush ();

    /* release GTK thread lock */
    gdk_threads_leave();

    return FLUID_OK;
}

/* Called when the windows are realized
 */
static void realize_cb (GtkWidget *widget, gpointer data) {
    /* now we can play the midi files, if any */
    fluid_player_play(player);
}

static gboolean delete_event( GtkWidget *widget,
                              GdkEvent  *event,
                              gpointer   data )
{
    /* If you return FALSE in the "delete-event" signal handler,
     * GTK will emit the "destroy" signal. Returning TRUE means
     * you don't want the window to be destroyed.
     * This is useful for popping up 'are you sure you want to quit?'
     * type dialogs. */

    g_print ("delete event occurred\n");

    /* Change TRUE to FALSE and the main window will be destroyed with
     * a "delete-event". */

    return TRUE;
}
```

```c
/* Another callback */
static void destroy( GtkWidget *widget,
                     gpointer    data )
{
    gtk_main_quit ();
}

int main(int argc, char** argv)
{

    /* set up the fluidsynth stuff */
    int i;
    fluid_settings_t* settings;

    fluid_audio_driver_t* adriver;
    settings = new_fluid_settings();
    fluid_settings_setstr(settings, "audio.driver", "alsa");
    fluid_settings_setint(settings, "synth.polyphony", 64);
    fluid_settings_setint(settings, "synth.reverb.active", FALSE);
    fluid_settings_setint(settings, "synth.sample-rate", 22050);
    synth = new_fluid_synth(settings);
    player = new_fluid_player(synth);

    lyrics = g_array_sized_new(FALSE, FALSE, sizeof(lyric_t *), 1024);

    /* Set the MIDI event callback to our own functions rather than the system default */
    fluid_player_set_playback_callback(player, event_callback, synth);

    /* Add an onload callback so we can get information from new data before it plays */
    fluid_player_set_onload_callback(player, onload_callback, NULL);

    adriver = new_fluid_audio_driver(settings, synth);
    /* process command line arguments */
    for (i = 1; i < argc; i++) {
        if (fluid_is_soundfont(argv[i])) {
            fluid_synth_sfload(synth, argv[1], 1);
        } else {
            fluid_player_add(player, argv[i]);
        }
    }

    // Gtk stuff now

    /* GtkWidget is the storage type for widgets */
    GtkWidget *window;
    GtkWidget *button;
    GtkWidget *lyrics_box;

    /* This is called in all GTK applications. Arguments are parsed
     * from the command line and are returned to the application. */
    gtk_init (&argc, &argv);
```

```
/* create a new window */
window = gtk_window_new (GTK_WINDOW_TOPLEVEL);

/* When the window is given the "delete-event" signal (this is given
 * by the window manager, usually by the "close" option, or on the
 * titlebar), we ask it to call the delete_event () function
 * as defined above. The data passed to the callback
 * function is NULL and is ignored in the callback function. */
g_signal_connect (window, "delete-event",
                  G_CALLBACK (delete_event), NULL);

/* Here we connect the "destroy" event to a signal handler.
 * This event occurs when we call gtk_widget_destroy() on the window,
 * or if we return FALSE in the "delete-event" callback. */
g_signal_connect (window, "destroy",
                  G_CALLBACK (destroy), NULL);

g_signal_connect (window, "realize", G_CALLBACK (realize_cb), NULL);

/* Sets the border width of the window. */
gtk_container_set_border_width (GTK_CONTAINER (window), 10);

// Gtk 3.0 deprecates gtk_vbox_new in favour of gtk_grid
// but that isn't in Gtk 2.0, so we ignore warnings for now
lyrics_box = gtk_vbox_new(TRUE, 1);
gtk_widget_show(lyrics_box);

char *str = "   ";
lyric_labels[0] = gtk_label_new(str);
lyric_labels[1] = gtk_label_new(str);

gtk_widget_show (lyric_labels[0]);
gtk_widget_show (lyric_labels[1]);

gtk_box_pack_start (GTK_BOX (lyrics_box), lyric_labels[0], TRUE, TRUE, 0);
gtk_box_pack_start (GTK_BOX (lyrics_box), lyric_labels[1], TRUE, TRUE, 0);

/* This packs the button into the window (a gtk container). */
gtk_container_add (GTK_CONTAINER (window), lyrics_box);

/* and the window */
gtk_widget_show (window);

/* All GTK applications must have a gtk_main(). Control ends here
 * and waits for an event to occur (like a key press or
 * mouse event). */
gtk_main ();

/* wait for playback termination */
fluid_player_join(player);
/* cleanup */
```

```
    delete_fluid_audio_driver(adriver);
    delete_fluid_player(player);
    delete_fluid_synth(synth);
    delete_fluid_settings(settings);
    return 0;
}
```

When run, it looks like Figure 27-1.

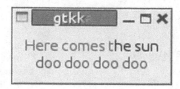

Figure 27-1. *Caption*

Playing a Background Video with Gtk

Chapter 15 showed how to play a background video with images (using pixbufs), text (using Cairo), and colored text (using Pango). You can extend that by adding in the dynamic text display for playing karaoke.

You can capture each lyric line in a structure, which keeps the whole line, the part that has been sung already, the Pango markup for the line, and the Pango attributes.

```
typedef struct _coloured_line_t {
    gchar *line;
    gchar *front_of_line;
    gchar *marked_up_line;
    PangoAttrList *attrs;
} coloured_line_t;
```

This is updated each time a MIDI lyric event occurs, in a thread listening to the FluidSynth sequencer.

A separate thread plays the video and on each frame overlays the frame image with the current and next lyric. This is set into a GdkImage for display by Gtk.

The program is gtkkaraoke_player_video_pango.c.

```
#include <fluidsynth.h>
#include <fluid_midi.h>
#include <string.h>

#include <gtk/gtk.h>

#include <libavcodec/avcodec.h>
#include <libavformat/avformat.h>
#include <libswscale/swscale.h>

// saving as pixbufs leaks memory
//#define USE_PIXBUF
```

```
/* run by
    gtkkaraoke_player_video_pango /usr/share/sounds/sf2/FluidR3_GM.sf2 /home/newmarch/Music/
karaoke/sonken/songs/54154.kar
*/

/*
 * APIs:
 * GString: https://developer.gnome.org/glib/2.28/glib-Strings.html
 * Pango text attributes: https://developer.gnome.org/pango/stable/pango-Text-Attributes.
html#pango-parse-markup
 * Pango layout: http://www.gtk.org/api/2.6/pango/pango-Layout-Objects.html
 * Cairo rendering: https://developer.gnome.org/pango/stable/pango-Cairo-Rendering.
html#pango-cairo-create-layout
 * Cairo surface_t: http://cairographics.org/manual/cairo-cairo-surface-t.html
 * GTK+ 3 Reference Manual: https://developer.gnome.org/gtk3/3.0/
 * Gdk Pixbufs: https://developer.gnome.org/gdk/stable/gdk-Pixbufs.html
 */

struct _lyric_t {
    gchar *lyric;
    long tick;


};
typedef struct _lyric_t lyric_t;

struct _lyric_lines_t {
    char *language;
    char *title;
    char *performer;
    GArray *lines; // array of GString *
};
typedef struct _lyric_lines_t lyric_lines_t;

GArray *lyrics;

lyric_lines_t lyric_lines;

typedef struct _coloured_line_t {
    gchar *line;
    gchar *front_of_line;
    gchar *marked_up_line;
    PangoAttrList *attrs;
#ifdef USE_PIXBUF
    GdkPixbuf *pixbuf;
#endif
} coloured_line_t;

coloured_line_t coloured_lines[2];

fluid_synth_t* synth;
```

```c
GtkWidget *image;
#if GTK_MAJOR_VERSION == 2
GdkPixmap *dbuf_pixmap;
#endif

int height_lyric_pixbufs[] = {300, 400}; // vertical offset of lyric in video

fluid_player_t* player;

int current_panel = 1;  // panel showing current lyric line
int current_line = 0;  // which line is the current lyric
gchar *current_lyric;   // currently playing lyric line
GString *front_of_lyric;  // part of lyric to be coloured red
//GString *end_of_lyric;    // part of lyrci to not be coloured

// Colours seem to get mixed up when putting a pixbuf onto a pixbuf
#ifdef USE_PIXBUF
#define RED blue
#else
#define RED red
#endif

gchar *markup[] = {"<span font=\"28\" foreground=\"RED\">",
                    "</span><span font=\"28\" foreground=\"white\">",
                    "</span>"};
gchar *markup_newline[] = {"<span foreground=\"black\">",
                            "</span>"};
GString *marked_up_label;

/* FFMpeg vbls */
AVFormatContext *pFormatCtx = NULL;
AVCodecContext *pCodecCtx = NULL;
int videoStream;
struct SwsContext *sws_ctx = NULL;
AVCodec *pCodec = NULL;

void markup_line(coloured_line_t *line) {
    GString *str =  g_string_new(markup[0]);
    g_string_append(str, line->front_of_line);
    g_string_append(str, markup[1]);
    g_string_append(str, line->line + strlen(line->front_of_line));
    g_string_append(str, markup[2]);
    printf("Marked up label \"%s\"\n", str->str);

    line->marked_up_line = str->str;
    // we have to free line->marked_up_line

    pango_parse_markup(str->str, -1,0, &(line->attrs), NULL, NULL, NULL);
    g_string_free(str, FALSE);
}
```

```
#ifdef USE_PIXBUF
void update_line_pixbuf(coloured_line_t *line) {
    //return;
    cairo_surface_t *surface;
    cairo_t *cr;

    int lyric_width = 480;
    int lyric_height = 60;
    surface = cairo_image_surface_create (CAIRO_FORMAT_ARGB32,
                                          lyric_width, lyric_height);
    cr = cairo_create (surface);

    PangoLayout *layout;
    PangoFontDescription *desc;

    // draw the attributed text
    layout = pango_cairo_create_layout (cr);
    pango_layout_set_text (layout, line->line, -1);
    pango_layout_set_attributes(layout, line->attrs);

    // centre the image in the surface
    int width, height;
    pango_layout_get_pixel_size(layout,
                                &width,
                                &height);
    cairo_move_to(cr, (lyric_width-width)/2, 0);

    pango_cairo_update_layout (cr, layout);
    pango_cairo_show_layout (cr, layout);

    // pull the pixbuf out of the surface
    unsigned char *data = cairo_image_surface_get_data(surface);
    width = cairo_image_surface_get_width(surface);
    height = cairo_image_surface_get_height(surface);
    int stride = cairo_image_surface_get_stride(surface);
    printf("Text surface width %d height %d stride %d\n", width, height, stride);

    GdkPixbuf *old_pixbuf = line->pixbuf;
    line->pixbuf = gdk_pixbuf_new_from_data(data, GDK_COLORSPACE_RGB, 1, 8, width, height,
stride, NULL, NULL);
    cairo_surface_destroy(surface);
    g_object_unref(old_pixbuf);
}
#endif

/**
 * This MIDI event callback filters out the TEXT and LYRIC events
 * and passes the rest to the default event handler.
 */
```

```
int event_callback(void *data, fluid_midi_event_t *event) {
    fluid_synth_t* synth = (fluid_synth_t*) data;
    int type = fluid_midi_event_get_type(event);
    int chan = fluid_midi_event_get_channel(event);
    if (synth == NULL) printf("Synth is null\n");

    //return 0;

    switch(type) {
    case MIDI_TEXT:
        printf("Callback: Playing text event %s (length %d)\n",
               (char *) event->paramptr, (int) event->param1);

        if (((char *) event->paramptr)[0] == '\\') {
            int next_panel = current_panel; // really (current_panel+2)%2
            int next_line = current_line + 2;
            gchar *next_lyric;

            if (current_line + 2 >= lyric_lines.lines->len) {
                return FLUID_OK;
            }
            current_line += 1;
            current_panel = (current_panel + 1) % 2;

            // set up new line as current line
            char *lyric =  event->paramptr;
            current_lyric = g_array_index(lyric_lines.lines, GString *, current_line)->str;
            front_of_lyric = g_string_new(lyric+1); // lose \
            printf("New line. Setting front to %s end to \"%s\"\n", lyric+1, current_lyric);

            coloured_lines[current_panel].line = current_lyric;
            coloured_lines[current_panel].front_of_line = lyric+1;
            markup_line(coloured_lines+current_panel);
#ifdef USE_PIXBUF
            update_line_pixbuf(coloured_lines+current_panel);
#endif
            // update label for next line after this one
            next_lyric = g_array_index(lyric_lines.lines, GString *, next_line)->str;

            marked_up_label = g_string_new(markup_newline[0]);

            g_string_append(marked_up_label, next_lyric);
            g_string_append(marked_up_label, markup_newline[1]);
            PangoAttrList *attrs;
            gchar *text;
            pango_parse_markup (marked_up_label->str, -1,0, &attrs, &text, NULL, NULL);

            coloured_lines[next_panel].line = next_lyric;
            coloured_lines[next_panel].front_of_line = "";
            markup_line(coloured_lines+next_panel);
```

```
#ifdef USE_PIXBUF
            update_line_pixbuf(coloured_lines+next_panel);
#endif
        } else {
            // change text colour as chars are played
            char *lyric = event->paramptr;
            if ((front_of_lyric != NULL) && (lyric != NULL)) {
                g_string_append(front_of_lyric, lyric);
                char *s = front_of_lyric->str;
                coloured_lines[current_panel].front_of_line = s;
                markup_line(coloured_lines+current_panel);
#ifdef USE_PIXBUF
                update_line_pixbuf(coloured_lines+current_panel);
#endif
            }
        }
        return  FLUID_OK;

    case MIDI_LYRIC:
        printf("Callback: Playing lyric event %d %s\n", (int) event->param1, (char *) event-
>paramptr);
        return  FLUID_OK;

    case MIDI_EOT:
        printf("End of track\n");
        exit(0);
    }
    return fluid_synth_handle_midi_event( data, event);
}

void build_lyric_lines() {
    int n;
    lyric_t *plyric;
    GString *line = g_string_new("");
    GArray *lines = g_array_sized_new(FALSE, FALSE, sizeof(GString *), 64);

    lyric_lines.title = NULL;

    for (n = 0; n < lyrics->len; n++) {
        plyric = g_array_index(lyrics, lyric_t *, n);
        gchar *lyric = plyric->lyric;
        int tick = plyric->tick;

        if ((strlen(lyric) >= 2) && (lyric[0] == '@') && (lyric[1] == 'L')) {
            lyric_lines.language =  lyric + 2;
            continue;
        }
```

```c
        if ((strlen(lyric) >= 2) && (lyric[0] == '@') && (lyric[1] == 'T')) {
            if (lyric_lines.title == NULL) {
                lyric_lines.title = lyric + 2;
            } else {
                lyric_lines.performer = lyric + 2;
            }
            continue;
        }

        if (lyric[0] == '@') {
            // some other stuff like @KMIDI KARAOKE FILE
            continue;
        }

        if ((lyric[0] == '/') || (lyric[0] == '\\')) {
            // start of a new line
            // add to lines
            g_array_append_val(lines, line);
            line = g_string_new(lyric + 1);
        } else {
            line = g_string_append(line, lyric);
        }
    }
    lyric_lines.lines = lines;

    printf("Title is %s, performer is %s, language is %s\n",
            lyric_lines.title, lyric_lines.performer, lyric_lines.language);
    for (n = 0; n < lines->len; n++) {
        printf("Line is %s\n", g_array_index(lines, GString *, n)->str);
    }

}


/**
 * This is called whenever new data is loaded, such as a new file.
 * Here we extract the TEXT and LYRIC events and just print them
 * to stdout. They could e.g. be saved and displayed in a GUI
 * as the events are received by the event callback.
 */
int onload_callback(void *data, fluid_player_t *player) {
    long ticks = 0L;
    lyric_t *plyric;

    printf("Load callback, tracks %d \n", player->ntracks);
    int n;
    for (n = 0; n < player->ntracks; n++) {
        fluid_track_t *track = player->track[n];
        printf("Track %d\n", n);
        fluid_midi_event_t *event = fluid_track_first_event(track);
```

```
      while (event != NULL) {
          switch (fluid_midi_event_get_type (event)) {
          case MIDI_TEXT:
          case MIDI_LYRIC:
              /* there's no fluid_midi_event_get_sysex()
                 or fluid_midi_event_get_time() so we
                 have to look inside the opaque struct
              */
              ticks += event->dtime;
              printf("Loaded event %s for time %ld\n",
                     (char *) event->paramptr,
                     ticks);
              plyric = g_new(lyric_t, 1);
              plyric->lyric = g_strdup(event->paramptr);
              plyric->tick = ticks;
              g_array_append_val(lyrics, plyric);
          }
          event = fluid_track_next_event(track);
      }
   }

   printf("Saved %d lyric events\n", lyrics->len);
   for (n = 0; n < lyrics->len; n++) {
       plyric = g_array_index(lyrics, lyric_t *, n);
       printf("Saved lyric %s at %ld\n", plyric->lyric, plyric->tick);
   }

   build_lyric_lines();

   return FLUID_OK;
}

static void overlay_lyric(cairo_t *cr,
                          coloured_line_t *line,
                          int ht) {
   PangoLayout *layout;
   int height, width;

   if (line->line == NULL) {
       return;
   }

   layout = pango_cairo_create_layout (cr);
   pango_layout_set_text (layout, line->line, -1);
   pango_layout_set_attributes(layout, line->attrs);
   pango_layout_get_pixel_size(layout,
                                &width,
                                &height);
   cairo_move_to(cr, (720-width)/2, ht);
```

```
        pango_cairo_update_layout (cr, layout);
        pango_cairo_show_layout (cr, layout);

        g_object_unref(layout);
}

static void pixmap_destroy_notify(guchar *pixels,
                                        gpointer data) {
        printf("Ddestroy pixmap\n");
}

static void *play_background(void *args) {
        /* based on code from
            http://www.cs.dartmouth.edu/~xy/cs23/gtk.html
            http://cdry.wordpress.com/2009/09/09/using-custom-io-callbacks-with-ffmpeg/
        */

        int i;
        AVPacket packet;
        int frameFinished;
        AVFrame *pFrame = NULL;

        int oldSize;
        char *oldData;
        int bytesDecoded;
        GdkPixbuf *pixbuf;
        AVFrame *picture_RGB;
        char *buffer;

#if GTK_MAJOR_VERSION == 2
        GdkPixmap *pixmap;
        GdkBitmap *mask;
#endif

        pFrame=avcodec_alloc_frame();

        i=0;
        picture_RGB = avcodec_alloc_frame();
        buffer = malloc (avpicture_get_size(PIX_FMT_RGB24, 720, 576));
        avpicture_fill((AVPicture *)picture_RGB, buffer, PIX_FMT_RGB24, 720, 576);

        while(av_read_frame(pFormatCtx, &packet)>=0) {
            if(packet.stream_index==videoStream) {
                //printf("Frame %d\n", i++);
                usleep(33670);  // 29.7 frames per second
                // Decode video frame
                avcodec_decode_video2(pCodecCtx, pFrame, &frameFinished,
                                        &packet);
                int width = pCodecCtx->width;
                int height = pCodecCtx->height;
```

```
    sws_ctx = sws_getContext(pCodecCtx->width, pCodecCtx->height, pCodecCtx->pix_
    fmt, pCodecCtx->width, pCodecCtx->height, PIX_FMT_RGB24, SWS_BICUBIC, NULL,
    NULL, NULL);

    if (frameFinished) {
        printf("Frame %d\n", i++);

        sws_scale(sws_ctx,  (uint8_t const * const *) pFrame->data, pFrame-
        >linesize, 0, pCodecCtx->height, picture_RGB->data, picture_RGB->linesize);

        pixbuf = gdk_pixbuf_new_from_data(picture_RGB->data[0], GDK_COLORSPACE_RGB,
        0, 8, 720, 480, picture_RGB->linesize[0], pixmap_destroy_notify, NULL);

        /* start GTK thread lock for drawing */
        gdk_threads_enter();

#define SHOW_LYRIC
#ifdef SHOW_LYRIC
        // Create the destination surface
        cairo_surface_t *surface = cairo_image_surface_create (CAIRO_FORMAT_ARGB32,
                                                            width, height);

        cairo_t *cr = cairo_create(surface);

        // draw the background image
        gdk_cairo_set_source_pixbuf(cr, pixbuf, 0, 0);
        cairo_paint (cr);

#ifdef USE_PIXBUF
        // draw the lyric
        GdkPixbuf *lyric_pixbuf = coloured_lines[current_panel].pixbuf;
        if (lyric_pixbuf != NULL) {
            int width = gdk_pixbuf_get_width(lyric_pixbuf);
            gdk_cairo_set_source_pixbuf(cr,
                                lyric_pixbuf,
                                (720-width)/2,
                                 height_lyric_pixbufs[current_panel]);
            cairo_paint (cr);
        }

        int next_panel = (current_panel+1) % 2;
        lyric_pixbuf = coloured_lines[next_panel].pixbuf;
        if (lyric_pixbuf != NULL) {
            int width = gdk_pixbuf_get_width(lyric_pixbuf);
            gdk_cairo_set_source_pixbuf(cr,
                                lyric_pixbuf,
                                (720-width)/2,
                                 height_lyric_pixbufs[next_panel]);
            cairo_paint (cr);
        }
```

```
#else

                overlay_lyric(cr,
                              coloured_lines+current_panel,
                              height_lyric_pixbufs[current_panel]);

                int next_panel = (current_panel+1) % 2;
                overlay_lyric(cr,
                              coloured_lines+next_panel,
                              height_lyric_pixbufs[next_panel]);
#endif
                pixbuf = gdk_pixbuf_get_from_surface(surface,
                                                     0,
                                                     0,
                                                     width,
                                                     height);

                gtk_image_set_from_pixbuf((GtkImage*) image, pixbuf);

                g_object_unref(pixbuf);        /* reclaim memory */
                //g_object_unref(layout);
                cairo_surface_destroy(surface);
                cairo_destroy(cr);
#else
        gtk_image_set_from_pixbuf((GtkImage*) image, pixbuf);
#endif /* SHOW_LYRIC */

                /* release GTK thread lock */
                gdk_threads_leave();
            }
        }
        av_free_packet(&packet);
    }
    sws_freeContext(sws_ctx);

    printf("Video over!\n");
    exit(0);
}

static void *play_midi(void *args) {
    fluid_player_play(player);

    printf("Audio finished\n");
    //exit(0);
}

/* Called when the windows are realized
 */
static void realize_cb (GtkWidget *widget, gpointer data) {
    /* start the video playing in its own thread */
    pthread_t tid;
    pthread_create(&tid, NULL, play_background, NULL);
```

```c
    /* start the MIDI file playing in its own thread */
    pthread_t tid_midi;
    pthread_create(&tid_midi, NULL, play_midi, NULL);
}

static gboolean delete_event( GtkWidget *widget,
                              GdkEvent  *event,
                              gpointer   data )
{
    /* If you return FALSE in the "delete-event" signal handler,
     * GTK will emit the "destroy" signal. Returning TRUE means
     * you don't want the window to be destroyed.
     * This is useful for popping up 'are you sure you want to quit?'
     * type dialogs. */

    g_print ("delete event occurred\n");

    /* Change TRUE to FALSE and the main window will be destroyed with
     * a "delete-event". */

    return TRUE;
}

/* Another callback */
static void destroy( GtkWidget *widget,
                     gpointer   data )
{
    gtk_main_quit ();
}

int main(int argc, char** argv)
{
    XInitThreads();

    int i;

    fluid_settings_t* settings;

    fluid_audio_driver_t* adriver;
    settings = new_fluid_settings();
    fluid_settings_setstr(settings, "audio.driver", "alsa");
    //fluid_settings_setint(settings, "lash.enable", 0);
    fluid_settings_setint(settings, "synth.polyphony", 64);
    fluid_settings_setint(settings, "synth.reverb.active", FALSE);
    fluid_settings_setint(settings, "synth.sample-rate", 22050);
    synth = new_fluid_synth(settings);
    player = new_fluid_player(synth);

    lyrics = g_array_sized_new(FALSE, FALSE, sizeof(lyric_t *), 1024);
```

```
/* Set the MIDI event callback to our own functions rather than the system default */
fluid_player_set_playback_callback(player, event_callback, synth);

/* Add an onload callback so we can get information from new data before it plays */
fluid_player_set_onload_callback(player, onload_callback, NULL);

adriver = new_fluid_audio_driver(settings, synth);

/* process command line arguments */
for (i = 1; i < argc; i++) {
    if (fluid_is_soundfont(argv[i])) {
        fluid_synth_sfload(synth, argv[1], 1);
    } else {
        fluid_player_add(player, argv[i]);
    }
}

/* FFMpeg stuff */

AVFrame *pFrame = NULL;
AVPacket packet;

AVDictionary *optionsDict = NULL;

av_register_all();

if(avformat_open_input(&pFormatCtx, "short.mpg", NULL, NULL)!=0) {
    printf("Couldn't open video file\n");
    return -1; // Couldn't open file
}

// Retrieve stream information
if(avformat_find_stream_info(pFormatCtx, NULL)<0) {
    printf("Couldn't find stream information\n");
    return -1; // Couldn't find stream information
}

// Dump information about file onto standard error
av_dump_format(pFormatCtx, 0, argv[1], 0);

// Find the first video stream
videoStream=-1;
for(i=0; i<pFormatCtx->nb_streams; i++)
    if(pFormatCtx->streams[i]->codec->codec_type==AVMEDIA_TYPE_VIDEO) {
        videoStream=i;
        break;
    }
if(videoStream==-1)
    return -1; // Didn't find a video stream
```

```
for(i=0; i<pFormatCtx->nb_streams; i++)
    if(pFormatCtx->streams[i]->codec->codec_type==AVMEDIA_TYPE_AUDIO) {
        printf("Found an audio stream too\n");
        break;
    }

// Get a pointer to the codec context for the video stream
pCodecCtx=pFormatCtx->streams[videoStream]->codec;

// Find the decoder for the video stream
pCodec=avcodec_find_decoder(pCodecCtx->codec_id);
if(pCodec==NULL) {
    fprintf(stderr, "Unsupported codec!\n");
    return -1; // Codec not found
}

// Open codec
if(avcodec_open2(pCodecCtx, pCodec, &optionsDict)<0) {
    printf("Could not open codec\n");
    return -1; // Could not open codec
}

sws_ctx =
    sws_getContext
    (
     pCodecCtx->width,
     pCodecCtx->height,
     pCodecCtx->pix_fmt,
     pCodecCtx->width,
     pCodecCtx->height,
     PIX_FMT_YUV420P,
     SWS_BILINEAR,
     NULL,
     NULL,
     NULL
    );

/* GTK stuff now */

/* GtkWidget is the storage type for widgets */
GtkWidget *window;
GtkWidget *button;
GtkWidget *lyrics_box;

/* This is called in all GTK applications. Arguments are parsed
 * from the command line and are returned to the application. */
gtk_init (&argc, &argv);

/* create a new window */
window = gtk_window_new (GTK_WINDOW_TOPLEVEL);
```

```
/* When the window is given the "delete-event" signal (this is given
 * by the window manager, usually by the "close" option, or on the
 * titlebar), we ask it to call the delete_event () function
 * as defined above. The data passed to the callback
 * function is NULL and is ignored in the callback function. */
g_signal_connect (window, "delete-event",
                  G_CALLBACK (delete_event), NULL);

/* Here we connect the "destroy" event to a signal handler.
 * This event occurs when we call gtk_widget_destroy() on the window,
 * or if we return FALSE in the "delete-event" callback. */
g_signal_connect (window, "destroy",
                  G_CALLBACK (destroy), NULL);

g_signal_connect (window, "realize", G_CALLBACK (realize_cb), NULL);

/* Sets the border width of the window. */
gtk_container_set_border_width (GTK_CONTAINER (window), 10);

lyrics_box = gtk_vbox_new(TRUE, 1);
gtk_widget_show(lyrics_box);

/*
char *str = "     ";
lyric_labels[0] = gtk_label_new(str);
str = "World";
lyric_labels[1] = gtk_label_new(str);
*/

image = gtk_image_new();

//image_drawable = gtk_drawing_area_new();
//gtk_widget_set_size_request (canvas, 720, 480);
//gtk_drawing_area_size((GtkDrawingArea *) image_drawable, 720, 480);

//gtk_widget_show (lyric_labels[0]);
//gtk_widget_show (lyric_labels[1]);

gtk_widget_show (image);

//gtk_box_pack_start (GTK_BOX (lyrics_box), lyric_labels[0], TRUE, TRUE, 0);
//gtk_box_pack_start (GTK_BOX (lyrics_box), lyric_labels[1], TRUE, TRUE, 0);
gtk_box_pack_start (GTK_BOX (lyrics_box), image, TRUE, TRUE, 0);
//gtk_box_pack_start (GTK_BOX (lyrics_box), canvas, TRUE, TRUE, 0);
//gtk_box_pack_start (GTK_BOX (lyrics_box), image_drawable, TRUE, TRUE, 0);

/* This packs the button into the window (a gtk container). */
gtk_container_add (GTK_CONTAINER (window), lyrics_box);

/* and the window */
gtk_widget_show (window);
```

```
/* All GTK applications must have a gtk_main(). Control ends here
 * and waits for an event to occur (like a key press or
 * mouse event). */
gtk_main ();

return 0;

/* wait for playback termination */
fluid_player_join(player);
/* cleanup */
delete_fluid_audio_driver(adriver);
delete_fluid_player(player);
delete_fluid_synth(synth);
delete_fluid_settings(settings);

return 0;
}
```

The application looks like Figure 27-2.

Figure 27-2. *Caption*

Conclusion

By extending FluidSynth, it can be made into a karaoke player in various ways. It is quite heavy in CPU usage, though. On my laptop, the final version runs at about 100 percent CPU.

■ ■ ■

## CHAPTER 28

TiMidity and Karaoke

TiMidity is a MIDI player, not a karaoke player. It is designed as a stand-alone application with a particular kind of extensibility. Out of the box it can sort of play karaoke but not well. This chapter looks at how to work with TiMidity to build a karaoke system.

By default it just plays the MIDI music, with the lyrics printed out.

```
$timidity ../54154.mid
Requested buffer size 32768, fragment size 8192
ALSA pcm 'default' set buffer size 32768, period size 8192 bytes
Playing ../54154.mid
MIDI file: ../54154.mid
Format: 1  Tracks: 1  Divisions: 30
No instrument mapped to tone bank 0, program 92 - this instrument will not be heard
#0001
@@OO@12
@Here Comes The Sun
@
@@Beatles
Here comes the sun
doo doo doo doo
Here comes the sun
I said it's alright
Little
darling
```

But it has a number of alternative interfaces that give different displays. If you run timidity with the -h (help) option, it will show a screen including something like this:

```
Available interfaces (-i, --interface option):
  -in        ncurses interface
  -ie        Emacs interface (invoked from `M-x timidity')
  -ia        XAW interface
  -id        dumb interface
  -ir        remote interface
  -iA        ALSA sequencer interface
```

The default interface is "dumb," but if you run with, say, the Xaw interface, you get a display like Figure 28-1.

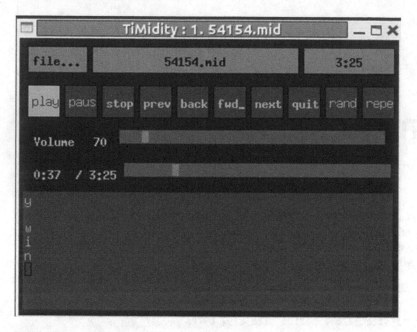

Figure 28-1. *TiMidity with Xaw interface*

There is, however, one unfortunate effect: the lyrics are displayed *before* they are due to be played! To get the lyrics played just as they should be sung, you need to turn on the --trace option. From the man page, "Toggles trace mode. In trace mode, TiMidity++ attempts to display its current state in real time." (You may find the link between documentation and behavior a little less than obvious.)

```
timidity --trace ../54154.mid
```

This now works fine for MIDI files; the lyrics are displayed when they should be sung. But it doesn't display the lyrics for KAR files. For that you need the --trace-text-meta option.

```
timidity --trace --trace-text-meta ../54154.kar
```

So, by this stage, TiMidity will display the lyrics on the screen in real time for karaoke files (and MIDI files with lyric events). To have your own control over this display, you need to build your own TiMidity interface.

TiMidity and Jack

In Chapter 17, I discussed playing MIDI files using Jack. Jack is designed to link audio sources and sinks in arbitrary configurations. By running qjackctl, you can link, for example, microphone outputs to speaker inputs. This is done by dragging capture_1 to playback_1, and so on, and it looks like Figure 28-2.

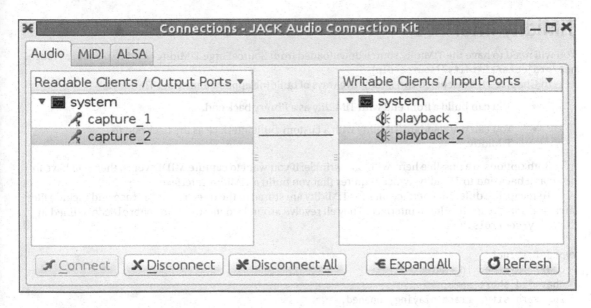

Figure 28-2. *qjackctl showing microphone to speakers*

If TiMidity is then run with Jack output, you get instant karaoke. You can also see the lyrics played in real time using the --trace option.

```
timidity -Oj --trace 54154.mid
```

The connections are shown in qjackctl in Figure 28-3.

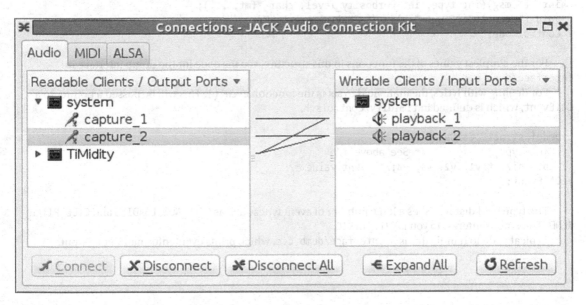

Figure 28-3. *qjackctl showing TiMidity*

The lyric display is klunky and will be improved later.

TiMidity Interface

You will need to have the TiMidity source downloaded from SourceForge TiMidity++ (http://sourceforge. net/projects/timidity/?source=dlp).

In Chapter 21, I discussed two alternative ways of building applications using TiMidity.

- You can build a front end with TiMidity as a library back end.

- You can use standard TiMidity with a custom-built interface as the back end to TiMidity.

Both options are possible here, with one wrinkle: if you want to capture MIDI events, then you have to do so as a back end to TiMidity, which requires that you build a TiMidity interface.

To recap, the different interface files for TiMidity are stored in the directory interface and include files such as dumb_c.c for the dumb interface. They all revolve around a data structure ControlMode defined in timidity/controls.h.

```
typedef struct {
  char *id_name, id_character;
  char *id_short_name;
  int verbosity, trace_playing, opened;

  int32 flags;

  int  (*open)(int using_stdin, int using_stdout);
  void (*close)(void);
  int (*pass_playing_list)(int number_of_files, char *list_of_files[]);
  int  (*read)(int32 *valp);
  int  (*write)(char *buf, int32 size);
  int  (*cmsg)(int type, int verbosity_level, char *fmt, ...);
  void (*event)(CtlEvent *ev);  /* Control events */
} ControlMode;
```

For the simplest values of the functions in this structure, see the code for the dumb interface in interface/dumb_c.c.

For dealing with lyrics, the main field to set is the function event(). This will be passed a pointer to a CtlEvent, which is defined in timidity/controls.h.

```
typedef struct _CtlEvent {
    int type;           /* See above */
    ptr_size_t v1, v2, v3, v4;/* Event value */
} CtlEvent;
```

The type field distinguishes a large number of event types such as CTLE_NOW_LOADING and CTLE_PITCH_BEND. The type of interest to you is CTLE_LYRIC.

Typical code to handle this is in interface/dumb_c.c, which prints event information to output.

```c
static void ctl_event(CtlEvent *e)
{
    switch(e->type) {
      case CTLE_LYRIC:
        ctl_lyric((int)e->v1);
        break;
    }
}

static void ctl_lyric(int lyricid)
{
    char *lyric;

    lyric = event2string(lyricid);
    if(lyric != NULL)
    {
        if(lyric[0] == ME_KARAOKE_LYRIC)
        {
            if(lyric[1] == '/' || lyric[1] == '\\')
            {
                fprintf(outfp, "\n%s", lyric + 2);
                fflush(outfp);
            }
            else if(lyric[1] == '@')
            {
                if(lyric[2] == 'L')
                    fprintf(outfp, "\nLanguage: %s\n", lyric + 3);
                else if(lyric[2] == 'T')
                    fprintf(outfp, "Title: %s\n", lyric + 3);
                else
                    fprintf(outfp, "%s\n", lyric + 1);
            }
            else
            {
                fputs(lyric + 1, outfp);
                fflush(outfp);
            }
        }
        else
        {
            if(lyric[0] == ME_CHORUS_TEXT || lyric[0] == ME_INSERT_TEXT)
                fprintf(outfp, "\r");
            fputs(lyric + 1, outfp);
            fflush(outfp);
        }
    }
}
```

Getting the List of Lyrics

The failing of the current interfaces in TiMidity with regard to karaoke is that while they can show the lyrics as they are played, they don't show the lyric lines and progressively highlight them as they are played. For that, you need the set of lyrics.

TiMidity in fact builds a list of lyrics and makes them accessible. It has a function event2string() that takes an integer parameter from 1 upward. For each value, it returns the string of a lyric or text event, finally returning NULL on the end of the list. The first character returned is a type parameter; the rest is the string. Using GLib functions, you can build up an array of lines for a KAR file with the following:

```
struct _lyric_t {
    gchar *lyric;
    long tick; // not used here
};
typedef struct _lyric_t lyric_t;

struct _lyric_lines_t {
    char *language;
    char *title;
    char *performer;
    GArray *lines; // array of GString *
};
typedef struct _lyric_lines_t lyric_lines_t;

GArray *lyrics;
lyric_lines_t lyric_lines;

static void build_lyric_lines() {
    int n;
    lyric_t *plyric;
    GString *line = g_string_new("");
    GArray *lines =  g_array_sized_new(FALSE, FALSE, sizeof(GString *), 64);

    lyric_lines.title = NULL;

    n = 1;
    char *evt_str;
    while ((evt_str = event2string(n++)) != NULL) {
        gchar *lyric = evt_str+1;

        if ((strlen(lyric) >= 2) && (lyric[0] == '@') && (lyric[1] == 'L')) {
            lyric_lines.language =  lyric + 2;
            continue;
        }

        if ((strlen(lyric) >= 2) && (lyric[0] == '@') && (lyric[1] == 'T')) {
            if (lyric_lines.title == NULL) {
                lyric_lines.title = lyric + 2;
            } else {
```

```
            lyric_lines.performer = lyric + 2;
        }
        continue;
    }

    if (lyric[0] == '@') {
        // some other stuff like @KMIDI KARAOKE FILE
        continue;
    }

    if ((lyric[0] == '/') || (lyric[0] == '\\')) {
        // start of a new line
        // add to lines
        g_array_append_val(lines, line);
        line = g_string_new(lyric + 1);
    } else {
        line = g_string_append(line, lyric);
    }
}
lyric_lines.lines = lines;

printf("Title is %s, performer is %s, language is %s\n",
        lyric_lines.title, lyric_lines.performer, lyric_lines.language);
for (n = 0; n < lines->len; n++) {
    printf("Line is %s\n", g_array_index(lines, GString *, n)->str);
}
}
```

The function `build_lyric_lines()` should be called from the `CTLE_LOADING_DONE` branch of `ctl_event()`.

TiMidity Options

If you choose to use TiMidity as the front end, then you need to run it with suitable options. These include turning tracing on and also dynamically loading your new interface. This can be done, for example, with the following for a "v" interface in the current directory:

```
timidity -d. -iv --trace  --trace-text-meta ...
.
```

The alternative is building a main program that calls TiMidity as a library. The command-line parameters to TiMidity then have to be included as hard-coded parameters in the application. One is easy: the `CtlMode` has a field `trace_playing` and setting it to 1 turns tracing on. Including text events as lyric events requires digging a bit deeper into TiMidity but just requires (shortly after initializing the library) the following:

```
extern int opt_trace_text_meta_event;
opt_trace_text_meta_event = 1;
```

Playing Lyrics Using Pango + Cairo + Xlib

I want to be able to play my karaoke files on the Raspberry Pi and similar systems on a chip (SOCs). Unfortunately, the Raspberry Pi has a grossly underpowered CPU, so I have ended up using a CubieBoard 2.

Anything involving heavy graphics is not possible on this CPU. All of the MIDI players hit close to (or over) 100 percent CPU usage just by themselves. So, the system discussed in the next section, showing background video, isn't feasible on the Raspberry Pi without the use of the GPU, which is discussed in my book *Raspberry Pi GPU Audio Video Programming*. The programs discussed in the sequel play fine on any current laptops and desktops.

In this section, you use TiMidity as the MIDI player with a minimal back end to display the lyrics as they are played. The lowest level of GUI support is used, namely, Xlib. This can be used to draw text using low-level Xlib calls such as XDrawImageString. This works fine with ASCII languages and, with appropriate font choices, with other languages in the ISO-8859 family.

Asian languages are harder to deal with in standard C. They involve 1- or 2-byte characters when using an encoding such as UTF-8. To manage these, it is easiest to switch to a library designed to handle them such, such as Cairo.

Cairo is good for drawing simple text. For example, for Chinese characters you have to find a font that will allow you to draw them. Alternatively, you can jump up one further level to Pango. Pango looks after all the font issues and produces glyphs that are sent to the X server.

That approach is adopted in the following interface, x_code.c.

The essential difference between the previous naive interface section and the Xlib interface of this section lies, of course, in the drawing. The function build_lyric_lines gives you access to the set of lines to render. Additional data types are required for Pango and Cairo as follows:

```
GArray *lyrics;
GString *lyrics_array[NUM_LINES];

lyric_lines_t lyric_lines;

typedef struct _coloured_line_t {
    gchar *line;
    gchar *front_of_line;
    gchar *marked_up_line;
    PangoAttrList *attrs;
} coloured_line_t;

int height_lyric_pixbufs[] = {100, 200, 300, 400}; // vertical offset of lyric in video
int coloured_text_offset;

// int current_panel = 1;  // panel showing current lyric line
int current_line = 0;  // which line is the current lyric
gchar *current_lyric;   // currently playing lyric line
GString *front_of_lyric;  // part of lyric to be coloured red
//GString *end_of_lyric;    // part of lyrci to not be coloured

gchar *markup[] = {"<span font=\"28\" foreground=\"RED\">",
                   "</span><span font=\"28\" foreground=\"white\">",
                   "</span>"};
gchar *markup_newline[] = {"<span foreground=\"black\">",
                           "</span>"};
GString *marked_up_label;
```

```
PangoFontDescription *font_description;

cairo_surface_t *surface;
cairo_t *cr;
```

The markup string will draw played text in red and unplayed text in white, while markup_newline will clear the previous line. The principal drawing functions are as follows:

```
static void paint_background() {
    cr = cairo_create(surface);
    cairo_set_source_rgb(cr, 0.0, 0.8, 0.0);
    cairo_paint(cr);
    cairo_destroy(cr);
}

static void set_font() {
    font_description = pango_font_description_new ();
    pango_font_description_set_family (font_description, "serif");
    pango_font_description_set_weight (font_description, PANGO_WEIGHT_BOLD);
    pango_font_description_set_absolute_size (font_description, 32 * PANGO_SCALE);
}

static int draw_text(char *text, float red, float green, float blue, int height, int offset)
{
    // See http://cairographics.org/FAQ/
    PangoLayout *layout;
    int width, ht;
    cairo_text_extents_t extents;

    layout = pango_cairo_create_layout (cr);
    pango_layout_set_font_description (layout, font_description);
    pango_layout_set_text (layout, text, -1);

    if (offset == 0) {
        pango_layout_get_size(layout, &width, &ht);
        offset = (WIDTH - (width/PANGO_SCALE)) / 2;
    }

    cairo_set_source_rgb (cr, red, green, blue);
    cairo_move_to (cr, offset, height);
    pango_cairo_show_layout (cr, layout);

    g_object_unref (layout);
    return offset;
}
```

The function to initialize X and Cairo is as follows:

```
static void init_X() {
    int screenNumber;
    unsigned long foreground, background;
    int screen_width, screen_height;
    Screen *screen;
    XSizeHints hints;
    char **argv = NULL;
    XGCValues gcValues;
    Colormap colormap;
    XColor rgb_color, hw_color;
    Font font;
    //char *FNAME = "hanzigb24st";
    char *FNAME = "-misc-fixed-medium-r-normal--0-0-100-100-c-0-iso10646-1";

    display = XOpenDisplay(NULL);
    if (display == NULL) {
        fprintf(stderr, "Can't open dsplay\n");
        exit(1);
    }
    screenNumber = DefaultScreen(display);
    foreground = BlackPixel(display, screenNumber);
    background = WhitePixel(display, screenNumber);

    screen = DefaultScreenOfDisplay(display);
    screen_width = WidthOfScreen(screen);
    screen_height = HeightOfScreen(screen);

    hints.x = (screen_width - WIDTH) / 2;
    hints.y = (screen_height - HEIGHT) / 2;
    hints.width = WIDTH;
    hints.height = HEIGHT;
    hints.flags = PPosition | PSize;

    window = XCreateSimpleWindow(display,
                                DefaultRootWindow(display),
                                hints.x, hints.y, WIDTH, HEIGHT, 10,
                                foreground, background);

    XSetStandardProperties(display, window,
                                "TiMidity", "TiMidity",
                                None,
                                argv, 0,
                                &hints);

    XMapWindow(display, window);
```

```
    set_font();
    surface = cairo_xlib_surface_create(display, window,
                              DefaultVisual(display, 0), WIDTH, HEIGHT);
    cairo_xlib_surface_set_size(surface, WIDTH, HEIGHT);

    paint_background();

    /*
    cr = cairo_create(surface);
    draw_text(g_array_index(lyric_lines.lines, GString *, 0)->str,
              0.0, 0.0, 1.0, height_lyric_pixbufs[0]);
    draw_text(g_array_index(lyric_lines.lines, GString*, 1)->str,
              0.0, 0.0, 1.0, height_lyric_pixbufs[0]);
    cairo_destroy(cr);
    */
    XFlush(display);
}
```

The key function is ctl_lyric, which is responsible for handling lyrics as they are played. If the lyric signals and end of line with \ or /, then it has to update the current_line. The next lines redraw the text of each line and then progressively step through the current line, coloring the first part red and the rest in white.

```
static void ctl_lyric(int lyricid)
{
    char *lyric;

    current_file_info = get_midi_file_info(current_file, 1);

    lyric = event2string(lyricid);
    if(lyric != NULL)
        lyric++;
    printf("Got a lyric %s\n", lyric);

    if ((*lyric == '\\') || (*lyric == '/')) {

        int next_line = current_line + NUM_LINES;
        gchar *next_lyric;

        if (current_line + NUM_LINES < lyric_lines.lines->len) {
            current_line += 1;

            // update label for next line after this one
            next_lyric = g_array_index(lyric_lines.lines, GString *, next_line)->str;

        } else {
            current_line += 1;
            lyrics_array[(next_line-1) % NUM_LINES] = NULL;
            next_lyric = "";
        }
```

```
    // set up new line as current line
    if (current_line < lyric_lines.lines->len) {
        GString *gstr = g_array_index(lyric_lines.lines, GString *, current_line);
        current_lyric = gstr->str;
        front_of_lyric = g_string_new(lyric+1); // lose      slosh
    }
    printf("New line. Setting front to %s end to \"%s\"\n", lyric+1, current_lyric);

    // Now draw stuff
    paint_background();

    cr = cairo_create(surface);

    int n;
    for (n = 0; n < NUM_LINES; n++) {

        if (lyrics_array[n] != NULL) {
            draw_text(lyrics_array[n]->str,
                      0.0, 0.0, 0.5, height_lyric_pixbufs[n], 0);
        }
    }
    // redraw current and next lines
    if (current_line < lyric_lines.lines->len) {
        if (current_line >= 2) {
            // redraw last line still in red
            GString *gstr = lyrics_array[(current_line-2) % NUM_LINES];
            if (gstr != NULL) {
                draw_text(gstr->str,
                          1.0, 0.0, 00,
                          height_lyric_pixbufs[(current_line-2) % NUM_LINES],
                          0);
            }
        }
        // draw next line in brighter blue
        coloured_text_offset = draw_text(lyrics_array[(current_line-1) % NUM_LINES]-
>str,
                0.0, 0.0, 1.0, height_lyric_pixbufs[(current_line-1) % NUM_LINES], 0);
        printf("coloured text offset %d\n", coloured_text_offset);
    }

    if (next_line < lyric_lines.lines->len) {
        lyrics_array[(next_line-1) % NUM_LINES] =
            g_array_index(lyric_lines.lines, GString *, next_line);
    }

    cairo_destroy(cr);
    XFlush(display);
```

```
    } else {
        // change text colour as chars are played
        if ((front_of_lyric != NULL) && (lyric != NULL)) {
            g_string_append(front_of_lyric, lyric);
            char *s = front_of_lyric->str;
            //coloured_lines[current_panel].front_of_line = s;

            cairo_t *cr = cairo_create(surface);

            // See http://cairographics.org/FAQ/
            draw_text(s, 1.0, 0.0, 0.0,
                      height_lyric_pixbufs[(current_line-1) % NUM_LINES],
                      coloured_text_offset);

            cairo_destroy(cr);
            XFlush(display);


        }
    }
}
```

The file x_code.c is compiled with the following:

```
CFLAGS =   $(shell pkg-config --cflags gtk+-$(V).0 libavformat libavcodec libswscale
libavutil )   -ITiMidity++-2.14.0/timidity/ -ITiMidity++-2.14.0/utils

LIBS =  -lasound -l glib-2.0 $(shell pkg-config --libs gtk+-$(V).0  libavformat libavcodec
libavutil libswscale) -lpthread -lX11

gcc  -fPIC $(CFLAGS) -c -o x_code.o x_code.c $(LIBS)
 gcc -shared -o if_x.so x_code.o $(LIBS)
```

Again, this uses a locally compiled and built version of TiMidity because the Ubuntu version crashes. It is run with the following:

```
TiMidity++-2.14.0/timidity/timidity -d. -ix --trace --trace-text-meta <KAR file>
```

Playing a Background Video with Gtk

In Chapter 27, I discussed a program to show lyrics overlaid onto a movie. Apart from the previous considerations, the rest of the application follows similarly to the FluidSynth case: build a set of lyric lines, display them using Pango over Gtk pixbufs, and when a new lyric event occurs, update the corresponding colors in the lyric line.

All of the dynamic action needs to occur out of the back end of TiMidity, particularly in the function `ctl_event`. Other parts such as initializing FFmpeg and Gtk must also occur in the back end when using standard TiMidity. If TiMidity is used as a library, this initialization could occur in the front or the back. For simplicity, you just place it all in the back in the file `video_code.c`.

As in the previous section, you have some initial data structures and values and will have an array of two lines of `coloured_line_t`.

```
struct _lyric_t {

    gchar *lyric;
    long tick;

};
typedef struct _lyric_t lyric_t;
```

```
struct _lyric_lines_t {
    char *language;
    char *title;
    char *performer;
    GArray *lines; // array of GString *
};
typedef struct _lyric_lines_t lyric_lines_t;

GArray *lyrics;

lyric_lines_t lyric_lines;

typedef struct _coloured_line_t {
    gchar *line;
    gchar *front_of_line;
    gchar *marked_up_line;
    PangoAttrList *attrs;
#ifdef USE_PIXBUF
    GdkPixbuf *pixbuf;
#endif
} coloured_line_t;

coloured_line_t coloured_lines[2];

GtkWidget *image;

int height_lyric_pixbufs[] = {300, 400}; // vertical offset of lyric in video

int current_panel = 1;  // panel showing current lyric line
int current_line = 0;   // which line is the current lyric
gchar *current_lyric;    // currently playing lyric line
GString *front_of_lyric;  // part of lyric to be coloured red
//GString *end_of_lyric;    // part of lyrci to not be coloured

// Colours seem to get mixed up when putting a pixbuf onto a pixbuf
#ifdef USE_PIXBUF
#define RED blue
#else
#define RED red
#endif

gchar *markup[] = {"<span font=\"28\" foreground=\"RED\">",
                   "</span><span font=\"28\" foreground=\"white\">",
b                  "</span>"};
gchar *markup_newline[] = {"<span foreground=\"black\">",
                           "</span>"};
GString *marked_up_label;
```

There are now essentially two blocks of code: one to keep the array of colored lines up-to-date as each new lyric is played and one to play the video with the colored lines on top. The first block has three functions: markup_line to prepare a string with the HTML markup, update_line_pixbuf to create a new pixbuf by applying the Pango attributes to the marked-up line, and ctl_lyric, which is triggered on each new lyric event.

The first two functions are as follows:

```
void markup_line(coloured_line_t *line) {
    GString *str =  g_string_new(markup[0]);
    g_string_append(str, line->front_of_line);
    g_string_append(str, markup[1]);
    g_string_append(str, line->line + strlen(line->front_of_line));
    g_string_append(str, markup[2]);
    printf("Marked up label \"%s\"\n", str->str);

    line->marked_up_line = str->str;
    // we have to free line->marked_up_line

    pango_parse_markup(str->str, -1,0, &(line->attrs), NULL, NULL, NULL);
    g_string_free(str, FALSE);
}

void update_line_pixbuf(coloured_line_t *line) {
    //return;
    cairo_surface_t *surface;
    cairo_t *cr;

    int lyric_width = 480;
    int lyric_height = 60;
    surface = cairo_image_surface_create (CAIRO_FORMAT_ARGB32,
                                          lyric_width, lyric_height);
    cr = cairo_create (surface);

    PangoLayout *layout;
    PangoFontDescription *desc;

    // draw the attributed text
    layout = pango_cairo_create_layout (cr);
    pango_layout_set_text (layout, line->line, -1);
    pango_layout_set_attributes(layout, line->attrs);

    // centre the image in the surface
    int width, height;
    pango_layout_get_pixel_size(layout,
                                &width,
                                &height);
    cairo_move_to(cr, (lyric_width-width)/2, 0);

    pango_cairo_update_layout (cr, layout);
    pango_cairo_show_layout (cr, layout);
```

```
    // pull the pixbuf out of the surface
    unsigned char *data = cairo_image_surface_get_data(surface);
    width = cairo_image_surface_get_width(surface);
    height = cairo_image_surface_get_height(surface);
    int stride = cairo_image_surface_get_stride(surface);
    printf("Text surface width %d height %d stride %d\n", width, height, stride);

    GdkPixbuf *old_pixbuf = line->pixbuf;
    line->pixbuf = gdk_pixbuf_new_from_data(data, GDK_COLORSPACE_RGB, 1, 8, width, height,
    stride, NULL, NULL);
    cairo_surface_destroy(surface);
    g_object_unref(old_pixbuf);
}
```

The function to handle each new lyric event needs to work out if a newline event has occurred, which is when the lyric is the single \ character. Then it needs to update the current_line index and also to replace the previous line by a new one. Once that is done, for all events the current line is marked and its pixmap generated for drawing. The ctl_lyric function is as follows:

```
static void ctl_lyric(int lyricid)
{
    char *lyric;

    current_file_info = get_midi_file_info(current_file, 1);

    lyric = event2string(lyricid);
    if(lyric != NULL)
        lyric++;
    printf("Got a lyric %s\n", lyric);
    if (*lyric == '\\') {
        int next_panel = current_panel; // really (current_panel+2)%2
        int next_line = current_line + 2;
        gchar *next_lyric;

        if (current_line + 2 >= lyric_lines.lines->len) {
            return;
        }
        current_line += 1;
        current_panel = (current_panel + 1) % 2;

        // set up new line as current line
        current_lyric = g_array_index(lyric_lines.lines, GString *, current_line)->str;
        front_of_lyric = g_string_new(lyric+1); // lose \
        printf("New line. Setting front to %s end to \"%s\"\n", lyric+1, current_lyric);

        coloured_lines[current_panel].line = current_lyric;
        coloured_lines[current_panel].front_of_line = lyric+1;
        markup_line(coloured_lines+current_panel);
#ifdef USE_PIXBUF
        update_line_pixbuf(coloured_lines+current_panel);
#endif
```

```
            // update label for next line after this one
            next_lyric = g_array_index(lyric_lines.lines, GString *, next_line)->str;

            marked_up_label = g_string_new(markup_newline[0]);

            g_string_append(marked_up_label, next_lyric);
            g_string_append(marked_up_label, markup_newline[1]);
            PangoAttrList *attrs;
            gchar *text;
            pango_parse_markup (marked_up_label->str, -1,0, &attrs, &text, NULL, NULL);

            coloured_lines[next_panel].line = next_lyric;
            coloured_lines[next_panel].front_of_line = "";
            markup_line(coloured_lines+next_panel);
            update_line_pixbuf(coloured_lines+next_panel);
        } else {
            // change text colour as chars are played
            if ((front_of_lyric != NULL) && (lyric != NULL)) {
                g_string_append(front_of_lyric, lyric);
                char *s = front_of_lyric->str;
                coloured_lines[current_panel].front_of_line = s;
                markup_line(coloured_lines+current_panel);
                update_line_pixbuf(coloured_lines+current_panel);
            }
        }
}

static gboolean draw_image(gpointer user_data) {
    GdkPixbuf *pixbuf = (GdkPixbuf *) user_data;

    gtk_image_set_from_pixbuf((GtkImage *) image, pixbuf);
    gtk_widget_queue_draw(image);
    g_object_unref(pixbuf);

    return G_SOURCE_REMOVE;
}
```

The function to play the video and overlay the colored lines has nothing essentially new. It reads a frame from the video and puts it into a pixbuf. Then for each of the lyric panels, it draws the colored line into the pixbuf. Finally, it calls gdk_threads_add_idle so that Gtk can draw the pixbuf in its main thread. The function play_background is as follows:

```
static void *play_background(void *args) {

    int i;
    AVPacket packet;
    int frameFinished;
    AVFrame *pFrame = NULL;
```

```
int oldSize;
char *oldData;
int bytesDecoded;
GdkPixbuf *pixbuf;
AVFrame *picture_RGB;
char *buffer;

pFrame=av_frame_alloc();

i=0;
picture_RGB = avcodec_frame_alloc();
buffer = malloc (avpicture_get_size(PIX_FMT_RGB24, 720, 576));
avpicture_fill((AVPicture *)picture_RGB, buffer, PIX_FMT_RGB24, 720, 576);

int width = pCodecCtx->width;
int height = pCodecCtx->height;

sws_ctx = sws_getContext(pCodecCtx->width, pCodecCtx->height, pCodecCtx->pix_fmt,
                         pCodecCtx->width, pCodecCtx->height, PIX_FMT_
                         RGB24,
                         SWS_BICUBIC, NULL, NULL, NULL);

while(av_read_frame(pFormatCtx, &packet)>=0) {
    if(packet.stream_index==videoStream) {
        //printf("Frame %d\n", i++);
        usleep(33670);  // 29.7 frames per second
        // Decode video frame
        avcodec_decode_video2(pCodecCtx, pFrame, &frameFinished,
                    &packet);

        if (frameFinished) {
            //printf("Frame %d\n", i++);

            sws_scale(sws_ctx,  (uint8_t const * const *) pFrame->data, pFrame-
            >linesize, 0,
                                    pCodecCtx->height, picture_RGB->data,
                                    picture_RGB->linesize);

            pixbuf = gdk_pixbuf_new_from_data(picture_RGB->data[0], GDK_COLORSPACE_RGB,
            0, 8,
                                    width, height, picture_RGB->linesize[0],
                                    pixmap_destroy_notify, NULL);

            // Create the destination surface
            cairo_surface_t *surface = cairo_image_surface_create (CAIRO_FORMAT_ARGB32,
                                                width, height);

            cairo_t *cr = cairo_create(surface);
```

```
                    // draw the background image
                    gdk_cairo_set_source_pixbuf(cr, pixbuf, 0, 0);
                    cairo_paint (cr);

                    // draw the lyric
                    GdkPixbuf *lyric_pixbuf = coloured_lines[current_panel].pixbuf;
                    if (lyric_pixbuf != NULL) {
                        int width = gdk_pixbuf_get_width(lyric_pixbuf);
                        gdk_cairo_set_source_pixbuf(cr,
                                                    lyric_pixbuf,
                                                    (720-width)/2,
                                                    height_lyric_pixbufs[current_panel]);
                        cairo_paint (cr);
                    }

                    int next_panel = (current_panel+1) % 2;
                    lyric_pixbuf = coloured_lines[next_panel].pixbuf;
                    if (lyric_pixbuf != NULL) {
                        int width = gdk_pixbuf_get_width(lyric_pixbuf);
                        gdk_cairo_set_source_pixbuf(cr,
                                                    lyric_pixbuf,
                                                    (720-width)/2,
                                                    height_lyric_pixbufs[next_panel]);
                        cairo_paint (cr);
                    }

                    pixbuf = gdk_pixbuf_get_from_surface(surface,
                                                         0,
                                                         0,
                                                         width,
                                                         height);
                    gdk_threads_add_idle(draw_image, pixbuf);

        /* reclaim memory */
                    sws_freeContext(sws_ctx);
                    g_object_unref(layout);
                    cairo_surface_destroy(surface);
                    cairo_destroy(cr);

            }
        }
        av_free_packet(&packet);
    }
    sws_freeContext(sws_ctx);

    printf("Video over!\n");
    exit(0);
}
```

It is run with the following:

```
TiMidity++-2.14.0/timidity/timidity -d. -iv --trace --trace-text-meta <KAR file>
```

In appearance, it looks like Figure 28-4.

Figure 28-4. Caption

Background Video with TiMidity as Library

The code for this follows the same structure as the code in Chapter 21. It is in the file gtkkaraoke_player_ video_pango.c.

```
#include <stdio.h>
#include <stdlib.h>

#include "sysdep.h"
#include "controls.h"

extern ControlMode   *video_ctl;
extern ControlMode   *ctl;

static void init_timidity() {
    int err;

    timidity_start_initialize();
```

```
    if ((err = timidity_pre_load_configuration()) != 0) {
        printf("couldn't pre-load configuration file\n");
        exit(1);
    }

    err += timidity_post_load_configuration();

    if (err) {
        printf("couldn't post-load configuration file\n");
        exit(1);
    }

    timidity_init_player();

    extern int opt_trace_text_meta_event;
    opt_trace_text_meta_event = 1;

    ctl = &video_ctl;
    //ctl->trace_playing = 1;
    //opt_trace_text_meta_event = 1;

}

#define MIDI_FILE "54154.kar"

static void *play_midi(void *args) {
    char *argv[1];
    argv[0] = MIDI_FILE;
    int argc = 1;

    timidity_play_main(argc, argv);

    printf("Audio finished\n");
    exit(0);
}

int main(int argc, char** argv)
{

    int i;

    /* TiMidity */
    init_timidity();
    play_midi(NULL);

    return 0;
}
```

Background Video with TiMidity as Front End

The interface needs to be built as a shared library with the following:

```
if_video.so: video_code.c
        gcc  -fPIC $(CFLAGS) -c -o video_code.o video_code.c $(LIBS)
        gcc -shared -o if_video.so video_code.o $(LIBS)
```

TiMidity is then run with options.

```
timidity -d. -iv --trace  --trace-text-meta
```

As before, it crashes TiMidity from the Ubuntu distro but works fine with TiMidity built from source in the current Linux environment.

Adding Microphone Input

At this stage you have a single application that can play a MIDI file, play a background movie, and display highlighted lyrics on top of the video. There is no microphone input to sing along.

Singing along can be handled either within this application or by an external process. If you want to include it in the current application, then you will have to build a mixer for two audio streams. Java does this in the Java Sound package, but in C you would need to do that yourself. It can be done in ALSA but would involve complex ALSA mixer code.

Jack makes it easy to mix audio, from different *processes*. The earlier section showed how to do that.

A long-term goal is to include scoring, and so on. However, that takes you into the realm of deep signal processing (identifying notes sung using algorithms such as YIN, for example), which is beyond the scope of this book.

Conclusion

This chapter showed you how to use TiMidity as a MIDI player for a karaoke system. On my laptop it uses about 35 percent of the CPU with Gtk 3.0.

CHAPTER 29

■■■

Jack and Karaoke

Jack is designed for professional audio. In this chapter you will apply the techniques from earlier chapters to building a karaoke system.

Using Jack Rack for Effects

Karaoke takes inputs from MIDI sources and from microphones. These are mixed together. Generally there is an overall volume control, but there is usually a volume control for the microphones as well. While the MIDI source should be passed straight through, it is common to apply a reverb effect to the microphones.

These are all effects that can be supplied by LADSPA modules (see Chapter 14). The Jack application jack-rack makes these plug-ins accessible to Jack applications so that LADSPA effects can be applied to Jack pipelines.

It is fairly straightforward to add a module to a session. Click the + button and choose from the enormous menu of effects. For example, choosing the Karaoke plug-in from the Utilities menu looks like Figure 29-1.

© Jan Newmarch 2017
J. Newmarch, *Linux Sound Programming*, DOI 10.1007/978-1-4842-2496-0_29

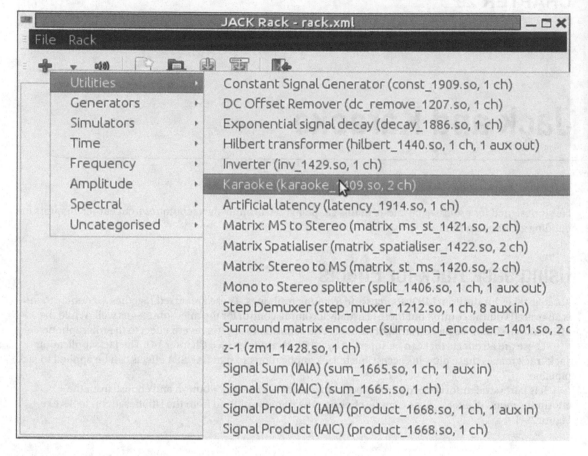

Figure 29-1. *Selecting Karaoke effect in Jack Rack*

The following are some of the modules that might be relevant:

- Karaoke (number 1409), which shows in the Utilities menu. This will attempt to remove center vocals from a music track.

- There are a number of reverb modules that appear in the Simulators ➤ Reverb menu.

  - GVerb

  - Plate reverb

  - TAP Reverberator (from the TAP plug-ins)

  The TAP Reverberator seems to be the most full featured (but is not guaranteed to be in real time).

- There are a number of amplifiers in the Amplitude ➤ Amplifiers menu.

Multiple modules can be applied in a single jack-rack application, and multiple applications can be run. For example, applying a volume control to a microphone and then applying reverb before sending it to the speakers can be done by adding the TAP reverberator and then one of the amplifiers. This looks like Figure 29-2.

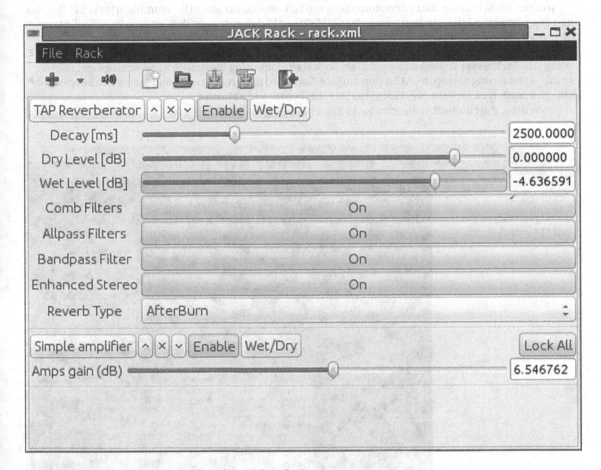

Figure 29-2. *Jack Rack with reverb and amplifier plug-ins*

I'm running this on a USB Sound Blaster TruStudioPro. This is only 16 bits, and I can't seem to find a suitable Jack hardware configuration. So, I'm running Jack by hand using a plug device, which Jack complains about but works anyway.

```
jackd -dalsa -dplughw:2 -r 48000
```

Although gladish can see it under its Jack configuration menu, I haven't managed to get gladish to accept the Sound Blaster as a setting. So far I can only manage to get Jack running under as a plug device, and gladish keeps swapping it back to a hardware device.

qjackctl does an OK job of saving and restoring sessions, starting jack-rack with its correct plug-ins and their settings, and linking it to the correct capture and playback ports.

Playing MIDI

The major synthesizer engines TiMidity and FluidSynth will output to ALSA devices. To bring them into the Jack world, Jack needs to be started with the -Xseq option or needs a2jmidid to be run.

You can try to manage the connections using the Jack session manager (for example, qjackctl). But this hits a snag using the MIDI synthesizers such as TiMidity or FluidSynth since they assume PulseAudio output rather than Jack output. Restoring a session fails to restore the synthesizer with Jack output.

You can try to manage the connections using LADSPA. Unfortunately, I have so far been unable to manage the Jack server settings using gladish. So, it starts Jack using the default ALSA settings and doesn't use the -Xseq setting to map the ALSA ports to Jack. You need to start a2jmidid, and then it can successfully manage a session of, for example, timidity, jack_keyboard, and a2jmidid.

Even then, the connection diagram looks like a mess (Figure 29-3).

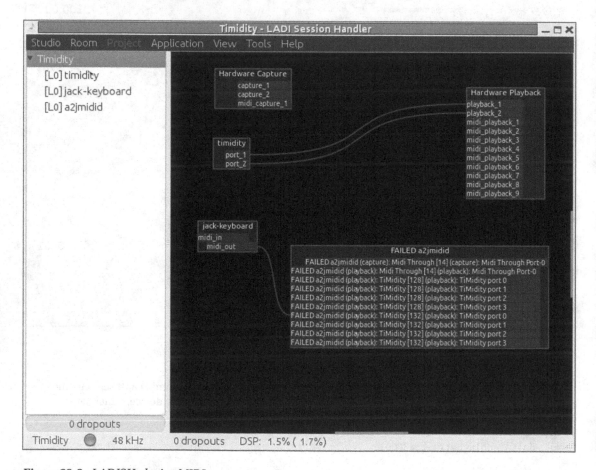

Figure 29-3. *LADISH playing MIDI*

TiMidity Plus Jack Rack

In Chapter 28, you used TiMidity with a Jack back end and an Xaw interface to give a basic karaoke system. You can now improve on that by using Jack Rack effects.

- Run TiMidity with Jack output and an Xaw interface, and synchronize the lyrics to the sound with this:

```
timidity -ia -B2,8 -Oj -EFverb=0 --trace --trace-text-meta
```

- Run Jack Rack with the TAP Reverberator and a volume control installed.

- Connect ports using qjackctl.

The resulting system looks like Figure 29-4.

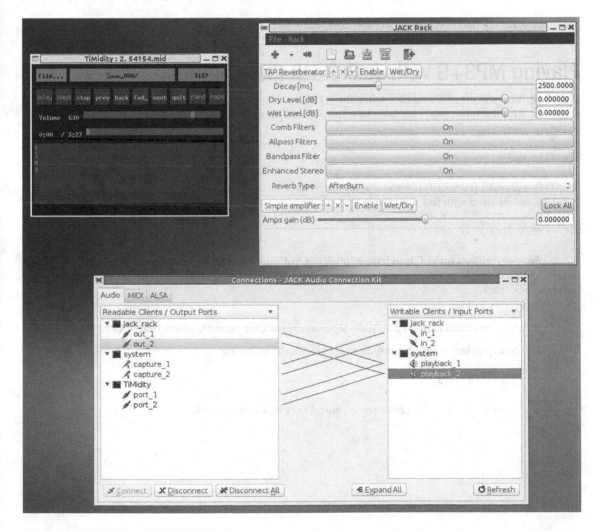

Figure 29-4. *TiMidity with Jack Rack*

Customizing TiMidity Build

The version of TiMidity from the Ubuntu distro crashes if I try to dynamically load another interface. As the code is stripped, it is not possible to find out why. So, to add a new interface, you need to build TiMidity from source.

The commands I now use are as follows:

```
./configure --enable-audio=alsa,jack \
            --enable-interface=xaw,gtk \
            --enable-server \
            --enable-dynamic
make clean
make
```

An interface with a key, say "k," can then be run with Jack output with the following:

```
timidity -d. -ik -Oj --trace  --trace-text-meta 54154.mid
```

Playing MP3+G with Jack Rack Pitch Shifting

The player VLC will play MP3+G files. Often the MP3+G is a zipped file containing both an MP3 file and s CDG file with the same root. This must be unzipped and then can be played by giving VLC the MP3 file name.

```
vlc file.mp3
```

This will pick up the CDG file and display the lyrics.
VLC can be used with Jack with the --aout jack option.

```
vlc --aout jack file.mp3
```

A common request for VLC is to have a "pitch control" mechanism. While it should be possible to add LADPSA pitch controls to VLC, no one has gotten around to it yet. But you can still add LADSPA effects through jack-rack.

The steps are as follows:

1. You may need to stop PulseAudio temporarily with, for example, pasuspender cat.

2. Start the Jack daemon running as usual with the following:

    ```
    jackd -d alsa
    ```

3. Start qjackctl so you have some control over Jack connections.

4. Start jack-rack. Using the + button, select Frequency ➤ Pitch shifters ➤ TAP Pitch Shifter. Don't forget to enable it; it should look like Figure 29-5.

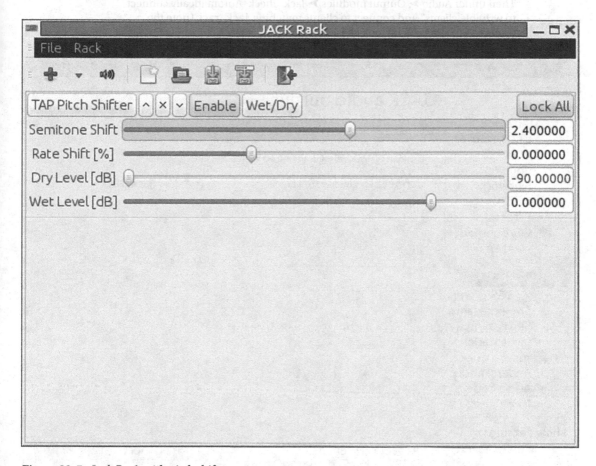

Figure 29-5. Jack Rack with pitch shifter

Note that in qjackctl, jack-rack shows as jack_rack (the minus has been replaced with an underscore), which is the proper Jack name of jack-rack. Connect the output of jack-rack to system.

5. Now start `vlc --aout jack` so you can set up the correct configuration. Choose Tools ➤ Preferences, and in "Show settings" set the radio button to All. Then under Audio ➤ Output modules ➤ Jack, check "Automatically connect to writable clients" and connect to clients matching `jack_rack` (note the underscore). This should look like Figure 29-6.

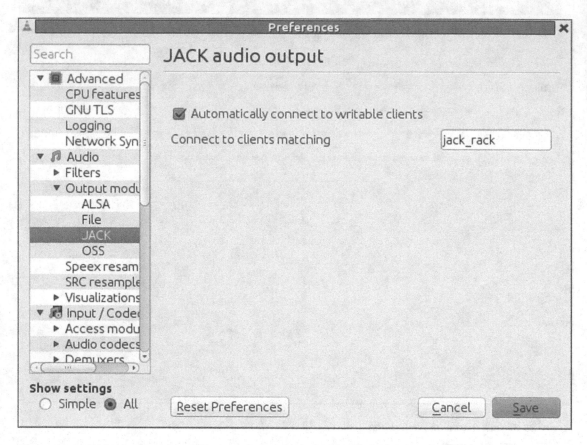

Figure 29-6. *VLC selecting output client*

6. The next time you start vlc with, for example, vlc --aout jack BST.mp3, qjackctl should look like Figure 29-7.

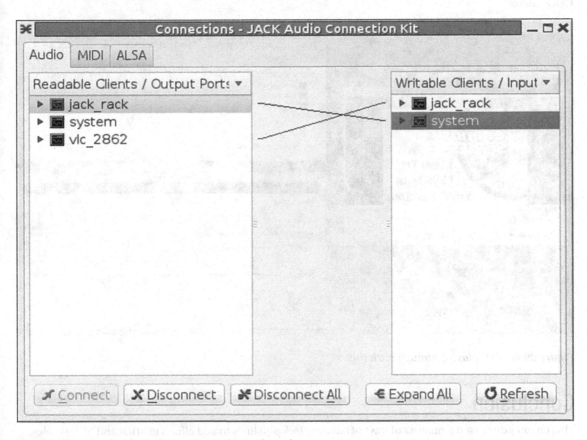

Figure 29-7. *qjackctl with VLC connected to Jack Rack*

The music should play through jack-rack where you can adjust the pitch.

Figure 29-8 shows the result of VLC playing MP3 audio through the pitch filter and also showing the CDG video.

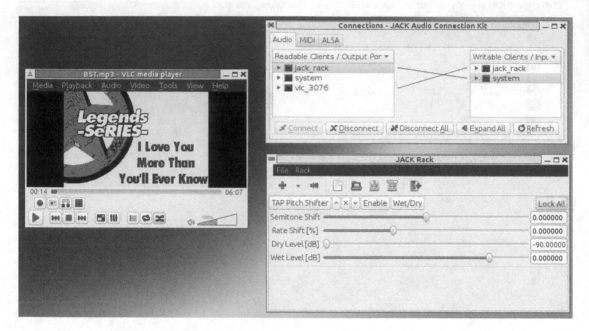

Figure 29-8. *VLC playing through pitch shifter*

Conclusion

This chapter discussed a number of ways of building Jack pipelines to add effects to MIDI and MP3+G files.

CHAPTER 30

Streaming Audio

Streaming audio generally involves sending audio from one node on a network to another node. There are a number of ways in which this can be done, using a number of formats. This chapter briefly discusses some of them.

HTTP

HTTP is the protocol underlying the Web. The protocol is agnostic to the content it carries. While it was originally designed to carry HTML documents, it is now used to transport image files, Postscript documents, PowerPoint files, and almost anything else. This includes media files, the subject of this book.

HTTP Servers

Content is delivered from a web site by means of HTTP servers. The most well-known of these is Apache, but in the Linux world Nginx and Lighttpd are also common. There are a number of proprietary servers as well.

An HTTP server can deliver static files stored on the server or construct content dynamically from, for example, a database connection.

HTTP Clients

There are many clients for HTTP streams, generally known as *user agents*. These include browsers as well as many of the audio players discussed earlier.

HTTP Browsers

Point your browser to the URL of an audio file and it will pass the content to a helper that will attempt to play the file. The browser will choose the helper based on the file extension of the URL or based on the content type of the file as delivered in the HTTP header from the HTTP server.

MPlayer

MPlayer is HTTP-aware. You just give the URL of the file.

```
mplayer http://localhost/audio/enigma/audio_01.ogg
```

© Jan Newmarch 2017
J. Newmarch, *Linux Sound Programming*, DOI 10.1007/978-1-4842-2496-0_30

VLC

VLC is also HTTP-aware. You just give the URL of the file.

```
vlc http://localhost/audio/enigma/audio_01.ogg
```

Streaming vs. Downloading

If you download a file from the Web, then you can play it once it has finished downloading. This means that play is delayed until the entire file has been saved into the local file system. Since it is now local, it can play without worrying about network delays. Here is a simple shell script to illustrate this:

```
wget -O tmp  http://localhost/audio/enigma/audio_01.ogg
mplayer tmp
rm tmp
```

The alternative is to read the resource from the Web and hand it as it is received to a player, using some sort of pipeline. This is fine as long as the pipeline is large enough to buffer enough of the resource so that it can cope with network delays. It is illustrated with the following:

```
wget -O - http://localhost/audio/enigma/audio_01.ogg | mplayer -
```

(Yes, I know, MPlayer can stream URLs directly; I'm just making a point here.)

HTML5

HTML5 is the latest version of HTML. HTML5 is a "living standard." Ugh! That means it isn't a standard at all, but just a label for a specification that is in a state of flux. There is now an audio element, <audio>, that is implemented by many browsers.

For example, the following HTML will try the Ogg file first, and if the client cannot play it, it will try the MP3 file, and if it cannot play that, then it will display the failure message:

```
<audio controls="controls"<
   <source src="audio_01.ogg" type="audio/ogg"<
     <source src="audio_01.mp3" type="audio/mpeg"<
       Your browser does not support the audio element.
   </audio<
```

Figure 30-1 shows what it looks like in the browser.

Figure 30-1. Caption

DLNA

Digital Living Network Alliance (DLNA) is designed for sharing digital media such as photos, audio, and video in a home network. It is built on top of the Universal Plug and Play (UPnP) protocol suite. This in turn is built on one of the uglier of the Internet standards, SOAP. UPnP itself compounds this poor choice of base technologies by using what can only be described as an appallingly badly engineered hack in order to handle media information. With its most complex data type being a string, UPnP buries complete XML documents inside these strings so that one XML document contains another XML document as an embedded string. Oh dear, better-quality engineers could surely have come up with better solutions than this!

UPnP is open in that it can describe many different home network devices and formats of data. DLNA restricts this to only a few "approved" types and then makes the specification private, only available after paying a fee.

Despite all this, an increasing number of devices are "DLNA enabled" such as TVs, BluRay players, and so on. It seems like DLNA is here to stay.

Matthew Panton in "DLNA for media streamers—what does it all mean?" (http://news.cnet.com/8301-17938_105-10007069-1.html) pointed out some further issues with DLNA, mainly relating to the supported file formats. The truth of his comments are illustrated by my latest purchase of a Sony BDP-S390 BluRay player. It supports LPCM (.wav) as required, but out of the optional MP3, WMA9, AC-3, AAC, and ATRAC3plus, it only supports MP3, AAC/HE-AAC (.m4a), and WMA9 Standard (.wma). And of course, Ogg is nowhere in any of the DLNA lists.

The site DLNA Open Source Projects (http://elinux.org/DLNA_Open_Source_Projects) lists a number of Linux DLNA players. I have successfully used the CyberGarage Java client and server and the MediaTomb server.

Icecast

Shoutcast is a proprietary piece of server software for Internet streaming of audio, which has set the standard for streaming. Icecast is the serious open source competitor, which is just as good in quality and superior as open source and which supports a larger variety of formats. To the receiver of a stream, Icecast is just an HTTP server. The back end is the interesting part, as Icecast uses the Shoutcast protocol to receive audio from a variety of sources such as online radio, microphones, or playlists.

IceS is one of the ways that Icecast can get its audio streams and is included in the distro. For further information, see the IceS v2.0 documentation (www.icecast.org/docs/ices-2.0.2/).

Flumotion

From the Flumotion site (www.flumotion.net/), "Flumotion Streaming Software allows broadcasters and companies to stream content live and on demand in all the leading formats from a single server. Flumotion also offers a streaming platform and WebTV, which reduce workflow and costs by covering the entire streaming value chain. This end-to-end yet modular solution includes signal acquisition, encoding, multi-format transcoding, streaming of contents, and state-of-the art interface design. The media back office allows for advanced content management and optimal monetization through rich media advertising."

Conclusion

This chapter gave a brief overview of some of the streaming mechanisms available. HTML5 embedding provides an easy way of including audio (and video) into web pages, while systems such as Icecast and Flumotion can be used for professional audio systems such as radio stations.

535

CHAPTER 31

Raspberry Pi

The Raspberry Pi (RPi) is a low-cost Linux computer developed with the intention of giving students entering university computer science courses a good, cheap environment in which to play. And it does! I've got a bunch of colleagues at work, well into middle-age, who have leapt upon it to play with. So far their kids haven't had a look, though....

Resources

Here are some resources:

- "Why is my audio (sound) output not working?" (http://raspberrypi. stackexchange.com/questions/44/why-is-my-audio-sound-output-not-working)

- Raspberry Pi GitHub sources (https://github.com/raspberryp)

- RPi VideoCore APIs (http://elinux.org/RPi_VideoCore_APIs)

- Linux Gizmos (http://linuxgizmos.com/) reporting on many systems on a chip (SoCs) including the RPi

- "Tutorial: VLC with hardware acceleration on Raspberry Pi" (http://intensecode. blogspot.com.au/2013/10/tutorial-vlc-with-hardware-acceleration.html?sho wComment=1405938529843#c6761170597378687078) by Helder Araujo Carneiro

- "Using direct textures on Android" (http://snorp.net/2011/12/16/android-direct-texture.html) and how to get from EGLImage to OpenGL texture

- "Raspberry Pi and real-time, low-latency audio" (http://wiki.linuxaudio.org/wiki/raspberrypi)

The Basics

The following sections cover the basics.

Hardware

The Raspberry Pi (RPi) 3 Model B has 1Gb RAM, four USB ports, WiFi and Bluetooth, and an Ethernet port. It has HDMI and analog audio and video outputs. The following is from the FAQ (www.raspberrypi.org/faqs):

J. Newmarch, *Linux Sound Programming*, DOI 10.1007/978-1-4842-2496-0_31

"All versions and revisions of the Raspberry Pi other than the Raspberry Pi 2B/3B use the Broadcom BCM2835. This contains an ARM1176JZFS with floating point, running at 700MHz, and a VideoCore 4 GPU. The GPU is capable of Blu-Ray-quality playback, using H.264 at 40MBits/s. It has a fast 3D core, accessed using the supplied OpenGL ES2.0 and OpenVG libraries. The Model 2B uses the Broadcom BCM2836. This contains a quad-core ARM Cortex-a7 processor with floating point and NEON, running at 900MHz, and the same VideoCore 4 GPU that is in the other models of Raspberry Pi. The Model 3B uses the Broadcom BCM2837, containing a quad-core ARM Cortex-A53 running at 1.2GHz. Its GPU capabilities are equivalent to the Pi 2."

The RPi has audio out through the HDMI port and also through an analog 3.5mm audio out. There is no audio in. However, there are USB ports, and a USB sound card can be plugged in, which is recognized by the Linux distros.

The CPU is an ARM CPU. You can find a simple overview of the differences between the ARM and Intel instruction sets in "ARM vs. x86 Processors: What's the Difference?" (`www.brighthub.com/computing/hardware/articles/107133.aspx`).

Alternative Single-Board Computers

There are many single-board computers. Wikipedia has a list of single-board computers (`http://en.wikipedia.org/wiki/List_of_single_board_computers`); they are all potential alternatives to the RPi. Here is just a quick selection:

Gumstix (`http://en.wikipedia.org/wiki/Gumstix`)

> This is a single-board computer that has been around for many years (I got one in 2004). It isn't high powered, but it isn't meant to be.

Arduino (`http://en.wikipedia.org/wiki/Arduino`)

> The Arduino is designed as a microcontroller for electronic projects. It uses an ARM Cortec-M3 CPU, which has even lower specs than the RPi.

UDOO (`www.udoo.org/`)

> UDOO attempts to marry the best of the RPi and Arduino with two CPUs into a single-board computer.

ODroid (`http://odroid.com/`)

> The ODroid U2 is a higher-powered system than the RPI, evaluated by Gigaom (`http://gigaom.com/2013/02/11/following-raspberry-pi-the-89-odroid-u2-continues-small-cheap-computing-movement/`). It is about double the price.

BeagleBone (`http://beagleboard.org/Products/BeagleBone%20Black`)

> The BeagleBone Black has a slightly better CPU (ARM Cortex-A8) than the RPi and is a bit more expensive.

Distros

Several Linux images are available from the Raspberry Pi site, and others are being developed elsewhere. I'm using the Debian-based image that essentially comes in two forms: with soft float using Debian and with hard float using the FPU, called Raspbian. The hard float image is required for decent sound processing, which is heavily floating-point dependent. There is a good article benchmarking these against each other at www.memetic.org/raspbian-benchmarking-armel-vs-armhf/. Another set of benchmarks is at http://elinux.org/RaspberryPiPerformance. Basically, these show that you should use the hard float version if you want good floating-point performance, and this is required for audio processing.

ELinux.org maintains a list of RPi distributions (http://elinux.org/RPi_Distributions). There are many standard Linux distros included here, such as Fedora, Debian, Arch, SUSE, Gentoo, and others. The RPi has gained traction as a media center based on the XBMC media center, and this is represented by distros such as Raspbmc and OpenElec.

So, how does it get along with the various audio tools discussed so far? It's a mixed bag.

No Sound

I plugged mine into a 29-inch ViewSonic monitor using the HDMI connectors. Initially I got no sound from either the 3.5mm analog output or the HDMI monitor. This is explained at "Why is my audio (sound) output not working?" (http://raspberrypi.stackexchange.com/questions/44/why-is-my-audio-sound-output-not-working). I edited the file /boot/config.txt and uncommented the line "hdmi_drive=2". I also used the following command, where n is 0=auto, 1=headphones, 2=hdmi to toggle between outputs:

```
sudo amixer cset numid=3 <n>
```

After that, the sound is fine.

ALSA

The Raspberry Pi uses the ALSA driver snd_bcm2835, and this can manage HDMI output. The command alsa-info is not present, but as this is a shell script, it can be copied from elsewhere and will run on the RPi. Some of the usual configuration files and commands on a larger distro are missing, but it shows on the Raspbian distro (with many omissions) for an RPi2.

```
!!################################
!!ALSA Information Script v 0.4.64
!!################################

!!Script ran on: Sun Nov 13 11:13:36 UTC 2016

!!ALSA Version
!!------------

Driver version:     k4.7.2-v7+
Library version:    1.0.28
Utilities version:  1.0.28

!!Loaded ALSA modules
!!-------------------
```

snd_bcm2835

```
!!Soundcards recognised by ALSA
!!-----------------------------

 0 [ALSA            ]: bcm2835 - bcm2835 ALSA
                        bcm2835 ALSA

!!Aplay/Arecord output
!!--------------------

APLAY

**** List of PLAYBACK Hardware Devices ****
card 0: ALSA [bcm2835 ALSA], device 0: bcm2835 ALSA [bcm2835 ALSA]
  Subdevices: 8/8
  Subdevice #0: subdevice #0
  Subdevice #1: subdevice #1
  Subdevice #2: subdevice #2
  Subdevice #3: subdevice #3
  Subdevice #4: subdevice #4
  Subdevice #5: subdevice #5
  Subdevice #6: subdevice #6
  Subdevice #7: subdevice #7
card 0: ALSA [bcm2835 ALSA], device 1: bcm2835 ALSA [bcm2835 IEC958/HDMI]
  Subdevices: 1/1
  Subdevice #0: subdevice #0

ARECORD

**** List of CAPTURE Hardware Devices ****

!!Amixer output
!!-------------

!!-------Mixer controls for card 0 [ALSA]

Card hw:0 'ALSA'/'bcm2835 ALSA'
  Mixer name    : 'Broadcom Mixer'
  Components    : ''
  Controls      : 6
  Simple ctrls  : 1
Simple mixer control 'PCM',0
  Capabilities: pvolume pvolume-joined pswitch pswitch-joined
  Playback channels: Mono
  Limits: Playback -10239 - 400
  Mono: Playback -2000 [77%] [-20.00dB] [on]
```

Sampled Audio Players

Earlier chapters have made extensive use of a number of audio tools. The RPi is still a Linux system, so you would expect that the audio tools behave normally on the RPi. But it is worth confirming!

MPlayer

MPlayer plays fine on the default ALSA modules, for MP3, OGG, and WAV files.

VLC

VLC attempts to play WAV files, but it is very broken up on the soft float distro. CPU usage is up around 90 percent, and it is quite unplayable. The soft distro is no longer used, for that kind of reason. The hard float distro can play MP3, OGG, and WAV files.

alsaplayer

The program alsaplayer plays files in formats such as Ogg-Vorbis and MP3 using the standard hard float distro.

omxplayer

The RPi has a GPU, and this can be used by omxplayer. It can play Ogg-Vorbis files with only 12 percent CPU usage and looks to be a good candidate for audio as well as video.

Is It X Using the CPU?

Apparently not just X: gnome-player works fine.

Sampled Audio Capture

The RPi does not have an audio-in or line-in port. I connected my Sound Blaster USB card through a powered USB hub. It shows up with arecord -l as follows:

```
**** List of CAPTURE Hardware Devices ****
card 1: Pro [SB X-Fi Surround 5.1 Pro], device 0: USB Audio [USB Audio]
  Subdevices: 1/1
  Subdevice #0: subdevice #0
```

So, to ALSA, it is device hw:1,0.

ALSA

The standard program arecord works if you get the options correct.

```
arecord -D hw:1,0 -f S16_LE -c 2 -r 48000 tmp.s16
Recording WAVE 'tmp.s16' : Signed 16 bit Little Endian, Rate 48000 Hz, Stereo
```

The resulting file can be played back using this:

```
aplay -D hw:1,1 -c 2 -r 48000 -f S16_LE tmp.s16
```

In Chapter X, I gave the source for a program called `alsa_capture.c`. When run with the following:

```
alsa_capture hw:1,0 tmp.s16
```

it records PCM data in stereo at 48,000Hz.

MIDI Players

While standard audio tools work fine, MIDI players are very heavy on the CPU. This section looks at customizing the common players to play OK.

TiMidity

TiMidity averages about 50 percent CPU on the RPi 2 and 38 percent CPU on the RPi 3. This may make it unusable if other applications (such as a GUI front end) are also in use.

To make the RPi more usable, in the `timidity.cfg` file, uncomment the following lines:

```
## If you have a slow CPU, uncomment these:
#opt EFresamp=d          #disable resampling
#opt EFvlpf=d            #disable VLPF
#opt EFreverb=d          #disable reverb
#opt EFchorus=d          #disable chorus
#opt EFdelay=d           #disable delay
#opt anti-alias=d        #disable sample anti-aliasing
#opt EWPVSETOZ           #disable all Midi Controls
#opt p32a                #default to 32 voices with auto reduction
#opt s32kHz              #default sample frequency to 32kHz
#opt fast-decay          #fast decay notes
```

This brings the CPU usage on the RP2 down to about 30 percent. (Thanks to Chivalry Timber, http://chivalrytimberz.wordpress.com/2012/12/03/pi-lights/.)

pykaraoke

This uses only 40 percent of the CPU and plays OK, even with a GUI.

FluidSynth/qsynth

On both the RPi2 and RPi3, CPU usage is up around 85 to 90 percent.

Scheduling

Sometimes FluidSynth complains about not being able to reset the scheduler. Aere Greenway (http://lists.gnu.org/archive/html/fluid-dev/2012-10/msg00018.html) suggests making the following security changes:

> You need to create a file (whose name starts with your user-ID) in the following folder: /etc/security/limits.d. For example, my user-ID is aere, so the file name I use is: aere. conf. The file needs to contain the following lines:

```
aere - rtprio 85
aere - memlock unlimited
```

Make sure to substitute your user ID in place of aere.

Noncauses

The following were suggested as causes of the problems but ultimately discarded:

- FluidSynth can be configured to use either doubles or floats. The default is doubles, and these are slow on ARM chips. Switching to floats didn't remove the problem peaks in CPU use.

- FluidSynth uses sound font files, and these are quite large. About 40MB is typical. Switching to smaller fonts didn't help; memory use was not the problem.

- Buffering is small in FluidSynth. The -z parameter can be used to make it larger. Buffering was not the problem, and changing it didn't help.

- A number of operations are known to be expensive in CPU. FluidSynth supports a number of interpolation algorithms, and these can be set using its command interpreter with, for example, interp 0 to turn off interpolation. Other expensive operations include reverb, polyphony, and chorus. Mucking around with any of these in isolation proved fruitless.

Solutions

The two solutions that I have found are

- polyphony=64 and reverb=false
- rate=22050, which brings CPU usage down to about 55 percent

Java Sound

I installed OpenJDK version 8, the default Java version currently. The program DeviceInfo was given in Chapter X. The output from this on the RPi is as follows:

```
Mixers:
   PulseAudio Mixer, version 0.02
     Mixer: org.classpath.icedtea.pulseaudio.PulseAudioMixer@144bcfa
```

```
    Source lines
      interface SourceDataLine supporting 42 audio formats, and buffers of 0 to 1000000 bytes
      interface Clip supporting 42 audio formats, and buffers of 0 to 1000000 bytes
    Target lines
      interface TargetDataLine supporting 42 audio formats, and buffers of 0 to 1000000 bytes
  ALSA [default], version 4.7.2-v7+
   Mixer: com.sun.media.sound.DirectAudioDevice@d3c617
    Source lines
      interface SourceDataLine supporting 84 audio formats, and buffers of at least 32 bytes
      interface Clip supporting 84 audio formats, and buffers of at least 32 bytes
    Target lines
  ALSA [plughw:0,0], version 4.7.2-v7+
   Mixer: com.sun.media.sound.DirectAudioDevice@1c63996
    Source lines
      interface SourceDataLine supporting 8 audio formats, and buffers of at least 32 bytes
      interface Clip supporting 8 audio formats, and buffers of at least 32 bytes
    Target lines
  ALSA [plughw:0,1], version 4.7.2-v7+
   Mixer: com.sun.media.sound.DirectAudioDevice@11210ee
    Source lines
      interface SourceDataLine supporting 8 audio formats, and buffers of at least 32 bytes
      interface Clip supporting 8 audio formats, and buffers of at least 32 bytes
    Target lines
  Port ALSA [hw:0], version 4.7.2-v7+
   Mixer: com.sun.media.sound.PortMixer@40e464
    Source lines
    Target lines
      PCM target port
```

Although this is using the PulseAudio mixer, PulseAudio isn't actually running (at this stage)! So, it can use only the ALSA interface.

The program PlayAudioFile was given in Chapter 9. This can play .wav files OK. But it can't play Ogg-Vorbis or MP3 files and throws an UnsupportedAudioFileException.

PulseAudio

PulseAudio installs OK from the repositories and runs with no problems. The output from pulsedevlist is as follows:

```
=======[ Output Device #1 ]=======
Description: bcm2835 ALSA Analog Stereo
Name: alsa_output.platform-bcm2835_AUDO.0.analog-stereo
Index: 0

=======[ Input Device #1 ]=======
Description: Monitor of bcm2835 ALSA Analog Stereo
Name: alsa_output.platform-bcm2835_AUDO.0.analog-stereo.monitor
Index: 0
```

Java MIDI

openJDK supports the Java MIDI devices. The program DeviceInfo reports the following:

```
MIDI devices:
    Name: Gervill, Decription: Software MIDI Synthesizer, Vendor: OpenJDK
        Device is a synthesizer
        Open receivers:

        Default receiver: com.sun.media.sound.SoftReceiver@10655dd

        Open receivers now:
            com.sun.media.sound.SoftReceiver@10655dd

        Open transmitters:
        No default transmitter
    Name: Real Time Sequencer, Decription: Software sequencer, Vendor: Sun Microsystems
        Device is a sequencer
        Open receivers:

        Default receiver: com.sun.media.sound.RealTimeSequencer$SequencerReceiver@12f0999

        Open receivers now:
            com.sun.media.sound.RealTimeSequencer$SequencerReceiver@12f0999

        Open transmitters:

        Default transmitter: com.sun.media.sound.RealTimeSequencer$SequencerTransmitter@65a77f

        Open transmitters now:
            com.sun.media.sound.RealTimeSequencer$SequencerTransmitter@65a77f
Default system sequencer is Real Time Sequencer
Default system synthesizer is Gervill
```

Programs like DumpSequence work OK. But the SimpleMidiPlayer hits 80 percent CPU usage and is unusable. So, any idea of a karaoke player using Java on the RPi is simply not good. There is a thread on the Raspberry Pi site discussing the problems with sound (www.raspberrypi.org/phpBB3/viewtopic.php?f=38&t=11009).

OpenMAX

Audio and video can be played on the Raspberry Pi using the OpenMAX IL toolkit. This has been implemented by Broadcom for its GPU used by the RPi. This is partly covered in Chapter 13 and is covered in depth in my book *Raspberry Pi GPU Audio and Video Programming*.

Conclusion

The Raspberry Pi is an exciting new toy to play with. There are many competitors on the block, but it has still sold more than ten million devices. This chapter covered some of the audio aspects of the device.

CHAPTER 32

Conclusion

These are my final words.

Where Did I Start?

The following were the starting points for all this:

- I have two karaoke machines, each with different capabilities.

- I wanted to build a "best of both worlds" machine from my computers.

- My initial attempt using the Java Sound API worked but suffered from latency, enough to make it unusable.

- Attempts to move any part of this Java solution to low-powered devices like the Raspberry Pi just failed miserably.

Where Did I Get To?

Well, I got most of the way there. I now have a system playing videos in the background and playing karaoke files using the TiMidity synthesizer. I didn't get scoring systems working, but that involves a further exploration into digital signal processing.

I actually got it all working on the Raspberry Pi, but that meant digging into the Raspberry Pi's GPU to handle the video effects, and I have dealt with its GPU programming in a separate book.

How Did I Get There?

Well, obviously I needed to play with sound. I started with the Java Sound API, and when that proved to have latency issues, I started hunting through all aspects of sound on Linux. That's why this book has sections on ALSA, Jack, PulseAudio, and more. I couldn't find the information I was looking for in a clear enough manner, so as I discovered more, I wrote it all down, and the result is this book.

I hope you find it to be of general value and not just something that fed my particular obsession. I've learned a tremendous amount in writing this book, and I feel confident that if you want to do anything with sound under Linux, then this book will give you at least some of the answers.

Regards, and good luck with your own projects!

© Jan Newmarch 2017
J. Newmarch, *Linux Sound Programming*, DOI 10.1007/978-1-4842-2496-0_32

APPENDIX A

■■■

Decoding the DKD Files on the Sonken Karaoke DVD

This chapter is about getting the information off my Sonken karaoke DVD so that I can start writing programs to play the songs. It is not directly involved in playing sound under Linux and can be skipped.

Introduction

I have two karaoke players, a Sonken MD-388 and a Malata MDVD-6619. Between the two of them, they have all the features I think I need from karaoke players, including the following:

- Selecting and playing tunes (of course!)

- A huge range of both Chinese and English-language songs (my wife is Chinese, and I am English)

- Both Mandarin and PinYin shown for the Chinese songs so that I can sing along too

- The notes of the melody displayed along with the notes that the singer is actually singing

- Scoring system showing different features

The Malata is really good in that it shows the notes of the melody and also shows the notes that you are singing. But it has a pathetic range of English songs and doesn't show the PinYin for the Chinese songs. The Songen has a good selection of both and shows the PinYin but doesn't show the notes and has a simplistic scoring system.

So, I want to take the songs off my Sonken DVD and play them either on the Malata or on my PC. Playing them on my PC is preferred because then I am limited only by the programs that I can write and am not so dependent on a vendor's machine. So, my immediate goal is to get the songs off the Sonken DVD and start playing them in the ways that I want.

The files on the Sonken DVD are in DKD format. This is an undocumented format probably standing for Digital Karaoke Disc. Many people have worked on this format, and there has been much discussion in forums such as Karaoke Engineering. These include "Understanding the HOTDOG files on DVD of California electronics" (http://old.nabble.com/Understanding-the-HOTDOG-files-on-DVD-of-California-electronics-td11359745.html), "Decoding JBK 6628 DVD Karaoke Disc" (http://old.nabble.com/Decoding-JBK-6628-DVD-Karaoke-Disc-td12261269.html) (these two links no longer seem to have any content, though), and "Karaoke Huyndai 99" (http://board.midibuddy.net/showpost.php?p=533722&postcount=31).

© Jan Newmarch 2017
J. Newmarch, *Linux Sound Programming*, DOI 10.1007/978-1-4842-2496-0_33

When I started looking at my disc, I went about it in a different direction than many of the posters in these forums. Also, the results in the forums were presented in an ad hoc and often confusing manner, as could be expected. So, I ended up re-inventing a lot of what had already been discovered, as well as coming up with some new stuff.

In hindsight, I could have saved myself weeks of work if I had paid proper attention to what was said in the forums. So, this appendix is my attempt to lay out the results in a simple and logical enough way so that people trying to do similar things with their own discs can easily work out what is applicable to their situation and what is different.

This chapter will cover the following:

- What files are on my DVD

- What each file contains (overview)

- Matching song titles to song numbers

- Finding the song data on the disc

- Extracting the song data

- Decoding the song data

This appendix is not complete, as there is still more to be discovered.

Format Shifting

Isn't it illegal to copy your DVDs? It's not in Australia, under the right conditions (see the Copyright Amendment Act 2006 FAQ at www.ag.gov.au/Copyright/Issuesandreviews/Pages/CopyrightAmendmentAct2006FAQs.aspx).

> Will I be able to copy my music collection onto my iPod? Yes. You can format-shift music that you own to devices such as an MP3 player, Xbox 360, or your computer.

I am just copying the music I legally bought with the Sonken DVD to my computer for personal use. That is within the Australian Copyright Amendment Act. You should check whether your country allows the same rights.

> *Don't ask for any copies of the files off my DVD. That would be illegal, and I'm not going to do it.*

Files on the DVD

My Sonken DVD contains these files:

```
BACK01.MPG
DTSMUS00.DKD
DTSMUS01.DKD
DTSMUS02.DKD
DTSMUS03.DKD
DTSMUS04.DKD
DTSMUS05.DKD
DTSMUS06.DKD
```

```
DTSMUS07.DKD
DTSMUS10.DKD
DTSMUS20.DKD
```

BACK01.MPG

This is the MP3 file that plays in the background.

DTSMUS00.DKD to DTSMUS07.DKD

These are the song files. The number of these depends on how many songs are on the DVD.

DTSMUS10.DKD

No one has worked out what this file is for yet.

DTSMUS20.DKD

This file contains the list of song number, song title, and artist as given in the song book. The song number in this file is one less than the song number in the book.

Decoding DTSMUS20.DKD

I'm on a Linux system, and I use Linux/Unix utilities and applications. Equivalents exist under other OSs such as Windows and Apple.

Song Information

The Unix command strings lists all the ASCII 8-bit encoded strings in a file that are at least four characters long. Running this command on all the DVD files shows that DTSMUS20.DKD is the only one with lots of English-language strings, and these strings are the song titles on the DVD.

A brief selection is as follows:

```
Come To Me
Come To Me Boy
Condition Of My Heart
Fly To The Sky
Cool Love
Count Down
Cowboy
Crazy
```

The actual strings that would show on your disc depend, of course, on the songs on it. You would need some English-language titles on it for this to work, of course!

To make further progress, you need a binary editor. I use `bvi`. emacs has a binary editor mode as well. Search using the editor for a song title you know is on the disc. For example, searching for the Beatles' "Here Comes the Sun" shows the following block:

```
000AA920  12 D3 88 48 65 72 65 20 43 6F 6D 65 73 20 54 68  ...Here Comes Th
000AA930  65 20 52 61 69 6E 20 41 67 61 69 6E 00 45 75 72  e Rain Again.Eur
000AA940  79 74 68 6D 69 63 73 00 1F 12 D3 89 48 65 72 65  ythmics.....Here
000AA950  20 43 6F 6D 65 73 20 54 68 65 20 53 75 6E 00 42   Comes The Sun.B
000AA960  65 61 74 6C 65 73 00 1B 12 D3 8A 48 65 72 65 20  eatles.....Here
000AA970  46 6F 72 20 59 6F 75 00 46 69 72 65 68 6F 75 73  For You.Firehous
```

The string "Here Comes the Sun" starts at 0xAA94C followed by a null byte. This is followed at 0xAA95F by the null-terminated "Beatles." Immediately before this is 4 bytes. The length of these two strings (including the null bytes) and the 4 bytes is 0x1F, and this is the first of the four preceding bytes. So, the block consists of a 4-byte header followed by a null-terminated song title followed by a null-terminated artist. Byte 1 is the length of the song information block including the 4-byte header.

Byte 2 of the header block is 0x12. jim75 at "Decoding JBK 6628 DVD Karaoke Disc" (http://old.nabble.com/Decoding-JBK-6628-DVD-Karaoke-Disc-td12261269.html) discovered the document JBK_Manual%5B1%5D.doc. In it is a list of country codes, shown here:

```
00 : KOREAN
01 : CHINESE( reserved )
02 : CHINESE
03 : TAIWANESE
04 : JAPANESE
05 : RUSSIAN
06 : THAI
07 : TAIWANESE( reserved )
08 : CHINESE( reserved )
09 : CANTONESE
12 : ENGLISH
13 : VIETNAMESE
14 : PHILIPPINE
15 : TURKEY
16 : SPANISH
17 : INDONESIAN
18 : MALAYSIAN
19 : PORTUGUESE
20 : FRENCH
21 : INDIAN
22 : BRASIL
```

The Beatles' song has 0x12 in byte 2 of the header, and this matches the country code in the table. This is confirmed by looking at other language files.

I discovered later that the WMA files have their own codes. So far I have seen the following:

```
83 : CHINESE WMA
92 : ENGLISH WMA
94 : PHILIPPINE WMA
```

I guess you can see a pattern with the earlier ones!

Bytes 3 and 4 of the header are 0xD389, which is 54153 in decimal. This is one less than the song number in the book (54154). So, bytes 3 and 4 are a 16-bit short integer, one less than the song index in the book.

This pattern is repeated throughout the file, so each record has this format.

Beginning/End of Data

There is a long sequence of bytes near the beginning of the file: "01 01 01 01 01 …." This finishes on my file at 0x9F23. By comparing the index number with those in my song book, I confirm this is the start of the Korean songs and probably the start of all songs. I haven't found any table giving me this start value.

Checking a number of songs gives me this table:

- English songs start at 60x9562D (song 24452, type 0x12)

- Cantonese at 0x8F5D2 (song 13701, type 3)

- Korean at 0x9F23 (song 37847, type 0)

- Indonesian at 0x11F942 (song 42002, type 0x17)

- Hindi at 0x134227 (song 45058, type 0x21)

- Philippine at 0xD5D20 (song 62775, type 0x14)

- Russian at 0x110428 (song 41012, type 5)

- Spanish at 0xF5145 (song 26487, type 0x16)

- Mandarin (1 character) at 0x413BE (song 1388, type 3)

I can't find the Vietnamese songs, though. There don't seem to any on my disc. My song book is lying! I guess there is some table somewhere giving these start points, but I haven't found it. These were all found by looking at my song book and then in the file.

The end of the block is signaled by a sequence of "FF FF FF FF …" at 0x136C92.

But there is a lot of stuff both before and after the song information block. I don't know what it means.

Chinese Songs

The first English song in my book is "Gump" by Al Wierd, song number 24452. In the table of contents file DTSMUS20.DK this is at 0x9562D (611885). The entry before this is "20 03 3A 04 CE D2 B4 F2 C1 CB D2 BB CD A8 B2 BB CB B5 BB B0 B5 C4 B5 E7 BB B0 B8 F8 C4 E3 00 00." The song code is "3A 04," in other words, 14852, which is song number 14853 (one offset, remember!). When I play that song on my karaoke machine, I'm in luck: the first character of the song is 我, which I recognize as the Chinese word "I" (in PinYin: wo3). Its encoding in the file is "CE D2." I've got Chinese input installed on my computer so I can search for this Chinese character.

A Google search for *Unicode value of* 我 shows me the following:

```
[RESOLVED] Converting Unicode Character Literal to Uint16 variable ...
www.codeguru.com › ... › C++ (Non Visual C++ Issues)
5 posts - 2 authors - 1 Jul 2011

I've determined that the unicode character '我' has a hex value of
0x6211 by looking it up on the "GNOME Character Map 2.32.1"
```

```
and if I do this....
```

Then looking up 0x6211 on Unicode Search (www.khngai.com/chinese/tools/codeunicode.php) gives gold.

```
Unicode        6211 (25105)
GB Code        CED2 (4650)
Big 5 Code     A7DA
CNS Code       1-4A3C
```

There's the CED2 in the second line as GB Code. So there you go: the character set is GB (probably GB2312 with EUC-CN encoding) with code for 我 as CED2.

Just to make sure, using the table by Mary Ansell at GB Code Table (www.ansell-uebersetzungen.com/gborder.html), the bytes "CE D2 B4 F2 C1 CB D2 BB CD A8 B2 BB CB B5 BB B0 B5 C4 B5 E7 BB B0 B8 F8 C4 E3" translate into "我 打 了 一 通 ...", which is indeed the song.

Other Languages

I'm not familiar with other language encodings so haven't investigated the Thai, Vietnamese, and so on. The Korean seems to be EUC-KR.

Programs

The earlier investigations by others have resulted programs in C or C++. These are generally stand-alone programs. I would like to build a collection of reusable modules, so I have chosen Java as an implementation language.

Java Goodies

Java is a good object-oriented language that supports good design. It includes a MIDI player and MIDI classes. It supports multiple language encodings so it is easy to switch from, say, GB-2312 to Unicode. It has good cross-platform GUI support.

Java Baddies

Java doesn't support unsigned integer types. This sucks *really* badly here since so many data types are unsigned for these programs. Even bytes in Java are signed. Here are some of the tricks:

- Make all types the next size up: byte to int, int to long, long to long. Just hope that unsigned longs aren't really needed.

- If you need an unsigned byte and you have an int and you need it to fit into 8 bits, cast to a byte and hope it's not too big.

- Typecast all over the place to keep the compiler happy, such as when a byte is required from an int, (byte) n.

- Watch signs all over the place. If you want to right shift a number, the operator >> preserves sign extensions, so, for example, in binary 1XYZ... shifts to 1111XYZ... You need to use >>>, which results in 0001XYZ.

- If you want to assign an unsigned byte to an int, watch signs again. You may need the following:

```
n = b ≥ 0 ? b : 256 - b
```

- To build an unsigned int from two unsigned bytes, signs will stuff you again: n = (b1 << 8) + b2 will get it wrong if either b1 or b2 is -ve. Instead, use the following:

```
n = ((b1 ≥ 0 ? b1 : 256 - b1) << 8) + (b2 ≥ 0 ? b2 : 256 - b2)
```

(No joke!)

Classes

The song class, SongInformation.java, contains information about a single song and is given here:

```java
public class SongInformation {

    // Public fields of each song record
    /**
     * Song number in the file, one less than in songbook
     */
    public long number;

    /**
     * song title in Unicode
     */
    public String title;

    /**
     * artist in Unicode
     */
    public String artist;

    /**
     * integer value of language code
     */
    public int language;

    public static final int  KOREAN = 0;
    public static final int  CHINESE1 = 1;
    public static final int  CHINESE2 = 2;
    public static final int  TAIWANESE3 = 3 ;
    public static final int  JAPANESE = 4;
    public static final int  RUSSIAN = 5;
```

```java
    public static final int  THAI = 6;
    public static final int  TAIWANESE7 = 7;
    public static final int  CHINESE8 = 8;
    public static final int  CANTONESE = 9;
    public static final int  ENGLISH = 0x12;
    public static final int  VIETNAMESE = 0x13;
    public static final int  PHILIPPINE = 0x14;
    public static final int  TURKEY = 0x15;
    public static final int  SPANISH = 0x16;
    public static final int  INDONESIAN = 0x17;
    public static final int  MALAYSIAN = 0x18;
    public static final int  PORTUGUESE = 0x19;
    public static final int  FRENCH = 0x20;
    public static final int  INDIAN = 0x21;
    public static final int  BRASIL = 0x22;
    public static final int  CHINESE131 = 131;
    public static final int  ENGLISH146 = 146;
    public static final int  PHILIPPINE148 = 148;

    public SongInformation(long number,
                           String title,
                           String artist,
                           int language) {
        this.number = number;
        this.title = title;
        this.artist = artist;
        this.language = language;
    }

    public String toString() {
        return "" + (number+1) + " (" + language + ") \"" + title + "\" " + artist;
    }

    public boolean titleMatch(String pattern) {
        // System.out.println("Pattern: " + pattern);
        return title.matches("(?i).*" + pattern + ".*");
    }

    public boolean artistMatch(String pattern) {
        return artist.matches("(?i).*" + pattern + ".*");
    }

    public boolean numberMatch(String pattern) {
        Long n;
        try {
            n = Long.parseLong(pattern) - 1;
            //System.out.println("Long is " + n);
        } catch(Exception e) {
            //System.out.println(e.toString());
```

```
            return false;
        }
        return number == n;
    }

    public boolean languageMatch(int lang) {
        return language == lang;
    }
}
```

The song table class, SongTable.java, holds a list of song information objects.

```java
import java.util.Vector;
import java.io.FileInputStream;
import java.io.*;
import java.nio.charset.Charset;

// public class SongTable implements java.util.Iterator {
// public class SongTable extends  Vector<SongInformation> {
public class SongTable {

    private static final String SONG_INFO_FILE = "/home/newmarch/Music/karaoke/sonken/
    DTSMUS20.DKD";
    private static final long INFO_START = 0x9F23;

    public static final int ENGLISH = 0x12;

    private static Vector<SongInformation> allSongs;

    private Vector<SongInformation> songs =
        new Vector<SongInformation>  ();

    public static long[] langCount = new long[0x23];

    public SongTable(Vector<SongInformation> songs) {
        this.songs = songs;
    }

    public SongTable() throws java.io.IOException,
                              java.io.FileNotFoundException {
        FileInputStream fstream = new FileInputStream(SONG_INFO_FILE);
        fstream.skip(INFO_START);
        while (true) {
            int len;
            int lang;
            long number;

            len = fstream.read();
            lang = fstream.read();
            number = readShort(fstream);
            if (len == 0xFF && lang == 0xFF && number == 0xFFFFL) {
```

```
                break;
            }
            byte[] bytes = new byte[len - 4];
            fstream.read(bytes);
            int endTitle;
            // find null at end of title
            for (endTitle = 0; bytes[endTitle] != 0; endTitle++)
                ;
            byte[] titleBytes = new byte[endTitle];
            byte[] artistBytes = new byte[len - endTitle - 6];

            System.arraycopy(bytes, 0, titleBytes, 0, titleBytes.length);
            System.arraycopy(bytes, endTitle + 1,
                            artistBytes, 0, artistBytes.length);
            String title = toUnicode(lang, titleBytes);
            String artist = toUnicode(lang, artistBytes);
            // System.out.printf("artist: %s, title: %s, lang: %d, number %d\n",
            artist, title, lang, number);
            SongInformation info = new SongInformation(number,
                                                        title,
                                                        artist,
                                                        lang);
            songs.add(info);

            if (lang > 0x22) {
                //System.out.println("Illegal lang value " + lang + " at song " + number);
            } else {
                langCount[lang]++;
            }
        }
        allSongs = songs;
    }

    public void dumpTable() {
        for (SongInformation song: songs) {
            System.out.println("" + (song.number+1) + " - " +
                            song.artist + " - " +
                            song.title);
        }
    }

    public java.util.Iterator<SongInformation> iterator() {
        return songs.iterator();
    }

    private int readShort(FileInputStream f)  throws java.io.IOException {
        int n1 = f.read();
        int n2 = f.read();
        return (n1 << 8) + n2;
    }
```

```java
private String toUnicode(int lang, byte[] bytes) {
    switch (lang) {
    case SongInformation.ENGLISH:
    case SongInformation.ENGLISH146:
    case SongInformation.PHILIPPINE:
    case SongInformation.PHILIPPINE148:
        // case SongInformation.HINDI:
    case SongInformation.INDONESIAN:
    case SongInformation.SPANISH:
        return new String(bytes);

    case SongInformation.CHINESE1:
    case SongInformation.CHINESE2:
    case SongInformation.CHINESE8:
    case SongInformation.CHINESE131:
    case SongInformation.TAIWANESE3:
    case SongInformation.TAIWANESE7:
    case SongInformation.CANTONESE:
        Charset charset = Charset.forName("gb2312");
        return new String(bytes, charset);

    case SongInformation.KOREAN:
        charset = Charset.forName("euckr");
        return new String(bytes, charset);

    default:
        return "";
    }
}

public SongInformation getNumber(long number) {
    for (SongInformation info: songs) {
        if (info.number == number) {
            return info;
        }
    }
    return null;
}

public SongTable titleMatches( String pattern) {
    Vector<SongInformation> matchSongs =
        new Vector<SongInformation>  ();

    for (SongInformation song: songs) {
        if (song.titleMatch(pattern)) {
            matchSongs.add(song);
        }
    }
    return new SongTable(matchSongs);
}
```

```java
public SongTable artistMatches( String pattern) {
    Vector<SongInformation> matchSongs =
        new Vector<SongInformation>  ();

    for (SongInformation song: songs) {
        if (song.artistMatch(pattern)) {
            matchSongs.add(song);
        }
    }
    return new SongTable(matchSongs);
}

  public SongTable numberMatches( String pattern) {
    Vector<SongInformation> matchSongs =
        new Vector<SongInformation>  ();

    for (SongInformation song: songs) {
        if (song.numberMatch(pattern)) {
            matchSongs.add(song);
        }
    }
    return new SongTable(matchSongs);
}

public String toString() {
    StringBuffer buf = new StringBuffer();
    for (SongInformation song: songs) {
        buf.append(song.toString() + "\n");
    }
    return buf.toString();
}

public static void main(String[] args) {
    // for testing
    SongTable songs = null;
    try {
        songs = new SongTable();
    } catch(Exception e) {
        System.err.println(e.toString());
        System.exit(1);
    }
    songs.dumpTable();
    System.exit(0);

    // Should print "54151 Help Yourself Tom Jones"
    System.out.println(songs.getNumber(54150).toString());

    // Should print "18062 伦巴(恋歌) 伦巴"
    System.out.println(songs.getNumber(18061).toString());

    System.out.println(songs.artistMatches("Tom Jones").toString());
```

```
        /* Prints
54151 Help Yourself Tom Jones
50213 Daughter Of Darkness Tom Jones
23914 DELILAH Tom Jones
52834 Funny Familiar Forgotten Feelings Tom Jones
54114 Green green grass of home Tom Jones
54151 Help Yourself Tom Jones
55365 I (WHO HAVE NOTHING) TOM JONES
52768 I Believe Tom Jones
55509 I WHO HAVE NOTHING TOM JONES
55594 I'll Never Fall Inlove Again Tom Jones
55609 I'm Coming Home Tom Jones
51435 It's Not Unusual Tom Jones
55817 KISS Tom Jones
52842 Little Green Apples Tom Jones
51439 Love Me Tonight Tom Jones
56212 My Elusive Dream TOM JONES
56386 ONE DAY SOON Tom Jones
22862 THAT WONDERFUL SOUND Tom Jones
57170 THE GREEN GREEN GRASS OF HOME TOM JONES
57294 The Wonderful Sound Tom Jones
23819 TILL Tom Jones
51759 What's New Pussycat Tom Jones
52862 With These Hands Tom Jones
57715 Without Love Tom Jones
57836 You're My World Tom Jones
        */

        for (int n = 1; n < langCount.length; n++) {
            if (langCount[n] != 0) {
                System.out.println("Count: " + langCount[n] + " of lang " + n);
            }
        }

        // Check Russian, etc
        System.out.println("Russian " + '\u0411');
        System.out.println("Korean " + '\u0411');
        System.exit(0);
    }
}
```

You may need to adjust the constant values in the file-based constructor for this to work properly for you.

A Java program using Swing to allow the display and searching of the song titles is SongTableSwing. java.

```
import java.awt.*;
import java.awt.event.*;
import javax.swing.event.*;
import javax.swing.*;
```

```java
import javax.swing.SwingUtilities;
import java.util.regex.*;
import java.io.*;

public class SongTableSwing extends JPanel {
    private DefaultListModel model = new DefaultListModel();
    private JList list;
    private static SongTable allSongs;

    private JTextField numberField;
    private JTextField langField;
    private JTextField titleField;
    private JTextField artistField;

    // This font displays Asian and European characters.
    // It should be in your distro.
    // Fonts displaying all Unicode are zysong.ttf and Cyberbit.ttf
    // See http://unicode.org/resources/fonts.html
    private Font font = new Font("WenQuanYi Zen Hei", Font.PLAIN, 16);
    // font = new Font("Bitstream Cyberbit", Font.PLAIN, 16);

    private int findIndex = -1;

    /**
     * Describe <code>main</code> method here.
     *
     * @param args a <code>String</code> value
     */
    public static final void main(final String[] args) {
        allSongs = null;
        try {
            allSongs = new SongTable();
        } catch(Exception e) {
            System.err.println(e.toString());
            System.exit(1);
        }

        JFrame frame = new JFrame();
        frame.setTitle("Song Table");
        frame.setSize(1000, 800);
        frame.setDefaultCloseOperation(JFrame.EXIT_ON_CLOSE);

        SongTableSwing panel = new SongTableSwing(allSongs);
        frame.getContentPane().add(panel);

        frame.setVisible(true);
    }

    public SongTableSwing(SongTable songs) {
```

```java
if (font == null) {
    System.err.println("Can't fnd font");
}

int n = 0;
java.util.Iterator<SongInformation> iter = songs.iterator();
while(iter.hasNext()) {
    model.add(n++, iter.next());
    // model.add(n++, iter.next().toString());
}

BorderLayout mgr = new BorderLayout();

list = new JList(model);
// list = new JList(songs);
list.setFont(font);
JScrollPane scrollPane = new JScrollPane(list);

setLayout(mgr);
add(scrollPane, BorderLayout.CENTER);

JPanel bottomPanel = new JPanel();
bottomPanel.setLayout(new GridLayout(2, 1));
add(bottomPanel, BorderLayout.SOUTH);

JPanel searchPanel = new JPanel();
bottomPanel.add(searchPanel);
searchPanel.setLayout(new FlowLayout());

JLabel numberLabel = new JLabel("Number");
numberField = new JTextField(5);

JLabel langLabel = new JLabel("Language");
langField = new JTextField(8);

JLabel titleLabel = new JLabel("Title");
titleField = new JTextField(20);
titleField.setFont(font);

JLabel artistLabel = new JLabel("Artist");
artistField = new JTextField(10);
artistField.setFont(font);

searchPanel.add(numberLabel);
searchPanel.add(numberField);
// searchPanel.add(langLabel);
// searchPanel.add(langField);
searchPanel.add(titleLabel);
```

```java
        searchPanel.add(titleField);
        searchPanel.add(artistLabel);
        searchPanel.add(artistField);

        titleField.getDocument().addDocumentListener(new DocumentListener() {
                public void changedUpdate(DocumentEvent e) {
                    // rest find to -1 to restart any find searches
                    findIndex = -1;
                    // System.out.println("reset find index");
                }
                public void insertUpdate(DocumentEvent e) {
                    findIndex = -1;
                    // System.out.println("reset insert find index");
                }
                public void removeUpdate(DocumentEvent e) {
                    findIndex = -1;
                    // System.out.println("reset remove find index");
                }
            }
        );
        artistField.getDocument().addDocumentListener(new DocumentListener() {
                public void changedUpdate(DocumentEvent e) {
                    // rest find to -1 to restart any find searches
                    findIndex = -1;
                    // System.out.println("reset insert find index");
                }
                public void insertUpdate(DocumentEvent e) {
                    findIndex = -1;
                    // System.out.println("reset insert find index");
                }
                public void removeUpdate(DocumentEvent e) {
                    findIndex = -1;
                    // System.out.println("reset insert find index");
                }
            }
        );

        titleField.addActionListener(new ActionListener(){
                public void actionPerformed(ActionEvent e){
                    filterSongs();
                }});
        artistField.addActionListener(new ActionListener(){
                public void actionPerformed(ActionEvent e){
                    filterSongs();
                }});
        numberField.addActionListener(new ActionListener(){
                public void actionPerformed(ActionEvent e){
                    filterSongs();
                }});
```

```
    JPanel buttonPanel = new JPanel();
    bottomPanel.add(buttonPanel);
    buttonPanel.setLayout(new FlowLayout());

    JButton find = new JButton("Find");
    JButton filter = new JButton("Filter");
    JButton reset = new JButton("Reset");
    JButton play = new JButton("Play");
    buttonPanel.add(find);
    buttonPanel.add(filter);
    buttonPanel.add(reset);
    buttonPanel.add(play);

    find.addActionListener(new ActionListener() {
            public void actionPerformed(ActionEvent e) {
                findSong();
            }
        });

    filter.addActionListener(new ActionListener() {
            public void actionPerformed(ActionEvent e) {
                filterSongs();
            }
        });

    reset.addActionListener(new ActionListener() {
            public void actionPerformed(ActionEvent e) {
                resetSongs();
            }
        });

    play.addActionListener(new ActionListener() {
            public void actionPerformed(ActionEvent e) {
                playSong();
            }
        });

}

public void findSong() {
    String number = numberField.getText();
    String language = langField.getText();
    String title = titleField.getText();
    String artist = artistField.getText();

    if (number.length() != 0) {
        try {

            long num = Integer.parseInt(number) - 1;
            for (int n = 0; n < model.getSize(); n++) {
                SongInformation info = (SongInformation) model.getElementAt(n);
                if (info.number == num) {
```

```java
                        list.setSelectedIndex(n);
                        list.ensureIndexIsVisible(n);
                        return;
                    }
                }
        } catch(Exception e) {
            System.err.println("Not a number");
            numberField.setText("");
        }

        return;
    }

    /*
    System.out.println("Title " + title + title.length() +
                        "artist " + artist + artist.length() +
                        " find start " + findIndex +
                        " model size " + model.getSize());
    if (title.length() == 0 && artist.length() == 0) {
        System.err.println("no search terms");
        return;
    }
    */

    //System.out.println("Search " + searchStr + " from index " + findIndex);
    for (int n = findIndex + 1; n < model.getSize(); n++) {
        SongInformation info = (SongInformation) model.getElementAt(n);
        //System.out.println(info.toString());

        if ((title.length() != 0) && (artist.length() != 0)) {
            if (info.titleMatch(title) && info.artistMatch(artist)) {
                // System.out.println("Found " + info.toString());
                    findIndex = n;
                    list.setSelectedIndex(n);
                    list.ensureIndexIsVisible(n);
                    break;
            }
        } else {
            if ((title.length() != 0) && info.titleMatch(title)) {
                // System.out.println("Found " + info.toString());
                findIndex = n;
                list.setSelectedIndex(n);
                list.ensureIndexIsVisible(n);
                break;
            } else if ((artist.length() != 0) && info.artistMatch(artist)) {
                // System.out.println("Found " + info.toString());
                findIndex = n;
                list.setSelectedIndex(n);
                list.ensureIndexIsVisible(n);
                break;
            }

        }
```

```java
        }

    }
}

public void filterSongs() {
    String title = titleField.getText();
    String artist = artistField.getText();
    String number = numberField.getText();
    SongTable filteredSongs = allSongs;

    if (allSongs == null) {
        // System.err.println("Songs is null");
        return;
    }

    if (title.length() != 0) {
        filteredSongs = filteredSongs.titleMatches(title);
    }
    if (artist.length() != 0) {
        filteredSongs = filteredSongs.artistMatches(artist);
    }
    if (number.length() != 0) {
        filteredSongs = filteredSongs.numberMatches(number);
    }

    model.clear();
    int n = 0;
    java.util.Iterator<SongInformation> iter = filteredSongs.iterator();
    while(iter.hasNext()) {
        model.add(n++, iter.next());
    }
}

public void resetSongs() {
    artistField.setText("");
    titleField.setText("");
    numberField.setText("");
    model.clear();
    int n = 0;
    java.util.Iterator<SongInformation> iter = allSongs.iterator();
    while(iter.hasNext()) {
        model.add(n++, iter.next());
    }
}
/**
 * "play" a song by printing its id to standard out.
 * Can be used in a pipeline this way
 */
public void playSong() {
    SongInformation song = (SongInformation) list.getSelectedValue();
    if (song == null) {
```

```
            return;
        }
        long number = song.number + 1;
        System.out.println("" + number);
    }

    class SongInformationRenderer extends JLabel implements ListCellRenderer {

        public Component getListCellRendererComponent(
                                            JList list,
                                            Object value,
                                            int index,
                                            boolean isSelected,
                                            boolean cellHasFocus) {
            setText(value.toString());
            return this;
        }
    }
}
```

When Play is selected, it will print the song ID to standard output for use in a pipeline.

The Data Files

The following sections will cover the data files.

General

The files DTSMUS00.DKD to DTSMUS07.DKD contain the music files. There are two formats for the music: Microsoft WMA files and MIDI files. In my song books, some songs are marked as having a singer. These turn out to be the WMA files. Those without a singer are MIDI files.

The WMA files are just that. The MIDI files are slightly compressed and have to be decoded before they can be played.

Each song block has at the beginning a section containing the lyrics. These are compressed and have to be decoded.

The data for one song forms a record of contiguous bytes. These records are collected into blocks, also contiguous. The blocks are separate. There is a "superblock" of pointers to these blocks. Part of the song number is an index into the superblock, selecting the block. The rest of the song number is an index of the record in the block.

My Route into This

I came backward into this and only arrived at understanding what others had accomplished after some time. So, in case it helps any others, here is my route.

I used the Unix command `strings` to discover the song information in DTSMUS10.DKD. On the other files it didn't seem to produce much. But there were ASCII strings in these files, and some were repeated. So, I wrote a shell pipeline to sort these strings and count them. The pipeline for one file was as follows:

```
strings DTSMUS05.DKD | sort |uniq -c | sort -n -r |less
```

This produced these results:

```
1229 :^y|
1018 j?wK
 843 ]/<
 756 Seh
 747 Ser
 747 \D+P
 674 :^yt
 234 IRI$
```

The results weren't inspiring. But when I looked inside the files to see where "Ser" was occurring, I also saw the following:

```
q03C3E230  F6 01 00 00 00 02 00 16 00 57 00 69 00 6E 00 64 .........W.i.n.d
03C3E240   00 6F 00 77 00 73 00 20 00 4D 00 65 00 64 00 69 .o.w.s. .M.e.d.i
03C3E250   00 61 00 20 00 41 00 75 00 64 00 69 00 6F 00 20 .a. .A.u.d.i.o.
03C3E260   00 39 00 00 00 24 00 20 00 34 00 38 00 20 00 6B .9...$. .4.8. .k
03C3E270   00 62 00 70 00 73 00 2C 00 20 00 34 00 34 00 20 .b.p.s.,. .4.4.
03C3E280   00 6B 00 48 00 7A 00 2C 00 20 00 73 00 74 00 65 .k.H.z.,. .s.t.e
03C3E290   00 72 00 65 00 6F 00 20 00 31 00 2D 00 70 00 61 .r.e.o. .1.-.p.a
03C3E2A0   00 73 00 73 00 20 00 43 00 42 00 52 00 00 00 02 .s.s. .C.B.R....
03C3E2B0   00 61 01 91 07 DC B7 B7 A9 CF 11 8E E6 00 C0 0C .a..............
03C3E2C0   20 53 65 72 00 00 00 00 00 00 00 40 9E 69 F8 4D  Ser.......@.i.M
```

Wow! *Two-byte* characters!

The `strings` command has options to look at, for example, 2-byte big-endian character strings. The command

```
strings -e b DTSMUS05.DKD
```

turned up this:

```
IsVBR
DeviceConformanceTemplate
WM/WMADRCPeakReference
WM/WMADRCAverageReference
WMFSDKVersion
```

```
9.00.00.2980
WMFSDKNeeded
0.0.0.0000
```

These are all part of the WMA format.

According to Gary Kessler's File Signatures Table (www.garykessler.net/library/file_sigs.html), the signature of a WMA file is given by the header shown here:

```
30 26 B2 75 8E 66 CF 11
A6 D9 00 AA 00 62 CE 6C
```

That pattern does occur, with the previous strings appearing some time later.

The spec for the ASF/WMA file format is at www.microsoft.com/download/en/details.aspx?displayl ang=en&id=14995, although you are advised not to read it in case you want to do anything open source with such files.

So, on that basis, I could identify the start of WMA files. The four bytes preceding each WMA file are the length of the file. From that I could find the *end* of the file, which turned out to be the start of a record for the *next* record containing some stuff and then the next WMA file.

In these records, I could see patterns I couldn't understand, but also from byte 36 on I could see strings like this:

```
AIN'T IT FUNNY HOW TIME SLIPS AWAY, Str length: 34

00000000  10 50 41 10 50 49 10 50 4E 10 50 27 10 50 54 10  .PA.PI.PN.P'.PT.
00000010  50 20 11 F1 25 12 71 05 04 61 05 05 51 21 13 01  P ..%.q..a..Q!..
00000020  02 05 91 2B 10 20 48 10 50 4F 10 50 57 13 40 00  ...+. H.PO.PW.@.
00000030  12 61 02 12 01 02 04 D1 05 04 51 3B 05 31 05 04  .a........Q;.1..
00000040  C1 29 10 20 50 10 51 45 10 21 28 10 21 1E 10 21  .). P.QE.!(.!..!
00000050  3A 14 F1 05 13 31 02 10 C1 0E 11 A1 58 15 A0 00  :....1......X...
00000060  15 70 00 13 A0 A9                                .p....
```

Can you see AIN'T (as .PA.PI.PN.P'.PT)?

But I couldn't figure out what the encoding was or how to find the table of song starts. That's when I was ready to look at the earlier stuff and understand how it applied to me. (See "Understanding the HOTDOG files on DVD of California electronics" (http://old.nabble.com/Understanding-the-HOTDOG-files-on-DVD-of-California-electronics-td11359745.html), "Decoding JBK 6628 DVD Karaoke Disc" (http://old.nabble.com/Decoding-JBK-6628-DVD-Karaoke-Disc-td12261269.html), and "Karaoke Huyndai 99" (http://board.midibuddy.net/showpost.php?p=533722&postcount=31).

The Superblock

The file DTSMUS00.DKD starts with a bunch of nulls. At 0x200 it starts to kick in with data. This was identified as the start of a "table of tables," in other words, a superblock. Each entry in this superblock is a 4-byte integer, which turns out to be an index to tables in the data files. The superblock is terminated by a sequence of nulls (for me at 0x5F4), and there are fewer than 256 indexes in the table.

The value of these superblock entries seems to have changed in different versions. In the JBK disc and also on mine, the values have to be multiplied by 0x800 to give a "virtual offset" in the data files.

To give meaning to this, on my disc at 0x200 is the following:

```
00000200  00 00 00 01 00 00 08 6C 00 00 0F C1 00 00 17 7A
00000210  00 00 1E 81 00 00 25 21 00 00 2B 8D 00 00 32 B7
```

So, the table values are 0x1, 0x86C, 0xFC1, 0x177A, ... The "virtual addresses" are 0x800, 0x436000 (0x86C * 0x800), and so on. If you go to these addresses, you'll see before the address is a bunch of nulls, and at that address is data.

I call them virtual addresses because there are eight data files on my DVD, and most addresses are larger than any of the files. The files (except the last) in my case are all 1065353216L bytes. The "obvious" solution works: the file number is address/file size, and the offset into the file is address percentage file size. You can check this by looking for the nulls before the address of each block.

Song Start Tables

Each of the tables indexed from the superblock is a table of song indexes. Each table contains 4-byte indexes. Each table has at most 0x100 entries or is terminated by a zero index. Each index is the offset from the table start of the beginning of a song entry.

Locating Song Entry from Song Number

Given a song number such as 54154, "Here Comes the Sun," you can now find the song entry. Reduce the song number by 1 to 54153. It is a 16-bit number. The top 8 bits are the index of the song index table in the superblock. The bottom 8 bits are the index of the song entry in the song index table.

Here is the pseudocode:

```
songNumber = get number for song from DTSMUS20.DKD
superBlockIdx = songNumber >>
indexTableIdx = songNumber & 0xFF

seek(DTSMUS00.DKD, superBlockIdx)
superBlockValue = read 4-byte int from DTSMUS00.DKD

locationIndexTable = superBlockValue * 0x800
fileNumber = locationIndexTable / fileSize
indexTableStart = locationIndexTable % fileSize
entryLocation = indexTableStart + indexTableIdx

seek(fileNumber, entryLocation)
read song entry
```

Song Entries

Each song entry has a header and is followed by two blocks that I call the information block and the song data block. Each header block has a 2-byte type code and a 2-byte integer length. The type code is either 0x0800 or 0x0000. The code signals the encoding of the song data: 0x0800 is a WMA file, while 0x0000 is a MIDI file.

If the type code is 0x0 such as the Beatles' "Help!" (song number 51765), then the information block has the length in the header block and starts 12 bytes further in. The song data block immediately follows this.

If the type code is 0x8000, then the information block starts 4 bytes in for the length given in the header. The song block starts on the next 16-byte boundary from the end of the information block.

The song block starts with a 4-byte header, which is the length of the song data for all types.

Song Data

If the song type is 0x8000, then the song data is a WMA file. All songs looked at have a singer included in this file.

If the song type is 0x0, then (from the book) there is no singer in the songs looked at. The file is encoded and decodes to a MIDI file.

Decoding MIDI Files

All files have a lyric block followed by a music block. The lyric block is compressed, and it has been discovered that this is LZW compression. This decompresses to a set of 4-byte chunks. The first two bytes are characters of the lyric. For 1-byte encodings such as English or Vietnamese, the first byte is one character, and the second is either zero or another character (two bytes such as \r\n). For two-byte encodings such as GB-2312, the two bytes form one character.

The next two bytes are the length of time the character string plays for.

Lyric Block

Each lyric block starts with strings such as ""#0001 @@00@12 @Help Yourself @ @@Tom Jones". The language code is in there as NN in @00@NN. The song title, writer, and singer are clear. (Note: these characters are all 4 bytes apart!) For English, it is 12 and so on.

Bytes 0 and 1 of each block are a character in the lyric. Bytes 2 and 3 are the duration of each character. To turn them into MIDI data, the durations have to be turned into the start/stop of each character.

My Java program to do this is SongExtracter.java.

```java
import java.io.*;
import javax.sound.midi.*;
import java.nio.charset.Charset;

public class SongExtracter {
    private static final boolean DEBUG = false;

    private String[] dataFiles = new String[] {
        "DTSMUS00.DKD", "DTSMUS01.DKD", "DTSMUS02.DKD",
        "DTSMUS03.DKD", "DTSMUS04.DKD", "DTSMUS05.DKD",
        "DTSMUS06.DKD", "DTSMUS07.DKD"};
    private String superBlockFileName = dataFiles[0];
    private static final String DATADIR = "/home/newmarch/Music/karaoke/sonken/";
    private static final String SONGDIR ="/home/newmarch/Music/karaoke/sonken/songs/";
    //private static final String SONGDIR ="/server/KARAOKE/KARAOKE/Sonken/";
    private static final long SUPERBLOCK_OFFSET = 0x200;
    private static final long BLOCK_MULTIPLIER = 0x800;
    private static final long FILE_SIZE = 0x3F800000L;

    private static final int SIZE_UINT = 4;
    private static final int SIZE_USHORT = 2;
```

```java
private static final int ENGLISH = 12;

public RawSong getRawSong(int songNumber)
    throws java.io.IOException,
            java.io.FileNotFoundException {
    if (songNumber < 1) {
        throw new FileNotFoundException();
    }

    // song number in files is one less than song number in books, so
    songNumber--;

    long locationIndexTable = getTableIndexFromSuperblock(songNumber);
    debug("Index table at %X\n", locationIndexTable);

    long locationSongDataBlock = getSongIndex(songNumber, locationIndexTable);

    // Now we are at the start of the data block
    return readRawSongData(locationSongDataBlock);

    //debug("Data block at %X\n", songStart);
}

private long getTableIndexFromSuperblock(int songNumber)
    throws java.io.IOException,
            java.io.FileNotFoundException {
    // index into superblock of table of song offsets
    int superBlockIdx = songNumber >> 8;

    debug("Superblock index %X\n", superBlockIdx);

    File superBlockFile = new File(DATADIR + superBlockFileName);

    FileInputStream fstream = new FileInputStream(superBlockFile);

    fstream.skip(SUPERBLOCK_OFFSET + superBlockIdx * SIZE_UINT);
    debug("Skipping to %X\n", SUPERBLOCK_OFFSET + superBlockIdx*4);
    long superBlockValue = readUInt(fstream);

    // virtual address of the index table for this song
    long locationIndexTable = superBlockValue * BLOCK_MULTIPLIER;

    return locationIndexTable;
}

/*
 * Virtual address of song data block
 */
private long getSongIndex(int songNumber, long locationIndexTable)
    throws java.io.IOException,
            java.io.FileNotFoundException {
```

```java
        // index of song into table of song ofsets
        int indexTableIdx = songNumber & 0xFF;
        debug("Index into index table %X\n", indexTableIdx);

        // translate virtual address to physical address
        int whichFile = (int) (locationIndexTable / FILE_SIZE);
        long indexTableStart =  locationIndexTable % FILE_SIZE;
        debug("Which file %d index into file %X\n", whichFile, indexTableStart);

        File songDataFile = new File(DATADIR + dataFiles[whichFile]);
        FileInputStream dataStream = new FileInputStream(songDataFile);
        dataStream.skip(indexTableStart + indexTableIdx * SIZE_UINT);
        debug("Song data index is at %X\n", indexTableStart + indexTableIdx*SIZE_UINT);

        long songStart = readUInt(dataStream) + indexTableStart;

        return songStart + whichFile * FILE_SIZE;
    }

    private RawSong readRawSongData(long locationSongDataBlock)
        throws java.io.IOException {
        int whichFile = (int) (locationSongDataBlock / FILE_SIZE);
        long dataStart =  locationSongDataBlock % FILE_SIZE;
        debug("Which song file %d  into file %X\n", whichFile, dataStart);

        File songDataFile = new File(DATADIR + dataFiles[whichFile]);
        FileInputStream dataStream = new FileInputStream(songDataFile);
        dataStream.skip(dataStart);

        RawSong rs = new RawSong();
        rs.type = readUShort(dataStream);
        rs.compressedLyricLength = readUShort(dataStream);
        // discard next short
        readUShort(dataStream);
        rs.uncompressedLyricLength = readUShort(dataStream);
        debug("Type %X, cLength %X uLength %X\n", rs.type, rs.compressedLyricLength,
        rs.uncompressedLyricLength);

        // don't know what the next word is for, skip it
        //dataStream.skip(4);
        readUInt(dataStream);

        // get the compressed lyric
        rs.lyric = new byte[rs.compressedLyricLength];
        dataStream.read(rs.lyric);

        long toBoundary = 0;
        long songLength = 0;
        long uncompressedSongLength = 0;
```

```java
        // get the song data
        if (rs.type == 0) {
            // Midi file starts in 4 bytes time
            songLength = readUInt(dataStream);
            uncompressedSongLength = readUInt(dataStream);
            System.out.printf("Song data length %d, uncompressed %d\n",
                              songLength, uncompressedSongLength);
            rs.uncompressedSongLength = uncompressedSongLength;

            // next word is language again?
            //toBoundary = 4;
            //dataStream.skip(toBoundary);
            readUInt(dataStream);
        } else {
            // WMA starts on next 16-byte boundary
            if( (dataStart + rs.compressedLyricLength + 12) % 16 != 0) {
                // dataStart already on 16-byte boundary, so just need extra since then
                toBoundary = 16 - ((rs.compressedLyricLength + 12) % 16);
                debug("Read lyric data to %X\n", dataStart + rs.compressedLyricLength + 12);
                debug("Length %X to boundary %X\n", rs.compressedLyricLength, toBoundary);
                dataStream.skip(toBoundary);
            }
            songLength = readUInt(dataStream);
        }

        rs.music = new byte[(int) songLength];
        dataStream.read(rs.music);

        return rs;
    }

    private long readUInt(InputStream is) throws IOException {
        long val = 0;
        for (int n = 0; n < SIZE_UINT; n++) {
            int c = is.read();
            val = (val << 8) + c;
        }
        debug("ReadUInt %X\n", val);
        return val;
    }

    private int readUShort(InputStream is) throws IOException {
        int val = 0;
        for (int n = 0; n < SIZE_USHORT; n++) {
            int c = is.read();
            val = (val << 8) + c;
        }
```

```java
        debug("ReadUShort %X\n", val);
        return val;
    }

    void debug(String f, Object ...args) {
        if (DEBUG) {
            System.out.printf("Debug: " + f, args);
        }
    }

    public Song getSong(RawSong rs) {
        Song song;
        if (rs.type == 0x8000) {
            song = new WMASong(rs);
        } else {
            song = new MidiSong(rs);
        }
        return song;
    }

    public static void main(String[] args) {
        if (args.length != 1) {
            System.err.println("Usage: java SongExtractor <song numnber>");
            System.exit(1);
        }

        SongExtracter se = new SongExtracter();
        try {
            RawSong rs = se.getRawSong(Integer.parseInt(args[0]));
            rs.dumpToFile(args[0]);

            Song song = se.getSong(rs);
            song.dumpToFile(args[0]);
            song.dumpLyric();
        } catch(Exception e) {
            e.printStackTrace();
        }
    }

    private class RawSong {
        /**
         * type == 0x0 is Midi
         * type == 0x8000 is WMA
         */
        public int type;
        public int compressedLyricLength;
        public int uncompressedLyricLength;
        public long uncompressedSongLength; // only needed for compressed Midi
        public byte[] lyric;
        public byte[] music;
```

```java
    public void dumpToFile(String fileName) throws IOException {
        FileOutputStream fout = new FileOutputStream(SONGDIR + fileName + ".lyric");
        fout.write(lyric);
        fout.close();

        fout = new FileOutputStream(SONGDIR + fileName + ".music");
        fout.write(music);
        fout.close();
    }
}

private class Song {
    public int type;
    public byte[] lyric;
    public byte[] music;
    protected Sequence sequence;
    protected int language = -1;

    public Song(RawSong rs) {
        type = rs.type;
        lyric = decodeLyric(rs.lyric,
                      rs.uncompressedLyricLength);
    }

    /**
     * Raw lyric is LZW compressed. Decompress it
     */
    public byte[] decodeLyric(byte[] compressedLyric, long uncompressedLength) {
        // uclen is short by at least 2 - other code adds 10 so we do too
        // TODO: change LZW to use a Vector to build result so we don't have to guess at
        length
        byte[] result = new byte[(int) uncompressedLength + 10];
        LZW lzw = new LZW();
        int len = lzw.expand(compressedLyric, compressedLyric.length, result);
        System.out.printf("uncompressedLength %d, actual %d\n", uncompressedLength,
        len);
        lyric = new byte[len];
        System.arraycopy(result, 0, lyric, 0, (int) uncompressedLength);
        return lyric;
    }

    public void dumpToFile(String fileName) throws IOException {
        FileOutputStream fout = new FileOutputStream(SONGDIR + fileName +
        ".decodedlyric");
        fout.write(lyric);
        fout.close();

        fout = new FileOutputStream(SONGDIR + fileName + ".decodedmusic");
```

```java
            fout.write(music);
            fout.close();

            fout = new FileOutputStream(SONGDIR + fileName + ".mid");
            if (sequence == null)  {
                System.out.println("Seq is null");
            } else {
                // type is MIDI type 0
                MidiSystem.write(sequence, 0, fout);
            }
    }

    public void dumpLyric() {
        for (int n = 0; n < lyric.length; n += 4) {
            if (lyric[n] == '\r') {
                System.out.println();
            } else {
                System.out.printf("%c", lyric[n] & 0xFF);
            }
        }
        System.out.println();
        System.out.printf("Language is %X\n", getLanguageCode());
    }

    /**
     * Lyric contains the language code as string @OO@NN in header section
     */
    public int getLanguageCode() {
        int lang = 0;

        // Look for @OO@NN and return NN
        for (int n = 0; n < lyric.length-20; n += 4) {
            if (lyric[n] == (byte) '@' &&
                lyric[n+4] == (byte) 'O' &&
                lyric[n+8] == (byte) 'O' &&
                lyric[n+12] == (byte) '@') {
                lang = ((lyric[n+16]-'0') << 4) + lyric[n+20]-'0';
                break;
            }
        }
        return lang;
    }

    /**
     * Lyric is in a language specific encoding. Translate to Unicode UTF-8.
     * Not all languages are handled because I don't have a full set of examples
     */
    public byte[] lyricToUnicode(byte[] bytes) {
        if (language == -1) {
            language = getLanguageCode();
        }
```

```java
        switch (language) {
        case SongInformation.ENGLISH:
            return bytes;

        case SongInformation.KOREAN: {
            Charset charset = Charset.forName("gb2312");
            String str = new String(bytes, charset);
            bytes = str.getBytes();
            System.out.println(str);
            return bytes;
        }

        case SongInformation.CHINESE1:
        case SongInformation.CHINESE2:
        case SongInformation.CHINESE8:
        case SongInformation.CHINESE131:
        case SongInformation.TAIWANESE3:
        case SongInformation.TAIWANESE7:
        case SongInformation.CANTONESE:
            Charset charset = Charset.forName("gb2312");
            String str = new String(bytes, charset);
            bytes = str.getBytes();
            System.out.println(str);
            return bytes;
        }
        // language not handled
        return bytes;
    }

    public void durationToOnOff() {

    }

    public Track createSequence() {
        Track track;

        try {
            sequence = new Sequence(Sequence.PPQ, 30);
        } catch(InvalidMidiDataException e) {
            // help!!!
        }
        track = sequence.createTrack();
        addLyricToTrack(track);
        return track;
    }

    public void addMsgToTrack(MidiMessage msg, Track track, long tick) {
        MidiEvent midiEvent = new MidiEvent(msg, tick);
```

```
                // No need to sort or delay insertion. From the Java API
                // "The list of events is kept in time order, meaning that this
                // event inserted at the appropriate place in the list"
                track.add(midiEvent);
        }

        /**
         * return byte as int, converting to unsigned if needed
         */
        protected int ub2i(byte b) {
            return  b >= 0 ? b : 256 + b;
        }

        public void addLyricToTrack(Track track) {
            long lastDelay = 0;
            int offset = 0;
            int data0;
            int data1;
            final int LYRIC = 0x05;
            MetaMessage msg;

            while (offset < lyric.length-4) {
                int data3 = ub2i(lyric[offset+3]);
                int data2 = ub2i(lyric[offset+2]);
                data0 = ub2i(lyric[offset]);
                data1 = ub2i(lyric[offset+1]);

                long delay = (data3 << 8) + data2;

                offset += 4;
                byte[] data;
                int len;
                long tick;

                //System.out.printf("Lyric offset %X char %X after %d with delay %d
                made of %d %d\n", offset, data0, lastDelay, delay, lyric[offset-1],
                lyric[offset-2]);

                if (data1 == 0) {
                    data = new byte[] {(byte) data0}; //, (byte) MetaMessage.META};
                } else {
                    data = new byte[] {(byte) data0, (byte) data1}; // , (byte) MetaMessage.META};
                }
                data = lyricToUnicode(data);

                msg = new MetaMessage();

                if (delay > 0) {
                    tick = delay;
                    lastDelay = delay;
                } else {
                    tick = lastDelay;
```

```
            }

            try {
                msg.setMessage(LYRIC, data, data.length);
            } catch(InvalidMidiDataException e) {
                e.printStackTrace();
                continue;
            }
            addMsgToTrack(msg, track, tick);
        }
    }

}

private class WMASong extends Song {

    public WMASong(RawSong rs) {
        // We want to decode the lyric, but just copy the music data
        super(rs);
        music = rs.music;
        createSequence();
    }

    public void dumpToFile(String fileName) throws IOException {
        System.out.println("Dumping WMA to " + fileName + ".wma");
        super.dumpToFile(fileName);
        FileOutputStream fout = new FileOutputStream(fileName + ".wma");
        fout.write(music);
        fout.close();
    }

}

private class MidiSong extends Song {

    private String[] keyNames = {"C", "C#", "D", "D#", "E", "F", "F#", "G", "G#", "A",
    "A#", "B"};

    public MidiSong(RawSong rs) {
        // We want the decoded lyric plus also need to decode the music
        // and then turn it into a Midi sequence
        super(rs);
        decodeMusic(rs);
        createSequence();
    }

    public void dumpToFile(String fileName) throws IOException {
        System.out.println("Dumping Midi to " + fileName);
        super.dumpToFile(fileName);
    }
```

```java
    public String getKeyName(int nKeyNumber)
    {
        if (nKeyNumber > 127)
            {
                return "illegal value";
            }
        else
            {
                int    nNote = nKeyNumber % 12;
                int    nOctave = nKeyNumber / 12;
                return keyNames[nNote] + (nOctave - 1);
            }
    }


    public byte[] decodeMusic(RawSong rs) {
        byte[]  compressedMusic = rs.music;
        long uncompressedSongLength = rs.uncompressedSongLength;

        // TODO: change LZW to use a Vector to build result so we don't have to guess at
        length
        byte[] expanded = new byte[(int) uncompressedSongLength + 20];
        LZW lzw = new LZW();
        int len = lzw.expand(compressedMusic, compressedMusic.length, expanded);
        System.out.printf("Uncompressed %d, Actual %d\n", compressedMusic.length, len);
        music = new byte[len];
        System.arraycopy(expanded, 0, music, 0, (int) len);

        return music;
    }


    public Track createSequence() {
        Track track = super.createSequence();
        addMusicToTrack(track);
        return track;
    }


    public void addMusicToTrack(Track track) {
        int timeLine = 0;
        int offset = 0;
        int midiChannelNumber = 1;

        /* From http://board.midibuddy.net/showpost.php?p=533722&postcount=31
           Block of 5 bytes :
           xx xx xx xx xx
           1st byte = Delay Time
           2nd byte = Delay Time when the velocity will be 0,
           this one will generate another midi event
           with velocity 0 (see above).
```

```
    3nd byte = Event, for example 9x : Note On for channel x+1,
    cx for PrCh, bx for Par, ex for Pitch Bend....
    4th byte = Note
    5th byte = Velocity
*/
System.out.println("Adding music to track");
while (offset < music.length - 5) {

    int startDelayTime = ub2i(music[offset++]);
    int endDelayTime = ub2i(music[offset++]);
    int event = ub2i(music[offset++]);
    int data1 = ub2i(music[offset++]);
    int data2 = ub2i(music[offset++]);

    int tick = timeLine + startDelayTime;
    System.out.printf("Offset %X event %X timeline %d\n", offset, event & 0xFF,
    tick);

    ShortMessage msg = new ShortMessage();
    ShortMessage msg2 = null;

    try {
        // For Midi event types see http://www.midi.org/techspecs/midimessages.
        php
        switch (event & 0xF0) {
        case ShortMessage.CONTROL_CHANGE:  // Control Change 0xB0
        case ShortMessage.PITCH_BEND:  // Pitch Wheel Change 0xE0
            msg.setMessage(event, data1, data2);
            /*
            writeChannel(midiChannelNumber, chunk[2], false);
            writeChannel(midiChannelNumber, chunk[3], false);
            writeChannel(midiChannelNumber, chunk[4], false);
            */
        break;

        case ShortMessage.PROGRAM_CHANGE: // Program Change 0xC0
        case ShortMessage.CHANNEL_PRESSURE: // Channel Pressure (After-touch)
        0xD0
            msg.setMessage(event, data1, 0);
            break;

        case 0x00:
            // case 0x90:
            // Note on
            int note = data1;
            int velocity = data2;

            /* We have to generate a pair of note on/note off.
               The C code manages getting the order of events
```

```
                    done correctly by keeping a list of note off events
                    and sticking them into the Midi sequence when appropriate.
                    The Java add() looks after timing for us, so we'll
                    generate a note off first and add it, and then do the note on
                */
                System.out.printf("Note on %s at %d, off at %d at offset %X channel
                %d\n",
                            getKeyName(note),
                            tick, tick + endDelayTime, offset, (event
                            &0xF)+1);
                // ON
                msg.setMessage(ShortMessage.NOTE_ON | (event & 0xF),
                        note, velocity);

                // OFF
                msg2 = new ShortMessage();
                msg2.setMessage(ShortMessage.NOTE_OFF  | (event & 0xF),
                        note, velocity);

                break;

            case 0xF0: // System Exclusive
                // We'll write the data as is to the buffer
                offset -= 3;
                // msg = SysexMessage();
                while (music[offset] != (byte) 0xF7) // bytes only go upto 127
                GRRRR!!!
                    {
                        //writeChannel(midiChannelNumber, midiData[midiOffset],
                        false);
                        System.out.printf("sysex: %x\n", music[offset]);
                        offset++;
                        if (offset >= music.length) {
                            System.err.println("Run off end of array while
                            processing Sysex");
                            break;
                        }
                    }
                //writeChannel(midiChannelNumber, midiData[midiOffset], false);
                offset++;
                System.out.printf("Ignoring sysex %02X\n", event);

                // ignore the message for now
                continue;
                // break;

            default:
                System.out.printf("Unrecognized code %02X\n", event);
```

```
                        continue;
                    }
                } catch(InvalidMidiDataException e) {
                    e.printStackTrace();
                }

                addMsgToTrack(msg, track, tick);
                if (msg2 != null ) {
                    if (endDelayTime <= 0) System.out.println("Start and end at same time");
                    addMsgToTrack(msg2, track, tick + endDelayTime);
                    msg2 = null;
                }

                timeLine = tick;
            }
        }
    }
}
```

The support classes are in LZW.java.

```
/**
 * Based on code by Mark Nelson
 * http://marknelson.us/1989/10/01/lzw-data-compression/
 */

public class LZW {

    private final int BITS = 12;                    /* Setting the number of bits to 12, 13*/
    private final int HASHING_SHIFT = (BITS-8);     /* or 14 affects several constants.    */
    private final int MAX_VALUE = (1 << BITS) - 1;  /* Note that MS-DOS machines need to   */
    private final int MAX_CODE = MAX_VALUE - 1;     /* compile their code in large model if*/
    /* 14 bits are selected.              */

    private final int TABLE_SIZE = 5021;            /* The string table size needs to be a */
    /* prime number that is somewhat larger*/
    /* than 2**BITS.                      */
    private final int NEXT_CODE = 257;

    private long[] prefix_code = new long[TABLE_SIZE];;       /* This array holds the
    prefix codes   */
    private int[] append_character = new int[TABLE_SIZE];     /* This array holds the
    appended chars */
    private int[] decode_stack; /* This array holds the decoded string */

    private int input_bit_count=0;
```

```java
    private long input_bit_buffer=0; // must be 32 bits
    private int offset = 0;

/*
** This routine simply decodes a string from the string table, storing
** it in a buffer.  The buffer can then be output in reverse order by
** the expansion program.
*/
/* JN: returns size of buffer used
 */
private int decode_string(int idx, long code)
{
    int i;

    i=0;
    while (code > (NEXT_CODE - 1))
        {
            decode_stack[idx++] = append_character[(int) code];
            code=prefix_code[(int) code];
            if (i++>=MAX_CODE)
                {
                    System.err.printf("Fatal error during code expansion.\n");
                    return 0;
                }
        }

    decode_stack[idx]= (int) code;

    return idx;
}
/*
** The following two routines are used to output variable length
** codes.  They are written strictly for clarity, and are not
** particularyl efficient.
*/

long input_code(byte[] inputBuffer, int inputLength, int dummy_offset, boolean
firstTime)
{
    long return_value;

    //int pOffsetIdx = 0;
    if (firstTime)
        {
            input_bit_count = 0;
            input_bit_buffer = 0;
        }

    while (input_bit_count <= 24 && offset < inputLength)
        {
```

```
        /*
        input_bit_buffer |= (long) inputBuffer[offset++] << (24 - input_bit_count);
        input_bit_buffer &= 0xFFFFFFFFL;
        System.out.printf("input buffer %d\n", (long) inputBuffer[offset]);
        */
        // Java doesn't have unsigned types. Have to play stupid games when mixing
        // shifts and type coercions
        long val = inputBuffer[offset++];
        if (val < 0) {
            val = 256 + val;
        }
        // System.out.printf("input buffer: %d\n", val);
        //if ( ((long) inpu) < 0) System.out.println("Byte is -ve???");
        input_bit_buffer |= (((long) val) << (24 - input_bit_count)) & 0xFFFFFFFFL;
        //input_bit_buffer &= 0xFFFFFFFFL;
        // System.out.printf("input bit buffer %d\n", input_bit_buffer);

        /*
        if (input_bit_buffer < 0) {
            System.err.println("Negative!!!");
        }
        */

        input_bit_count  += 8;
    }

    if (offset >= inputLength && input_bit_count < 12)
        return MAX_VALUE;

    return_value      = input_bit_buffer >>> (32 - BITS);
    input_bit_buffer <<= BITS;
    input_bit_buffer &= 0xFFFFFFFFL;
    input_bit_count  -= BITS;

    return return_value;
}

void dumpLyric(int data)
{
    System.out.printf("LZW: %d\n", data);
    if (data == 0xd)
        System.out.printf("\n");
}

/*
** This is the expansion routine.  It takes an LZW format file, and expands
** it to an output file.  The code here should be a fairly close match to
** the algorithm in the accompanying article.
*/

public int expand(byte[] intputBuffer, int inputBufferSize, byte[] outBuffer)
```

```
{
     long next_code = NEXT_CODE;/* This is the next available code to define */
     long new_code;
     long old_code;
     int character;
     int string_idx;

     int offsetOut = 0;

     prefix_code       = new long[TABLE_SIZE];
     append_character = new int[TABLE_SIZE];
     decode_stack      = new int[4000];

     old_code= input_code(intputBuffer, inputBufferSize, offset, true);  /* Read in the
     first code, initialize the */
     character = (int) old_code;             /* character variable, and send the first */
     outBuffer[offsetOut++] = (byte) old_code;         /*
     code to the output file          */
     //outTest(output, old_code);
     // dumpLyric((int) old_code);

     /*
     **  This is the main expansion loop.  It reads in characters from the LZW file
     **  until it sees the special code used to inidicate the end of the data.
     */
     while ((new_code=input_code(intputBuffer, inputBufferSize, offset, false))
     != (MAX_VALUE))
         {
             // dumpLyric((int)new_code);
             /*
             ** This code checks for the special STRING+CHARACTER+STRING+CHARACTER+STRING
             ** case which generates an undefined code.  It handles it by decoding
             ** the last code, and adding a single character to the end of the decode
             ** string.
             */

             if (new_code>=next_code)
                 {
                     if (new_code > next_code)
                         {
                             System.err.printf("Invalid code: offset:%X new:%X
                             next:%X\n", offset, new_code, next_code);
                             break;
                         }

                     decode_stack[0]= (int) character;
                     string_idx=decode_string(1, old_code);
                 }
             else
                 {
                     /*
                     ** Otherwise we do a straight decode of the new code.
```

```
                */
                string_idx=decode_string(0,new_code);
            }

        /*
        ** Now we output the decoded string in reverse order.
        */
        character=decode_stack[string_idx];
        while (string_idx >= 0)
            {
                int data = decode_stack[string_idx--];
                outBuffer[offsetOut] = (byte) data;
                //outTest(output, *string--);

                if (offsetOut % 4 == 0) {
                    //dumpLyric(data);
                }

                offsetOut++;
            }

        /*
        ** Finally, if possible, add a new code to the string table.
        */
        if (next_code > 0xfff)
            {
                next_code = NEXT_CODE;
                System.err.printf("*");
            }

        // test code
        if (next_code > 0xff0 || next_code < 0x10f)
            {
                Debug.printf("%02X ", new_code);
            }

        prefix_code[(int) next_code]=old_code;
        append_character[(int) next_code] = (int) character;
        next_code++;

        old_code=new_code;
    }
Debug.printf("offset out is %d\n", offsetOut);
return offsetOut;
}
}
```

Here is SongInformation.java:

```
public class SongInformation {
```

```java
// Public fields of each song record
/**
 *  Song number in the file, one less than in songbook
 */
public long number;

/**
 * song title in Unicode
 */
public String title;

/**
 * artist in Unicode
 */
public String artist;

/**
 * integer value of language code
 */
public int language;

public static final int  KOREAN = 0;
public static final int  CHINESE1 = 1;
public static final int  CHINESE2 = 2;
public static final int  TAIWANESE3 = 3 ;
public static final int  JAPANESE = 4;
public static final int  RUSSIAN = 5;
public static final int  THAI = 6;
public static final int  TAIWANESE7 = 7;
public static final int  CHINESE8 = 8;
public static final int  CANTONESE = 9;
public static final int  ENGLISH = 0x12;
public static final int  VIETNAMESE = 0x13;
public static final int  PHILIPPINE = 0x14;
public static final int  TURKEY = 0x15;
public static final int  SPANISH = 0x16;
public static final int  INDONESIAN = 0x17;
public static final int  MALAYSIAN = 0x18;
public static final int  PORTUGUESE = 0x19;
public static final int  FRENCH = 0x20;
public static final int  INDIAN = 0x21;
public static final int  BRASIL = 0x22;
public static final int  CHINESE131 = 131;
public static final int  ENGLISH146 = 146;
public static final int  PHILIPPINE148 = 148;

public SongInformation(long number,
                       String title,
                       String artist,
                       int language) {
    this.number = number;
```

```
            this.title = title;
            this.artist = artist;
            this.language = language;
        }

        public String toString() {
            return "" + (number+1) + " (" + language + ") \"" + title + "\" " + artist;
        }

        public boolean titleMatch(String pattern) {
            // System.out.println("Pattern: " + pattern);
            return title.matches("(?i).*" + pattern + ".*");
        }
        public boolean artistMatch(String pattern) {
            return artist.matches("(?i).*" + pattern + ".*");
        }

        public boolean numberMatch(String pattern) {
            Long n;
            try {
                n = Long.parseLong(pattern) - 1;
                //System.out.println("Long is " + n);
            } catch(Exception e) {
                //System.out.println(e.toString());
                return false;
            }
            return number == n;
        }

        public boolean languageMatch(int lang) {
            return language == lang;
        }
    }
```

Here is Debug.java:

```
public class Debug {

    public static final boolean DEBUG = false;

    public static void println(String str) {
        if (DEBUG) {
            System.out.println(str);
        }
    }

    public static void printf(String format, Object... args) {
        if (DEBUG) {
            System.out.printf(format, args);
        }
```

```
        }
}
```

To compile these, run this:

```
javac SongExtracter.java LZW.java Debug.java SongInformation.java
```

Run this with the following:

```
java SongExtracter <song number >
```

The program to convert these MIDI files to karaoke KAR files is KARConverter.java.

```
    /*
 * KARConverter.java
 *
 * The output from decodnig the Sonken data is not in
 * the format required by the KAR "standard".
 * e.g. we need @T for the title,
 * and LYRIC events need to be changed to TEXT events
 * Tempo has to be changed too
 *
 */

import java.io.File;
import java.io.FileOutputStream;
import java.io.IOException;

import javax.sound.midi.MidiSystem;
import javax.sound.midi.InvalidMidiDataException;
import javax.sound.midi.Sequence;
import javax.sound.midi.Track;
import javax.sound.midi.MidiEvent;
import javax.sound.midi.MidiMessage;
import javax.sound.midi.ShortMessage;
import javax.sound.midi.MetaMessage;
import javax.sound.midi.SysexMessage;
import javax.sound.midi.Receiver;

public class KARConverter {
    private static int LYRIC = 5;
    private static int TEXT = 1;

    private static boolean firstLyricEvent = true;

    public static void main(String[] args) {
        if (args.length != 1) {
            out("KARConverter: usage:");
            out("\tjava KARConverter <file>");
```

```java
        System.exit(1);
    }
    /*
     *      args[0] is the common prefix of the two files
     */
    File    inFile = new File(args[0] + ".mid");
    File    outFile = new File(args[0] + ".kar");

    /*
     *      We try to get a Sequence object, which the content
     *      of the MIDI file.
     */
    Sequence        inSequence = null;
    Sequence        outSequence = null;
    try {
        inSequence = MidiSystem.getSequence(inFile);
    } catch (InvalidMidiDataException e) {
        e.printStackTrace();
        System.exit(1);
    } catch (IOException e) {
        e.printStackTrace();
        System.exit(1);
    }

    if (inSequence == null) {
        out("Cannot retrieve Sequence.");
    } else {
        try {
            outSequence = new Sequence(inSequence.getDivisionType(),
                                      inSequence.getResolution());
        } catch(InvalidMidiDataException e) {
            e.printStackTrace();
            System.exit(1);
        }

        createFirstTrack(outSequence);
        Track[]      tracks = inSequence.getTracks();
        fixTrack(tracks[0], outSequence);
    }
    FileOutputStream outStream = null;
    try {
        outStream = new FileOutputStream(outFile);
        MidiSystem.write(outSequence, 1, outStream);
    } catch(Exception e) {
        e.printStackTrace();
        System.exit(1);
    }
}

public static void fixTrack(Track oldTrack, Sequence seq) {
    Track lyricTrack = seq.createTrack();
    Track dataTrack = seq.createTrack();
```

```java
        int nEvent = fixHeader(oldTrack, lyricTrack);
        System.out.println("nEvent " + nEvent);
        for ( ; nEvent < oldTrack.size(); nEvent++) {
            MidiEvent event = oldTrack.get(nEvent);
            if (isLyricEvent(event)) {
                event = convertLyricToText(event);
                lyricTrack.add(event);
            } else {
                dataTrack.add(event);
            }
        }
    }

    public static int fixHeader(Track oldTrack, Track lyricTrack) {
        int nEvent;

        // events at 0-10 are meaningless
        // events at 11, 12 should be the language code,
        // but maybe at 12, 13
        nEvent = 11;
        MetaMessage lang1 = (MetaMessage) (oldTrack.get(nEvent).getMessage());
        String val = new String(lang1.getData());
        if (val.equals("@")) {
            // try 12
            lang1 = (MetaMessage) (oldTrack.get(++nEvent).getMessage());
        }
        MetaMessage lang2 = (MetaMessage) (oldTrack.get(++nEvent).getMessage());
        String lang = new String(lang1.getData()) +
            new String(lang2.getData());
        System.out.println("Lang " + lang);
        byte[] karLang = getKARLang(lang);

        MetaMessage msg = new MetaMessage();
        try {
            msg.setMessage(TEXT, karLang, karLang.length);
            MidiEvent evt = new MidiEvent(msg, OL);
            lyricTrack.add(evt);
        } catch(InvalidMidiDataException e) {
        }

        // song title is next
        StringBuffer titleBuff = new StringBuffer();
        for (nEvent = 15; nEvent < oldTrack.size(); nEvent++) {
            MidiEvent event = oldTrack.get(nEvent);
            msg = (MetaMessage) (event.getMessage());
            String contents = new String(msg.getData());
            if (contents.equals("@")) {
                break;
            }
            if (contents.equals("\r\n")) {
                continue;
            }
```

```java
            titleBuff.append(contents);
}
String title = "@T" + titleBuff.toString();
System.out.println("Title '" + title +"'");
byte[] titleBytes = title.getBytes();

msg = new MetaMessage();
try {
    msg.setMessage(TEXT, titleBytes, titleBytes.length);
    MidiEvent evt = new MidiEvent(msg, OL);
    lyricTrack.add(evt);
} catch(InvalidMidiDataException e) {
}

// skip the next 2 @'s
for (int skip = 0; skip < 2; skip++) {
    for (++nEvent; nEvent < oldTrack.size(); nEvent++) {
        MidiEvent event = oldTrack.get(nEvent);
        msg = (MetaMessage) (event.getMessage());
        String contents = new String(msg.getData());
        if (contents.equals("@")) {
            break;
        }
    }
}

// then the singer
StringBuffer singerBuff = new StringBuffer();
for (++nEvent; nEvent < oldTrack.size(); nEvent++) {
    MidiEvent event = oldTrack.get(nEvent);
    if (event.getTick() != 0) {
        break;
    }
    if (! isLyricEvent(event)) {
        break;
    }

    msg = (MetaMessage) (event.getMessage());
    String contents = new String(msg.getData());
    if (contents.equals("\r\n")) {
        continue;
    }
    singerBuff.append(contents);
}
String singer = "@T" + singerBuff.toString();
System.out.println("Singer '" + singer +"'");

byte[] singerBytes = singer.getBytes();

msg = new MetaMessage();
try {
```

```java
                msg.setMessage(1, singerBytes, singerBytes.length);
                MidiEvent evt = new MidiEvent(msg, 0L);
                lyricTrack.add(evt);
        } catch(InvalidMidiDataException e) {
        }


        return nEvent;
    }

    public static boolean isLyricEvent(MidiEvent event) {
        if (event.getMessage() instanceof MetaMessage) {
            MetaMessage msg = (MetaMessage) (event.getMessage());
            if (msg.getType() == LYRIC) {
                return true;
            }
        }
        return false;
    }

    public static MidiEvent convertLyricToText(MidiEvent event) {
        if (event.getMessage() instanceof MetaMessage) {
            MetaMessage msg = (MetaMessage) (event.getMessage());
            if (msg.getType() == LYRIC) {
                byte[] newMsgData = null;
                if (firstLyricEvent) {
                    // need to stick a \ at the front
                    newMsgData = new byte[msg.getData().length + 1];
                    System.arraycopy(msg.getData(), 0, newMsgData, 1, msg.getData().length);
                    newMsgData[0] = '\\';
                    firstLyricEvent = false;
                } else {
                    newMsgData = msg.getData();
                    if ((new String(newMsgData)).equals("\r\n")) {
                        newMsgData = "\\".getBytes();
                    }
                }
                try {
                    /*
                    msg.setMessage(TEXT,
                                    msg.getData(),
                                    msg.getData().length);
                    */
                    msg.setMessage(TEXT,
                                    newMsgData,
                                    newMsgData.length);
                } catch(InvalidMidiDataException e) {
                    e.printStackTrace();
                }
            }
        }
        return event;
    }
}
```

```java
public static byte[] getKARLang(String lang) {
    System.out.println("lang is " + lang);
    if (lang.equals("12")) {
        return "@LENG".getBytes();
    }

    // don't know any other language specs, so guess
    if (lang.equals("01")) {
        return "@LCHI".getBytes();
    }
    if (lang.equals("02")) {
        return "@LCHI".getBytes();
    }
    if (lang.equals("08")) {
        return "@LCHI".getBytes();
    }
    if (lang.equals("09")) {
        return "@LCHI".getBytes();
    }
    if (lang.equals("07")) {
        return "@LCHI".getBytes();
    }
    if (lang.equals("")) {
        return "@L".getBytes();
    }
    if (lang.equals("")) {
        return "@LENG".getBytes();
    }
    if (lang.equals("")) {
        return "@LENG".getBytes();
    }
    if (lang.equals("")) {
        return "@LENG".getBytes();
    }
    if (lang.equals("")) {
        return "@LENG".getBytes();
    }
    if (lang.equals("")) {
        return "@LENG".getBytes();
    }

    return ("@L" + lang).getBytes();
}

public static void copyNotesTrack(Track oldTrack, Sequence seq) {
    Track newTrack = seq.createTrack();

    for (int nEvent = 0; nEvent < oldTrack.size(); nEvent++)
        {
            MidiEvent event = oldTrack.get(nEvent);
```

```java
                newTrack.add(event);
            }
        }

    public static void createFirstTrack(Sequence sequence) {
        Track track = sequence.createTrack();
        MetaMessage msg1 = new MetaMessage();
        MetaMessage msg2 = new MetaMessage();

        byte data[] = "Soft Karaoke".getBytes();
        try {
            msg1.setMessage(3, data, data.length);
        } catch(InvalidMidiDataException e) {
            e.printStackTrace();
            return;
        }
        MidiEvent event = new MidiEvent(msg1, 0L);
        track.add(event);

        data = "@KMIDI KARAOKE FILE".getBytes();
        try {
            msg2.setMessage(1, data, data.length);
        } catch(InvalidMidiDataException e) {
            e.printStackTrace();
            return;
        }
        MidiEvent event2 = new MidiEvent(msg2, 0L);
        track.add(event2);
    }

    public static void output(MidiEvent event)
    {
        MidiMessage    message = event.getMessage();
        long           lTicks = event.getTick();
    }

    private static void out(String strMessage)
    {
        System.out.println(strMessage);
    }
}

/*** KARConverter.java ***/
```

Playing MIDI Files

The MIDI files extracted from the disc can be played using standard MIDI players such as TiMidity. The lyrics are included, and the melody line is in MIDI channel 1. I've written a batch of Java programs using Swing and also the Java Sound framework, which can play and do things to MIDI files. At the same time as playing MIDI files, I can also do cool karaoke things such as show the lyrics, show the notes that should be played, and show progress through the lyrics.

Playing WMA Files

WMA files are "evil." They are based on two Microsoft proprietary formats. The first is the Advanced Systems Format (ASF) file format, which describes the "container" for the music data. The second is the Windows Media Audio 9 codec.

ASF is the primary problem. Microsoft has a published specification (www.microsoft.com/en-us/download/details.aspx?id=14995) that is strongly antagonistic to anything open source. The license states that if you build an implementation based on that specification, then you:

- Cannot distribute the source code

- Can only distribute the object code

- Cannot distribute the object code except as part of a "solution" (in other words, libraries seem to be banned)

- Cannot distribute your object code for no charge

- Cannot set your license to allow derivative works

What's more, you are not allowed to begin any new implementation after January 1, 2012, and it is already January 2017!

Just to make it a little worse, Microsoft has patent 6041345, "Active stream format for holding multiple media streams" (www.google.com/patents/US6041345), which was filed in 1997. The patent appears to cover the same ground as many other such formats that were in existence at the time, so the standing of this patent (were it to be challenged) is not clear. However, it has been used to block the GPL-licensed project VirtualDub (www.advogato.org/article/101.html) from supporting ASF. The status of patenting a file format is a little suspect anyway but may become a little clearer after Oracle wins or loses its claim to patent the Java API.

The FFmpeg project (http://ffmpeg.org/) has nevertheless done a clean-room implementation of ASF, reverse-engineering the file format and not using the ASF specification at all. It has also reverse-engineered the WMA codec. This allows players such as MPlayer and VLC to play ASF/WMA files. FFmpeg itself can also convert from ASF/WMA to better formats such as Ogg Vorbis.

There is no Java handler for WMA files, and given the license, there is unlikely to be one unless it is based on FFmpeg.

The WMA files that I have extracted from the DVD have the following characteristics:

- Each file has two channels.

- Each channel carries a mono signal.

- The right channel carries all the instruments, the backing vocals, and also the lead singer.

- The left channel carries all the instruments and backing vocals but not the lead singer.

The Sonken player plays the right channel if no one is singing into the microphone but switches to the left channel (effectively muting the lead singer) as soon as someone sings into a microphone. It's simple and effective.

The lyrics are still there in the track data as MIDI and can be extracted as before. They can be played by a MIDI player. I have no idea (yet) how to synchronize playing the MIDI and the WMA files.

KAR Format

The resultant MIDI files are not in KAR format. This means that karaoke players such as pykaraoke may have problems playing them. It is not too hard to convert the files to this format: loop through the sequence, writing or modifying MIDI events as appropriate. The program is not very exciting but is downloadable as KARConverter.

Playing Songs with pykar

One of the simplest ways to play karaoke MIDI files is by using pykar (www.kibosh.org/pykaraoke/). Regrettably, the songs ripped from the Sonken disc do not play properly. This is because of a mixture of bugs in pykar and features required that are not supplied. The problems and their solutions follow.

Tempo

Many MIDI files will set the tempo explicitly using the meta event Set Tempo, 0x51. These files often do not. pykar expects a MIDI file to include this event and otherwise defaults to a tempo of zero beats per minute. As might be expected, this throws out all timing calculations performed by pykar.

As the Sonic Spot (www.sonicspot.com/guide/midifiles.html) explains, "If no set tempo event is present, 120 beats per minute is assumed." It gives a formula for calculating the appropriate tempo value, which is 60000000/120.

This requires one change to one pykaraoke file: change line 190 of pykar.py from this:

```
sele.Tempo = [(0, 0)]
```

to this:

```
self.Tempo = [(0, 500000)]
```

Language Encoding

The file pykdb.py claims that cp1252 is the default character encoding for karaoke files and uses a font called DejaVuSans.t, which is appropriate for displaying such characters. This encoding adds in various European symbols such as á in the top 128 bits of a byte, in addition to standard ASCII.

I'm not sure where pykaraoke got that information from, but it certainly doesn't apply to Chinese karaoke. I don't know what encodings Chinese, Japanese, Korean, and so on, use, but my code dumps them out as Unicode UTF-8. A suitable font for Unicode is Cyberbit.ttf. (See the "Fonts" chapter in my lecture notes on Global Software at http://jan.newmarch.name/i18n/.)

The file pykdb.py needs the following lines:

```
self.KarEncoding = 'cp1252'  # Default text encoding in karaoke files
self.KarFont = FontData("DejaVuSans.ttf")
```

changed to the following:

```
self.KarEncoding = 'utf-8'  # Default text encoding in karaoke files
self.KarFont = FontData("Cyberbit.ttf")
```

and a copy of Cyberbit.tt copied to the directory /usr/share/pykaraoke/fonts/.

Songs with No Notes

Some songs on the disc have no MIDI notes, as this is all in a WMA file. The MIDI file has only the lyrics. pykaraoke only plays up to the last note, which is at zero! So, no lyrics are played.

Conclusion

This chapter discussed basically a forensics issue: how to get information off a DVD when the format of the files is not known. It doesn't have anything directly to do with playing sound, although it does give me a big source of files that I have already paid for.

Index

A

aconnect, 344, 348
AdaptableMidiPlayer.java, 342
AdjustableMidiPlayer.java, 340
Advanced Linux Sound Architecture (ALSA)
    aplay/arecord, 23
    applications, 32
    audio file, 46–48
    captured sound, 52
    configuration files, 27, 29
    configuration space information, 40
    devices/aliases, 24–27, 177
    hardware cards and devices, 34
    initialization, 46
    interrupts, 52
    managing latency, 52
    MPlayer, 33
    parameters, 49
    programs, 33
    resources, 21
    software parameters, 53–55
    speaker-test, 22
    TiMidity, 33
    user space tools, 21
    VLC, 33
Advanced Systems Format (ASF), 13, 599
Alpha channel, 308
alsactl control program, 22
alsa-info (collect information), 27
alsamixer command, 21
alsa_sink component, 259–260
amp program, 291
analyseplugin amp, 280
Application libraries, 302
Application programming interface (API)
    asynchronous
        client sources, 133–138
        file playing, 93–101
        I/O callbacks, 101–112
        latency controlling, 112–120
        list of devices, 79, 81–84

        microphone to speaker, 120–125
        PulseAudio server, 78
        sources and sinks, 84–88
        stream recording, 89–93
        structure, 78
        volume on devices, 126–128
    default output device, 71
    file recording, 73, 75–76
    functions, 70–71
    playing file, 71–73
    source-sink, 76–77
applyplugin command, 278
AttributedLyricPanel, 420
Audacity, 9, 163
Audio
    analog and sampled signals, 1, 2
    analysis, 1
    audio_decode component, 248
    audio_render device and component, 260, 262
    AudioFormat, 197
    AudioInputStream, 197, 199, 206
    device, 28
    digital signals, 1
    frame, 2
    jitter, 4
    latency, 3
    mixing, 5
    overrun and underrun, 3
    PCM stream, 2
    ports, 245
    production, sounds, 1
    sample format, 2
AudioSystem class, 197
Australian Copyright Amendment Act, 550

B

Bellagio code
    implementation, 258
    library, 238, 246
    output, 241–242

Get the eBook for only $4.99!

Why limit yourself?

Now you can take the weightless companion with you wherever you go and access your content on your PC, phone, tablet, or reader.

Since you've purchased this print book, we are happy to offer you the eBook for just $4.99.

Convenient and fully searchable, the PDF version enables you to easily find and copy code—or perform examples by quickly toggling between instructions and applications.

To learn more, go to http://www.apress.com/us/shop/companion or contact support@apress.com.

Printed in the United States
By Bookmasters

Printed in the United States
By Bookmasters